1 MONTH OF
FREE
READING

at
www.ForgottenBooks.com

By purchasing this book you are eligible for one month membership to ForgottenBooks.com, giving you unlimited access to our entire collection of over 1,000,000 titles via our web site and mobile apps.

To claim your free month visit:
www.forgottenbooks.com/free920677

ISBN 978-0-265-99569-3
PIBN 10920677

OF THE

GENERAL ASSEMBLY

OF THE

COMMONWEALTH OF PENNSYLVANIA,

PASSED AT THE

SESSION OF 1893,

IN THE

ONE HUNDRED AND SEVENTEENTH YEAR OF INDEPENDENCE,

TOGETHER WITH

A Proclamation by the Governor, declaring that he has filed certain Bills in the Office
of the Secretary of the Commonwealth with his objections thereto, and a List
of Charters of Corporations organized under the Corporation
Act of one thousand eight hundred and seventy-four,
and the Supplements thereto.

BY AUTHORITY.

HARRISBURG:
EDWIN K. MEYERS, STATE PRINTER.
1893.

JURISPRUDENCE

LAWS

OF THE

Commonwealth of Pennsylvania.

No. 1.

AN ACT

Making an appropriation to pay the expenses incurred by the special committee, appointed at the session of the Legislature in one thousand eight hundred and ninety-one, to investigate the causes of the recent failures of incorporated and private banks.

SECTION 1. *Be it enacted, &c.*, That the sum of six thousand three hundred and eighty-four dollars and ninety cents, or so much thereof as may be necessary, be and is hereby appropriated out of any money in the treasury not otherwise appropriated for the payment of the expenses of the joint committee of the Senate and House of Representatives appointed to inquire into recent failures of incorporated and private banks, authorized by resolution of January twenty-first, one thousand eight hundred and ninety-one, as follows:

For hotel bills at Philadelphia, Harrisburg and Pittsburg, three thousand six hundred and ten dollars and sixty cents.

For Sergeant-at-Arms serving writs and mileage, one thousand and forty dollars and fifty cents.

For clerk and messenger, three hundred and forty-nine dollars and eighty cents.

For stenographer and typewriter, seven hundred and twenty dollars.

FOR MEMBERS OF THE COMMITTEE.

M. F. Sando, extra car fare, sleeping berths, telegrams et cetera, one hundred and fifty-seven dollars.

W. P. Morrison, extra car fare, sleeping berths, telegrams et cetera, one hundred and seventy-five dollars.

J. William Flad, extra car fare, sleeping berths, telegrams et cetera, one hundred and seventy-six dollars.

H. B. Packer, extra car fare, sleeping berths, telegrams et cetera, one hundred and fifty-six dollars.

How payable

To be paid by warrant drawn by the Auditor General in favor of the chairman of the joint committee, upon an itemized statement furnished by the chairman.

APPROVED—The 2d day of March, A. D. 1893.

ROBT. E. PATTISON.

No. 2.

AN ACT

Making an appropriation to pay the necessary and general expenses incurred in investigating and preparing reports upon appropriation bills for the session of the Legislature of one thousand eight hundred and ninety-one.

$10,250.00 appropriated for committee of House of Representatives

SECTION 1. *Be it enacted, &c.,* That the sum of ten thousand two hundred and fifty dollars, or so much thereof as may be necessary, is hereby specifically appropriated out of any moneys not already appropriated to pay the expenses of the Committee on Appropriations of the House of Representatives of the session of one thousand eight hundred and ninety-one, (1891), for the general and necessary expenses incurred in investigating appropriation bills, including clerical services, extra car fares, hotel bills, carriage hire, typewriting and other services; the said sum so appropriated to be paid

How payable

on the warrant of the Auditor General upon vouchers furnished him by the chairman of said committee, as follows:

Items.

Richard S. Fleckwir, one thousand dollars.

James S. Fruit, three hundred and fifty-two dollars and thirty-eight cents.

W. T. Marshall, three hundred and eighty-three dollars and four cents.

A. C. Baldwin, three hundred and sixty-two dollars and thirty-nine cents.

David A. Boyer, three hundred and eighty-three dollars and forty-nine cents.

W. E. Burdick, three hundred and seventy-two dollars and seventy-eight cents.

E. A. Coray, two hundred and ninety-one dollars.

M. B. Lemon, four hundred and thirty-five dollars and seventy-nine cents.

George T. Losey, three hundred and fifty-four dollars and sixty-nine cents.

Austin L. Taggart, two hundred and sixty-six dollars and thirty-nine cents.

W. B. Flickinger, four hundred and twenty-two dollars and ninety-eight cents.

P. M. Lytle, four hundred and three dollars.

A. P. McDonald, three hundred and ninety-two dollars.

W. P. Morrison, four hundred and fifteen dollars and sixty-eight cents.

Richard Patterson, three hundred and eighty-six dollars and thirty-eight cents.

W. Scott Mullen, three hundred and eighty dollars.

D. C. Titman, three hundred and thirty dollars and eighty-nine cents.

J. E. Woodmansee, two hundred and eighty-eight dollars and eighty-nine cents.

Samuel Wherry, four hundred and thirty-six dollars and sixty nine cents.

John H. Fow, four hundred and fifty-five dollars and twenty-nine cents.

M. F. Sando, three hundred and twenty dollars and fifty-eight cents.

Charles R. Gentner, three hundred and sixty-one dollars and forty cents.

J. H. Holt, three hundred and thirty-six dollars and eighty-nine cents.

J. W. Flad, four hundred and fifty-eight dollars.

W. H. Robbins, three hundred and twenty-nine dollars and thirty-eight cents.

N. M. Lesh, three hundred and thirty dollars and thirty-four cents.

Total ten thousand two hundred and fifty dollars.

SECTION 2. For the payment of the expenses of the committee on appropriations of the Senate for the session of one thousand eight hundred and ninety-one, incurred in visiting and examining schools, asylums, hospitals, reformatories and prisons supported in whole or in part by the State, two thousand eight hundred and twenty four dollars and seventy-two cents. $2,824.00 appropriated for committee of Senate.

For services of Pullman and hotel car and supplies furnished, one thousand six hundred and forty-six dollars and thirty-two cents. Items.

For entertainment and carriage hire at Hotel Lafayette, Philadelphia, four hundred and seventy-nine dollars and sixty-five cents.

For money advanced in payment of hotel bills outside of Philadelphia, supplies furnished and sundries for which no receipts were taken, five hundred and forty-eight dollars and seventy-five cents.

For J. H. Myers, clerical service, one hundred and fifty dollars.

The said sum to be paid by the State Treasurer on warrant drawn by the Auditor General, on the statement rendered him by the chairman of said committee. How payable

APPROVED—The 2d day of March, A. D. 1893.

ROBT. E. PATTISON.

No. 3.

AN ACT

To repeal section eleven of an act, entitled "An act to regulate the practice of pharmacy and sale of poisons, and to prevent adulterations in drugs and medicinal preparations, in the State of Pennsylvania," approved the twenty-fourth day of May, Anno Domini one thousand eight hundred and eighty-seven.

SECTION 1. *Be it enacted, &c.*, That section eleven of an act, entitled "An act to regulate the practice of pharmacy and sale of poisons, and to prevent adulterations in drugs and medicinal preparations, in the State of Pennsylvania," approved the twenty-fourth day of May, Anno Domini one thousand eight hundred and eighty-seven, which reads as follows :

"Any graduate of an accredited medical college, who has had not less than three years' continuous practice since the date of his diploma, and who is registered as a practitioner of medicine and surgery, under the act, entitled 'An act to provide for the registration of all practitioners of medicine and surgery,' approved the eighth day of June, Anno Domini one thousand eight hundred and eighty-one, may be registered under this act without examination and be granted a certificate, which shall entitle him to conduct and carry on the retail drug or apothecary business as proprietor or manager thereof, subject to fees provided in sections three and four of this act," be and the same is hereby repealed.

APPROVED—The 14th day of March, A. D. 1893.

ROBT. E. PATTISON.

No. 4.

AN ACT

To provide for the re-equipment of the National Guard of Pennsylvania and making an appropriation therefor.

Duty of the Adjutant General.

SECTION 1. *Be it enacted, &c.*, That the Adjutant General under the direction and supervision of the State Military Board be required to purchase and issue to the National Guard of Pennsylvania such uniform great coats, blankets, knapsacks or clothing bags, canteens and straps, meat cans, tincups, knives, forks, spoons, shoes, blue flannel shirts and cartridge belts, as may be necessary to complete the equipment of the said National Guard of Pennsylvania ; such articles to conform as nearly as may be in style and pattern with similar articles in use by the United States army.

$163 600.00 appropriated

SECTION 2. That the sum of one hundred sixty-three thousand six hundred dollars, or as much thereof as may be necessary, be and the same is hereby appropriated out of any moneys in the treasury not otherwise appropriated for said purchase provided for in the first section of this act, the said appropriation to be paid on warrants drawn by the Adjutant General on the State Treasurer, countersigned by the Auditor General, after having been approved by the State Military Board. How payable

APPROVED—The 28th day of March, A. D. 1893.

ROBT. E. PATTISON.

No. 5.

AN ACT

Defining fraternal beneficial and relief societies and their status, authorizing them to create subordinate lodges and to pay benefits upon the sickness, disability or death of their members from funds collected by dues and assessments therein, providing for their registration in the office of the Insurance Commissioner, and requiring that they shall make annual reports to him, and exempting them from taxation and from the supervision of the Insurance Commissioner.

SECTION 1. *Be it enacted, &c.*, That it shall be lawful for any corporation, society or voluntary association now or hereafter formed or organized and carried on for the sole benefit of its members and their beneficiaries and not for profit, to have and create subordinate lodges with ritualistic form of work and a representative form of government and to issue certificates of membership, make provision for the payment of benefits in case of sickness, disability or death of its members, subject to their compliance with its constitution and laws in which the fund from which the payment of such benefits shall be made, and the expenses of such association shall be defrayed and shall be derived from assessments or dues collected from its members, and in which the payment of death benefits shall be to families, heirs, blood relatives, affianced husband or affianced wife of or to persons dependent upon the member. Fraternal bene-ficial society de-fined

Such corporation, society or voluntary association now existing, or hereafter formed or organized, shall be and is hereby declared to be a fraternal beneficial society and shall be governed by this act, and shall be exempt from the provisions of insurance laws of this State, and no law hereafter passed shall be applied to them unless they be expressly designated therein. All funds of such fraternal beneficial societies shall be exempt from the State tax on money at interest.

SECTION 2. Within sixty days after the passage of this act all supreme or grand or other bodies which may be known to constitute the head of any fraternal beneficial society doing business within this Common- Shall file copy of constitution with Insurance Com-missioner

wealth, as provided in the first section of this act, shall
file through its proper officers or representatives with
the Insurance Commissioner a copy of their constitution and general laws, and annually any alterations,
changes or amendments, whose duty it shall be to register them without charge in the Insurance Department
as fraternal beneficial societies, and when so registered
they shall be exempt from any and all fees and taxes
imposed by existing laws upon insurance companies reporting to said department.

Shall be exemp from fees and taxes.

SECTION 3. The executive officers of each such supreme or grand lodge of any fraternal beneficial society
doing busines in this Commonwealth shall, on or before
the first day of March of each year, make a report under
oath on a blank to be provided by the Insurance Commissioner, which report shall be printed as a part of
his annual report of the operations of said society in
this Commonwealth for the preceding fiscal year ending December thirty-first, in form as follows:

Shall make annual report to Insurance Commissioner.

I.

Form of report

Name of the society or association, with its principal
office or place of business.

II.

INCOME.

First. Annual dues.
Second. Assessments.
Third. All other sources.
Fourth. Total income during the year.

III.

EXPENDITURES.

First. Losses and claims paid.
Second Salary and other compensation of officers.
Third. Rent.
Fourth. Office expenses.
Fifth. All other expenditures.

IV.

ASSETS.

First. Real estate.
Second. Loans on mortgages.
Third. Bonds and stock owned absolutely.
Fourth. Cash in office or bank.
Fifth. Due from members on assessments called or
pending collection.
Sixth. All other assets (stating character).

V.

LIABILITIES.

First. Losses and claims unpaid.
Second. Salaries due and unpaid.
Third. Borrowed money.
Fourth All other liabilities (stating character).

VI.

EXHIBIT OF MEMBERSHIP.

First. Total members in good standing December thirty-first, one thousand ——— hundred and ———. Number.

Second. Total number of members received by initiation or readmission during the year. Number.

Third. Total. Number.

Fourth. Deduct members retiring by withdrawal or suspension during the year. Number.

Fifth. Deduct members who have died during the year. Number.

Sixth. Total members in good standing December thirty-first, one thousand ——— hundred and —— ——. Number.

SECTION 4. Any fraternal beneficial society failing to register as required by the second section of this act, or to make the report required by the third section of this act, shall be prohibited from doing business in this State, and the officers of societies violating these requirements shall be deemed guilty of a misdemeanor and upon conviction shall be fined not exceeding one hundred dollars for each offense: *Provided always,* That nothing in this act shall be so construed as to give the Insurance Commissioner any supervision or authority in any matter or thing whatsoever pertaining to the business of any fraternal society as prescribed in the first section of this act, other than is expressly provided for in the second and third sections hereof: *And provided further,* That all beneficial and relief associations formed by churches, societies, classes, firms or corporations with or without ritualistic form of work, the privileges and membership in which are confined to the members of such churches, societies or classes and to the members and employés of such firms or corporations, shall be exempt from the provisions of this act: *And provided further,* That this act shall not apply to any secret fraternal beneficial society, order or association which has for one of its objects the payment of a sum not exceeding a certain amount at the expiration of a fixed period.

APPROVED—The 6th day of April, A. D. 1893.

ROBT. E. PATTISON.

Marginal notes:
Penalty for failure to register or to make report.

Power of Insurance Commissioner.

Certain associations exempt from the provisions of this act.

No. 6.

AN ACT

Regulating the organization and incorporation of secret fraternal beneficial societies, orders or associations and protecting the rights of members therein.

WHEREAS, Fraternal beneficial societies, orders or associations have for many years been in existence in this Commonwealth;

And Whereas, The said societies when properly managed are beneficial to the laboring and business classes, but by reason of there being no statutory provisions regulating the conduct of their affairs the citizens of this Commonwealth are unprotected from fraudulent schemes and plans and from the mismanagement of officers and promoters of such societies, orders and associations, now therefore;

SECTION 1. *Be it enacted, &c.,* That from and after the passage of this act, any fifteen or more persons, nine of whom shall be citizens and residents of this Commonwealth, having associated themselves as a secret fraternal beneficial society, order or association, may be incorporated under the provisions of this act and when so incorporated the said corporation shall have the following powers:

Number of persons who may organize.

GENERAL POWERS.

General powers

First. To have succession by its corporate name perpetually, subject to the power of the General Assembly under the Constitution of this Commonwealth.

Second. To maintain and defend judicial proceedings.

Third. To make and use a common seal and alter the same at pleasure.

Fourth. To be capable of taking, receiving, purchasing, holding and transferring real and personal property for the purpose of its incorporation and for no other purpose.

Fifth. To elect, appoint and remove the officers and agents for the management of its business and carrying out its objects and to allow them a suitable compensation.

Sixth. To make a constitution and general laws for the management of its affairs, not inconsistent with the Constitution and laws of this State, and to alter and amend the same when necessary. When so made, altered or amended, the said constitution and general laws shall be the law governing such society, order or association and its officers, subordinate lodges, councils or bodies and the members in their relations to such society, order or association in all their acts.

Seventh. To provide in the constitution and general laws for the payment to its members of sick, disability or death claims in such amounts as may be authorized and directed by said constitution and general laws. And also to provide for the payment in not less than five years, to members whose beneficiary or distribution period may then expire, of such sum not exceeding the maximum amount named in the beneficiary certificates as the constitution and general laws in force at the expiration of said period may authorize and direct.

Eighth. To collect from its members by admission fees, dues and assessments the funds necessary to carry on its operations and provide for the payment of its benefits, which assessments shall be made in manner and form as provided by its constitution and general laws.

Ninth. To carry on its operations through supreme and subordinate bodies or lodges and to issue beneficiary or relief certificates in accordance with its constitution and general laws.

Tenth. To enter into any obligation necessary for the transaction of its affairs.

SECTION 2. The charter of such intended corporation must be subscribed by five or more persons citizens of this Commonwealth and shall set forth : *Charter and what it shall set forth.*

First. The name of the corporation.

Second. The purpose for which it is formed.

Third. The place where its principal office is to be located.

Fourth. The names and residences of the subscribers.

Fifth. The number and names of its officers with the term or terms of years for which they have been chosen, and also the names of not less than six directors, managers or members of an executive committee who, together with the president of the society, order or association, shall form a board of directors, managers or executive committee, with the term or terms of years for which each is to serve.

NOTICE TO BE GIVEN.

SECTION 3. Notice of the intention to apply for any such charter shall be inserted in two newspapers of general circulation printed in the proper county for three weeks, setting forth briefly the character and object of the corporation to be formed and the intention to make application therefor. *Publication of notice.*

CERTIFICATES.

SECTION 4. The said certificates of incorporation shall be acknowledged by at least five of those who subscribed to them, before any officer authorized to take the acknowledgements of deeds in the Commonwealth of Pennsylvania, to be their act and deed, and the same being duly certified under the hand and official seal of the said officer shall be presented to a law judge of the county in which the principal office of the corporation *Certificates of incorporation, how prepared.* *To whom presented.*

is located, accompanied by proof of the publication of the notice of such application, who is hereby authorized to peruse and examine said instrument and if the same shall be found to be in the proper form and within the purposes named in this act he shall endorse thereon these facts, and shall order and decree thereon **Approval of charter.** that the charter is approved and that upon the recording of the said charter and order the subscribers thereto and their associates shall be a corporation for the purposes and upon the terms therein stated, and said order and charter shall be recorded in the office for the recording of deeds in and for the county aforesaid and from thence-forth the persons named therein and subscribing the same and their associates and successors shall be a corporation by the name therein given. No **What is required before corporation shall engage in business.** such corporation, however, shall engage in business until at least twenty-five persons have subscribed in writing to be beneficiary members therein in the aggregate amount of at least five thousand dollars, and have each paid in one full assessment in cash amounting in the aggregate to at least one per centum of the amount in which they are beneficiary, nor until a certificate signed and sworn to by three of the highest officers of the corporation has been filed with the Insurance Commissioner stating that the requirements of this section have been complied with.

ANNUAL REPORTS.

Annual report must be filed with Insurance Commissioner. SECTION 5. Every such fraternal society, order or association incorported under or accepting the provisions of this act shall, on or before the first day of March of each year, make and file with the Insurance Commissioner a report of its affairs and operations during the year ending on the thirty-first day of December immediately preceding; such report shall be upon blank forms to be provided by the Insurance Commissioner and shall be verified under oath by the duly authorized officers of such society, order or association and shall be in lieu of all other reports required by any other law; the said report shall contain answers to the following questions:

What report shall contain. First. Number of members admitted during the year and number of beneficiary certificates issued.

Second. Amount of benefits named in said certificates.

Third. Number of benefit liabilities incurred during the year.

Fourth. Number of benefit liabilities paid during the year.

Fifth. The amount received from each assessment during the year and the number of assessments levied.

Sixth. Total amount paid members, beneficiaries, legal representatives or heirs.

Seventh. Number and kinds of claims compromised or resisted and brief statement of reasons.

Eighth. Does the corporation charge annual or other periodical dues or admission fees.

Ninth. Total amount of salaries paid to officers.

Tenth. Has the society a reserve fund.

Eleventh. If so, how is it created and for what purpose, the amount thereof and how invested.

Twelfth. If the custody and investment of said reserve fund is entrusted to any trust companies or corporations in the Commonwealth of Pennsylvania, state the name of said corporation or corporations, the capital stock of the same, the amount of capital stock paid in, the surplus, if any, and the place of business of said corporation or corporations.

Thirteenth. If the custody and investment of said reserve fund is entrusted to any of the officers of the said secret fraternal beneficial society give the names and residences of the said officers, the names and residences of their sureties, the amount of their bonds and the place or person with whom the said bonds are deposited.

Fourteenth. State the amount of said reserve fund.

Fifteenth. Number of certificates of membership lapsed during the year.

Sixteenth. Number in force at beginning and end of year.

Seventeenth. Date of organization and incorporation and county where incorporated.

All such societies, orders or associations, together with their books, papers and vouchers, shall be subject to visitation and inspection by the Insurance Commissioner or such person or persons as he may at any time designate. Any such society, order or association refusing or neglecting to make such report to the Insurance Commissioner may, upon the suit of the Commonwealth, be enjoined by the court of common pleas of Dauphin county from carrying on any business until such report shall be made Visitation and inspection by Insurance Commissioner.

Failure to file report.

SECTION 6. Every officer of any corporation accepting the provisions of or doing business under this act shall give bond with sufficient surety for the faithful performance of his duties, and for the safe custody of the moneys and securities and other property which may be in his possession and control, which bond shall be for such amount as the board of directors, managers, executive committee or supreme governing body may require : *Provided, however,* That when the reserve funds of any corporation organized hereunder or accepting the provisions hereof are deposited for investment with any trust companies or financial corporations, chartered by the Commonwealth of Pennsylvania, the officers of said corporation so depositing its reserve funds need not be bonded for any of the moneys or securities in the custody or possession of said trust com- Every officer shall give bond.

No bond to be given when reserve fund is deposited with Trust Company

panies or financial corporations. The Insurance Commissioner shall have the power and authority at all
times to examine said bonds at the place of business of
the corporation, and there to inquire of and receive
answers from the officers of the corporation as to their
knowledge of the financial standing of the surety or
sureties on any of said bonds.

SECTION 7. Any beneficial society, order or association heretofore incorporated under any act of the General Assembly of the Commonwealth of Pennsylvania
for beneficial or protective purposes to its members
from funds collected therein, and which has been carrying on the operations of a secret fraternal society, order
or association, and any unincorporated society, order
or association which has been carrying on said operations, shall have and enjoy the rights and privileges
conferred by this act, upon filing with the Insurance
Commissioner a certificate or declaration signed by its
supreme officers accepting the provisions of this act
and agreeing to abide by all the requirements herein
made : *Provided, however*, That nothing in this act shall
apply to any incorporated or unincorporated fraternal
beneficial society not accepting the provisions hereof
or be so construed as to compel any such society to accept its provisions or become incorporated thereunder.

APPROVED—The 6th day of April, A. D. 1893.

ROBT. E. PATTISON.

-- —

No. 7.

AN ACT

To enable eleemosynary corporations to secure their property from
liability to be wasted or incumbered by managers or beneficiaries
of the estate.

WHEREAS, Corporations for religious purposes have
been established in this Commonwealth and well-dis-
posed persons have from time to time contributed
funds for the foundation of the said charities, and these
funds are liable to be diverted by imprudence, mismanagement or fraud of the persons for the time being
constituting the governing body of the corporation or
charities.

SECTION 1. *Be it enacted, &c.*, That any corporation
or trustees for charitable uses owning any property
dedicated to religious or charitable purposes, such as
churches, school houses, parsonages, hospitals, almshouses and the like, may, for the purpose of protecting
the said property from liability to debt thereafter contracted on the part of the corporation or persons having the control or management of the charity, vest
their property in trustees upon trust for the use of the

congregation or members of the corporation for the time being as places of worship, or for use as school houses or residence for the minister or pastor of the congregation, or for the maintenance of any charity, and when the trustees shall be so vested by deeds duly recorded, the property thus conveyed, so long as it is used for the purposes above mentioned and is not used for any secular purpose or for a purpose from which profits are derived, shall not be liable to any debts, contracts or engagements of the corporation or congregation thereafter made or entered into, but shall be deemed and taken to be freed therefrom in the same manner and with like effects as if the same had been conveyed or devised to the trustees by a stranger in trust for the uses of the congregation or corporation, but so that the same shall not be liable to their debts, contracts or engagements nor to their control for any purpose other than for the uses of the same as places of worship, or as free schools or schools from which no pecuniary profits are derived, or as a residence for the minister or pastor of the congregation. or for the maintenance of the charitable purpose for which it was dedicated or intended by the donors or contributors. *When so conveyed shall not be liable to any debts.*

SECTION 2. All trustees and officers of corporations having the management of property for charitable uses which is held in trust under the provisions of section one, contracting debts or causing them to be contracted in the improvement of the property by building thereon shall be personally liable for the debts thus contracted, unless they shall have notified the persons with whom the contract is made that the property is not liable for the debts contracted in building thereon, but there shall be no liability to anyone but to the person with whom a contract is made by the trustees or corporation. *Trustees and officers shall be personally liable unless they shall notify contractor*

APPROVED—The 10th day of April, A. D. 1893.

ROBT. E. PATTISON.

No. 8.

A FURTHER SUPPLEMENT

To an act regulating lateral railroads, changing the method of assessing damages to land owners in certain cases.

SECTION 1. *Be it enacted, &c.*, That the first section of an act of Assembly, entitled "Supplement to an act regulating lateral railroads," approved the eighteenth day of April, one thousand eight hundred and sixty-five, which reads as follows, to wit:

"That the act, entitled 'An act regulating lateral railroads,' passed May fifth, one thousand eight hundred and thirty-two, and the several supplements thereto, shall be construed to authorize the construction *Act of May 5, 1832, amended.*

of a single or double track railroad, with the necessary
sidings, wharves, schutes, machinery, fixtures and appurtenances, for the transfer and delivery of limestone,
iron ore, coal and other minerals, from said lateral
railroad, on to any public or locomotive road, the damages to the owners of the land to be ascertained and
paid in the same manner as under the general railroad law : *Provided*, That not any of said roads shall
exceed five (5) miles in length," be and the same is
hereby amended to read as follows, namely :

That the act, entitled "An act regulating lateral railroads," passed May fifth, one thousand eight hundred
and thirty-two, and the several supplements thereto,
shall be construed to authorize the construction of a
single or double track railroad with the necessary sidings, wharves, schutes, machinery, fixtures and appurtenances for the transfer and delivery of limestone,
iron ore, coal and other minerals from said lateral rail-

How damage shall
be ascertained.

road on to any public or locomotive road, the damages
to the owners of the lands shall be ascertained by six
disinterested and judicious men resident in the said
county, to be appointed by the court, who shall proceed in the same manner as is provided and directed by
the first section of the act of May fifth, one thousand
eight hundred and thirty-two, entitled "An act regulating lateral railroads," and when the damages shall
have been finally ascertained and determined they shall
be paid : *Provided*, That not any of said roads shall
exceed five miles in length.

APPROVED—The 14th day of April, A. D. 1898.

ROBT. E. PATTISON.

No. 9.

AN ACT

Rendering women eligible to office of notary public.

SECTION 1. *Be it enacted, &c.*, That from and after
the passage of this act women being twenty-one years
of age and citizens of this Commonwealth shall be eligible to the office of notary public.

SECTION 2. That whenever any female notary shall
marry she shall, before the performance of any notarial act, return her commission to the Governor,
stating the fact of her marriage and giving her married
name, and the Governor shall thereupon issue to her
a new commission conforming to the change of name
covering the term for which she was originally commissioned without requiring any payment to the Commonwealth other than that originally made, and upon
the issuing of said new commission the notary thus

commissioned shall give a new bond according to the change of name with security as required by existing laws.

APPROVED—The 14th day of April, A. D. 1893.

ROBT. E. PATTISON.

No. 10.

AN ACT

Amending section seventy-six of an act to consolidate, revise and amend the penal laws of this Commonwealth, approved March thirty-one, one thousand eight hundred and sixty, increasing the maximum punishment for the first conviction of murder in the second degree to twenty years.

SECTION 1. *Be it enacted, &c.*, That section seventy-six of an act, entitled "An act to consolidate, revise and amend the penal laws of this Commonwealth," approved March thirty-first, one thousand eight hundred and sixty which now reads as follows, namely:

"Every person duly convicted of the crime of murder of the second degree, shall, for the first offense, be sentenced to undergo an imprisonment, by separate or solitary confinement, not exceeding twelve years, and for the second offense, for the period of his natural life" is hereby amended so as to read as follows, namely:

Every person duly convicted of the crime of murder of the second degree shall, for the first offense, be sentenced to undergo an imprisonment by separate or solitary confinement not exceeding twenty years, and for the second offense for the period of his natural life.

APPROVED—The 14th day of April, A. D. 1893.

ROBT. E. PATTISON.

No. 11.

AN ACT

To provide for the erection of a fire-proof building for the State Departments, State Library, Archives, Battle Flags of the State, Art Treasures and Geological Collections, and to authorize changes and improvements in the Capitol and Department buildings, and making appropriations therefor.

WHEREAS, The present library room is entirely insufficient in size for the convenient occupancy and use of the large and constantly increasing State Library, and the State is exposed to the imminent and continuing risk of great and irreparable loss from the destruction of said library by fire;

And whereas, There is no place now provided for

2—LAWS.

the safe-keeping of the archives and early records of
the State Department, but the same are inaccessible
and liable to loss as well as in great danger of destruction by fire;

And whereas, The State is the owner of valuable
historic paintings now scattered and exposed to injury
for want of a proper place for their preservation and
display;

And whereas, The Geological Survey Commission
has accumulated an extensive, interesting and valuable collection of geological and mineralogical specimens from all parts of the State, for the safe keeping
and exhibition of which no provision has been made
therefor;

Who shall have charge of the work. SECTION 1. *Be it enacted, &c.*, That the Board of Commissioners of Public Grounds and Buildings, consisting
of the Governor, Auditor General and State Treasurer,
shall carry into effect the provisions of this act and
are hereby empowered to select a location within the
Capitol grounds, adopt plans and proceed to erect a
fire-proof building for the State Departments, State
Library, Archives, Battle Flags of the State, Art Treasures and Geological and Mineralogical collections, and
provide for heating and ventilating the same, and for
this purpose shall have full power to employ such
architects and pay the same, also advertise for proposals and give contract or contracts to the lowest reasonable bidder or bidders.

Erection and furnishing of the building. SECTION 2. Said Commissioners shall proceed to
erect and complete said Department and Library
building at as early a date as practicable, compatible
with the economical, substantial and skilful execution
of the work, and when completed shall furnish the same
with such cases, desks and furniture as may be necessary. When said building is ready for occupancy
said Commissioners shall direct and procure the re-
Removal of Library etc. moval thereto of the State Library and of such of the
archives, paintings, maps, deeds, battle flags and other
memorials as they shall deem proper, and shall also cause
to be placed therein the ornithological. geological and
mineralogical collections the State Geological Commission, or such part thereof as may seem proper.

Commission shall remodel State Library room and hall of House. SECTION 3. Upon the completion of said Department
and Library building said Commission shall remodel
the present State Library room, and convert the same
into such rooms for the occupancy of such officers of
the State Government or committees of the Legislature
as they shall deem best, and shall remodel and reconstruct the present hall of the House of Representatives
in such manner as in their proper judgment shall best
secure proper ventilation and a more commodious and
convenient place of meeting for said House of Repre-
May improve wings of Capitol building. sentatives. Said Commission shall have power to make
such alterations, repairs and improvements to either

or both wings and to other portions of the present Capitol buildings as may seem necessary to secure proper and convenient accommodations for the Senate and House of Representatives and their officers, and as to said other portions for such officers of the State as may occupy the same. Said Commission may, if demed best, connect said Capitol building with the present Department buildings, and may alter and repair said Department buildings in such manner as may be deemed best to accommodate such officers of the State as may occupy the same. Said Commission may furnish said Capitol and Department building with such cases, desks, shelving and furniture as may be necessary, and shall have full power for the purpose contained in this section to employ such architects, superintendents, mechanics and laborers and puchase material and make contracts as to them seem necessary and proper.

May furnish Capitol and Department building, and employ architects and laborers.

SECTION 4. Upon the completion of said Department and Library building the said Commissioners shall designate the offices and rooms to be occupied by the several State Departments, and shall assign the offices and rooms in the Capitol and Department buildings now in use to such public officials and State Boards as now exist or may hereafter be created, in such manner as may be deemed best for the public service.

Shall assign offices and rooms.

SECTION 5. To carry out the provisions of this act the following sums are hereby appropriated namely :

For the erection and furnishing, as herein provided, of said fire-proof State Department and Library building, the sum of five hundred thousand dollars, or so much thereof as may be necessary.

$500,000.00 appropriated for Department building.

For remodeling the present Library room and hall of the House of Representatives and for such other additions, alterations. repairs and furnishing of and to the present Capitol and Department buildings as provided in section three, the sum of one hundred and twenty-five thousand dollars, or so much thereof as may be necessary.

$125,000.00 appropriated for remodeling etc., of Capitol building.

Said appropriation to be paid by the State Treasurer upon warrants drawn by the Auditor General in the rsual manner from time to time, as the progress of the work shall require, vouchers for the same being frst produced and filed.

How payable.

SECTION 6. Said Commissioners shall receive no compensation for their services and shall make report to the next Legislature.

No compensation to Commissioners.

APPROVED—The 14th day of April, A. D. 1893.

ROBT. E. PATTISON.

No. 12.

AN ACT

Making an appropriation for the payment of the salary of the Superintendent of Banking and the payment of clerk hire and the payment of contingent expenses of the Banking Department for the years ending May thirty-first, one thousand eighth hundred and ninety-two and one thousand eight hundred and ninety-three.

$14,800.00 appropriated.

How payable.

Items.

SECTION 1. *Be it enacted, &c.*, That the sum of fourteen thousand eight hundred dollars, or so much thereof as may be necessary, be and the same is hereby appropriated to be paid on warrant drawn by the Auditor General in the usual manner, upon the presentation of duly authenticated vouchers, for the purpose of paying the salary of the Superintendent of Banking and his clerks and the expenses of the Banking Department, under the provision of the act approved June eighth, one thousand eight hundred and ninety-one. That the gross sum of money so appropriated be applied as follows:

Six thousand dollars for the payment of the salary of the Superintendent of Banking from the twenty-fifth day of November, one thousand eight hundred and ninety-one to the thirty-first day of May, one thousand eight hundred and ninety-three.

Six thousand three hundred dollars, or so much thereof as may be necessary, for the payment of clerk hire from the time of their appointment to the thirty-first day of May, one thousand eight hundred and ninety-three.

Two thousand five hundred dollars, or so much thereof as may be necessary, for the payment of the contingent expenses of the Banking Department from the date of the appointment of the Superintendent to the thirty-first day of May, one thousand eight hundred and ninety-three.

APPROVED—The 14th day of April, A. D. 1893.

ROBT. E. PATTISON.

No. 13.

AN ACT

To provide for the better protection of female insane patients in transit.

SECTION 1. *Be it enacted, &c.*, That whenever any indigent female insane patient is to be removed from any county almshouse to a State hospital or asylum for the insane, or from one State hospital or asylum for the insane to another State hospital or asylum, or from the home of such indigent patient to an almshouse, hospital or asylum, or when returned from such institution to her home, it shall be the duty of the court under whose order such patient is committed, or of the commissioners of tne county or the overseers of the poor of the district to which such patient is chargeable (if not committed by the court), to provide a female attendant for every female patient in transit at the expense of the proper county or poor district unless such patient is accompanied by a member of her family.

APPROVED —The 14th day of April, A. D. 1893.

ROBT. E. PATTISON.

No. 14.

AN ACT

Making an appropriation to defray the expenses incurred in establishing the right of the Superintendent of Public Instruction to his office.

SECTION 1. *Be it enacted, &c.*, That the sum of eighteen hundred dollars, or so much thereof as may be necessary, be and the same is hereby appropriated to pay the expenses incurred in establishing the right of the Superintendent of Public Instruction to his office in the courts of Dauphin county and before the supreme court of Pennsylvania, between the twenty-eighth day of May, one thousand eight hundred and ninety-one and the fourth day of January, one thousand eight hundred and ninety-two, and the Auditor General is hereby directed to draw his warrant on the State Treasurer for the same in favor of D. J. Waller, Jr., then Superintendent of Public Instruction, whenever the proper vouchers shall have been submitted to and approved by the Auditor General.

$1,800.00 appropriated.

How payable.

APPROVED—The 14th day of April, A. D. 1893.

ROBT. E. PATTISON.

No. 15.

AN ACT

To facilitate the labors of the Judges of the court of common pleas of the county in which the seat of government is or may be located, in the disposition of the business of the Commonwealth, by providing suitable clerical assistance.

SECTION 1. *Be it enacted, &c.*, That to facilitate the labors of the judges of the court of common pleas of the county in which the seat of government is or may be located in the disposition of the business of the Commonwealth, the said judges are hereby authorized to employ the help of stenographers, typewriters and

other clerks, provided the cost of such help shall not
exceed the sum of one thousand dollars per annum for
each of said judges, the cost of such help to be paid by
the judge employing the same, and shall be repaid to
him by the State Treasurer upon his certificate of the
amount paid by him during the preceding three months
for such help.

APPROVED—The 17th day of April, A. D. 1893.

ROBT. E. PATTISON.

No. 16.

AN ACT

To amend an act, entitled "An act to provide for the regulation
and inspection of buildings within the city of Philadelphia, and
for the better preservation of life and property," approved the
seventh day of May, Anno Domini one thousand eight hundred
and fifty-five, as to the amount of the bond which the inspector
shall be required to furnish for the faithful performance of his
duties and providing for the cancellation thereof.

SECTION 1. *Be it enacted, &c.*, That section second of
an act, entitled "An act to provide for the regulation
and inspection of buildings in the city of Philadelphia,
and for the better preservation of life and property,"
approved the seventh day of May, Anno Domini one
thousand eight hundred and fifty-five, which now reads
as follows:

Section 2. act of
May 7, 1855, cited
for amendment.

"That every such inspector, before he enters upon
the duties of his office, shall be required to take and
subscribe, before some person authorized by law to administer the same, the following oath or affirmation: I
do solemnly and sincerely swear or affirm, (as the case
may be), that I am duly qualified, as required by section first, to act as inspector of buildings, and that I
will faithfully, impartially and truly execute and perform the duties of an inspector of buildings in the city
of Philadelphia, and see that the buildings inspected
by me are built as required by the laws of the Commonwealth, according to the best of my judgment and
abilities, which said oath or affirmation shall be reduced to writing and filed in the office of the Prothonotary of the court of common pleas of said city and
county, and shall be entered on the record in said
office; every such person shall, moreover, before entering on the duties of his office, execute a bond to the
Commonwealth in the sum of ten thousand dollars,
with one or more sureties, to be approved by the said
court, or two of the judges thereof in vacation, conditioned for the faithful performance of the duties imposed upon him by law, which bond shall be for the use
of any or all persons who may be aggrieved by the acts
or neglect of such inspector," shall be and the same is
amended so as to read in the following manner:

SECTION 2. That every such inspector, before he enters upon the duties of his office, shall be required to make and subscribe before some person authorized by law to administer the same, the following oath or affirmation : I do solemnly and sincerely swear or affirm, (as the case may be), that I am duly qualified, as required by section first, to act as an inspector of buildings, and that I will faithfully, impartially and truly execute and perform the duties of an inspector of buildings in the city of Philadelphia, and see that the buildings inspected by me are built as required by the laws of this Commonwealth, according to the best of my judgment and abilities. Which said oath or affirmation shall be reduced to writing and filed in the office of the Prothonotary of the court of common pleas of said city and county, and shall be entered on the record in said office ; every such person shall, moreover, before entering on the duties of his office, execute a bond to the Commonwealth in the sum of five thousand dollars with one or more sureties to be approved by the said court, or by two of the judges thereof in vacation, conditioned for the faithful performance of the duties imposed upon him by law, which bond shall be for the use of any and all persons who may be aggrieved by the acts or neglect of such inspector ; and the bond hereinbefore provided for, conditioned for the faithful performance of his duties, shall be cancelled and marked satisfied of record by the city solicitor, upon the request of the director of public safety, who shall first certify that the accounts of such inspector are correct and that there is no default, and no claim has come to his knowledge from or on behalf of any person or persons alleged to have been aggrieved by the acts or neglect of such inspector.

Oath of inspector.

Oath shall be filed and recorded.

Inspector shall execute a bond to the Commonwealth.

Conditions of bond.

When bond shall be cancelled.

APPROVED—The 18th day of April, A. D. 1893.

ROBT. E. PATTISON.

No. 17.

AN ACT

Relative to the admission and instruction of children of soldiers of the late war of the rebellion in the common schools of districts outside of those in which their parents, guardians or others entitled to their custody may reside.

SECTION 1. *Be it enacted, &c.*, That any child or children of any person who was a soldier in the service of the United States in the late war of the rebellion being, or who shall be, temporarily or otherwise within any school district of the Commonwealth shall, upon application, be entitled to admission and instruction the same as resident children, in the proper common school of such district, and notwithstanding such child or children may have or shall come into such district for the purpose of attendance at such school, and the residence of the parents, guardian or other person or persons entitled by law to the custody of such child or children be in another district.

Approved—The 18th day of April, A. D. 1893.

ROBT. E PATTISON.

--- --- ---

No. 18.

AN ACT

To prevent county superintendents of common schools from engaging in the profession of teaching during their term of office, unless it shall be done without compensation.

Section 1. *Be it enacted, &c.*, That from and after the passage of this act it shall be unlawful for any person holding the office of county superintendent of common schools to engage in the business or profession of teaching in any of the schools of the Commonwealth, unless it be done without any other compensation than that paid them as county superintendent.

Section 2. Any violation of the provisions of this act on the part of any county superintendent shall be deemed a sufficient cause for removal from office by the State Superintendent of Public Instruction.

Approved—The 26th day of April, A. D. 1893.

ROBT. E. PATTISON.

--- --- ---

No. 19

AN ACT

To provide for the licensing and regulation of lying-in hospitals.

Board of Health shall license lying in hospital.

Section 1. *Be it enacted, &c.*, That it shall be lawful for the board of health of any locality to license any person or persons, other than an institution duly incorporated for such purpose, to establish and keep a lying-in hospital, ward or other private place for the reception, care and treatment of women in labor, upon written application filed with the said board, accompanied by the endorsement of six or more reputable persons, citizens of the county where such hospital may be situated, who shall certify to the respectability of the applicant and that the hospital, hospital ward or other private place shall only be used for legitimate, moral and charitable purposes; and if, after due inquiry of such board of health, it is believed that the applicant is a proper person and the premises are suitable and properly arranged for such purpose, the said board of health shall grant a license for the purpose above mentioned upon the payment of a fee of five dollars. Such license shall continue in force for a period of two years, subject, however, to be revoked by the board of health granting the same upon the violation of the rules and regulations enacted by the said board of health for the government of said hospitals, hospital wards or other private places. The proprietor of every such hospital, hospital ward or other private place kept for lying-in purposes shall keep a record in a book for that purpose, containing the full name and address of each person admitted, the date of admission, the date of birth of every child, the date of its removal and the place to which such child shall be removed. Such hospital, hospital ward or other private place shall be subject to the visitation or inspection at any time by the board of health granting the said license, or any special officer that may be appointed for that purpose by the court of common pleas, upon the petition of any society, for the prevention of cruelty to children of the proper county.

How long such license shall continue in force.

Proprietor shall keep record.

Visitation of such hospital by Board of Health or officer.

SECTION 2. The proprietor of every hospital, hospital ward or other private place for lying-in purposes to which a license has been granted according, to section one of this act shall, within five days after the birth of any child, report to the said board of health the date and place of such birth, the name, sex and color of the child.

Births shall be reported to Board of Health

SECTION 3. Whoever shall violate the provisions of section one of this act by keeping a hospital, hospital ward or other private place for lying-in purposes for hire or reward, without license, shall be guilty of a misdemeanor, and for the first offense, upon conviction thereof, shall be punished by a fine not exceeding one hundred dollars, and for the second offense, upon conviction thereof, shall be punished by a fine not exceeding two hundred dollars and imprisonment of not more than one year, or either or both, at the discretion of the court.

Penalties for violation of the provisions of this act.

SECTION 4. All acts or parts of acts inconsistent herewith are hereby repealed.

Repeal.

APPROVED—The 26th day of April, A. D. 1893.

ROBT. E. PATTISON.

No. 20.

AN ACT

Directing the board of revision of taxes in cities of the first class to add to the assessment books and to the duplicates thereof in the hands of the receiver of taxes, real estate which has ceased to be exempt from taxation, and subjecting such real estate to taxation for the proportionate part of the year during which it is not exempt.

SECTION 1. *Be it enacted, &c.*, That whenever any real estate in the cities of the first class in this Commonwealth, which has been exempt from taxation under the law, shall cease to be occupied and used for the purpose or purposes which entitled it to such exemption, it shall be the duty of the board of revision of taxes to add said real estate to the assessment books and to the duplicates thereof in the hands of the receiver of taxes, as taxable for the portion of the year commencing at the time when the right to exemption ceased, and said real estate shall thereupon become subject to taxation at the tax rate fixed for the year for the proportionate part of the year during which it is not entitled to exemption.

APPROVED—The 26th day of April, A. D. 1893.

ROBT. E. PATTISON.

No. 21.

AN ACT

To provide that municipal corporation shall not be required to file affidavits of defense in actions of assumpsit.

SECTION 1. *Be it enacted, &c.*, That municipal corporations shall not be required to file affidavits of defense in actions of assumpsit.

SECTION 2. All laws or parts of laws inconsistent herewith are hereby repealed.

APPROVED—The 26th day of April, A. D. 1893.

ROBT. E. PATTISON.

No. 22.

AN ACT

Providing for the appointment of a receiver in cases where corporations have been dissolved by judgment of ouster upon proceedings of quo warranto.

Court may appoint a receiver.

SECTION 1. *Be it enacted, &c.*, That whenever any corporation incorporated under the laws of this Commonwealth shall be dissolved by judgment of ouster upon proceedings by quo. warranto in any court of competent jurisdiction, the said court, or in vacation any one of the law judges thereof, shall have power to appoint a receiver, who shall have all the powers of a receiver appointed by a court of chancery, to take possession of all the estate, both real and personal thereof, and make distribution of the assets among the persons entitled to receive the same according to law. The

Such receiver shall supersede assignee of corporation in possession.

powers of such receiver may continue as long as the court deems necessary for said purposes and he shall be held to supersede an assignee of the corporation in possession.

SECTION 2. The provisions of this act shall also apply to any corporation that has been heretofore dissolved by judgment of ouster upon proceedings of quo warranto in any court of competent jurisdition, the affairs of which have not been settled and adjusted.

APPROVED—The 26th day of April, A. D. 1893. ·

ROBT. E. PATTISON.

Shall apply to corporation heretofore dissolved.

No. 23.

A SUPPLEMENT

To an act approved August the seventh, one thousand eight hundred and eighty-three, entitled "An act to designate the several Judicial Districts of the Commonwealth as required by the Constitution," constituting Lawrence county as a separate judicial district.

SECTION 1. *Be it enacted, &c.*, That from and after September first, one thousand eight hundred and ninety-three, the county of Lawrence be and the same is hereby detached from the seventeenth judicial district and henceforth shall constitute a separate judicial district, which is hereby designated as the fifty-first judicial district, and shall have one judge learned in the law.

Lawrence county constituted the fifty-first judicial district.

SECTION 2. That the president judge of the seventeenth judicial district shall be the president judge of the said fifty-first judicial district, and the additional law judge in said seventeenth judicial district shall be the president judge of the seventeenth judicial district, and the office of additional law judge in the seventeenth judicial district as provided by the act of Assembly, affirmed August seventh, one thousand eight hundred eighty-three, is hereby abolished.

President Judges.

SECTION 3. That all acts or parts of acts, general or special, inconsistent herewith be and the same are hereby repealed so far as the same relate to Butler and Lawrence counties.

Repeal.

APPROVED—The 28th day of April, A. D. 1893.

ROBT. E. PATTISON.

No. 24.

AN ACT

To amend an act, entitled "An act relating to marriage licenses, providing for officers herein indicated to issue licenses for parties to marry," approved the twenty-third day of June, Anno Domini one thousand eight hundred and eighty-five, relating to the county wherein to secure the license.

SECTION 1. *Be it enacted, &c.*, That so much of section one of the act, entitled "An act relating to mar-

Part of section 1, act of June 23, 1885 amended.

riage licenses, providing for officers herein indicated to issue licenses for parties to marry," approved the twenty-third day of June, Anno Domini one thousand eight hundred and eighty-five, which reads as follows:

"That from and after the first day of October, Anno Domini one thousand eight hundred and eighty-five, no person, within this Commonwealth, shall be joined in marriage, until a license shall have been obtained for that purpose, from the clerk of the orphans' court, in the county, where the marriage is performed" be and the same is hereby amended so as to read as follows:

Where license shall be obtained. SECTION 1. That from and after the first day of October, Anno Domini, one thousand eight hundred and ninety-five, no person within this Commonwealth shall be joined in marriage, until a license shall have been obtained for that purpose from the clerk of the orphans' court in the county wherein either of the contracting parties resides, or in the county where the marriage is performed: *Provided*, That one or both of the applicants shall be identified to the satisfaction of the clerk applied to for such license. A license so issued shall **Where ceremony may be performed.** authorize the marriage ceremony to be performed in any county of this Commonwealth: *Provided, however*, **Duplicate certificate to be filed in county where ceremony is performed.** That a duplicate, as provided for in section one in the marriage license act of June twenty-third, one thousand eight hundred and eight-five, shall in all cases, by the person solemnizing said marriage, be returned duly signed to the clerk of the orphans' court of the county in which the marriage is solemnized, and shall by him be recorded as provided in the fourth section of said act of June twenty-third, one thousand eight hundred and eighty-five.

APPROVED—The 1st day of May, A. D. 1893.

ROBT. E. PATTISON.

No. 25.

AN ACT

To amend section one of an act, entitled "An act making the first Monday in September in each year a legal holiday, to be known as 'Labor holiday,'" approved the twenty-fifth day of April, Anno Domini one thousand eight hundred and eighty-nine, changing the same to the first Saturday of September.

SECTION 1. *Be it enacted, &c.*, That the first section of the act, entitled "An act making the first Monday in September in each year a legal holiday, to be known as 'Labor holiday,'" approved the twenty-fifth day of April, Anno Domini one thousand eight hundred and eighty-nine, which reads as follows:

"SECTION 1. *Be it enacted by the Senate and House of Representatives of the Commonwealth of Pennsylvania in in General Assembly met and is hereby enacted by the authority of the same,* That the first Monday of September in each year, after the passage of this act, shall be a holiday to be known as 'Labor holiday,'" shall be so amended as to read and be as follows:

That the first Saturday of September in each year, after the passage of this act, shall be a holiday to be known as "Labor holiday."

SECTION 2. That all acts or parts of acts inconsistent herewith be and the same are hereby repealed.

APPROVED—The 1st day of May, A. D. 1893.

ROBT. E. PATTISON.

No. 26.

AN ACT

To extend the jurisdiction of the courts of this Commonwealth having equity powers, so as to embrace all litigation between stockholders and parties claiming to be stockholders of corporations, and between creditors and stockholders and creditors and the corporation.

SECTION 1. *Be it enacted, &c.,* That the several courts of common pleas of this Commonwealth having the powers of a court of chancery, shall have jurisdiction of all litigation and disputes between stockholders and parties claiming to be stockholders, and between creditors and stockholders and creditors and the corporation, of all corporations within this State; and in the proceedings before the court in such case, the service of process upon the company shall be held and considered as a service upon one of the principal defendants, as provided in the first section of the act of April sixth, one thousand eight hundred and fifty-ninth, relating to equity jurisdition and proceedings.

APPROVED—The 4th day of May, A. D. 1893.

ROBT. E. PATTISON.

No. 27.

AN ACT

To amend an act, entitled "An act to provide for the establishment and maintenance of a home for disabled and indigent soldiers and sailors of Pennsylvania." further regulating the admission of inmates to said hom

SECTION 1. *Be it enacted, &c.,* That section six of the act, entitled "An act to provide for the establishment and maintenance of a home for disabled and indigent soldiers and sailors of Pennsylvania," which reads as follows:

Section repealed.

"That the soldiers, sailors or marines who shall be
entitled to admission in this home, shall be those only
who, at the time of their enlistment in the army or
navy, were citizens of Pennsylvania or served in some
Pennsylvania organization, where honorably discharged
from the service of the United States, who are in indigent circumstances, and from any disabilities (not received in any illegal act) are unable to support themselves by manual labor, and who cannot gain admission
into the homes for soldiers and sailors provided by the
Government of the United States," be and the same is
hereby amended to read as follows:

**Who shall be en-
titled to admission.**   That the soldiers, sailors or marines who shall be entitled to admission in this home, shall be those only,
who, at the time of their enlistment in the army or
navy, were citizens of Pennsylvania or served in some
Pennsylvania organization, or those who, for five
years immediately preceding the date of their application for admission, were citizens of Pennsylvania
who were honorably discharged from the service of
the United States, who are in indigent circumstances,
and from any disabilities (not received in any illegal
act) are unable to support themselves by manual labor,
and who are unable to gain admission into the homes
for soldiers and sailors provided by the Government of
the United States.

APPROVED—The 4th day of May, A. D. 1893.

ROBT. E. PATTISON.

No. 28.

AN ACT

Amending the ninth clause of the fifth section of the act, entitled
"An act to restrain and regulate the sale of vinous, spirituous,
malt or brewed liquors, or any admixtures thereof," approved
the thirteenth day of May, Anno Domini one thousand eight
hundred and eighty-seven, authorizing bondsmen from any part
of the county to execute a bond, and fixing the amount thereof.

**Ninth clause of the
fifth section
amended, act of
May 13, 1887.**   SECTION 1. *Be it enacted, &c.,* That the ninth clause
of the fifth section of the act, entitled "An act to restrain and regulate the sale of vinous, spirituous, malt
or brewed liquors or any admixtures thereof," approved
the thirteenth day of May, Anno Domini one thousand
eight hundred and eighty-seven, which reads as follows:

"Ninth. The names of no less than two reputable
freeholders of the ward or township where the liquor is
to be sold, who will be his, her or their sureties on the
bond which is required, and a statement that each of
said sureties is a bona fide owner of real estate in the
said county worth, over and above all incumbrances,
the sum of two thousand dollars and that it would sell

for that much at public sale, and that he is not engaged in the manufacture of spirituous, vinous, malt or brewed liquors," be and the same is hereby amended so it shall read as follows:

Ninth. The names of no less than two reputable freeholders of the county where the liquor is to be sold, who will be his, her or their sureties on the bond which is required, and a statement that each of said sureties is a bona fide owner of real estate in said county worth, over and above all incumbrances, the sum of two thousand dollars, and that it would sell for that much at public sale, and that he is not engaged in the manufacture of spirituous, vinous, malt or brewed liquors: *Provided*, That when any person is surety on more than one bond, he shall certify that he is worth four thousand dollars over and above all incumbrances and over and above any previous bonds he may be on as surety.

APPROVED—The 4th day of May, A. D. 1893.

ROBT. E. PATTISON.

What is required of sureties on bond.

Surety on more than one bond.

No. 29.

AN ACT

Detaching the county of Lebanon from the twelfth judicial district and erecting the same into a separate judicial district.

WHEREAS, The federal census, taken in the year one thousand eight hundred and ninety, shows that the poulation of the county of Lebanon exceeds forty thousand, and it therefore appears that the said county has become entitled, by virtue of the fifth section of Article five of the Constitution, to be a separate judicial district. Now, therefore:

SECTION 1. *Be it enacted, &c.*, That from and after the first Monday of January, one thousand eight hundred and ninty-four, the said county of Lebanon shall be detached from the twelfth judicial district and shall constitute a separate judicial district, to be known as the fifty-first judicial district, which said district shall have one judge learned in the law as president judge thereof. The Governor is hereby authorized and directed to appoint one person, learned in the law, to serve as president judge of the said fifty-first district, from the first Monday of January, one thousand eight hundred and ninety-four, until the first Monday of January, one thousand eight hundred and ninety-five, and the qualified electors of the said fifty-first district shall, at the general election in November, one thousand eight hundred and ninety-four, elect one person, learned in the law, to be the president judge of the said fifty-first district for the term of ten years from the said first Monday of January, one thousand eight hundred and ninety-five.

Lebanon county constituted the fifty-first judicial district.

Governor shall appoint a President Judge.

The two judges, learned in the law, now in commission in the said twelfth judicial district, shall remain judges of said twelfth district, which shall continue to be composed of the county of Dauphin, and to be entitled to have and elect two judges, learned in the law.

APPROVED—The 4th day of May, A. D. 1893.

In giving my approval to the foregoing bill I deem it only fair to the General Assembly, and to the people of the Commonwealth, that I should express the considerations which have moved me to approved a measure, the effect of which is to add another to the total number of judges of the courts in the Commonwealth, contrary to my frequently expressed conviction that a too "rapid increase in the number of judges has detracted from the dignity of the judicial office without adding to the efficiency of the courts; or raising them in public esteem."

The effect of this bill is to erect Lebanon county, with 48,131 population—and a tendency toward increase in population and business—into a separate judicial district. While the constitution provides that a county of this population "shall constitute a separate judicial district, and shall elect one judge learned in the law." I am not convinced that the judicial business of the county of Lebanon is adequate to engage the entire time and attention of one judge. Its peculiar geographical location, situated as it is, between four large counties, each constituting separate judicial districts with two or more judges, renders it impossible to form it with any other county or counties into a convenient single district, and I am constrained to permit its erection into a separate judicial district, not alone by the mandate of the constitution, but by the conviction that the largely increased and increasing business of the Dauphin county court requires the exclusive attention of two judges in the district which it comprises.

The population of Dauphin county, under the last census, was 96,977, an increase of over 20,000 in the preceding decade with more than a corresponding increase in the elements which give rise to litigation. It considerably exceeds in population Northampton county, which has long had two judges, is nearly even with that of York, which has been for some years a double district, and has 7,600 more population than Chester, which has for years had two judges. The district which has comprised Dauphin and Lebanon counties has more population than Berks county, with three judges, Lackawanna with three judges, and almost as much as Schulykill with three judges. By the erection of Lebanon county into a separate district the two associate judges in that county will hereafter be dispensed with.

Moreover, the court of Dauphin county is empowered with special and peculiar jurisdiction, not only of vast importance to the Commonwealth and of great dignity and responsibility, but which has imposed upon it rapidly increasing labors of great magnitude. By numerous and successive acts of the Legislature, the court of common pleas of Dauphin county has been clothed with jurisdiction throughout the State for the purpose of hearing and determining all suits, claims and demands whatever at law and in equity in which the Commonwealth may be a party plaintiff, for accounts, unpaid balances, unpaid liens, taxes, penalties and all other causes of action, real, personal and mixed.

The experience of the past few years, the records of the auditing, fiscal and law departments of the State Government, and the reports of the Attorney General, all prove how enormously the litigations to which the Commonwealth is a party has increased. A comparison of the report of the law department for the year 1883 and 1884, with the report for 1891 and 1892, illustrates most vividly the extent of this increase. The total number of claims received for collection for the years 1883 and 1884 was $40,486.47. The same claims for the years 1891 and 1892 amounted to $1,387,927.83. The collections, largely made through suits in the Dauphin county courts for the first named two years were $274,355.93; for the last period, $874,506.70. I have at hand no record of the number of appeals taken from the settlements of the auditing and fiscal officers to the Dauphin county court for the earlier years, but the record of the past few years shows how rapidly litigation thus instituted has been increasing. In 1889 they numbered 74; in 1892 there were 127; already during the present year 108 appeals have been taken, and it is estimated that, owing to the questions arising under the revenue bill of 1891, the total number of appeals for 1893 will be not less than 300. The continuing popular demand and legislative agitation for changes in the revenue laws give promise of incessant litigation of this character.

It is also worthy of consideration that many of the cases of the Commonwealth, subject to this jurisdiction, not only involve new and peculiar questions arising in the construction of the tax statutes, but they are decisive of momentous interests to the Commonwealth and upon them hangs the collection or the failure to secure millions of dollars of revenues.

It is to be remembered, too, that almost without exception, the Commonwealth cases are tried before the court without a jury, and this custom, which is admirably suited to this class of business, imposes much additional labor on the trial judges. All the evidence must be sifted and weighed, offers and objections must be considered and disposed of in writing, and the facts must be stated in a detailed and orderly manner. The value to the supreme court of this preliminary work cannot be overestimated. Instead of being confronted with a voluminous record, bristling with exceptions, and hard to understand the cause of its complexity, the record is now put into such a shape by the court below that the precise questions are instantly seen, and thus the labors and intelligent action of the appellate court are greatly facilitated. All of this work, however, is new in the last ten years and has added very much indeed to the labors of the Dauphin county court.

Besides the tax question of this vast interest, with the settlement of which the Dauphin county court must, in the first instance deal, many cases peculiar to its jurisdiction arise at the instance of the Commonwealth in the construction and enforcement of the corporation laws generally, involving writs of quo warranto, injunctions and other equity proceedings, the regulation and dissolution of insurance companies, the construction of the election laws and the numerous special cases which have arisen, and are likely to arise continually under the ballot reform act and its proposed amendments, clothing this court with authority to hear and determine objections to the validity of certificates and nomination papers for the entire State.

In view of all this, I am of the opinion that the volume of work imposed upon the court of common pleas of Dauphin county, is not only far greater in extent but of vaster consequence, in every view of it, than that which is committed to the jurisdition of any other two judges in the Commonwealth. The district is especially fortunate at present in the incumbency and prospective long tenure of two jurists of notable learning, capacity and integrity, which fact is not without consideration in my approval of this measure.

ROBT. E. PATTISON.

No. 30.

AN ACT

To prohibit members of boards of control of school districts in cities of the second class from holding any office of emolument under or being employed by said boards.

SECTION 1. *Be it enacted, &c.*, That from and after the passage of this act it shall be unlawful for any director or member of the board of control of school districts in any city of the second class within this Commonwealth, to hold the office of secretary of said board, or be employed by said board, while a member thereof, in any capacity in which any compensation is attached.

SECTION 2. All laws or parts of laws inconsistent herewith are hereby repealed.

APPROVED—The 10th day of May, A. D. 1893.

ROBT. E. PATTISON.

No. 31.

AN ACT

To amend an act, entitled "An act to provide for the licensing of transient retail merchants in cities, boroughs and townships," empowering councils to increase the maximum license.

SECTION 1. *Be it enacted, &c.*, That section one of an act, entitled "An act to provide for the licensing of transient retail merchants in cities, boroughs and townships," approved the fourth day of May, Anno Domini one thousand eight hundred and eighty-nine, which reads as follows, namely:

"That hereafter every person, whether principal or agent, not engaged in a permanent business in any city, borough or township of this Commonwealth, but entering into, beginning, or desiring to begin a transient retail business in such city, borough or township, for the sale of any goods, wares or merchandise whatsoever, whether the same shall be represented or held forth to be bankrupt, assignees, or about to quit business, or of goods damaged by fire, water or otherwise, or by any attractive or conspicuous advertisement whatsoever, shall take out a license for the same from the proper authorities of said city, borough or township. The amount of such license in any city or borough shall be fixed by ordinance, duly passed by the council of such city or borough, and the amount of such license in any township shall be fixed by the county treasurer, and to be paid into the school fund of such township, to be used for school purposes, which license shall not be less than twenty-five dollars, nor exceed the sum of one hundred dollars per month; said license to be renewed monthly during the continuance of such sales; and upon failure of said person or persons so to secure license, he or they shall be fined in a sum not less than one hundred dollars, to be collected as all other fines are by law collectible, and in default of payment of said fines and costs, be imprisoned in the jail of said city or county for a period not exceeding thirty days," be and the same is hereby amended so that the said section one shall read as follows, namely:

That hereafter every person, whether principal or agent, not engaged in permanent business in any city, borough or township of this Commonwealth, but entering into, beginning or desiring to begin, a transient retail business in such city, borough or township for the sale of any goods, wares or merchandise whatsoever, whether the same shall be represented or held forth to be bankrupt, assignees, or about to quit business, or of goods damaged by fire, water or otherwise, or by any attractive or conspicuous advertisement whatsoever, shall take out a license for the same from the proper authorities of the said city, borough or township. The amount of such license in any city or bor-

[marginal notes]
Section one, act of May 4, 1889, cited for amendment.

License must be obtained for transient retail business.

Who shall fix amount of such license.

ough shall be fixed by ordinance, duly passed by the council of such city or borough, and the amount of such license in any township shall be fixed by the county treasurer and to be paid into the school fund of such township to be used for school purposes, which license shall not be less than twenty-five dollars, nor exceed the sum of one thousand dollars per month; said license to be renewed monthly during the continuance of said sales, and upon failure of said person or persons so to secure license, he or they shall be fined in a sum not less than one hundred dollars, to be collected as all other fines are by law collectible, and in default of payment of said fines and costs, to be imprisoned in the jail of said city or county for a period not exceeding thirty days.

APPROVED—The 10th day of May, A. D. 1893.

ROBT. E. PATTISON.

Minimum and maximum amount of license.

Penalty for failure to procure such license.

No. 32.

AN ACT

Relating to the naturalization of aliens and prohibiting the payment of the expenses connected therewith by officers and members of political organizations and by candidates.

SECTION 1. *Be it enacted, &c.,* That on and after the passage of this act the certificates of naturalization shall be printed on parchment; and it shall be unlawful for any officer or any member of any committee or organization of any political party, or any candidate for office nominated by any political party or nomination papers or for any person in behalf of said committee, organization or candidate to pay or furnish the money to pay, or in any way to become responsible for the payment of the fees and expenses directly or indirectly incurred by an alien in attending upon any court for the purpose of and in obtaining his naturalization papers.

SECTION 2. Any person violating the provisions of the first section of this act shall, upon conviction in a summary proceeding before any city magistrate, alderman or justice of the peace, who are hereby given jurisdiction to try said offenders in a summary way, for each offense, pay a fine of fifty dollars, which, when collected, shall be paid into the county treasury of the county wherein the offense was committed.

SECTION 3. If any person convicted in the manner prescribed in the second section of this act and sentenced to pay a fine or fines shall refuse or fail to forthwith pay said fine or fines and costs to the city magistrate, alderman or justice of the peace before whom he is convicted, or give satisfactory security to be approved by said magistrate, alderman or justice of the

Certificates shall be printed on parchment.

Payment of fees.

Penalty for violation of provisions of section one.

Shall be committed to county jail if payment of fine is refused.

peace to pay the same within ten days, he shall be committed to county jail, there to be held one day for every five dollars of the fine or fines which he has been sentenced to pay : *Provided, however,* That said imprisonment shall not prevent the collection of said fine or fines and costs by legal process. **Proviso.**

APPROVED—The 10th day of May, A. D. 1893.

ROBT. E. PATTISON.

No. 33.

AN ACT

To prevent deception and fraud by owners or agents who may have control of any stallion kept for service, by proclaiming or publishing fraudulent or false pedigrees or records, and to protect such owners or agents in the collection of fees for services of such stallions.

SECTION 1. *Be it enacted, &c.,* That every owner or agent who may have the custody or control of any stallion, who shall charge a fee for the services of such stallion, shall, before advertising or offering such services to the public for any fee, reward or compensation, file with the clerk of the court of quarter sessions of the county in which such owner or owners, agent or agents reside, or in which such stallion shall be kept for service, a written statement giving the name, age, pedigree and record, if known, and if not known, then that the same is unknown, the description, terms and condition upon which such stallion will serve. Upon filing such statement, the clerk of the court of quarter sessions for the county shall issue a certificate or license to the owner or owners, agent or agents having the custody and control of such stallion, that such a statement has been filed in his office. The clerk of the court of quarter sessions to receive one dollar for each and every certificate so issued, and the county commissioners are hereby authorized and required to furnish registration books and blanks for such purposes. The owners, agent or agents of the owners of such stallion shall then post a written or printed copy of the statement, so filed with such clerk of the court of quarter sessions, in a conspicuous place in each locality in which said stallion shall be kept for service. *Statement of pedigree etc., must be filed in court of Quarter Sessions.* *Clerk shall issue a license.* *Commissioners shall furnish registration books* *Owner must post copy of statement.*

SECTION 2. Every owner or agent who shall file, proclaim or publish a false or fraudulent pedigree or record or statement of any kind regarding any stallion, or who shall neglect or refuse to comply with the provisions of section one of this act, shall forfeit all fees for the services of such stallion, and the person or persons who may be deceived or defrauded by such false or fraudulent pedigree or record or statement may sue *Owner shall forfeit fees for service if false pedigree is published.*

and recover, in any court of competent jurisdiction, such damages as may be shown to have been sustained by reason of such false and fraudulent representation.

Collection of fees for service.

SECTION 3. Whenever the owner or agent of an owner or owners of any stallion shall have complied with the foregoing provisions of this act, the amount agreed upon between the parties at the time of service, or in the event of no such agreement having been entered into between them, then in such an amount as specified for service fee of such stallion or stallions in the state ment hereinbefore required to be filed with the clerk of the court of quarter sessions of said counties, may be collected in the same manner as other debts are now collected.

APPROVED—The 10th day of May, A. D. 1893.

ROBT. E. PATTISON

No. 34.

AN ACT

Making it a misdemeanor for any person to represent or advertise himself as the agent of an unauthorized or fictitious insurance company within this Commonwealth.

Company of any other state or government which has not complied with laws of this state.

SECTION 1. *Be it enacted, &c.*, That any person or persons representing or advertising himself or themselves as the agent or agents of any insurance company of any other state or government, which has not complied with the laws of this State, by poster, circular letter or in any other way or manner, shall be deemed

Penalty for representing such company.

to be guilty of a misdemeanor, and upon conviction shall be sentenced to pay a fine of not more than one thousand dollars, at the discretion of the court.

Fictitious or spurious company.

SECTION 2. That any person or persons representing or advertising himself or themselves as the agent or agents of any fictitious or spurious insurance company by poster, circular letter or in any other way or man-ner, shall be deemed to be guilty of a misdemeanor,

Penalty for representing such company.

and on conviction shall be sentenced to pay a fine of not more than five hundred dollars and undergo im-prisonment not more than three years, at the discre-tion of the court.

Repeal.

SECTION 3. That all acts or parts of acts inconsistent herewith are hereby repealed.

APPROVED—The 10th day of May, A. D. 1893.

ROBT. E. PATTISON.

No. 35.

A SUPPLEMENT

To an act relative to the supervision and control of hospitals and houses in which the insane are placed for treatment or detention, approved the eight day of May, Anno Domini one thousand eight hundred and eighty-three.

SECTION 1. *Be it enacted, &c.*, That section thirty-four of the act of Assembly, approved the eighth day of May, Anno Domini one thousand eight hundred and eighty-three, which reads as follows:

"Persons voluntarily placing themselves in any of the houses provided for in this act, may be detained for the time they shall specify by an agreement signed by them, at the time of their admission, but not exceeding seven days; and they may, from time to time, renew the authority to detain them for a time not exceeding seven days from such renewal, but no agreement shall be deemed to authorize a detention, unless signed in the presence of some adult person attending as a friend of the person detained, in the presence of, and also by the person in charge of the house or the medical attendant," be and the same is hereby amended to read as follows:

Persons voluntarily placing themselves in any of the houses provided for in this act, and who may be suffering from nervous diseases threatening mental disorder, may be received for a period of one month or less, by an agreement, which shall also specify the time, signed by them at the time of admisison, and they may renew said agreement at the end of one month, but no agreement shall be deemed to authorize their remaining, unless signed in the presence of some adult persons attending as a friend of the person applying in the presence of and also by the medical attendant.

APPROVED—The 10th day of May, A. D. 1893.

ROBT. E. PATTISON.

Section 34, act of May 8, 1883, amended.

How persons may be admitted.

No. 36.

AN ACT

To authorize the State Superintendent of Public Instruction to grant permanent State teachers' certificates to graduates of recognized literary and scientific colleges.

SECTION 1. *Be it enacted, &c.*, That after the passage of this act, the State Superintendent of Public Instruction be empowered to and shall grant, without examination, permanent State teachers' certificates to all applicants therefor, who are graduates of recognized iterary or scientific colleges legally empowered to con-

Who shall receive state teachers certificates.

fer the degrees of Bachelor of Arts (B. A.), Master of Arts (M. A.), Bachelor of Science (B. S.), Master of Science and Bachelor of Philosophy (Ph. B.), and whose course of study embraces not less than four collegiate years: *Provided*, Said applicants are at least

Conditions under which certificates shall be issued.

twenty-one years of age and have taught at least three full annual terms in the public schools of the Commonwealth: *Provided further*, That each applicant shall produce to the said State Superintendent of Public Instruction a certificate from the school board or boards, countersigned by the County Superintendent of the same county where he or she last taught, showing that the said applicant is a person of good moral character; has been successful as a teacher in the public schools during said term: *And provided further*, That said certificates shall be granted by the State Superintendent of Public Instruction, after having received satisfactory evidence from the said applicants that they have complied with the requirements of this act.

Powers of Superintendent of Public Instruction.

SECTION 2. That the forms of application shall be submitted by applicants, and the certificates to be issued in accordance with the provisions of this act shall be prescribed and determined by the Superintendent of Public Instruction, and he shall have authority to annul such certificates granted by himself or predecessors in office, upon complaint duly proven, of incompetency, cruelty, negligence or immorality on the part of the holder thereof.

Repeal.

SECTION 3. All acts or parts of acts inconsistent herewith are hereby repealed.

APPROVED—The 10th day of May, A. D. 1893.

ROBT. E. PATTISON.

No. 37.

AN ACT

To repeal an act, entitled "An act to attach Henry Sanders and Jonathan Sanders to Center township, Snyder county, for school purposes," approved the tenth day of February, Anno Domini one thousand eight hundred and sixty-five.

SECTION 1. *Be it enacted, &c.*, That the act of Assembly, entitled "An act to attach Henry and Jonathan Sanders to Center township, Snyder county, for school purposes," approved the tenth day of February, Anno Domini one thousand eight hundred and sixty-five, be and the same is hereby repealed.

APPROVED—The 10th day of May, A. D. 1893.

ROBT. E. PATTISON.

No. 38.

AN ACT

To provide for the election, qualification and compensation of auditors in the independent school districts of this Commonwealth.

SECTION 1. *Be it enacted, &c.*, That on and after the passage of this act there shall be elected in each independent school district of this Commonwealth three auditors, one to serve for one year, one for two years and one for three years, and annually thereafter, one each year, to serve for the term of three years, to audit and adjust the several school accounts of said district. Three auditors shall be elected.

SECTION 2. That the auditors in said independent school district shall be qualified and shall perform the duties as township and borough auditors are now required by law to do. Duties.

SECTION 3. That from and after the passage of this act the compensation of each independent school district auditor shall be two dollars per diem for each day necessarily employed in the duties of his office, which shall be paid out of the school funds of said district. Compensation.

APPROVED—The 10th day of May, A. D. 1893.

ROBT. E. PATTISON.

—————

No. 39.

AN ACT

To protect the life and limbs of those employed in the construction of new buildings in this Commonwealth.

SECTION 1. *Be it enacted, &c.*, That on and after the passage of this act it shall be the duty of the party or parties having charge of the construction of any new building hereafter erected in this Commonwealth, to have the joists or girders of each floor above the third story covered with rough scaffold boards or other suitable material, as the buildng progresses, so as to sufficiently protect the workmen either from falling through such joists or girders, or to protect the workmen or others who may be under or below each floor from falling bricks, tools, mortar or other substances whereby accidents happen, injuries occur and life and limb are endangered. Joists or girders to be covered.

SECTION 2. That for every violation of this act a penalty, not exceeding one hundred dollars for each floor of joists or girders left uncovered, shall be imposed, to be collected as fines and penalties are usually collected. Penalty for violation.

APPROVED—The 11th day of May, A. D. 1893.

ROBT. E. PATTISON.

No. 40.

AN ACT

To authorize corporations organized for profit under the laws of Pennsylvania, to make allowances or pensions to employés for faithful and long continued service, who, in such service, have become old, infirm or disabled.

SECTION 1. *Be it enacted, &c.*, That from and after the passage of this act corporations organized for profit under the laws of the Commonwealth of Pennsylvania may, out of the earnings of said corporations, grant allowances or pensions to employés for faithful and long continued service, who have, in such service, become old, infirm or disabled:

Provided, That the provisions of this act shall not apply to any director or officer of any such company or corporation.

APPROVED—The 11th day of May, A. D. 1893.

ROBT. E. PATTISON.

———

No. 41.

AN ACT

To amend an act, entitled "An act to amend the eleventh section of an act, entitled 'An act dividing the cities of this State into three classes, regulating the passage of ordinances, providing for contracts for supplies and work for said cities, authorizing the increase of indebtedness, and the creation of a sinking fund to redeem the same, defining and punishing certain offenses in all of said cities, and providing for the incorporation and government of the cities of the third class,'" approved the twenty-sixth day of May, Anno Domini one thousand eight hundred and ninety-one, repealing that part of said section which authorizes councils to draw by lot, yearly, certain municipal bonds.

Section 11, act of May 26. 1891. amended.

SECTION 1. *Be it enacted, &c.*, That the eleventh section of an act, entitled "An act to amend the eleventh section of an act, entitled 'An act dividing the cities of this State into three classes, regulating the passage of ordinances, providing for contracts for supplies and work for said cities, authorizing the increase of indebtedness, and the creation of a sinking fund to redeem the same, defining and punishing certain offenses in all of said cities, and providing for the incorporation and government of cities of the third class,'" approved the twenty-sixth day of May, Anno Domini one thousand eight hundred and ninety one, and which reads as follows:

"SECTION 11. That for the purpose of creating a sinking fund for the gradual extinguishment of the bonds and funded debt of the respective cities of this Commonwealth, the councils of each thereof shall annually (until payment of the bonds and funded debt be fully provided for) levy and collect, in addition to the other taxes of said corporation, a tax of not less than one mill and not exceeding three mills upon the assessed value of the taxable property of each of said cities, to be called the sinking fund tax, which shall be paid into the city treasury and shall be applied towards the extinguishment of said bonds and funded debt in the order of the date of issue thereof, and to no other purpose whatever.

"And the commissioners of the sinking fund shall annually draw, by lot, a number of said bonds equal in amount to the taxes so paid into the city treasury, and shall give public notice by advertisement in at least two newspapers, if there be so many published in said city, once a week for three weeks prior to the said drawing, of the time and place thereof, and shall give notice in like manner and also ten days'notice by mail, to the registered holders thereof of the number of such bonds as may be drawn and of the time and place at which such bonds shall be redeemed at par and accrued interest, and from and after such time all interest on such bonds shall cease.

"The councils of any city of the first class, the debt of which now exceeds seven per centum upon the assessed value of the taxable property therein, shall be and they are hereby authorized to increase the said debt one per centum upon such valuation: *Provided*, That no money shall hereafter be borrowed on the faith and credit of said cities, unless the ordinance or other authority authorizing the same shall have been introduced at one stated meeting of the common council and the draft thereof published in at least two of the newspapers of the city, daily, four weeks before the final consideration and passage thereof by the said common council, and at any stated meetings of the select council, held at least one week after the final consideration of any such ordinance by the common council, the select council may consider and act upon any such ordinance; but the select council shall not originate any ordinance or other authority for borrowing money, and no loan shall be authorized without a vote of two-thirds of the whole number of members of each council: *And provided also*, That the specific purpose or purposes for which the said loan is authorized shall be distinctly set out in the said ordinance, and that the moneys received for said loan shall not be used for any purpose other than those so stated: *And provided further*, That the said city shall, at or before the time of authorizing the said loan, provide for the collection of an annual tax sufficient to pay the interest and also the principal of the said loan within thirty years, and said bonds when so redeemed shall be cancelled,"be amended to read as follows:

Council shall levy a tax not exceeding three mills.

SECTION 11. That for the purpose of creating a sinking fund for the gradual extinguishment of the bonds and funded debt of the respective cities of this Commonwealth, the council of each thereof shall, annually (until payment of the bonds and funded debt be fully provided for) levy and collect, in addition to the other taxes of said corporation, a tax of not less than one mill and not exceeding three mills upon the assessed value of the taxable property of each of said cities, to be called the sinking fund tax, which shall be paid into the city treasury and shall be applied towards the extinguishment of said bonds and funded debt in the order of the date of issue thereof, and to no other purpose whatever.

Cities of first class may increase debt one per centum.

The councils of any city of the first class, the debt of which now exceeds seven per centum upon the assessed value of the taxable property therein, shall be and they are hereby authorized to increase the said debt one per centum upon such valuation : *Provided*, That no money shall hereafter be borrowed on the faith and credit of said cities, unless the ordinance or other authority authorizing the same shall have been introduced at one stated meeting of the common council and the draft thereof published in at least two of the newspapers of the city, daily, four weeks before the final consideration and passage thereof by the said common council, and at any stated meetings of the select council held at least one week after the final consideration of any such ordinance by the common council, the select council may consider and act upon any such ordinance ; but the select council shall not originate any ordinance or other authority for borrowing money, and no loan shall be authorized without a vote of two-thirds of the whole number of members elected to each council : *And provided also*, That the specific purpose or purposes for which the said loan is authorized shall be distinctly set out in the said ordinance, and that the moneys received for said loan shall not be used for any purposes other than those as stated : *And provided further*, That the said city shall, at or before the time of authorizing the said loan, provide for the collection of an annual tax sufficient to pay the interest and also the principal of the said loan within thirty years, and said bonds when so redeemed shall be cancelled.

Introduction and publication of ordinance.

Select councils cannot originate and two-third vote necessary to authorize loan.

Specific purpose of loan must be set out.

Shall provide for the collection of a tax to pay interest, and also the principal.

APPROVED—The 11th day of May, A. D. 1893.

ROBT. E. PATTISON.

No. 42.

AN ACT

To enable borough councils to establish boards of health.

Town council or burgess shall appoint a Board of Health to consist of five persons.

SECTION 1. *Be it enacted, &c.*, That it shall be the duty of the president of the town council, or burgess where he is the presiding officer, of every borough in this Commonwealth, within six months after the passage of this act, to nominate and by and with the consent of the council to appoint a board of health of such borough to consist of five persons not members of the council, one of whom shall be a reputable physician of not less than two years' standing in the practice of his profession. At the first appointment the president of the town council, or burgess where he is the presiding officer, shall designate one of the members to serve for one year, one to serve for two years, one to serve for three years, one to serve for four years and one to serve for five years, and thereafter one member of said board shall be appointed annually to serve for five years. The board shall be appointed by districts to be fixed by the town council, representing as equally as may be all portions of the borough. The members shall serve without compensation.

Length of term of first appointees.

Shall be appointed by districts.

SECTION 2. The duties, responsibilities, powers and prerogatives of said board shall be identical with those assigned to boards of health of cities of the third class, by sections three, four, five, six and seven of article eleven of the act of May twenty-third, one thousand eight hundred and eighty-nine, entitled "An act providing for the incorporation and government of cities of the third class," which reads as follows, due allowance being made for the difference in the municipal government of cities and boroughs:

Duties, etc., of board, how regulated.

SECTION 3. The members of the board shall severally take and subscribe the oath prescribed for borough officers, and shall annually organize by the choice of one of their number as president. They shall elect a secretary, who shall keep the minutes of their proceedings and perform such other duties as may be directed by the board, and a health officer who shall execute the orders of the board, and for that purpose the said health officer shall have and exercise the powers and authority of a policeman of the borough. The secretary and the health officer shall receive such salary as may be fixed by the board, and shall hold their offices during the pleasure of the board. They shall severally give bond to the borough in such sums as may be fixed by ordinance, for the faithful discharge of their duties, and shall also take and subscribe the oath required by the members of the board. All fees which shall be collected or received by the board, or by any officer thereof in his official capacity, shall be paid over into the borough treasury monthly, together with all penalties which shall be recovered for the violation of any regulation of the board. The president and secretary shall have full power to administer oaths or affirmations in any proceedings or investigation touching the regulations of the board, but shall not be entitled to receive any fee therefor.

Members to be sworn and shall organize annually.

Secretary and his duties.

Salaries.

Bonds.

Fees to be paid into borough treasury.

President and Secretary shall have power to administer oaths.

SECTION 4. The said board of health shall have power, and it shall be their duty, to make and enforce all need-

Powers and duties of board as to infectious diseases.

ful rules and regulations to prevent the introduction
and spread of infectious or contagious diseases, by the
regulation of intercourse with infected places, by the
arrest, separation and treatment of infected persons,
and persons who shall have been exposed to any infectious or contagious disease, and by abating and removing all nuisances which they shall deem prejudicial to
'the public health ; to enforce vaccination, to mark infected houses or places, to prescribe rules for the construction and maintenance of house drains, waste-pipes,
soil pipes and cess-pools, and to make all such other
regulations as they shall deem necessary for the pres-

May establish hospitals. ervation of the public health. They shall also have
power with the consent of the councils in case of the
prevalence of any contagious or infectious disease
within the borough to establish one or more hospitals
and to make provision and regulations for the manage-

May appoint district physicians and sanitary agents. ment of the same. The board may in such cases appoint
as many ward or district physicians and other sanitary
agents as they may deem necessary, whose salaries
shall be fixed by the board before their appointment.

Duties of all practicing physicians. It shall be the duty of all physicians practicing within
the borough to report to the secretary of said board of
health the names and residences of all persons coming
under their professional care afflicted with such contagious or infectious disease, in the manner directed by
the said board.

Abatement of nuisances. SECTION 5. The said board of health shall have
power, as a body or by committee, as well as the health
officer, together with his subordinates, assistants and
workmen, under and by order of the said board, to enter
at any time upon any premises in the borough upon
which there is suspected to be any infectious or contagious disease, or nuisance detrimental to the public
health, for the purpose of examining and abating the
same ; and all written orders for the removal of nuisance
issued to the said health officer by order of said board,
attested by the secretary, shall be executed by him and

Costs and expenses. his subordinates and workmen, and the cost and expenses thereof shall be recoverable from the owner or
owners of the premises from which the nuisance shall
be removed, or from any person or persons causing or
maintaining the same, in the same manner as debts of
like amount are now by law collected.

May maintain system of registration of marriages, births and deaths. SECTION 6. The said board of health shall have power
to create and maintain a complete and accurate system
of the registration of all marriages, births and deaths,
which may occur within the borough, and to compel
obedience to the same upon the part of all physicians
and other medical practitioners, clergymen, magistrates,
undertakers, sextons and all other persons from whom
information for such purposes may properly be required.

Board shall publish necessary rules and regulations. The board shall make and cause to be published, all necessary rules and regulations for carrying into effect the
powers and functions with which they are hereby in-

vested, which rules and regulations, when approved by the borough council and chief burgess, and when advertised in the same manner as other ordinances, shall have the force of ordinances of the borough, and all penalties for the violation thereof, as well as expenses necessarily incurred in carrying the same into effect, shall be recoverable for the use of the borough, in the same manner as penalties for the violation of borough ordinances, subject to the like limitation as to the amount thereof.

How penalties etc, shall be recovered.

SECTION 7. It shall be the duty of the board of health to submit annually to the council before the commencement of the fiscal year, an estimate of the probable receipts and expenditures of the board during the ensuing year, and the council shall then proceed to make such appropriation · thereto as they shall deem necessary : and the said board shall, in the month of January of each year, submit a report in writing to the council of its operations for the preceding year, with the necessary statistics thereof, together with such information or suggestions relative to the sanitary condition and requirements of the borough as it may deem proper, and the council shall publish the same in its official journal. It shall also be the duty of the board to communicate to the State Board of Health, at least annually, notice of its organization and membership, and copies of all its reports and publications, together with such sanitary information as may from time to time be required by said State Board.

Board shall submit estimate of probable receipts and expenditures.

Shall submit an annual report.

Communication with State Board of Health

SECTION 8. All acts or parts of act inconsistent with or contrary to the provisions of this act are hereby repealed.

Repeal

APPROVED—-The 11th day of May, A. D. 1893.

ROBT. E. PATTISON.

No. 43.
AN ACT

To repeal an act, entitled "An act to extend the provisions of an act laying a tax on dogs in the borough of West Chester and certain townships in the county of Chester, and for other purposes," approved the fourteenth day of April, one thousand eight hundred and forty-six, to the township of Honeybrook in the county of Chester.

SECTION 1. *Be it enacted, &c.*, That the act of Assembly approved the ninth day of April. one thousand eight hundred and seventy-two, entitled "An act to extend the provisions of an act laying a tax on dogs in the borough of West Chester, and certain township in the county of Chester, and for other purposes," be and the same is hereby repealed, so far as it relates to the township of Honeybrook in the county of Chester.

APPROVED—The 15th day of May, A. D. 1893.

ROBT. E. PATTISON.

No. 44.

AN ACT

To authorize meadow companies controlling contiguous districts to be consolidated into one company.

Two or more companies may consolidate by agreement. SECTION 1. *Be it enacted, &c.,* That where the districts of two or more meadow companies are contiguous to each other, it shall be lawful for them to consolidate their franchises and corporate rights and to become one company, by an agreement duly executed and recorded in the office for recording of deeds in each county in which the districts of said meadow companies shall extend.

Manner of consolidation where lands of a company lie in more than one county. SECTION 2. It shall also be lawful for the court of common pleas of any county in which the major part of the lands of any meadow company may lie, upon the application of the said company, to decree the consolidation of said company with any other meadow company controlling contiguous territory, whenever in the opinion of said court such consolidation would enure to the public interest; and the said decree shall be recorded in the office for recording deeds in each county into which the districts of said meadow companies shall extend.

Name of consolidated company. SECTION 3. In case of consolidation of two or more meadow companies by agreement or by decree as aforesaid, the consolidated company shall be known by the name and be subject to all the provisions of the charter of that one of the original companies which controlled the larger territory prior to the consolidation.

APPROVED—The 15th day of May, A. D. 1893.

ROBT. E. PATTISON.

No. 45.

AN ACT

To repeal an act, entitled "A supplement to the act, entitled 'An act to diminish the number of justices of the peace and supervisors in the township of South Coventry, Chester county,'" approved the sixth day of March, one thousand eight hundred and forty-nine.

SECTION 1. *Be it enacted, &c.,* That the act, entitled "A supplement to the act, entitled 'An act to diminish the number of justices of the peace and supervisors in the township of South Coventry, Chester county,'" approved the sixth day of March, Anno Domini one thousand eight hundred and forty-nine, be and the same is hereby repealed.

APPROVED—The 15th day of May, A. D. 1893.

ROBT. E. PATTISON.

No. 46.

AN ACT

To repeal an act, entitled "An act relative to roads and supervisors in the townships of Pennsbury and Pocopson, Chester county, and George township, Fayette county," approved March twenty-second, one thousand eight hundred and fifty.

SECTION 1. *Be it enacted, &c.*, That so much of the act of Assembly approved the twenty-second day of March, one thousand eight hundred and fifty, entitled "An act relative to roads and supervisors in the townships of Pennsbury and Pocopson, Chester county, and George township, Fayette county," is hereby repealed, so far as it relates to the township of Pennsbury, Chester county.

APPROVED—The 15th day of May, A. D. 1893.

ROBT. E. PATTISON.

No. 47.

AN ACT

For the establishment and government of a State Naval Militia.

SECTION 1. *Be it enacted, &c.*, That when, in conformity with the military code, an enrollment of persons subject to military duty shall be made, there shall be separately enrolled and designated as Naval Militia in such districts as the Commander-in-Chief may designate, all seafaring men of whatsoever calling or occupation, and all men engaged in navigation of the rivers, lakes and other waters, all persons engaged in the construction and management of ships and crafts, or any part thereof, upon such waters, together with ship owners, members of yacht clubs and all other associations for aquatic pursuits, and all ex-officers and former enlisted men of the United States Navy subject to the existing qualifications for and exemption from enrollment for Military Service in the National Guard. *(Who shall be enrolled as Naval Militia.)*

SECTION 2. As a part of the Naval National Guard authorized by law, and in addition to the National Guard, there may be Naval Battalions organized by voluntary enlistment for the defense of the coasts, lakes and harbors. In time of peace there shall not be maintained more than two such battalions organized as herein provided, and which shall constitute a regiment to be known as the Naval Force of the State of Pennsylvania; but the Commander-in-Chief shall have power in case of war, insurrection, invasion or imminent danger thereof to increase the said force beyond such limit of two battalions and to organize the same as the exigencies of the service may require. The Commander-i *(Naval battalions may be organized. But two battalions in time of peace, which may be increased in time of war. Powers of the Commander-in-Chief.)*

4—LAWS.

Chief may alter, annex, divide, consolidate or disband the said Naval Force or any battalions or divisions thereof, whenever, in his judgment, the efficiency of the State service will be thereby increased.

Officers of Naval Force and of the battalions.

SECTION 3. The Naval Force shall be commanded by a Captain who shall be chosen and commissioned as soon as two battalions are fully organized. To each battalion there shall be one commander who shall command the same, one lieutenant-commander to act as executive officer and one lieutenant to act as navigator. Each battalion shall consist of four divisions or companies, and an engineer corps to each division; there shall be one lieutenant to command the same, two lieutenants, junior grade, two ensigns and forty-two petty officers and seamen as a minimum and eighty-four pettty officers and seamen as a maximum to each engineer corps; there shall be allowed one lieutenant to command the same, one ensign and twelve petty officers and seamen as a minimum and twenty petty officers and seamen as a maximum to each battalion and division thereof; there shall be allowed such and so many petty officers as the Commander-in-Chief may from time to time determine.

Staff of captain.

SECTION 4. The captain shall have power to appoint a staff to consist of one aide, one ordnance officer, one chief of engineers, one paymaster and one surgeon, each with the rank of lieutenant. The commanding officer of each battalion shall have power to appoint a staff to consist of one aide, one paymaster and one surgeon, each with the rank of lieutenant, junior grade, and one assistant surgeon with the rank of ensign.

Staff of commanding officer of battalion.

How officers shall be chosen and shall qualify.

SECTION 5. Commissioned and non-commissioned officers of the Naval Force shall be chosen and shall qualify as required by the existing military code of Pennsylvania for officers of the same relative rank in the National Guard. The rank given in this act is naval rank as the same now exists in the Navy in the United States.

Rank.

Duty and pay of officers and enlisted men.

SECTION 6. Officers and enlisted men of the Naval Force shall perform such duty or service as may be ordered by the Commander in-Chief, and shall be paid the same compensation as is allowed to officers and enlisted men, have the same relative rank or position in the National Guard for performing similar duty or service, but they shall not receive any compensation from the State for duty performed by way of instruction or drill or otherwise, for which they shall receive compensation from the United States. The uniform of the Naval Force and the insignia and designation of grade and rank shall be prescribed by the Commander-in-Chief, who may change and modify the same from time to time.

Uniform.

Discipline, duty and exercises.

SECTION 7. The system of discipline, routine of duty and exercises of the Naval Force shall conform generally with the existing laws governing the National

Guard of the State of Pennsylvania, so far as the same may apply to the Naval Force, and where the same does not apply the discipline, duty and exercises, shall conform generally to the laws, customs and usages governing the Navy of the United States. The Commander-in-Chief is hereby authorized to make such rules and regulations from time to time as he may deem expedient for the government, assignment and instruction of the Naval Force, but such regulations shall conform to this act and as nearly as practicable to those governing the United States Navy and when promulgated they shall have the same force and effect as the provisions of this act. The Naval Force shall be subject to the articles and regulations for the government of the United States Navy, to the same extent as members of the National Guard are subject to the articles of war and regulations for the government of the United States Army. *Commander-in-Chief may make certain rules.* *How far U. S. Navy regulations apply.*

SECTION 8. The appointment, composition and powers of naval boards, delinquency courts, courts of inquiry and courts martial shall be as is now provided for the Military Code of Pennsylvania for similar bodies in the National Guard. *Naval boards, delinquency courts etc.*

SECTION 9. The divisions of each battalion in the Naval Force shall be considered the equivalents of companies of the National Guard and shall receive the same allowances for armory rent, for rifle practice, for clothing and equipment as are received by such companies. The battalions shall be treated as battalions in the National Guard, and shall be entitled to all allowances of such battalions for armory rent, rifle practice, clothing and equipment. The Naval Force, when organized, shall be entitled to all the privileges and allowances of a regiment of the National Guard. The word "armory" as used in this act and in the Military Code of Pennsylvaina shall be held to include a vessel anchored, moored or secured to the land while used only as an armory for the purposes of instruction, drill or defense. *Allowances for divisions of each battalion.* *Allowances for each battalion.* *The word "armory" defined*

SECTION 10. The members of each battalion and division of the Naval Force may form themselves into an organization and adopt by-laws in the same manner, with the same powers and subject to the same limitations, as are now prescribed for members of companies in the National Guard. *By-laws.*

SECTION 11. The act, entitled "An act to constitute a battalion to be known as the Naval Battalion of the National Guard of Pennsylvania," approved the twenty-sixth day of April, Anno Domini one thousand eight hundred and eighty-nine, is hereby repealed. *Repeal of act of April 6, 1889*

APPROVED—The 15th day of May, A. D. 1893.

ROBT. E. PATTISON.

No. 48.

AN ACT

Relating to bituminous coal mines, and providing for the lives, health, safety and welfare of persons employed therein.

ARTICLE I.

Survey Maps and Plans.

Shall make map of mine.

SECTION 1. *Be it enacted, &c.*, That the operator or superintendent of every bituminous coal mine shall make, or cause to be made by a competent mining engineer or surveyor, an accurate map or plan of such coal mine, not smaller than a scale of two hundred feet to an inch, which map shall show as follows:

What shall be shown on map.

First. All measurements of said mine in feet or decimal parts thereof.

Second. All the openings, excavations, shafts, tunnels, slopes, planes, main-entries, cross-entries, rooms et cetera, in proper numerical order in each opened strata of coal in said mine.

Third. By darts or arrows made thereon by a pen or pencil the direction of air currents in the said mine.

Fourth. An accurate delineation of the boundary lines between said coal mine and all adjoining mines or coal lands, whether owned or operated by the same operator or other operator, and the relation and proximity of the workings of said mine to every other adjoining mine or coal lands.

Fifth. The elevation above mean tide at Sandy Hook of all tunnels and entries, and of the face of working places adjacent to boundary lines at points not exceeding three hundred feet apart.

Sixth. The bearings and lengths of each tunnel or entry and of the boundary or property lines. The said map or plan, or a true copy thereof, shall be kept in the general mine office by the said operator or superintendent for use of the mine inspectors and for the inspection of any person or persons working in said mine, whenever said person or persons shall have cause to fear that any working place is becoming dangerous by reason of its proximity to other workings that may contain water or dangerous gas.

Map must be corrected every six months.

SECTION 2. At least once in every six months, or oftener if necessary, the operator or superintendent of each mine shall cause to be shown accurately on the map or plan of said coal mine, all the excavations made therein during the time elapsing since such excavations were last shown upon said map or plan; and all parts of said mine which were worked out or abandoned during said elapsed period of time shall be clearly indicated by colorings on said map or plan; and whenever any of

Workings abandoned and workings completed must be put on map immediately

the workings or excavations of said coal mine have been driven to their destination, a correct measurement of all such workings or excavations shall be made promptly and recorded in a survey book prior to the removal of the pillars or any part of the same from such workings or excavations.

SECTION 3. The operator or superintendent of every coal mine shall, within six month after the passage of this act, furnish the mine inspector of the district in which said mine is located with a correct copy, on tracing muslin or sun print, of the map or plan of said mine hereinbefore provided for. And the inspector of the district shall, at the end of each year or twice a year if he requires it, forward said map or plan to the proper person at any particular mine, whose duty it shall be to place or caused to be placed on said map or plan all extensions and worked out or abondoned parts of the mine during the preceding six or twelve months, as the case may be, and return the same to the mine inspector within thirty days from the time of receiving it. The copies of the maps or plans of the several coal mines of each district as hereinbefore required to be furnished to the mine inspector shall remain in the care of the inpector of the district in which the said mines are situated, as official records, to be transferred by him to his successor in office; but it is provided that in no case shall any copy of the same be made without the consent of the operator or his agent.

SECTION 4. If any superintendent or operator of mines shall neglect or fail to furnish to the mine inspector any copies of maps or plans as hereinbefore required by this act, or if the mine inspector shall believe that any map or plan of any coal mine made or furnished in pursuance of the provisions of this act is materially inaccurate or imperfect, then, in either case, the mine inspector is hereby authorized to cause a correct survey and map or plan of said coal mine to be made at the expense of the operator thereof, the cost of which shall be recoverable from said operator as other debts are recoverable by law: *Provided however*, That if the map or plan which may be claimed by the mine inspector to be inaccurate shall prove to be correct, then the Commonwealth shall be liable for the expense incurred by the mine inspector in causing to be made said test survey and map, and the costs thereof, ascertained by the Auditor General by proper vouchers and satisfactory proofs, shall be paid by the State Treasurer upon warrants which the said Auditor General is hereby directed to draw for the same.

ARTICLE II.

SECTION 1. It shall not be lawful for the operator, superintendent or mine foreman of any bituminous coal mine to employ more than twenty persons within said coal mine, or permit more than twenty persons to be employed therein at any one time, unless they are in

---

Marginal notes:

Mine inspector must be furnished with map.

Inspector shall have map corrected.

Maps, &c., shall remain in care of the inspector, and be transferred by him to his successor.

Copy of maps shall not be made without consent of owner.

If operator fails to furnish map, or if same be incorrect, the inspector shall have new map made at expense of operator.

If original map shall prove to be correct, the Commonwealth shall be liable for the expense of test survey and map.

Where twenty persons are employed, there must be at least two openings to surface.

communication with at least two available openings to the surface from each seam or stratum of coal worked in such mine exclusive of the furnace upcast, shaft or slope : *But provided*, That in any mine operated by shaft or slope and ventilated by a fan, if the air shaft shall be divided into two compartments, one of them may be used for an air-way and the other for the purpose of egress and ingress from and into said mine by the persons therein employed and the same shall be considered a compliance with the provisions of this section hereinbefore set forth. And there shall be cut out or around the side of every hoisting shaft, or driven through the solid strata at the bottom thereof, a traveling way not less than five feet high and three feet wide to enable persons to pass the shaft in going from one side of it to the other without passing over or under the cage or other hoisting apparatus.

Except where the air shaft shall be divided into two compartments.

Travelling way shall be provided around or through strata at bottom of shaft.

SECTION 2. The shaft or outlet, other than the main shaft or outlet, shall be separated from the main outlet and from the furnace shaft by natural strata at all points by a distance of not less than one hundred and fifty feet (except in all mines opened prior to June thirtieth, one thousand eight hundred and eighty-five, where such distances may be less, if, in the judgment of the mine inspector, one hundred and fifty feet is impracticable). If the mine be worked by drift, two openings, exclusive of the furnace upcast shaft, and not less than thirty feet apart shall be required (except in drift mines opened prior to June thirtieth, one thousand eight hundred and eighty-five, where the mine inspector of the district shall deem the same impracticable). Where the two openings shall not have been provided as required hereinbefore by this act, the mine inspector shall cause the second to be made without delay ; and in no case shall furnace ventilation be used where there is only one opening into the mine.

Separation of shaft or outlet from main outlet and furnace shaft.

Two openings required if mine be worked by drift.

If but one opening is provided.

SECTION 3. Unless the mine inspector shall deem it impracticable, all mines shall have at least two entries or other passage ways, one of which shall lead from the main entrance and the other from the other opening into the body of the mine, and said two passage ways shall be kept well drained and in a safe condition for persons to travel therein throughout their whole length so as to obtain, in cases of emergency, a second way for egress from the workings. No part of said workings shall at any time be driven more than three hundred feet in advance of the aforesaid passage ways, except entries, air ways or other narrow work, but should an opening to the surface be provided from the interior of the mine, the passage ways aforesaid may be made and maintained therefrom into the working part of the mine, and this shall be deemed sufficient compliance with the provisions of this act relative thereto ; said two passage ways shall be separated by pillars of coal or other strata of sufficient strength and width.

Each mine shall have two entries.

No workings shall be driven more than 300 feet in advance of passage ways.

Two passage ways shall be separated by pillars or strata.

SECTION 4. Where necessary to secure access to the two passage ways required in section three of article two of this act in any slope mine where the coal seam inclines and has workings on both sides of said slope, there shall be provided an overcast for the use of persons working therein, the dimensions of which shall not be less than four feet wide and five feet high. Said overcast shall connect the workings on both sides of said slope and the intervening strata between the slope and the overcast shall be of sufficient strength and thickness at all points for its purpose: *Provided*, That if said overcast be substantially constructed of masonry or other incombustible material it shall be deemed sufficient. *(Overcast shall be provided.)* *(Construction of overcast.)*

SECTION 5. When the opening or outlet, other than the main opening, is made and does not exceed seventy-five feet in vertical depth, it shall be set apart exclusively for the purpose of ingress to or egress from the mine by any person or persons employed therein; it shall be kept in a safe and available condition and free from steam and dangerous gases and all other obstructions, and if such opening is a shaft it shall be fitted with safe and convenient stairs with steps of an average tread of ten inches and nine inches rise, not less than two feet wide and to not exceed an angle of sixty degrees descent with landings of not less than eighteen inches wide and four feet long, at easy and convenient distances: *Provided*, That the requirements of this section shall not be applicable to stairways in use prior to June thirtieth, one thousand eight hundred and eighty-five, when, in the judgment of the mine inspector, they are sufficiently safe and convenient. And water coming from the surface or out of the strata in the shaft shall be conducted away by rings, casing or otherwise and be prevented from falling upon persons who are ascending or descending the stairway of the shaft. *(Opening or outlet, and how same shall be kept, when not exceeding seventy-five feet in depth.)* *(Shall be fitted with stairs.)* *(Proviso.)* *(Water shall be conducted away.)*

SECTION 6. Where any mine is operated by a shaft which exceeds seventy-five feet in vertical depth, the persons employed in said mine shall be lowered into and raised from said mine by means of machinery, and in any such mine the shaft, other than the main shaft, shall be supplied with safe and suitable machinery for hoisting and lowering persons, or with safe and convenient stairs for use in cases of emergency by persons employed in said mine: *Provided*, That any mine operated by two shafts, and where safe and suitable machinery is provided at both shafts for hoisting coal or persons, shall have sufficiently complied with the requirements of this section. *(Where shaft exceeds seventy-five feet in depth.)* *(Proviso)*

SECTION 7. At any mine, where one of the two openings required hereinbefore is a slope and is used as a traveling way, it shall not have a greater angle of descent than twenty degrees and may be of any depth. *(Where one of the two openings is a slope.)*

SECTION 8. The machinery used for lowering or raising the employés into or out of the mine and the stairs used for ingress and egress shall be kept in a safe condition, and inspected once each twenty-four hours by a competent person employed for that purpose. And such machinery and the method of its inspection shall be approved by the mine inspector of the district in which the mine is situated.

Machinery for hoisting, &c., and stairs in shaft must be inspected every twenty-four hours.

Machinery must be approved by mine inspector.

ARTICLE III.

Hoisting Machinery, Safety Catches, Signaling Apparatus et cetera.

Metal speaking and signalling tube must be maintained in every shaft.

SECTION 1. The operator or superintendent shall provide and maintain, from the top to bottom of every shaft where persons are raised or lowered, a metal tube suitably adapted to the free passage of sound through which conversation may be held between persons at the top and bottom of said shaft, and also a means of signaling from the top to the bottom thereof, and shall provide every cage or gear carriage used for hoisting or lowering persons with a sufficient overhead covering to protect those persons when using the same, and shall provide also for each said cage or carriage a safety catch approved by the mine inspector. And the said operator or superintendent shall see that flanges, with a clearance of not less than four inches, when the whole of the rope is wound on the drum, are attached to the sides of the drum of every machine that is used for lowering and hoisting persons in and out of the mine, and also that adequate brakes are attached to the drum. At all shafts safety gates, to be approved by the mine inspector of the district, shall be so placed as to prevent persons from falling into the shaft.

Cage must have an overhead covering.

Drum and brakes of hoisting machine.

Safety gates.

Coupling chain

SECTION 2. The main coupling chain attached to the socket of the wire rope shall be made of the best quality of iron and shall be tested by weights or otherwise to the satisfaction of the mine inspector of the district wherein the mine is located, and bridle chains shall be attached to the main hoisting rope above the socket, from the top cross-piece of the carriage or cage, so that no single chain shall be used for lowering or hoisting persons into or out of the mines.

Bridle chain.

Number of persons to be lowered or hoisted, shall be regulated by mine inspector and notice shall be posted.

SECTION 3. No greater number of persons shall be lowered or hoisted at any one time than may be permitted by the mine inspector of the district, and notice of the number so allowed to be lowered or hoisted at any one time shall be kept posted up by the operator or superintendent in conspicuous places at the top and bottom of the shaft, and the aforesaid notice shall be signed by the mine inspector of the district.

Machinery shall be fenced off.

SECTION 4. All machinery about mines from which any accident would be liable to occur shall be properly fenced off by suitable guard railing.

ARTICLE IV.

SECTION 1. The operator or superintendent of every bituminous coal mine, whether shaft, slope or drift, shall provide and hereafter maintain ample means of ventilation for the circulation of air through the main entries, cross-entries and all other working places to an extent that will dilute, carry off and render harmless the noxious or dangerous gases generated in the mine, affording not less than one hundred cubic feet per minute for each and every person employed therein; but in a mine where fire-damp has been detected the minimum shall be one hundred and fifty cubic feet per minute for each person employed therein, and as much more in either case as one or more of the mine inspectors may deem requisite.

SECTION 2. After May thirtieth, one thousand eight hundred and ninety-four, not more than sixty-five persons shall be permitted to work in the same air current: *Provided*, That a larger number, not exceeding one hundred, may be allowed by the mine inspector where, in his judgment, it is impracticable to comply with the foregoing requirement; and mines where more than ten persons are employed shall be provided with a fan furnace or other artificial means to produce the ventilation, and all stoppings between main intake and return air-ways hereinafter built or replaced shall be substantially built with suitable material, which shall be approved by the inspector of the district.

SECTION 3. All ventilating fans shall be kept in operation continuously night and day, unless operations are indefinitely suspended, except written permission is given by the mine inspector of the district to stop the same, and the said written permission shall state the particular hours the said fan may not be in operation, and the mine inspector shall have power to withdraw or modify such permission as he may deem best, but in all cases the fan shall be started two hours before the time to begin work. When the fan may be stopped by permission of the mine inspector a notice printed in the various languages used by persons employed in the mine, stating at what hour or hours the fan will be stopped, shall be posted by the mine foreman in a conspicuous place at the entrance or entrances to the mine.

Said printed notices shall be furnished by the mine inspector and the cost thereof borne by the State: *Provided*, That should it at any time become necessary to stop the fan on account of accident or needed repairs to any part of the machinery connected therewith, or by reason of any other unavoidable cause, it shall then be the duty of the mine foreman or any other officials in charge, after first having provided, as far as possible, for the safety of the persons employed in the mine, to order said fan to be stopped so as to make the necessary repairs or to remove any other difficulty that

[Margin notes: Ventilation of slope or drift. — Minimum number of cubic feet per minute. — Number of persons permitted to work in same air current. — Proviso. — Ventilating fans. — Stopping of fans. — Notices to be posted when fans are stopped. — Notices to be furnished by mine inspector. — Sudden stopping of fans.]

Ventilating furnaces.

may have been the cause of its stoppage. And all ventilating furnaces in mines shall, for two hours before the appointed time to begin work and during working hours, be properly attended by a person employed for that purpose. In mines generating fire-damp in sufficient quantities to be detected by ordinary safety lamps, all main air bridges or overcasts made after the passage of this act shall be built of masonry or other incombustible material of ample strength or be driven through the solid strata.

Air bridges and overcasts in mines generating fire damp.

Ventilating doors.

In all mines the doors used in guiding and directing the ventilation of the mine shall be so hung and adjusted that they will close themselves, or be supplied with spring or pulleys so that they cannot be left standing open, and an attendant shall be employed at all principal doors through which cars are hauled, for the purpose of opening and closing said doors when trips of cars are passing to and from the workings, unless an approved self-acting door is used, which principal doors shall be determined by the mine inspector or mine foreman. A hole for shelter shall be provided at each door so as to protect said attendant from being run over by the cars while attending to his duties, and persons employed for this purpose shall at all times remain at their post of duty during working hours: *Provided*, That the same person may attend two doors where the distance between them is not more than one hundred feet. On every inclined plane or road in any mine where haulage is done by machinery and where a door is used, an extra door shall be provided to be used in case of necessity.

Hole for shelter.

Proviso.

Extra doors.

ARTICLE V.

Safety Lamps, Fire Bosses et cetera.

Standing gas in mines generating fire damps.

Accumulation of explosive gas not allowed to exist.

SECTION 1. All mines generating fire-damp shall be kept free of standing gas in all working places and roadways. No accumulation of explosive gas shall be allowed to exist in the worked out or abandoned parts of any mine when it is practicable to remove it, and the entrance or entrances to said worked out and abandoned places shall be properly fenced off and cautionary notices shall be posted upon said fencing to warn persons of danger.

Mines generating explosive gas and fire damp.

SECTION 2. In all mines wherein explosive gas has been generated within the period of six months next preceding the passage of this act, and also in all mines where fire-damp shall be generated, after the passage of this act, in sufficient quantities to be detected by the ordinary safety lamp, every working place without exception and all roadways shall be carefully examined immediately before each shift by competent person or persons appointed by the superintendent and mine foreman for that purpose. The person or persons making such examination shall have received a fire boss certificate of competency required by this act, and shall' use no light other than that enclosed in a safety lamp while making said examination. In all cases said examination shall be begun within three hours prior to the appointed time of each shift commencing to work, and it shall be the duty of the said fire boss, at each examination, to leave at the face and side of every place so examined, evidence of his presence. And he shall also, at each examination, inspect the entrance or entrances to the worked out or abandoned parts which are adjacent to the roadways and working places of the mine where fire-damp is likely to accumulate, and where danger is found to exist he shall place a danger signal at the entrance or entrances to such places, which shall be sufficient warning for persons not to enter said place.

SECTION 3. In any place that is being driven towards or in dangerous proximity to an abandoned mine or part of a mine suspected of containing inflammable gases, or which may be inundated with water, bore holes shall be kept not less than twelve feet in advance of the face, and on the sides of such working places, said side holes to be drilled diagonally not more than eight feet apart, and any place driven to tap water or gas shall not be more than ten feet wide, and no water or gas from an abandoned mine or part of a mine and no bore hole from the surface shall be tapped until the employés, except those engaged at such work, are out of the mine and such work to be done under the immediate instruction of the mine foreman.

SECTION 4. The fire boss shall, at each entrance to the mine or in the main intake air-way near to the mine entrance, prepare a permanent station with the proper danger signal designated by suitable letters and colors placed thereon, and it shall not be lawful for any person or persons, except the mine officials in cases of necessity, and such other persons as may be designated by them, to pass beyond said danger station until the mine has been examined by the fire boss as aforesaid and the same, or certain parts thereof, reported by him to be safe, and in all mines where operations are temporarily suspended the superintendent and mine foreman shall see that a danger signal be placed at the mine entrance or entrances, which shall be a sufficient warning to persons not to enter the mine, and if the ordinary circulation of air through the mine be stopped each entrance to said mine shall be securely fenced off and a danger signal shall be displayed upon said fence and any workman or other person, (except those persons hereinbefore provided for), passing by any danger signal into the mine before it has been examined and reported to be safe as aforesaid, shall be deemed guilty of a misdemeanor and it shall be the duty of the

Marginal notes:

Examination to be made by fire boss.

Time of examination.

Shall mark places examined.

Shall examine worked out or abandoned parts and place danger signal.

Bore holes in places driven towards abandoned mines, or mines which may contain gases.

Permanent station with proper danger signal at entrance to mine.

Placing of danger signals when operations are temporarily suspended.

If circulation of air is stopped entrance shall be fenced off.

Penalty for passing danger signal.

fire boss, mine foreman, superintendent or any employé of the mine to forthwith notify the mine inspector, who shall enter proceedings against such person or persons as provided for in section two of article twenty-one of this act.

SECTION 5. All entries, tunnels, air-ways, traveling ways and other working places of a mine where explosive gas is being generated in such quantities as can be detected by the ordinary safety lamp, and pillar workings and other working places in any mine where a sudden inflow of said explosive gas is likely to be encountered, (by reason of the subsidence of the overlying strata or from other causes), shall be worked exclusively with locked safety lamps. The use of open

lights is also prohibited in all working places, roadways or other parts of the mine through which firedamp might be carried in the air current in dangerous quantities. In all mines or parts of mines worked with

locked safety lamps, the use of electric wires and electric currents is positively prohibited, unless said wires and machinery and all other mechanical devices attached thereto and connected therewith are constructed and protected in such a manner as to secure freedom from the emission of sparks or flame therefrom into the atmosphere of the mine.

SECTION 6. After January first, one thousand eight hundred and ninety-four, the use of the common Davy safety lamp for general work in any bituminous coal mine is hereby prohibited, neither shall the Clanny lamp be so used unless its gauze is thoroughly protected by a metallic shield, but this act does not prohibit the use of the Davy and Clanny lamps by the mine officials for the purpose of examining the workings for gas.

SECTION 7. All safety lamps used for examining mines or for working therein shall be the property of the operator, and shall be in the care of the mine foreman, his assistant or fire boss or other competent person, who shall clean, fill, trim, examine and deliver the same, locked, in a safe condition, to the men when entering the mine before each shift and shall receive the same from the men at the end of each shift, for which service a charge not exceeding cost of labor and mate-

rial may be made by the operator. A sufficient number of safety lamps, but not less than twenty-five per centum of those in use, shall be kept at each mine where gas has at any time been generated in sufficient quantities to be detected by an ordinary safety lamp,

for use in case of emergency. It shall be the duty of every person who knows his safety lamp to be injured or defective to promptly report such fact to the party authorized herein to receive and care for said lamps, and it shall be the duty of that party to promptly report such fact to the mine foreman.

ARTICLE VI.

Mine Foreman and His Duties.

SECTION 1. In order to better secure the proper venti- Inside overseer shall be employed to be called mine foreman, who shall look after ventilation. lation of the bituminous coal mines and promote the health and safety of the persons employed therein, the operator or superintendent shall employ a competent and practical inside overseer for each and every mine, to be called mine foreman; said mine foreman shall Requirements for mine foreman. have passed an examination and obtained a certificate of competency or of service as required by this act and shall be a citizen of the United States and an experienced coal miner, and said mine foreman shall devote the whole of his time to his duties at the mine when in operation, or in case of his necessary absence, an assistant chosen by him, and shall keep a careful watch over Duties. the ventilating apparatus and the air-ways, traveling ways, pump and pump timbers and drainage, and shall often instruct, and as far as possible, see that as the miners advance their excavations all dangerous coal, slate and rock overhead are taken down or carefully secured against falling therein, or on the traveling and hauling ways, and that sufficient props, caps and timbers of suitable size are sent into the mine when required, and all props shall be cut square at both ends, and as near as practicable to a proper length for the places where they are to be used, and such props, caps and timbers shall be delivered in the working places of the mine.

SECTION 2. Every workman in want of props or tim- Props or timbers and cap pieces. bers and cap pieces shall notify the mine foreman or his assistant of the fact at least one day in advance, giving the length and number of props or timbers and cap pieces required, but in cases of emergency the timbers may be ordered immediately upon the discovery of any danger. (The place and manner of leaving the orders for the timber shall be designated and specified in the rules of the mine.) And if, from any If timbers cannot be supplied when needed, work shall be stopped. cause, the timbers cannot be supplied when required, he shall instruct the persons to vacate all said working places until supplied with the timber needed, and shall see that all water be drained or hauled out of all working places before the miner enters and as far as practicable kept dry while the miner is at work.

SECTION 3. It shall be the duty of the mine foreman Cut-throughs for ventilation. to see that proper cut-throughs are made in all the rooms, pillars at such distances apart as in the judgment of the mine inspector may be deemed requisite, not more than thirty-five nor less than sixteen yards each, for the purpose of ventilation, and the ventilation How ventilation shall be conducted. shall be conducted through said cut-throughs into the rooms by means of check doors made of canvas or other suitable material, placed on the entries or in other suitable places, and he shall not permit any room to be opened in advance of the ventilating current.

Should the mine inspector discover any room, entry, air-way or other working places being driven in advance of the air current contrary to the requirements of this section, he shall order the workmen working in such places to cease work at once until the law is complied with.

SECTION 4. In all hauling roads, on which hauling is done by animal power, and whereon men have to pass to and from their work, holes for shelter, which shall be kept clear of obstruction, shall be made at least every thirty yards and be kept whitewashed, but shelter holes shall not be required in entries from which rooms are driven at regular intervals not exceeding fifty feet, where there is a space four feet between the wagon and rib, it shall be deemed sufficient for shelter. On all hauling roads whereon hauling is done by machinery, and all gravity or inclined planes inside mines upon which the persons employed in the mine must travel on foot to and from their work, such shelter holes shall be cut not less than two feet six inches into the strata and not more than fifteen yards apart, unless there is a space of at least six feet from the side of the car to the side of the roadway, which space shall be deemed sufficient for shelter:

Provided, That this requirement shall not apply to any parts of mines, which parts were opened prior to the passage of this act, if deemed impracticable by the mine inspector.

SECTION 5. The mine foreman shall measure the air current at least once a week at the inlet and outlet and at or near the faces of the entries, and shall keep a record of such measurements. An anemometer shall be provided for this purpose by the operator of the mine.

It shall be the further duty of the mine foreman to require the workmen to use locked safety lamps when and where required by this act.

SECTION 6. The mine foreman shall give prompt attention to the removal of all dangers reported to him by the fire boss or any other person working in the mine, and in mines where a fire boss is not employed,

the said mine foreman or his assistant shall visit and examine every working place therein at least once every alternate day while the miners of such place are or should be at work, and shall direct that each and every working place be properly secured by props or timbers, and that no person shall be directed or permitted to work in an unsafe place unless it be for the purpose of making it safe:

Provided, That if the owner or operator of any mine employing a fire boss shall require the mine foreman to examine every working place every alternate day, then it shall be the duty of the mine foreman to do so.

SECTION 7. When the mine foreman is unable personally, to carry out all the requirements of this act as pertaining to his duties, he shall employ a compe-

teut person or persons not objectionable to the operator, to act as his assistant or assistants, who shall act
under his instructions, and in all mines where fire-
damp is generated the said assistant or assistants shall
possess a certificate of competency as mine foreman or
fire boss.

SECTION 8. A suitable record book, with printed head
lines, prepared by and approved by the mine inspector,
the same to be provided at the expense of the Commonwealth, shall be kept at each mine generating explosive gases, and immediately after each examination
of the mine made by the fire boss or fire bosses, a record of the same shall be entered in said book, signed
by the person or persons making such examination,
which shall clearly state the nature and location of any
danger which he or they may have discovered, and the
fire boss or fire bosses shall immediately report such
danger and the location of the same to the mine foreman, whose duty it shall be to remove the danger or
cause the same to be done forthwith as far as practicable, and the mine foreman shall also each day countersign all reports entered by the fire boss or fire bosses.
At all mines the mine foreman shall enter in a book
provided as above by the mine inspector, a report of
the condition of the mine signed by himself, which
shall clearly state any danger that may have come
under his observation during the day, and shall also
state whether he has a proper supply of material on
hand for the safe working of the mine, and whether all
requirements of the law are strictly complied with.
He shall, once each week, enter or cause to be entered
plainly, with ink, in said book, a true record of all air
measurements required by this act, and such book
shall, at all times, be kept at the mine office for examination by the mine inspector of the district and any
other person working in the mines.

Record book shall be provided for making record of examinations by mine inspector.

Danger shall be reported to the mine foreman.

Record of air measurements.

ARTICLE VII.

Timbers and Other Mine Supplies et cetera.

SECTION 1. It shall be the duty of the superintendent,
on behalf and at the expense of the operator, to keep
on hand at the mines at all times, a full supply of all
materials and supplies required to preserve the health
and safety of the employés as ordered by the mine foreman and required by this act. He shall, at least once a
week, examine and countersign—(which countersigna-
ture of the superintendent shall be held, under this act,
to have no further bearing than the evidence of the
fact that the mine superintendent has read the matter
entered on the book)—all reports entered in the mine
record book, and if he finds that the law is being vio-
lated in any particular, he shall order the mine foreman to comply with its provisions forthwith. If from

Full supply of materials &c., required to preserve the health of employees shall be kept on hand.

Superintendent shall examine and countersign all reports.

If necessary supplies cannot be procured. men shall be withdrawn from mine.

any cause he cannot procure the necessary supplies or material as aforesaid, he shall notify the mine foreman, whose duty it shall be to withdraw the men from the mine or part of mine until such supplies or material are received.

Superintendent shall not obstruct mine foreman or other officials.

SECTION 2. The superintedent of the mine shall not obstruct the mine foreman or other officials in their fulfillment of any of the duties required by this act. At mines where superintendents are not employed, the duties that are herein prescribed for the superintendent shall devolve upon the mine foreman.

ARTICLE VIII.

Steam Boilers, Stables, Regulations for the Use of Oil, Powder et cetera.

Ventilating fan in mine where gas has been detected.

SECTION 1. After the passage of this act, it shall be unlawful to place a main or principal ventilating fan inside of any bituminous coal mine wherein explosive gas has been detected or in which the air current is contaminated with coal dust. No stationary steam boiler shall be placed in any bituminous coal mine, unless said steam boiler be placed within fifty feet from the bottom of an up-cast shaft, which shaft shall not be less than twenty-five square feet in area, and after May thirtieth, one thousand eight hundred and ninety-five, no stationary steam boiler shall be permitted to remain in any bituminous coal mine, only as aforesaid.

Stationary steam boiler in mine.

Horse or mule stables in mine and construction thereof.

SECTION 2. It shall not be lawful, after the passage of this act, to provide any horse or mule stables inside of bituminous coal mines, unless said stables are excavated in the solid strata or coal seams and no wood or other combustible material shall be used excessively in the construction of said stables, unless surrounded by or incased by some incombustible material. The air current used for ventilating said stable shall not be intermixed with the air current used for ventilating the working parts of the mine, but shall be conveyed directly to the return air current, and no open light shall be permitted to be used in any stable in any mine.

Ventilation of stables.

Hay or straw taken into mine.

SECTION 3. No hay or straw shall be taken into any mine, unless pressed and made up into compact bales, and all hay or straw taken into the mines as aforesaid shall be stored in a storehouse excavated in the solid strata or built in masonry for that purpose After January first, one thousand eight hundred and ninety-four, no horse or mule stable or storehouse, only as aforesaid, shall be permitted in any bituminous coal mine.

Regulation for stables after January 1, 1894.

Explosive oil shall not be used.

SECTION 4. No explosive oil shall be used or taken into bituminous coal mines for lighting purposes, and oil shall not be stored or taken into the mines in quantities exceeding five gallons. The oiling or greasing of cars inside of the mines is strictly forbidden unless the place where said oil or grease is used is thoroughly

Oiling or greasing of cars inside of mine.

cleaned at least once every day to prevent the accumulation of waste oil or grease on the roads or in the drains at that point. Not more than one barrel of lubricating oil shall be permitted in the mine at any one time   Only a pure animal or pure cotton-seed oil or oils, that shall be as free from smoke as a pure animal or pure cotton-seed oil, shall be used for illuminating purposes in any bituminous mine. Any person found knowingly using explosive or impure oil, contrary to this section, shall be prosecuted as provided for in section two of article twenty-one of this act.

SECTION 5. No powder or high explosive shall be stored in any mine, and no more of either article shall be taken into the mine at any one time than is required in any one shift, unless the quantity be less than five pounds, and in all working places where locked safety lamps are used blasting shall only be done by the consent and in the presence of the mine foreman, his assistant or fire boss, or any competent party designated by the mine foreman for that purpose; whenever the mine inspector discovers that the air in any mine is becoming vitiated by the unnecessary blasting of the coal, he shall have the power to regulate the use of the same and to designate at what hour of the day blasting may be permitted.

ARTICLE IX.

Opening for Drainage et cetera, on Other Lands.

SECTION 1. If any person, firm or corporation is, or shall hereafter be, seized in his or their own right, of coal lands, or shall hold such lands under lease and shall have opened or shall desire to open a coal mine on said land, and it shall not be practicable to drain or ventilate such mines or to comply with the requirements of this act as to ways of ingress and egress or traveling ways by means of openings on lands owned or held under lease by him, them or it, and the same can be done by means of openings on adjacent lands, he, they or it may apply by petition to the court of quarter sessions of the proper county, after ten days' notice to the owner or owners, their agent or attorney, setting forth the facts under oath or affirmation particularly describing the place or places where such opening or openings can be made, and the pillars of coal or other material necessary for the support of such passage way and such right of way to any public road as may be needed in connection with such opening, and that he or they cannot agree with the owner or owners of the land as to the amount to be paid for the privilege of making such opening or openings, whereupon the said court shall appoint three disinterested and competent citizens of the county to view the ground designated and lay out from the point or points mentioned

Lubricating oil.

Oil to be used for illuminating purposes.

Penalty for using explosive or impure oil

Powder shall not be stored in mine.

Blasting in mine.

Proceedings to provide necessary drainage or ventilation where it is necessary to take lands other than those of owner or lessee.

Court shall appoint viewers.

in such petition, a passage or passages not more than eighty feet area, by either drift, shaft or slope, or by a combination of any of said methods, by any practicable and convenient route, to the coal of such person, firm or corporation, preferring in all cases an opening through the coal strata where the same is practicable.

Viewers shall assess damages.

The said viewers shall, at the same time, assess the damages to be paid by the petitioner or petitioners to the owner or owners of such lands for the coal or other valuable material to be removed in the excavation and construction of said passage, also for such coal or other valuable material necessary to support the said passage, as well as for a right of way not exceeding fifteen feet in width from any such opening to any public road, to enable persons to gain entrance to the mine through such opening or to provide therefrom, upon the surface, a water course of suitable dimensions to a natural water stream to enable the operator to discharge the water from said mine if such right of way shall be desired by the petitioner or petitioners, which damages shall be fully paid before such opening is made.

Recording.

The proceedings shall be recorded in the road docket of the proper county, and the pay of viewers shall be the same

Pay of viewers.

as in roadcases : if exceptions be filed they shall be disposed of by the court as speedily as possible, and both parties to have the right to take depositions as in road cases. If, however, the petitioner desires to

Proceedings where petitioners desires to proceed before decision of viewers.

make such openings or roads or water way before the final disposition of such exceptions, he shall have the right to do so by giving bond, to be approved by the court securing the damages as provided by law in the case of lateral railroads.

On request of fifty miners. owner or operator must procure right of way.

SECTION 2. It shall be compulsory upon the part of the mine owner or operator to exercise the powers granted by the provisions of the last preceding section for the procuring of a right of way on the surface from the opening of a coal mine to a public road or public roads, upon the request in writing of fifty miners employed in the mine or mines of such owner or operator:

Proviso.

Provided however, That with such request satisfactory security be deposited with the mine owner or operator by said petitioners, being coal miners, to fully and sufficiently pay all costs, damages and expenses caused by such proceedings and in paying for such right of way.

Water accumulating in large or dangerous quantities may be removed.

SECTION 3. In any mine or mines, or parts thereof, wherein water may have been allowed to accumulate in large and dangerous quantities, putting in danger the adjoining or adjacent mines and the lives of the miners working therein, and when such can be tapped and set free and flow by its own gravity to any point

Method of removal.

of drainage. it shall be lawful for any operator or person having mines so endangered, with the approval of the inspector of the district, to proceed and remove the said danger by driving a drift or drifts protected by bore holes as provided by this act, and in removing said danger it shall be lawful to drive across property lines if needful. And it shall be unlawful for any person to dam or in any way obstruct the flow of any water from said mine or parts thereof, when so set free, on any part of its passage to point of drainage.

SECTION 4. No operator shall be permitted to mine coal within fifty feet of any abandoned mine containing a dangerous accumulation of water, until said danger has been removed by driving a passage way so as to tap and drain off said water as provided for in this act: *Provided*, That the thickness of the barrier pillars shall be greater, and shall be in proportion of one foot of pillar thickness to each one and one-quarter foot of waterhead, if, in the judgment of the engineer of the property and that of the district mine inspector, it is necessary for the safety of the persons working in the mine. *Shall not mine coal within fifty feet of abandoned mine or of water.* *Proviso*

SECTION 5. All operators of bituminous coal mines shall keep posted, in a conspicuous place at their mines, the general and special rules embodied in and made part of this act, defining the duties of all persons employed in or about said mine, which said rules shall be printed in the English language and shall also be printed in such other language or languages as are used by any ten persons working therein. It shall be the duty of the mine inspector to furnish to the operator printed copies of such rules and such translations thereof as are required by this section, and to certify their correctness over his signature. The cost thereof shall be borne by the State. *General and special rules shall be posted.* *Mine inspector shall furnish printed copies of rules.* *Cost of copies.*

ARTICLE X.

Inspectors, Examining Boards et cetera.

SECTION 1. The board of examiners appointed to examine candidates for the office of mine inspectors, under the provisions of the act to which this is a supplement, shall exercise all the powers granted and perform all the duties required by this supplementary act, and at the expiration of their term of office, and every four years thereafter, the Governor shall appoint, as hereinafter provided, during the month of January, two mining engineers of good repute and three other persons, who shall have passed successful examinations qualifying them to act as mine inspectors or mine foremen in mines generating fire-damp, who shall be citizens of this Commonwealth and shall have attained the age of thirty years and shall have had at least five years of practical experience in the bituminous mines of Pennsylvania, and who shall not be serving at that time in any official capacity at mines, which five persons shall constitute a board of examiners, whose duty it shall be to inquire into the character and qualifica- *Governor shall appoint Board of Examiners.* *Qualifications of members of board.* *Duties.*

tion of candidates for the office of inspector of mines under the provisions of this act.

SECTION 2. The examining board, so constituted, shall meet on the first Tuesday of March following their appointment, in the city of Pittsburg, to examine applicants for the office of mine inspector : *Provided however*, The examining board shall meet two weeks previous to the aforesaid time for the purpose of preparing questions et cetera, and when called together by the Governor on extra occasions at such time and place as he may designate, and after being duly organized and having taken and subscribed before any officer authorized to administer the same the following oath, namely : "We, the undersigned, do solemnly swear (or affirm) that we will perform the duties of examiners of applicants for the appointment as inspectors of bituminous coal mines to the best of our abilities, and that in recommending or rejecting said applicants we will be governed by the evidence of the qualifications to fill the position under the law creating the same, and not by any consideration of political or personal favor ; that we will certify all whom we may find qualified according to the true intent and meaning of the act and none others."

SECTION 3. The general examination shall be in writing and the manuscript and other papers of all applicants, together with the tally sheets and the solution of each question as given by the examining board, shall be filed with the Secretary of Internal Affairs as public documents, but each applicant shall undergo an oral examination pertaining to explosive gases and safety lamps, and the examining board shall certify to the Governor the names of all such applicants which they shall find competent to fill this office under the provisions of this act, which names, with the certificates and their percentages and the oaths of the examiners, shall be mailed to the Secretary of the Commonwealth and be filed in his office. No person shall be certified as competent whose percentage shall be less than ninety per centum, and such certificate shall be valid only when signed by four of the members of the examining board.

SECTION 4. The qualifications of candidates for said office of inspectors of mines to be inquired into and certified by said examiners shall be as follows, namely : They shall be citizens of Pennsylvania, of temperate habits, of good repute as men of personal integrity and shall have attained the age of thirty years, and shall have had at least five years of practical experience in working of or in the workings of the bituminous mines of Pennsylvania immediately preceding their examination, and shall have had practical experience with fire-damp inside the mines of this country, and upon examination shall give evidence of such theoretical as well as practical knowledge and general intelligence respecting mines and mining and the working and ventilation thereof, and all noxious mine gases, and will satisfy the examiners of their capability and fitness for the duties imposed upon inspectors of mines by the provisions of this act. And the examining board shall, immediately after the examination, furnish to each person who came before it to be examined a copy of all questions whether oral or written, which were given at the examination, on printed slips of paper and to be marked solved, right, imperfect or wrong, as the case may be, together with a certificate of competency to each candidate who shall have made at least ninety per centum. *Examining board shall furnish copy of all questions.*

SECTION 5. The board of examiners may, also, at their meeting, or when at any time called by the Governor together for an extra meeting, divide the bituminous coal regions of the State into inspection districts, no district to contain less than sixty nor more than eighty mines, and as nearly as possible equalizing the labor to be performed by each inspector, and at any subsequent calling of the board of examiners this division may be revised as experience may prove to be advisable. *Board may divide the region into inspection districts.*

SECTION 6. The board of examiners shall each receive ten dollars per day for each day actually employed, and all necessary expenses, to be paid out of the State Treasury. Upon the filing of the certificate of the examining board in the office of the Secretary of the Commonwealth, the Governor, shall, from the names so certified, commission one person to be inspector of mines for each district as fixed by the examiners in pursuance of this supplementary act, whose commission shall be for a full term of four years from the fifteenth day of May following: *Always provided however,* The highest candidate or candidates in percentage shall have priority to be commissioned for a full term or unexpired term before those candidates of lower percentage, and in case of a tie in percentage the oldest candidate shall be commissioned. *Compensation of board.* *Governor shall commission one person for each district.* *Highest candidate shall have priority.*

SECTION 7. As often as vacancies occur in said offices of inspectors of mines, the Governor shall commission for the unexpired term, from the names on file, the highest in percentage in the office of the Secretary of the Commonwealth, until the number shall be exhausted, and whenever this may occur, the Governor shall cause the aforesaid board of examiners to meet and they shall examine persons who may present themselves for the vacant office of mine inspector as herein provided, and the board of examiners shall certify to the Governor all persons who shall have made ninety per centum in said examination, one of whom to be commissioned by him according to the provisions of this act for the office of mine inspector for the unexpired term, and any vacancy that may occur in the examining board. *Vacancies in office of inspector.* *Vacancy in examining board.*

amining board shall be filled by the Governor of this Commonwealth.

SECTION 8. Each inspector of mines shall receive for his services an annual salary of three thousand dollars and actual traveling expenses, to be paid quarterly by the State Treasurer upon warrant of the Auditor General, and each mine inspector shall keep an office in the district for which he is comissioned and he shall be permitted to keep said office at his place of residence: *Provided,* A suitable apartment or room be set off for that purpose. Each mine inspector is hereby authorized to procure such instruments, chemical tests and stationery and to incur such expenses of communication from time to time, as may be necessary to the proper discharge of his duties under this act, at the cost of the State, which shall be paid by the State Treasurer upon accounts duly certified by him and audited by the proper department of the State.

SECTION 9. All instruments, plans, books, memoranda. notes and other material pertaining to the office shall be the property of the State, and shall be delivered to their successors in office. In addition to the expenses now allowed by law to the mine inspectors in enforcing the several provisions of this act, they shall be allowed all necessary expenses by them incurred in enforcing the several provisions of said law in the respective courts of the Commonwealth, the same to be paid by the State Treasurer on warrants drawn by the Auditor General after auditing the same; all such accounts presented by the mine inspector to the Auditor General shall be itemized and first approved by the court before which the proceedings were instituted.

SECTION 10. Each mine inspector of bituminous coal mines shall, before entering upon the discharge of his duties, give bond in the sum of five thousand dollars. with sureties to be approved by the president judge of the distrct in which he resides, conditional for the faithful discharge of his duties to, and take an oath or affirmation to discharge his duties impartially and with fidelity to the best of his knowledge and ability. But no person who shall act as manager or agent of any coal mine, or as a mining engineer, or is interested in operating any coal mine shall, at the same time act as mine inspector of coal mines under this act.

SECTION 11. Each inspector of bituminous coal mines shall devote the whole of his time to the duties of his office. It shall be his duty to examine each mine in his district as often as possible, but a longer period of time than three months shall not elapse between said examination, to see that all the provisions of this act are observed and strictly carried out. and he shall make a record of all examinations of mines, showing the condition in which he finds them, especially with reference to ventilation and drainage, the number of persons employed in each mine, the extent to which the law is obeyed and progress made in the improvement of mines, the number of serious accidents and the nature thereof, the number of deaths resulting from injuries received in or about the mines with the cause of such accident or death, which record completed to the thirty-first day of December of each and every year, shall, on or before the fifteenth day of March following, be filed in the office of the Secretary of Internal Affairs, to be by him recorded and included in the annual report of his department.

Filing report in office of Secretary of Internal Affairs.

SECTION 12. It shall be the duty of the mine inspector, on examination of any mine, to make out a written or partly written and partly printed report of the condition in which he finds such mine and post the same in the office of the mine or other conspicuous place. The said report shall give the date of the visit, the number of cubic feet of air in circulation and where measured, and that he has measured the air at the cut through of one or more rooms in each heading or entry, and such other information as he shall deem necessary, and the said report shall remain posted in the office or conspicuous place for one year and may be examined by any person employed in or about the mine.

Posting of report of the condition of mines.

Contents of report.

SECTION 13. In case the inspector becomes incapacitated to perform the duties of his office or receives a leave of absence from the same from the Governor, it shall be the duty of the judge of the court of common pleas of his district to appoint, upon said mine inspector's application or that of five miners or five operators of said inspector's district, some competent person, recommended by the board of examiners, to fill the office of inspector until the said inspector shall be able to resume the duties of his office, and the person so appointed shall be paid in the same manner as is hereinbefore provided for the inspector of mines.

In case of the absence of inspector court shall appoint a competent person to fill vacancy.

ARTICLE XI.

Inspectors' Powers et cetera.

SECTION 1. That the mine inspectors may be enabled to perform the duties herein imposed upon them, they shall have the right at all times to enter any bituminous coal mine to make examinations or obtain information, and upon the discovery of any violation of this act, they shall institute proceedings against the person or persons at fault under the provisions of section two of article twenty-one of this act. In case, however, where, in the judgment of the mine inspector of the district, any mine or part of mine is in such dangerous condition as to jeopardize life or health, he shall at once notify two of the mine inspectors of the other districts, whereupon they shall at once proceed to the mine where the danger exists and examine into the matter, and if, after full investigation thereof, they shall be agreed in the

Inspectors shall have the right, at at all times, to enter any bituminous mine to make examinations

Procedure in case inspector finds mine in a dangerous condition.

opinion that there is immediate danger, they shall instruct the superintendent of the mine in writing to remove such condition forthwith, and in case said superintendent shall fail to do so, then they shall apply, in the name of the Commonwealth, to the court of common pleas of the county, or in case the court shall not be in session, to a judge of the said court in chambers in which the mine may be located for an injunction to suspend all work in and about said mine, whereupon said court or judge shall at once proceed to hear and determine speedily the same, and if the cause appear to be sufficient after hearing the parties and their evidence, as in like cases, shall issue its writ to restrain the working of said mine until all cause of danger is removed, and the cost of said proceedings shall be borne by the owner, lessee or agent of the mine : *Provided,* That if said court shall find the cause not sufficient, then the case shall be dismissed and the costs shall be borne by the county wherein said mine is located

Proviso.

Article XII.

Inquests et cetera.

Coroner of county shall be notified if loss of life occurs.

SECTION 1. Whenever, by reason of any explosion or other accidents in any bituminous coal mine or the machinery connected therewith, loss of life or serious personal injury shall occur, it shall be the duty of the person having charge of such mine to give notice thereof forthwith to the mine inspector of the district and also to the coroner of the county, if any person is killed.

If inquest is held mine inspector shall be notified.

SECTION 2. If the coroner shall determine to hold an inquest he shall notify the mine inspector of the district of the time and place of holding the same, who shall offer such testimony as he may deem necessary to thoroughly inform the said inquest of the cause of the death, and the said mine inspector shall have authority at any time to appear before such coroner and jury and question or cross-question any witness, and in choosing a jury for the purpose of holding such inquest it shall be the duty of the coroner to empanel a jury, no one of which shall be directly or indirectly interested.

Jury shall not be interested.

Mine inspector shall immediately go to the scene of the accident.

SECTION 3. It shall be the duty of the mine inspector, upon being notified of any fatal accident as herein provided, to immediately repair to the scene of the accident and make such suggestion as may appear necessary to secure the safety of any persons who may be endangered, and if the results of the accident do not require an investigation by the coroner the said mine inspector shall proceed to investigate and ascertain the cause of the accident and make a record thereof, which he shall file as provided for, and to enable him to make the investigation he shall have power to compel the attendance of persons to testify and to administer oaths

If no inquest is necessary the mine inspector shall investigate.

or affirmations, and if it is found upon investigation that the accident is due to the violation of any provisions of this act by any person, other than those who may be deceased, the mine inspector may institute proceedings against such person or persons as provided for in section two of article twenty-one of this act.

SECTION 4. The cost of such investigation shall be paid by the county in which the accident occurred in the same manner as costs of inquests held by the coroners or justices of the peace are paid.

Cost of such investigations to be paid by the county

ARTICLE XIII.

Neglect or Incompetence of Inspectors.

SECTION 1. The court of common pleas in any county or district, upon a petition signed by not less than fifteen reputable citizens who shall be miners or operators of mines, and with the affidavit of one or more of said petitioners attached setting forth that any inspector of mines neglects his duties or is incompetent or that he is guilty of a malfeasance in office, shall issue a citation in the name of the Commonwealth to the said mine inspector to appear on not less than fifteen days' notice, upon a day fixed, before said court, at which time the court shall proceed to inquire into and investigate the allegations of the petitioners.

Procedure in the investigation of an incompetent inspector.

SECTION 2. If the court find that the said mine inspector is neglectful of his duties or incompetent to perform the duties of his office or that he is guilty of malfeasance in office, the court shall certify the same to the Governor, who shall declare the office of said mine inspector vacant and proceed in compliance with the provisions of this act to supply the vacancy; the costs of said investigation shall, if the charges are sustained, be imposed upon the mine inspector, but if the charges are not sustained they shall be imposed upon the petitioners.

If found incompetent, court shall certify same to Governor.

Costs of proceeding.

ARTICLE XIV.

Discretionary Powers of Inspectors, Arbitration et cetera.

SECTION 1. The mine inspector shall exercise a sound discretion in the enforcement of the provisions of this act, and if the operator, owner, miners, superintendent, mine foreman or other persons employed in or about the mine as aforesaid shall not be satisfied with any decision the mine inspector may arrive at in the discharge of his duties under this act, which said decision shall be in writing signed by the mine inspector, the said owner, operator, superintendent, mine foreman or other person specified above shall either promptly comply therewith or within seven days from date thereof appeal from such decision to the court of quar-

Proceedings when operator, owner or others are not satisfied with decision of mine inspector.

ter sessions of the county wherein the mine is located, and said court shall speedily determine the question involved in said decision and appeal and the decision of said court shall be binding and conclusive.

Court may appoint three persons to examine mine or other cause of complaint.

SECTION 2. The court or the judge of said court in chambers may, in its discretion, appoint three practical, reputable, competent and disinterested persons whose duty it shall be, under instuctions of the said court, to forthwith examine such mine or other cause of complaint and report, under oath, the facts as they exist or may have been, together with their opinions thereon, within thirty days after their appointment. The report of said board shall become absolute unless exceptions thereto shall be filed within ten days after the notice of the filing thereof by the owner, operator, mine superintendent. mine foreman, mine inspector and other persons, as aforesaid, and if exceptions are filed the court shall at once hear and determine the same and the decision shall be final and conclusive.

Payment of costs.

SECTION 3. If the court shall finally sustain the decision of the mine inspector then the appellant shall pay all costs of such proceedings, and if the court shall not sustain the decision of the mine inspector then such

Proviso.

costs shall be paid by the county : *Provided*, That no appeal from any decision made by any mine inspector which can be immediately complied with shall work as a supersedeas to such decision during the pendency of such appeal, but all decisions shall be in full force until reversed or modified by the proper court.

ARTICLE XV.

Examinations of Mine Foreman and Fire Bosses.

Court shall appoint an Examining Board.

SECTION 1. On the petition of the mine inspector the court of common pleas in any county in said district shall appoint an examining board of three persons, consisting of a mine inspector, a miner and an operator or superintendent, which said miner shall have received a certificate of competency as mine foreman in mines generating explosive gases, and the members of said examining board shall be citizens of this Commonwealth, and the persons so appointed shall after being duly organized take and subscribe before an officer au-

Oath of board.

thorized to administer the same the following oath namely : "We the undersigned do solemnly swear (or affirm) that we will perform the duties of examiners of applicants for the position of mine foreman and fire bosses of bituminous coal mines to the best of our abilities, and that in certifying or rejecting said applicants we will be governed by the evidence of the qualifications to fill the position under the law creating the same and not by any consideration of personal favor: that we will certify all whom we may find qualified and none others."

SECTION 2. The examining board shall examine any Examinations. person applying thereto as to his competency and qualifications to discharge the duties of mine foreman or fire boss.

Applicants for mine foreman or fire boss certificates Qualifications of applicants. shall be at least twenty-three years of age, and shall have had at least five years practical experience, after fifteen years of age, as minors superintendent at or inside of the bituminous mines of Pennsylvania and shall be citizens of this Commonwealth and men of good moral character and of known temperate habits.

The said board shall be empowered to grant certifi- Granting of certificates. cates of competency of two grades, namely : certificates of first grade, to persons who have had experience in First grade. mines generating explosive gases and who shall have the necessary qualifications to fulfill the duties of mine foreman in such mines; and certificates of second Second grade grade, to persons who give satisfactory evidence of their ability to act as mine foreman in mines not generating explosive gases.

SECTION 3. The said board of examiners shall meet Meeting of board at the call of the mine inspector and shall grant certifi- Granting of certificates. cates to all persons whose examination shall disclose their fitness for the duties of mine foreman as above classified, or fire boss, and such certificates shall be sufficient evidence of the holder's competency for the duties of said position so far as relates to the purposes of this act : *Provided*, That all persons holding certifi- Proviso. cates of competency granted under the provisions of the act to which this is a supplement shall continue to act under this act : *And provided further*, That any per- Any person acting under former act. may continue to act. son acting as mine foreman upon a certificate of service under the act to which this is a supplement may continue to act in the same capacity at any mine where the general conditions affecting the health and safety of the persons employed do not differ materially from those at the mine in which he was acting when said certificate was granted : *Provided however*, That if Proviso. such mine foreman leaves his present employer and secures employment elsewhere at any mine where in the judgment of the mine inspector of the district the conditions affecting the health and safety of the persons employed do differ materially from those at the mine at which he was employed when his certificate was granted, it shall then be the duty of the mine inspector of the district in which he has secured employment to serve written protest against such mine foreman's employment to the operator of said mine.

SECTION 4. The examining board shall hold their Term and compensation of Examining Board. office for a period of four years from their appointment and shall receive five dollars per day for each day necessarily employed and mileage at the rate of three cents per mile for each mile necessarily traveled, and all other necessary expenses connected with the examination shall be paid by the Commonwealth. Each ap-

Fee to be paid by applicant.

Annual examinations.

plicant before being examined shall pay the examining board the sum of one dollar, and one dollar additional for each certificate granted, which shall be for the use of the Commonwealth. The foregoing examination shall be held annually in each inspection district.

ARTICLE XVI.

Suspension of Certificates of Mine Foreman and Fire Bosses.

Fire boss must have certificate of competency.

SECTION 1. No person shall act as fire boss in any bituminous coal mines, unless granted a certificate of competency by any one of the several examining boards. All applicants applying to any of the examining boards for fire boss certificates shall undergo an oral exmination in the presence of explosive gas, and such certificate shall only be granted to men of good moral character and of known temperate habits, and it shall be unlawful for any operator or superintendent to employ any person as fire boss who has not obtained such certificate of competency as required by this act.

Proceeding in case foreman or fire boss shall neglect his duty.

SECTION 2. If the mine foreman or fire boss shall neglect his duties, or has incapacitated himself by drunkenness, or has been incapacitated by any other cause for the proper performance of said duties, and the same shall be brought to the knowledge of the operator or superintendent it shall be the duty of such operator or superintendent to discharge such delinquent at once and notify the inspector of the district of such action, whereupon it shall be the duty of said inspector to inform the court of common pleas of the county who shall issue a citation in the name of the Commonwealth to the said operator, superintendent, mine foreman or fire boss to appear at not less than fifteen days' notice upon a day fixed before said court, at which time the court shall proceed to inquire into and investigate the allegations. If the court finds that the allegations are true it shall notify the examining board of such finding and instruct the said board to withdraw the certificate of such delinquent during any period of time that said court may deem sufficient, and at the expiration of such time he shall be entitled to a re examination.

ARTICLE XVII.

Employment of Boys and Females.

SECTION 1. No boy under the age of twelve years, or any woman or girl of any age, shall be employed or permitted to be in the workings of any bituminous coal mine for the purpose of employment, or for any other purpose; and no boy under the age of sixteen shall be permitted to mine or load coal in any room, entry or other working place, unless in company with a person over sixteen years of age. If the mine inspector or mine foreman has reason to doubt the fact of any particular boy being as old as this act requires for the service which said boy is performing at any mine it shall be the duty of said mine inspector or mine foreman to report the fact to the superintendent, giving the name of said boy, and the said superintendent shall at once discharge the said boy.

ARTICLE XVIII.

Stretchers.

SECTION 1. It shall be the duty of operators or superintendents to keep at the mouth of the drift, shaft, or slope, or at such other place about the mine as shall be designated by the mine inspector, a stretcher properly constructed, and a woolen and a waterproof blanket in good condition for use in carrying away any person who may be injured at the mine: *Provided,* That where more than two hundred persons are employed two stretchers and two woolen and two waterproof blankets shall be kept. And in mines generating fire damp a sufficient quantity of linseed or olive oil bandages and linen shall be kept in store at the mines for use in emergencies, and bandages shall be kept at all mines.

ARTICLE XIX.

Annual Reports.

SECTION 1. On or before the twenty-fifth day of January in each year the operator or superintendent of every bituminous coal mine shall send to the mine inspector of the district in which said mine is located a correct report, specifying with respect to the year ending the thirty-first day of December preceding, the name of the operator and officers of the mine and the quantity of coal mined. The report shall be in such form and give such information regarding said mine as may be from time to time required and prescribed by the mine inspector of the district. Blank forms for such reports shall be furnished by the Commonwealth.

ARTICLE XX.

RULES GENERAL AND SPECIAL.

Additional duties of Mine Foreman.

SECTION 1. *Rule* 1. The mine foreman shall attend personally to his duties in the mine and carry out all the instructions set forth in this act and see that the regulations prescribed for each class of workmen under his charge are carried out in the strictest manner possible and see that any deviations from or infringements of any of them are promptly adjusted.

Mine foreman shall attend personally.

Air-ways.

Rule 2. He shall cause all stoppings along the airways to be properly built.

Width of entries.

Rule 3. He shall see that the entries at such places where road grades necessitate sprags or brakes to be applied or removed shall have a clear level width of not less than two and one-half feet between the side of car and the rib to allow the driver to pass his trip safely and keep clear of the cars there.

Blasting.

Rule 4. He shall direct that all miners undermine the coal properly before blasting it and that blasting shall be done at only such hours as he shall direct and shall order the miners to set sprags under the coal when necessary for safety while undermining at distances not exceeding seven feet apart, and he shall not allow the improper drawing of pillars.

Furnace fire where fire-damp is generated.

Rule 5. In mines where fire damp is generated when the furnace fire has been put out it shall not be relighted, except in his presence or that of his assistant acting under his instructions.

Accident to ventilating fan or machinery.

Rule 6. In case of accident to a ventilating fan or its machinery, or to the fan itself, whereby the ventilation of the mine would be seriously interrupted it shall be his duty to order the men to immediately withdraw from the mine and not allow their return to their work until the ventilation has been restored and the mine has been thoroughly examined by him or his assistant and reported to be safe.

Dangerous places must be fenced off.

Rule 7. He shall see that all dangerous places are properly fenced off and proper danger signal boards so hung on such fencing that they may be plainly seen; he shall also travel all air roads and examine all the accessible openings to old workings as often as is necessary to insure their safety.

Book or sheets to be provided for record of props, &c.

Rule 8. He shall provide a book or sheet to be put in some convenient place, or places, upon which shall be made a place for the numbers used by the miners with space sufficient to each number so that the miners can write plainly the quantity of props, their approximate length and the number of caps and other timbers which they require, together with the date of the order. Said book or sheets shall be preserved for thirty days from their date.

Duties of Fire Boss.

Rule 9. He shall enter the mine before the men have entered it, and before proceeding to examine the same he shall see that the air current is traveling in its proper course, and if all seems right, he shall proceed to examine the workings.

Rule 10. He shall not allow any person, except those duly authorized, to enter or remain in any part of the mine through which a dangerous accumulation of gas is being passed in the ventilating current from any other part of the mine.

Rule 11. He shall frequently examine the edge and accessible parts of new falls and old gobs and air courses and he shall report at once any violation of this act to the mine foreman.

Duties of Miners.

Rule 12. He shall examine his working place before beginning work and take down all dangerous slate, or otherwise make it safe by properly timbering the same before commencing to dig or load coal, and in mines where fire bosses are employed, he shall examine his place to see whether the fire boss has left the proper marks indicating his examination thereof, and he shall at all times be very careful to keep his working place in a safe condition during working hours.

Must keep his working place in safe condition.

Rule 13. Should he at any time find his place becoming dangerous, either from gas or roof, or from any unusual condition which may have arisen, he shall at once cease working, and inform the mine foreman or his assistant of such danger, and before leaving such place he shall place some plain warning at the entrance thereto to warn others from entering into the danger.

If place becomes dangerous he shall cease working and inform foreman.

Rule 14. It shall be the duty of every miner to mine his coal properly and to set sprags under the coal while undermining to secure it from falling and, after each blast, he shall exercise great care in examining the roof and coal and shall secure them safely before beginning work.

Shall mine his coal properly, &c.

Rule 15. When places are liable to generate sudden volumes of fire damp, or where locked safety lamps are used, no miner shall be allowed to fire shots except under the supervision and with the consent of the mine foreman, or his assistant, or other competent person designated by the mine foreman for that purpose.

Shall not fire shots except under direction of foreman in certain places.

Duties of Drivers.

Rule 16. When a driver has occasion to leave his trip he must be careful to see that it is left, when possible, in a safe place, secure from cars or other danger, or from endangering drivers of trips following.

Rule 17. The driver must take great care while taking his trips down grades to have the brakes or sprags so adjusted that he can keep the cars under control and prevent them from running onto himself or others.

Driver must have cars under control.

Rule 18. He shall not leave any cars standing where they may materially obstruct the ventilating current, except in case of accident to the trip.

Cars in ventilating currents.

Duties of Trip Riders or Runners.

Rule 19. He shall exercise great care in seeing that all hitchings are safe for use and see that all the trip is coupled before starting, and should he at any time see any material defect in the rope, link or chain, he

shall immediately remedy such defect or, if unable to
do so, he shall detain the trip and report the matter to
the mine foreman.

Duties of Engineer.

Must watch machinery.

Rule 20. It shall be the duty of the engineer to keep
a careful watch over his engine and all machinery
under his charge and see that the boilers are properly
supplied with water, cleaned and inspected at proper
intervals, and that the steam pressure does not exceed
at any time the limit allowed by the superintendent.

Know signals.

Rule 21. He shall make himself acquainted with the
signal codes provided for in this act.

Engine house and engine.

Rule 22. He shall not allow any unauthorized person
to enter the engine house, neither shall he allow any
person to handle or run the engine, without the permission of the superintendent.

Keep engine under control.

Rule 23. When workmen are being raised or lowered
he shall take special precautions to keep the engine
well under control.

Locomotive engineer.

Rule 24. The locomotive engineer must keep a sharp
lookout ahead of his engine and sound the whistle or
alarm bell frequently when coming near the partings
or landings; he must not exceed the speed allowed
by the mine foreman or superintendent. He must not
allow any person, except his attendants, to ride on the
engine or on the full cars.

Duties of Firemen.

Rule 25. Every fireman and other person in charge
of a boiler or boilers for the generation of steam shall
keep a careful watch of the same; he shall see that
the steam pressure does not at any time exceed the
limit allowed by the superintendent; he shall frequently try the safety valve and shall not increase the
weight on the same; he shall maintain a proper depth
of water in each boiler, and if anything should happen
to prevent this, he shall report the same without
delay to the superintendent, or other person designated
by the superintendent, and take such other action as
may, under the particular circumstances, be necessary
for the protection of life and preservation of property.

Duties of Fan Engineer.

Rule 26. The engineer in charge of any ventilating
fan must keep it running at such speed as the mine
foreman directs in writing. In case of accident to the
boiler or fan machinery, not requiring the immediate
withdrawal of the men from the mine by reason of
serious interruption of the ventilation, he shall invari-
ably notify the mine foreman. If ordinary repairs of
the fan or machinery becomes necessary, he must give

timely notice to the mine foreman and await his instructions before stopping it. He shall also examine at the beginning of each shift all the fan bearings, stays and other parts, and see that they are kept in proper working order. Should it become impossible to run the fan or necessary to stop it to prevent destruction, he shall then at once stop it and notify the mine foreman immediately and give immediate warning to persons in the mine.

Duties of Furnace Men.

Rule 27. The furnace man must attend to his duties with regularity, and in case he should be likely to be off work for any reason whatever, he must give timely notice to the mine foreman.

Rule 28. The furnace man must at all times keep a clear, brisk fire and the fire must not be smothered with coal or slack during working hours, nor shall he allow ashes to accumulate excessively on or under the bars, or in the approaches to the furnace, and ashes shall be cooled before being removed.

Rule 29. The furnace man must promptly obey the instructions of the mine foreman.

SHAFTS AND SLOPES.
Duties of Hookers-on.

Rule 30. The hookers-on at the bottom of any slope shall be very careful to see that the cars are properly coupled to a rope or chain and that the safety catch or other device is properly attached to the cars before giving the signal to the engineer

Duties of Cagers.

Rule 31. The cager at the bottom of any shaft shall not attempt to withdraw the car until the cage comes to rest, and when putting the full car on the cage, he must be very careful to see that the springs or catches are properly adjusted so as to keep the car in its proper place before giving the signal to the engineer.

Rule 32. At every shaft or slope mine in which provision is made in this act for lowering and hoisting persons, a headman and footman shall be designated by the superintendent or mine foreman, who shall be at their proper places from the time that persons begin to descend until all the persons who may be at the bottom of said shaft or slope, when quitting work, shall be hoisted; such headman and footman shall personally attend to the signals and see that the provisions of this act in respect to lowering or hoisting persons in shafts or slopes shall be complied with. *(Headman and footman.)*

Rule 33. He shall not allow any tools to be placed on the same cage with men or boys, nor on either cage when persons are being hoisted out of the mine or be- *(Tools shall not be placed in cage when persons are being hoisted or lowered.)*

6—LAWS.

ing lowered into the mine, except when for the purpose of repairing the shaft or machinery therein. The men shall place their tools in cars provided for that purpose which car, or cars, shall be hoisted or lowered before and after the men have been hoisted or lowered. And he shall immediately inform the mine foreman of any violation of this rule.

Rule 34. He shall also see that no driver, or other person, ascends the shaft with any horse or mule, unless the said horse or mule is secured in a suitable box, or safely penned, and only the driver in charge of said horse or mule shall accompany it in any case.

Duties of Top Man.

Shall inspect machinery daily.

Rule 35. The top man of any slope, or incline plane, shall be very careful to close the safety block, or other device, as soon as the cars have reached the landing so as to prevent any loose or runaway cars from descending the slope, or incline plane, and in no case shall such safety block, or other device, be withdrawn until the cars are coupled to the rope or chain, and the proper signal given. He shall carefully inspect, daily, all the machinery in and about the check house and the rope used for lowering the coal and promptly report any defect discovered to the superintendent, and shall use great care in attaching securely the wagons or cars to the rope and carefully lower the same down the incline. He shall ring the alarm bell in case of accident, and when necessary, immediately set free to act the drop logs or safety switch.

Springs or keeps must be in good order.

Rule 36. The top man of any shaft shall see that the springs or keeps for the cage to rest upon are kept in good working order, and when taking the full car off, he must be careful that no coal or other material is allowed to fall down the shaft.

Must be at his proper place

Rule 37. He shall be at his proper place from the time that persons begin to descend until all the persons who may be at the bottom of said shaft or slope, when quitting work, shall be hoisted. Such headman and footman shall personally attend to the signals and see that the provisions of this act in respect to lowering and hoisting persons in shafts or slopes shall be complied with.

Shall personally attend to signals.

Tools shall not be placed in same cage with men or boys.

Rule 38. He shall not allow any tools to be placed on the same cage with men or boys, nor on either cage when persons are being lowered into the mine, except when for the purpose of repairing the shaft or the machinery therein. The men shall place their tools in cars provided for that purpose, which car or cars shall be lowered before and after the men have been lowered.

Driver with horse or mule descending shaft.

Rule 39. He shall also see that no driver, or other person, descends the shaft with any horse or mule unless the said horse or mule is secured in a suitable

box or safely penned, and only the driver in charge
of said horse or mule shall accompany it in any case.

GENERAL RULES.

Rule 40. If any person shall receive any injury in or
about the mine and the same shall come within the
knowledge of the mine foreman, and if he shall be of
opinion that the injured person requires medical
or surgical treatment, he shall see that said injured
person receives the same, and in case of inability of
such injured person to pay therefor the same shall be
borne by the county. The mine foreman shall report
monthly to the mine inspector of the district on blanks
furnished by said inspector for that purpose all accidents resulting in personal injury. *Treatment of injured persons.*

Monthly reports of accidents.

Rule 41. No unauthorized person shall enter the
mine without permission from the superintendent or
mine foreman.

Rule 42. No person in a state of intoxication shall be
allowed to go into or loiter about the mine. *Intoxicated person.*

Rule 43. All employés shall inform the mine foreman,
or his assistant, of the unsafe condition of any working place, hauling roads or traveling ways, or of damage to doors, brattices or stoppings, or of obstructions
in the air passages when known to them. *Foreman shall be
notified of unsafe
condition of any
part of mine.*

Rule 44. No person shall be employed to blast coal,
rock or slate, unless the mine foreman is satisfied that
such a person is qualified by experience to perform the
work with ordinary care. *Blasting coal rock
or slate.*

Rule 45. The mine superintendent, or mine foreman,
shall cause to be constructed safety blocks, or some
other device, for the purpose of preventing cars from
falling into the shaft, or running away on slopes or
incline planes; and safety switches, drop logs or other
device shall be used on all slopes and incline planes;
and said safety blocks, safety switches or other device must be maintained in good working order. *Safety blocks.*

Rule 46. Every workman employed in the mine shall
examine his working place before commencing work,
and after any stoppage of work during the shift, he
shall repeat such examination. *Examination of
working places.*

Rule 47. No person shall be allowed to travel on foot
to or from his work on any incline plane, dilly or locomotive roads, when other good roads are provided for
that purpose. *Traveling to or
from work.*

Rule 48. Any employé or other person who shall
wilfully deface, pull down or destroy any notice board,
danger signal, general or special rules or mining laws,
shall be prosecuted as provided for in section two,
article twenty-one of this act. *Destroying notices,
signals, etc.*

Rule 49. No powder or high explosive shall be taken
into the mine in greater quantities than required for
use in one shift, unless such quantity be less than five *Powder in mine.*

pounds, and all powder shall be carried into the mine in metallic canisters.

Powder in tipple or weighing office.

Rule 50. Powder in quantities exceeding twenty-five pounds, or other explosives in quantities exceeding ten pounds, shall not be stored in any tipple or any weighing office, nor where workmen have business to visit. and no naked lights shall be used while weighing and giving out powder.

Tampering with signal wires.

Rule 51. All persons, except those duly authorized, are forbidden to meddle or tamper in any way with any electric or signal wires in or about the mines.

Hoisting or lowering persons in shaft.

Rule 52. No greater number of persons shall be hoisted or lowered at any one time in any shaft than is permitted by the mine inspector, and whenever said number of persons shall arrive at the bottom of the shaft in which persons are regularly hoisted or lowered, they shall be furnished with an empty cage and be hoisted, and in cases of emergency, a less number shall be promptly hoisted. Any person or persons crowding or pushing to get on or off the cages shall be deemed guilty of a misdemeanor.

New workman shall be informed of rules.

Rule 53. Each workman, when engaged, shall have his attention directed to the general and special rules by the person employing him.

Nuisance must not be committed.

Rule 54. Workmen and all other persons are expressly forbidden to commit any nuisance or throw into, deposit, or leave coals or dirt, stones or other rubbish in the air-way or road so as to interfere with, pollute or hinder the air passing into and through the mine.

Key for safety lamps.

Rule 55. No one, except a person duly authorized by the mine foreman, shall have in his possession a key or other instrument for the purpose of unlocking any safety lamp in any mine where locked safety lamps are used.

Fencing abandoned slope.

Rule 56. Every abandoned slope, shaft, air hole or drift shall be properly fenced around or across its entrance.

Who shall have safety lamp in mine.

Rule 57. No safety lamps shall be intrusted to any person for use in mines until he has given satisfactory evidence to the mine foreman that he understands the proper use thereof and danger of tampering with the same.

Riding on loaded or empty cars.

Rule 58. No person shall ride upon or against any loaded car or cage in any shaft or slope in or about any bituminous coal mine; no person other than the trip runner shall be permitted to ride on empty trips on any slope, inclined plane or dilly road, when the speed of the cars exceeds six miles per hour. The transportation of tools in and out of the mine shall be under the direction of the mine foreman.

Transportation of tools.

Rule 59. No persons other than the drivers or trip runners shall be permitted to ride on the full cars.

Coal dust to be sprinkled.

Rule 60. In mines where coal dust has accumulated to a dangerous extent, care shall be exercised to prevent said dust from floating in the atmosphere by sprinkling it with water, or otherwise, as far as practicable.

Rule 61. In cutting of clay veins, spars or faults in entries, or other narrow workings going into the solid coal in mines where explosive gases are generated in dangerous quantities, a bore hole shall be kept not less than three feet in advance of the face of the work, or an advance of any shot hole drilled for a blast to be fired therein. Bore holes in clay veins, &c.

Rule 62. The engineer placed in charge of an engine whereby persons are hoisted out of or lowered into any mine shall be a sober and competent person and not less than twenty-one years of age. Engineer must be sober and competent

Rule 63. When a workman is about to fire a blast he shall be careful to notify all persons who might be endangered thereby, and shall give sufficient alarm so that any person or persons approaching shall be warned of the danger. Firing a blast

Rule 64. In every shaft or slope where persons are hoisted or lowered by machinery as provided by this act, a topman and cager shall be appointed by the superintendent or mine foreman. Topman and cager

Rule 65. Whenever a workman shall open a box containing powder or other explosives, or while in any manner handling the same, he shall first place his lamp not less than five feet from such explosive and in such a position that the air current cannot convey sparks to it, and he shall not smoke while handling explosives. Handling of powder.

Rule 66. An accumulation of gas in mines shall not be removed by brushing. Brushing of gas not allowed.

Rule 67. When gas is ignited by blast or otherwise, the person having charge of the place where the said gas is ignited, shall immediately extinguish it if possible, and if unable to do so shall immediately notify the mine foreman or his assistant of the fact. Workmen must see that no gas blowers are left burning upon leaving their working places. Gas ignited.

Rule 68. All ventilating fans used at mines shall be provided with recording instruments by which the number of revolutions or the effective ventilating pressure of the fan shall be registered and the registration with its date for each and every day shall be kept in the office of the mine for future reference for one year from its date. Ventilating fans.

Rule 69. Where the clothing or wearing apparel of employés become wet by reason of working in wet places in the mines, it shall be the duty of the operator or superintendent of each mine, at the request in writing of the mine inspector, who shall make such request upon the petition of any five miners of any one mine in the district working in the aforesaid wet places, to provide a suitable building which shall be convenient to the principal entrances of such mine for the use of the persons employed in wet places therein for the pur- Clothing becoming wet in mine.

pose of washing themselves and changing their clothes when entering the mine and returning therefrom. The said building shall be maintained in good order and be properly lighted and heated and shall be provided with facilities for persons to wash. If any person or persons shall neglect or fail to comply with the provisions of this article or maliciously injure or destroy or cause to be injured or destroyed the said building or any part thereof, or any of the appliances or fittings used for supplying light and heat therein, or doing any act tending to the injury or destruction thereof, he or they shall be deemed guilty of an offense against this act.

Signals to be used in shafts or slopes.

Rule 70. In all shafts and slopes where persons, coal or other material are hoisted by machinery the following code of signals shall be used:

One rap or whistle to hoist coal or other material.

One rap or whistle to stop cage or car when in motion.

Two raps or whistles to lower cage or car.

Three raps or whistles when persons are to be hoisted and for engineer to signal back ready when persons are to be hoisted, after which persons shall get on the cage or car, then one rap shall be given to hoist.

Four raps or whistles to turn on steam to the pumps.

But a variation from the above code of signals may be used by permission of the mine inspector: *Provided*, That in any such case such changed code shall be printed and posted.

Shall not go into any old shaft or abandoned mine.

Rule 71. No person or persons shall go into any old shaft or abandoned parts of the mine or into any other place which is not in actual course of working without permission from the mine foreman, nor shall they travel to and from their work except by the traveling way assigned for that purpose.

Steam pipes in hauling or traveling ways.

Rule 72. No steam pipes through which high pressure steam is conveyed for the purpose of driving pumps or other machinery shall be permitted on traveling or haulage ways, unless they are encased in asbestos, or some other suitable non-conducting material, or are so placed that the radiation of heat into the atmosphere of the mine will be prevented as far as possible.

Ventilation where locomotive is used

Rule 73. Where a locomotive is used for the purpose of hauling coal out of a mine, the tunnel or tunnels through which the locomotive passes shall be properly ventilated and kept free as far as practicable of noxious gases, and a ventilating apparatus shall be provided by the operator to produce such ventilation when deemed necessary and practicable to do so by the mine inspector.

Mining out pillars.

Rule 74. No inexperienced person shall be employed to mine out pillars unless in company with one or more experienced miners and by their consent.

Article XXI.

Penalties.

Section 1. Any person or persons whomsoever, who shall intentionally or carelessly injure any shaft, safety lamp, instrument, air course or brattice, or obstruct or throw open air ways, or take matches for any purpose, or pipes or other smokers' articles beyond any station inside of which locked safety lamps are used, or injure any part of the machinery, or open a door in the mine and not close it again immediately or open any door which opening is forbidden, or disobey any order given in carrying out the provisions of this act, or do any other act whatsoever whereby the lives or the health of persons or the security of the miners or the machinery is endangered, shall be deemed guilty of a misdemeanor and may be punished in a manner provided for in this article.

Section 2. The neglect or refusal to perform the duties required to be performed by any section of this act by the parties therein required to perform them, or the violation of any of the provisions or requirements hereof, shall be deemed a misdemeanor and shall, upon conviction thereof in the court of quarter sessions of the county wherein the misdemeanor was committed, be punishable by a fine not exceeding five hundred dollars or imprisonment in the county jail for a period not exceeding six months, or both, at the discretion of the court. *(Penalty for neglect or refusal to perform duties required by any section of this act.)*

Section 3. That for any injury to person or property occasioned by any violation of this act, or any failure to comply with its provisions by any owner, operator or superintendent of any coal mine or colliery, a right of action shall accrue to the party injured against said owner or operator for any direct damages he may have sustained thereby, and in case of loss of life by reason of such neglect or failure aforesaid, a right of action shall accrue to the widow and lineal heirs of the person whose life shall be lost for like recovery of damages for the injury they shall have sustained. *(Action for injury occasioned by violation of this act by owner.)*

Article XXII.

Definition.

Section 1. *Coal Mine.* In this act the term "coal mine" includes the shafts, slopes, adits, drifts or inclined planes connected with excavations penetrating coal stratum or strata, which excavations are ventilated by one general air current or divisions thereof and connected by one general system of mine railroads over which coal may be delivered to one or more common points outside the mine, when such is operated by one operator. *(Coal mine.)*

Excavations and workings.

Excavations and Workings. The term "excavations and workings" includes all the excavated parts of a mine, those abandoned as well as the places actually being worked, also all underground workings and shafts, tunnels and other ways and openings, all such shafts, slopes, tunnels and other openings in the course of being sunk or driven, together with all roads, appliances, machinery and material connected with the same below the surface.

Shaft.

Shaft. The term "shaft" means a vertical opening through the strata and which is or may be used for the purpose of ventilation or drainage or for hoisting men or material or both in connection with the mining of coal.

Slope.

Slope. The term "slope" means an incline way or opening used for the same purpose as a shaft.

Operator.

Operator. The term "operator" means any firm, corporation or individual operating any coal mine or part thereof.

Superintendent.

Superintendent. The term "superintendent" means the person who shall have, on behalf of the operator, immediate supervision of one or more mines.

Bituminous.

Bituminous Mines. The term "bituminous" coal mine shall include all coal mines in the State not now included in the anthracite boundaries.

Mine employing less than ten persons in any one period.

The provisions of this act shall not apply to any mine employing less than ten persons in any one period of twenty-four hours.

ARTICLE XXIII.

Repeal.

SECTION 1. That all acts or parts of acts inconsistent herewith be and the same are hereby repealed.

APPROVED—The 15th day of May, A. D. 1893.

ROBT. E. PATTISON.

No. 49.

AN ACT

To revive and continue in force provisions of an act, entitled "An act to extend the time during which corporations may hold and convey the title to real estate heretofore bought under execution, or conveyed to them in satisfaction of debts and now remaining in their hands unsold," approved the twenty-sixth day of May, Anno Domini one thousand eight hundred and eighty-seven.

SECTION 1. *Be it enacted, &c.,* That the provisions of the act, entitled "An act to extend the time during which corporations may hold and convey the title to real estate heretofore bought under execution, or conveyed to them in satisfaction of debts and now remaining in their hands unsold," approved the twenty-sixth day of May, Anno Domini one thousand eight hundred and eighty-seven, which provides "that the time during which all corporations are authorized by law and their charters to hold and convey real estate acquired by them under execution, or in satisfaction of debts, be and the same is hereby extended to all property heretofore bought and now held by such corporations for and during a further period of five years from and after the expiration of the time during which, as aforesaid, they are now so authorized to hold and convey the same," be and the same are hereby revived, continued and extended for a further period of five years from and after the time for which they are now authorized by law to hold the same.

APPROVED—The 18th day of May, A. D. 1893.

ROBT. E. PATTISON.

———

No. 50.

AN ACT

To encourage and authorize the formation of co-operating banking associations where the profits derived from the business, after paying all legitimate expenses, shall accrue to the depositors and borrowers of the association in proportion to their deposits or loans.

SECTION 1. *Be it enacted, &c.*, That co-operative banking associations may be incorporated under this act upon compliance with the requirements of section eleven, article sixteen, State Constitution, when ten or more persons of lawful age, citizens of this Commonwealth, who shall have associated themselves together by written articles of association for the purpose of carrying on a co-operative banking business where the profits derived from the business shall, after paying all legitimate expenses, be divided pro rata among the depositors and borrowers of the bank in proportion to their deposits or loans to each class, one-half of the net profits; and a dividend not to exceed six per centum per annum on original subscribed stock may be considered legitimate expenses. *(margin: May be incorporated. Conditions to be complied with.)*

SECTION 2. That such persons so associating may adopt any corporate name indicating their co-operative character and which has not been previously adopted by any other corporation formed under this act: *Provided*, The last three words of such name shall be Co-operative Banking Association, and it shall not be lawful to use in such name either of the words "society" or "company," and that any violation of this proviso by any corporation formed under this act shall render each member thereof personally liable for all its debts. *(margin: Corporate name. Last three words of name. What words must not be used in name. Penalty for violation.)*

That before any company formed under this act shall commence its business its articles of association shall be filed and recorded in the office of the Secretary of the Commonwealth, and two copies of said articles *(margin: Proceedings necessary before company shall commence business.)*

shall be made which the said Secretary of the Commonwealth shall certify by his official signature and the seal of this Commonwealth as being correct copies of said articles so filed and recorded; one of said certified copies shall be filed and recorded in the office of the clerk of the county in which the office of the association shall be located and the said clerk shall certify by his official signature and seal of his office that the **Certified copies of articles of association shall be evidence in courts.** said certified copy of said articles has been filed and recorded in his office, and the other certified copy of said articles shall be held by the association named therein, and the said articles or copies thereof, duly certified by either of the aforesaid officers, may be used as evidence in all courts and places of the incorporation of as well as for or against such association, and the said Secretary of the Commonwealth and the said county **Fees for filing and recording papers.** clerk shall be paid for said filing and recording and certifying at the rate of ten cents for each hundred words contained in said articles, and after such articles of association shall have been made, filed and recorded as herein required, the person signing the same and **Shall be deemed a body corporate.** such other persons, partnerships or corporations who shall, from time to time, own or possess any share in the stock capital of such association, and their several successors and assigns, shall be deemed and taken to be a body corporate and by the name and for the purposes mentioned in such articles of association.

How articles of association shall be prepared, and what shall be set forth therein. SECTION 3. That the articles of association shall be signed by the persons originally associating themselves together and shall be acknowledged by at least five of them before a notary public, and shall state distinctly (a) the name by which this association shall be known, (b) the place in this State where its principal office is to be located, (c) the purpose or object for which it is formed, (d) amount of its stock capital, (e) the amount of each share of stock of such capital, such shares not to exceed ten dollars per share, and how such share may be paid for, (f) the amount of capital that will be actually paid in before commencing business; also amount of preferred stock to be assigned to stockholders who may hereafter earn stock from custom dividends, (g) whether, and if so to what extent, loans or deposits of money are to be received for use in its business, (h) the terms upon which persons may become members, (i) on what days in January regular annual meetings of the members are to be held, (j) such other matters not repugnant to this act as may be deemed proper and necessary, (k) the term of its existence not to exceed twenty years, and (l) names of the first associates, their respective residences and the **Approved by superintendent of the Banking Department.** number of shares held by each of them. No such association shall commence business until the financial standing, responsibility and character of the original stockholders shall have been approved and certified by the Superintendent of the Banking Department of the Commonwealth.

SECTION 4. That the stock capital of any such asso- *Stock capital.* ciation shall consist of the amounts standing to the credit of the members on account of the shares allotted to them, certificates of which shall be issued from time to time as shares shall be fully paid up or earned.

SECTION 5. It shall be the duty of such company to *Shall exhibit list of stockholders, etc.* exhibit in some conspicuous place in its principal office at all times a list of stockholders and the amount of stock held by each stockholder, the amount of stock subscribed or earned at the time of each last annual meeting; also the amount of preferred stock which shall not be a liability stock only as it becomes assigned to individual stockholders.

SECTION 6. It shall be the duty of the auditors to *Duty of auditors.* audit all books, papers and vouchers of the company annually, or at any time when called upon in writing so to do by the president or any ten of the stockholders, or twenty of the depositors when joined by at least five of the stockholders, and each of these audits shall be rendered in writing which shall give a statement of the as- *Contents of statement.* sets and liabilities of said company; also a detailed statement of the character and nature of all the notes and securities held by the association, and such statement shall be posted conspicuously in the office.

SECTION 7. No profits shall be paid out to any stock- *When profits shall be paid to stockholders.* holder until the total registered amount of stock shall be fully paid in cash, or earned from the net profits of the company.

SECTION 8. It shall be lawful, if the by-laws so pro- *Minor may hold shares and make loans.* vide, for any minor to take and hold shares in, or to make loans or deposits of money to or with any such corporation, and for such association to pay any minor any moneys that may be due to him in respect of any shares, loans or deposits standing in his name, and his receipt therefor shall be in all respects valid in law, but such *Shall not hold office.* minor shall not be eligible to hold any office in such association though he may be subject to its by-laws and vote at any meeting of its members.

SECTION 9. Depositors and borrowers to whom divi- *Withdrawal of dividends.* dends are due shall not withdraw the same, but shall take full paid stock in lieu thereof, until the registered and preferred stock of the company becomes fully paid up, and as each share of stock becomes fully paid up this class of stockholders may become voting members, *Voting members.* but each shareholder shall be entitled to but one vote on each share of stock.

The company shall be controlled by a board of six *Directors of the company.* directors who shall serve for three years, two of which shall be elected annually, and provision shall be made at the first election to elect two to serve one year, two to serve two years, and two for three years. Said direc- *President and secretary, powers of.* tors shall elect a president and secretary from their number and said directors shall have full control of all employés and business of the association, subject to by-laws, but no employé shall be a director. The by-laws shall provide rules and regulations for the loaning or discounting of the capital and deposits of the association and the nature of its securities and no loan shall be made to any individual, firm or company, either singly or collectively, in excess of ten per centum of the deposits of the association at the time of making such loan, and any violation of this provision will render the person or cashier so making liable upon his bond and the directors sanctioning such a loan will render them individually liable, unless a protest be entered at the first monthly meeting subsequent to the making of such loan.

Two auditors shall be elected annually by the stockholders from their number at their annual meeting in January, and one auditor shall be elected by the depositors from their number on first Monday of each December, notice of which election shall be posted conspicuously in the bank room for at least three weeks prior to the election of such auditor, all of which shall serve for one year.

SECTION 10. That the members shall be severally and jointly liable for all deposits, debts for labor, or service of any kind performed for such association, and for any other debts lawfully incurred under the provisions of this act; each of the members shall be liable to twice the amount of his subscribed or earned stock capital, and no more, but no suit shall be brought or any execution issued against any member individually until a judgment be first obtained for such deposits, labor, services, or other lawful debts against such association and execution thereon be returned unsatisfied, in whole or in part, and in case any member shall be compelled to pay any such judgment, or any part thereof, beyond his pro rata liability therefor, he shall have the right to call upon all the members to pay their pro rata share of the same, or up to their pro rata liability therefor, and may sue them jointly, or severally, or any member of them, and recover in such action the ratable amount due from the member or members so sued.

SECTION 11. That any such association may take, hold, lease and convey such real estate as may be necessary for the purpose of its organization, and may sue and be sued in its corporate name, and may submit any matter in dispute to arbitration, and shall have a common seal, which shall not be altered or imitated, and shall bear the corporate name of, together with such device or motto as may be adopted by such association, and such seal shall be impressed upon the articles of association.

SECTION 12. That any person appointed to any position in any such association requiring the receipt, payment, management, or use of money belonging to such association, shall, before entering upon the discharge

---

Marginal notes:

By-laws.

Loans shall not exceed ten per centum of deposits of association.

Violation of this provision.

Two auditors shall be elected annually.

Liability for deposits and debts.

When suit may be brought for deposits, &c.

May hold real estate, and sue and be sued.

Shall have common seal.

Any person appointed to a position shall give bond.

of his duties, become bound with two or more good and
sufficient sureties, or insurance bonds, in such sum and
form as the directors shall require and approve; and
the directors may also require from any other employés of such association, bonds with good and sufficient sureties for the faithful discharge of duties.

SECTION 13. That the first meeting of any such association may be called by a notice signed by any two of
the associates who signed its articles of association,
setting forth the time and place and objects of such
meetings, such notice to be mailed to the address of
each associate, at least four days clear prior to such
meeting, and a majority of such associates at such
meeting shall be competent to make all such by-laws
as they may deem necessary for the proper management of the association, so that any such by-laws are
not repugnant to or inconsistent with the provisions of
this act, or any law of the State or United States, and
to elect such officers as are heretofore provided by this
act, and such officers shall hold office until their successors shall have been elected and installed.

First meeting and how it may be called.

A majority of associates may do business.

SECTION 14. That any association may alter or amend
its articles of association and may alter or rescind any
by-laws, or make any additional by-laws with the consent of the majority of its members present at a special
meeting convened for such purpose, but the notice calling such meeting shall set forth fully and clearly the
proposed alterations, amendment, recision or addition;
and any alteration or amendment of the articles of association shall be approved, filed, recorded and certified
in the same manner as the original articles of association.

Amendment of articles of association, etc.

This act shall take effect immediately.

APPROVED—The 18th day of May, A. D. 1893.

ROBT. E. PATTISON.

No. 51.

AN ACT

To amend the first section of an act, entitled "An act authorizing
school directors to purchase school books out of the district fund,"
approved June twenty-fifth, one thousand eight hundred and
eighty-five, by requiring school directors, or controllers, to furnish
school books and other school supplies free of cost.

SECTION 1. *Be it enacted, &c.*, That section first of an
act, entitled "An act authorizing school directors to
purchase school books out of the district funds," approved June twenty-fifth, one thousand eight hundred
and eighty-five, which reads as follows:

Section 1, act of June 25, 1885, cited for amendment.

"That school directors, or controllers, may purchase
text books for use in the public schools of their respective school districts out of the school funds of the dis-

trict, and when so procured, the necessary books shall be supplied free of cost to each pupil for use in the schools of said district, subject to the orders of the directors thereof, whose duty it shall be to provide for the safe keeping and care of the books which shall be returned at the close of the annual school term in each year, or as the board may direct," be and the same is hereby amended so as to read as follows:

School directors shall purchase text books out of school funds of district.

SECTION 1. That school directors, or controllers, shall purchase text books and other necessary school supplies for use in the public schools of their respective school districts, as such new text books and supplies are required in addition to those at present in use in the hands of pupils or owned by the school districts, out of the school fund of the district, and when so procured,

Books and supplies shall be furnished free.

the necessary books and school supplies shall be furnished free of cost for use in the schools of said district, subject to the orders of the directors or controllers therof, whose duty it shall be to provide for the return of, and for the safe keeping and care of the

Shall be returned at close of annual term.

books, which shall be returned at the close of the annual school term in each year, or as the board may direct.

APPROVED—The 18th day of May, A. D. 1893.

ROBT. E. PATTISON.

No. 52.

AN ACT

To establish a Medical Council, and three State Boards of Medical Examiners, to define the powers and duties of said Medical Council and said State Boards of Medical Examiners, to provide for the examination and licensing of practitioners of medicine and surgery, to further regulate the practice of medicine and surgery, and to make an appropriation for the Medical Council.

WHEREAS, The safety of the public is endangered by incompetent physicians and surgeons, and due regard for public health and the preservation of human life demands that none but competent and properly qualified physicians and surgeons shall be allowed to practice their profession.

Medical Council established, and who shall be members thereof.

SECTION 1. *Be it enacted, &c.*, That there shall be established a Medical Council of Pennsylvania, consisting of the Lieutenant Governor, the Attorney General, the Secretary of Internal Affairs, the Superintendent of Public Instruction and the President of the State Board of Health and Vital Statistics, and the Presidents of the three State Boards of Medical Examiners provided for in this act.

Name of council.

SECTION 2. The said council shall be known by the name and style of the Medical Council of Pennsylvania, and may make and adopt all necessary rules and

Rules.

regulations and by laws not inconsistent with the Constitution and the laws of this Commonwealth, or of the United States, and shall have power to locate and maintain an office within this State for the transaction of business; five members of the said council shall constitute a quorum for the transaction of business.

Office of council.

SECTION 3. The said council shall organize at Harrisburg within ten days from the date of the organization of three boards of medical examiners, and shall elect from its own number a president and a secretary who shall also act as treasurer, both of whom shall hold their offices for one year, or until their successors are chosen.

When council shall organize and where.

Officers

SECTION 4. The members of the said council shall receive no salary, except the secretary and treasurer who shall receive a salary of not over five hundred dollars, and who shall file with the president of the council a bond in the sum of one thousand dollars conditioned for the faithful performance of his duties. The necessary expenses of the said council shall be paid out of the appropriation made in section sixteen of this act, and any balance remaining from the appropriation after the disbursements herein specified shall be paid into the Treasury of the Commonwealth.

Salary of secretary and treasurer.

They shall file a bond.

Expenses, how paid.

SECTION 5. The said medical council shall hold two stated meetings in each year at Harrisburg and may hold special meetings at such times and places as it may deem proper. It shall supervise the examinations conducted by the three State Boards of Medical Examiners of all applicants for license to practice medicine and surgery in this Commonwealth, and shall issue licenses to practice medicine and surgery to such applicants as have presented satisfactory and properly certified copies of licenses from State Boards of Medical Examiners, or State Boards of Health of other States, as provided for in section thirteen of this act, or as have successfully passed the examination of one of the three State Boards of Medical Examiners, but all such examinations shall be made by the State Boards of Medical Examiners established in section six of this act. And the said medical council shall have no power, duty or function, except such powers, duties and functions as pertain to the supervision of the examinations of applicants for licenses to practice medicine and surgery and to the issuing of licenses to such applicants as have successfully passed the examination of one of the State Boards of Medical Examiners, or have presented satisfactory and properly certified copies of licenses from State Boards of Medical Examiners, or State Boards of Health of other States, as provided for in section thirteen of this act.

Council shall hold two meetings each year.

It shall supervise examinations of State boards and shall issue licenses

It shall have no power except supervision.

SECTION 6. It is further enacted, that from and after the first day of March, Anno Domini one thousand eight hundred and ninety-four, there shall be and continue to be three separate boards of medical examiners for the State of Pennsylvania, one representing the

Shall be three boards of examiners after March 1, 1894.

Medical Society of the State of Pennsylvania, one representing the Homeopathic Medical Society of the State of Pennsylvania, one representing the Eclectic Medical Society of the State of Pennsylvania.

Number of members and length of term of

Each board shall consist of seven members, and each of said members shall serve for a term of three years from the first day of March next after his appointment, with the exception of those first apointed, who shall serve as follows namely : Two of each board for one year, two of each board for two years, and three of each board for three years, from the first day of March, Anno Domini one thousand eight hundred and ninety-four.

Governor shall appoint the members of boards from lists presented.

The Governor shall appoint the members of said boards of examiners, respectively, from the full lists of the members of the said medical societies, which lists shall, on or before the first day of January, one thousand eight hundred and ninety-four, and annually thereafter, be transmitted to the Governor under the seal and signed by the secretary of the society so nominating.

When boards shall be appointed.

From these lists of nominees respectively the Governor shall, during the month of January, Anno Domini one thousand eight hundred and ninety-four, appoint three separate boards of medical examiners, each board to be composed exclusively of members of the same medical society.

If medical societies fail to submit lists.

In case of failure of any or all of said medical societies to submit lists, as aforesaid, the Governor shall appoint members in good standing of the corresponding society, or societies, entitled to nominate without other restriction.

Each appointee must be a registered physician of ten years' practice in this State.

Each one of the said appointees must be a registered physician in good standing and shall have practiced medicine or surgery under the laws of this State for a period of not less than ten years prior to such appointment.

Vacancies in board. Removal of members.

The Governor shall fill vacancies, by death or otherwise, for unexpired terms of said examiners from the respective lists submitted by the said medical societies, and may remove any member of any of said boards for continued neglect of the duties required by this act, or on recommendation of the medical society of which said members may be in affiliation, for unprofessional or dishonorable conduct.

Governor shall designate length of term of first appointees.

When and how appointments shall be made.

The Governor shall in his first appointments designate the number of years for which each appointee shall serve. The appointments of successors to those members whose term of office will expire on the first day of March of each year shall be made by the Governor during the month of January of such year, upon the same conditions and requirements as hereinbefore specified with reference to the appointment of three separate examining boards, each to be composed exclusively of members of the same medical school and society as hereinbefore provided.

Name of boards.

SECTION 7. Said boards shall be known by the name and style of Boards of Medical Examiners of the State of Pennsylvania. Every person who shall be appointed to serve on either of said boards shall receive a certificate of appointment from the Secretary of the Commonwealth.

Each of said boards shall be authorized to take testimony concerning all matters within its jurisdiction, and the presiding officer for the time being of either of said boards, or of any of the committees thereof, may issue subpœnas and administer oaths to witnesses. Each of said boards of examiners shall make and adopt all necessary rules, regulations and by-laws, not inconsistent with the Constitution and laws of this State, or of the United States, whereby to perform the duties and transact the business required under the provisions of this act; said rules, regulations and by-laws to be subject to the approval of the Medical Council of Pennsylvania established by this act.

SECTION 8. From the fees provided by this act the respective boards may pay, not to exceed said income, all proper expenses incurred by its provisions, and if any surplus above said expenses shall remain at the end of any year it shall be apportioned among said examiners pro rata according to the number of candidates examined by each : *Provided*, That the medical council shall keep separate accounts of all fees received from physicians applying for licenses to practice medicine and surgery and shall not devote any such fees to the uses of the council, or to the uses or remuneration of any other examining board than that of the society with which the physician who pays the fee wishes to be affiliated.

SECTION 9. The first meeting of each of the examining boards repectively shall be held on the first Tuesday of April, one thousand eight hundred and ninty-four, suitable notice in the usual form being given with the notice of their appointment by the Secretary of the Commonwealth to each of the members thereof, specifying the time and place of meeting.

At the first meeting of each of the boards respectively an organization shall be effected by the election, from their own membership, of a president and secretary. For the purpose of examining applicants for license each of said boards of medical examiners shall hold two or more stated or special meetings in each year, due notice of which shall be made public at such times and places as they may determine. At said stated or special meetings a majority of the members of the board shall constitute a quorum thereof, but the examination may be conducted by a committe of one or more members of the board of examiners duly authorized by said boards.

SECTION 10. The several boards of medical examiners shall, not less than one week prior to each examination, submit to the Medical Council of Pennsylvania questions for thorough examinations in anatomy, physiology, hygiene, chemistry, surgery, obstetrics, path-

7—LAWS.

Marginal notes:

Certificate of appointment.

May take testimony, issue subpœnas and administer oaths

Rules and by-laws.

Expenses shall be paid from fees.

Council shall keep account of all fees.

First meeting of examining boards.

Organization of boards.

Meetings and notice thereof.

Quorum.

Questions of boards shall be submitted to the council.

ology, diagnosis, therapeutics, practice of medicine and materia medica; from the lists of questions so submitted the council shall select the questions for each examination, and such questions for each examination shall be the same for all candidates, except that in the departments of therapeutics, practice of medicine and materia medica, the questions shall be in harmony with the teachings of the school selected by the candidate.

SECTION 11. Said examinations shall be conducted in writing in accordance with the rules and regulations prescribed by the Medical Council of Pennsylvania and shall embrace the subjects named in section ten of this act. After each such examination the board having charge thereof shall, without unnecessary delay, act upon the same. An official report of such action signed by the president, secretary and each acting member of said board of medical examiners, stating the examination, average of each candidate in each branch, the general average and the result of the examination, whether successful or unsuccessful, shall be transmitted to the medical council. Said report shall embrace all the examination papers, questions and answers thereto. All such examination papers shall be kept for reference and inspection for a period of not less than five years.

SECTION 12. On receiving from any of said boards of medical examiners such official report of the examination of any applicant for license, the medical council shall issue forthwith to each applicant who shall have been returned as having successfully passed said examination, and who shall have been adjudged by the medical council to be duly qualified for the practice of medicine, a license to practice medicine and surgery in the State of Pennsylvania. The medical council shall require the same standard of qualifications from all candidates, except in the departments of therapeutics practice of medicine and materia medica, in which the standard shall be determined by each of the boards respectively. Every license to practice medicine and surgery issued pursuant to this act shall be subscribed by the officers of the medical council and by each medical examiner who reported the licentiate as having successfully passed said examinations. It shall also have affixed to it by the person authorized to affix the same, the seal of this Commonwealth.

Before said license shall be issued it shall be recorded in a book to be kept in the office of the medical council, and the number or the book and page therein containing said recorded copy shall be noted upon the face of said license. Said records shall be open to public inspection, under proper restrictions as to their safe keeping, and in all legal proceedings shall have the same weight as evidence that is given to the conveyance of land.

SECTION 13. From and after the first day of July, Anno Domini one thousand eight hundred and ninety-four, any person not theretofore authorized to practice

Marginal notes:
Subjects for examination.
Examinations shall be conducted in writing.
Official report of examinations shall be transmitted by the board to the council.
Contents of report.
Examination papers shall be kept five years.
Council shall issue license.
Same standard of qualifications from all candidates.
License shall be subscribed by officers of council and examiner.
And shall have the seal of the Commonwealth attached.
License shall be recorded in office of council.
Public inspection.
Legal proceedings.
Application for license, how made, and what shall be contained therein.

medicine and surgery in this State, and desiring to enter upon such practice, may deliver to the secretary of the medical council, upon the payment of a fee of twenty-five dollars, a written application for license, together with satisfactory proof that the applicant is more than twenty-one years of age, is of good moral character, has obtained a competent common school education, and has received a diploma conferring the degree of medicine from some legally incorporated medical college of the United States, or a diploma or license conferring the full right to practice all the branches of medicine and surgery in some foreign country; applicants who have received their degree in medicine after the first day of July, one thousand eight hundred and ninety-four, must have pursued the study of medicine for at least three years, including three regular courses of lectures, in different years, in some legally incorporated medical college, or colleges, prior to the granting of said diploma, or foreign license, and after the first day of July, eighteen hundred and ninety-five, such applicants must have pursued the study of medicine for at least four years, including three regular courses of lectures, in different years, in some legally incorporated medical college, or colleges, prior to the granting of said diploma or foreign license. Such proof shall be made, if required, upon affidavit. Upon the making of said payment and proof the medical council, if satisfied with the same, shall issue to said applicant an order for examination before such one of the State Boards of Medical Examiners as the applicant for license may select. In case of failure at any such examination the candidate, after the expiration of six months and within two years, shall have the privilege of a second examination by the same board to which application was first made without the payment of an additional fee: *And it is further provided*, That applicants examined and licensed by State Boards of Medical Examiners or State Boards of Health of other States, on payment of a fee of fifteen dollars to the medical council, and on filing in the office of the medical council a copy of said license certified by the affidavit of the president or secretary of such board showing also that the standard of acquirements adopted by said State Board of Medical Examiners or State Board of Health, is substantially the same as is provided by sections eleven, twelve and thirteen of this act, shall without further examination receive a license conferring on the holder thereof all the rights and privileges provided by sections fourteen and fifteen of this act.

Section 14. From and after the first day of March, Anno Domini one thousand eight hundred and ninety-four, no person shall enter upon the practice of medicine or surgery in the State of Pennsylvania, unless he or she has complied with the provisions of this act, and

[marginal notes:]
Affidavit may be required.
Order for examination.
In case of failure at examination, second examination may be had.
Applicants having license from other states.
Conditions on which they can receive a license without further examination.
Act shall go into effect March 1. 1894.

shall have exhibited to prothonotary of the court of common pleas of the county in which he or she desires to practice medicine or surgery, a license duly granted to him or her as hereinbefore provided, whereupon he or she shall be entitled upon the payment of one dollar to be duly registerd in the office of the prothonotary of the court of common pleas in the said county, and any person violating any of the provisions of this act shall be guilty of a misdemeanor, and upon conviction thereof in the court of quarter sessions of the county wherein the offense shall have been committed, shall pay a fine of not more than five hundred dollars for each offense.

SECTION 15. Nothing in this act shall be construed to interfere with or punish commissioned medical officers serving in the army or navy of the United States, or in the United States Marine Hospital service while so commisioned, or medical examiners of relief departments of railroad companies while so employed, or any one while actually serving as a member of the resident medical staff of any legally incorporated hospital, or any legally qualified and registered dentist exclusively engaged in the practice of denistry, or shall interfere with or prevent the dispensing and sales of medicines or medical appliances by apothecaries, pharmacists, or interfere with the manufacture of artificial eyes, limbs or orthopedical instruments or trusses of any kind for fitting such instruments on persons in need thereof, or any lawfully qualified physicians and surgeons residing in other States or countries, meeting registered physicians of this State in consultation or any physician or surgeon residing on the border of a neighboring State and duly authorized under the laws thereof to practice medicine and surgery therein whose practice extends into the limits of this State: *Provided*, That such practitioner shall not open an office, or appoint a place to meet patients or receive calls, within the limits of Pennsylvania, or physicians duly registered in one county of this State called to attend cases in another county but not residing or opening an office therein. And nothing in this act shall be construed to prohibit the practice of medicine and surgery within this Commonwealth by any practitioner who shall have been duly registered before the first day of March, Anno Domini one thousand eight hundred and ninety-four, according to the terms of the act, entitled "An act to provide for the registration of all practitioners of medicine and surgery," approved the eight day of June, Anno Domini one thousand eight hundred and eighty-one, and one such registry shall be sufficient warrant to practice medicines and surgery in any county in this Commonwealth.

SECTION 16. The sum of two thousand dollars is hereby appropriated out of any moneys in the State Treasury not otherwise appropriated for the salary of the secretary and treasurer of said medical council and the necessary expenses of said council, one thousand dollars thereof for the year begining January one, one thousand eight hundred and ninety-four, and one thousand dollars thereof for the year beginning January one, one thousand eight hundred and'ninety-five.

SECTION 17. All acts or parts of acts of Assembly inconsistent herewith shall be and are hereby repealed. *Acts repealed.*

APPROVED—The 18th day of May, A. D. 1893.

ROBT. E. PATTISON.

No. 53.

AN ACT

To amend section six of the act, entitled "A further supplement to the act regulating elections in this Commonwealth," approved the thirtieth day of January, one thousand eight hundred and seventy-four, extending the power of the several courts of common pleas of the Commonwealth to appoint election officers in certain cases.

SECTION 1. *Be it enacted, &c.*, That section six of the act, entitled "A further supplement to the act regulating elections in this Commonwealth," approved the thirtieth day of January, one thousand eight hundred and seventy-four, which reads as follows, to wit: "In all election districts where a vacancy exists by reason of the disqualification of the officer, or otherwise, in an election board heretofore appointed, or where any new district shall be formed the judge or judges of the court of common pleas of the proper county shall, ten days before any general or special election, appoint competent persons to fill said vacancies and to conduct the election in said new districts, and in the appointment of inspectors in any election district both shall not be of the same political party, and the judge of elections shall in all cases be of the political party having the majority of votes in said district as nearly as the said judge or judges can ascertain the fact, and in case of the disagreement of the judges as to the selection of inspectors the political majority of the judges shall select one of such inspectors and the minority judge or judges shall select the other," be amended so as to read as follows: In all election districts where a vacancy exists by reason of the disqualification of the officer, or by removal, resignation, death or other cause, in an election board heretofore elected or appointed, the judge or judges of the court of common pleas of the proper county, upon proof furnished that such vacancy or vacancies exist, shall at any time before any general, municipal or special election appoint competent persons to fill said vacancies to conduct the election in said districts, and in the appointment of inspectors in any election district

Section 6, Act of January 30, 1874, cited for amendment.

Judge of court of common pleas shall appoint person to fill vacancy in election board.

How board shall be divided politically and how appointed.

both shall not be of the same political party, and the judge of election shall in all cases be of the political party having the majority of votes in said district as nearly as the said judge or judges can ascertain the fact, and in case of the disagreement of the judges as to the selection of inspectors the political majority of the judges shall select one of such inspectors and the minority judge or judges select the other.

APPROVED—The 18th day of May, A. D. 1893.

ROBT. E. PATTISON.

No. 54.

AN ACT

To provide for the immediate printing, distribution, filing and keeping of unbound copies of the laws of this Commonwealth as they are enacted from time to time.

Secretary of the Commonwealth shall transmit copies of laws to prothonotaries.

SECTION 1. *Be it enacted, &c.*, That on and after the passage of this act it shall be the duty of the Secretary of the Commonwealth of Pennsylvania, within ten days after the signing of any bill by the Governor whereby it becomes a law, to transmit by mail one copy of said law to the prothonotary of each court of common pleas in the State, said laws to be in uniform unbound leaves and consecutively numbered.

Prothonotaries shall keep such copies on file.

SECTION 2. It shall be the duty of the prothonotaries of said courts to file and keep in their respective offices such copies of the laws for a period of one year from the date of the reception of the first of the said laws enacted in one year in such manner that they shall be accessible to the public during the office hours of the said prothonotaries: *Provided*, That this act shall not affect existing laws relative to the printing and distribution of the pamphlet laws.

APPROVED—The 18th day of May, A. D. 1893.

ROBT. E. PATTISON.

No. 55.

AN ACT

To establish boards of arbitration to settle all questions of wages and other matters of variance between capital and labor.

WHEREAS, The great industries of this Commonwealth are frequently suspended by strikes and lockouts resulting at times in criminal violation of the law and entailing upon the State vast expense to protect life and property and preserve the public peace:

And whereas, No adequate means exist for the adjustment of these issues between capital and labor, employers and employés, upon an equitable basis where each party can meet together upon terms of equality to settle the rates of compensation for labor and establish rules and regulations for their branches of industry in harmony with law and a generous public sentiment: Therefore,

SECTION 1. *Be it enacted, &c.*, That whenever any differences arise between employers and employés in the mining, manufacturing or transportation industries of the Commonwealth which cannot be mutually settled to the satisfaction of a majority of all parties concerned, it shall be lawful for either party, or for both parties jointly, to make application to the court of common pleas wherein the service is to be performed about which the dispute has arisen to appoint and constitute a board of arbitration to consider, arrange and settle all matters at variance between them which must be fully set forth in the application, such application to be in writing and signed and duly acknowledged before a proper officer by the representatives of the persons employed as workmen, or by the representatives of a firm, individual or corporation, or by both, if the application is made jointly by the parties, such applicants to be citizens of the United States, and the said application shall be filed with the record of all proceedings had in consequence thereof among the records of said court. *Court of common pleas, on application, may appoint board of arbitration. when differences cannot be mutually settled.*

Such application must be in writing, and duly acknowledged.

Applicants must be citizens of the United States.

SECTION 2. That when the application duly authenticated has been presented to the court of common pleas, as aforesaid, it shall be lawful for said court, if in its judgment the said application allege matters of sufficient importance to warrant the intervention of a board of arbitrators in order to preserve the public peace, or promote the interests and harmony of labor and capital, to grant a rule on each of the parties to the alleged controversy, where the application is made jointly, to select three citizens of the county of good character and familiar with all matters in dispute to serve as members of the said board of arbitration which shall consist of nine members all citizens of this Commonwealth; as soon as the said members are appointed by the respective parties to the issue, the court shall proceed at once to fill the board by the selection of three persons from the citizens of the county of well known character for probity and general intelligence, and not directly connected with the interests of either party to the dispute, one of whom shall be designated by the said judge as president of the board of arbitration. *When application is made jointly. each party shall appoint three arbitrators, and court shall appoint three.*

Persons appointed by the court shall not be connected with interests of either party.

Where but one party makes application for the appointment of such board of arbitration the court shall give notice by order of court to both parties in interest, requiring them each to appoint three persons as members of said board within ten days thereafter, and in case either party refuse or neglects to make such appointment the court shall thereupon fill the board by the selection of six persons who, with the three named *When application is made by but one party, court may appoint six persons.*

by the other party in the controversy, shall constitute said board of arbitration.

Court shall appoint one member as secretary.

The said court shall also appoint one of the members thereof secretary to the said board who shall also have a vote and the same powers as any other member, and shall also designate the time and place of meeting of the said board. They shall also place before them copies of all papers and minutes of proceedings to the case or cases submitted to them.

Board shall be sworn

Shall consider records and determine their rules, and shall sit with closed doors until organization is consummated. Powers of president.

SECTION 3. That when the board of arbitrators has been thus appointed and constituted and each member has been sworn or affirmed and the papers have been submitted to them, they shall first carefully consider the records before them and then determine the rules to govern their proceedings; they shall sit with closed doors until their organization is consummated after which their proceedings shall be public. The president of the board shall have full authority to preserve order at the sessions and may summon or appoint officers to assist and in all ballotings he shall have a vote.

May send for persons, books and papers and enforce their presence.

Failure to appear shall be a misdemeanor.

It shall be lawful for him at the request of any two members of the board to send for persons, books and papers, and he shall have power to enforce their presence and to require them to testify in any matter before the board, and for any willful failure to appear and testify before said board, when requested by the said board, the person or persons so offending shall be guilty of a misdemeanor, and on conviction thereof in the court of quarter sessions of the county where the offense is committed, shall be sentenced to pay a fine not exceeding five hundred dollars and imprisonment not exceeding thirty days, either or both, at the discretion of the court.

Penalty.

When board is organized sessions shall be open.

SECTION 4. That as soon as the board is organized the president shall announce that the sessions are opened and the variants may appear with their attorneys and counsel, if they so desire, and open their case, and in all proceedings the applicant shall stand as plantiff, but when the application is jointly made, the employés shall stand as plantiff in the case, each party in turn shall be allowed a full and impartial hearing and may examine experts and present models, drawings, statements and any proper matter bearing on the case, all of which shall be carefully considered by the said board in arriving at their conclusions, and the decision of the said board shall be final and conclusive of all matters brought before them for adjustment, and the said board of arbitration may adjourn from the place designated by the court for holding its sessions, when it deems it expedient to do so, to the place or places where the dispute arises and hold sessions and personally examine the workings and matters at variance to assist their judgment.

Applicant shall be plaintiff, but in joint application employés shall be plaintiff.

Decision of board shall be final and conclusive.

Board may hold meeting at place where dispute arises.

Compensation of members of board.

SECTION 5. That the compensation of the members of the board of arbitration shall be as follows, to wit:

each shall receive four dollars per diem and ten cents per mile both ways between their homes and the place of meeting by the nearest comfortable routes of travel to be paid out of the treasury of the county where the arbitration is held, and witnesses shall be allowed from the treasury of the said county the same fees now allowed by law for similar services.

SECTION 6. That the board of arbitrators shall duly execute their decision which shall be reached by a vote of a majority of all the members by having the names of those voting in the affirmative signed thereon and attested by the secretary, and their decisions, together with all the papers and minutes of their proceedings, shall be returned to and filed in the court aforesaid for safe keeping.

SECTION 7. All laws and parts of laws inconsistent with the provisions of this act be and the same are hereby repealed.

APPROVED—The 18th day of May, A. D. 1893.

ROBT. E. PATTISON.

No. 56.

AN ACT

Authorizing and directing county commissioners of the several counties of this Commonwealth to procure, bind and preserve weekly newspapers published within their respective counties.

WHEREAS, The county newspapers have become valuable as mediums of information, social, legal and political, and are referred to quite frequently for the facts embodied in their pages ; hence the preservation of the same will be of great value in the future as faithful records of past occurrences;

SECTION 1. *Be it enacted, &c.*, That the county com- missioners of the several counties of this Commonwealth are hereby authorized and directed to subscribe for three weekly newspapers, if so many be published within their respective counties, to procure the binding of the same in separate volumes, and keep them in their offices as books of reference for the use of the public.

SECTION 2. It shall be the duty of each member com- posing a board of county commissioners to select one of the said newspapers referred to in section one, when three or more are published in said county, where less than three are published within the county the commissioners shall have all such newspapers so bound.

SECTION 3. All expenses necessary to carry this act into effect shall be paid out of the county treasury.

APPROVED--The 18th day of April, A. D. 1893.

ROBT. E. PATTISON.

No. 57.

AN ACT

To repeal the second section of an act, entitled "Supplement to an act to incorporate the Philadelphia and Delaware River railroad company," approved April fourth, one thousand eight hundred and fifty-four.

SECTION 1. *Be it enacted, &c.*, That so much of an act, entitled "Supplement to an act to incorporate the Philadelphia and Delaware River Railroad Company," approved April fourth, one thousand eight hundred and fifty-four, as reads as follows, namely: "It shall be the duty of said company at its own expense to erect upon their said road on either side of the said crossing, one gate to be kept securely closed under the care and supervision of some sober and competent person to be appointed by the said company, which person shall be permanently stationed at the said crossing, whose duty it shall be to open the said gate for the passage of the cars of the said company only when the same can be done without danger of collision with any of the trains passing over the road of the said Reading railroad: *Provided*, Every violation of the provisions of this section, information and proof thereof having been made before any alderman of the city of Philadelphia, the said Delaware River Railroad Company shall pay a fine of one hundred dollars, one-half to go to the city treasury and the other half to the informer, and the informer shall be a competent witness in the case," being the second section of the said act be and the same is hereby repealed.

APPROVED—The 18th day of May, A. D. 1893.
                         ROBT. E. PATTISON.

(marginal note: Section 2, act of April 4, 1854, cited for repeal.)

No. 58.

AN ACT

To empower the court of quarter sessions of any county of this Commonwealth to fix the place of holding the general election.

SECTION 1. *Be it enacted, &c.*, That it shall be lawful for the court of quarter sessions of the proper county at any time, for any reason that may seem proper to the court upon a petition of at least ten qualified electors of any election district, and upon such notice to the county commissioners as the court may direct, to change the polling place of said district: *Provided however*, That the court may, in its discretion, direct that an election shall be held to settle the question as to where said polling place shall be located.

SECTION 2. That all acts inconsistent herewith are hereby repealed.

APPROVED—The 18th day of May, A. D. 1893.
                         ROBT. E. PATTISON.

No. 59.

AN ACT

To repeal an act approved the sixth day of April, Anno Domini one thousand eight hundred and fifty-four, entitled "An act supplementary to an act relating to roads, highways and bridges," approved the thirteenth day of April, Anno Domini one thousand eight hundred and forty-three.

SECTION 1. *Be it enacted, &c.*, That the act approved the sixth day of April, Anno Domini one thousand eight hundred and fifty-four, entitled An act supplementary to an act, entitled "An act relating to roads, highways and bridges," approved the thirteenth day of April, one thousand eight hundred and forty-three, which reads as follows: "That the exemptions of the act approved the thirteenth day of April, Anno Domini one thousand eight hundred and forty-three, relating to roads and bridges in the counties of Bedford, Washington, Westmoreland, Tioga, Potter, Cambria, Somerset, Armstrong, Allegheny and Susquehanna, be and the same is hereby extended to the county of Erie," be and the same is hereby repealed.

APPROVED—The 18th day of May, A. D. 1893.

ROBT. E. PATTISON.

No. 60.

AN ACT

Providing that voters in this Commonwealth shall cast their ballots at polling places inside the election district in which they are domiciled and making it the duty of the courts of quarter sessions of the several counties to carry out the provisions of the same.

SECTION 1. *Be it enacted, &c.*, That from and after the passage of this act it shall not be lawful for any voter in this Commonwealth, except when in actual military service of this State, or the United States, at any election authorized by law to cast his ballot at any polling place outside the lawfully designated election district in which he is domiciled.

Shall not vote outside election district.

SECTION 2. It shall be the duty of the several courts of quarter sessions of the several counties of the Commonwealth to designate the polling places within the election districts in the manner now provided by law.

Court shall fix polling places

APPROVED—The 18th day of April, A. D. 1893.

ROBT. E. PATTISON.

No. 61.

AN ACT

To amend an act, entitled "A supplement to the act, entitled 'An act for acknowledging deeds,'" passed March eighteenth, one thousand seven hundred and seventy-five, requiring the recording of certain conveyances and designating the time within which they shall be recorded.

SECTION 1. *Be it enacted, &c.*, That section one of an act, entitled "A supplement to an act, entitled 'An act for acknowledging and recording of deeds,'" passed the eighteenth day of March, Anno Domini one thousand seven hundred and seventy-five, which reads as follows, namely :

" WHEREAS, by the different and secret ways of conveying lands, tenements and hereditaments, such as are ill-disposed have it in their power to commit frauds, whereof divers persons may be injured in their purchase and mortgages by prior and secret conveyances, and fraudulent incumbrances :

" For remedy whereof, be it enacted, all deeds and conveyances, which from after the publication hereof, shall be made and executed within this province, of or concerning any lands, tenements or hereditaments, in this province, whereby the same may be in any way affected in law or equity, shall be acknowledged by one for the grantors, or bargainors, or proved by one or more of the subscribing witnesses of such deed, before one of the judges of the supreme court, or one of the justices of the court of common pleas of the county where the lands conveyed lie, and shall be recorded in the office for recording of deeds in the county where such lands or hereditaments are lying and being, within six months after the execution of such deeds and conveyances ; and every such deed and conveyance that shall at any time after the publication hereof be made and executed, and which shall not be proved and recorded as aforesaid, shall be adjudged fraudulent and void against any subsequent purchaser or mortgagee for a valuable consideration, unless such deed or conveyance be recorded as aforesaid, before the proving and recording of the deed or conveyance under which subsequent purchaser or mortgagee shall claim," be and is hereby amended as follows :

WHEREAS, by the different and secret ways of conveying lands, tenements and hereditaments, such as are ill-disposed, have it in their power to commit frauds, by means whereof divers persons may be injured in their purchases, mortgages, debts and credits against said grantors by prior and secret conveyances, and fraudulent incumbrances :

For remedy whereof, be it enacted, that all deeds and conveyances, which, from and after the passage of this act, shall be made and executed within this Commonwealth of or concerning any lands, tenements or hereditaments in this Commonwealth, or whereby the title to the same may be in any way affected in law or equity, shall be acknowledged by the grantor, or grantors, bargainor, or bargainors, or proved by one or more of the subscribing witnesses thereto before one of the judges of the supreme court, or before one of the judges of the court of common pleas, or recorder of deeds, prothonotary, or clerk of any court of record, justice of the peace or notary public of the county wherein said conveyed lands lie, and shall be recorded in the office for the recording of deeds where such lands, tenements or hereditaments are lying and being, within ninety days after the execution of such deeds or conveyance, and every such deed and conveyance that shall at any time after the passage of this act be made and executed in this Commonwealth, and which shall not be proved and recorded as aforesaid, shall be adjudged fraudulent, and void against any subsequent purchaser or mortgagee for a valid consideration, or any creditor of the grantor or bargainor, in said deed of conveyance, and all deeds or conveyances that may have been made and executed prior to the passage of this act, having been duly proved and acknowledged as now directed by law, which shall not be recorded in the office for recording of deeds in the county where said lands and tenements and hereditaments are lying and being, within ninety days after the date of the passage of this act, shall be adjudged fraudulent, and void as to any subsequent purchaser for a valid consideration, or mortgagee, or creditor of the grantor, or bargainor therein.

By whom acknowledged.

Who shall take acknowledgment.

Shall be recorded within ninety days.

If not proved and recorded shall be void against subsequent purchasers, etc.

Deeds, etc., proved prior to this act.

SECTION 2. That section two of said act which reads as follows: "All such deeds and conveyances, which shall be executed out of this province, after the publication of this act, and acknowledged or proved in manner as directed by the laws heretofore for that purpose made, or proved by one or more of the subscribing witnesses, before a Supreme Judge of this province, shall be recorded in the office for the recording of deeds in the county where the lands and hereditaments specified in such deed or deeds do lie, within the space of twelve months after the execution thereof, otherwise every such deed or conveyance shall be adjudged fraudulent against any purchaser for a valuable consideration, unless such deed or conveyance be recorded as aforesaid, before the proving and recording of the deed or conveyance under which subsequent purchaser or mortgagee shall claim," be and the same is hereby amended as follows:

Section 2, act of March 18, 1775, cited for repeal.

All such deeds and conveyances which shall be made and executed out of this Commonwealth after the passage of this act, and acknowledged and proved in manner as directed by the laws for that purpose heretofore made, shall be recorded in the office for the recording

Deeds, etc., proved out of this Commonwealth shall be recorded within six months.

of deeds in the county where the lands and hereoita-
ments specified in such deed or deeds do lie, within
the space of six months from the execution thereof,
otherwise every such deed or conveyance shall be adjudged fraudulent and void against any subsequent
purchaser or mortgagee for a valuable consideration,
and against any creditor of the bargainor, or grantor,
in such deed.

APPROVED—The 19th day of May, A. D. 1893.

ROBT. E. PATTISON.

No. 62.

AN ACT

Relating to judicial sales and the preservation of the lien of mortgages.

Liens of certain
mortgages shall not
be destroyed by any
judicial sale.

SECTION 1. *Be it enacted, &c.*, That when the lien of
a mortgage upon real estate is, or shall be, prior to all
other liens upon the same property, except other mortgages, ground rents, assessments and municipal claims,
whose lien though afterward accruing has by law given
it the lien of such mortgage shall not be destroyed, or
in anywise affected by any judicial or other sale whatsoever, except as hereinafter stated, whether such sale
be made by virtue or authority of any order or decree
of any orphans' or other court, or of any writ of execu-

Shall not apply to
unseated lands.

tion, or otherwise, howsoever: *Provided*, That this
section shall not apply to cases of mortgages upon
unseated lands or sales of the same for taxes.

Real estate of a de-
cedent may be freed
in certain action.

SECTION 2. That whenever the application for an
order or decree of the sale of real estate shall be made
by an executor or administrator for the purpose of paying the debts of the decedent, it shall and may be lawful for the orphans' court having jurisdiction of such
petition to decree a sale of the premises freed and
discharged from the lien of a mortgage, or mortgages,
as mentioned in the first section of this act, if the
holder, or holders, of such mortgage, or mortgages, by
writing filed in said court, shall consent to the sale being so made, that the sale should be made freed and
discharged from the lien of the mortgage or mortgages
as aforesaid.

APPROVED—The 19th day of May, A. D. 1893.

ROBT. E. PATTISON.

No. 63.

AN ACT

Designating general election days, that is the third Tuesday of February and the first Tuesday after the first Monday of November of each year, as legal half holidays from twelve o'clock noon until midnight of such days, and providing for the payment, acceptance and protesting of bills, notes, drafts, checks and other negotiable paper, on such days.

SECTION 1. *Be it enacted, &c.*, That the third Tuesday of February of each year, and the first Tuesday after the first Monday of November of each year, be and the same are hereby designated as legal half holidays from twelve o'clock noon until midnight of such days, and shall for all purposes whatsoever as regards the presenting for payment or acceptance, and as regards the protesting and giving notice of the dishonor of bills of exchange, checks, drafts and promissory notes, made after the passage of this act, be treated and considered as the first day of the week, commonly called Sunday, and as public holidays, and half holidays, and all such bills, checks, drafts and notes, otherwise presentable for acceptance or payment on any of the said days, shall be deemed to be payable and be presentable for acceptance or payment at or before twelve o'clock noon on such half holidays.

Certain days designated as legal half holidays.

APPROVED—The 23d day of May, A. D. 1893.

ROBT. E. PATTISON.

No. 64.

AN ACT.

To authorize certain banks to improve and derive rent from buildings held by them for banking purposes.

SECTION 1. *Be it enacted, &c.*, That it shall be lawful for such banks of this Commonwealth as have heretofore erected buildings for banking purposes to further expend such sums, not in excess of one-half of their surplus fund, as may be necessary to renew or replace such buildings with such new or additional structures as may be suitable and convenient for the transaction of their banking business, and to lease from time to time such portions or apartments of said buildings as are not required for banking purposes, and to receive rents for use of the same.

APPROVED—The 23d day of May, 1893.

ROBT. E. PATTISON.

No. 65.

AN ACT

To prohibit the use of any adulteration or imitation of dairy products in any charitable or penal institution, being supplementary to an act, entitled "An act for the protection of the public health and to prevent adulteration of dairy products and fraud in the sale thereof," approved May twenty-one, Anno Domini one thousand eight hundred and eighty-five.

Shall not furnish to inmates any substance made or sold contrary to act of May 21 1885. SECTION 1. *Be it enacted, &c.,* That it shall not be lawful for any charitable or penal institution in the State of Pennsylvania to use, or furnish to its inmates, any substance, the manufacture or sale of which is prohibited by section one of the act, entitled "An act for the protection of the public health and to prevent adulteration of dairy products and fraud in the sale thereof," approved May twenty-first, Anno Domini one thousand eight hundred and eighty-five.

Purchase of any such substance shall be a misdemeanor SECTION 2. That any officer, agent, steward or other official of any such charitable or penal institution, who shall knowingly buy any substance the manufacture or sale of which is prohibited by section one of the said act of May twenty-one, Anno Domini one thousand eight hundred and eighty-five, for use in such charitable or penal institution, or who shall knowingly cause such substance to be used by the inmates of such charitable or penal institution, shall be deemed guilty **Penalty.** of a misdemeanor, and upon conviction shall be punished by a fine not exceeding one thousand dollars, or imprisonment not exceeding two years for each offense, or either or both at the discretion of the court.

Selling or offering for sale such substance to any institution shall be a misdemeanor. SECTION 3. Every person who shall knowingly sell or offer for sale, to any officer, agent, steward or other official of any charitable or penal institution, any substance, the manufacture or sale of which is prohibited by section one of the said act of May twenty-first, Anno Domini one thousand eight hundred and eighty-five, for use in such charitable or penal institution, shall be deemed guilty of a misdemeanor, and upon conviction, shall be punished by a fine not exceeding one thousand dollars, or by imprisonment not exceeding two years, or either or both at the discretion of the court.

APPROVED—The 23d day of May, A. D. 1893.

ROBT. E. PATTISON.

No. 66.

AN ACT

To provide for the continuation of the publication of the Pennsylvania Archives.

SECTION 1 *Be it enacted, &c.*, That the Secretary of the Commonwealth is hereby directed to have prepared for publication ten additional volumes of the third series of Archives, comprising the documents and papers connected with the affairs of the Provincial and State Governments of a date prior to the war of one thousand eight hundred and twelve and fourteen, and that copies of all such papers as may be required by the editor thereof shall be furnished by the department in which they are on record without expense. — *Secretary of the Commonwealth directed to have prepared for publication ten additional volumes of Archives.*

SECTION 2. That the editor of the aforesaid volumes directed to be published shall be paid for his services in selecting and arranging of the copy, reading the proofs, making indices, the sum of five hundred dollars upon the completion of each volume. — *Editor shall be paid $500 on completion of each volume.*

SECTION 3. The number of copies to be printed of each volume to be uniform in printing and binding, as in previous series, shall be two thousand, one complete set thereof to be furnished each member of the Legislature of one thousand eight hundred and ninety-three, the Governor and heads of all departments, the remaining copies to be sold by the Secretary of the Commonwealth at one dollar per volume: *Provided also*, That copies may be furnished by the Governor to such of the incorporated libraries in Pennsylvania as he may deem proper. — *Number of copies and style of printing and binding. Distribution of copies.*

SECTION 4. That a general index of the second series of Pennsylvaia Archives be prepared under the direction of the Secretary of the Commonwealth to be published uniform with the series and numbered volume twenty, and the sum of one thousand dollars is hereby appropriated for the preparation thereof. — *General index of second series to be prepared. $1,000 appropriated*

APPROVED—The 23d day of May, A. D. 1893.

ROBT. E. PATTISON.

No. 67.

AN ACT

To authorize the election of a chief burgess for three years in the several boroughs of this Commonwealth who shall not be eligible to the office for the next succeeding term, and providing that such officer shall not be a member of the town council, giving him the power to veto ordinances, providing for the election of a presiding officer of councils and abolishing the office of assistant burgess.

SECTION 1. *Be it enacted, &c.*, That the qualified voters of every borough in the Commonwealth of Pennsylvania shall, on the third Tuesday of February, Anno — *Chief burgess shall be elected for three years.*

8—LAWS.

Domini one thousand eight hundred and ninety-four, and triennially thereafter, vote for and elect a properly qualified person for chief burgess in each of said boroughs who shall serve for the term of three years, and shall not be eligible to the office for the next succeeding term.

SECTION 2. Such chief burgess shall not hold any other borough office or appointment during the term for which he is elected, nor be a member of, nor preside at the meetings of the town council of said borough. But said meetings shall be presided over by a president of council to be at the annual organization thereof elected by such council from among their number. And in the absence of such president shall be presided over by a president pro tempore.

SECTION 3. Every ordinance and resolution which shall be passed by said council shall be presented to the chief burgess of such borough, if he approve, he shall sign it, but if he shall not approve, he shall return it with his objections to said council at the next regular meeting thereof when said objections shall be entered at large in the minute book, and said council shall proceed to a reconsideration of such ordinance or resolution. If after such reconsideration two-thirds of all the members elected to said council shall vote to pass such ordinance or resolution, it shall become and be of as full force and effect as if said chief burgess had signed it, but in such cases the votes of the members of council shall be determined by the yeas and nays and the names of the members voting shall be entered on the minutes of said council: *Provided*, That when the number of councilmen is less than nine a majority of council and one vote more shall be required to pass an ordinance over the veto. If such ordinance or resolution shall not be returned by the chief burgess at the next regular meeting of said council after the same shall have been presented to him, the same shall likewise become and be in as full force and effect as he had signed it: *Provided*, That before any ordinance shall come into force and effect as aforesaid the same shall be recorded in the borough ordinance book with the certificate of the secretary and be advertised as heretofore required by law.

SECTION 4. That from and after the passage of this act the office of assistant burgess in all of the boroughs of this Commonwealth shall be and the same is hereby abolished.

SECTION 5. All acts or parts of acts inconsistent herewith are hereby repealed.

APPROVED—The 23d day of May, A. D. 1893.

ROBT. E. PATTISON.

No. 68.

AN ACT

Relative to a Forestry Commission and providing for the expenses thereof.

SECTION 1. *Be it enacted, &c.*, That the Governor be authorized to appoint two persons as a commission, one of whom is to be a competent engineer, one a botanist practically acquainted with the forest trees of the Commonwealth, whose duty it shall be to examine and report upon the conditions of the slopes and summits of the important water sheds of the State for the purpose of determining how far the presence or absence of the forest cover may be influential in producing high and low water stages in the various river basins, and to report how much timber remains standing of such kinds as have special commercial value, how much there is of each kind, as well also as to indicate the part or parts of the State where each grows naturally, and what measures if any are being taken to secure a supply of timber for the future. It shall further be the duty of said commission to suggest such measures in this connection as have been found of practical service elsewhere in maintaining a proper timber supply, and to ascertain as nearly as is practicable what proportion of the State not now recognized as mineral land is unfit for remunerative agriculture and could with advantage be devoted to the growth of trees. *(margin: Governor shall appoint two persons as a commission. Duty of commission.)*

SECTION 2. The said commission shall also ascertain what wild lands, if any, now belong to the Commonwealth, their extent, character and location, and report the same together with a statement of what part or parts of such lands would be suitable for a States Forest Reserve, and further, should the lands belonging to the Commonwealth be insufficient for such purpose, then to ascertain and report what other suitable lands there may be within the State, their extent, character and value. The final report of the said commission shall be presented to the Legislature not later than March fifteenth, one thousand eight hundred and ninety-five. *(margin: Shall ascertain wild lands belonging to Commonwealth. State Forest Reserve. Final report of commission.)*

SECTION 3. The said commission shall have power to appoint one competent person to act as statistician whose duties shall be to compile the statistics collected by said commission under their direction and supervision, whose salary shall be one thousand dollars per annum with necessary expenses to be paid in the same manner as is hereinafter provided for the payment of the Forestry Commission. *(margin: Commission may appoint a statistician. Salary.)*

SECTION 4. The commissioners appointed hereunder shall be entitled to receive by quarterly payments a compensation as follows: The engineer twenty-five hundred dollars ($2,500) per annum, the botanist twenty-five hundred dollars ($2,500) per annum, with *(margin: Compensation of commission.)*

$20,000 appropriated

How payable.

necessary expenses for each, and the sum of twenty thousand dollars ($20,000), or so much as is necessary, is hereby appropriated out of any money in the Treasury, not otherwise appropriated, to be paid by warrant drawn by the Auditor General.

APPROVED—The 23d day of May, A. D. 1893.

ROBT. E. PATTISON.

No. 69.

AN ACT

Giving authority to the Commissioners of the Sinking Fund to to pay certain moneys out of the Sinking Fund to the commissioners of the Sinking Fund of the City of Philadelphia.

WHEREAS, The Commissioners of the Sinking Fund of the Commonwealth sold in January, one thousand eight hundred and ninety-two, three hundred thousand dollars of United States four per centum registered bonds to the Commissioners of the Sinking Fund of the City of Philadelphia.

And whereas, The said bonds were not transferred on the books of the United States Treasurer at Washington, District of Columbia, until after three months' interest was due on the same.

And whereas, Said interest was paid to the fiscal agent of the State and is now in the State Tresaury; therefore,

SECTION 1. *Be it enacted, &c.,* That the State Treasurer is hereby authorized to pay the sum of three thousand dollars out of the sinking fund to the Commissioners of the Sinking Fund of the City of Philadelphia.

APPROVED—The 23d day of May, A. D. 1893.

ROBT. E. PATTISON.

No. 70.

AN ACT

Limiting the liability of poor districts.

SECTION 1. *Be it enacted, &c.,* That hereafter no poor district in this Commonwealth shall be held or adjudged liable to any person for or on account of relief of any kind or nature whatsoever afforded by him to any poor, sick or destitute person for more than ten days immediatey preceding the time when an order for the relief of such poor person shall have been procured and delivered to the overseers of the poor of the district wherein such relief shall have been afforded.

APPROVED—The 23d day of May, A. D. 1893.

ROBT. E. PATTISON.

No. 71.

AN ACT

To regulate and establish the fees to be charged by justices of the
peace, aldermen, magistrates and constables in this Commonwealth.

WHEREAS, No general fee bill for justices of the
peace has been enacted since the act increasing the jurisdiction of justices ;

And whereas, No uniform fee bill for the several
counties throughout the Commonwealth of Pennsylvania now exists relating to justices of the peace, magistrates, aldermen and constables ; therefore,

SECTION 1. *Be it enacted, &c.,* That there shall be uniformity throughout the Commonwealth in the charges
of justices of the peace, aldermen, magistrates and constables, and that their fees shall be as follows, to wit :
That from and after the passage of this act the fees of
justices of the peace, magistrates and aldermen, shall
be :

For information or complaint on behalf of the Commonwealth, fifty cents.

Docket entry of action on behalf of the Commonwealth, twenty-five cents.

Warrant, mittimus or capias on behalf of the Commonwealth, fifty cents.

Writing an examination or confession of defendant,
fifty cents.

Hearing in criminal cases, fifty cents.

Administering oath or affidavit in criminal or civil
cases, ten cents.

Taking recognizance in criminal case, fifty cents.

Transcript in criminal cases, including certificate,
fifty cents.

Entering judgment on conviction for fine, fifty cents.

Recording conviction, twenty-five cents.

Warrant to levy fine or forfeiture, thirty cents.

Bail piece and return supersedeas, thirty cents.

Discharge of jailor, thirty-five cents.

Entering discontinuance in case of an assault and
battery, fifty cents.

Entering complaint of master, mistress or an apprentice, thirty cents.

Notice to master, mistress or apprentice, twenty-five
cents.

Hearing parties, fifty cents.

Holding inquisition under landlord and tenant act,
or in case of forcible entry. each day, each justice, two
dollars.

Process et cetera to sheriff, each justice, seventy-five
cents.

Recording proceedings, each justice, one dollar and
fifty cents.

Writ of restitution, each justice, seventy five cents.

Warrant to appraise damages, thirty cents

*Establishing uni-
form fees in all
counties of the
Commonwealth for
justices of the
peace, magistrates
and aldermen.*

Warrant to sell strays, thirty cents.

Warrant to appraise swine, thirty-five cents.

Receiving and entering return of appraisement of swine, twenty-five cents.

Publishing proceedings of appraisers of swine, seventy-five cents.

Entering action in civil case, twenty-five cents.

Summons or subpœna, twenty-five cents.

Capias in civil case, fifty cents.

Every additional name after the first, all witnesses names to be in one subpœna unless separate subpoenas be requested by the parties, ten cents.

Subpoena duces tecum, twenty-five cents.

Entering return of summons, twenty-five cents.

Entering capias and bail bond, twenty-five cents.

Every continuance of a suit, twenty cents.

Trial and judgment in case, fifty cents.

Taking bail or plea of freehold, twenty-five cents.

Entering satisfaction, fifteen cents.

Entering discontinuance of suit, fifteen cents.

Entering amicable suit, fifty cents.

Entering rule to take deposition of witnesses, fifteen cents.

Rule to take depositions, twenty-five cents.

Entering return of rule in any case, fifteen cents.

Interrogatories annexed to rule to take depositions, twenty-five cents.

Entering rule to refer, fifteen cents.

Rule of reference, twenty-five cents.

Notice to each referee, twenty-five cents.

Entering report of referees and judgment thereon, thirty cents.

Written notice in any case, twenty-five cents.

Execution, thirty cents.

Entering return of execution, fifteen cents.

Scire facias in any case, thirty-five cents.

Opening judgment for a rehearing, twenty-five cents.

Transcription of judgment and certificate, fifty cents.

Return of proceedings on certiorari or appeals, including recognizances, one dollar.

Receiving the amount of a judgment and paying the same over, if not exceeding ten dollars, twenty-five cents.

If exceeding ten, and not exceeding forty dollars, fifty cents.

If exceeding forty, and not exceeding sixty dollars, seventy-five cents.

If exceeding sixty, and not exceeding one hundred dollars, one dollar.

And a like amount on each one hundred up to three hundred.

Every search service to which no fees are attached, twenty cents.

Affidavit in case of attachment, thirty cents.

Entering action in case of attachment, twenty-five cents.

Attachment in any case, thirty-five cents.

Recognizance, fifty cents.

Interrogatories, thirty-five cents.

Rule on garnishee, twenty-five cents.

Return of rule on garnishee, twenty-five cents.

Bond in case of attachment, fifty cents.

Entering return and appointing freeholders, twenty-five cents.

Advertisement, each, twenty-five cents.

Order to sell goods, thirty-five cents.

Order for the relief of a pauper, each justice, fifty cents.

Entering transcript of judgment from another justice or alderman, fifty cents.

Order for the removal of a pauper, each justice or alderman, one dollar.

Order to seize goods for the maintenance of wife and children, fifty cents.

Order for premium for wolf, fox or other scalps to be paid by the county, twenty-five cents.

Every acknowledgment or probate of deed, or other instrument of writing, for first name, fifty cents.

Each additional name after the first, twenty-five cents.

Taking and signing acknowledgment of indenture of an apprentice, fifty cents.

Assignment and making record of indenture, fifty cents.

Cancelling indenture, fifty cents.

Comparing and signing tax duplicates, each alderman, seventy-five cents.

Marrying each couple, making record thereof and certificates to the parties, five dollars.

Certificate of approbation of two justices to the binding as apprentice of a person by the directors of the poor, each justice, thirty-five cents.

Certificate to obtain land warrant, seventy-five cents.

Swearing or affirming county commissioner, assessor, director of the poor, or other township officer, or county officer, and certificate, fifty cents. Administering oaths or affirmations in any case not herein provided for, twenty-five cents.

Justifying parties on bonds for tavern licenses, one dollar.

Entering complaint in landlord and tenant proceedings, act one thousand eight hundred and thirty, twenty-five cents.

Issuing process in landlord and tenant proceedings, act one thousand eight hundred and thirty, twenty-five cents.

Hearing and determining case in landlord and tenant proceedings, act one thousand eight hundred and thirty, fifty cents.

Record of proceedings in landlord and tenant proceedings, act one thousand eight hundred and thirty, fifty cents.

Writ of possession (and return) in landlord and tenant proceedings, act one thousand eight hundred and thirty, fifty cents.

When more than one magistrate is required in landlord and tenant proceedings the above fees shall be charged by each magistrate.

Entering complaint in landlord and tenant proceedings, act one thousand eight hundred and sixty-three, seventy-five cents.

Issuing process in landlord and tenant proceedings, act one thousand eight hundred and sixty-three, seventy-five cents.

Hearing and determining case, act one thousand eight hundred and sixty-three, one dollar.

Record of proceedings, act one thousand eight hundred and sixty-three, one dollar and fifty cents.

Issuing writ of restitution (and return), act one thousand eight hundred and sixty-three, one dollar.

The fees for services under the laws of the United States shall be as follows:

For certificate of protection, fifty cents.

For certificate of lost protection, twenty-five cents.

Warrant, twenty-five cents.

Commitment, twenty-five cents.

Summons for seamen in admiralty case, twenty-five cents.

Hearing thereon with docket entry, fifty cents.

For certificate to clerk of the district court to issue admiralty process, twenty-five cents.

For affidavits of claims and copies thereof, twenty-five cents.

The fees for services not herein specially provided shall be the same as for similar services.

Uniform fees for constables.

SECTION 2. That from and after the passage of this act the fees to be received by constables in this Commonwealth shall be as follows: For executing warrant on behalf of the Commonwealth, one dollar; for taking body into custody, or conveying to jail on mittimus or warrant, one dollar; for arresting a vagrant, disorderly person, or other offender against the laws (without warrant), and bringing before a justice, seventy-five cents; for levying a fine or forfeiture on a warrant, fifty cents; for serving subpœna, fifty cents; for taking the body into custody on mittimus where bail is afterwards entered before the prisoner is delivered to the jailor, one dollar; for serving summons notices on reference suitor, master or mistress, or apprentice personally, each fifty cents; for serving by leaving a copy, fifty cents; for executing attachment personally, fifty cents; for arresting on capias one dollar; for taking bail bond on capias or for delivery of goods, fifty cents; for notifying plaintiff where defendant has been arrested on capias to be paid by plaintiff, twenty-five cents; for executing landlord's warrants, fifty cents; for taking inventory of goods (each item), two cents; for levying or distraining goods and selling the same, for each dollar not exceeding one hundred dollars, three cents; and for each dollar above one hundred dollars, two cents; (and one half of said commission shall be allowed where the money is paid after levy without sale but no commission shall in any case be taken on more than the real debt and then only for the money actually received by the constable and paid over to the creditor); for advertising the same, one dollar; for copy of vendue paper when demanded, each item, two cents; for putting up notice of distress at mansion house, or at any other place on the premises, twenty-five cents; for serving *scire facias* personally, fifty cents; for serving by leaving a copy, fifty cents; for executing bail piece, one dollar; for traveling expenses on an execution returned *nulla bona* and *non est inventus* where the constable has been at the defendant's last residence, each mile, ten cents; for traveling expenses in all other cases, each mile, ten cents; for executing order for the removal of a pauper, seventy-five cents; for traveling expenses in said removal, each mile circular, fifteen cents; for serving execution, fifty cents; for serving execution on a writ of restitution, two dollars; for serving execution on a writ of possesion, two dollars; for serving summons in landlord and tenant proceedings, one dollar; for serving notice in landlord and tenant proceedings, fifty cents; for taking inventory of goods on an execution (each item), two cents; for serving search warrant, one dollar; for serving capias execution, one dollar; constable and appraisers personally, each, one dollar on appraisement.

SECTION 3. That all acts or parts of acts in force at the date of the passage of this act inconsistent with its provisions are hereby repealed. *Repeal.*

APPROVED—The 23d day of May, A. D. 1893.

ROBT. E. PATTISON.

———

No. 72.

AN ACT

To amend an act. entitled "An act prescribing the mode of fixing the salaries of county superintendents of common schools," approved the twenty-ninth day of April, Anno Domini one thousand eight hundred and seventy-eight, amending first section thereof by fixing the minimum salaries to be paid said superintendents.

SECTION 1. *Be it enacted, &c.,* That section one of an act, entitled "An act prescribing the mode of fixing salaries of county superintendents of common schools," approved the twenty-ninth day of April, Anno Domini one thousand eight hundred and seventy-eight, which reads as follows:

Section 1, act of April 29, 1878, cited for amendment.

"SECTION 1. *Be it enacted by the Senate and House of Representatives of the Commonwealth of Pennsylvania in General Assembly met, and it is hereby enacted by the authority of the same,* That the salary of each county superintendent of common schools, elected according to law, in the year one thousand eight hundred and seventy-eight, and thereafter, shall be four dollars and fifty cents for each school in his jurisdiction at the time of his election to be paid out of the general fund appropriated for common schools: *Provided,* That the salary of a county superintendent shall in no case be less than eight hundred dollars, nor more than two thousand dollars per annum, and in counties with over one hundred schools it shall not be less than one thousand dollars: *And provided further,* That conventions of school directors, when assembled for the purpose of electing a county superintendent, may vote him a salary greater than the amount he would receive by this act, such increase to be in all cases taken from the school fund of the county thus voting. That in all counties having over one hundred and ninety schools, or twelve hundred square miles of territory, or a school term exceeding seven and one half months, the salaries of said superintendents shall not be less than fifteen hundred dollars," be and the same is hereby amended so as to read as follows:

Salary of county superintendent of schools.

SECTION 1. That the salary of each superintendent of common schools elected according to law, in the year one thousand eight hundred and ninety-three, and thereafter, shall be four dollars and fifty cents for each school in his jurisdiction at the time of his election, to be paid out of the general fund appropriated for

Minimum and maximum salary.

common schools: *Provided,* That the salary of a county superintendent shall in no case be less than one thousand dollars nor more than two thousand dollars per annum: *And provided further,* That conventions of

Directors may increase.

school directors when assembled for the purpose of electing a county superintendent may vote him a salary greater than the amount he would receive by this act, such increase to be, in all cases, taken from the school fund of the county thus voting. That in all

Minimum salary in certain counties.

counties having over one hundred and ninety schools, or twelve hundred square miles of territory, or a school term exceeding seven and one-half months, the salaries of said superintendents shall not be less than fifteen hundred dollars.

APPROVED—The 23d day of May, A. D. 1893.

ROBT. E. PATTISON.

No. 73.

AN ACT

To authorize councils of cities of the first class to place on the plans of public streets of such cities all streets laid out and opened prior to June sixth, one thousand eight hundred and seventy-one, and which are less than thirty feet in width, or have dead ends, or do not extend in a straight line from one street to another.

SECTION 1. *Be it enacted, &c.*, That the councils of all cities of the first class are hereby authorized to place on the city plan of public streets of such cities, all streets which were laid out and opened prior to June sixth, one thousand eight hundred and seventy-one, and which are less than thirty feet in width, or have dead ends, or which do not extend in a straight line from one street to another, whereupon such streets shall become public streets; and all acts or parts of acts inconsistent herewith be and the same are hereby repealed.

Councils shall place certain streets on city plan

Repeal.

APPROVED –The 23d day of May, A. D. 1893.

ROBT. E. PATTISON.

—————

No. 74.

AN ACT

Authorizing the Governor of this Commonwealth to appoint five persons to make inquiry and examine into and make report to the next session of this Legislature, at its next regular session, the advisability of erecting suitable tablets, marking the various forts erected as a defense against the Indians by the early settlers of this Commonwealth prior to the year one thousand seven hundred and eighty-three.

SECTION 1. *Be it enacted, &c.*, That on and after thirty days from the passage of this act, the Governor of this Comomnwealth is hereby authorized and required to appoint five persons to make inquiry in relation to the various forts erected by the early settlers of this Commonwealth prior to the year one thousand seven hundred and eighty-three, as a defense against the Indians. Said five persons are hereby authorized to make inquiry and examination as to the number and location of said forts and the propriety of erecting tablets to mark said forts and do such things as they may deem best to carry out the provisions of this act, and make report to the next regular session of the Legislature of this Comomnwealth within thirty days after it shall convene.

Governor shall appoint a commission.

Which shall make inquiry and examination as to forts erected prior to 1783, as a defense against the Indians and report to next session of the Legislature.

SECTION 2 The persons appointed to serve in making such examination and report shall be allowed no compensation for their services, only such actual expenses as they shall incur in making such examination

Commissioners shall receive no compensation, but actual expenses shall be allowed.

and report and such railroad fare, not exceeding three cents per mile for each mile actually traveled thereon, and such other expenses of other conveyance as may be necessary in making such investigation and report.

How expenses shall be paid.

An itemized account and statement whereof shall be certified to by the Governor and attested by the Auditor General of the Commonwealth before paid by the Treasurer, which shall accompany the report to the Legislature.

APPROVED—The 23d day of May, A. D. 1893.

ROBT. E. PATTISON.

No. 75.

AN ACT

To abolish commissioners of public buildings, and to place all public buildings heretofore under the control of such commissioners, under the control of the Department of Public Works in cities of the first class.

Commissioners for the erection, etc., of public buildings abolished.

SECTION 1. *Be it enacted, &c.,* That commissioners created by any special act of Assembly for the erection and construction of public buildings required to accommodate the courts and for municipal purposes in cities of the first class in this Commonwealth are

Erection, etc., under direction of the Department of Public Works.

hereby abolished, and the erection, completion, construction, repair, removal and protection of all public buildings heretofore under the control of such commissioners in said cities shall be under the direction, control and administration of the Department of Public Works.

Act of August 5, 1870, and part of section 1, article 4, act of June 1, 1885, repealed.

SECTION 2. An act, entitled "An act to provide for the erection of all the public buildings required to accommodate the courts and for all municipal purposes in the city of Philadelphia, and to require the appropriation by said city of Penn Square, at Broad and Market streets, to the Academy of Fine Arts, the Academy of Natural Science, the Franklin Institute and the Philadelphia Library, in the event of the said squares not being selected by a vote of the people as the site for the public buildings for said city," approved the fifth day of August, one thousand eight hundred and seventy, and so much of section one, article four of an act, entitled "An act to provide for the better government of cities of the first class in this Commonwealth," approved the first day of June, one thousand eight hundred and eighty-five, as reads as follows: "That nothing in this section contained shall be construed to repeal or conflict with any special acts of Assembly providing for the erection and construction of public buildings," and all laws and parts of laws inconsistent herewith shall be and the same hereby are repealed: *Provided,* That nothing in this section contained shall be construed to repeal or conflict with an act, entitled "An act appropriating ground for public purposes in the city of Philadelphia," approved the twenty-sixth day of March, one thousand eight hundred and sixty-seven.

APPROVED—The 24th day of May, A. D. 1893.

ROBT. E. PATTISON.

No. 76.

AN ACT

Providing for monthly returns and payments by county and city officers and prothonotaries of the Supreme Court of moneys received by them for the use of the Commonwealth.

SECTION 1. *Be it enacted, &c.*, That on the first Monday July next, and on the first Monday of each month thereafter, it shall be the duty of each county and city officer to render to the Auditor General and State Treasurer, under oath or affirmation, monthly returns of all moneys received for the use of the Commonwealth, designating under proper heads, the sources from which said moneys were received, and to pay the said moneys into the State Treasury.

The returns herein required from county and city officers and prothonotaries of the Supreme Court, except those rendered by city and county treasurers, shall include fees received during the month from all sources.

SECTION 2. Any officer who shall refuse or neglect, for the period of ten days after the same shall become due, to make the return and payment as required by the preceding section of this act shall forfeit his fees and commissions on the whole amount of money collected during the month, and shall be subject to a penalty of ten per centum which shall be added to the amount of the tax found due.

SECTION 3. The Auditor General or State Treasurer, or either of them, or any agent appointed by them or either of them, are hereby authorized to examine the books and accounts of any county or city officer who shall refuse or neglect to make the return and payment as required by the first section of this act, and upon information obtained from such examination the Auditor General and State Treasurer shall settle an account against such officer in the usual manner for the settlement of public accounts, and in the settlement of said accounts shall add not to exceed fifty per centum to the amount of the tax to provide for any losses which might otherwise result to the Commonwealth from neglect or refusal of the said officer to furnish the return.

SECTION 4. If the amount of an account settled in accordance with the preceding section of this act shall not be paid into the State Treasury within fifteen days from the date of settlement of said account, then the same shall be placed in the hands of the Attorney General for collection and shall bear interest from fifteen days after date of settlement, at the rate of twelve per centum per annum, and if the Auditor General and State Treasurer, or either of them, shall deem it conducive to the public interest to proceed immediately upon said account against the sureties of the said officer, they shall so instruct the Attorney General, who shall proceed in accordance with such direction received from them, or either of them.

Account shall then bear 12 per centum interest.

May proceed against sureties of officer.

SECTION 5. All acts or parts of acts inconsistent herewith, or which are substantially re-enacted hereby, shall be and the same are hereby repealed, saving, preserving and excepting unto the Commonwealth the right to collect any taxes accrued or accruing under said repealed acts or parts of acts.

Repeal.

Commonwealth reserves certain rights.

APPROVED—The 24th day of May, A. D. 1893.

ROBT. E. PATTISON.

No. 77.

AN ACT

Defining to whom the benefit certificates issued by fraternal societies paying benefits upon the death of their members by mutual assessment shall be paid, where the person or member dies without leaving a person designated to receive the same.

SECTION 1. *Be it enacted, &c.*, That from and after the passage of this act any benefit certificate or certificates now or hereafter issued by any corporation, society or voluntary association now or hereafter formed or organized and carried on for the sole benefit of its members and their beneficiaries and not for profit, when any person or persons shall have been designated by the members as his beneficiary or beneficiaries shall die prior to the death of the member without any new designation, and no provision is made by the laws of the society as to who shall take the share designated to go to such deceased beneficiary or beneficiaries, in all such cases the amount or share designated to be paid to such deceased beneficiary or beneficiaries shall be payable to the widow and children of such deceased member, if any, share and share alike, and in case none such be living, then to such other relatives of such deceased members, and in such proportions as they are entitled to receive under a distribution of the personal estate by the laws of the domicile of such member.

APPROVED—The 24th day of May, A. D. 1893.

ROBT. E. PATTISON.

No. 78.

AN ACT

Requiring all deeds of sheriffs to be recorded in the offices of the prothonotaries of the several courts of common pleas of the Commonwealth.

SECTION 1. *Be it enacted, &c.*, That from and after the passage of this act all deeds of sheriffs, being duly acknowledged, shall be recorded in full in the office of the prothonotary of the court of common pleas of the county where the lands lie, and the records thereof, or duly certified copies thereof, shall be evidence in all cases where the original deeds would be evidence. And it shall be the duty of the prothonotaries of the several courts of common pleas of the counties aforesaid to record said deeds in books to be by them kept for that purpose, and to index the same both in the name of the grantee and the name of the person as whose property the lands were sold, for which services they shall receive as fees from the grantee one cent for every eight words, or part thereof.

Sheriffs' deeds shall be recorded by prothonotary.

Fees for recording.

APPROVED—The 24th day of May, A. D. 1893.

ROBT. E. PATTISON.

No. 79.

AN ACT

To amend the fifth section of an act, entitled "An act to carry into effect section five of the Constitution relative to the salaries of county officers and the payment of fees received by them into the State or county treasury, in counties containing over one hundred and fifty thousand inhabitants," approved the thirty-first day of March, Anno Domini one thousand eight hundred and seventy-six, requiring the payment of salaries of county officers, their deputies and clerks, in offices wherein fees are no longer by law collected or received, to be made on the first secular day of the month succeeding that in which said services were rendered.

SECTION 1. *Be it enacted, &c.*, That section five of an act, entitled "An act to carry into effect section five of the Constitution, relative to the salaries of county officers and the payment of fees received by them into the State or county treasury, in counties containing over one hundred and fifty thousand inhabitants," approved the thirty-first day of March, Anno Domini one thousand eight hundred and seventy-six, which reads as follows:

Section 5. act of March 31, 1876, cited for repeal.

"All county officers within the counties to which this act applies, whether elected by the people or appointed according to law, and their several deputies and clerks shall be paid for their services by fixed and specific salaries, which shall be a charge upon the treasury of the county to which each shall respectively belong to the extent (except as hereinafter provided) of the fees collected and paid in by each officer respectively, or earned where fees are chargeable upon the county treasury ; and said salaries shall be paid monthly, except as herein otherwise provided, on the second Monday of the month succeeding that in which his services were rendered, but no warrant shall be drawn for the payment of any of said officers, his deputies or clerks, who shall not have filed the receipt and transcript provided for in this act," be and the same is hereby amended so as to read as follows, namely :

Officers, deputies and clerks shall be paid a fixed salary.

All county officers within the counties to which this act applies, whether elected by the people or appointed according to law, and their several deputies and clerks, shall be paid for their services by fixed and specific salaries which shall be a charge upon the treasury of the county to which each shall respectively belong to the extent (except as hereinafter provided) of the fees collected and paid in by each officer respectively, or

When salaries shall be paid.

earned where fees are chargeable upon the county treasury, and said salaries shall be paid monthly, except as herein otherwise provided, on the second Monday of the month succeeding that in which his services

When warrants shall be drawn.

were rendered ; but no warrant shall be drawn for the payment of any of said officers, his deputies or clerks, who shall not have filed the receipt and transcript pro-

Proviso as to payment of salary.

vided for in this act : *Provided however*, That all county officers, their deputies and clerks, in offices wherein fees are no longer by law collected or received, shall be paid said salaries on the first secular day of the month succeeding that in which said services were rendered.

APPROVED—The 24th day of May, A. D. 1893.

ROBT. E. PATTISON.

— —

No. 80.

AN ACT

Relating to the private sale of real estate in assignments for the benefit of creditors.

Court may decree and approve a private sale.

SECTION 1. *Be it enacted, &c.*, That from and after the passage of this act, it shall and may be lawful for the several courts of common pleas of this Commonwealth, in all cases where under existing laws the court has power to order the public sale of real estate assigned for the benefit of creditors, may decree and approve a private sale or may confirm a private sale returned under an order for a public sale, if, in the opinion of the court, under all the circumstances, as good or a better price can be obtained at private than at public sale, upon such notice being given to all lien creditors in such manner as the court may direct.

SECTION 2. All acts or parts of acts inconsistent with *Repeal.* the provisions of this act be and the same are hereby repealed.

APPROVED—The 24th day of May, A. D. 1893.

ROBT. E. PATTISON.

———

No. 81.

AN ACT

To amend the thirty-second section of an act, entitled "An act relating to elections in this Commonwealth," approved the second day of July, Anno Domini one thousand eight hundred and thirty-nine, providing for mileage for Presidential electors and increasing the contingent expenses of said electors.

SECTION 1. *Be it enacted, &c.,* That the thirty-second section of an act, entitled "An act relating to elections in this Commonwealth," approved the second day of July, Anno Domini one thousand eight hundred and thirty-nine, which reads as follows:

"SECTION 32. Every elector aforesaid shall receive *Section 32, act of* from the State Treasury the sum of three dollars for *July 2, 1839, cited for amendment.* every day spent in traveling to, remaining at, and returning from the place of meeting aforesaid. And the contingent expenses of the electoral college, not exceeding fifty dollars in amount, shall likewise be paid by the State Treasurer, in both cases upon warrants drawn by the presiding officer of the college," be and the same is hereby amended to read:

SECTION 32. Every elector aforesaid shall receive *Compensation of electors.* from the State Treasury the sum of three dollars for every day spent in traveling to, remaining at, and returning from the place of meeting aforesaid, and shall be entitled to mileage at the rate of three cents per mile to and from their homes, to be computed by the ordinary mail route between their homes and the place of meeting aforesaid. And the contingent expenses of the electoral college, not exceeding one hundred *Contingent expenses of electoral college.* dred dollars in amount, shall likewise be paid by the State Treasurer, in both cases upon warrants drawn by the presiding officer of the college.

APPROVED—The 24th day of May, A. D. 1893.

ROBT. E. PATTISON.

———

No. 82.

AN ACT

To empower boroughs and cities to establish a police pension fund, to take property in trust therefor and regulating and providing for the regulation of the same.

SECTION 1 *Be it enacted, &c.,* That the several bor- *Boroughs and cities may establish a police pension fund.* oughs and cities of this Commonwealth, incorporated

9—LAWS.

by general or special laws, shall have power to establish by ordinance a police pension fund to be maintained by an equal and proportionate monthly charge against each member of the police force which shall not exceed annually three per centum of the pay of such member, which fund shall be under the direction of councils or committee to the direction of such officers of the city or borough as may be designated by councils, and applied under such regulations as councils may by ordinance presribe for the benefit of such members of the police force as shall receive honorable discharge therefrom by reason of age or disability and the families of such as may be injured or killed in the service, but such allowances as shall be made to those who are retired by reason of the disabilities of age shall be in conformity with a uniform scale.

Such ordinance may prescribe a minimum period of continuous service, not less than twenty years, after which members of the force may be retired from active duty, and such members as retired shall be subject to service from time to time as a police reserve until unfitted for such service, when they may be finally discharged by reason of age or disability.

Payments made under the provisions of this section shall not be a charge on any other fund in the treasury of the city or borough, or under its control, save the police pension fund herein provided for. The basis of the apportionment of the pension shall be determined by the rate of the monthly pay of the member at the date of death, honorable discharge, or retirement, and shall not in any case exceed in any year one-half the annual pay of such member computed at such monthly rate.

SECTION 2. It shall be competent for any such city or borough to take by gift, grant, devise or bequest, any money or property, real, personal or mixed, in trust for the benefit of such pension fund, and the care, management, investment and disposal of such trust funds or property shall be vested in such officer or officers of such city or borough for the time being as the said city or borough may designate, and such care, management and disposal shall likewise be directed by ordinance and the said trust funds shall be governed thereby, subject to such directions not inconsistent therewith as the donors of such funds and property may prescribe.

SECTION 3. Whenever any person shall become entitled to receive a benefit from the police pension fund, and shall have been admitted to participate therein, he shall not be deprived of his right to an equal and proportionate participation therein upon the basis upon which he first became entitled thereto, save from one or more of the following causes, that is to say, conviction of a crime or misdemeanor, becoming an habitual drunkard, becoming a non-resident of the State, or

Marginal notes:

How the fund shall be maintained and under whose direction it shall be.

How applied.

Minimum period of continuous service for members of force.

Final discharge.

Payments shall not be a charge on any other fund of borough or city

Basis of apportionment of pension.

May take gift, etc., in trust for the fund.

Care and management of any such trust.

Termination of right to participate in the fund, and how regulated.

failing to comply with same general regulation relating to the management of said fund which may be made by ordinance, and which may provide that a failure to comply therewith shall terminate the right to participate in the pension fund after such due notice and hearing as shall be prescribed by ordinance.

APPROVED—The 24th day of May, A. D. 1893.

ROBT. E. PATTISON.

— — —

No. 83.

AN ACT

To prohibit the employment of any minor under the age of fourteen years in or about elevators.

SECTION 1. *Be it enacted, &c.*, That no person, firm or corporation shall employ or permit any minor under the age of fourteen years to have the care, custody, management or operation of any elevator. Any person, firm or corporation, employing any minor under the age of fourteen years to operate, manage, or otherwise have the care or custody of an elevator, shall be guilty of a misdemeanor, and upon conviction thereof, shall be sentenced to pay a fine of not less than twenty-five dollars nor more than one hundred dollars.

APPROVED—The 24th day of May, A. D. 1893.

ROBT. E. PATTISON.

— — —

No. 84.

AN ACT

To amend an act, entitled "To settle title to real estate," approved the eighth day of March, Anno Domini one thousand eight hundred and eighty-nine, by designating the manner in which notices may be served.

SECTION 1. *Be it enacted, &c.*, That section one of an act, entitled "An act to settle title to real estate," approved the eighth day of March, Anno Domini one thousand eight hundred and eighty-nine, which reads as follows :

"That whenever any person not being in possession thereof shall claim an interest in, or title to, real estate, it shall be lawful for any person in possession thereof, claiming title to the same, to make application to the court of common pleas of the proper county, whereupon a rule shall be granted upon said person not in possession to bring his or her action of ejectment within six months from service of such rule upon him or her, or show why the same cannot be so brought, which rule may be made returnable to any term, or return day of such court, and be served and returned as writs of

Section 1, act of March 8, 1889, cited for amendment.

summons are by law served and returned, and shall be
entered of record and indexed as actions of ejectment
are now indexed in the courts of the Commonwealth,"
be amended so as to read as follows:

Party in possession may obtain rule on party not in possession but claiming title, to bring action.

That whenever any person not being in posession
thereof shall claim an interest in, or title to, real
estate, it shall be lawful for any person in possession
thereof claiming title to the same, to make application
to the court of common pleas of the proper county,
whereupon a rule shall be granted upon said person
not in possession to bring his or her action of ejectment within six months from the service of such rule
upon him or her, or show cause why the same cannot

When rule returnable. How served.

be so brought, which rule may be made returnable to any
term, or return day of such court, and be served and returned as writs of summons are by law served and re-

Service when parties reside outside the county.

turned: *Provided however,* When parties claiming, but
not in possession, reside without the county where the
land lies and within the Commonwealth, in such case the
sheriff of the county in which such writ shall issue,
shall have power to execute the same, and when parties

Or outside the State.

claiming, reside outside of the State, it shall be lawful
for any person to serve notice of said application on
such parties, and upon affidavit and satisfactory proof
being made of such service had, the court may proceed
as fully and effectually as if the same had been made
by the sheriff within the jurisdiction of such court, and

Shall be entered of record.

shall be entered of record and indexed as actions of
ejectment are now indexed in the courts of the Commonwealth.

APPROVED—The 25th day of May, A. D. 1893.

ROBT. E. PATTISON.

No. 85.

AN ACT

To repeal the eighth section of an act, entitled "An act to incor
porate the Schuylkill county agriculture society; relative to a
school district in Schuylkill county; to an election district in
said county; to the daily pay of the commissioners of Berks
county; to reporter of the decisions of the Supreme Court; to
the collection of school taxes in certain townships in Crawford
and Allegheny counties; to the estate of Joseph Parker Norris,
deceased; to the Keystone Life and Health Insurance Company; to tavern licenses in Philadelphia city and county; to the
estate of Polly Dunlap, of Clearfield county; to the sale of a lot
of ground by the overseers of the public schools of the city and
county of Philadelphia," approved the fourteenth day of April,
one thousand eight hundred and fifty-one.

SECTION 1. *Be it enacted, &c.,* That the eighth section
of the act, entitled "An act to incorporate the
Schuylkill County Agricultural Society; relative to a
school district in Schuylkill county; to an election dis-

trict in said county; to the daily pay of the commissioners of Berks county; to the reporter of the decisions
of the Supreme Court; to the collection of school taxes in
certain townships in Crawford and Allegheny counties;
to the estate of Joseph Parker Norris, deceased; to
the Keystone Life and Health Insurance Company; to
tavern licenses in Philadelphia city and county; to the
estate of Polly Dunlap of Clearfield county; to the sale
of a lot of ground by the overseers of the public schools
of the city and county of Philadelphia," approved the
fourteenth day of April, one thousand eight hundred
and fifty-one, which reads as follows:

"That a tax of fifty cents for the reporter of the decis- *Section 8, act of*
ions of the Supreme Court be and the same is hereby *April 14, 1857, re-*
imposed on each writ of error and on appeals to the *pealed.*
said court on writs of certiorari and on cases removed
into the Supreme Court from the court of *nisi prius* in
Philadephia, and the same amount of tax for the said
reporter is hereby imposed on all such cases not now
pending or which shall have been decided during the
present session of the said court at Philadelphia, the
same to be taxed by the prothonotary in the several
bills of costs," be and the same is hereby repealed.

APPROVED—The 25th day of May, A. D. 1893.

ROBT. E. PATTISON.

———

No. 86.

AN ACT

Providing that whenever it shall happen that a receipt given by a
warehouseman, warehousing company, storage or deposit company, or wharfinger, has become lost, mislaid or destroyed, the
court, on the petition of the owner of such receipt, may, in its
discretion, order that the goods, wares, merchandise, petroleum,
grain, flour, produce, commodity, or other property for which it
was given, shall be delivered without the production or return
of such receipt.

WHEREAS, It frequently happens that the rightful
owners of receipts issued by warehousemen, warehousing companies, storage or deposit companies and
wharfingers lose or mislay such receipts, or that such
receipts become destroyed, and such rightful owners
being therefore unable to produce or return the same
are unable to obtain possession or control of the goods,
wares, merchandise, petroleum, grain, flour, or other
produce, commodity or property for which such receipts
were given, thus leading to great embarrassment and
inconvenience, and it is desirable that relief against
this evil should be afforded, therefore,

SECTION 1. *Be it enacted, &c.*, That where any receipt
given or issued by any warehouseman, warehousing
company, storage or deposit company, or wharfinger,

Where receipt given has been lost or destroyed owner may present petition to court of common pleas, praying for an order on the company to deliver up the goods.

Contents of Petition.

has become lost, mislaid or destroyed, it shall be lawful for the person claiming to be the owner of such receipt to present to the court of common pleas of the county wherein said warehouseman, warehousing company, storage or deposit company, or wharfinger, issuing such receipt shall have his, their or its principal office, or place of business, a petition verified by the oath or affirmation of the petitioner, setting forth all the material facts, including the date of the receipt as accurately as the same can be ascertained, a description of the goods, wares, merchandise, petroleum, grain, flour, or other produce commodity or property for which the receipt was given, and a statement of the value thereof, the name of the person or party to whom the receipt was given, the manner in which the petitioner obtained title to such receipt, the date at which he acquired title and whether such title be absolute or in trust, or otherwise qualified, the date of the loss, mislaying or destruction as far as the same can be furnished, and a statement that the petitioner is unable by reason thereof to return such receipt, or to produce the same, and praying for an order on such warehouseman, warehousing company, storage or deposit company, or wharfinger who issued the same, to deliver up to the petitioner the goods, wares, merchandise, petroleum, grain, flour, or other produce, commodity or property for which such receipt was issued and given, without the petitioner being required to produce or return such receipt: whereupon

Court shall cause a citation to issue, directed to the company to appear and show cause why petition should not be granted.

the court shall cause a citation to issue directed to the warehouseman, warehousing company, storage or deposit company, or wharfinger, issuing such receipt, and to such other person or persons, if any, as to the court may seem to have an interest in the matter, requiring them to appear on a day certain to be fixed by the court and show cause why the prayer of said petition should not be granted and why the order and decree prayed for should not be entered.

Court, after due consideration, may grant prayer of petition.

SECTION 2. On the return of such citation the court may, in its discretion, after due consideration, grant the prayer of such petition and may order and direct the warehouseman, warehousing company, storage or deposit company, or wharfinger who issued such receipt, to deliver up to the petitioner the goods, wares, merchandise, petroleum, grain, flour, or other produce, commodity or property for which such receipt was given without requiring the production or return of such receipt: *Provided however*, That the petitioner

The petitioner shall first execute a bond and file same.

shall first execute and file in the office of the prothonotary or clerk of said court a bond with one or more sureties to be approved by the court, which bond shall be taken in the name of the Commonwealth of Pennsylvania for the use and benefit of all parties in interest,

Amount of bond shall be fixed by the court

and shall be taken in such sum as shall be fixed by the court, after due consideration, as to the value of the goods and property so ordered to be delivered as well as to the other circumstances of the case. And upon the filing of such bond and on the entering of such order and decree by the court said warehouseman, warehousing company, storage or deposit company, or wharfinger who issued such receipt, shall deliver up to the petitioner the goods, wares, merchandise, petroleum, grain, flour, or other commodity or produce or property for which such receipt was given, without requiring the production or return of such receipt, and shall be fully released and discharged of and from all liability and responsibility whatsoever to any and all persons or parties whomsoever by reason of so doing, and should any person or party be injured by such order or decree, his or their recourse shall be solely upon such bond or against the wrongdoer whose action procured such order or decree.

Company shall deliver up the goods after bond is filed and decree entered.

And shall be fully released.

And further provided, That no such decree or order shall in anywise impair or affect any right, lien or claim that such warehouseman, warehousing company, storage or deposit company, or wharfinger, may or shall have upon or against such goods, wares, merchandise, petroleum, grain, flour, or other produce, commodity or property for advances, loans, payments, storage, work or services whatsoever.

Such decree shall not impare any lien of company against such goods.

SECTION 3. The bond herein provided for shall be conditioned that the petitioner shall indemnify all parties interested against any and all loss, or damage, which may accrue to him, her or them, by reason of any order or decree granted or entered on the prayer of such petition as aforesaid, or by reason of any delivery made upon or under the same, and whenever injury shall be sustained by any person or party under or by reason of such order, decree or delivery, actions of debt or of *scire facias* may be instituted on said bond, as often as the circumstances may require, against the petitioner, his surety or sureties, and their respective heirs, executors or administrators, and in each case a judgment shall be entered and execution shall be issued only for such damage as the party plaintiff may have sustained together with the costs of suit.

Conditions of bond

Any person injured may institute action of debt or scire facias.

SECTION 4. The costs of such proceeding, together with a reasonable allowance to be fixed by the court for counsel fee to the respondents, shall in every case arising hereunder be fully paid by the petitioner before the respondents shall be required to comply with the order or decree made upon such petition.

Costs of these proceedings and council fee to respondents shall be paid by petitioner.

APPROVED—The 25th day of May, A. D. 1893.

ROBT. E. PATTISON.

No. 87.

AN ACT

To validate affidavits, acknowledgements and other notarial acts heretofore or hereafter performed by notaries public of this Commonwealth outside of the place within which they have been commissioned to reside, but within the Commonwealth.

SECTION 1. *Be it enacted, &c.*, That all affidavits, acknowledgments or other notarial acts heretofore performed, or which shall hereafter be performed, by notaries public of this Commonwealth outside the place within which they have been commissioned to reside, but within the Commonwealth otherwise in conformity with the requirements of the law, shall be valid to all intents and purposes as if the same had been performed according to previously existing laws of the Commonwealth: *Provided however*, That no case heretofore judicially decided, or now pending, shall be affected by this act.

APPROVED—The 25th day of May. A. D. 1893.

ROBT. E. PATTISON.

No. 88.

AN ACT

For the taxation of dogs and the protection of sheep.

Tax on dogs shall be assessed, levied and collected annually.

SECTION 1. *Be it enacted, &c.*, That from and after the passage of this act there shall be assessed, levied and collected, in the same manner in which other taxes are now assessed, levied and collected, annually in each of the townships, boroughs and cities of this Commonwealth, from the owners or keepers of dogs, taxes

Amount of tax on each dog.

to the following amount namely : For each male dog, a sum to be fixed by the county commissioners of their respective counties, and councilmen of their respective cities, of not more than two dollars, and for each female dog, a sum of not more than four dollars, excepting such female dog be spayed, in which case the amount of tax so levied and collected shall be equal

Shall be paid to the County or City Treasurer, and applied to loss of sheep by dogs.

to that upon male dogs as hereinbefore provided, to be paid to the treasurer of the county or city in which the same is collected to be kept by him separate and apart from other taxes, the same to be a fund from which persons sustaining loss or damage to sheep by a dog or dogs, and the necessary costs therefor may be indemnified as hereinafter provided: *Provided further*, That no dogs shall be assessed until they arrive at the age of four months.

Assessors shall make return of the number of dogs and names of owners.

SECTION 2. The assessors in each township, borough and city, shall, for the purpose of levying and collecting such taxes, annually, at the time of assessing other taxable property within the respective townships, boroughs and cities, ascertain and return to the county commissioners of their county, and councilmen of their respective cities, a true statement of all the dogs in their townships, boroughs and cities, respectively, the names of the persons owning or keeping such dogs and how many of each sex is owned or kept by each person and how many of such female dogs so owned or kept are spayed, such commissioners in each county, and councilmen of their respective cities, shall annually levy a tax upon each dog so returned and within the discretion so given to such commissioners and councilmen to such an amount as will in their judgment create a sufficient fund from which all loss or damage caused to sheep within the respective counties, or cities, by a dog, or dogs, during each current year may be paid, together with all necessary expenses incurred in the adjustment of claims as hereinafter provided.

Commissioners and Councilmen shall levy tax annually in such amount as will create sufficient fund to meet loss or damage caused to sheep.

SECTION 3. That whenever any person shall sustain any loss or damage to sheep by a dog, or dogs, in any township, borough or city, such person his or her agent or attorney may complain to any justice of the peace, magistrate or alderman of such township, borough or city, in writing to be signed by the person making such complaint, stating therein when, where and how, such damage was done and by whose dog or dogs, if known, whereupon the justice of the peace, magistrate or alderman, to whom such complaint shall be made, shall notify the township, borough or city auditors, or controllers, of such claim, and such township, borough or city auditors shall at once examine the place where the alleged loss or damage was sustained and the sheep injured or killed, if practicable, and they shall examine under oath or affirmation to be administered by one of them, any witness called before them by subpœna which the said auditors are hereby authorized to issue, and after making diligent inquiry in relation to such claim, shall determine and report to such justice, magistrate or alderman in writing, whether any such damage has been sustained and the amount thereof, and who was the owner or keeper of such dog or dogs, if known, by which such damage was done, and if the dog or dogs are destroyed that caused the damage, if known, then the owner or keeper of said dog or dogs shall be exempt from further claim. Such report so made shall be signed by a majority of the auditors and delivered to the justice, magistrate or alderman, before whom such claim has been made: *Provided*, That any owner of dog or dogs refusing to kill his dog or dogs, after having received due notice from the constable or police through the justice of the peace, magistrate or alderman before whom such claim has been made of the damage done by his dog or dogs, shall be liable for all damage and cost of the same.

How damage for loss of sheep shall be recovered.

Auditors or controllers shall examine and ascertain amount of damage to sheep.

Shall make report to justice, magistrate or alderman.

If owner shall refuse to kill dogs causing the damage, he shall be liable for amount of same and costs.

SECTION 4. That upon receiving such report the said justice, magistrate or alderman, shall immediately make

Officer shall certify the report.

a certificate thereto, signed and sealed by him, that such appraisement was regularly and duly made by such auditors or controllers, and if by such report it

If damage has been sustained, he shall deliver report to claimant or his attorney, who shall deliver same to commissioners or councilmen.

appears that any damage has been sustained by such complainant, the said justice, magistrate or alderman, shall deliver such report and all papers relating to the case to such claimant, his or her agent or attorney, upon payment of the costs up to that time hereinafter provided to be delivered to the county commissioners or councilmen or cities where such damage has been sustained to be filed in their office.

Commissioners or councilmen shall draw warrant for amount of damages and costs.

SECTION 5. That upon the commissioners of the county and councilmen of cities receiving such report, if it shall appear thereby that a certain amount of damage has been sustained by the claimant to sheep by a dog or dogs, they shall immediately draw their order on the treasurer of such county or city in favor of the claimant for the amount of loss or damage such claimant has sustained according to such report, with necessary and

Fund from which paid.

proper costs incurred as aforesaid, to be paid out of the fund raised or to be raised by taxes on dogs as hereinbefore provided: *Provided further*, That no

Effort must be made to ascertain whose dogs did such damage.

person shall receive an order for any claim until he or she has been qualified according to law before said justice of the peace, magistrate or alderman, before whom claim was made that due diligence was made to ascertain whose dog or dogs did such damage.

Method of procedure, when owner of dogs causing the damage does not kill them.

SECTION 6. If, in the report of the auditors or controllers made in accordance with the provisions of section three, the name of the owner or owners of any dog or dogs having caused loss or damage to sheep shall be definitely and conclusively shown, who have not complied with section three of this act, then it shall be the duty of the county commissioners or city councilmen to notify such owner or keeper immediately to kill said dog or dogs, and upon failure of such owner or keeper to comply with such order within a period of ten days, then it shall become the duty of the constable or police of the respective township, borough or city, in which said dog or dogs are kept, upon notice from said commis-

Fee of constable for killing dogs, and how same shall be paid.

sioners to kill the said dog or dogs, for which service he shall be entitled to one dollar for each dog so killed, to be paid out of the county or city fund that is kept for the purpose of paying loss or damage to sheep, upon a certified statement that such dog or dogs were killed by him to the commissioner or councilmen who shall issue such order on the treasurer of the county or city, unless payment has been made by the owner or keeper of dog or dogs causing such damage as provided for in section three.

All dog shall be personal property, and subjects of larceny.

SECTION 7. That all dogs in this Commonwealth shall hereafter be personal property and subjects of larceny, and the owner or keeper of any dog shall be liable to the county commissioners or the councilmen for all loss or damage to sheep by such dog, with all necessary costs incurred in recovering and collecting such damages, unless the foregoing provisions are complied with.

SECTION 8. That justices of the peace, magistrates or aldermen, for the special service under the provisions of this act, shall be entitled to one dollar for each case, and the auditors or controllers, each one dollar per day for the time necessarily spent by them in investigating each claim, to be paid by the claimant in each case: *Provided*, That in all cases where damages are awarded the fees paid by claimants shall be included in the amount of such damages.

Fees of officers in proceedings under this act.

Proviso

SECTION 9. That at the end of each year if any such treasurer shall have in his hands moneys collected for the payment of claims as hereinbefore mentioned, more than two hundred dollars, after the payment of all such claims, he shall immediately pay the same into the county or city fund to be used for county or city purposes.

How balance in hands of treasurer at end of year shall be disposed of

SECTION 10. All acts or supplements of acts inconsistent with the provisions of this act are hereby repealed: *Provided*, That this act shall not repeal or affect the provisions of any special law relating to the same subject in any county, township, borough, or city in this Commonwealth.

Repeal of general laws.

Shall not effect special law.

APPROVED—The 25th day of May, A. D. 1893.

ROBT. E. PATTISON.

No. 89.

AN ACT

Authorizing cities of the Commonwealth of Pennsylvania to enter upon, take, use and appropriate private property for the construction of piers, abutments, fills, slopes and approaches for bridges crossing rivers within the corporate limits thereof, and providing the manner in which compensation shall be made.

SECTION 1. *Be it enacted, &c.*, That it shall be lawful, and the right is hereby given to the cities of this Commonwealth to enter upon, take, use and appropriate private property for the purpose of constructing and maintaining all such piers, abutments, fills, slopes and approaches as shall be found necessary in the erection, construction and maintenance of such bridges as shall be authorized and constructed by such cities, within their corporate limits, over any stream or river which shall separate any parts or portions of such city.

Cities may take private property for the construction and maintenance of bridges.

SECTION 2. If the compensation and damages arising from any such taking, using and appropriating of private property cannot be agreed upon by the owners thereof and such cities, it shall be lawful for such city to tender the bond thereof as security to the party claiming or entitled to any damages, or to the attorney or agent of

If compensation cannot be agreed upon, cities shall tender bond.

any absent person, or to the agent or other officers of a corporation, or to the guardian or committee of any one **Condition of bond.** under legal incapacity, the condition of which shall be that the said city shall pay, or cause to be paid, such amount of damages as the party shall be entitled to receive, after the same shall be agreed upon or assessed in the manner provided by this act. In case the party **Proceedings when security tendered is not accepted.** or parties claiming damages refuse, or do not accept the security so tendered, the said city shall then give the party, his, or their agent, attorney, guardian or committee, written notice of the time when the same will be presented in the court for approval, and thereafter the said city may present said security to the court of common pleas of the county where the lands or other property are situated, and when approved, the said security shall be filed in said court for the benefit of those interested, and recovery may be had thereon for the amount of damages assessed, if the same be not paid, or cannot be made by execution on the judgment in the issue formed to try the question, and upon the approval of said security said city may proceed with the said work.

If compensation has not been agreed upon, court on application shall appoint viewers. SECTION 3. In case the compensation for damages accruing from such appropriation have not been agreed upon any court of common pleas of the proper county, or any law judge thereof in vacation, on application thereto by said city or any person interested, shall appoint three discreet and disinterested freeholders as viewers and appoint a time, not less than ten nor more than twenty days thereafter, when said viewers shall meet upon the property and view the same and the premises affected **Viewers shall give notice of first meeting.** thereby. The said viewers shall give at least ten days' personal notice of the time of their first meeting upon the owners, agents, attorneys or representatives thereof, if the same reside within the county in which such city is located, otherwise by handbills posted upon the premises or by such other notice as the court shall direct. **Viewers shall be sworn** The said viewers having been duly sworn or affirmed faithfully, justly and impartially to decide and true report to make concerning all matters and things to be submitted to them and in relation to which they are author-**Shall hear all parties interested and determine damages.** ized to inquire under the provisions of this act, and having viewed the premises or examined the property shall hear all parties interested and their witnesses and shall estimate and determine the damages for the property taken, injured or destroyed, to whom the same are payable, and having due regard to the advantages and dis-**Shall give notice when report will be exhibited** advantages; they shall give at least ten days notice thereof in the manner herein provided to all parties interested of the time and place when said viewers will meet and exhibit said report and hear all exceptions **Shall make report to the court, and file plan therewith.** thereto. After making whatever changes are deemed necessary the said viewers shall make report to the court, showing the damages, if any allowed, and file therewith a plan showing the location of said bridge, or bridges, the properties taken, injured or destroyed, and the names of the persons to whom such damages are payable.

SECTION 4. Upon the report of said viewers, or any two of them, being filed in said court any party may, within thirty days thereafter, file exceptions to the same, and the court shall have power to confirm said report, or to modify, change, or otherwise correct the same, or refer the same back to the same or new viewers with like power as to their report. Or within thirty days from the filing of any report in court, or the final action of the court upon the exceptions, any party whose property is taken, injured or destroyed, may appeal and demand a trial by jury, and any party interested therein may, within thirty days after final decree, have an appeal to the Supreme Court. If no exceptions are filed, or no demands made for trial by jury within the said thirty days after the filing of said report, the same shall become absolute. The said court of common pleas shall have power to order what notices shall be given in connection with any part of said proceedings and may make all such orders as it may deem requisite.

Exceptions to report.

Court may correct or refer back to viewers.

Trial by jury may be demanded.

Appeal to Supreme Court.

When report shall become absolute.

SECTION 5. The viewers provided for in the foregoing sections may be appointed before, or at any time after, the entry, taking appropriation, or injury of any property or materials for constructing said bridge or bridges.

When viewers may be appointed.

The costs of the viewers and all court costs incurred in the proceedings aforesaid shall be defrayed by the said city, and each of the said viewers shall be entitled to a sum, not exceeding five dollars per day, for every day necessarily employed in performance of the duties herein prescribed.

All costs shall be paid by the city

APPROVED—The 26th day of May, A. D 1893.

ROBT. E. PATTISON.

No. 90.

AN ACT

Amending an act, entitled "An act defining evidence of stock ownership in corporations, and for determining the right to vote thereon," approved May seventh, one thousand eight hundred and eighty-nine, further defining evidence of stock ownership and the right to vote thereon.

SECTION 1. *Be it enacted, &c.,* That sections first and second of an act, entitled "An act defining evidence of stock ownership in corporations, and for determining the right to vote thereon," approved the seventh day of May, Anno Domini one thousand eight hundred and eighty-nine, which read as follows:

"SECTION 1. *Be it enacted by the Senate and House of Representatives of the Commonwealth of Pennsylvania in General Assembly met, and it is hereby enacted by the authority of the same,* That the certificate of stock and transfer books, or either, of any corporation within this Commonwealth, shall be prima facie evidence of the right to vote thereon by the person named therein as the owner, either personally or by proxy. If however objection is taken at the time the ballot is tendered by an actual stockholder, setting out in writing under oath that the stock is not owned absolutely and bona fide by the person in whose name it stands in the certificate, or on the transfer books, and who in person or by proxy is in fact offering to vote thereon, it shall be the duty of the judges of election to inquire and determine summarily whether the name given in the certificate, or standing on the transfer books, is that of the absolute and bona fide owner thereof, or of a holder of the same, as executor, administrator, guardian, or as trustee created by last will and testament, or by decree of court. If not then the vote or votes so tendered shall be rejected.

"SECTION 2. In cases where, by the terms of the preceding section, the person in whose name the stock stands in the certificate, or on the transfer books, is not permitted to vote, the beneficial owner thereof, including a person who has transferred stock to a trustee as collateral for loan, reserving in the conveyance the right to vote upon the stock, shall upon furnishing evidence of ownership, satisfactory to the judges of election, be entitled to vote," shall be and the same are hereby amended so as to read as follows:

SECTION 1. *Be it enacted by the Senate and House of Representatives of the Commonwealth of Pennsylvania in General Assembly met, and it is hereby enacted by the authority of the same,* That the certificate of stock and transfer books, or either, of any corporation of this Commonwealth, shall be prima facie evidence of the right of the person named therein to vote thereon as the owner,

either personally or by due proxy. If however objection is taken by an actual stockholder at the time the ballot is tendered, accompanied by a written statement under oath that the person in whose name such stock stands on such certificate, or transfer books, and who is offering to vote thereon either in person or by proxy, is not the owner thereof, either in his own right or as active trustee with the character of his trusteeship disclosed on the face of said certificate, or transfer books, in connection with his

name, it shall be the duty of the judges of election to inquire and determine summarily whether the facts are as represented in such statement, and if so, the vote or

votes so tendered shall be rejected: *Provided however,* That nothing in this section shall be held to prohibit executors, administrators, guardians or trustees created by last will and testament, or by decree of court, from voting on stock standing in the name of a decedent, minor or other beneficiary.

SECTION 2 That in cases where, under the terms of the preceding section, the person named in the certificate, or transfer books, is not permitted to vote, the beneficial owner of such stock shall have the right to vote thereon upon furnishing to the judges of election satisfactory evidence of ownership.

Beneficial owner of stock shall have a right to vote.

SECTION 3. That as between the pledgeor and the pledgee of capital stock pledged to secure a specific loan with a fixed period or periods of maturity, the right to vote shall be determined as follows: First, By the written agreement of the pledgeor and pledgee. Second, In all other instances the pledgeor shall be held to be the owner and entitled to the right to vote.

Right of pledgeor and pledgee to vote

APPROVED—The 26th day of May, A. D. 1893.

ROBT. E. PATTISON.

No. 91.

AN ACT

To extend the limitation of actions to a right to mine iron ore in lands in this Commonwealth, where the same has not been exercised for a period of twenty-one years.

SECTION 1. *Be it enacted, &c.,* That when any person or persons claiming to have or to hold the right to mine iron ore in any lands in this Commonwealth by conveyance, lease, reservation in a deed, or any other writing, and where the said right to mine iron ore has at any time been exercised and the iron ore in such lands has been exhausted and such right of mining has been subsequently abandoned, and after such abandonment has not been entered upon and exercised for a period of twenty-one years, it shall be lawful for the owner or owners of the land to petition the court of common pleas in and for the county where the land is located for a decree for the extinguishment of said right: *Provided,* That before said petition is presented to said court, personal notice of such application or petition, shall be given fifteen days prior to the presenting said application or petition to the owner or owners of said right, if he, she or any of them reside within the limits of said county, and if they do not reside in said county, then notice of said application shall be published in at least one newspaper published in said county for four successive weeks immediately prior to the term of court at which such application or petition is to be presented, and a copy of the newspaper in which said notice is first published, shall be sent directed to the owner or owners of said right to their nearest postoffice, if such can be ascertained.

When right to mine iron ore on lands has been abandoned after ore is exhausted owner of land may petition court of common pleas for extinguishment of right.

Personal notice must be given to owner of right if he resides within the county.

Notice by publication must be given if owner of right does not reside in county.

SECTION 2. Upon such application or petition being presented to the court, verified by the affidavit of the

How petition may be verified.

owner of the land that said right has not been entered upon and exercised for a period of twenty-one years, and that he and those under whom he claims has been in the adverse possession for the period of twenty one years, and notice of the application having been given as required by section first of this act, and it being also shown to the court by the affidavit of two or more disinterested witnesses that said right has not been entered upon or exercised for a period of twenty-one years, and that the iron ore in the lands sought to be released has been sub-

Court may make decree.

stantially exhausted, it shall be lawful for said court to make a decree releasing said land from the charge upon it and extinguishing the said right or reservation, unless the owner or owners of said land appear and show cause why such a decree should not be entered, and no action

When act shall take effect.

thereafter shall be sustained to enforce said right: *Provided*, That this act shall not take effect within one year from its passage: *Provided further*, That the provisions

How far provisions of act shall extend.

contained in this act shall only be extended to those rights which have already been exercised and to those lands in which the iron ore has been exhausted.

APPROVED—The 26th day of May, A. D. 1893.

ROBT E. PATTISON.

No. 92.

AN ACT

To amend the first section of an act, entitled "An act fixing the pay of road commissioners, road and bridge viewers and reviewers, and appointed commissioners to run township lines and to divide boroughs into wards and township division lines, and surveyors of this Commonwealth," approved the thirteenth day of May, Anno Domini one thousand eight hundred and seventy-four, providing that such commissioners, viewers and surveyors shall be paid by the proper county, or by the petitioners, as the court shall by order direct.

Section 1. Act of May 13, 1874, cited for amendment.

SECTION 1. *Be it enacted, &c.*, That the first section of the said act of Assembly which reads as follows, namely : "That from and after the passage of this act the pay of the viewers and reviewers of roads and bridges, commissioners of roads, and of commissioners appointed to run township lines and to divide boroughs into wards and township division lines in the several counties of this Commonwealth, shall be two dollars ($2), and the pay of surveyors for that purpose shall be four dollars ($4), for every day necessarily employed in the duties of their office," be and the same is hereby amended to read as follows namely :

Pay of viewers and reviewers

That the pay of viewers and reviewers of roads and bridges, commissioners of roads, and of commissioners appointed to run township lines and to divide boroughs into wards and township division lines in the several counties of this Commonwealth, shall be two dollars, and

the pay of surveyors for that purpose shall be four dol- Pay of surveyors
lars for every day necessarily employed in the duties of
their office, and the same shall be paid by the proper By whom paid.
county, or by the petitioners asking for their appointment, as the court shall by order direct when such proceedings are ended.

APPROVED—The 26th day of May, A D. 1893.

ROBT. E. PATTISON.

No. 93.

AN ACT

Regulating the fee to be charged for filing petitions for the adoption of minors and entering order of court thereon.

SECTION 1. *Be it enacted, &c.*, That the fees to be received by the several prothonotaries of the courts of
common pleas for filing petitions for the adoption of
minors and entering the order of court thereon, shall be
twenty-five cents for each petition so filed, and it shall be
the duty of the prothonotary to furnish to the adopting
parent a copy of the proceedings certified under the seal
of the court, for an additional fee of fifty cents for each
copy so furnished.

APPROVED—The 26th day of May, A. D. 1893.

ROBT. E. PATTISON.

No. 94.

AN ACT

Making an appropriation to the Southern Home for Destitute Children of Philadelphia.

SECTION 1. *Be it enacted, &c.*, That the sum of seven $7,000.00 appropri-
ated.
thousand dollars, or so much thereof as may be neces-
sary, is hereby specifically appropriated to the Southern
Home for Destitute Children, of Philadelphia, for the
purpose of maintenance for the two fiscal years commencing June first, one thousand eight hundred and
ninety-three.

The said appropriation to be paid on the warrant of How payable.
the Auditor General on a settlement made by him and
the State Treasurer, but no warrant shall be drawn on
settlement made until the directors or managers of said
institution shall have made, under oath to the Auditor
General, a report containing a specifically itemized state- Itemized state-
ment.
ment of the receipts from all sources and the expenses of
said institution during the previous quarter, with the
cash balance on hand, and the same is approved by him
and the State Treasurer; nor until the Treasurer shall have
sufficient money in the treasury, not otherwise appropriated, to pay the quarterly installments due said institution, and unexpended balances of sums appropriated

Unexpended balances shall revert to State Treasury.

for specific purposes shall not be used for other purposes, whether specific or general, and shall revert to the State Treasury at the close of the two fiscal years.

APPROVED—The 26th day of May, A. D. 1893.

ROBT. E. PATTISON.

No. 95.

AN ACT

To amend the first section of an act, entitled "A further supplement to an act, entitled 'An act for the regulation and continuance of a system of education by common schools,' approved the eighth day of May, Anno Domini one thousand eight hundred and fifty-four, so as to enable certain school districts to establish, maintain and operate a public high school," so as to enable boroughs not divided into wards for school purposes to establish, maintain and operate public high schools.

SECTION 1. *Be it enacted, &c.,* That section one of an act, entitled "A further supplement to an act, entitled 'An act for the regulation and continuance of a system of education by common schools,' approved the eighth day of May, one thousand eight hundred and fifty-four, so as to enable certain school districts to establish, maintain and operate a public high school," which reads as follows:

Section 1 Act of May 8, 1854 cited for amendment.

"SECTION 1. *Be it enacted by the Senate and House of Representatives of the Commonwealth of Pennsylvania in General Assembly met, and it is hereby enacted by the authority of the same.* That the board of controllers of school districts which are composed of cities or boroughs divided into wards for school purposes shall, in addition to the powers and duties conferred or enjoined by the act of the eighth day of May, one thousand eight hundred and fifty-four, and the supplements thereto, possess the following powers and perform the following duties:

Clause 1. They may establish a public high school.

Clause 2. They shall admit to said public high school all children under the age of twenty-one years residing within said school district, who shall be found qualified for admission thereto after having undergone such an examination as shall be prescribed by the said board of controllers: *Provided,* Said board of controllers shall have power to prescribe the terms upon which other children than those residing in said district shall be allowed to attended said public high school.

Clause 3. They shall exercise a general supervision over said public high school, appoint all the teachers therefor, fix the amount of their salaries and shall have power to dismiss any teacher at any time for incompetency, cruelty, negligence, immorality, or other cause; they may suspend or expel from said school all pupils found guilty, on full examination and hearing, of refractory or incorrigible bad conduct, and shall have power to make all proper regulations and rules for the government and discipline of said school.

Clause 4. Said board of controllers shall visit said public high school, by at least one of their number, at least once in each week and cause the results of such visit to be entered on the minutes of said board of controllers.

Clause 5 They shall direct what branches of learning shall be taught and what books shall be used in said public high school.

Clause 6. The said board of controllers shall not employ any person as teacher in said public high school unless such person shall produce such a certificate as would entitle him or her to teach in the ward schools, which certificate shall set forth the branches of learning which the holder thereof is qualified to teach, and provided no teacher shall be employed in teaching any branch of learning other than those enumerated in his or her certificate.

Clause 7. The said board of controllers shall maintain and operate said public high school, not exceeding ten months in each year, and shall pay all the necessary expenses thereof by drafts on the treasurer of said board, signed by the president and attested by the secretary thereof.

Clause 8. They shall have power to purchase, procure and hold, such real and personal property as may be necessary for the establishment and support of said public high school and the same to sell, alien and dispose of, when no longer necessary for the purposes aforesaid: *Provided,* Said real estate shall not exceed one hundred thousand dollars.

Clause 9. They shall cause suitable lots of ground to be procured and suitable buildings to be erected thereon for the accommodation of said public high school, and shall keep the same in repair, and shall cause to be rented a suitable building for the temporary accommodation of said public high school until a suitable permanent building can be obtained.

Clause 10. Whenever said board of controllers shall be unable to procure an eligible site for the erection of said public high school by agreement of the owner or owners of the land, it shall and may be lawful for said board of controllers to enter upon and occupy sufficient ground for such purpose, but before doing so said board of controllers shall tender to such owner or owners the bond of said school district conditioned for the payment of the damages suffered by such owner or owners by reason of such entry and occupancy when finally ascertained, if the owner refuse to accept said bond, or cannot be found, or is not *sui juris,* the same shall then be presented to the court of common pleas of the proper county for its approval, after notice to the property owner by advertisement in a newspaper of said county at least once a week for three weeks. Upon the approval of said bond, and its being filed, the right of said board of controllers to enter upon said land shall be complete.

Either said board of controllers, or said owner or owners of said land, may within twenty days from the approval of said bond, apply by petition to the court of common pleas of the proper county for the appointment of viewers, and thereupon said court shall appoint three disinterested citizens of said county, and not owners of property or residents of said school district, and appoint a time not less than twenty or more than thirty days thereafter, when the said viewers shall meet upon and view said premises, of the time of which meeting ten days' notice shall be given to the viewers and the opposite party, and the said viewers, or any two of them, having been first sworn or affirmed faithfully, justly and impartially to decide and a true report to make concerning all matters and things to be submitted to them, and having viewed the premises and having made a just and fair computation of the advantages and disadvantages, shall estimate and determine whether any, and if any, what amount of damages has been or may be sustained and to whom payable, and make report thereof to said court, and when the damages are finally ascertained either by the confirmation of said report by the court, or the verdict of the jury, judgment shall be entered thereon, and if the amount thereof shall not be paid within thirty days from the entry of such judgment, execution may issue thereon as in other cases of judgment against school districts, and such viewers shall each be entitled to the sum of one dollar and fifty cents for each day necessarily employed in the performance of the duties herein prescribed, to be paid by the school district.

Clause 11. The councils of any such city or borough referred to in the first section of this act shall, at any time, not oftener than once in each school year, levy a special tax for such amount as the said board of controllers may by resolution duly passed fix and determine, to be called, "The public high school building tax," not exceeding the amount of one mill in any one year, to be applied solely to the purpose of purchasing or paying for the ground and the erection of a school building thereon and the repair of the same, which tax shall be levied and collected at the same time and in the same manner and with like authority as other taxes are levied and collected for school purposes in the respective districts to which this act shall apply.

Clause 12. That for the purpose of erecting such school building, or purchasing or procuring grounds whereon to erect such school buildings, as provided by this act, it shall be lawful for said board of controllers to borrow money at a rate of interest not exceeding six per centum, and issue bonds therefor in sums not less than one hundred dollars, which bonds may be registered in such manner as the said board of controllers may hereafter provide," shall be and the same is hereby amended so as to read as follows:

That the board of controllers or directors of school districts which are composed of cities or boroughs divided into wards for school purposes, or boroughs not divided into wards for school purposes, having a population of five thousand or over, shall, in addition to the powers and duties conferred or enjoined by the act of the eighth day of May, one thousand eight hundred and fifty-four, and the supplements thereto, possess the following powers and perform the following duties: *(margin: Additional powers conferred on board of controllers or directors of school districts.)*

Clause 1. They may establish a public high school. *(margin: May establish high school.)*

Clause 2. They shall admit to said public high school all children under the age of twenty-one years residing within said school district, who shall be found qualified for admission thereto after having undergone such an examination as shall be prescribed by the said board of controllers: *Provided,* Said board of controllers or directors shall have power to prescribe the terms upon which other children than those residing in said district shall be allowed to attend said public high school. *(margin: Who shall be admitted to said high school.)*

Clause 3 They shall exercise a general supervision over said public high school, appoint all the teachers therefor, fix the amount of their salaries, and shall have power to dismiss any teacher at any time for incompetency, cruelty, negligence, immorality, or other cause; they may suspend or expel from said school all pupils found guilty, on full examination and hearing, of refractory or incorrigible bad conduct, and shall have power to make all proper regulations and rules for the government and discipline of said school. *(margin: Shall exercise general supervision over high school. Powers over teachers and pupils)*

Clause 4. Said board of controllers or directors shall visit said public high school, by at least one of their number, at least once in each week and cause the results of such visit to be entered on the minutes of said board of controllers. *(margin: Visitation.)*

Clause 5. They shall direct what branches of learning shall be taught and what books shall be used in said public high school. *(margin: Branches to be taught and books used.)*

Clause 6. The said board of controllers or directors shall not employ any person as teacher in said public high school unless such person shall produce such a certificate as would entitle him or her to teach in the ward schools, which certificate shall set forth the branches of learning which the holder thereof is qualified to teach, and provided no teacher shall be employed in teaching any branch of learning other than those enumerated in his or her certificate. *(margin: Qualifications of teachers.)*

Clause 7. The said board of controllers or directors shall maintain and operate said public high school, not exceeding ten months in each year, and shall pay all the necessary expenses thereof by drafts on the treasurer of said board signed by the president and attested by the secretary thereof *(margin: Maximum length of term. Payment of expenses.)*

Power to hold or convey real estate.

Clause 8. They shall have power to purchase, procure and hold such real and personal property as may be necessary for the establishment and support of said public high school, and the same to sell, alien and dispose of, when no longer necessary for the purposes aforesaid: *Provided*, Said real estate shall not exceed one hundred thousand dollars.

Value of real estate.

Grounds and buildings.

Clause 9. They shall cause suitable lots of ground to be procured and suitable buildings to be erected thereon for the accommodation of said public high school, and shall keep the same in repair, and shall cause to be rented a suitable building for the temporary accommodation of said public high school until a suitable, permanent building can be obtained.

When proper site cannot be procured. ground may be entered upon and occupied.

Clause 10. Whenever said board of controllers or directors shall be unable to procure an eligible site for the erection of said public high school by agreement of the owner or owners of the land, it shall and may be lawful for said board of controllers or directors to enter upon and occupy sufficient ground for such purpose, but before doing so, said board of controllers or directors

Shall tender bond before entry.

shall tender to such owner or owners the bond of said school district conditioned for the payment of the damages suffered by said owner or owners by reason of such entry and occupancy when finally ascertained; if the owner refuse to accept said bond, or cannot be found, or is not *sui juris*, the same shall then be presented to

Or shall present bond to court of common pleas, after notice by publication.

to the court of common pleas of the proper county for its approval, after notice to the property owner by advertisement in a newspaper of said county at least once a week for three weeks. Upon the approval of said

When right to enter shall be complete.

bond, and its being filed, the right of said board of controllers or directors to enter upon said land shall be complete.

Petition for appointment of viewers.

Either said board of controllers or directors, or said owner or owners of said land may, within twenty days from the approval of said bond, apply by petition to the court of common pleas of the proper county for the appointment of viewers, and thereupon said court shall appoint three disinterested citizens of said county, and not owners of property or residents in said school district, and appoint a time not less than twenty or more than

When viewers shall meet.

thirty days thereafter, when said viewers shall meet upon and view said premises, of the time of which meeting ten days' notice shall be given to the viewers and the opposite party, and the said viewers, or any two of them,

Viewers shall be sworn.

having been first duly sworn or affirmed faithfully, justly and impartially to decide and a true report to make concerning all matters and things to be submitted to them, and having viewed the premises, and having made a just and fair computation of the advantages and

Shall estimate damage, and report to court.

disadvantages, shall estimate and determine whether any, and if any, what amount of damages has been or may be sustained, and to whom payable, and make report thereof to said court, and when the damages are finally ascertained, either by the confirmation of said report by the court, or the verdict of the jury, judgment shall be entered thereon, and if the amount thereof shall not be paid within thirty days from the entry of such judgment, execution may issue thereon as in other cases of judgments against school districts, and such viewers shall each be entitled to the sum of one dollar and fifty cents for each day necessarily employed in the performance of the duties herein prescribed, to be paid by the school district.

Clause 11. The councils of any such city or boroughs divided into wards for school purposes referred to in the first section of this act, shall at any time, not oftener than once in each school year, levy a special tax for such amount as the said board of controllers or directors may by resolution duly passed fix and determine, to be called, "The public high school building tax," not exceeding the amount of one mill in any one year; boroughs not divided into wards for school purposes mentioned in this act shall levy and collect said high school tax as they levy and collect other school tax, without the intervention of the borough council aforesaid, to be applied solely to the purpose of purchasing or paying for the ground and the erection of a school building thereon and the repair of the same, which tax shall be levied and collected at the same time and in the same manner and with like authority as other taxes are levied and collected for school purposes in the respective districts to which this act shall apply.

Clause 12. That for the purpose of erecting such school building, or purchasing or procuring grounds whereon to erect such school building as provided by this act, it shall be lawful for said board of controllers or directors to borrow money at a rate of interest not exceeding six per centum, and issue bonds therefor, in sums not less than one hundred dollars, which bonds may be registered in such manner as the said board of controllers or directors may hereafter provide: *Provided,* That this act shall not apply to school districts governed by special act of Assembly.

APPROVED—The 26th day of May, A. D. 1893.

ROBT. E. PATTISON.

No. 96.

AN ACT.

To enlarge the powers of the State Board of Agriculture, to authorize the said Board to enforce the provisions of the act, entitled "An act for the protection of the public health, and to prevent adulteration of dairy products and fraud in the sale thereof," approved May twenty-one, Anno Domini one thousand eight hundred and eighty-five, and of other acts in relation to dairy products; to authorize the appointment of an agent of the said Board who shall be known as the "Dairy and Food Commissioner," and to define his duties and fix his compensation, being supplementary to an act, entitled "An act to establish a State Board of Agriculture," approved May eighth, Anno Domini one thousand eight hundred and seventy-six.

Enforcement of provisions of Act of May 21, 1885, and of other laws, regulating the adulteration of dairy products.

SECTION 1. *Be it enacted, &c.*, That the State Board of Agriculture be and is hereby empowered and charged with the enforcement of the provisions of the act, entitled "An act for the protection of the public health, and to prevent the adulteration of dairy products and fraud in the sale thereof," approved May twenty-one, Anno Domini one thousand eight hundred and eighty-five, and with the enforcement of the various provisions of all other laws now enacted, or hereafter to be enacted, prohibiting or regulating the adulteration or imitation of butter, cheese or other dairy products.

Appointment of "Dairy and Food Commissioner."

SECTION 2. That for the purpose of securing the enforcement of the provisions of the said laws concerning dairy products the president of the said State Board of Agriculture be and is hereby authorized and empowered to appoint an agent of the said board, who shall be known by the name and title of the "Dairy and Food

Term of office.

Salary.

Commissioner," who shall hold his office for the term of two years, or until his successor shall be duly appointed and qualified, and shall receive a salary of two thousand dollars per annum and his necessary expenses incurred in the discharge of his official duties under this act. The

Agent shall be charged with enforcement of the laws.

said agent shall be charged under the direction of the said board with the execution and enforcement of all laws now enacted, or hereafter to be enacted, in relation to the adulteration or imitation of dairy products.

How assistants shall be appointed.

SECTION 3. That the said agent of the said board, the said Dairy and Food Commissioner, is hereby authorized and empowered, subject to the approval of the said State Board of Agriculture, to appoint and fix the compensation of such assistants, agents, experts, chemists, detectives and counsel, as may be deemed by him necessary for the proper discharge of the duties of his office, and for the discovery and prosecution of violations

Proviso as to expenses.

of the said laws: *Provided*, That the entire expenses of the said agent and of all his assistants, agents, experts, chemists, detectives and counsel (salaries included), shall not exceed the sum appropriated for the purposes of this act.

SECTION 4. That the said agent of the State Board of Agriculture and such assistants, agents, experts, chemists, detectives and counsel, as he shall duly authorize for the purpose, shall have full access, egress and ingress, to all places of business, factories, farms, buildings, carriages, cars, vessels and cans, used in the manufacture, transportation and sale of any dairy products, or of any adulteration or imitation thereof. They shall also have power and authority to open any package, can or vessel, containing dairy products, or any adulteration or imitation thereof, which may be manufactured, sold or exposed for sale, in violation of any of the provisions of any act now enacted or which may be hereafter enacted in relation to dairy products, or the adulteration or imitation thereof, and they shall also have power to take from such package, can or vessel, samples for analysis. *(Powers of agent and his assistants.)*

SECTION 5. That all penalties and costs received by the said State Board of Agriculture for violations of the said act of May twenty-one, Anno Domino one thousand eight hundred and eighty-five, and of other acts now enacted or hereafter to be enacted, prohibiting or regulating the adulteration or imitation of butter, cheese or other dairy products, shall be appropriated by the said board to the payment only of the necessary expenses incurred by the said Dairy and Food Commissioner and his assistants and agents in the investigation, discovery and prosecution of violations of the said act. *(Penalties and costs received shall be appropriated to payment of necessary expenses by the commissioner and assistants.)*

SECTION 6. That all charges, accounts and expenses of the the said Commissioner, and of all the assistants, agents, experts, chemists, detectives and counsel employed by him, shall be paid by the Treasurer of the State in the same manner as other accounts and expenses of the said State Board of Agriculture are now paid as provided by law. *(How charges, accounts and expenses shall be paid.)*

SECTION 7. That the said Commissioner shall make annual reports of his work and proceedings and shall report in detail the number and names of the assistants, agents, experts, chemists, detectives and counsel employed by him, with their expenses and disbursements, the number of prosecutions, the number of convictions and the penalties recovered in each case, which report shall be presented to the said State Board of Agriculture at its annual meeting. *(Commissioner shall make annual reports.)*

APPROVED—The 26th day of May, A. D. 1893.

ROBT. E. PATTISON.

No. 97.

AN ACT

Authorizing cities of the Commonwealth of Pennsylvania to purchase, maintain, use and condemn, bridges erected and in use over rivers and streams separating or dividing any part or district of such cities, and providing the manner in which compensation shall be made.

WHEREAS, In cities of this Commonwealth sections or districts thereof are divided and separated from each other by rivers and streams of water, rendering bridges necessary for the connection of the same in order that the inhabitants may have access to each part.

And whereas, Many of such bridges have been erected and are operated by private corporations and the tolls thereon have become burdensome to the people, and it is desirable such cities should have the ownership of and control of such bridges to make the same free for the people, therefore;

Bridges may be purchased or taken by city in certain cases. SECTION 1. *Be it enacted*, &c., That whenever any city of this Commonwealth shall be divided or separated in any of its territorial sections or parts by intervening rivers or streams of water it shall be lawful, and the right is given to such city or cities, to purchase, enter upon, take, use, hold and appropriate such bridge or bridges, together with the approaches and appurtenances thereto, lying within the corporate limits of such cities as shall have been erected and now in use over such rivers or streams of water so dividing and separating the sec-

Ordinance to do so. tions or parts aforesaid. Whenever the councils of such cities shall determine upon the purchase, appropriation or condemnation of such bridge or bridges, approaches and appurtenances, it shall be so expressed by ordinance or joint resolution of such councils.

City shall tender bond if compensation cannot be agreed upon. SECTION 2. If the compensation to be paid for such bridge cannot be agreed upon between the owners thereof and such cities, it shall be lawful for such city, or cities, to tender the bond thereof as security to the person, firm or corporation claiming or entitled to compensation, or to the attorney or agent of any absent person, or to the agent or officers of a corporation, or to the guardian or committee

Conditions of bond. of any one under legal incapacity, the conditions of which shall be that the said city shall pay or cause to be paid such amount of damages or compensation as the person, firm or corporation, as the case may be, shall be entitled to receive

If bond is refused, city may present security to court. after the same shall be agreed upon or assessed in the manner provided in this act; in case the party or parties claiming damages or compensation refuse or do not accept the security so tendered, such city shall then give the party, his or their agent, attorney, guardian or committee, written notice of the time when the same will be

If security is approved same shall be filed in said court, and recovery may be had thereon. presented in the court for approval, and thereafter the said city may present said security to any court of common pleas of the county wherein such bridges are located

and used, and when approved, the said security shall be
filed in said court for the benefit of those interes'ed, and
recovery may be had thereon for the amount of damages
or compensation assessed, if the same be not paid, or
cannot be made by execution on the judgment in the
issue formed to try the question, and upon the approval *City may enter upon such bridge*
of said security said city may enter upon, appropriate,
take, hold, use and control such bridge or bridges. *When viewers shall be appointed.*

SECTION 3. In case the compensation for damages accruing from such appropriation, taking, holding and
using, have not been agreed upon, any court of common
pleas of the proper county, or any law judge thereof in
vacation, on application thereto by said city or any person interested, shall appoint three discreet and disinterested freeholders as viewers, and appoint a time not less
than ten nor more than twenty days thereafter, when said *Meeting of viewers.*
viewers shall meet and view the said bridges. The said
viewers shall give at least ten days' notice in writing of
the time of their first meeting to the owners, agents, officers, attorneys or representatives of the persons interested, or such other notice as the court may direct. *They shall be sworn.*

The said viewers having been first duly sworn or affirmed faithfully, justly and impartially, to decide and
true report to make concerning all matters and things to
be submitted to them and in relation to which they are
authorized to inquire under the provisions of this act, and
having viewed the property and structure, shall hear all *Shall determine damages.*
parties interested and their witnesses and shall estimate
and determine the damages for the property so taken,
appropriated, held and used, to whom the same are payable; they shall give at least ten days' notice thereof, in
the manner herein provided, to all parties interested of *Report shall be ex-hibited.*
the time and place when said viewers will meet and ex-
hibit said report and hear all exceptions thereto. *Report shall be made to the court and plan filed with same.*

After making whatever changes are deemed right and
proper the said viewers, or any two of them, shall make
report to the court, showing the amount of damages or
compensation allowed, and to whom payable, and shall
file therewith a plan showing the location of said bridge,
or bridges, so taken and appropriated. *Exceptions to re-port.*

SECTION 4. Upon the report of said viewers, or any two
of them, being filed in said court, any party interested
may, within thirty days thereafter, file exceptions to the
same, and the said court shall have power to confirm said *Court may confirm, correct or refer re-port back to*
report or to modify change or otherwise correct the same, *viewers.*
or refer the same back to the same or new viewers with
like power as to their report. Or within thirty days from
the filing of such report in court any party interested *Appeal from report.*
may appeal and demand a trial by jury, and any party
so interested may, within thirty days after final decree,
have an appeal to the Supreme Court. If no exceptions
are filed, or no demand made for trial by jury within said
thirty days after the filing of said report, the same shall
become absolute.

The said court of common pleas shall have power to

order what notices shall be given in connection with any part of said proceedings and may make all such orders as it may deem requisite.

SECTION 5. The viewers provided for in the foregoing sections may be appointed before, or at any time after,
the entry upon, taking and appropriating of such property. They shall have power to administer oaths or affirmations to all parties and witnesses.

The costs of the viewers and all court costs incurred in the proceedings aforesaid shall be defrayed by said city, and each of the said viewers shall be entitled to a sum not exceeding five dollars per day for every day necessarily employed in performance of the duties herein prescribed.

APPROVED—The 26th day of May, A. D. 1893.

ROBT. E. PATTISON.

No. 98.

AN ACT

To repeal the Lenox road law in the township of Choconut, in the county of Susquehanna.

SECTION 1. *Be it enacted, &c.,* That the act approved the eighteenth day of February, one thousand eight hundred and sixty-nine, extending the Lenox road law, approved the third day of March, one thousand eight hundred and forty-seven, to the township of Choconut, in the county of Susquehanna, be and the same is hereby repealed.

APPROVED—The 26th day of May, A. D. 1893.

ROBT. E. PATTISON.

No. 99.

AN ACT

To repeal an act, entitled "An act relating to the sprinkling of a part of Front street, in the borough of Catasauqua," approved the twenty-seventh day of February, Anno Domini one thousand eight hundred and sixty-five.

SECTION 1. *Be it enacted, &c.,* That the act of Assembly, entitled "An act relating to the sprinkling of a part of Front street, in the borough of Catasauqua," approved the twenty-seventh day of February, Anno Domini one thousand eight hundred and sixty-five, be and the same is now hereby repealed.

APPROVED—The 26th day of May, A. D. 1893.

ROBT. E. PATTISON.

No. 100.

AN ACT

Making an appropriation to the Pennsylvania Prison Society.

SECTION 1. *Be it enacted, &c.*, That the sum of six thousand dollars, or so much thereof as may be necessary, be and the same is hereby specifically appropriated to the Pennsylvania Prison Society for the two fiscal years beginning June first, one thousand eight hundred and ninety-three, for the relief of prisoners discharged from the Eastern Penitentiary.

The said appropriation to be paid on the warrant of the Auditor General on a settlement made by him and the State Treasurer, but no warrant shall be drawn on settlement made until the directors or managers of said society shall have made under oath to the Auditor General a report containing a specifically itemized statement of the receipts from all sources, and expenses of said society, during the previous quarter, with the cash balance on hand, and the same is approved by him and the State Treasurer, nor until the Treasurer shall have sufficient money in the treasury, not otherwise appropriated, to pay the quarterly installments due said society; and unexpended balances of sums appropriated for specific purposes shall not be used for other purposes, whether specific or general, and shall revert to the State Treasury at the close of the two fiscal years.

APPROVED—The 26th day of May, A. D. 1893.

ROBT. E. PATTISON.

$6,000.00 appropriated.

How payable.

Itemized statement.

Unexpended balance shall revert to the State Treasury

No. 101.

AN ACT

To repeal an act, entitled "An act to attach part of Washington township to the borough of Edenboro for school purposes," approved the ninth day of February, one thousand eight hundred and fifty-nine.

SECTION 1. *Be it enacted, &c.*, That the act, entitled "An act to attach part of Washington township to the borough of Edenboro for school purposes" approved the ninth day of February, one thousand eight hundred and fifty-nine, published in the annual reports of that year on pages twenty-eight, twenty-nine and thirty, be and the same is hereby repealed.

APPROVED—The 26th day of May, A. D. 1893.

ROBT. E. PATTISON.

No. 102.

AN ACT

To repeal an act, approved the seventeenth day of April, Anno Domini one thousand eight hundred and sixty-seven, entitled "An act to extend the provisions of an act to prohibit the issuing of licenses within certain boroughs in the counties of Armstrong, Potter, Indiana and Perry, or within two miles of the same in the counties in which such boroughs are located, approved the twenty-seventh day of March, one thousand eight hundred and sixty-six, to the boroughs of West Newton and Mount Pleasant in the county of Westmoreland, in so far as the same relates to the borough of Mount Pleasant in the county of Westmoreland.

Act of March 7, 1866, repealed so far as same relates to Mt. Pleasant. Westmoreland county.

SECTION 1. *Be it enacted, &c.*, That the act of Assembly approved the seventeenth day of April, Anno Domini one thousand eight hundred and sixty-seven, entitled "An act to extend the provisions of an act to prohibit the issuing of licenses within certain boroughs in the counties of Armstrong, Potter, Indiana and Perry, or within two miles of the same in the counties in which such boroughs are located, approved the twenty-seventh day of March, one thousand eight hundred and sixty-six, to the boroughs of West Newton and Mount Pleasant in the county of Westmoreland," which reads as follows:

"SECTION 2. That the provisions of an act, entitled 'An act to prohibit the issuing of licenses within certain boroughs in the counties of Armstrong, Potter, Indiana and Perry, or within two miles of the same in the counties in which said boroughs are located, approved the twenty-seventh day of March, Anno Domini one thousand eight hundred and sixty-six, are hereby extended to the boroughs of West Newton and Mount Pleasant in the county of Westmoreland,' be and the same is hereby repealed so far as the same relates to the borough of Mount Pleasant in the county of Westmoreland."

APPROVED—The 26th day of May, A. D. 1893.

ROBT. E. PATTISON.

No. 103.

AN ACT

Authorizing water companies to re-locate roads destroyed, and to acquire land to preserve water supply from contamination.

If public road is occupied or overflowed, company shall reconstruct the same at their own expense.

Location to be approved by court.

SECTION 1. *Be it enacted, &c.*, That whenever any water company incorporated for the purpose of supplying water to the public shall have found, or shall find it necessary in storing water to occupy and flow with water portion of any turnpike or any public road in this Commonwealth, the said company shall cause the same to be reconstructed forthwith, at their own proper expense, on a favorable location to be approved by the court of quarter sessions of the proper county, and in as perfect a manner as the original road, and are authorized to condemn land for that purpose whenever an agreement as to price cannot be had with the owners. May condemn land

SECTION 2. That any such water company shall be and is hereby empowered to acquire and hold by purchase, or condemnation, such lands along and contiguous to streams of water, or reservoirs from which water is taken for public use, as may be necessary to preserve them from contamination: *Provided*, That no land shall be taken for the uses mentioned in this act until just compensation shall have been made for property taken, injured or destroyed, which shall be paid or secured before such taking, injury or destruction: *And provided further*, That any owner of land along said streams shall have the use of the water for farming and domestic purposes, with free ingress and egress at all times to such streams. Company may purchase or condemn lands. Proviso as to compensation Use of water by owner of land.

SECTION 3. The damage incurred in changing the location of any turnpike or public road as authorized by the first section of this act, and in acquiring lands to preserve water supply from contamination as authorized by the second section of this act, shall be ascertained and paid by such water company in the same manner as is provided for in regard to the taking of lands, waters, materials, property and franchises, for the public purposes of such water company, and no lands, property or franchises, shall be taken for the uses mentioned in this act until just compensation shall have been paid or secured therefor. How damages for land taken for road are to be ascertained.

APPROVED—The 26th day of May, A. D. 1893.

ROBT. E. PATTISON.

No. 104.

AN ACT

Making an appropriation of three thousand dollars for the purchase of law books for the use of the Supreme Court.

SECTION 1. *Be it enacted, &c.,* That the sum of three thousand dollars, or so much thereof as may be necessary, be and the same is hereby specifically appropriated for the purchase of law books for the use of the Supreme Court in the city hall in Philadelphia. Such books to be selected by the justices of said court. $3,000 00 appropriated

The said appropriation to be paid on the warrant of the Auditor General on a settlement made by him and the State Treasurer, upon an itemized voucher, certified to by the Chief Justice, that the books have been purchased and delivered in said rooms. How payable.

APPROVED—The 26th day of May, A. D. 1893.

ROBT. E. PATTISON.

No. 105.

AN ACT

Making an appropriation to Robert A. Packer Hospital, at Sayre, Pennsylvania.

$10,000.00 appropriated.

SECTION 1. *Be it enacted, &c.,* That the sum of ten thousand dollars, or so much thereof as may be necessary, be and the same is hereby specifically appropriated to the Robert A. Packer Hospital, at Sayre, for the two fiscal years beginning June first, one thousand eight hundred and ninety-three, for the purpose of erecting and furnishing an additional ward to said hospital and repairing and improving the present building.

How payable.

The said appropriation to be paid on the warrant of the Auditor General on a settlement made by him and the State Treasurer, but no warrant shall be drawn on settlement made until the directors or managers of said institution shall have made, under oath to the Auditor General, a report containing a specifically itemized statement of the receipts from all sources and expense of said institution, together with a specifically itemized statement of the cost of said building, furnishing and improvements during the previous quarter, with the cash balance on hand, and the same is approved by him and the State Treasurer, nor until the Treasurer shall have sufficient money in the treasury, not otherwise appropriated, to pay the quarterly installments due said institution; and unexpended balances of sums appropriated for specific purposes shall not be used for other purposes, whether specific or general, and shall revert to the State Treasury at the close of the two fiscal years.

Itemized statement.

Unexpended balances shall revert to the State Treasury.

APPROVED—The 26th day of May, A. D. 1893.

ROBT. E. PATTISON.

No. 106.

AN ACT

Making an appropriation for the support of the Pennsylvania Institution for the Instruction of the Blind.

$60,000.00 appropriated.

SECTION 1. *Be it enacted, &c.,* That the sum of sixty thousand dollars, or so much thereof as may be necessary, be and the same is hereby specifically appropriated to the Pennsylvania Institution for the Instruction of the Blind for the two fiscal years beginning June first, one thousand eight hudred and ninety-three, for the maintenance and education of one hundred and seventy pupils, to be paid in proportion to the number of indigent blind pupils from the several counties of the Commonwealth at the annual rate of one hundred and seventy-five dollars per pupil.

How payable.

The said appropriation to be paid on the warrant of the Auditor General on a settlement made by him and the State Treasurer, but no warrant shall be drawn on settlement made until the directors or managers of said institution shall have made, under oath to the Auditor General, a report containing a specifically itemized statement of the receipts from all sources and expenses of said institution, together with the names and residence of each pupil chargeable under this act during the previous quarter, with the cash balance on hand, and the same is approved by him and the State Treasurer, nor until the Treasurer shall have sufficient money in the treasury, not otherwise appropriated, to pay the quarterly installments due said institution; and unexpended balances of sums appropriated for specific purposes shall not be used for other purposes, whether specific or general, and shall revert to the State Treasury at the close of the two fiscal years.

Itemized statement.

Unexpended balances shall revert to the State Treasury.

APPROVED—The 27th day of May, A. D. 1893.

ROBT. E. PATTISON.

No. 107.

AN ACT

Making an appropriation to the Eastern State Penitentiary.

SECTION 1. *Be it enacted, &c.,* That the following sums, or so much thereof as may be necessary, be and the same are hereby specifically appropriated to the Eastern State Penitentiary for the two fiscal years beginning June first, one thousand eight hundred and ninety-three, for the following purposes namely:

For salaries of officers, ninety-four thousand dollars, or so much thereof as may be necessary. *For salaries $94,-000.00.*

For repairs, three thousand dollars, or so much thereof as may be necessary. *Repairs $3,000.00.*

For library books and stationery, one thousand dollars, or so much thereof as may be necessary. *Library &c., $1,-000.00.*

For each discharged convict from the city of Philadelphia, or whose residence is within fifty miles thereof, the sum of five dollars, and for each discharged convict whose residence is over fifty miles from the penitentiary, the sum of ten dollars. *For discharged convicts.*

The said appropriation to be paid on the warrant of the Auditor General on a settlement made by him and the State Treasurer, but no warrant shall be drawn on settlement made until the directors or managers of said institution shall have made, under oath to the Auditor General, a report containing a specifically itemized statement of the receipts from all sources and expenses of said institution, together with a specifically itemized statement of the cost of repairs, library books, gratuities et cetera, during the previous quarter, with the cash balance on hand, and the same is approved by him and the State Treasurer, nor until the Treasurer shall have sufficient *How payable.*

Itemized statement.

Unexpended balances shall revert to the State Treasury. money in the treasury, not otherwise appropriated, to pay the quarterly installments due said institution; and unexpended balances of sums appropriated for specific purposes shall not be used for other purposes, whether specific or general, and shall revert to the State Treasury at the close of the two fiscal years.

APPROVED—The 27th day of May, A. D. 1893.

ROBT. E. PATTISON.

No. 108.

AN ACT

Making an appropriation for the support of State pupils in the Western Pennsylvania Institution for the instruction of the Deaf and Dumb, and to aid in the construction of a sewer for the proper drainage of the buildings.

SECTION 1. *Be it enacted, &c.,* That the sum of ninety-one thousand four hundred dollars, or so much thereof as may be necessary, be and the same is hereby specifically appropriated to the Western Pennsylvania Institution for the Deaf and Dumb for the two fiscal years beginning June first, one thousand eight hundred and ninety-three, for the following purposes namely:

$91,400.00 total appropriated.

The sum of eighty-six thousand four hundred dollars, or so much thereof as may be necessary, for expenses incurred in the education and maintenance of one hundred and eighty indigent deaf and dumb children from the several counties of this Commonwealth, at the annual rate of two hundred and forty dollars per capita, and the sum of five thousand dollars, or so much thereof as may be necessary, for the construction of a sewer necessary to secure proper drainage for the building of said institution.

$86,400 00 for education and maintenance.

Rate per capita.

$5,000.00 for sewer.

How payable.

The said appropriation to be paid on the warrant of the Auditor General on a settlement made by him and the State Treasurer, but no warrant shall be drawn on settlement made until the directors or managers of said institution shall have made, under oath to the Auditor General, a report containing a specifically itemized statement of the receipts from all sources and expenses of said institution, together with the name and residence of the pupils chargeable under this act, and a specifically itemized statement of the cost of said sewer during the previous quarter, with the cash balance on hand, and the same is approved by him and the State Treasurer, nor until the Treasurer shall have sufficient money in the treasury, not otherwise appropriated, to pay the quarterly installments due said institution; and unexpended balances of sums appropriated for specific purposes shall not be used for other purposes, whether specific or general, and shall revert to the State Treasury at the close of the two fiscal years.

Itemized statement

Unexpended balances shall revert to the State Treasury.

APPROVED—The 27th day of May, A. D. 1893.

ROBT. E. PATTISON.

No. 109.

AN ACT

Making appropriations to the Western Pennsylvania Institution
for the Blind at Pittsburgh.

SECTION 1. *Be it enacted, &c.*, That the following sums,
or so much thereof as may be necessary, be and the same
are hereby specifically appropriated and made payable
in quarterly payments commencing June first, Anno
Domini one thousand eight hundred and ninety-three,
to the Western Pennsylvania Institution for the Blind.

For the education and maintenance of forty State
pupils for the fiscal year commencing June first, Anno
Domini one thousand eight hundred and ninety three,
the sum of ten thousand four hundred dollars, or so much
thereof as may be necessary, upon the basis of two hundred and sixty dollars per pupil, and for a boiler-house
and laundry building, smoke-stack, engine, pumps, washing machines and other laundry fixtures, the sum of ten
thousand dollars, or so much thereof as may be necessary.

For the education and maintenance of fifty-two State
pupils for the fiscal year commencing June first, Anno
Domini one thousand eight hundred and ninety-four, the
sum of thirteen thousand five hundred and twenty dollars,
or so much thereof as may be necessary, upon a basis of
two hundred and sixty dollars per pupil. For boilers,
steam pipes, radiators and other steam-heating apparatus for the proper heating of the new institution building, the sum of ten thousand dollars, or so much thereof
as may be necessary, and for school apparatus, furniture
et cetera, the sum of three thousand dollars, or so much
thereof as may be necessary.

SECTION 2. To reimburse the trustees of said institution for moneys expended over and above the amount
appropriated, pro rata, by the General Assemby for the
education and maintenance of State pupils for the year
commencing June first, Anno Domini one thousand eight
hundred and ninety-one, the sum of one thousand one
hundred and sixty-two dollars and ninety-nine cents, or
so much thereof as may be necessary, said sum to be
made payable at the same time and along with sums
appropriated and made payable by the first section of
this act for the first quarter of the year commencing
June first, Anno Domini one thousand eight hundred and
ninety-three.

The said appropriation to be paid on the warrant of
the Auditor General on a settlement made by him and
the State Treasurer, but no warrant shall be drawn on
settlement made until the directors or managers of said
institution shall have made, under oath to the Auditor
General, a report containing a specifically itemized statement of the receipts from all sources and expenses of
said institution, together with a specifically itemized
statement of the names and residence of the pupils

*$10,400.00 for educa-
tion of forty State
pupils in 1893.*

*$10,000.00 for boiler
house &c..*

*$13,520.00 for educa-
tion of fifty-two
State pupils in 1894.*

*$10,000.00 for heat-
ing.*

*$3,000.00 for school
apparatus.*

*$1,162.99 to re-im-
burse trustees.*

How payable

*Itemized state-
ment.*

chargeable under this act and the cost of said improvements et cetera during the previous quarter, with the cash balance on hand, and the same is approved by him and the State Treasurer, nor until the treasurer shall have sufficient money in the treasury, not otherwise appropriated, to pay the quarterly installments due said institution; and unexpended balances of sums appropriated for specific purposes shall not be used for other purposes, whether specific or general, and shall revert to the State Treasury at the close of the two fiscal years.

APPROVED—The 27th day of May, A. D. 1893.

ROBT. E. PATTISON.

No. 110

AN ACT

To provide for the current expenses of the Board of Public Charities for the two fiscal years commencing on the first day of June, Anno Domini one thousand eight hundred and ninety-three.

SECTION 1. *Be it enacted, &c.*, That the following sums, or so much thereof as may be necessary, be and are hereby specifically appropriated for defraying the expenses of the Board of Public Charities for the two fiscal years commencing on the first day of June, Anno Domini one thousand eight hundred and ninety-three.

Items.

For salary of general agent and secretary of the board for two years, six thousand dollars, or so much thereof as may be necessary.

For employment of necessary clerical aid for two years, four thousand dollars, or so much thereof as may be necessary.

For postage, telegrams, express charges, office rent and incidental expenses for two years, one thousand five hundred dollars, or so much thereof as may be necessary.

For traveling expenses of the commissioners and the general agent and secretary, and to pay the cost and the legal expenses of investigating abuses in institutions which come under the supervision of the board, and for removing persons improperly confined in prisons, almshouses or other places, for two years, four thousand dollars, or so much thereof as may be necessary.

For messenger service, fuel, light, cleaning and caring for offices for two years, six hundred dollars, or so much thereof as may be necessary.

For salary of the secretary of the Committee on Lunacy, as fixed by statute, for two years, six thousand dollars, or so much thereof as may be necessary.

For the employment of necessary clerical aid for the Committee on Lunacy for two years, three thousand three hundred dollars, or so much thereof as may be necessary.

For postage, telegrams, express charges, and incidental expenses for two years, eight hundred dollars, or so much thereof as may be necessary.

For traveling expenses of the Committee on Lunacy and the secretary thereof, necessarily entailed in carrying out the provisions of the act of May eighth, one thousand eight hundred and eighty-three, and to defray the cost and the legal expenses in investigating cases of abuse in the institutions under their supervision, for two years, three thousand six hundred dollars, or so much thereof as may be necessary.

For rent of offices, fuel and light, for two years, eight hundred dollars, or so much thereof as may be necessary.

The said appropriation to be paid on the warrant of the Auditor General on a settlement made by him and the State Treasurer, upon itemized vouchers duly certified to by the president and secretary of said board. All moneys appropriated under this act, and remaining unexpended at the close of the two fiscal years, shall revert to the State Treasury.

APPROVED—The 27th day of May, A. D. 1893.

ROBT. E. PATTISON.

Marginal notes: How payable. Itemized vouchers. Amount unexpended shall revert to State Treasury.

No. 111.

AN ACT

Making an appropriation for the State Hospital for Injured Persons of the Middle Coal Field.

SECTION 1. *Be it enacted, &c.* That the following sums, or so much thereof as may be necessary, be and are specifically appropriated to the State Hospital for Injured Persons of the Middle Coal Field for the two fiscal years commencing June first, Anno Domini one thousand eight hundred and ninety-three, to be paid in equal quarterly installments, except for the sums appropriated for ice house, isolating ward and steam boiler.

For the erection of an ice house, three hundred dollars.

For the erection of an isolating ward, one thousand dollars.

For the purchase and putting in of an additional steam boiler, one thousand dollars.

For salaries of officers and employes, and for the support and maintenance of the institution for the two fiscal years commencing June first, Anno Domini one thousand eight hundred and ninety-three, thirty-five thousand dollars, or so much thereof as may be necessary: *Provided,* That the treasurer of said institution shall make, under oath, a monthly report to the Auditor General of the Commonwealth, containing an itemized statement of the income and expenses of the institution, showing the amount of provisions, articles et cetera furnished the institution, the price paid and the name of the person or persons furnishing the same, and the date upon which the same was furnished during the previous month, and unless such itemized report is made, approved by both

Marginal notes: When amounts appropriated are payable. Items. $35,000.00 appropriated for salaries and maintenance. Treasurer shall make monthly report to Auditor General.

the Auditor General and the State Treasurer, the State Treasurer is hereby directed not to pay any more money to said institution until such report is made and approved as aforesaid: *And provided,* That the superintendent

shall, after the passage of this act, for two consecutive weeks, and yearly thereafter for the same length of time, commencing on the second Monday in March, advertise in three newspapers of general circulation for bids to furnish all needed supplies for the year beginning June first, next ensuing. Said superintendent shall furnish promptly on application to all persons desiring to bid, an itemized list of the kind and probable amount required.

The board of trustees shall award the contract for supplies to the lowest and best bidder, taking such security for the faithful performance of the contract as they deem necessary.

The said appropriation to be paid on the warrant of the Auditor General on a settlement made by him and the State Treasurer, but no warrant shall be drawn on settlement made until the directors or managers of said institution shall have made, under oath to the Auditor General, a report containing a specifially itemized state-

ment of the receipts from all sources and expenses of said institution, together with a specifically itemized statement of the cost of the improvements during the previous quarter, with the cash balance on hand, and the same is approved by him and the State Treasurer, nor until the Treasurer shall have sufficient money in the treasury, not otherwise appropriated, to pay the quarterly installments due said institution; and unexpended balances of sums

appropriated for specific purposes shall not be used for other purposes, whether specific or general, and shall revert to the State Treasury at the close of two fiscal years.

APPROVED—The 27th day of May, A. D. 1893.

ROBT. E. PATTISON.

No. 112.

AN ACT

Making an appropriation towards the maintenance of the Pennsylvania Nautical School Ship located at the port of Philadelphia.

SECTION 1. *Be it enacted, &c.,* That the sum of twenty-six thousand dollars, or so much thereof as may be necessary, be and the same is hereby specifically appropriated to the board of directors of the Pennsylvania Nautical School Ship toward the maintenance of the Pennsylvania Nautical School Ship, located at the port of Philadelphia, for the two fiscal years commencing on the first day of June, one thousand eight hundred and ninety-three:

Provided, That the city of Philadelphia shall appropriate twenty thousand dollars per annum toward the maintenance of said Pennsylvania Nautical School Ship, and that the fact of such appropriation shall be certified to the Auditor General by the mayor of the city of Philadelphia before the amounts hereinbefore appropriated, or any part thereof, shall be paid:

Provided further, That quarterly statements of the expenditures of the said board of directors for the maintenance of the said Pennsylvania Nautical School Ship shall be rendered to the controller of the city of Philadelphia and, when certified by him, submitted to the Auditor General of the Commonwealth, and no part of the moneys hereinbefore appropriated shall be paid until the said statement for the previous quarter shall have been submitted to the Auditor General, as herein provided, and approved by him.

The said appropriation to be paid on the warrant of the Auditor General on a settlement made by him and the State Treasurer, but no warrant shall be drawn on settlement made until the board of directors or managers of said Pennsylvania Nautical School Ship shall have made, under oath to the Auditor General, a report containing a specifically itemized statement of the receipts from all sources and expenses of said Pennsylvania Nautical School Ship during the previous quarter, with the cash balance on hand, and the same is approved by him and the State Treasurer, nor until the Treasurer shall have sufficient money in the treasury, not otherwise appropriated, to pay the quarterly installments due said Pennsylvania Nautical School Ship; and unexpended balances of sums appropriated for specific purposes shall not be used for other purposes, whether specific or general, and shall revert to the State Treasury at the close of the two fiscal years.

APPROVED—The 27th day of May, A. D. 1893.

ROBT. E. PATTISON.

No. 113.

AN ACT

Making an appropriation to the Pennsylvania Museum and School of Industrial Art.

SECTION 1. *Be it enacted, &c.* That the sum of twenty thousand dollars, or so much thereof as may be necessary, be and the same is hereby specifically appropriated to the Pennsylvania Musuem and School of Industrial Art for the two fiscal years beginning June first, one thousand eight hundred and ninety-three, for the general maintenance of the said Pennsylvania Museum and School of Industrial Art, and any portion of the said appropriation may be used for the purchase of looms and other machinery necessary for instruction in weaving

Marginal notes:

Provided that the City of Philadelphia shall appropriate $20,000.00.

Quarterly statement to controller of City of Philadelphia, who shall certify same to Auditor General.

How payable.

Itemized statement.

Unexpended balances shall revert to the State Treasury.

$20,000.00 appropriated.

Part may be used for purchase of looms, &c.,

and textile design, and other arts pertaining to the industries of the State: *Provided,* That in such school there shall be maintained a free scholarship of one pupil from each county in the State to be filled by nomination of the Governor of the Commonwealth.

Free scholarships.

How payable

The said appropriation to be paid on the warrant of the Auditor General on a settlement made by him and the State Treasurer, but no warrant shall be drawn on settlement made until the directors or managers of said institution shall have made, under oath to the Auditor General, a report containing a specifically itemized statement of the receipts from all sources and expenses of said institution during the previous quarter, with the cash balance on hand, and the same is approved by him and the State Treasurer, nor until the Treasurer shall have sufficient money in the treasury, not otherwise appropriated, to pay the quarterly installments due said institution; and unexpended balances of sums appropriated for specific purposes shall not be used for other purposes, whether specific or general, and shall revert to the State Treasury at the close of the two fiscal years.

Itemized statement.

Unexpended balances shall revert to the State Treasury.

APPROVED—The 27th day of May, A. D. 1893.

ROBT. E. PATTISON.

No. 114.

AN ACT

Making an appropriation to the State Hospital for Injured Persons of the bituminous and semi-bituminous coal regions of Pennsylvania at Blossburg, Tioga county, Pennsylvania.

$16,000 00 appropriated.

SECTION 1. *Be it enacted, &c.,* That the sum of sixteen thousand dollars, or so much thereof as may be necessary, be and the same is hereby specifically appropriated to the State Hospital for Injured Persons of the bituminous and semi-bituminous coal regions of Pennsylvania at Blossburg, Tioga county, for the two fiscal years beginning June first, one thousand eight hundred and ninety-three, as follows: for the purpose of maintenance of said hospital, the sum of twelve thousand dollars, or so much thereof as may be necessary; for the purpose of making necessary improvements to said hospital, the sum of four thousand dollars, or so much thereof as may be necessary.

For maintenance.

For improvements.

How payable

The said appropriation to be paid on the warrant of the Auditor General on a settlement made by him and the State Treasurer, but no warrant shall be drawn on settlement made until the directors or managers of said institution shall have made, under oath to the Auditor General, a report containing a specifically itemized statement of the receipts from all sources and expenses of said institution, together with a specifically itemized statement of the cost of improvements during the previous quarter, with the cash balance on hand, and the

Itemized statement

same is approved by him and the State Treasurer, nor until the Treasurer shall have sufficient money in the treasury, not otherwise appropriated, to pay the quarterly installments due said institution; and unexpended balances of sums appropriated for specific purposes shall not be used for other purposes, whether specific or general, and shall revert to the State Treasury at the close of the two fiscal years. Unexpended balances to revert the State Treasury.

APPROVED—The 27th day of May, A. D. 1893.

ROBT. E. PATTISON.

No. 115.

AN ACT

To provide for the support of the National Guard and Naval Force for the years, Anno Domini one thousand eight hundred and ninety-three, and one thousand eight hundred and ninety-four.

SECTION 1. *Be it enacted, &c.*, That the following sums, or so much thereof as may be necessary, be and the same are hereby specifically appropriated for the support of the National Guard and Naval Force: The sum of three hundred and twenty thousand dollars, or so much thereof as may be necessary, for the year beginning June first, one thousand eight hundred and ninety-three, and the sum of three hundred and twenty thousand dollars, or so much thereof as may be necessary, for the year beginning June first, one thousand eight hundred and ninety-four, to be paid out of any money in the treasury not otherwise appropriated. The said appropriation to be paid on the warrant of the Adjutant General, countersigned by the Auditor General, upon properly itemized vouchers, duly approved by the State Military Board. All moneys appropriated under this act, and remaining unexpended at the close of each fiscal year, shall revert to the State Treasury. $320,000.00 for the first year. $320,000.00 for the second year. How payable. Itemized statement. Unexpended balances.

APPROVED—The 27th day of May, A. D. 1893.

ROBT. E. PATTISON.

No. 116.

AN ACT

To provide for the current expenses of the State Board of Agriculture.

SECTION 1. *Be it enacted, &c.*, That the following sums be and are hereby specifically appropriated for the current expenses of the State Board of Agriculture for the two fiscal years commencing June first, one thousand eight hundred and ninety-three.

For the salary of the Secretary of the Board, twenty-five hundred dollars per annum, or so much thereof as may be authorized by law. Items.

For clerical assistance, salary of messenger, postage, express charges, and other necessary office expenses, one thousand five hundred dollars per annum, or so much thereof as may be necessary.

For the actual and necessary expenses of the members of the board, two thousand dollars per annum, or so much thereof as may be necessary.

For the actual and necessary expenses of local or farmers' institutes and for the traveling expenses of the secretary, nine thousand five hundred dollars per annum, or so much thereof as may be necessary.

For the necessary expense of preventing the spread of contagious disease (not otherwise provided for) among domestic animals, one thousand dollars per annum, or so much thereof as may be necessary.

How payable.

Itemised statement.

Unexpended balances.

The said appropriation to be paid on the warrant of the Auditor General on a settlement made by him and the State Treasurer, upon itemized vouchers duly certified by the Secretary of the State Board of Agriculture. All moneys appropriated under this act, and remaining unexpended at the close of each fiscal year, shall revert to the State Treasury.

APPROVED—The 27th day of May, A. D. 1893.

ROBT. E. PATTISON.

No. 117.

AN ACT

Making an appropriation to the Western State Penitentiary.

SECTION 1. *Be it enacted, &c.,* That the following sums, or so much thereof as may be necessary, be and the same are hereby specifically appropriated to the Western State Penitentiary for the several objects hereinafter named for the two fiscal years commencing on the first day of June, Anno Domini one thousand eight hundred and ninety-three, to be paid out of any moneys in the State Treasury

$120,000.00 for salaries.

$20,500.00 for steam boilers, &c..

$15,000.00 to complete wing.

$7,200.00 for female building.

$3,000.00 for extra repairs.

$3,000.00 for insurance.
$1,000.00 for books. &c .

For each discharged prisoner.

not otherwise appropriated, as follows namely : For salaries of officers, one hundred and twenty thousand dollars, or so much thereof as may be necessary; for additional steam boilers, repairing old boilers, pipes and fittings, twenty thousand five hundred dollars, or so much thereof as may be necessary; to complete south wing, fifteen thousand dollars, or so much thereof as may be necessary; to complete female cell building, seven thousand and two hundred dollars, or so much thereof as may be necessary; for extraordinary repairs, three thousand dollars, or so much thereof as may be necessary; for insurance of buildings, three thousand dollars, or so much thereof as may be necessary; for books and stationery for prisoners, one thousand dollars, or so much thereof as may be necessary; for each discharged prisoner whose residence is in the city of Pittsburgh, or within fifty miles thereof, the sum of five dollars; for each discharged prisoner whose residence is more than fifty miles from the penitentiary, the sum of ten dollars.

The said appropriation to be paid on the warrant of the Auditor General on a settlement made by him and the State Treasurer, but no warrant shall be drawn on settlement made until the directors or managers of said institution shall have made, under oath to the Auditor General, a report containing a specifically itemized statement of the receipts from all sources and expenses of said institution, together with a specifically itemized statement of the cost of said improvements, insurance et cetera, during the previous quarter, with the cash balance on hand and the same is approved by him and the State Treasurer, nor until the Treasurer shall have sufficient money in the treasury, not otherwise appropriated, to pay the quarterly installments due said institution; and unexpended balances of sums appropriated for specific purposes shall not be used for other purposes, whether specific or general, and shall revert to the State Treasury at the close of the two fiscal years.

How payable.

Itemized statement.

Unexpended balances shall revert to the State Treasury.

APPROVED—The 27th day of May, A. D. 1893.

ROBT. E. PATTISON.

No. 118.

AN ACT

Providing for the erection of the Pennsylvania Soldiers Orphans' Industrial School; the purchase of land and the erection and equipment of the building and buildings necessary therefor; making appropriations for such purposes, erection and equipment, and the maintenance of children admitted therein, placing the care of the same in the commission now known as the Commission of Soldiers' Orphan Schools of the State of Pennsylvania, and regulating the admissions to the said Pennsylvania Soldiers Orphans' Industrial School and the said Soldiers' Orphan Schools.

SECTION 1. *Be it enacted, &c.*, That there shall be erected, at some point within the State easily accessible, a building or buildings to be known as the Pennsylvania Soldiers Orphans' Industrial School.

Erection of buildings authorized.

SECTION 2. That the commission now in charge of the Soldiers' Orphan Schools are empowered to purchase not more than one hundred acres of ground, the title of which shall be vested in the Commonwealth, and to erect buildings thereon, equipping the same with shops, tools et cetera, for industrial training, as well as for the educational course, and for the maintenance of the soldiers' orphans, first taking security for the faithful performance of all contracts and for the completion of the building and buildings in a substantial, good and workmanlike manner.

Commission empowered to purchase ground, erect buildings, &c..

Security for faithful performance of all contracts.

SECTION 3. The said commission as now constituted shall continue until the third Wednesday in January, one

thousand eight hundred and ninety-seven, at which time
there shall be appointed by the president *pro tempore*
of the Senate, two members thereof, and by the speaker
of the House, three members thereof, to serve for two
years, and the Commander of the Department of Pennsylvania Grand Army of the Republic shall then recommend to the Governor, five honorably discharged soldiers
for the appointment, who, if approved by the Governor,
shall be appointed to serve for two years. The Governor shall be a member *ex-officio* of the said commission.
At the expiration of the said terms of the said appointees
their successors shall be appointed in like manner and
for like term. Vacancies occurring in the membership of
the said commission shall be filled by the appointing
powers as above set forth.

SECTION 4. The said commission shall elect from their
own number a president, secretary, financial secretary
and treasurer, and shall employ all necessary clerks,
teachers and employés, necessary for the proper conduct
and care of the schools.

SECTION 5. The said commission shall have full power
to continue the soldiers' orphan schools as now constituted, or if necessary, change either, any, or all of them
to other localities, until such time or times as the Pennsylvania Soldiers Orphans' Industrial School shall be completed, or sufficiently advanced to accommodate said
orphans, when the commission shall close all of the said
soldiers' orphans schools.

SECTION 6. The said commission, under such rules and
forms of application as it may adopt, shall be and is
hereby authorized to admit to said soldiers' orphan
school, or to the Pennsylvania Soldiers Orphans' Industrial Schools, soldiers' orphans of parents residents of
this State for a continuous period of not less than five
years prior to their application, who shall be under fourteen years of age, to be educated and maintained therein,
until they shall severally become sixteen years of age,
unless sooner discharged for cause by order of the commission.

SECTION 7. Preference in admission shall be as follows:

First. Full orphans, the children of honorably discharged soldiers, sailors or marines, who served in the
war for the suppression of the rebellion and were members of Pennsylvania commands, or having served in the
commands of other States, or of the United States, were
residents of Pennsylvania at the time of enlistment.

Second. Children of such honorably discharged soldiers, sailors or marines, as above, whose father may be
deceased and mother living.

Third. Children of such honorably discharged soldiers,
sailors or marines, as above, whose parents may either,
or both, be permanently disabled.

SECTION 8. In order that the benefits of industrial
training may be given to the children now in its soldiers'
orphans schools and who may arrive at an age to be dis-

charged at or about the time of the opening of the said Soldiers Orphans' Industrial School, the said commission is hereby empowered to extend the time of the discharge of such children, who may be fifteen and sixteen years of age, for the space of two years additional.

SECTION 9. The per capita rate of the appropriation for the education and maintenance of the children admitted in the Pennsylvania Soldiers Orphans' Industrial School shall not exceed the sum of two hundred dollars per annum. *Maximum appropriation per capita.*

SECTION 10. No compensation shall be allowed any member of the said commission, except such reasonable expenses as they may incur in the performance of their duties; and no member of said commission shall be directly or indirectly interested financially in any school under care of said commission, or in the education and maintenance of said soldiers' orphans, nor in furnishing supplies to or for the same, nor in the purchase of lands, erection of buildings, or equipment of the same. *No compensation to members of commission, except expenses. Members of commission shall not be interested, financially or otherwise in schools, &c.,*

SECTION 11. The said commission shall, on or before the third Wednesday in January of each year, present to the Legislature, under oath, a detailed report of the financial transaction of the preceding year, setting forth in detail the amount of all moneys, or other property, received on account of such Pennsylvania Soldiers Orphans' Industrial School, and an itemized statement of the disbursements thereof. *Commission shall make annual report to Legislature.*

SECTION 12. That the year for all provisions under this act shall begin on the first day of June in each year and end on the thirty-first day of May of the year then next succeeding. *When the year shall begin.*

SECTION 13. To carry out the provisions of this act the following sums of money are hereby specifically appropriated, out of any money in the treasury not otherwise appropriated, which sums shall be paid to the treasurer of the Commission of Soldiers' Orphan Schools, who shall first be required to give a bond in the sum to be named by the said commission with security for the proper application of such moneys. *Appropriation of money and bond of Treasurer.*

First. For the establishing, building, furnishing and fitting up of said Pennsylvania Soldiers' Orphan Industrial School, as hereinbefore provided, with the sum of one hundred and fifty thousand dollars, or so much thereof as may be necessary. *$150,000.00 for building, &c.,*

Second. For the education and maintenance of the children admitted to said Soldiers' Orphan Industrial School for the year ending May thirty-first, one thousand eight hundred and ninety-four, the sum of ten thousand dollars, or so much thereof as may be necessary. *$10,000.00 for education and maintenance first year.*

Third. For the education and maintenance of the children admitted to said Soldiers' Orphan Industrial School for the year ending May thirty-first, one thousand eight hundred and ninety-five, the sum of fifty thousand dollars, or so much thereof as may be necessary. *$50,000.00 for education and maintenance.*

Fourth. For the expenses of the commission as herein-

$3,000.00 for expenses of commission.

How payable.

Unexpended balance for first year

before provided, the sum of three thousand dollars, or so much thereof as may be necessary.

SECTION 14. All moneys to be paid on the warrant of the Auditor General drawn on the State Treasurer upon requisition approved and certified to by the said commission.

SECTION 15. Any balance remaining unexpended for the year one thousand eight hundred and ninety-four, shall be available for the year one thousand eight hundred and ninety-five, in addition to the sum of fifty thousand dollars herein appropriated for that year.

Repeal.

SECTION 16. That all acts or parts of acts inconsistent with the provisions of this act be and the same are hereby repealed.

APPROVED—The 27th day of May, A. D. 1893.

ROBT. E. PATTISON.

No. 119.

AN ACT

Relative to the appointing of special deputies, marshals or policemen, by sheriffs, mayors or other persons authorized by law to make such appointments, and by individuals, associations or corporations, incorporated under the laws of this State, or any other State of the United States, and making it a misdemeanor for persons to exercise the functions of such officers without authority.

Citizens of this Commonwealth must be appointed.

· SECTION 1. *Be it enacted, &c.,* That no sheriff of a county, mayor of a city, or other person authorized by law to appoint special deputies, marshals or policemen in this Commonwealth to preserve the public peace and prevent or quell public disturbances, and no individuals, association, company or corporation incorporated under the laws of this State, or of any other State of the United States, and doing business in this State, shall hereafter appoint or employ as such special deputy, marshal or policeman, any person who shall not be a citizen of this Commonwealth.

Misdemeanor to falsely represent oneself as an officer.

SECTION 2. That any person who shall in this Commonwealth without due authority pretend or hold himself out to any one as a deputy sheriff, marshall, policeman, constable or peace officer, shall be deemed guilty of a misdemeanor.

Misdemeanor to violate provisions of this act.

Penalty.

Penalty for company or association.

SECTION 3. Any person or persons, company or association, or any person in the employ of such company or association, violating any of the provisions of this act, shall be guilty of a misdemeanor, and upon conviction thereof, shall be sentenced to pay a fine not exceeding five hundred dollars or undergo an imprisonment not exceeding one year, or both, or either, at the discretion of the court: *Provided,* That if any company or association be convicted under this act it shall be sentenced to pay a fine not exceeding five thousand dollars: *Provided further,* That the provisions of this act shall not be construed as applying to policemen, constables or specials appointed by municipalities for municipal purposes. Who shall be exempt from provisions of act.

APPROVED—The 29th day of May, A. D. 1893
ROBT. E. PATTISON.

No. 120.

AN ACT

Providing for the insurance of public buildings and making an appropriation therefor.

SECTION 1. *Be it enacted, &c.,* That the sum of seven thousand dollars, or so much thereof as may be necessary, is hereby appropriated for the payment of perpetual insurance on the public buildings, and the further sum of seven thousand dollars, or so much thereof as may be necessary, for insuring the contents of said buildings for a term of five years from the fifteenth day of March, one thousand eight hundred and ninety-three, or as soon thereafter as the policies are executed and delivered to the Board of Public Grounds and Buildings, and the said board is hereby authorized to receive estimates for and designate the companies in which said insurance shall be placed. $7,000 00 appropriated for perpetual insurance. $7 000.00 for insuring contents of buildings.

The said appropriation to be paid on the warrant of the Auditor General on a settlement made by him and the State Treasurer. How payable.

APPROVED—The 29th day of May, A. D. 1893.
ROBT. E. PATTISON.

No. 121.

AN ACT

To repeal sections one and three of an act, entitled "An act authorizing the borough of Bellevue, Allegheny county, to levy an extra tax and to prohibit the sale of liquors within said borough," approved the twenty-second day of March, Anno Domini one thousand eight hundred and sixty-nine.

SECTION 1. *Be it enacted, &c.,* That the first section of the act, entitled "An act authorizing the borough of Bellevue, Allegheny county, to levy an extra tax and to prohibit the sale of liquors within said borough," which reads as follows:

"SECTION 1. That the burgess and town council of the borough of Bellevue, in the county of Allegheny, be and they are hereby authorized and required to levy a special tax, not exceeding fifteen mills on the dollar of the assessed value of all property made taxable for state and county purposes, in addition to the borough tax now authorized, the said tax to be expended in making, Section 1 and 3 Act of March 22. 1869, cited for repeal.

grading and repairing the roads and streets, side walks and crossings, in said borough, and to be in lieu of all other assessments in the general act regulating boroughs authorized to be made for like purposes," also section three of said act which reads as follows:

"SECTION 3. That hereafter all taxes payable in the borough of Bellevue, in the county of Allegheny, shall be paid to the treasurer of said borough within such time and subject to the same provisions of law as are enacted and govern the payment of taxes to the treasurer of said county of Allegheny," be and the same are hereby repealed.

APPROVED—The 29th day of May, A. D. 1893.

ROBT. E. PATTISON.

No. 122.

AN ACT

To repeal the seventh section of an act, entitled "A supplement to an act, entitled 'An act to enlarge the jurisdiction of justices of the peace in the county of Erie,' approved February eighteenth, one thousand eight hundred and sixty-nine, passed March twenty-eighth, one thousand eight hundred and seventy."

Section 7. Act of March 28. 1870, cited for repeal.

SECTION 1. *Be it enacted, &c.*, That so much of an act, entitled "A supplement to an act, entitled 'An act to enlarge the jurisdiction of justices of the peace in the county of Erie,' approved February eighteeth, one thousand eight hundred and sixty-nine," passed March twenty-eighth, one thousand eight hundred and seventy, as reads as follows, namely: "The only remedy which the party aggrieved by any act of the justice or the jury done under the provisions of this act, or the act to which this is a supplement, shall be by an appeal to the court of common pleas of Erie county within twenty days after final judgment: *Provided*, That if the defendant shall prove to the satisfation of a judge of said court that he had no knowledge of the proceedings before the justice until the twenty days for appeal had expired, and that no summons was legally served upon him, said judge may order a writ of certiorari to be issued, and upon the defendant entering into recognizance, with sufficient surety to pay the debt and costs in case the proceedings before the justice shall be affirmed, all proceedings before the justice shall be stayed until the determination of the court on the writ of certiorari," being the seventh section of the said act, be and the same is hereby repealed.

APPROVED—The 29th day of May, A. D. 1893.

ROBT. E. PATTISON.

No. 123.

AN ACT

Making an appropriation to the trustees of the State Hospital for the Insane for the Southeastern district of Pennsylvania at Norristown, Pennsylvania.

SECTION 1. *Be it enacted, &c.,* That the sum of forty-two thousand dollars, or so much thereof as may be necessary, be and the same is hereby specifically appropriated to the State Hospital for the Insane for the Southeastern district of Pennsylvania at Norristown, Pennsylvania, for the two fiscal years commencing June first, one thousand eight hundred and ninety-three, for the following purposes, namely : $42,000.00 appropriated.

For replacing the wooden coal shed with a brick building and a cold storage system, ten thousand dollars, or so much thereof as may be necessary. Items.

For replacing steam pipes and pipe covering, five thousand dollars, or so much thereof as may be necessary.

For an electrical light plant, twenty thousand dollars, or so much thereof as may be necessary.

For sinking artesian wells for the purpose of supplying the hospital with pure water, seven thousand dollars, or so much thereof as may be necessary.

The said appropriation to be paid on the warrant of the Auditor General on a settlement made by him and the State Treasurer, but no warrant shall be drawn on settlement made until the trustees of said institution shall have made, under oath to the Auditor General, a report containing a specifically itemized statement of the receipts from all sources and expenses of said institution, together with an itemized statement of the cost of said improvements during the previous quarter, with the cash balance on hand, and the same is approved by him and the State Treasurer, nor until the Treasurer shall have sufficient money in the treasury, not otherwise appropriated, to pay the quarterly installments due said institution; and unexpended balances of sums appropriated for specific purposes shall not be used for other purposes, whether specific or general, and shall revert to the State Treasury at the close of the two fiscal years. How payable. Itemized statement. Unexpended balances shall revert to the State Treasury.

APPROVED—The 29th day of May, A. D. 1893.

ROBT. E. PATTISON.

No. 124.

AN ACT

Making an appropriation for the erection and furnishing of a Shad Hatchery on the Delaware River.

SECTION 1. *Be it enacted, &c.,* That the sum of three thousand dollars, or so much thereof as may be necessary, be and the same is hereby specifically appropriated to the $3,000.00 appropriated.

12—Laws.

State Fishery Commissioners for the purchase or lease of a site and the erection and furnishing of a shad hatchery on the Delaware river.

How payable

The said appropriation to be paid on the warrant of the Auditor General on a settlement made by him and the State Treasurer, but no warrant shall be drawn on settlement made until the Fish Commissioners shall have made, under oath to the Auditor General, a report con-

Itemized statement.

taining a specifically itemized statement of the cost of said shad hatchery and furnishing, with the cash balance on hand, and the same is approved by him and the State Treasurer, nor until the Treasurer shall have sufficient money in the treasury, not otherwise appropriated, to pay the amount due said Fish Commissioners; and unex-

Unexpended balances shall revert to the State Treasury.

pended balances of sums appropriated for specific purposes shall not be used for other purposes, whether specific or general, and shall revert to the State Treasury at the close of the fiscal year.

APPROVED—The 29th day of May, A. D. 1893.

ROBT. E. PATTISON.

No. 125.

AN ACT

Making an appropriation to the Pennsylvania State Lunatic Hospital at Harrisburg, Pennsylvania.

$100,000.00 appropriated for rebuilding central portion of main building.

SECTION 1. *Be it enacted, &c.,* That the sum of one hundred thousand dollars, or so much thereof as may be necessary, be and the same is hereby specifically appropriated to the trustees of the Pennsylvania State Lunatic Hospital located at Harrisburg for the purpose of tearing down and removing the central portion of the main building of said hospital and rebuilding and completing the same in accordance with plans and specifications to be drawn under the supervision of the board of trustees of said hospital, and approved by the State Board of Public Charities. The building shall be of the best design for the construction of such an institution without expensive architectral adornment or unduly large or costly administrative accommodations, and as nearly fire-proof as possible, and no changes to be made in said plans of construction without the consent of the Board of Public Charities: *Pro-*

How plans shall be drawn.

vided, That the said plans shall be drawn with a view to tearing down, removing and replacing either, or both, of the wings of said main buildings, at some future time, without interfering with the said new central main building.

Superintendent of construction shall be appointed.

SECTION 2. The said trustees in order to provide for the proper and economical construction of said building shall, with the approval of the Governor and Board of Public Charities, appoint a superintendent of construction and fix the salary thereof: *And it is further provided,* That the total cost of tearing down and removing the present building and rebuilding and completing the new building shall not exceed one hundred thousand dollars.

Total cost.

SECTION 3. Said trustees shall proceed to erect said building and complete the same within two years from the passage of this act, and shall make report to the Board of Public Charities of the amount of money expended by them and of the progress made in the erection of the buildings, quarterly at least, and oftener, if so required by the board.

Shall complete the building within two years.

SECTION 4 The said trustees shall make, under oath, by their president or treasurer a quarterly report to the Auditor General and to the Board of Public Charities, containing a specifically itemized statement of the expenditures for tearing down, removing and rebuilding of said central portion of main building, together with the balance on hand at the close of the quarter and, unless such itemized report is made and approved by the Board of Public Charities, Auditor General and State Treasurer, the State Treasurer is hereby directed not to pay any more money to said institution for the purposes herein set forth, until such report is made and approved as aforesaid: *And it is further provided,* That a copy of the contracts entered into in accordance with the provisions of this act shall be filed with the Auditor General, and that any unexpended balance on hand at the close of two fiscal years from the passage of this act shall revert to the State Treasury.

Quarterly report to Auditor General Board of Public Charities.

Approval of report.

Copy of contract shall be filed with Auditor General.

Unexpended balances shall revert to the State Treasury.

APPROVED—The 29th day of May, A. D. 1893.

ROBT. E. PATTISON.

No. 126.

AN ACT.

Providing for the complete compilation of the corporation laws from one thousand eight hundred and seventy-four to one thousand eight hundred and ninety-three, together with all laws relating to railroads, beginning with the act of one thousand eight hundred and forty-nine, making an appropriation therefor and providing for the distribution of the same.

SECTION 1. *Be it enacted, &c.,* That the sum of one thousand dollars, or so much thereof as may be necessary, be and the same is hereby specifically appropriated, out of any money in the treasury not otherwise appropriated, for the compilation, revising, proof reading, copying, classifying, indexing and digesting, of all the

$1,000.00 appropriated.

general corporation laws of Pennsylvania, from one thousand eight hundred and seventy-four to one thousand eight hundred and ninety-three, inclusive. Said compilation also to include the act regulating railroad companies, approved February nineteenth, one thousand eight hundred and forty-nine, and all subsequent acts of Assembly from that time to the year one thousand eight hundred and ninety-three, which refer to such corporations.

Who shall make compilation.

SECTION 2. That said compilation shall be made by the corporation department of the State Department, and the

Payment of appropriation.

sum hereby appropriated shall be settled by the Auditor General and State Treasurer on the presentation of the proper specifically itemized vouchers upon the completion of the work.

How copies shall be printed, bound and distributed.

SECTION 3. That three thousand copies of said compilation shall be printed and bound in cloth, and the head of each department of the State, each member of the present Senate and each member of the present House of Representatives, shall be entitled to a copy of the same, and the balance shall be deposited in the office of the Secretary of the Commonwealth and sold for one dollar a copy, and the proceeds thereof turned into the State Treasury.

APPROVED—The 29th day of May, A. D. 1893.

ROBT. E. PATTISON.

No. 127.

AN ACT

To provide for a deficiency arising under provisions of an act, approved June first, one thousand eight hundred and ninety-one, entitled "An act to carry out the provisions of an act relating to to the care and treatment of the indigent insane," approved the thirteenth day of June, one thousand eight hundred and eighty-three, and making an appropriation therefor.

$65,000.00 appropriated.

SECTION 1. *Be it enacted, &c.,* That the sum of sixty-five thousand dollars, or so much thereof as may be necessary, be and the same is hereby specifically appropriated to provide for deficiency for the care and treatment of the indigent insane as prescribed by the act, approved June thirteenth, one thousand eight hundred and

When payable.

eighty-three: *Provided, also,* That no payment shall be made on account of the care and treatment of the insane until the Secretary of the Board of Public Charities shall certify to the Auditor General that the quarterly report of the cost of such care and treatment contains no charge except for maintenance.

APPROVED—The 30th day of May, A. D. 1893.

ROBT. E PATTISON.

No. 128.

A SUPPLEMENT

To an act, entitled "An act to fix the salaries of the several State officers of the Commonwealth, the number of clerks to be employed in the several departments and their compensation, and providing for the incidental expenses of said department," approved May fourteenth, one thousand eight hundred and seventy-four, providing for an increase in the salary of the Superintendent of Public Instruction, Deputy Attorney General, Auditor General and Secretary of Internal Affairs.

SECTION 1. *Be it enacted, &c.*, That the first section of an act, entitled "An act to fix the salaries of the several State officers of this Commonwealth, the number of clerks to be employed in the several departments and their compensation, and providing for the incidental expenses of said departments," approved May fourteenth, Anno Domini one thousand eight hundred and seventy four, which reads as follows:

Section 1, Act of
May 14, 1874. cited
for amendment.

"SECTION 1. *Be it enacted by the Senate and House of Representatives of the Commonwealth of Pennsylvania in General Assembly met, and it is hereby enacted by the authority of the same,* That the salaries of the several officers of this Commonwealth, enumerated herein, are hereby fixed, and shall be as follows:

Governor, ten thousand dollars.

Lieutenant Governor, three thousand dollars.

Attorney General, three thousand five hundred dollars.

Deputy Attorney General, one thousand eight hundred dollars.

Secretary of the Commonwealth, four thousand dollars.

Deputy Secretary of the Commonwealth, two thousand five hundred dollars.

Auditor General, three thousand dollars.

Secretary of Internal Affairs, three thousand dollars.

Adjutant General, two thousand five hundred dollars.

State Treasurer, five thousand dollars.

Superintendent of Public Instruction, two thousand five hundred dollars.

State Librarian, one thousand eight hundred dollars.

Assistant State Librarian, nine hundred dollars.

Superintendent of Public Printing, one thousand six hundred dollars.

Superintendent of Public Grounds and Buildings, one thousand four hundred dollars.

The Commissioner of Bureau of Statistics and the Surveyor General shall each receive a salary of two thousand five hundred dollars.

The salary of the Surveyor General shall continue until this office is merged in the office of the Secretary of the Internal Affairs.

The recorder and clerk of the Board of Pardons shall each receive the sum of five hundred dollars per annum, and each member of the board, five hundred dollars per annum, to date from the first day of January, Anno Domini one thousand eight hundred and seventy-four, and the same shall be, and continue annually, the salary of said recorder and clerk and of each of the members of said board, as designated by the Constitution of the Commonwealth, until otherwise provided by law," shall be amended to read as follows:

Salaries of the several officers of this Commonwealth.

SECTION 1. *Be it enacted by the Senate and House of Representatives of the Commonwealth of Pennsylvania in General Assembly met, and it is hereby enacted by the authority of the same,* That the salaries of the several officers of this Commonwealth enumerated herein are hereby fixed and shall be as follows:

Governor, ten thousand dollars.

Lieutenant Governor, three thousand dollars.

Attorney General, three thousand five hundred dollars.

Deputy Attorney General, four thousand dollars.

Secretary of the Commonwealth, four thousand dollars.

Deputy Secretary of the Commonwealth, two thousand five hundred dollars.

Auditor General, four thousand dollars.

Secretary of Internal Affairs, four thousand dollars.

Adjutant General, two thousand five hundred dollars.

State Treasurer, five thousand dollars.

Superintendent of Public Instruction, four thousand dollars.

Superintendent of Public Printing, one thousand six hundred dollars.

Superintendent of Public Grounds and Buildings, one thousand four hundred dollars.

The Commissioner of Bureau of Statistics shall receive a salary of two thousand five hundred dollars.

The recorder and clerk of the Board of Pardon shall each receive the sum of five hundred dollars per annum, and each member of the board five hundred dollars per annum, to date from the first day of January, Anno Domini one thousand eight hundred and seventy-four, and the same shall be, and continue annually, the salary of said recorder and clerk of each of the members of said board, as designated by the Constitution of the Commonwealth, until otherwise provided by law.

APPROVED—The 30th day of May, A. D. 1893.

ROBT. E. PATTISON.

No. 129.

AN ACT

To repeal an act, entitled "A supplement to the act laying a tax on dogs in certain townships in the county of Chester," so far as relates to taxing dogs in West Marlborough township, Chester county.

SECTION 1. *Be it enacted, &c.,* That so much of the Act of Assembly, approved the ninth day of March, one thousand eight hundred and fifty-five, entitled "A supplement to the act laying a tax on dogs in certain towships in the county of Chester as relates to the taxing of dogs in West Marlborough township, Chester county," be and the same is hereby repealed.

APPROVED—The 30th day of May, A. D. 1893.

ROBT. E. PATTISON.

No. 130.

AN ACT

Providing for the acquisition by the State of certain ground at Valley Forge for a public park, and making an appropriation therefor.

SECTION 1. *Be it enacted, &c.,* That for the purpose of perpetuating and preserving the site on which the Continental Army under which General George Washington was encamped in winter quarters at Valley Forge during the winter, one thousand seven hundred and seventy-seven and one thousand seven hundred and seventy-eight, the title to and ownership in the ground covering said site, including Forts Washington and Huntingdon, and the entrenchments adjacent thereto, and the adjoining grounds, in all not exceeding two hundred and fifty acres, but not including therein the property known as Washington's headquarters and now owned by the Centenial and Memorial Association of Valley Forge, the location and boundaries thereof to be fixed by the commissioners hereafter mentioned, shall be vested in the State of Pennsylvania, to be laid out, preserved and maintained forever, as a public place or park by the name of Valley Forge, so that the same and the fortifications thereon may be maintained as nearly as possible in their original condition as a military camp, and may be preserved for the enjoyment of the people of the said State.

Grounds at Valley Forge shall be vested in the State.

Boundaries to be fixed by the commissioners.

Shall be a public park by the name of Valley Forge.

SECTION 2. That ten citizens of the State be appointed by the Governor for the term of five years, who are hereby constituted commissioners of said park. As often as a vacancy occurs, either by expiration of term or otherwise, the Governor may fill said vacancy, either for

Governor shall appoint ten commissioners and may fill vacancies.

another term of five years or for the expired term as the case may be. The said commissioners shall organize, annually, on the first Monday of June, by the election of a president and secretary to serve for one year, but they shall receive no compensation for their service as commissioners.

Organization of commissioners.

SECTION 3. That the owners of the said ground by the first section of this act appropriated for public purposes, shall be paid for the same by the State of Pennsylvania according to the value which shall be ascertained by a jury of disinterested freeholders to be appointed by the court of quarter sessions of the county in which said grounds lie, upon the petition of the said commissioners; and if the said commissioners shall delay petitioning, as aforesaid, for the period of sixty days after notice is given of their taking possession of said ground, then said jury shall be appointed upon the petition of any person whose property shall be so taken: *Provided however*, That in any case the said commissioners may negotiate and agree with the owners of any part of said ground as to the price thereof, and said price shall be reported to court of quarter sessions, and if approved and confirmed by said court, shall be binding on said State: *And provided further*, That whenever it shall be necessary to have recourse to a jury to assess the damages for any property to be taken, as aforesaid, the said jury shall consist of such number, and shall proceed, and their award shall be reviewed and enforced in the same manner as now provided by law in the taking of land for the opening of roads in said county, and the sum of twenty-five thousand dollars, or so much thereof as may be necessary, is hereby specifically appropriated for the purchase or condemnation money of said lands and making the said forts and entrenchments accessible to the public by such means as may be deemed necessary, and for the necessary expenses incident thereto.

Owners of ground shall be paid by the State.

Value to be ascertained by a jury.

If commissioners agree as to the price.

How jury shall proceed.

$25,000.00 appropriated.

SECTION 4. That the commissioners of the said park, after they shall have secured possession of the said grounds, shall adopt plans for the improvement, preservation and maintenance thereof, and shall have power to carry the same into execution, and all moneys expended shall be under their supervision; but no contracts shall be made for said improvement unless an appropriation therefor shall have been first made by the Legislature.

Commissioners shall adopt plans etc..

Shall have power to carry same into execution.

Contracts

SECTION 5. After the said premises shall have, as aforesaid, passed into the possession of the Commonwealth, they may at any time or times hereafter be used as a camping ground for the National Guard of Pennsylvania. Whenever the Governor, acting as Commander-in-Chief, shall direct said commissioners to open the grounds and park for the accommodation of the said guard, or any portion thereof, it shall be the duty of the commissioners to make all necessary arrangements for such camps, to provide for sufficient water supply and drainage, and during such camps to relinquish to the commanding

Premises may be used as a camping ground for the National Guard.

Commissioners shall open grounds for Guard whenever Governor shall direct.

officer, for the time being, all police control over and through the said park and grounds

The said appropriation to be paid on the warrant of the Auditor General on a settlement made by him and the State Treasurer, but no warrant shall be drawn on settlement made until the commissioners of said park shall have made, under oath to the Auditor General, a report containing a specifically itemized statement of the cost of said ground and improvements, and the same is approved by him and the State Treasurer, nor until the Treasurer shall have sufficient money in the treasury, not otherwise appropriated, to pay the amount due said commissioners under this act; and unexpended balances of sums appropriated for specific purposes shall not be used for other purposes, whether specific or general, and shall revert to the State Treasury at the close of the fiscal years.

APPROVED—The 30th day of May, A. D. 1893.

ROBT. E. PATTISON.

Police control of grounds shall be under direction of commanding officer during encampment.

How appropriation shall be paid.

Itemized statement.

Unexpended balances shall revert to State Treasury.

No. 131.

AN ACT

Relating to affidavits of defense in the several courts of common pleas of this Commonwealth, and authorizing the plantiff or plantiffs in all actions to take judgment for the amount admitted to be due by the defendant or defendants in such actions.

SECTION 1. *Be it enacted, &c.*, That in all cases now pending, or hereafter to be commenced, in the several courts of this Commonwealth in which affidavits of defense have been, or may be filed to part of the claim of the plaintiff or plaintiffs, the plaintiff or plaintiffs may take judgment for the amount admitted to be due and have execution for the collection of the same, and the cases shall be proceeded in for the recovery of the balance of the demand of the plaintiff or plaintiffs, if anything more should be justly due to such plaintiff or plaintiffs.

APPROVED—The 31st day of May, A. D. 1893.

ROBT. E. PATTISON.

No. 132.

AN ACT

To repeal an act passed the twenty-seventh day of March, Anno Domini one thousand seven hundred and eighty-four, entitled "An act to regulate fences and to appoint appraisers in each township in the counties of Bedford, Westmoreland, Washington and Fayette, and to encourage the raising of swine," so far as its provisions relate to or affect the county of Armstrong.

SECTION 1. *Be it enacted, &c.*, That an act passed the twenty-seventh day of March, Anno Domini one thousand seven hundred and eighty-four, entitled "An act to regulate fences and to appoint appraisers in each township in the counties of Bedford, Westmoreland, Washington and Fayette, and to encourage the raising of swine," so far as its provisions relate to or affect the county of Armstrong, be and the same is hereby repealed.

APPROVED—The 31st day of May, A. D. 1893.

ROBT. E. PATTISON.

No. 133.

AN ACT

To repeal an act, entitled "An act laying a tax on dogs in certain townships in the county of Chester, relative to elections in West Philadelphia and to assessors in Millerstown, Perry county," so far as relates to taxing dogs in Tredyffrin township, Chester county.

SECTION 1. *Be it enacted, &c.*, That so much of the act of Assembly, approved the eleventh day of March, one thousand eight hundred and fifty, entitled "An act laying a tax on dogs in certain townships in the county of Chester, relative to elections in West Philadelphia and to assessors in Millerstown, Perry county," as relates to the taxing of dogs in Tredyffrin township, Chester county, be and the same is hereby repealed.

APPROVED—The 31st day of May, A. D. 1893.

ROBT. E. PATTISON

No. 134.

AN ACT

To repeal an act, entitled "An act relative to the expenditure of the road taxes in Fayette county and for other purposes, approved the fifth day of May, Anno Domini one thousand eight hundred and thirty-two, and for other purposes," approved March eleventh, one thousand eight hundred and forty-five, so far as relates to Pennsbury township, Chester county.

SECTION 1. *Be it enacted, &c.*, That so much of the act of Assembly, approved March eleventh, one thousand eight hundred and forty-five, entitled "An act relative to the expenditure of the road taxes in Fayette county and for other purposes, approved the fifth day of May, Anno Domini one thousand eight hundred and thirty-two, and other purposes," be and the same is hereby repealed so far as it relates to Pennsbury township, Chester county.

APPROVED—The 31st day of May, A. D. 1893.

ROBT. E. PATTISON.

No. 135.

AN ACT

Repealing an act relating to sheriff sales in Luzerne county, so far as it requires publication of the notice of sheriff sale in newspapers at the county seat.

SECTION 1. *Be it enacted, &c*, That from and after the passage of this act, the act, entitled "An act relating to sheriff sales in the county of Luzerne," approved the eighteenth day of April, Anno Domini one thousand eight hundred and sixty-one, as follows:

"That from and after the passage of this act, in all cases of sheriff sales of real estate in the county of Luzerne, the publication of notice of said sales shall be made in any two newspapers published at the county seat of said county, as may be directed by the attorney or party issuing or having charge of the writs upon which direction shall be endorsed on the præcipe to the prothonotary and by him endorsed on the writ, and so much of any law as is inconsistent herewith is hereby repealed, so far as relates to said county," be and the same is hereby repealed, so far as it requires publication of the notice of sheriff's sales in newspapers at the county seat.

APPROVED—The 31st day of May, A. D. 1893.

ROBT. E. PATTISON.

No. 136.

AN ACT

Making an appropriation for medals of honor.

WHEREAS, In order to commemorate the valor and patriotism of the "Worth Infantry" and "York Rifles", two volunteer militia companies from York, York county, Pennsylvania, which participated and took part in helping to suppress the late rebellion:

SECTION 1. *Be it enacted, &c.*, That the sum of three hundred dollars, or so much thereof as may be necessary, is hereby specifically appropriated for the purpose of procuring a suitable medal with commemorating devices for each of the surviving members, or their heirs, of the Worth Infantry and the York Rifles, of York, Pennsylvania, who went from the State of Pennsylvania into active service, fully armed and equipped, on the nineteenth day of April, one thousand eight hundred and sixty-one. $300.00 appropriated.

Who shall receive medals.

SECTION 2. That the Auditor General, Adjutant General and State Treasurer of the State of Pennsylvania be and are hereby authorized and directed to secure a medal of honor, with suitable device or devices, to be presented to each soldier at such time and place as may be determined on within one year from the passage of this act, and the State Treasurer is hereby authorized to pay on a warrant of the Auditor General the cost of the same out of any money in the treasury, not otherwise appropriated. Who shall prepare devices for medals.

Payment of cost of procuring same.

APPROVED—The 31st day of May, A. D. 1891.

ROBT. E. PATTISON.

No. 137.

AN ACT

Requiring all public records within this Commonwealth to be kept in the English language.

Act shall go into effect July 1, 1898.

Section 1. *Be it enacted, &c.*, That from and after the first day of July, Anno Domini one thousand eight hundred and ninety-three, any and all person or persons, who shall offer for probate any will or codicil, or who shall offer any deed, mortgage, agreement, lease or release, commission, power of attorney, or any other written or printed instrument to be recorded in any register's or recorder's office, or court of record, within this Commonwealth, or to be filed in said office or court as required by law, and which shall be in any other than the English language, shall furnish at his, her or their expense, the register, clerk of the orphans' court, recorder, prothonotary, or other person in charge of such office wherein the **Sworn translation shall be furnished, which shall be attached to original paper.** same is to be filed or recorded, with a sworn translation in English of such written or printed instrument thus offered, and the person in charge of said office shall attach or cause to be attached such translation to the original and file both the original and the translation of record in his office in all cases where filing is now or hereafter may be required by law, but in all cases where recording is now or hereafter may be required both the original and translation in English shall be recorded.

Papers not conforming to this act shall not be filed or recorded.

Section 2. The clerk or person in charge of such records shall not file or mark filed, record or mark recorded, any written or printed instrument in violation of this act, nor shall any paper filed or recorded in violation of this act be notice to any person in any legal proceeding whatever, nor be received or considered in evidence in any proceeding at law or equity.

Repeal

Section 3. That all acts or parts of acts inconsistent herewith be and the same are hereby repealed.

Approved—The 31st day of May, A. D. 1893.

ROBT. E. PATTISON.

No. 138.

AN ACT.

Designating the days and half days to be observed as legal holidays, and for the payment, acceptance and protesting of bills, notes, drafts, checks and other negotiable paper on such days.

Days and half days to be observed as legal holidays.

Section 1. *Be it enacted, &c.*, That the following days and half days, namely: the first day of January, commonly called New Year's day; the twenty-second day of February, known as Washington's birthday; Good Friday; the thirtieth day of May, known as Memorial day; the fourth of July, called Independence Day; the first Saturday of September, known as Labor day; the first Tuesday after the first Monday of November, Election day; the twenty-fifth day of December, known as Christmas day; and every Saturday after twelve o'clock noon until twelve o'clock midnight, each of which Saturdays is hereby designated a half holiday, and any day appointed or recommended by the Governor of this State or the President of the United States as a day of thanksgiving or fasting and prayer or other religious observance shall, for all purposes whatever as regards the presenting for payment or acceptance, and as regards the protesting and giving notice of the dishonor of bills of exchange, checks, drafts and promissory notes, made after the passage of this act, be treated and considered as the first day of the week, commonly called Sunday, and as public holidays and half holidays, and all such bills, checks, drafts and notes otherwise presentable for acceptance or payment on any of the said days shall be deemed to be payable and be presentable for acceptance or payment on the secular or business day next succeeding such holiday or half holiday, except checks, drafts, bills of exchange and promissory notes, payable at sight, or on demand, which would otherwise be payable at any half holiday Saturday, shall be deemed to be payable at or before twelve o'clock noon of such half holiday: *Provided however*, That for the purpose of protesting or otherwise holding liable any party to any bill of exchange, check, draft or promissory note, and which shall not have been paid before twelve o'clock noon of any Saturday designated a half holiday, as aforesaid, a demand or acceptance or payment thereof shall not be made and notice of protest or dishonor thereof shall not be given until the next succeeding secular or business day: *And provided further*, That when any person, firm, corporation or company, shall on any Saturday designated a half holiday, receive for collection any check, bill of exchange, draft or promissory note, such person, firm, corporation or company, shall not be deemed guilty of any neglect or omission of duty, nor incur any liability in not presenting for payment, or acceptance, or collection, such check, bill of exchange, draft or promissory note on that day: *And provided further*, That in construing this section every Saturday designated a half holiday shall, until twelve o'clock noon, be deemed a secular or business day, and the days and half holidays, aforesaid so designated as holidays and half holidays, shall be considered as public holidays and half holidays for all purposes whatsoever as regards the transaction of business: *And provided further*, That nothing herein contained shall be construed to prevent or invalidate the entry, issuance, service or execution of any writ, summons, confession of judgment, or other legal process whatever on any of the Saturday afternoons herein designated as holidays, nor to prevent any bank from keeping its doors open or transacting its business on any of the said Saturday afternoons if, by a vote of its directors, it shall elect to do so.

Shall be treated as Sunday in presentation of bills, drafts, notes, &c.,

Proviso as to protesting. &c.,

Proviso as to non-presentation for payment on Saturday.

Shall be considered as public holidays and half holidays for all purposes as to transaction of business.

Execution of writs, &c., shall not be prevented on Saturday afternoons.

Banks may keep their doors open.

Mond ay to be observed when certain holidays fall on Sunday.

SECTION 2. Whenever the first day of January, the twenty-second day of February, the fourth of July, or the twenty-fifth day of December, shall any of them occur on Sunday, the following day, Monday, shall be deemed and declared a public holiday. All bills of exchange, checks, drafts or promissory notes falling due on any of the Mondays so observed as holidays, shall be due and payable on the next succeeding secular or business day, and all Mondays so observed as holidays shall, for all purposes whatever as regards the presenting for payment ·or acceptance, and as regards the protesting and giving notice of the dishonor of bills of exchange, checks, drafts and promissory notes, made after the passage of this act, be treated and considered as is the first day of the week, commonly called Sunday. When the thirtieth day of May falls on Sunday, the day preceding it, Saturday, shall be observed as the holiday, and payment of bills of exchange, checks, draft and promissory notes, due and payable on such holiday, shall be made on the next succeeding secular or business day.

Payment of checks, &c., on such days.

Saturday to be observed when May thirtieth fall on Sunday.

Checks, notes, &c., which may become due on Sunday shall be payable on next business day.

SECTION 3. All bills of exchange, checks, drafts and promissory notes made after the passage of this act, which by the terms thereof shall be payable on the first day of the week, commonly called Sunday, shall be deemed to be and shall be payable on the next succeeding secular or business day.

Shall be regarded as business days for all other purposes than those mentioned in this act.

SECTION 4. That all the days and half days herein designated as legal holidays shall be regarded as secular or business days for all other purposes than those mentioned in this act.

APPROVED —The 31st day of May, A. D. 1893.

ROBT. E. PATTISON.

No. 139.

AN ACT

Making an appropriation for the purchase of copies of "An Index to Local Legislation in Pennsylvania from Anno Domini seventeen hundred to Anno Domini eighteen hundred and ninety two," compiled by Giles D. Price.

WHEREAS, The enactment of local laws constitute an important part of the Legislation of Pennsylvania, affecting the government of counties, cities, boroughs and townships, the support of the poor, the maintenance of roads and bridges, the construction of fences and party walls, the administration of justice, the titles to lands and the rights of citizens generally;

And whereas, The local legislation relating to a subject or locality cannot be ascertained excepting by a laborious search through the indices of the several pamphet laws (about seventy or more in number) compiled without uniformity of plan and in many instances incorrect;

And whereas, The sale of an index to local legislation of Pennsylvania would be too small to warrant the publication of the same by unaided private enterprise;

And whereas, It would seem to be the duty of the State to aid in securing to its people a convenient and certain method of ascertaining what the law is relating to matters of so much importance, therefore,

SECTION 1. *Be it enacted, &c.,* That the sum of two thousand five hundred dollars be and the same is hereby specifically appropriated for the purchase of five hundred copies of a work, entitled "An Index to Local Legislation in Pennsylvania from Anno Domini seventeen hundred to Anno Domini eighteen hundred and ninety two," compiled by Giles D. Price:" *Provided,* That two hundred and fifteen copies thereof shall be for the use of the members and officers of the House of Representatives of the sessions of one thousand eight hundred and ninety-three, one hundred and fifty copies for the use of the members and officers of the Senate of the session one thousand eight hundred and ninety-three, thirty-five copies for the use of the several Executive departments at Harrisburg and one hundred copies for the use of the law judges of the several courts of this Commonwealth, said books to contain about six hundred pages, to be printed on good paper, with good and sufficient binding. Said books to be delivered to the Secretary of the Commonwealth for distribution. The said appropriation to be paid on the warrant of the Auditor General on a settlement made by him and the State Treasurer upon the certificate of the Secretary of the Commonwealth that the said books have been delivered.

$2,500.00 appropriated to purchase 500 copies.

Distribution of copies.

Size and style of each.

How appropriation shall be paid.

We do certify that the bill, "An act making an appropriation for the purchase of copies of 'An Index to Local Legislation in Pennsylvania, from A. D. 1700 to A. D. 1892,' compiled by Giles D. Price," which has been disapproved by the Governor and returned with his objections to the Senate in which it originated, was passed by a two-thirds vote of all the members of the Senate on the thirtieth day of May, Anno Domini one thousand eight hundred and ninety-three, and the foregoing is the act so passed by the Senate.

LOUIS A. WATRES,
President of the Senate.
E. W. SMILEY,
Clerk of the Senate.

HARRISBURG, PA., *May 31, 1893.*

We do certify that the bill, entitled "An act making an appropriation for the purchase of copies of 'An Index to Local Legislation in Pennsylvania, from A. D. 1700 to A. D. 1892,' compiled by Giles D. Price," which has been disapproved by the Governor and returned with his objections to the Senate in which it originated, was passed by a two-thirds vote of all the members of the House of Representatives on the thirty-first day of May, Anno

Domini one thousand eight hundred and ninety-three, and the foregoing is the act so passed by the House of Representatives.

C. C. THOMPSON,
Speaker of the House of Representatives.
CHARLES E. VOORHEES,
Chief Clerk of the House of Representatives.
HARRISBURG, PA., *May 31, 1893.*

No. 140.

AN ACT

Making an appropriation for the payment of the expenses of the Committee on Centennial Affairs of the House of Representatives incurred in carrying out the terms of the resolution adopted March thirteenth, one thousand eight hundred and ninety-three, directing the said committee to examine the accounts and correspondence of the World's Fair Commission.

$480.00 appropriated.

SECTION 1. *Be it enacted, &c.,* That the sum of four hundred and eighty dollars, or so much thereof as may be necessary, be and the same is hereby specifically appropriated for the payment of the expenses of the Committee on Centennial Affairs of the House of Representatives incurred in carrying out the terms of the resolution adopted March thirteen, one thousand eight hundred and ninety-three, directing the said committee to examine the accounts and correspondence of the World's Fair Commission, for the following purposes, namely:

Items.

S. C. Osman, for stenographic services, one hundred dollars.

W. K. Buckingham, for services as clerk and incidental expenses, three hundred and eighty dollars.

How payab'e.

The said appropriation to be paid on the warrant of the Auditor General on a settlement made by him and the State Treasurer, upon specifically itemized vouchers to be furnished by the chairman of said committee.

APPROVED—The 2d day of June, A. D. 1893.

ROBT. E. PATTISON.

No. 141

AN ACT.

Making an appropriation for the State Normal Schools of this Commonwealth.

$130,000.00 appropriated for year beginning June 1, 1893.

SECTION 1. *Be it enacted, &c.,* That for the several State Normal Schools organized and accepted as such under the laws of this Commonwealth, the sum of one hundred and thirty thousand dollars be and the same is hereby specifically appropriated for the school year beginning the first Monday of June, Anno Domino one thousand eight hundred and ninety-three; and further, that a like sum be and is hereby specifically appropriated for the school year beginning on the first Monday of June, Anno Domini one thousand eight hundred and ninety-four. The said sums to be distributed equally among the thirteen State Normal Schools of the Commonwealth, and to be paid on the warrant of the Superintendent of Public Instruction on the receipt of the annual financial statement and the report of the several schools.

Like sum for year beginning June 1, 1894.

To be equally distributed among schools.

How and when payable.

APPROVED—The 2d day of June, A. D. 1893.

                    ROBT. E. PATTISON.

No. 142.

AN ACT

Making an appropriation to the State Normal School of the Fourth District of Pennsylvania located at East Stroudsburg.

SECTION 1. *Be it enacted, &c.,* That the sum of twenty-five thousand dollars, or so much thereof as may be necessary, be and the same is hereby specifically appropriated to the State Normal School of the Fourth Normal School district of Pennsylvania, located at East Stroudsburg, Monroe county, for the two fiscal years beginning June first, one thousand eight hundred and ninety three, for the purpose of completing the buildings, furnishing the same and providing the necessary library and apparatus: *Provided,* That before the said money shall be paid the trustees of said school shall cause a mortgage to be placed upon the grounds and buildings of the institution for the amount hereby appropriated, to be executed to the Commonwealth, creating a lien upon said property: *Provided further,* That a policy of insurance shall be placed upon the school property for the benefit of the Commonwealth for a sum not less than two-thirds of the value of the same.

$25,000 appropriated.

Purpose of appropriation.

Mortgage to be placed on ground and buildings.

Insurance of property.

The said appropriation to be on the warrant of the Auditor General on a settlement by him and the State Treasurer, but no warrant shall be drawn on settlement made until the trustees of said Normal School shall have made, under oath to the Auditor General, a report containing specifically itemized statement of the receipts from all sources and expenses of said Normal School, together with a specifically itemized statement of the expenditures for building, furnishing and library, with apparatus, during the previous quarter, with the cash balance on hand, and the same is approved by him and the State Treasurer, nor until the Treasurer shall have sufficient money in the treasury, not otherwise appropriated, to pay the quarterly installments due said Normal School; and unexpended balances of sums appropriated for specific purposes shall not be used for

How payable

Itemized statement.

Unexpended balances shall revert to the State Treasury.

13—LAWS.

other purposes, whether specific or general, and shall revert to the State Treasurer at the close of the two fiscal years.

APPROVED—The 2d day of June, A. D. 1893.

ROBT. E. PATTISON.

No. 143.

AN ACT

Making an appropriation to the Cumberland Valley State Normal School at Shippensburg, Cumberland county.

$50,000.00 appropriated.

SECTION 1. *Be it enacted, &c.,* That the sum of fifty thousand dollars, or so much thereof as may be necessary, be and the same is hereby specifically appropriated to the State Normal School located at Shippensburg, Cumberland county, for the two fiscal years beginning June first, one thousand eight hundred and ninety-three,

Purpose of appropriation.

for the purpose of erecting an additional building for the dormitories and repairing and rearranging the present building: *Provided,* That no part of the money herein appropriated shall become available until the trustees of

Mortgage to be placed on grounds and buildings.

said Normal School shall cause a mortgage to be placed upon the grounds and buildings for the amount of money herein appropriated, to be executed to the Commonwealth, creating a lien upon said property, and that the

Insurance of property.

school property shall be insured for the benefit of the Commonwealth for a sum of not less than two-thirds of the value of the same.

How payable.

The said appropriation to be paid on the warrant of the Auditor General on a settlement made by him and the State Treasurer, but no warrant shall be drawn on settlement made until the directors or managers of said Normal School shall have made, under oath to the Auditor General, a report containing a specifically itemized

Itemized statement

statement of the receipts from all sources and expenses of said Normal School, together with a specifically itemized statement of the cost of said building and repairs during the previous quarter, with the cash balance on hand, and the same is approved by him and the State Treasurer, nor until the Treasurer shall have sufficient money in the treasury, not otherwise appropriated, to pay the quarterly installments due said Normal School; and unex-

Unexpended balances shall revert to the State Treasury.

pended balances of sums appropriated for specific purposes shall not be used for other purposes, whether specific or general, and shall revert to the State Treasury at the close of the two fiscal years.

APPROVED—The 2d day of June, A. D. 1893.

ROBT. E. PATTISON.

No. 144.

AN ACT

Making an appropriation to the State Normal School of the Eighth Normal School district located at Lock Haven, Pennsylvania.

SECTION 1. *Be it enacted, &c.*, That the sum of eleven thousand five hundred dollars, or so much thereof as may be necessary, be and the same is hereby specifically appropriated to the Central Normal School Association of the State of Pennsylvania in the Eighth Normal School district at Lock Haven, Clinton county, for the fiscal year beginning June first, one thousand eight hundred and ninety-three, for the purchase of land necessary to secure a full supply of water for the school, and for the erection of an engine house wherein to provide steam, heat and power to distribute heat and light to the buildings of the institution and to pump the supply of water, and for any machinery or attachments that may be necessary therefor: *Provided,* That before any part of the money herein appropriated shall become available, the trustees of said school shall cause a mortgage to be placed upon the grounds and buildings for the amount of money herein appropriated, to be executed to the Commonwealth, creating a lien upon said property: *Provided further,* That the school property shall be insured for the benefit of the Commonwealth for a sum not less than two-thirds of the value of the same.

The said appropriation to be paid on the warrant of the Auditor General on a settlement made by him and the State Treasurer, but no warrant shall be drawn on settlement made until the trustees of said Normal School shall have been made, under oath to the Auditor General, a report containing a specifically itemized statement of the receipts from all sources and expenses of said Normal School, together with a specifically itemized statement of the cost of said land and new building, during the previous quarter, with the cash balance on hand, and the same is approved by him and the State Treasurer, nor until the Treasurer shall have sufficient money in the treasury, not otherwise appropriated, to pay the quarterly installments due said Normal School; and unexpended balances of sums appropriated for specific purposes shall not be used for other purposes, whether specific or general, and shall revert to the State Treasury at the close of the fiscal year.

APPROVED—The 2d day of June, A D. 1893.

ROBT. E. PATTISON.

(Margin notes:) $11,500.00 appropriated. Purpose of appropriation. Mortgage to be placed on grounds and buildings. Insurance of property. How payable. Itemized statement. Unexpended balances shall revert to the State Treasury.

No. 145.

AN ACT

Making an appropriation to Slippery Rock State Normal School in
the Eleventh district of Pennsylvania.

\$40,(00.00 total appropriation.

SECTION 1. *Be it enacted, &c.* That the sum of forty
thousand dollars, or so much thereof as may be necessary, be and the same is hereby specifically appropriated
to the Slippery Rock State Normal School located at
Slippery Rock, Butler county, and being in the Eleventh
State Normal School district, for the two fiscal years beginning June first, one thousand eight hundred and
nine-three, for the following purposes, namely:

\$20,000.00 to complete building.

\$20,000 00 for extension to ladies dormitory.

The sum of twenty thousand dollars, or so much
thereof as may be necessary, for completing the building
now in course of erection, and the sum of twenty thousand dollars, or so much thereof as may be necessary, for
making an extension to the northwest corner of the ladies'
dormitory: *Provided*, That no part of the money herein
appropriated shall become available until the trustees of

Mortgage to be placed on grounds and buildings.

said school shall cause a mortgage to be placed upon the
grounds and buildings for the amount of money herein
appropriated, to be executed to the Commonwealth,
creating a lien upon the said property: *Provided further*,

Insurance of property.

That the property of the school shall be insured for the
benefit of the Commonwealth for a sum not less than
two-thirds of the value of the same.

How payable

The said appropriation to be paid on the warrant of
the Auditor General on a settlement made by him and
the State Treasurer, but no warrant shall be drawn on
settlement made until the trustees of said Normal
School shall have made, under oath to the Auditor General, a report containing a specifically itemized state-

Itemized statement.

ment of the receipts from all sources and expenses of
said Normal School, together with a specifically itemized
statement of the said new buildings, during the previous quarter, with the cash balance on hand, and the same
is approved by him and the State Treasurer, nor until
the Treasurer shall have sufficient money in the treasury,
not otherwise appropriated, to pay the quarterly instal-

Unexpended balances shall revert to the State Treasury.

ments due said Normal School; and unexpended balances
of sums appropriated for specific purposes shall not
be used for other purposes, whether specific or general,
and shall revert to the State Treasury at the close of the
two fiscal years.

APPROVED—The 2d day of June, A. D. 1898.

ROBT. E. PATTISON.

No. 146.

AN ACT

Making an appropriation to the State Normal School of the Thirteenth District of Pennsylvania, located at Clarion.

SECTION 1. *Be it enacted, &c.,* That the sum of fifty-five thousand dollars, or so much thereof as may be necessary, be and the same is hereby specifically appropriated to the State Normal School of the Thirteenth district of Pennsylvania, located at Clarion, in the county of Clarion, for the two fiscal years beginning June first, one thousand eight hundred and ninety-three, for the following purposes, namely : The sum of thirty-five thousand dollars, or so much thereof as may be necessary, for the erection and equipment of a model school building, and the sum of twenty thousand dollars, or so much thereof as may be necessary, for the erection and equipment of a building for steam heating, electric lighting and laundry purposes: *Provided,* That before any part of the money herein appropriated shall become available, the trustees of the said Normal School shall cause a mortgage to be placed upon the grounds and buildings for the amount of money herein appropriated, to be executed to the Commonwealth, creating a lien upon said property : *Provided further,* That the school property shall be insured for the benefit of the Commonwealth for a sum not less than two-thirds of the value of the same: *And be it further provided,* That the sum of twelve thousand dollars appropriated to said school under an act of Assembly, approved the sixteenth day of June, one thousand eight hundred and ninety-one, shall not be drawn from the State Treasury, but be permitted to lapse and revert into the treasury upon the first day of June, one thousand eight hundred and ninety-three, or if it has or shall be so drawn before that time, said sum shall be deducted from the amount herein appropriated for the erection of a model school building.

The said appropriation to be paid on the warrant of the Auditor General on a settlement made by him and the State Treasurer, but no warrant shall be drawn on settlement made until the trustees of said Normal School shall have made, under oath to the Auditor General, a report containing a specifically itemized statement of the receipts from all sources and expenses of said Normal School, together with a specifically itemized statement of the cost of said new buildings and the equipment of the same, during the previous quarter, with the cash balance on hand, and the same is approved by him and the State Treasurer, nor until the Treasurer shall have sufficient money in the treasury, not otherwise appropriated, to pay the quarterly instalments due said Normal School ; and unexpended balances of sums appropriated

[Margin notes:]
$55,000.00 total appropriation.

Items.

Mortgage to be placed on grounds and buildings.

Property shall be insured.

Proviso as to appropriation of 1891.

How payable.

Itemised statement.

Unexpended balances shall revert to the State Treasury.

for specific purposes shall not be used for other purposes, whether specific or general, and shall revert to the State Treasury at the close of the two fiscal years.

APPROVED—The 2d day of June, A. D. 1893.

ROBT. E. PATTISON.

No. 147.

AN ACT.

Making an appropriation to the Pennsylvania Industrial Reformatory at Huntingdon.

SECTION 1. *Be it enacted, &c.,* That the following sums, or so much thereof as may be necessary, be and the same are hereby specifically appropriated to the Pennsylvania Industrial Reformatory at Huntingdon, for the two fiscal years, commencing on the first day of June, one thousand eight hundred and ninety-three, for the following specific purposes, namely:

Salaries.

For salaries of officers and employés, the sum of one hundred and eight thousand dollars, or so much thereof as may be necessary.

Deficiencies of salaries.

For deficiencies of salaries for the year one thousand eight hundred and ninety-two, consequent upon the employment of additional force on the passage of the eight hour law, the sum of ten thousand dollars, or so much thereof as may be necessary.

Insurance.

For insurance of buildings, the sum of fifteen hundred dollars, or so much thereof as may be necessary.

Rent of farm.

For rent of farm, two years, the sum of one thousand dollars, or so much thereof as may be necessary.

Heating, &c

For heating, lighting and ventilating the buildings, shops and approaches thereto, the sum of fifteen thousand dollars, or so much thereof as may be necessary.

Library, Postage, &c.

For library books, postage and stationery for prisoners, the sum of one thousand five hundred dollars, or so much thereof as may be necessary.

School books and maps.

For school books, maps and apparatus for reformatory schools, the sum of eight hundred dollars, or so much thereof as may be necessary.

Lectures.

For lectures and special school instruction, the sum of five hundred dollars, or so much thereof as may be necessary.

Tools and material.

For tools and material for mechanical instruction, the sum of five thousand dollars, or so much thereof as may be necessary.

Replacing of buildings.

For replacing buildings destroyed by fire, the sum of fifteen thousand dollars, or so much thereof as may be necessary.

Engines, &c

For engines, shafting, pulleys, belting and tools for the same, the sum of six thousand dollars, or so much thereof as may be necessary.

For water pipes, plumbing and hose in same, the sum **Plumbing.** of one thousand dollars, or so much thereof as may be necessary.

For fitting up hospital, the sum of one thousand dol- **Hospital** lars, or so much thereof as may be necessary.

For additional equipment to prisoners' kitchen, the **Kitchen.** sum of five hundred dollars, or so much thereof as may be necessary.

For additional water supply and piping the same to **Additional water** the institution, and for repairs to the present reservoir, **supply.** the sum of six thousand five hundred dollars, or so much thereof as may be necessary.

For changing flush pipes in cell houses "A", "B" and **Flush pipes and** "C" and putting in vacuum chambers and steam coils **ventilation of cells.** for ventillating cells, the sum of one thousand eight hundred dollars, or so much thereof as may be necessary.

For the erection of a green house, and the erection of **Green house and** an ice house, the sum of one thousand one hundred dol- **ice house.** lars, or so much thereof as may be necessary.

For the erection of porches on general superinten- **Erection of** dent's and deputy superintendent's residences, the sum **porches.** of six hundred and thirty dollars, or so much thereof as may be necessary.

For the erection of safety walls around the railroad **Safety walls.** and wagon gates, the sum of one thousand seven hundred dollars, or so much thereof as may be necessary.

For each discharged or paroled prisoner, whose resi- **Discharged or pa-** dence is within fifty miles of Huntingdon, five dollars, **roled prisoners** and for each discharged or paroled prisoner, whose residence is more than fifty miles from Huntingdon, ten dollars.

The said appropriation to be paid on the warrant of **How payable.** Auditor General on a settlement made by him and the State Treasurer, but no warrant shall be drawn on settlement made until the directors or managers of said institution shall have made, under oath to the Auditor General, a report containing a specifically itemized state- **Itemized state-** ment of the receipts from all sources and the expenses **ment.** of said institution and costs of buildings, improvements, repairs and so forth, during the previous quarter, and the same is approved by him and the State Treasurer, nor until the Treasurer shall have sufficient money in the treasury, not otherwise appropriated, to pay the quarterly instalments due said institution; and unexpended balances of sums appropriated for specific pur- **Unexpended bal-** poses shall not be used for other purposes, whether **ances shall revert** specific or general, and shall revert to the State Treas- **Treasury.** ury at the close of the two fiscal years.

APPROVED—The 2d day of June, A. D. 1893.

ROBT. E. PATTISON.

No. 148.

AN ACT

Making an appropriation to the Pittsburg Hospital for Children at Pittsburgh.

$4,000.00 appro-
priated for mainte-
nance.

SECTION 1. *Be it enacted, &c.,* That the sum of four thousand dollars, or so much thereof as may be necessary, be and the same is hereby specifically appropriated to the Pittsburgh Hospital for Children at Pittsburgh, for the two fiscal years beginning June first, one thousand eight hundred and ninety-three, for the purpose of maintenance.

How payable.

The said appropriation to be paid on the warrant of the Auditor General on a settlement made by him and the State Treasurer, but no warrant shall be drawn on settlement made until the directors or managers of said institution shall have made, under oath to the Auditor

Itemized state-
ment

General, a report containing a specifically itemized statement of the receipts from all sources and expenses of said institution during the previous quarter, with the cash balance on hand, and the same is approved by him and the State Treasurer, nor until the Treasurer shall have sufficient money in the treasury, not other-wise appropriated, to pay the quarterly installments

Unexpended bal-
ances shall revert
to the State
Treasury.

due said institution; and unexpended balances of sums appropriated for specific purposes shall not be used for other purposes, whether specific or general, and shall revert to the State Treasury at the close of the two fiscal years.

APPROVED--The 2d day of June, A. D. 1893.

　　　　　　　　ROBT. E. PATTISON.

No. 149.

AN ACT

Making an appropriation to the Wills' Eye Hospital of Philadelphia.

$20,000.00 total ap-
propriation.

SECTION 1. *Be it enacted, &c.,* That the sum of twenty thousand dollars, or so much thereof as may be necessary, is hereby specifically appropriated to the Wills' Eye Hospital of Philadelphia, for the two fiscal years beginning June first, one thousand eight hundred and ninety-three. for the following purposes namely:

Items.

The sum of ten thousand dollars, or so much thereof as may be necessary, for the purpose of erecting a new hospital building, and the sum of ten thousand dollars, or so much thereof as may be necessary, for the purpose of maintenance of said hospital.

How payable.

The said appropriation to be paid on the warrant of the Auditor General on a settlement made by him and the State Treasurer, but no warrant shall be drawn on settlement made until the directors or managers of said institution shall have made, under oath to the Auditor

General, a report containing a specifically itemized Itemized statement. statement of the receipts from all sources and expenses of said institution, together with a specifically itemized statement of the cost of said new building during the previous quarter, with the cash balance on hand, and the same is approved by him and the State Treasurer, nor until the Treasurer shall have sufficient money in the treasury, not otherwise appropriated, to pay the quarterly installments due said institution; and unexpended balances of sums appropriated for specific purposes shall not be used for other purposes, whether specific or general, and shall revert to the State Treasury at the close of the two fiscal years. Unexpended balances shall revert to the State Treasury.

APPROVED—The 2d day of June, A. D. 1893.

ROBT. E. PATTISON.

No. 150.

AN ACT

Making an appropriation to Roselia Foundling Asylum and Maternity Hospital of Pittsburgh.

SECTION 1. *Be it enacted, &c.*, That the sum of ten thousand dollars, or so much thereof as may be necessary, be and the same is hereby specifically appropriated to the Roselia Foundling Asylum and Maternity Hospital of Pittsburgh for the purpose of maintenance of said institution for the two fiscal years beginning June first, one thousand eight hundred and ninety-three. $10.000.00 appropriated for maintenance.

The said appropriation to be paid on the warrant of the Auditor General on a settlement made by him and the State Treasurer, but no warrant shall be drawn on settlement made until the directors or managers of said institution shall have made, under oath to the Auditor General, a report containing a specifically itemized statement of the receipts from all sources and expenses of said institution during the previous quarter, with the cash balance on hand, and the same is approved by him and the State Treasurer, nor until the Treasurer shall have sufficient money in the treasury, not otherwise appropriated, to pay the quarterly installments due said institution; and unexpended balances of sums appropriated for specific purposes, shall not be used for other purposes, whether specific or general, and shall revert to the State Treasury at the close of the two fiscal years. How payable. Itemized statement. Unexpended balances shall revert to the State Treasury.

APPROVED—The 2d day of June, A. D. 1893.

ROBT. E. PATTISON.

No. 151.

AN ACT

Making an appropriation to the Trustees of the University of Pennsylvania.

SECTION 1. *Be it enacted, &c.*, That the sum of one hundred thousand dollars, or so much thereof as may be necessary, be and the same is hereby specifically appropriated to the trustees of the University of Pennsylvania for the two fiscal years beginning June first, one thousand eight hundred and ninety-three, for the following purposes, namely :

The sum of sixty thousand dollars, or so much thereof as may be necessary, for the purpose of assisting in the erection and equipment of a new hospital building.

The sum of twenty thousand dollars, or so much thereof as may be necessary, for maintenance of indigent patients.

And the sum of twenty thousand dollars, or so much thereof as may be necessary, for the purpose of assisting in the erection and equipment of a new maternity building.

Provided, That no part of the money herein appropriated for the erection and equipment of new buildings shall become available, until the treasurer of the University of Pennsylvania shall have certified, under oath to the Auditor General, that the sum of eighty thousand dollars, exclusive of the value of the ground, has been subscribed by private contributors and paid in cash into the treasury of the University of Pennsylvania for the specific purpose of assisting in the erection and equipment of a new hospital building and maternity ward.

The said appropriation to be paid on the warrant of the Auditor General on a settlement made by him and the State Treasurer, but no warrant shall be drawn on settlement made until the trustees or managers of said institution shall have made, under oath, a report to the Auditor General containing a specifically itemized statement of the receipts from all sources and the expenses of said institution and cost of said buildings during the previous quarter, with the cash balance on hand, and the same has been approved by him and the State Treasurer, nor until the Treasurer shall have sufficient money in the treasury, not otherwise appropriated, to pay the quarterly installment due said institution; and unexpended balances of sums appropriated for specific purposes shall not be used for other purposes, whether specific or general, and shall revert to the State Treasury at the close of the two fiscal years.

APPROVED—The 2nd day of June, A. D. 1893.

ROBT. E. PATTISON.

Marginal notes:

$100,000.00 total appropriation.

Items.

When appropriation shall become available.

How payable.

Itemized statement.

Unexpended balances shall revert to the State Treasury.

No. 152.

AN ACT

Making an appropriation to the Philadelphia Polyclinic and College for Graduates in Medicine.

SECTION 1. *Be it enacted, &c.*, That the sum of seventy thousand dollars, or so much thereof as may be necessary, be and the same is hereby specifically appropriated to the Philadelphia Polyclinic and College for Graduates in Medicine for the two fiscal years beginning June first, one thousand eight hundred and ninety-three, for the following purpose, namely : $70,000.00 total appropriation.

For the erection and furnishing of a new hospital building, the sum of fifty thousand dollars, or so much thereof as may be necessary ; for maintenance of said hospital, the sum of twenty thousand dollars, or so much thereof as may be necessary. Items

The said appropriation to be paid on the warrant of the Auditor General on a settlement made by him and the State Treasurer, but no warrant shall be drawn on settlement made until the directors or managers of said institution shall have made, under oath to the Auditor General, a report containing a specifically itemized statement of the receipts from all sources and expenses of said institution, together with a specifically itemized statement of the cost of said new building and furnishing during the previous quarter, with the cash balance on hand, and the same is approved by him and the State Treasurer, nor until the Treasurer shall have sufficient money in the treasury, not otherwise appropriated, to pay the quarterly installments due said institution ; and unexpended balances of sums appropriated for specific purposes shall not be used for other purposes, specific or general, and shall revert to the State Treasury at the close of the two fiscal years. How payable. Itemized statement. Unexpended balances shall revert to the State Treasury.

APPROVED—The 2nd day of June, A. D. 1893.

ROBT. E. PATITSON.

No. 153.

AN ACT

Making an appropriation to the Shenango Valley Hospital in the city of New Castle, Pennsylvania.

SECTION 1. *Be it enacted, &c.*, That the sum of ten thousand dollars, or so much thereof as may be necessary, be and the same is hereby specifically appropriated to the Shenango Valley Hospital, located in the city of New Castle, Pennsylvania, for the following purposes, namely : $10,000.00 total appropriation

The sum of four thousand dollars, or so much thereof as may be necessary, to assist in the erection, furnish- Items and when payable.

ing and equipping of a suitable hospital building, said sum to be paid when the president of the board of trustees shall have certified to the Auditor General, under oath, that said building has been furnished and equipped and ready to receive patients; and the sum of five thousand dollars, or so much thereof as may be necessary, for the maintenance of said hospital for the two fiscal years beginning June first, one thousand eight hundred and ninety-three.

How payable.

The said appropriation to be paid on the warrant of the Auditor General on a settlement made by him and the State Treasurer, but no warrant shall be drawn on settlement made until the directors or managers of said institution shall have made, under oath to the Auditor

Itemized statement.

General, a report containing a specifically itemized statement of the receipts from all sources and expenses of said institution, together with a specifically itemized statement of the cost of said building, furnishing and equipping during the previous quarter, with the cash balance on hand, and the same is approved by him and the State Treasurer, nor until the Treasurer shall have sufficient money in the treasury, not otherwise appropriated, to pay the quartely installments

Unexpended balances shall revert to the State Treasury.

due said instituion; and unexpended balances of sums appropriated for specific purposes shall not be used for other purposes, whether specific or general, and shall revert to the State Treasury at the close of the two fiscal years.

APPROVED—The 2nd day of June, A. D. 1893.

ROBT. E. PATTISON.

No. 154.

AN ACT

Making an appropriation to the Pottstown Hospital.

$18,000.00 total appropriation.

SECTION 1. *Be it enacted, &c.*, That the sum of eighteen thousand dollars, or so much thereof as may be necessary, be and the same is hereby specificaly appropriated to the Pottstown Hospital of Pottstown, Pennsylvania, for the two fiscal years beginning June first, one thousand eight hundred and ninety-three, for the following purposes, namely: for maintenance of said

Items.

hospital, the sum of eight thousand dollars, or so much thereof as may be necessary, and for the completion and equipment of the said hospital, the sum of ten thousand dollars, or so much thereof as may be necessary.

How payable.

The said appropriation to be paid on the warrant of the Auditor General on a settlement made by him and the State Treasurer, but no warrant shall be drawn on settlement until the directors or managers of said institution shall have made, under oath to the Auditor Gen-

eral, a report containing a specifically itemized state- *Itemized statement.*
ment of the receipts from all sources and expenses of
said institution, together with a specifically itemized
statement of the cost of the improvements and equipments during the previous quarter, with the cash balance on hand, and the same is approved by him and
the State Treasurer, nor until the Treasurer shall have
sufficient money in the treasury, not otherwise appropriated, to pay the quarterly installments due said in-
stitution; and unexpended balances of sums appropri- *Unexpended balances shall revert to the State Treasury.*
ated for specific purposes shall not be used for other
purposes, whether specific or general, and shall revert
to the State Treasury at the close of the two fiscal
years.

APPROVED—The 2nd day of June, A. D. 1893.

ROBT. E. PATTISON.

No. 155.

AN ACT

To make an appropriation to the Pennsylvania Working Home
for Blind Men.

SECTION 1. *Be it enacted, &c.*, That the sum of forty- *$45,000.00 total appropriation.*
five thousand dollars, or so much thereof as may be
necessary, be and the same is hereby specifically appropriated to the Pennsylvania Working Home for
Blind Men at Philadelphia, Pennsylvania, for the two
fiscal years beginnng June first, one thousand eight
hundred and ninety-three, for the following purposes,
namely: The sum of twenty-five thousand dollars, or so *Items*
much thereof as may be necessary, for the purpose of
extending workshops, purchase of tools and machinery,
and the sum of twenty thousand dollars, or so much
thereof as may be necessary, for the purpose of instruction, maintenance and employment in handicraft of
blind men, inhabitants of the State.

The said appropriation to be paid on the warrant of *How payable*
the Auditor General on a settlement made by him and
the State Treasurer, but no warrant shall be drawn on
settlement made until the directors or managers of said
institution shall have made, under oath to the Auditor
General, a report containing a specifically itemized
statement of the receipts from all sources and expenses
of said institution, together with a specifically item- *Itemized statement.*
ized statement of the cost of improvements, tools, ma-
chinery et cetera during the previous quarter, with the
cash balance on hand, and the same is approved by
him and the State Treasurer, nor until the Treasurer
shall have sufficient money in the treasury, not otherwise appropriated, to pay the quarterly installments
due said institution; and unexpended balances of sums *Unexpended balances shall revert to the State Treasury.*
appropriated for specific purposes shall not be used for

other purposes, whether specific or general, and shall revert to the State Treasury at the close of the two fiscal years.

APPROVED—The 2nd day of June, A. D. 1893.

ROBT. E. PATTISON.

No. 156.

AN ACT

Making an appropriation to assist in the erection, furnishing and maintenance of a hospital in the city of McKeesport, Allegheny county, Pennsylvania.

$25,000.00 total appropriation.

SECTION 1. *Be it enacted, &c.*, That the sum of twenty-five thousand dollars, or so much thereof as may be necessary, be and the same is hereby specificaly appropriated to the McKeesport hospital in the city of Mc Keesport for the two fiscal years beginning June first, one thousand eight hundred and ninety-three, for the following purposes, namely: The sum of twenty thousand dollars, or so much thereof as may be necessary, to aid in the completion of the building now being erected in said city, and the sum of five thousand dollars, or so much thereof as may be necessary, for the purpose of maintenance of said hospital.

Items.

How payable.

The said appropriation to be paid on the warrant of the Auditor General on a settlement made by him and the State Treasurer, but no warrant shall be drawn on settlement made until the directors or managers of said institution shall have made, under oath to the Auditor General, a report containing a specifically itemized statement of the receipts from all sources and expenses of said institution, together with a specifically itemized statement of the cost of said building during the previous quarter, with the cash balance on hand, and the same is approved by him and the State Treasurer, nor until the Treasurer shall have sufficient money in the treasury, not otherwise appropriated, to pay the quarterly installments due said institution; and unexpended balances of sums appropriated for specific purposes shall not be used for other purposes, whether specific or general, and shall revert to the State Treasury at the close of the two fiscal years.

Itemized statement.

Unexpended balances shall revert to the State Treasury.

APPROVED—The 2nd day of June, A. D. 1893.

ROBT. E. PATTISON.

No. 157.

AN ACT

Making an appropriation to the Sharon and Sharpsville Hospital.

$5,000.00 appropriated for erection of building.

SECTION 1. *Be it enacted, &c.*, That the sum of five thousand dollars, or so much thereof as may be necessary, is hereby specifically appropriated to the Sharon and Sharpsville hospital, in or near the borough of Sharon, Pennsylvania, to aid in erecting and furnishing of a suitable hospital building for the medical and surgical care of sick and injured persons, indigent or otherwise, and without discrimination in respect to religion, nationality or color.

Said appropriation to be paid in equal quarterly installments during the two fiscal years beginning June first, one thousand eight hundred and ninety-three. The further sum of two thousand dollars, or so much thereof as may be necessary, for the furnishing of said hospital, to be paid when said hospital is comple ed and furnished, and the further sum of two thousand dollars, or so much thereof as may be necessary, for maintenance of said hospital, to be paid in equal quarterly payments during the fiscal year beginning June first, one thousand eight hundred and ninety-four: *Provided*, That no part of the appropriation herein made shall become available until the treasurer of said institution shall have certified, under oath to the Auditor General, that the sum of seven thousand dollars, exclusive of the value of the grounds, has been subscribed and paid in cash into the treasury of said institution, by private subscriptions, for the purpose of assisting the erection of said hospital.

The said appropriation to be paid on the warrant of the Auditor General on a settlement made by him and the State Treasurer, but no warrant shall be drawn on settlement made until the directors or managers of said institution shall have made, under oath to the Auditor General, a report containing a specifically itemized statement of the income and expenses of said institution, together with a specifically itemized statement of the cost of erecting and furnishing said building during the previous quarter, with the cash balance on hand, and the same is approved by him and the State Treasurer, nor until the Treasurer shall have sufficient money in the treasury, not otherwise appropriated, to pay the quarterly installments due said institution; and unexpended balances of sums appropriated for specific purposes shall not be used for other purposes, whether specific or general, and shall revert to the State Treasury at the close of the two fiscal years.

APPROVED—The 2nd day of June, A. D. 1893.

ROBT. E. PATTISON.

Marginal notes:

Payment of same.

$2,000.00 for furnishing.

$2,000.00 for maintenance.

When appropriations shall become available.

How payable.

Itemized statement.

Unexpended balances shall revert to the State Treasury.

No. 158.

AN ACT

Making an appropriation to the Childrens' Aid Society of Western Pennsylvania.

$10,000.00 appropriated

SECTION 1. *Be it enacted, &c.*, That the sum of ten thousand dollars, or so much thereof as may be necessary, be and the same is hereby specifically appropriated to the Children's Aid Society of Western Pennsylvania for the purpose of maintenance and prosecution of its work for the two fiscal years beginning June first, one thousand eight hundred and ninety-three.

How payable.

The said appropriation to be paid on the warrant of the Auditor General on a settlement made by him and the State Treasurer, but no warrant shall be drawn on settlement made until the directors or managers of said society shall have made, under oath to the Auditor General, a report containing a specifically itemized statement of the receipts from all sources and expenses of said society during the previous quarter, with the cash balance on hand, and the same is approved by him and the State Treasurer, nor until the Treasurer shall have sufficient money in the treasury, not otherwise appropriated, to pay the quarterly instalments due said society; and unexpended balances of sums appropriated for specific purposes shall not be used for other purposes, whether specific or general, and shall revert to the State Treasury at the close of the two fiscal years.

Itemized statement.

Unexpended balances shall revert to the State Treasury.

APPROVED—The 2d day of June, A. D. 1893.

ROBT. E. PATTISON.

No. 159.

AN ACT

Making an appropriation to the Homeopathic Medical and Surgical Hospital and Dispensary of Pittsburgh.

$59,520.65 total appropriation.

SECTION 1. *Be it enacted, &c.*, That the sum of fifty-nine thousand five hundred and twenty dollars and sixty-five cents, or so much thereof as may be necessary, be and the same is hereby specifically appropriated to the Homeopathic Medical and Surgical Hospital and Dispensary of Pittsburgh for the following purposes, namely:

$50,000.00 for maintenance.

The sum of fifty thousand dollars, or so much thereof as may be necessary, for the purpose of maintenance of said hospital for the two fiscal years beginning June first, one thousand eight hundred and ninety-three, and the sum of nine thousand five hundred and twenty dollars and sixty-five cents, or so much thereof as may be necessary, for the purpose of paying a defi-

$9,520.65 for paying deficit.

cit in the maintenance account of said institution for the two fiscal years ending May thirty-first, one thousand eight hundred and ninety-three: *Provided*, That in consideration of this appropriation there shall be ten free beds maintained, which shall be filled upon certificate of the mayor or poor board of the proper city or county on presentation of such certificate to the officers of the hospital, in the order in which applications are made, after examination as to the propriety of such certificates being given.

The said appropriation to be paid on the warrant of the Auditor General on a settlement made by him and the State Treasurer, but no warrant shall be drawn on settlement made until the directors or managers of said institution shall have made, under oath to the Auditor General, a report containing a specifically itemized statement of the receipts from all sources and expenses of said institution during the previous quarter, with the cash balance on hand, and the same is approved by him and the State Treasurer, nor until the Treasurer shall have sufficient money in the treasury, not otherwise appropriated, to pay the quarterly instalments due said institution; and unexpended balances of sums appropriated for specific purposes shall not be used for other purposes, whether specific or general, and shall revert to the State Treasury at the close of the two fiscal years.

APPROVED—The 2d day of June, A. D. 1893.

ROBT. E. PATTISON.

———

No. 160.

AN ACT

Making an appropriation to the Memorial Hospital Association of Monongahela City, Pennsylvania.

SECTION 1. *Be it enacted, &c.*, That the sum of ten thousand dollars be and the same is hereby specifically appropriated to the Memorial Hospital Association of Monongahela City to aid in erecting a suitable hospital building for the medical and surgical care of injured persons, indigent or otherwise, and without discrimination in respect to religion, nationality or color.

Said appropriation to be paid in equal quarterly instalments of twelve hundred and fifty dollars during the two fiscal years beginning June first, one thousand eight hundred and ninety-three; and the further sum of two thousand dollars, or so much thereof as may be necessary, is hereby specifically appropriated for the furnishing of said hospital to be paid in equal quarterly payments during the fiscal year beginning June first, one thousand eight hundred and ninety-four: *Provided*, That no part of the appropriations herein

14—LAWS.

made shall become available until the treasurer of said
association shall have certified, under oath to the Auditor General, that the sum of ten thousand dollars, exclusive of the value of the ground, has been subscribed
and paid in cash into the treasury of said association
by private subscriptions for the purpose of assisting
in the erection of said hospital.

The said appropriation to be paid on the warrant of
the Auditor General on a settlement made by him and
the State Treasurer, but no warrant shall be drawn on
settlement made until the directors or managers of
said institution shall have made, under oath to the Auditor General, a report containing a specifically itemized statement of the income and expenses of erecting and furnishing said building during the previous
quarter, with the cash balance on hand, and the same
is approved by him and the State Treasurer, nor until
the Treasurer shall have sufficient money in the treasury, not otherwise appropriated, to pay the quarterly
instalments due said institution; and unexpended
balances of sums appropriated for specific purposes
shall not be used for other purposes, whether specific
or general, and shall revert to the State Treasury at
the close of the two fiscal years.

APPROVED—The 2d day of June, A. D. 1893.

ROBT. E. PATTISON.

No. 161.

AN ACT

Making an appropriation to the Carbondale Hospital Association
of the city of Carbondale, County of Lackawanna, Pennsylvania.

SECTION 1. *Be it enacted, &c.*, That the sum of twelve
thousand dollars, or so much thereof as may be necessary, be and the same is hereby specifically appropriated to the Carbondale Hospital Association of the
city of Carbondale, Pennsylvania, for the two fiscal
years beginning June first, one thousand eight hundred and ninety-three, for the following purposes,
namely: The sum of six thousand dollars, or so much
thereof as may be necessary, for the purpose of maintenance, and the sum of six thousand dollars, or so
much thereof as may be necessary, for the purpose of
assisting in completion and equipping of said hospital.
The said appropriation to be paid on the warrant of
the Auditor General on a settlement made by him and
the State Treasurer, but no warrant shall be drawn on
settlement made until the directors or managers of
said institution shall have made, under oath to the Auditor General, a report containing a specifically itemized statement of the income and expenses of said institution, together with an itemized statement of the

cost and expense of completing and equipping said institution during the previous quarter, with the cash
balance on hand, and the same is approved by him
and the State Treasurer, nor until the Treasurer shall
have sufficient money in the treasury, not otherwise
appropriated, to pay the quarterly instalments due
said institution; and unexpended balances of sums ap- *Unexpended bal-*
propriated for specific purposes shall not be used for *ances shall revert to the State Treas-*
other purposes, whether specific or general, and shall *ury.*
revert to the State Treasurer at the close of the two fiscal years.

APPROVED—The 2d day of June, A. D. 1893.

No. 162.

AN ACT

Making an appropriation to the Pittsburgh News Boys' Home.

SECTION 1. *Be it enacted, &c.*, That the sum of ten *$10,000.00 appropri-*
thousand dollars, or so much thereof as may be nec- *ated.*
essary, be and the same is hereby specifically appropriated to the Pittsburgh News Boys' Home for the
purpose of maintenance for the two fiscal years beginning June first, one thousand eight hundred and ninety-
three.

The said appropriation to be paid on the warrant of *How payable.*
the Auditor General on a settlement made by him and
the State Treasurer, but no warrant shall be drawn on
settlement made until the directors or managers of said
institution shall have made, under oath to the Auditor
General, a report containing a specifically itemized *Itemized state-*
statement of the receipts from all sources and expenses *ment.*
of said institution during the previous quarter, with
the cash balance on hand, and the same is approved by
him and the State Treasurer, nor until the Treasurer
shall have sufficient money in the treasury, not otherwise appropriated, to pay the quarterly instalments
due said institution; and unexpended balances of sums *Unexpended bal-*
appropriated for specific purposes shall not be used for *ances shall revert to the State Treas-*
other purposes, whether specific or general, and shall *ury.*
revert to the State Treasury at the close of the two
fiscal years.

APPROVED—The 2d day of June, A. D. 1893.

ROBT. E. PATTISON.

No. 163.

AN ACT

Making an appropriation to the Allegheny County Association for
the Prevention of Cruelty to Children and Aged Persons.

SECTION 1. *Be it enacted, &c.*, That the sum of one *$1,200.00 appropri-*
thousand two hundred dollars, or so much thereof as *ated.*

may be necessary, be and the same is hereby specifically appropriated to the Allegheny County Association for the Prevention of Cruelty to Children and Aged
Persons for the purpose of support and maintenance
for the two fiscal years beginning June first, one thousand eight hundred and ninety-three.

How payable.

The said appropriation to be paid on the warrant of
the Auditor General on a settlement made by him and
the State Treasurer, but no warrant shall be drawn on
settlement made until the directors or managers of said
association shall have made, under oath to the Auditor

Itemized statement

General, a report containing a specifically itemized
statement of the receipts from all sources and expenses
of said association during the previous quarter, with
the cash balance on hand, and the same is approved
by him and the State Treasurer, nor until the Treasurer shall have sufficient money in the treasury,
not otherwise appropriated, to pay the quarterly in-

Unexpended bal-
ances shall revert
to the State Treas-
ury.

stalments due said association; and unexpended balances of sums appropriated for specific purposes shall
not be used for other purposes, whether specific or
general, and shall revert to the State Treasury at the
close of the two fiscal years.

APPROVED—The 2d day of June, A. D. 1893.

ROBT. E. PATTISON.

No. 164.

AN ACT

Making an appropriation to the Old Ladies' Home of Philadel-
delphia, in Pennsylvania.

$4,000.00 appropri-
ated.

SECTION 1. *Be it enacted, &c.*, That the sum of four
thousand dollars, or so much thereof as may be necessary, be and the same is hereby specifically appropriated to the Old Ladies' Home of Philadelphia, in
Pennsylvania, for the purpose of maintenance for the
two fiscal years beginning June first, one thousand
eight hundred and ninety-three.

How payable.

The said appropriation to be paid on the warrant of
the Auditor General on a settlement made by him and
the State Treasurer, but no warrant shall be drawn on
settlement made until the directors or managers of
said institution shall have made, under oath to the Aud-

Itemized statement

itor General, a report containing a specifically itemized statement of the receipts from all sources and expenses of said instituion during the previous quarter,
with the cash balance on hand, and the same is approved by him and the State Treasurer, nor until
the Treasurer shall have sufficient money in the treasury, not otherwise appropriated, to pay the quarterly

Unexpended bal-
ances shall revert to
the State Treasury.

instalments due said institution; and unexpended balances of sums appropriated for specific purposes shall

not be used for other purposes, whether specific or general, and shall revert to the State Treasury at the close of the two fiscal years.

APPROVED—The 2d day of June, A. D. 1893.

ROBT. E. PATTISON.

No. 165.

AN ACT

Making an appropriation for the repair of the great stone bridge over the Youghiogheny river at Somerfield, Pennsylvania.

SECTION 1. *Be it enacted, &c.,* That the sum of one thousand five hundred dollars, or so much thereof as may be needed, be and the same is hereby specifically appropriated for the purpose of repairing said bridge over the Youghiogheny river at Somerfield, Pennsylvania, the .point at which said National (now State) road crosses said river. $1,500.00 appropriated.

SECTION 2. The superintendents of said road, John A. Brownfield, of Fayette county, and John McDowell, of Washington county, are hereby empowered and directed to cause said repairs to be made as soon as practicable, by such persons as they may deem proper to employ. Superintendents shall cause repairs to be made.

The said appropriation to be paid on the warrant of the Auditor General on a settlement made by him and the State Treasurer, but no warrant shall be drawn on settlement made until the superintendent of said National turnpike shall have made, under oath to the Auditor General, a report containing a specifically itemized statement of the expense of said repairs and the same is approved by him and the State Treasurer, nor until the Treasurer shall have sufficient money in the treasury, not otherwise appropriated, to pay the amount due; and unexpended balances of sums appropriated for specific purposes shall not be used for other purposes, whether specific or general, and revert to the State Treasury at the close of the two fiscal years. How payable. Itemized statement. Unexpended balances shall revert to the State Treasury.

APPROVED—The 2d day of June, A. D. 1893.

ROBT. E. PATTISON.

No. 166.

AN ACT

Making an appropriation for the purpose of assisting in the erection, furnishing and maintenance of a hospital in the borough of West Chester, Chester county, Pennsylvania.

SECTION 1. *Be it enacted, &c.,* That the sum of five thousand dollars, or so much thereof as may be necessary, be and the same is hereby specifically appro- $5,000.00 appropriated for completion.

priated to the West Chester hospital towards the completion, and the sum of two thousand dollars, or so
much thereof as may be necessary, towards the furnishing of a suitable building in the borough of West Chester, Chester county, Pennsylvania, for the purpose of a
general hospital for the county of Chester and regions
adjacent, to be opened to all classes without distinction of color or creed, wherein all injured or sick persons can receive suitable care and surgical or medical
treatment, and where no case of injury or sickness shall
be refused on account of inability to pay expenses so
long as there may be accommodation in said hospital:
Provided, That no part of this appropriation shall be
paid by the State Treasurer until the treasurer of the
board of trustees of said hospital shall have certified,
under oath to the Auditor General, that the sum of five
thousand dollars, exclusive of the value of the ground,
has been subscribed and paid in cash into the treasury
towards the erection and furnishing of the said hospital, and that the said hospital has become the owner in
fee simple of real estate to be used for hospital purposes, costing not less than four thousand dollars.

SECTION 2. That the further sum of three thousand
dollars, or so much thereof as may be necessary, be and
the same is hereby specifically appropriated to the said
hospital for maintenance for the two fiscal years
commencing on the first day of June, one thousand
eight hundred and ninety-three: *Provided*, That no
part of the moneys hereby appropriated for maintenance shall be paid by the State Treasurer until the
president of the board of trustees of said hospital shall
have certified, under oath to the Auditor General, that
the said hospital building is fully constructed, completed and furnished.

The said appropriation to be paid on the warrant of
the Auditor General on a settlement made by him and
the State Treasurer, but no warrant shall be drawn on
settlement made until the directors or managers of
said institution shall have made, under oath to the
Auditor General, a report containing a specifically
itemized statement of the income and expenses of said
institution, together with a specifically itemized statement of the cost of said building and the furnishing of
the same during the previous quarter, the cash balance
on hand, and the same is approved by him and the
State Treasurer, nor until the Treasurer shall have sufficient money in the treasury, not otherwise appropriated, to pay the quarterly instalments due said institution; and unexpended balances of sums appropriated for specific purposes shall not be used for other
purposes, whether specific or general, and shall revert
to the State Treasury at the close of the two fiscal
years.

APPROVED—The 2d day of June, A. D. 1893.

ROBT. E. PATTISON.

No. 167.

AN ACT

Making an appropriation to the St Luke's Hospital of South Bethlehem, Pennsylvania.

SECTION 1. *Be it enacted, &c.*, That the sum of eight thousand dollars, or so much thereof as may be necessary, be and the same is hereby specifically appropriated to the St. Luke's Hospital of South Bethlehem, Pennsylvania, for the purpose of maintenance for the two fiscal years beginning June first, one thousand eight hundred and ninety-three. $8,000.00 appropriated.

The said appropriation to be paid on the warrant of the Auditor General on a settlement made by him and the State Treasurer, but no warrant shall be drawn on settlement made until the directors or managers of said institution shall have made, under oath to the Auditor General, a report containing a specifically itemized account of the receipts from all sources and expenses of said institution during the previous quarter, with the cash balance on hand, and the same is approved by him and the State Treasurer, nor until the Treasurer shall have sufficient money in the treasury, not otherwise appropriated, to pay the quarterly instalments due said institution; and unexpended balances of sums appropriated for specific purposes shall not be used for other purposes, whether specific or general, and shall revert to the State Treasury at the close of the two fiscal years. How payable. Itemized statement. Unexpended balances shall revert to the State Treasury.

APPROVED—The 2d day of June, A. D. 1893.

ROBT. E. PATTISON.

No. 168.

AN ACT

Making an appropriation to the Allegheny General Hospital of Allegheny City.

SECTION 1. *Be it enacted, &c.*, That the sum of thirty thousand dollars, or so much thereof as may be necessary, be and the same is hereby specifically appropriated for the maintenance of the Allegheny General Hospital of Allegheny City for the two fiscal years beginning June first, one thousand eight hundred and ninety-three. $30,000.00 appropriated.

The said appropriation to be paid on the warrant of the Auditor General on a settlement made by him and the State Treasurer, but no warrant shall be drawn on settlement made until the directors or managers of said institution shall have made, under oath to the Auditor General, a report containing a specifically itemized statement of the receipts from all sources and expenses of said institution during the previous quarter, with How payable. Itemized statement.

the cash balance on hand, and the same is approved by him and the State Treasurer, nor until the Treasurer shall have sufficient money in the treasury, not otherwise appropriated, to pay the quarterly instalments due said institution; and unexpended balances of sums appropriated for specific purposes shall not be used for other purposes, whether specific or general, and shall revert to the State Treasury at the close of the two fiscal years.

Unexpended balances shall revert to the State Treasury.

APPROVED—The 2d day of June, A. D. 1893.

ROBT. E. PATTISON.

No. 169.

AN ACT

Making an appropriation to the Bethesda Home of the city of Pittsburgh.

$3,000.00 appropriated.

SECTION 1. *Be it enacted, &c.*, That the sum of three thousand dollars, or so much thereof as may be necessary, be and the same is hereby specifically appropriated to the Bethesda Home of the city of Pittsburgh, (a corporation formed for the purpose of rescuing fallen women and protecting tempted and defenseless girls), for the purpose of maintenance for the two fiscal years beginning June first, one thousand eight hundred and ninety-three.

How payable.

The said appropriation to be paid on the warrant of the Auditor General on a settlement made by him and the State Treasurer, but no warrant shall be drawn on settlement made until the directors or managers of said institution shall have made, under oath to the Auditor General, a report containing a specifically itemized statement of the receipts from all sources and expenses of said institution during the previous quarter, with the cash balance on hand, and the same is approved by him and the State Treasurer, nor until the Treasurer shall have sufficient money in the treasury, not otherwise appropriated, to pay the quarterly instalments due said institution; and unexpended balances of sums appropriated for specific purposes shall not be used for other purposes, whether specific or general, and shall revert to the State Treasury at the close of the two fiscal years.

Itemized statement.

Unexpended balances shall revert to the State Treasury.

APPROVED—The 2d day of June, A. D. 1893.

ROBT. E. PATTISON.

No. 170.

AN ACT

Making an appropriation to the Philadelphia Lying-in Charity.

SECTION 1. *Be it enacted, &c.,* That the sum of five thousand dollars, or so much thereof as may be necessary, be and the same is hereby specifically appropriated to the Philadelphia Lying-in Charity, for the purpose of maintenance, for the two fiscal years beginning June first, one thousand eight hundred and ninety-three. $5,000.00 appropriated.

The said appropriation to be paid on the warrant of the Auditor General on a settlement made by him and the State Treasurer, but no warrant shall be drawn on settlement made until the directors or managers of said institution shall have made, under oath to the Auditor General, a report containing a specifically itemized statement of the receipts from all sources and expenses of said institution during the previous quarter, with the cash balance on hand, and the same is approved by him and the State Treasurer, nor until the Treasurer shall have sufficient money in the treasury, not otherwise appropriated, to pay the quarterly instalments due said institution; and unexpended balances of sums appropriated for specific purposes shall not be used for other purposes, whether specific or general, and shall revert to the State Treasury at the close of the two fiscal years. How payable.
Itemized statement.
Unexpended balances shall revert to the State Treasury.

APPROVED—The 2d day of June, A. D. 1893.

ROBT. E. PATTISON.

No. 171.

AN ACT

Making an appropriation to the Rosine Home of Philadelphia.

SECTION 1. *Be it enacted, &c.,* That the sum of two thousand dollars, or so much thereof as may be necessary, be and the same is hereby specifically appropriated toward the maintenance of the Rosine Home of Philadelphia for the two fiscal years commencing June first, one thousand eight hundred and ninety-three. $2,000.00 appropriated.

The said appropriation to be paid on the warrant of the Auditor General on a settlement made by him and the State Treasurer, but no warrant shall be drawn on settlement made until the directors or managers of said institution shall have made, under oath to the Auditor General, a report containing a specifically itemized statement of the receipts from all sources and expenses of said institution during the previous quarter, with the cash balance on hand, and the same is approved by him and the State Treasurer, nor until the Treasurer How payable.
Itemized statement.

shall have sufficient money in the treasury, not otherwise appropriated, to pay the quarterly instalments due said institution; and unexpended balances of sums appropriated for specific purposes shall not be used for other purposes, whether specific or general, and shall revert to the State Treasury at the close of the two fiscal years.

APPROVED—The 2d day of June, A. D. 1893.

ROBT. E. PATTISON.

' No. 172.

AN ACT

Making an appropriation to the Western Temporary Home.

SECTION 1. *Be it enacted, &c.*, That the sum of three thousand four hundred dollars, or so much thereof as may be necessary, be and the same is hereby specifically appropriated to the board of managers of the Western Temporary Home for the two fiscal years commencing June first, one thousand eight hundred and ninety-three, for the following purposes, namely : The sum of two thousand four hundred dollars, or so much thereof as may be necessary, for the purpose of maintenance, and the sum of one thousand dollars for heating apparatus, to be paid in equal quarterly instalments, except the one thousand dollars for heating plant, which shall be paid for when completed, out of any money in the treasury, not otherwise appropriated.

The said appropriation to be paid on the warrant of the Auditor General on a settlement made by him and the State Treasurer, but no warrant shall be drawn on settlement made until the directors or managers of said instituton shall have made, under oath to the Auditor General, a report containing a specifically itemized statement of the receipts from all sources and expenses of said institution, together with a specifically itemized statement of the cost of said heating apparatus, during the previous quarter, with the cash balance on hand, and the same is approved by him and the State Treasurer, nor until the Treasurer shall have sufficient money in the treasury, not otherwise appropriated, to pay the quarterly instalments due said institution; and unexpended balances of sums appropriated for specific purposes shall not be used for other purposes, whether specific or general, and shall revert to the State Treasury at the close of the two fiscal years.

APPROVED—The 2d day of June, A. D. 1893.

ROBT. E. PATTISON.

Margin notes:
Unexpended balances shall revert to the State Treasury.

$1,400.00 total appropriation.

$2,400.00 for maintenance.

$1,000.00 for heating apparatus.

How payable.

Itemized statement.

Unexpended balances shall revert to the State Treasury.

No. 173.

AN ACT

Making an appropriation to the Aged and Infirm Colored Woman's Home at Pittsburgh.

SECTION 1. *Be it enacted, &c.*, That the sum of three thousand dollars, or so much thereof as may be necessary, is hereby specifically appropriated to the Home for Aged and Infirm Colored Women for maintenance and care of the inmates for the two fiscal years commencing June first, one thousand eight hundred and ninety-three. $3,000.00 appropriated.

The said appropriation to be paid on the warrant of the Auditor General on a settlement made by him and the State Treasurer, but no warrant shall be drawn on settlement made until the directors or managers of said institution shall have made, under oath to the Auditor General, a report containing a specifically itemized statement of the receipts from all sources and expenses of said institution during the previous quarter, with the cash balance on hand, and the same is approved by him and the State Treasurer, nor until the Treasurer shall have sufficient money in the treasury, not otherwise appropriated, to pay the quarterly instalments due said institution; and unexpended balances of sums appropriated for specific purposes shall not be used for other purposes, whether specific or general, and shall revert to the State Treasury at the close of the two fiscal years. How payable.
Itemized statement.
Unexpended balances shall revert to the State Treasury.

APPROVED—The 2d day of June, A. D. 1893.
ROBT. E. PATTISON.

No. 174.

AN ACT

Making an appropriation to the Maternity Hospital in the city of Philadelphia for maintenance.

SECTION 1. *Be it enacted, &c.*, That the sum of five thousand dollars, or so much thereof as may be necessary, be and the same is hereby specifically appropriated to the Maternity Hospital in the city of Philadelphia for the purpose of maintenance for the two fiscal years commencing June first, Anno Domini one thousand eight hundred and ninety-three. $5,000.00 appropriated.

The said appropriation to be paid on the warrant of the Auditor General on a settlement made by him and the State Treasurer, but no warrant shall be drawn on settlement made until the directors or managers of said institution shall have made, under oath to the Auditor General, a report containing a specifically itemized statement of the receipts from all sources and expenses How payable.
Itemized statement.

of said institution during the previous quarter, with the cash balance on hand, and the same is approved by him and the State Treasurer, nor until the Treasurer shall have sufficient money in the treasury, not otherwise appropriated, to pay the quarterly instalments due said institution; and unexpended balances of sums appropriated for specific purposes shall not be used for other purposes, whether specific or general, and shall revert to the State Treasury at the close of the two fiscal years.

APPROVED—The 2d day of June, A. D. 1893.

ROBT. E. PATTISON.

Unexpended balances shall revert to the State Treasury.

No. 175.

AN ACT

Making an appropriation to the Mercy Hospital of the city of Pittsburgh.

$20,000.00 appropriated.

SECTION 1. *Be it enacted, &c.*, That the sum of twenty thousand dollars, or so much thereof as may be necessary, be and the same is hereby specifically appropriated to the Mercy Hospital of the city of Pittsburgh for the maintenance of said hospital for the two fiscal years beginning June first, Anno Domini one thousand eight hundred and ninety-three.

How payable.

The said appropriation to be paid on the warrant of the Auditor General on a settlement made by him and the State Treasurer, but no warrant shall be drawn on settlement made until the directors or managers of said institution shall have made, under oath to the Auditor General, a report containing a specifically itemized statement of the receipts from all sources and expenses of said institution during the previous quarter, with the cash balance on hand, and the same is approved by him and the State Treasurer, nor until the Treasurer shall have sufficient money in the treasury, not otherwise appropriated, to pay the quarterly instalments due said institution; and unexpended balances of sums appropriated for specific purposes shall not be used for other purposes, whether specific or general, and shall revert to the State Treasury at the close of the two fiscal years.

Itemized statement.

Unexpended balances shall revert to the State Treasury.

APPROVED—The 2d day of June, A. D. 1893.

ROBT. E. PATTISON.

No. 176.

AN ACT

Making an appropriation to the Pennsylvania Society to Protect Children from Cruelty.

$7,000.00 appropriated.

SECTION 1. *Be it enacted, &c.*, That the sum of seven thousand five hundred dollars, or so much thereof as may be necessary, be and the same is hereby specifically appropriated to the Pennsylvania Society to Protect Children from Cruelty, for the purpose of assisting in the prosecution of its work, for the two fiscal years beginning June first, one thousand eight hundred and ninety-three.

The said appropriation to be paid on the warrant of the Auditor General on settlement made by him and the State Treasurer, but no warrant shall be drawn on settlement made until the directors or managers of said society shall have made, under oath to the Auditor General, a report containing a specifically itemized statement of the receipts from all sources and expenses of said society during the previous quarter, with the cash balance on hand, and the same is approved by him and the State Treasurer, nor until the Treasurer shall have sufficient money in the treasury, not otherwise appropriated, to pay the quarterly instalments due said society; and unexpended balances of sums appropriated for specific purposes shall not be used for other purposes, whether specific or general, and shall revert to the State Treasury at the close of the two fiscal years.

APPROVED—The 2d day of June, A. D. 1893.

ROBT. E. PATTISON.

How payable.

Itemized statement,

Unexpended balances shall revert to the State Treasury.

No. 177

AN ACT

Making an appropriation to the Meadville City Hospital in Meadville, Pennsylvania.

SECTION 1. *Be it enacted, &c.,* That the sum of five thousand dollars, or so much thereof as may be necessary, be and the same is hereby specifically appropriated to the Meadville City Hospital at Meadville, Pennsylvania, for the two fiscal years beginning June first, one thousand eight hundred and ninety-three, for the purpose of maintenance.

The said appropriation to be paid on the warrant of the Auditor General on a settlement made by him and the State Treasurer, but no warrant shall be drawn on settlement made until the directors or managers of said institution shall have made, under oath to the Auditor General, a report containing a specifically itemized statement of the receipts from all sources and expenses of said institution during the previous quarter, with the cash balance on hand, and the same is approved by him and the State Treasurer, nor until the Treasurer shall have sufficient money in the treasury, not otherwise appropriated, to pay the quarterly instalments due said institution: and unexpended balances of sums appropriated for specific purposes shall not be

$5,000.00 appropriated.

How payable.

Itemized statement.

used for other purposes, whether specific or general, and shall revert to the State Treasury at the close of the two fiscal years.

APPROVED—The 2d day of June, A. D. 1893.

ROBT. E. PATTISON.

No. 178.

AN ACT

Making an appropriation to the South Side Hospital of Pittsburgh.

SECTION 1. *Be it enacted, &c.*, That the sum of nine thousand dollars, or so much thereof as may be necessary, be and the same is hereby specifically appropriated to the South Side Hospital of Pittsburgh, for the purpose of maintenance, to be paid as follows, namely : The sum of three thousand dollars, or so much thereof as may be necessary, during the fiscal year beginning June first, one thousand eight hundred and ninety-three, and the sum of six thousand dollars, or so much thereof as may be necessary, during the fiscal year beginning June first, one thousand eight hundred and ninety-four.

The said appropriation to be paid on the warrant of the Auditor General on a settlement made by him and the State Treasurer, but no warrant shall be drawn on settlement made until the directors or managers of said institution shall have made, under oath to the Auditor General, a report containing a specifically itemized statement of the receipts from all sources and expenses of said institution, together with a specifically itemized statement of the cost of said building during the previous quarter, with the cash balance on hand, and the same is approved by him and the State Treasurer, nor until the Treasurer shall have sufficient money in the treasury, not otherwise appropriated, to pay the quarterly instalments due said institution ; and unexpended balances of sums appropriated for specific purposes shall not be used for other purposes, whether specific or general, and shall revert to the State Treasury at the close of each fiscal year.

APPROVED—The 2d day of June, A. D. 1893.

ROBT. E. PATTISON.

No. 179.

AN ACT

Making an appropriation to the Spencer Hospital at Meadville, Pennsylvania.

SECTION 1. *Be it enacted, &c.*, That the sum of five thousand dollars, or so much thereof as may be necessary, be and the same is hereby specifically appropriated to the Spencer Hospital at Meadville, Pennsylvania, for the two fiscal years beginning June first, one thousand eight hundred and ninety-three, for the purpose of maintenance.

The said appropriation to be paid on the warrant of the Auditor General on a settlement made by him and the State Treasurer, but no warrant shall be drawn on settlement made until the directors or managers of said institution shall have made, under oath to the Auditor General, a report containing a specifically itemized statement of the receipts from all sources and expenses of said institution during the previous quarter, with the cash balance on hand, and the same is approved by him and the State Treasurer, nor until the Treasurer shall have sufficient money in the treasury, not otherwise appropriated, to pay the quarterly instalments due said institution; and unexpended balances of sums appropriated for specific purposes shall not be used for other purposes, whether specific or general, and shall revert to the State Treasury at the close of the two fiscal years.

APPROVED—The 2d day of June, A. D. 1893.

ROBT. E. PATTISON.

How payable.

Itemized statement.

Unexpended balances shall revert to the State Treasury.

No. 180.

AN ACT

Making an appropriation to the Home of the Ladies of the Grand Army of the Republic at Hawkins' Station, Allegheny county, Pennsylvania.

SECTION 1. *Be it enacted, &c.*, That the sum of three thousand dollars, or so much thereof as may be necessary, be and the same is hereby specifically appropriated to the Home of the Ladies of the Grand Army of the Republic at Hawkins' Station, Allegheny county, Pennsylvania, for the purpose of maintenance for the two fiscal years commencing June first, one thousand eight hundred and ninety-three.

The said appropriation to be paid on the warrant of the Auditor General on a settlement made by him and the State Treasurer, but no warrant shall be drawn on settlement made until the directors or managers of said institution shall have made, under oath to the Auditor General, a report containing a specifically itemized statement of the receipts from all sources and expenses of said institution during the previous quarter, with the cash balance on hand, and the same is approved by him and the State Treasurer, nor until the Treasurer shall have sufficient money in the treasury, not otherwise appropriated, to pay the quarterly instalments due said institution; and unexpended balances

$3,000.00 appropriated.

How payable.

Itemized statement.

of sums appropriated for specific purposes shall not
be used for other purposes, whether specific or general,
and shall revert to the State Treasury at the close of
the two fiscal years.

APPROVED—The 2d day of June, A. D. 1893.

ROBT. E. PATTISON.

No. 181.

AN ACT

Making an appropriation to the State Normal School of the Fifth
District of Pennsylvania, located at Mansfield, Tioga county,
Pennsylvania.

SECTION 1. *Be it enacted, &c.*, That the sum of forty
thousand dollars, or so much thereof as may be necessary, be and the same is hereby specifically appro-
prated to the State Normal School of the Fifth District of Pennsylvania, located at Mansfield, Tioga
county, Pennsylvania, for the special purpose of erecting, enlarging and remodeling school bulidings and
furnishing the same, and improving the sanitary
condition of buildings, for the two fiscal years beginning June first, one thousand eight hundred and
ninety-three : *Provided*, That before the said money
shall be paid the trustees of said school shall cause a
mortgage to be placed upon the said grounds and
buildings for the amount of money hereby appropriated, to be executed to the Commonwealth, creating a
lien upon said property : *Provided further*, That the
school property shall be insured for the benefit of the
Commonwealth for a sum not less than two-thirds of
the value of the same.

The said appropriation to be paid on the warrant of
the Auditor General on a settlement made by him and
the State Treasurer, but no warrant shall be drawn on
settlement made until the trustees of said institution
shall have made, under oath to the Auditor General, a
report containing a specifically itemized statement of
the receipts from all sources and expenses of said institution, together with a specifically itemized statement of the cost of said buildings and improvements
during the previous quarter, with the cash balance on
hand, and the same is approved by him and the State
Treasurer, nor until the Treasurer shall have sufficient
money in the treasury, not otherwise appropriated, to
pay the quarterly instalments due said institution ; and
unexpended balances of sums apppropriated for specific purposes shall not be used for other purposes,
whether specific or general, and shall revert to the State
Treasury at the close of the two fiscal years.

APPROVED—The 2d day of June, A. D. 1893.

ROBT. E. PATTISON.

No. 182.

AN ACT

Making an appropriation to provide for the expenses required by an act, entitled "An act to provide for the continuance of the education and maintenance of the destitute orphans of the deceased soldiers, sailors and marines, and the destitute children of permanently disabled soldiers, sailors and marines of the State," approved May twenty-fifth, one thousand eight hundred and eighty-nine.

SECTION 1. *Be it enacted, &c.*, That the following sums, or so much thereof as may be necessary, be and the same are hereby specifically appropriated to the commission of soldiers' orphan schools for the several objects hereinafter named, for the year commencing on the first day of June, one thousand eight hundred and ninety-three, and for the year commencing on the first day of June, one thousand eight hundred and ninety-four, to be paid out of any moneys in the treasury, not otherwise appropriated.

Appropriations made for two years

For the salary of the chief clerk, eighteen hundred dollars per annum, or so much thereof as may be necessary.

$1,800.00 for salary of chief clerk.

For the salary of one other clerk, fourteen hundred dollars per annum, or so much thereof as may be necessary.

$1,400.00 for clerk.

For the salaries of the male and female inspectors, if the commission shall deem it advisable to continue them, twenty-eight hundred dollars per annum, or so much thereof as may be necessary, and six hundred dollars per annum for their traveling expenses, or so much thereof as may be necessary.

$2,800.00 for salaries of inspectors

For postage, telegrams and express charges, four hundred dollars per annum, or so much thereof as may be necessary.

$400.00 for postage, &c.

For transferring pupils and the expense attending the consolidation of the schools, one thousand dollars per annum, or so much thereof as may be necessary.

$1,000.00 for transferring pupils, &c.

For funeral expenses, three hundred dollars per annum, or so much thereof as may be necessary.

$300.00 for funeral expenses.

For traveling expenses of the commission and clerks, three thousand dollars per annum, or so much thereof as may be necessary.

$3,000.00 for traveling expenses.

For furniture and miscellaneous expenses in the schools and including the office of the commission, three thousand dollars per annum, or so much thereof as may be necessary.

$3,000.00 for furniture, &c.

For partial relief of soldiers' orphans remaining in the care of surviving parents, relatives or guardians, in accordance with section eight of an act, approved April ninth, one thousand eight hundred and sixty-seven, one hundred dollars per annum, or so much thereof as may be necessary.

$100.00 for partial relief of certain orphans.

15—LAWS.

For the education and maintenance, including clothing, of the orphans or destitute children admitted to such institutions as may be selected for them by the commission, for the years ending May thirty-first, one thousand eight hundred and ninety-four and May thirty-first, one thousand eight hundred and ninety-five, the sum of one hundred and ninety thousand dollars, or so much thereof as may be necessary: *Pro*

vided, That the maximum per capita rate for such education and maintenance shall not exceed the sum of one hundred and forty dollars per annum, and any surplus remaining to the credit of the said commission at the close of the year ending May thirty-first, one thousand eight hundred and ninety-three, shall revert to the State Treasury.

The said appropriation to be paid on the warrant of the Auditor General on a settlement made by him and the State Treasurer, but no warrant shall be drawn on settlement made until the commission of soldiers' orphan schools shall have made, under oath to the Auditor General, a report containing a specifically item-

ized statement of the receipts from all sources and expenses of said schools during the previous quarter, with the cash balance on hand, and the same is approved by him and the State Treasurer, nor until the Treasurer shall have sufficient money in the treasury, not otherwise appropriated, to pay the quarterly instal-

ments due said commission; and unexpended balances of sums appropriated for specific purposes shall not be used for other purposes, whether specific or general, and shall revert to the State Treasury at the close of the two fiscal years.

APPROVED—The 2d day of June, 1893.

ROBT. E. PATTISON.

No. 183.

AN ACT

Making an appropriation to the State Hospital for the Insane at Warren, Pennsylvania.

SECTION 1. *Be it enacted, &c.,* That the sum of ten thousand dollars, or so much thereof as may be necessary, be and the same is hereby specifically appropriated to the State Hospital for the Insane at Warren, Pennsylvania, for the two fiscal years beginning June first, one thousand eight hundred and ninety-three, to

enable the trustees to erect a building for a Turkish bath, a gymnasium, a reading room and museum, and such other rooms as may be required for the diversion and occupation of the female patients.

The said appropriation to be paid on the warrant of the Auditor General on a settlement by him and the

State Treasurer. but no warrant shall be drawn on settlement made until the trustees of said institution shall have made, under oath to the Auditor General, a report containing a specifically itemized statement of the receipts from all sources and expenses of said institution, together with a specifically itemized statement of the cost of said building during the previous quarter, with the cash balance on hand, and the same is approved by him and the State Treasurer, nor until the Treasurer shall have sufficient money in the treasury, not otherwise appropriated, to pay the quarterly instalments due said institution; and unexpended balances of sums appropriated for specific purposes shall not be used for other purposes, whether specific or general, and shall revert to the State Treasury at the close of the two fiscal years.

Itemized statement.

Unexpended balances shall revert to the State Treasury.

APPROVED—The 2d day of June, A. D. 1893.

ROBT. E. PATTISON.

No. 184.

AN ACT

Making an appropriation for salaries of officers and employes of the Pennsylvania Reform School at Morganza, Pennsylvania, and to pay for permanent improvements et cetera.

SECTION 1. *Be it enacted, &c.*, That the sum of seventy-six thousand eight hundred and thirty-one dollars and thirty-seven cents, or so much thereof as may be necessary, be and the same is hereby specifically appropriated to the Pennsylvania Reform School, for the two fiscal years commencing June first, one thousand eight hundred and ninety-three, for the following specific purposes:

$76,831.37 total appropriation.

For the payment of salaries of officers and employés, the sum of fifty thousand dollars, or so much thereof as may be necessary.

Salaries.

For insurance, the sum of one thousand five hundred and nineteen dollars and thirty-seven cents, or so much thereof as may be necessary.

Insurance.

For material for painting, glazing and general repairs, the sum of four thousand dollars, or so much thereof as may be necessary.

Painting, &c.

For brick for gutters, the sum of five hundred dollars, or so much thereof as may be necessary.

Brick for gutters.

For equipment and instruction in industrial school, the sum of ten thousand dollars, or so much thereof as may be necessary.

Equipment and instruction.

For improved pavements, the sum of three thousand dollars, or so much thereof as may be necessary.

Improved pavements.

For laundry machinery, the sum of two thousand one hundred and twelve dollars, or so much thereof as may be necessary.

Laundry machinery.

Steam heating.

For steam heating improvements, the sum of one thousand five hundred dollars, or so much thereof as may be necessary.

Plumbing

For sanitary plumbing, the sum of one thousand dollars, or so much thereof as may be necessary.

Electric alarm system

For equipment in electric alarm system, the sum of four hundred dollars, or so much thereof as may be necessary.

Engine and boiler.

For engine and boiler for stone crusher, the sum of eight hundred dollars, or so much thereof as may be necessary.

Paint shop.

For material to build paint shop, the sum of five hundred dollars, or so much thereof as may be necessary.

Cooling house.

For cooling house, the sum of one thousand five hundred dollars, or so much thereof as may be necessary.

How payable

The said appropriation to be paid on the warrant of the Auditor General on a settlement made by him and the State Treasurer, but no warrant shall be drawn on settlement made until the directors or managers of said institution shall have made, under oath to the Auditor General, a report containing a specifically

Itemized statement.

itemized statement of the receipts from all sources and expenses of said institution, together with a specifically itemized statement of the cost of improvements, machinery, insurance, material purchased and so forth during the previous quarter, with the cash balance on hand, and the same is approved by him and the State Treasurer, nor until the Treasurer shall have sufficient money in the treasury, not otherwise appropriated, to pay the quarterly instalments due said institution;

Unexpended balances shall revert to the State Treasury.

and unexpended balances of sums appropriated for specific purposes shall not be used for other purposes, whether specific or general, and shall revert to the State Treasury at the close of the two fiscal years.

APPROVED—The 2d day of June, A. D. 1893.

ROBT. E. PATTISON.

No. 185.

AN ACT

Making an appropriation to the Medical and Surgical Department of the Western Pennsylvania Hospital at Pittsburgh.

$90,000.00 appropriated.

SECTION 1. *Be it enacted, &c.,* That the sum of ninety thousand dollars, or so much thereof as may be necessary, be and the same is hereby specifically appropri-

Purpose of appropriation.

ated to the Medical and Surgical Department of the Western Pennsylvania Hospital, for the payment of the salaries of officers, wages of employés, and the maintenance of patients, for the two fiscal years commencing June first, one thousand eight hundred and ninety-three.

The said appropriation to be paid on the warrant of the Auditor General on a settlement made by him and the State Treasurer, but no warrants shall be drawn on settlement made until the directors or managers of said institution shall have made, under oath to the Auditor General, a report containing a specifically itemized statement of the receipts from all sources and expenses of said institution during the previous quarter, with the cash balance on hand, and the same is approved by him and the State Treasurer, nor until the Treasurer shall have sufficient money in the treasury, not otherwise appropriated, to pay the quarterly instalment due said institution; and unexpended balances of sums appropriated for specific purposes shall not be used for other purposes, whether specific or general, and shall revert to the State Treasury at the close of the two fiscal years.

APPROVED—The 2d day of June, A. D. 1893.

ROBT. E. PATTISON.

No. 186.

AN ACT

Making an appropriation to the trustees of the Cottage State Hospitals for Injured Persons of the bituminous and semi-bituminous coal regions of Pennsylvania, located at Connellsville, Fayette county.

SECTION 1. *Be it enacted, &c.*, That the sum of twelve thousand one hundred and twenty-five dollars, or so much thereof as may be necessary, is hereby specifically appropriated to the trustees of the Cottage State Hospital for Injured Persons of the bituminous and semi-bituminous coal regions of Pennsylvania, located in Connellsville, Fayette county, out of any money in the treasury, not otherwise appropriated, for the following purposes:

The sum of ten thousand dollars, or so much thereof as may be necessary, for the purpose of maintenance during the two fiscal years beginning June first, one thousand eight hundred and ninety-three, to be paid in quarterly instalments.

And the further sum of two thousand one hundred and twenty-five dollars, or so much thereof as may be necessary, to be used in making necessary improvements in connection with said hospital building and grounds, said sum to be paid in equal quarterly payments during the fiscal year beginning June first, one thousand eight hundred and ninety-three, as follows:

For picket fence (already built), four hundred dollars.

For painting hospital inside and outside, five hundred dollars.

For one hundred and fifty feet of stone wall, coping and iron fence, five hundred dollars.

For one hundred and fifty feet of curbing, one hundred and twenty-five dollars.

For one hundred and thirty-five yards paving, four hundred and fifty dollars.

For shed for horses in inclement weather, one hundred and fifty dollars.

How payable

The said appropriation to be paid on the warrant of the Auditor General on a settlement made by him and the State Treasurer, but no warrant shall be drawn on settlement made until the directors or managers of said institution shall have made, under oath to the Auditor General, a report containing a specifically itemized statement of the receipts from all sources and expenses

Itemized statement.

of said institution, together with a specifically itemized statement of the cost of said improvements during the previous quarter, with the cash balance on hand, and the same is approved by him and the State Treasurer, nor until the Treasurer shall have sufficient money in the treasury, not otherwise appropriated, to pay the quarterly instalments due said institution; and unex-

Unexpended balances shall revert to the State Treasury.

pended balances of sums appropriated for specific purposes shall not be used for other purposes, whether specific or general, and shall revert to the State Treasury at the close of the two fiscal years.

APPROVED—The 2d day of June, A. D. 1893.

ROBT. E. PATTISON.

No. 187.

AN ACT

Making an appropriation to the Children's Industrial Home at Harrisburg.

$5,500.00 total appropriation.

SECTION 1. *Be it enacted, &c.*, That the sum of five thousand five hundred dollars, or so much thereof as may be necessary, be and the same is hereby specifically appropriated to the Children's Industrial Home at Harrisburg, for the following purpose, namely: The

$900.00 for fire escape.

sum of nine hundred dollars, or so much thereof as may be necessary, for the purpose of erecting a fire escape

$600.00 for fence.

on said Home, and the sum of six hundred dollars, or so much thereof as may be necessary, for the purpose of erecting a fence around the grounds of said Home,

$4 000.00 for maintenance.

and the sum of four thousand dollars, or so much thereof as may be necessary, for the purpose of maintenance of said Home for the two fiscal years beginning June first, one thousand eight hundred and ninety-three.

How payable.

The said appropriation to be paid on the warrant of the Auditor General on a settlement made by him and the State Treasurer, but no warrant shall be drawn on settlement made until the directors or managers of said institution shall have made, under oath to the Auditor General, a report containing a specifically itemized statement of the receipts from all sources and expenses of said institution, together with a specifically itemized statement of the cost of erecting fire escape and fence during the previous quarter, with the cash balance on hand, and the same is approved by him and the State Treasurer, nor until the Treasurer shall have sufficient money in the treasury, not otherwise appropriated, to pay the quarterly instalments due said institution ; and unexpended balances of sums appropriated for specific purposes shall not be used for other purposes, whether specific or general, and shall revert to the State Treasury at the close of the two fiscal years.

APPROVED—The 2d day of June, A. D. 1893.

ROBT. E. PATTISON.

No. 188.

AN ACT

Making an appropriation to the Home for Friendless Children for the city and county of Lancaster.

SECTION 1. *Be it enacted, &c.*, That the sum of three thousand dollars, or so much thereof as may be necessary, be and the same is hereby specifically appropriated to the Home for Friendless Children for the city and county of Lancaster, toward the maintenance, education and support of homeless, destitute and vagrant children in said home, for the two fiscal years beginning June first, one thousand eight hundred and ninety-three.

The said appropriation to be paid on the warrant of the Auditor General on a settlement made by him and the State Treasurer, but no warrant shall be drawn on settlement made until the directors or managers of said institution shall have made, under oath to the Auditor General, a report containing a specifically itemized statement of the receipts from all sources and expenses of said institution during the previous quarter, with the cash balance on hand, and the same is approved by him and the State Treasurer, nor until the Treasurer shall have sufficient money in the treasury, not otherwise appropriated, to pay the quarterly instalments due said institution ; and unexpended balances of sums appropriated for specific purposes shall not be used for other purposes, whether specific or general, and shall revert to the State Treasury at the close of the two fiscal years.

APPROVED—The 2d day of June, A. D. 1893.

ROBT. E. PATTISON.

No. 189.

AN ACT

Making an appropriation to the Home of the Friendless in the city of Erie.

$5,000.00 appropriated.

SECTION 1. *Be it enacted, &c.*, That the sum of five thousand dollars, or so much thereof as may be necessary, be and the same is hereby specifically appropriated to the Home for the Friendless of Erie, for the two fiscal years beginning June first, one thousand eight hundred and ninety-three, for the purpose of maintenance.

How payable.

The said appropriation to be paid on the warrant of the Auditor General on a settlement made by him and the State Treasurer, but no warrant shall be drawn on settlement made until the manager or managers of said institution shall have made, under oath to the Auditor

Itemized statement.

General, a report containing a specifically itemized statement of the receipts from all sources and expenses of said society during the previous quarter, with the cash balance on hand, and the same is approved by him and the State Treasurer, nor until the Treasurer shall have sufficient money in the treasury, not otherwise appropriated, to pay the quarterly instalments due said

Unexpended balances shall revert to the State Treasury.

institution; and unexpended balances of sums appropriated for specific purposes shall not be used for other purposes, whether specific or general, and shall revert to the State Treasury at the close of the two fiscal years.

APPROVED—The 2d day of June, A. D. 1893.

ROBT. E. PATTISON.

No. 190.

AN ACT

Making an appropriation to the Charity Hospital of Montgomery county, Pennsylvania, for maintenance.

$6,000.00 appropriated.

SECTION 1. *Be it enacted, &c.*, That the sum of six thousand dollars, or so much thereof as may be necessary, be and the same is hereby specifically appropriated to the Charity Hospital of Montgomery county, Pennsylvania, located at Norristown, for the purpose of maintenance of said hospial for the two fiscal years beginning June first, one thousand eight hundred and ninety-three.

How payable.

The said appropriation to be paid on the warrant of the Auditor General on a settlement made by him and the State Treasurer, but no warrant shall be drawn on settlement made until the directors or managers of said institution shall have made, under oath to the Auditor

Itemized statement

General, a report containing a specifically itemized

statement of the receipts from all sources and expenses of said institution during the previous quarter, with the cash balance on hand, and the same is approved by him and the State Treasurer, nor until the Treasurer shall have sufficient money in the treasury, not otherwise appropriated, to pay the quarterly instalments due said institution; and unexpended balances of sums appropriated for specific purposes shall not be used for other purposes, whether specific or general, and shall revert to the State Treasury at the close of the two fiscal years.

Unexpended balances shall revert to the State Treasury.

APPROVED—The 2d day of June, A. D. 1893.

ROBT. E. PATTISON.

No. 191.

AN ACT

Making an appropriation to the Oil City Hospital, located at Oil city, county of Venango, Pennsylvania.

SECTION 1. *Be it enacted, &c.,* That the sum of ten thousand dollars, or so much thereof as may be necessary, be and the same is hereby specifically appropriated to the Oil City Hospital, located at Oil City, Pennsylvania, for the two fiscal years beginning June first, one thousand eight hundred and ninety-three, for the following purposes, namely: The sum of six thousand dollars, or so much thereof as may be necessary, to assist in the erection, furnishing and equipping of a hospital building, and the sum of four thousand dollars, or so much thereof as may be necessary, for the purpose of maintenance.

$10,000.00 total appropriation.

Items.

The said appropriation to be paid on the warrant of the Auditor General on a settlement made by him and the State Treasurer, but no warrant shall be drawn on settlement made until the directors or managers of said institution shall have made, under oath to the Auditor General, a report containing a specifically itemized statement of the receipts from all sources and expenses of said institution, together with a specifically itemized statement of the cost of building, furnishing and equipping during the previous quarter, with the cash balance on hand, and the same is approved by him and the State Treasurer, nor until the Treasurer shall have sufficient money in the treasury, not otherwise appropriated, to pay the quarterly instalments due said institution; and unexpended balances of sums appropriated for specific purposes shall not be used for other purposes, whether specific or general, and shall revert to the State Treasury at the close of the two fiscal years.

How payable.

Itemized statement.

Unexpended balances shall revert to State Treasury.

APPROVED—The 2d day of June, A. D. 1893.

ROBT. E. PATTISON.

No. 192.

AN ACT

Making an appropriation to the Women's Homeopathic Association of Pennsylvania.

$5,000.00 appropriated.

SECTION 1. *Be it enacted, &c.,* That the sum of five thousand dollars, or so much thereof as may be necessary, be and the same is hereby specifically appropriated to the Women's Homeopathic Association of Pennsylvania, for the purpose of maintenance of the hospitals owned and conducted by said association, for the two fiscal years beginning June first, one thousand eight hundred and ninety-three.

How payable.

Itemized statement.

Unexpended balances shall revert to the State Treasury.

The said appropriation to be paid on the warrant of the Auditor General on a settlement made by him and the State Treasurer, but no warrant shall be drawn on settlement made until the directors or managers of said association shall have made, under oath to the Auditor General, a report containing a specifically itemized statement of the receipts from all sources and expenses of said association during the previous quarter, with the cash balance on hand, and the same is approved by him and the State Treasurer, nor until the Treasurer shall have sufficient money in the Treasury, not otherwise appropriated, to pay the quarterly instalments due said association; and unexpended balances of sums appropriated for specific purposes shall not be used for other purposes, whether specific or general, and shall revert to the State Treasury at the close of the two fiscal years.

APPROVED—The 2d day of June, A. D. 1893.

ROBT. E. PATTISON.

No. 193.

AN ACT

Making an appropriation to the Conemaugh Valley Memorial Hospital.

$10,000.00 appropriated.

SECTION 1. *Be it enacted, &c.,* That the sum of ten thousand dollars, or so much thereof as may be necessary, is hereby specifically appropriated to the Conemaugh Valley Memorial Hospital at Johnstown, for the purpose of maintenance, for the two fiscal years commencing the first day of June, one thousand eight hundred and ninety-three.

How payable.

Itemized statement.

The said appropriation to be paid on the warrant of the Auditor General on a settlement made by him and the State Treasurer, but no warrant shall be drawn in settlement made until the directors or managers of said institution shall have made, under oath to the Auditor General, a report containing a specifically itemized statement of the receipts from all sources and expenses

of said institution during the previous quarter, with
the cash balance on hand, and the same is approved by
him and the State Treasurer, nor until the Treasurer
shall have sufficient money in the treasury, not otherwise appropriated, to pay the quarterly instalments
due said institution; and unexpended balances of sums Unexpended bal-
ances shall revert
to the State Treas-
ury.
appropriated for specific purposes shall not be used
for other purposes, whether specific or general, and
shall revert to the State Treasury at the close of the
two fiscal years.

APPROVED—The 2d day of June, A. D. 1893.

ROBT. E. PATTISON.

No. 194.

AN ACT

**Making an appropriation to the Philadelphia Orthopedic Hospital
and Infirmary for Nervous Diseases of the city of Philadelphia.**

SECTION 1. *Be it enacted, &c.*, That the sum of ten $10,000.00 total ap-
propriation.
thousand dollars, or so much thereof as may be nec-
essary, be and the same is hereby specifically appropriated to the Philadelphia Orthopedic Hospital and
Infirmary for Nervous Diseases of the city of Philadelphia for the two fiscal years beginning June first, one
thousand eight hundred and ninety-three, for the following purposes, namely :

The sum of five thousand dollars, or so much thereof Items.
as may be necessary, for the purpose of maintenance
of said hospital, and the sum of five thousand dollars,
or so much thereof as may be necessary, for improving and furnishing the new building.

The said appropriation to be paid on the warrant of How payable.
the Auditor General on a settlement made by him and
the State Treasurer, but no warrant shall be drawn on
settlement made until the directors or mangers of said
institution shall have made, under oath to the Auditor
General, a report containing a specifically itemized
statement of the receipts from all sources and expenses
of said institution, together with a specifically item- Itemized state-
ment.
ized report of the cost of improving and furnishing new
building during the previous quarter, with the cash
balance on hand, and the same is approved by him and
the State Treasurer, nor until the Treasurer shall have
sufficient money in the treasury, not otherwise appropriated, to pay the quarterly instalments due said
institution; and unexpended balances of sums appro- Unexpended bal-
ances shall revert
to the State Treas-
ury.
propriated for specific purposes shall not be used for
other purposes, whether specific or general, and shall
revert to the State Treasury at the close of the two fiscal years.

APPROVED—The 2d day of June, A. D. 1893.

ROBT. E. PATTISON.

No. 195.

AN ACT

Making an appropriation to the Williamsport Hospital of the city Williamsport.

$10,000.00 total appropriation.

SECTION 1. *Be it enacted, &c.*, That the sum of ten thousand dollars, or so much thereof as may be necessary, be and the same is hereby specifically appropriated to the Williamsport Hospital of the city of Williamsport for the two fiscal years beginning June first, one thousand eight hundred and ninety-three, for the following purposes, namely:

Items.

The sum of eight thousand dollars, or so much thereof as may be necessary, for maintenance of said hospital, and the sum of two thousand dollars, or so much thereof as may be necessary, for the purpose of aiding in the erection and completion of new buildings and making necessary improvements.

How payable.

The said appropriation to be paid on the warrant of the Auditor General on a settlement made by him and the State Treasurer, but no warrant shall be drawn on settlement made until the directors or managers of said institution shall have made, under oath to the Auditor

Itemized statement.

General, a report containing a specifically itemized statement of the receipts from all sources and expenses of said institution, together with a specifically itemized statement of the cost of said new buildings and improvements during the previous quarter, with the cash balance on hand, and the same is approved by him and the State Treasurer, nor until the Treasurer shall have sufficient money in the treasury, not otherwise appropriated, to pay the quarterly instalments due

Unexpended balances shall revert to the State Treasury.

said institution; and unexpended balances of sums appropriated for specific purposes shall not be used for other purposes, whether specific or general, and shall revert to the State Treasury at the close of the two fiscal years.

APPROVED—The 2d day of June, A. D. 1893.

ROBT. E. PATTISON.

No. 196.

AN ACT

Making an appropriation to the Home for the Friendless of the city of Williamsport.

$5,000.00 appropriated.

SECTION 1. *Be it enacted, &c.*, That the sum of five thousand dollars, or so much thereof as may be necessary, to be paid in four equal, quarterly instalments during the fiscal year beginning June first, one thousand eight hundred and ninety-three, be and the same is hereby specifically appropriated to the Home for the Friendless Association of the city of Williamsport, Pennsylvaina, for the purpose of erecting an addition and for making other necessary improvements to the Home for the Friendless in said city : *Provided,* That the plans for the said improvements and addition shall be first approved by the State Board of Public Charities. Proviso.

The said appropriation to be paid on the warrant of the Auditor General on a settlement made by him and the State Treasurer, but no warrant shall be drawn on settlement made until the directors or managers of said institution shall have made, under oath to the Auditor General, a report containing a specifically itemized statement of the receipts from all sources and expenses of said institution, together with a specifically itemized statement of the cost of said improvements during the previous quarter, with the cash balance on hand, and the same is approved by him and the State Treasurer, nor until the Treasurer shall have sufficient money in the treasury, not otherwise appropriated, to pay the quarterly instalments due said institution ; and unexpended balances of sums appropriated for specific purposes shall not be used for other purposes, whether specific or general, and shall revert to the State Treasury at the close of the fiscal years. How payable

Itemized statement.

Unexpended balances shall revert to the State Treasury.

APPROVED—The 2d day of June, A. D. 1893.

ROBT. E. PATTISON.

No. 197.

AN ACT

Making an appropriation to the Midnight Mission of Philadelphia.

SECTION 1. *Be it enacted, &c.,* That the sum of one thousand dollars, or so much thereof as may be necessary, be and the same is hereby specifically appropriated to the Midnight Mission of Philadelphia, for the purpose of maintenance, for the two fiscal years beginning June first, one thousand eight hundred and ninety-three. $1,000.00 appropriated.

The said appropriation to be paid on the warrant of the Auditor General on a settlement made by him and the State Treasurer, but no warrant shall be drawn on settlement made until the directors or managers of said institution shall have made, under oath to the Auditor General, a report containing a specifically itemized statement of the receipts from all sources and expenses of said institution during the previous quarter, with the cash balance on band, and the same is approved by him and the State Treasurer, nor until the Treasurer shall have sufficient money in the treasury, not otherwise appropriated, to pay the quarterly How payable.

Itemized statement

instalments due said institution; and unexpended balances of sums appropriated for specific purposes shall not be used for other purposes, whether specific or general, and shall revert to the State Treasury at the close of the two fiscal years.

APPROVED—The 2d day of June, A. D. 1893.

ROBT. E. PATTISON.

No. 198.

AN ACT

Making an appropriation to Rush Hospital for Consumption and Allied Diseases.

SECTION 1. *Be it enacted, &c.,* That the sum of ten thousand dollars, or so much thereof as may be necessary, be and the same is hereby specifically appropriated to the Rush Hospital for Consumption and Allied Diseases, for the maintenance of the said hospital, for the two fiscal years commencing June first, one thousand eight hundred and ninety-three.

The said appropriation to be paid on the warrant of the Auditor General on a settlement made by him and the State Treasurer, but no warrant shall be drawn on settlement made until the directors or managers of said institution shall have made, under oath to the Auditor General, a report containing a specifically

itemized statement of the receipts from all sources and expenses of said institution during the previous quarter, with the cash balance on hand, and the same is approved by him and the State Treasurer, nor until the Treasurer shall have sufficient money in the treasury, not otherwise appropriated, to pay the quarterly

instalments due said institution; and unexpended balances of sums appropriated for specific purposes shall not be used for other purposes, whether specific or general, and shall revert to the State Treasury at the close of the two fiscal years.

APPROVED—The 2d day of June, A. D. 1893.

ROBT. E. PATTISON.

No. 199.

AN ACT

Making an appropriation to the Altoona Hospital.

SECTION 1. *Be it enacted, &c.,* That the sum of nineteen thousand dollars, or so much thereof as may be necessary, be and the same is hereby specifically appropriated to the Altoona Hospital for the two fiscal years beginning June first, one thousand eight hundred and ninety-three, for the following purposes, namely :

The sum of nine thousand dollars, or so much thereof as may be necessary, for the maintenance of said hospital, and the sum of ten thousand dollars, or so much thereof as may be necessary, for the purpose of assisting in the erection and furnishing of an additional ward to said hospital : *Provided*, That no part of the money herein appropriated for the erection and furnishing of an additional ward shall become available until the treasurer of said hospital shall have certified, under oath to the Auditor General, that the sum of ten thousand dollars has been subscribed and paid in cash into the treasury of said hospital by private subscriptions for the purpose of assisting in the erection and furnishing of the said additional ward.

The said appropriation to be paid on the warrant of the Auditor General on a settlement made by him and the State Treasurer, but no warrant shall be drawn on settlement made until the directors or managers of said institution shall have made, under oath to the Auditor General, a report containing a specifically itemized statement of the receipts from all sources and expenses of said institution, together with a specifically itemized statement of the cost of said additional ward and furnishing the same during the previous quarter, with the cash balance on hand, and the same is approved by him and the State Treasurer, nor until the Treasurer shall have sufficient money in the treasury, not otherwise appropriated, to pay the quarterly instalments due said institution; and unexpended balances of sums appropriated for specific purposes shall not be used for other purposes, whether specific or general, and shall revert to the State Treasury at the close of the two fiscal years.

APPROVED--The 2d day of June, A. D. 1893.

ROBT. E. PATTISON.

Marginal notes: Items. / Private subscriptions to be certified to before appropriations can be paid. / How payable. / Itemized statement. / Unexpended balances shall revert to the State Treasury.

No. 200.

AN ACT

Making an appropriation to the Hospital Department of the Hahnemann Medical College and Hospital of Philadelphia.

SECTION 1. *Be it enacted, &c.*, That the sum of thirty-three thousand five hundred and forty-six dollars, or so much thereof as may be necessary, be and the same is hereby specifically appropriated to the Hahnemann Medical College and Hospital of Philadelphia for the two fiscal years beginning June first, one thousand eight hundred and ninety-three, for the following purposes, namely :

The sum of twenty-five thousand dollars, or so much

Marginal notes: $33,546.00 appropriated. / Items.

240

thereof as may be necessary, for the purpose of the maintenance of the hospital department of said institution, and the sum of eight thousand five hundred and forty-six dollars, or so much thereof as may be necessary, for the purpose of paying a deficit in the hospital maintenance account of said institution for the two fiscal years ending May thirty-first, one thousand eight hundred and ninety-three.

How payable.

The said appropriation to be paid on the warrant of the Auditor General on a settlement by him and the State Treasurer, but no warrant shall be drawn on settlement made until the directors or managers of said institution shall have made, under oath to the Auditor General, a report containing a specifically itemized statement of the receipts from all sources and expenses of said institution during the previous quarter, with the cash balance on hand, and the same is approved by him and the State Treasurer, nor until the Treasurer shall have sufficient money in the treasury, not otherwise appropriated, to pay the quarterly instalments due said institution; and unexpended balances of sums appropriated for specific purposes shall not be used for other purposes, whether specific or general, and shall revert to the State Treasury at the close of the two fiscal years.

Itemized statement.

Unexpended balances shall revert to the State Treasury.

APPROVED—The 2d day of June. A. D. 1893.

ROBT. E. PATTISON.

No. 201.

AN ACT

Making an appropriation to the Kensington Hospital for Women in Philadelphia.

$5,000.00 appropriated.

SECTION 1. *Be it enacted, &c.*, That the sum of five thousand dollars, or so much thereof as may be necessary, be and the same is hereby specifically appropriated to the Kensington Hospital for Women in Philadelphia, for the purpose of maintenance, for the two fiscal years beginning June first, one thousand eight hundred and ninety-three.

How payable.

The said appropriation to be paid on the warrant of the Auditor General on a settlement made by him and the State Treasurer, but no warrant shall be drawn on settlement made until the directors or managers of said institution shall have made, under oath to the Auditor General, a report containing a specifically itemized statement of the receipts from all sources and expenses of said institution during the previous quarter, with the cash balance on hand, and the same is approved by him and the State Treasurer, nor until the Treasurer shall have sufficient money in the treasury not otherwise appropriated, to pay the quarterly instal-

Itemized statement

ments due said institution; and unexpended balances of sums appropriated for specific purposes shall not be used for other purposes, whether specific or general, and shall revert to the State Treasury at the close of the two fiscal years.

APPROVED—The 2d day of June, A. D. 1893.

ROBT. E. PATTISON.

Unexpended balances shall revert to the State Treasury.

No. 202.

AN ACT

Making an appropriation to the Hospital Department of the Jefferson Medical College of Philadelphia.

SECTION 1. *Be it enacted, &c.,* That the sum of one hundred and ten thousand dollars, or so much thereof as may be necessary, be and the same is hereby specifically appropriated to the Jefferson Medical College of Philadelphia for the two fiscal years beginning June first, one thousand eight hundred and ninety-three, for the following purposes, namely: The sum of one hundred thousand dollars, or so much thereof as may be necessary, to aid in the erection and equipment of a new hospital building, and the sum of ten thousand dollars, or so much thereof as may be necessary, for the maintenance of said hospital: *Provided,* That no part of the money herein appropriated for the erection and equipment of a hospital building shall become available until the treasurer of said hospital shall have filed a statement, under oath with the Auditor General, that the sum of one hundred thousand dollars has been subscribed by private contributions, and paid in cash into the treasury of said hospital, for the purpose of aiding in the erection and equipping of said new hospital building, and that the hospital is the owner in fee simple, clear of all incumbrances, of the property on which said new hospital building is to be erected: *Provided further,* That the said hospital shall maintain forever not less than one hundred free beds for the reception and care of indigent sick or maimed persons from any of the counties of the Commonwealth, who shall be received and treated free of all charge or expense whatsoever.

The said appropriation to be paid on the warrant of the Auditor General on a settlement made by him and the State Treasurer, but no warrant shall be drawn on settlement made until the directors or managers of said institution shall have made, under oath to the Auditor General, a report containing a specifically itemized statement of the receipts from all sources and expenses of said institution, together with a specifically itemized statement of the cost of said new building and equipping the same during the previous quarter,

$110,000.00 total appropriation.

Items.

Amount of private subscriptions required before appropriation shall be available.

Must maintain 100 free beds.

How payable.

Itemized statement.

16—LAWS.

with the cash balance on hand, and the same is approved by him and the State Treasurer, nor until the Treasurer shall have sufficient money in the treasury, not otherwise appropriated, to pay the quarterly instalments due said institution; and unexpended balances of sums appropriated for specific purposes shall not be used for other purposes, whether specific or general, and shall revert to the State Treasury at the close of the two fiscal years.

Unexpended balances shall revert to the State Treasury.

APPROVED—The 2d day of June, A. D. 1893.

ROBT. E. PATTISON.

No. 203.

AN ACT

Making an appropriation to the Home for the Friendless at Harrisburg, Pennsylvania.

$2,500.00 appropriated.

SECTION 1. *Be it enacted, &c.*, That the sum of two thousand five hundred dollars, or so much thereof as may be necessary, be and the same is hereby specifically appropriated towards the maintenance of the inmates of the Home for the Friendless located at Harrisburg for the two fiscal years beginning June first, one thousand eight hundred and ninety-three.

How payable.

The said appropriation to be paid on the warrant of the Auditor General on a settlement made by him and the State Treasurer, but no warrant shall be drawn on settlement made until the directors or managers of said institution shall have made, under oath to the Auditor General, a report containing a specifically itemized statement of the receipts from all sources and expenses of said institution during the previous quarter, with the cash balance on hand, and the same is approved by him and the State Treasurer, nor until the Treasurer shall have sufficient money in the treasury, not otherwise appropriated, to pay the quarterly instalments due said institution; and unexpended balances of sums appropriated for specific purposes shall not be used for other purposes, whether specific or general, and shall revert to the State Treasury at the close of the two fiscal years.

Itemized statement.

Unexpended balances shall revert to the State Treasury.

APPROVED—The 2d day of June, A. D. 1893.

ROBT. E. PATTISON.

No. 204.

AN ACT

Making an appropriation to the Lackawanna Hospital in the city of Scranton.

$27,000.00 total appropriation.

SECTION 1. *Be it enacted, &c.*, That the sum of twenty-seven thousand dollars, or so much thereof as may be necessary, be and the same is hereby specifically ap-

propriated to the Lackawanna Hospital of the city of
Scranton for the following purposes, namely: The **Items.**
sum of twenty thousand dollars, or so much thereof as
may be necessary, for the purpose of maintenance for
the two fiscal years beginning June first, one thousand
eight hundred and ninety-three; the sum of four thousand five hundred dollars, or so much thereof as may
be necessary, for necessary repairs and improvements
to old buildings and improving the ventilation of the
same, and the sum of two thousand five hundred dollars, or so much thereof as may be necessary, for re-
plumbing and building water closets, bath rooms et
cetera, for women's ward to be paid upon the comple
tion of said improvements.

The said appropriation to be paid on the warrant to **How payable.**
the Auditor General on a settlement made by him and
the State Treasurer, but no warrant shall be drawn on
settlement made until the directors or managers of said
institution shall have made, under oath to the Auditor
General, a report containing a specifically itemized **Itemized state-**
statement of the receipts from all sources and expenses **ment.**
of said institution, together with a specifically itemized statement of the cost of said improvements during
the previous quarter, with the cash balance on hand,
and the same is approved by him and the State Treasurer, nor until the Treasurer shall have sufficient money
in the treasury not otherwise appropriated, to pay the
quarterly instalments due said institution; and unex- **Unexpended bal-**
pended balances of sums appropriated for specific pur- **ances shall revert
to the State Treas-**
poses shall not be used for other purposes, whether **ury.**
specific or general, and shall revert to the State Treasury at the close of the two fiscal years.

APPROVED—The 2d day of June, A. D. 1893.

ROBT. E. PATTISON.

No. 205.

AN ACT

Making an appropriation to the Hamot Hospital Association in
the city of Erie.

SECTION 1. *Be it enacted, &c.*, That the sum of six **$6,000.00 appropri-**
thousand dollars, or so much thereof as may be neces- **ated.**
sary, be and the same is hereby specifically appropriated to the Hamot Hospital Association in the city of
Erie, for the purpose of maintenance, for the two fiscal
years beginning June first, one thousand eight hundred and ninety-three.

The said appropriation to be paid on the warrant of **How payable.**
the Auditor General on a settlement made by him and
the State Treasurer, but no warrant shall be drawn on
settlement made until the directors or managers of said
institution shall have made, under oath to the Auditor

General, a report containing a specifically itemized statement of the receipts from all sources and expenses of said institution during the previous quarter, with the cash balance on hand, and the same is approved by him and the State Treasurer, nor until the Treasurer shall have sufficient money in the treasury, not otherwise appropriated, to pay the quarterly instalments due said institution; and unexpended balances of sums appropriated for specific purposes shall not be used for other purposes, whether specific or general, and shall revert to the State Treasury at the close of the two fiscal years.

APPROVED—The 2d day of June, A. D. 1893.

ROBT. E. PATTISON.

No. 206.

AN ACT

Making an appropriation to the Chester Hospital at Chester, Pennsylvania.

SECTION 1. *Be it enacted, &c.*, That the sum of ten thousand dollars, or so much thereof as may be necessary, and the same is hereby specifically appropriated to the Chester Hospital at Chester, Pennsylvania, for the two fiscal years beginning June first, one thousand eight hundred and ninety-three, for the following purposes, namely:

For maintenance, the sum of eight thousand dollars, or so much thereof as may be necessary.

For completion of buildings and improvements of grounds, the sum of two thousand dollars, or so much thereof as may be necessary, which sum shall be payable immediately on the warrant of the Auditor General on a settlement made by him and the State Treasurer, after the managers of the said institution shall have filed with the Auditor General a sworn itemized statement of the cost of said improvements of grounds and completion of building.

The said appropriation for maintenance to be paid on the warrant of the Auditor General on a settlement made by him and the State Treasurer, but no warrant shall be drawn on settlement made until the directors or managers of said institution shall have made, under oath, a specifically itemized statement of the receipts from all sources and expenses of said institution during the previous quarter, with a cash balance on hand, and the same is approved by him and the State Treasurer, nor until the Treasurer shall have sufficient money in the treasury, not otherwise appropriated to pay the quarterly instalments due said institution; and unexpended balances of sums appropriated for specific purposes shall not be used for other purposes, whether specific or general, and shall revert to the State Treasury at the close of the two fiscal years.

APPROVED—The 2d day of June, A. D. 1893.

ROBT. E. PATTISON.

No. 207.

AN ACT

Making an appropriation to the Penn Asylum for Indigent Widows and Single Women.

SECTION 1. *Be it enacted, &c.*, That the sum of ten thousand dollars, or so much thereof as may be necessary, be and the same is hereby specifically appropriated to the Penn Asylum for Indigent Widows and Single Women, situate on Belgrade street above Susquehanna avenue, Philadelphia, for the two fiscal years beginning June first, one thousand eight hundred and ninety-three, for the purpose of purchasing property and building an infirmary.

The said appropriation to be paid on the warrant of the Auditor General on a settlement made by him and the State Treasurer, but no warrant shall be drawn on settlement made until the directors or managers of said institution shall have made, under oath to the Auditor General, a report containing a specifically itemized statement of the receipts from all sources and expenses of said institution, together with a specifically itemized statement of the cost of said property and building during the previous quarter with the cash balance on hand, and the same is approved by him and the State Treasurer, nor until the Treasurer shall have sufficient money in the treasury, not otherwise appropriated, to pay the quarterly instalments due said institution; and unexpended balances of sums appropriated for specific purposes shall not be used for other purposes, whether specific or general, and shall revert to the State Treasury at the close of the two fiscal years.

APPROVED—The 2d day of June, A. D. 1893.

ROBT. E. PATTISON.

[marginal notes: $10,000 00 appropriated. How payable. Itemized statement. Unexpended balances shall revert to the State Treasury.]

No. 208.

AN ACT

Making an appropriation to the Children's Homeopathic Hospital of the city of Philadelphia.

SECTION 1. *Be it enacted, &c.*, That the sum of eight thousand dollars, or so much thereof as may be necessary, be and the same is hereby specifically appropriated to the Children's Homeopathic Hospital of the city of Philadelphia for the two fiscal years commenc-

[marginal note: $8,000.00 appropriated.]

ing June first, one thousand eight hundred and ninety-three, for the maintenance of indigent patients treated in said hospital.

How Payable.
The said appropriation to be paid on the warrant of the Auditor General on a settlement made by him and the State Treasurer, but no warrant shall be drawn on settlement made until the directors or managers of said institution shall have made, under oath to the Auditor General, a report containing a specifically itemized statement of the receipts from all sources and expenses of said institution during the previous quarter, with the cash balance on hand, and the same is approved by him and the State Treasurer, nor until the Treasurer shall have sufficient money in the treasury, not otherwise appropriated, to pay the quarterly instalments due said institution; and unexpended balances of sums appropriated for specific purposes shall not be used for other purposes, whether specific or general, and shall revert to the State Treasury at the close of the two fiscal years.

Itemized statement.

Unexpended balances shall revert to the State Treasury.

APPROVED—The 2d day of June, A. D. 1893.

ROBT. E. PATTISON.

No. 209.

AN ACT

Making an appropriation to the Gynecean Hospital in the city of Philadelphia.

$20,000.00 appropriated.
SECTION 1. *Be it enacted, &c.*, That the sum of twenty thousand dollars, or so much thereof as may be necessary, be and the same is hereby specifically appropriated to the Gynecean Hospital in the city of Philadelphia, for the purpose of maintenance, for the two fiscal years beginning June first, one thousand eight hundred and ninety-three.

How payable
The said appropriation to be paid on the warrant of the Auditor General on a settlement made by him and the State Treasurer, but no warrant shall be drawn on settlement made until the directors or managers of said institution shall have made, under oath to the Auditor General, a report containing a specifically itemized statement of the receipts from all sources and expenses of said institution during the previous quarter, with the cash balance on hand, and the same is approved by him and the State Treasurer, nor until the Treasurer shall have sufficient money in the treasury, not otherwise appropriated, to pay the quarterly instalments due said institution; and unexpended balances of sums appropriated for specific purposes shall not be used for other purposes, whether specific or general, and shall revert to the State Treasury at the close of the two fiscal years.

Itemized statement.

Unexpended balances shall revert to the State Treasury.

APPROVED—The 2d day of June, A. D. 1893.

ROBT. E. PATTISON.

No. 210.

AN ACT

Making an appropriation to the Philadelphia Home for Infants, for support and maintenance.

SECTION 1. *Be it enacted, &c.*, That the sum of four thousand dollars, or so much thereof as may be necessary, be and the same is hereby specifically appropriated to the Philadelphia Home for Infants, for support and maintenance of homeless and destitute poor children in said home, for the two fiscal years beginning June first, one thousand eight hundred ninety-three. $4,000.00 appropriated.

The said appropriation to be paid on the warrant of the Auditor General on a settlement made by him and the State Treasurer, but no warrant shall be drawn on settlement made until the directors or managers of said institution shall have made, under oath to the Auditor General, a report containing a specifically itemized statement of the receipts from all sources and expenses of said institution during the previous quarter, with the cash balance on hand, and the same is approved by him and the State Treasurer, nor until the Treasurer shall have sufficient money in the treasury, not otherwise appropriated, to pay the quarterly instalments due said institution; and unexpended balances of sums appropriated for specific purposes shall not be used for other purposes, whether specific or general, and shall revert to the State Treasury at the close of the two fiscal years. How payable.

Itemized statement.

Unexpended balances shall revert to the State Treasury.

APPROVED—The 2d day of June, A. D. 1893.

ROBT. E. PATTISON.

No. 211.

AN ACT

Making an appropriation to the Western Home for Poor Children of the city of Philadelphia, for the erection of an Infirmary.

SECTION 1. *Be it enacted, &c.*, That the sum of four thousand dollars, or so much thereof as may be necessary, be and the same is hereby specifically appropriated to the Western Home for Poor Children of the city of Philadelphia, Pennsylvania, for the two fiscal years beginning June first, one thousand eight hundred and ninety-three, for the purpose of erecting an Infirmary upon the lot, separate and apart from the main building. $4,000.00 appropriated.

The said appropriation to be paid on the warrant of the Auditor General on a settlement made by him and the State Treasurer, but no warant shall be drawn on settlement made until the directors or managers of said institution shall have made, under oath to the Auditor General, a report accompanied with a copy of the con- How payable.

tract containing a specifically itemized statement of the receipts from all sources and expenses of said institution, together with an itemized statement of cost of erecting Infirmary during the previous quarter, with the cash balance on hand, and the same is approved by him and the State Treasurer, nor until the Treasurer shall have sufficient money in the treasury, not otherwise appropriated, to pay the quarterly instalments

due said institution; and unexpended balances of sums appropriated for specific purposes shall not be used for other purposes, whether specific or general, and shall revert to the State Treasury at the close of the two fiscal years.

APPROVED—The 2d day of June, A. D. 1893.

ROBT. E. PATTISON.

No. 212.

AN ACT

Making an appropriation to the State Hospital for Injured Persons at Mercer, Mercer county, Pennsylvania.

SECTION 1. *Be it enacted, &c.*, That the sum of nine thousand dollars, or so much thereof as may be necessary, be and the same is hereby specifically appropriated to the State Hospital for Injured Persons at Mercer, Mercer county, Pennsylvania, for salaries of employés and maintenance, for the two fiscal years beginning June first, one thousand eight hundred and ninety-three.

The said appropriation to be paid on the warrant of the Auditor General on a settlement made by him and the State Treasurer, but no warrant shall be drawn on settlement made until the trustees of said institution shall have made, under oath to the Auditor General, a report containing a specifically itemized state-

ment of the receipts from all sources and expenses of said institution during the previous quarter, with the cash balance on hand, and the same is approved by him and the State Treasurer, nor until the Treasurer shall have sufficient money in the treasury, not otherwise appropriated, to pay the quarterly instalments due said institution; and unexpended balances of sums

appropriated for specific purposes shall not be used for other purposes, whether specific or general, and shall revert to the State Treasury at the close of the two fiscal years.

APPROVED—The 2d day of June. A. D. 1893.

ROBT. E. PATTISON.

No. 213.

AN ACT

Making an appropriation to the Women's Hospital of Philadelphia.

SECTION 1. *Be it enacted, &c.*, That the sum of fifteen thousand dollars, or so much thereof as may be necessary, be and the same is hereby specifically appropriated to the Women's Hospital of Philadelphia, to be used in the erection, completion and furnishing of a suitable new hospital building, sufficient to accommodate one hundred and fifty patients, on the ground of said Women's hospital, to be used for the purpose of a general hospital and dispensary, to be open to all classes without the distinction of race, color or creed, and that no case of sickness or injury shall be refused admission on account of the inability of the applicant to pay expenses, so long as there may be accommodations in said hospital: *Provided*, That before any part of this appropriation shall become available, the treasurer of said hospital shall certify, under oath to the Auditor General, that the sum of twenty-five thousand dollars, exclusive of the value of the grounds, has been subscribed and paid in cash into the treasury of said hospital towards the erection, completion and furnishing of said new hospital building. ·

The said appropriation to be paid on the warrant of the Auditor General on a settlement made by him and the State Treasurer, but no warrant shall be drawn on settlement made until the directors or managers of said institution shall have made, under oath to the Auditor General, a report containing a specifically itemized statement of the receipts from all sources and expenses of said institution, together with an itemized statement of the cost of said new building during the previous quarter, with the cash balance on hand, and the same is approved by him and the State Treasurer, nor until the Treasurer shall have sufficient money in the treasury, not otherwise appropriated, to pay the quarterly instalments due said institution; and unexpended balances of sums appropriated for specific purposes shall not be used for other purposes, whether specific or general, and shall revert to the State Treasury at the close of the two fiscal years.

APPROVED—The 2d day of June, A. D. 1893.

ROBT. E. PATTISON.

(Marginal notes:)
$15,000.00 appropriated.

Conditions incident to the appropriation.

Proviso as to amount of private subscriptions before appropriation shall become available.

How payable.

Itemized statement.

Unexpended balances shall revert to the State Treasury.

No. 214.

AN ACT

Making an appropriation to the Pittston Hospital Association.

$17,000.00 total appropriation.

SECTION 1. *Be it enacted, &c.*, That the sum of seventeen thousand dollars, or so much thereof as may be necessary, be and the same is hereby specifically appropriated to the Pittston Hospital Association for the two fiscal years beginning June first, one thousand eight hundred and ninety-three, for the following purposes, namely:

Items.

The sum of ten thousand dollars, or so much thereof as may be necessary, for the purpose of maintenance of said hospital; and the sum of seven thousand dollars, or so much thereof as may be necessary, for the purpose of constructing a sewer, erecting fences and grading the grounds.

How payable.

The said appropriation to be paid on the warrant of the Auditor General on a settlement made by him and the State Treasurer, but no warrant shall be drawn on settlement made until the directors or managers of said institution shall have made, under oath to the Auditor General, a report containing a specifically itemized statement of the receipts from all sources and expenses of said institution, together with a specifically itemized report of the cost of said sewer, fencing and grading said grounds during the previous quarter, with the cash balance on hand, and the same is approved by him and the State Treasurer, nor until the Treasurer shall have sufficient money in the treasury, not otherwise appropriated, to pay the quarterly instalments due said institution; and unexpended balances of sums appropriated for specific purposes shall not be used for other purposes, whether specific or general, and shall revert to the State Treasury at the close of the two fiscal years.

Itemized statement.

Unexpended balances shall revert to the State Treasury.

APPROVED—The 2d day of June, A. D. 1893.

ROBT. E. PATTISON.

No. 215.

AN ACT

Making an appropriation to the Pennsylvania Institution for the Deaf and Dumb.

$274,000.00 total appropriation.

SECTION 1. *Be it enacted, &c.*, That the sum of two hundred and seventy-four thousand dollars, or so much thereof as may be necessary, be and the same is hereby specifically appropriated to the Pennsylvania Institution for the Deaf and Dumb for the two fiscal years beginning June first, one thousand eight hundred and ninety-three, for the following purposes, namely:

The sum of two hundred and thirty-four thousand dollars, or so much thereof as may be necessary, for expenses incurred in the education and maintenance of four hundred and fifty indigent deaf and dumb children from the several counties of the Commonwealth, at an annual rate of two hundred and sixty dollars per capita. *$234,000.00 for education and maintenance.*

The sum of ten thousand dollars, or so much thereof as may be necessary, for furniture and equipment of new buildings at Mount Airy. *$10,000.00 for furniture.*

The sum of fifteen thousand dollars, or so much thereof as may be necessary, for erection of walls and fences and improvements of the grounds surrounding said buildings at Mount Airy. *$15,000.00 for walls and fences.*

The sum of fifteen thousand dollars, or so much thereof as may be necessary, for the erection of a hospital building, separate and apart from the other buildings of said institution at Mount Airy : *Provided,* That no part of this appropriation shall become available until the management of this institution shall have filed with the State Board of Public Charities and the Auditor General a declaration that hereafter all pupils received into this institution, under sixteen years of age, who have not been pupils in another institution of a similar character, shall be taught exclusively by the oral method, unless physically incapable of being taught by such method. *$15,000.00 for a hospital building.* *Pupils must be taught by oral method.*

The said appropriation to be paid on the warrant of the Auditor General on a settlement made by him and the State Treasurer, but no warrant shall be drawn on settlement made until the directors or managers of said institution shall have made, under oath to the Auditor General, a report containing a specifically itemized statement of the receipts from all sources and expenses of said institution, together with a specifically itemized statement of the cost of furniture and equipments of new buildings, improvements of grounds and hospital buildings et cetera, and the names and residence of pupils chargeable under this act during the previous quarter, with the cash balance on hand, and the same is approved by him and the State Treasurer, nor until the Treasurer shall have sufficient money in the treasury, not otherwise appropriated, to pay the quarterly instalments due said institution : and unexpended balances of sums appropriated for specific purposes shall not be used for other purposes, whether specific or general, and shall revert to the State Treasury at the close of the two fiscal years. *How payable.* *Itemized statement.* *Unexpended balances shall revert to the State Treasury.*

Approved—The 2d day of June, A. D. 1893.

ROBT. E. PATTISON.

No. 216.

AN ACT

Making an appropriation to the Harrisburg Hospital.

$20,000.00 appropriated.

SECTION 1. *Be it enacted, &c..* That the sum of twenty thousand dollars, or so much thereof as may be necessary, be and the same is hereby specifically appropriated to the Harrisburg Hospital for the two fiscal years beginning June first, one thousand eight hundred and ninety-three, for the following purposes, namely:

Items.

The sum of ten thousand dollars, or so much thereof as may be necessary, for the purchase of land adjacent to property of the hospital on Front street in the city of Harrisburg; and the sum of ten thousand dollars, or so much thereof as may be necessary, for the erection of an addition to the present hospital build-

Proviso before appropriation shall become available.

ing: *Provided*, That before any part of said appropriation shall become available, the treasurer of said hospital shall file with the Auditor General a sworn statement, setting forth the fact that the hospital has received by gift from the owner a piece of property of the present value of six thousand dollars, lying adjacent to the hospital property, and the title to which is vested in the hospital in fee simple free of all incumbrances.

How payable.

The said appropriation to be paid on the warrant of the Auditor General on a settlement made by him and the State Treasurer, but no warrant shall be drawn on settlement made until the directors or managers of said institution shall have made, under oath to the Auditor General, a report containing a specifically item-

Itemized statement.

ized statement of the receipts from all sources and expenses of said institution, together with an itemized statement of the cost of addition to present hospital et cetera, during the previous quarter, with the cash balance on hand, and the same is approved by him and the State Treasurer, nor until the Treasurer shall have sufficient money in the treasury, not otherwise appropriated, to pay the quarterly instalments due

Unexpended balances shall revert to the State Treasury.

said institution; and unexpended balances of sums appropriated for specific purposes shall not be used for other purposes, whether specific or general, and shall revert to the State Treasury at close of the two fiscal years.

APPROVED—The 2d day of June, A. D. 1893.

ROBT. E. PATTISON.

No. 217.

AN ACT

Making an appropriation to the State Hospital for Injured Persons of the anthracite coal region of Pennsylvania, near Ashland.

SECTION 1. *Be it enacted, &c.*, That the following sums, or so much thereof as may be necessary, be and are hereby specifically appropriated to the State Hospital for injured persons of the anthracite coal region of Pennsylvania for the two fiscal years commencing June first, Anno Domini one thousand eight hundred and ninety-three, to be paid in equal quarterly instalments, except the sums appropriated for dining room and enlarging kitchen and dormitories, for extension to corridor, for leveling and cementing floors and for improvements to light supply, out of any money in the treasury, not otherwise appropriated.

For dining room and enlarging kitchen and dormitories, seven thousand dollars, or so much thereof as may be necessary. $7,000.00 for kitchen.

For extension to corridor, two thousand five hundred dollars, or so much thereof as may be necessary. $2,500.00 for corridor.

For leveling and cementing floors, one thousand dollars, or so much thereof as may be necessary. $1,000.00 for floors.

For improvements to light supply, fifteen hundred dollars, or so much thereof as may be necessary. $1,500.00 for light.

For salaries of officers and employés and for the support and maintenance of the institution, for the two fiscal years commencing June first, Anno Domini one thousand eight hundred and ninety-three, sixty-four thousand dollars, or so much thereof as may be necessary: *Provided*, That the superintendent shall, after the passage of this act, for three consecutive weeks, and yearly hereafter for the same length of time, commencing on the second Monday of March, advertise in three newspapers of general circulation for bids to furnish all needed supplies for the year beginning June first, next ensuing. Said superintendent shall furnish promptly on application, to all persons desiring to bid, an itemized list of the kind and probable amount required. The board of trustees shall, at a stated meeting, open such lists and award the contract for supplies to the lowest and best bidder, taking such security for the faithful performance of such contract as they may deem necessary. $64,000.00 for salaries.

Superintendent shall advertise for bids to furnish supplies.

Trustees shall open bids and award contract.

The said appropriation to be paid on the warrant of the Auditor General on a settlement made by him and the State Treasurer, but no warrant shall be drawn on settlement made until the trustees of said institution shall have made, under oath to the Auditor General, a report containing a specifically itemized statement of the receipts from all sources and expenses of said institution, together with a specifically itemized statement of the cost of said improvements during the pre- How payable.

Itemised statement.

vious quarter, with the cash balance on hand, and the same is approved by him and the State Treasurer, nor until the Treasurer shall have sufficient money in the treasury, not otherwise appropriated, to pay the quarterly instalments due said institution; and unexpended balances of sums appropriated for specific purposes shall not be used for other purposes, whether specific or general, and shall revert to the State Treasury at the close of the two fiscal years.

Unexpended balances shall revert to the State Treasury.

APPROVED—The 2d day of June, A D. 1893.

ROBT. E. PATTISON.

No. 218.

AN ACT

Making an appropriation to the German Hospital, Philadelphia.

$20,000.00 appropriated.

SECTION 1. *Be it enacted, &c.*, That the sum of twenty thousand dollars, or so much thereof as may be necessary, be and the same is hereby specifically appropriated to the German Hospital of Philadelphia, for the maintenance of said hospital, for the two fiscal years commencing June first, one thousand eight hundred and ninety-three.

How payable.

The said appropriation to be paid quarterly on the warrant of the Auditor General on a settlement made by him and the State Treasurer, but no warrant shall be drawn on settlement made until the directors or managers of said institution shall have been made, under oath to the Auditor General, a report containing a

Itemized statement.

specifically itemized statement of the receipts from all sources and the expenses of said institution during the previous quarter, with the cash balance on hand, and the same is approved by him and the State Treasurer, nor until the Treasurer shall have sufficient money in the treasury, not otherwise appropriated, to pay the

Unexpended balances shall revert to the State Treasury.

quarterly instalments due the institution; and unexpended balances of sums appropriated for specific purposes shall not be used for other purposes, whether specific or general, and shall revert to the State Treasury at the close of the two fiscal years.

APPROVED—The 2d day of June, A. D. 1893.

ROBT. E. PATTISON.

No. 219.

AN ACT

To establish an emergency fund to be used, as occasion may require, in the suppression of epidemics, the prevention of disease and protection of human life in time of disease or disasters, and making an appropriation therefor.

$50,000.00 appropriated for emergency fund.

SECTION 1 *Be it enacted, &c.*, That the sum of fifty thousand dollars be and the same is hereby specifically appropriated and set apart, out of any money in the treasury not otherwise appropriated, for the purpose of creating an emergency fund to be used as occasion may require by the State Board of Health in the suppression of epidemics, prevention of diseases and protection of human life in times of disease or disaster, beyond the relief of individual and organized charity. The money herein appropriated shall be held in the Treasury of the Commonwealth, and whenever the State Board of Health shall determine that the public health is threatened, either by epidemic or as a result of great disaster, to such an extent that the local authorities and individual or organized charity are unable to meet the emergency, they shall pass a resolution to that effect, stating all the facts in the case and the reasons for considering that State aid is needed, and to what amount, and transmit the same to the Governor. If the resolution and the reasons therein set forth shall meet with the approval of the Governor, Auditor General and State Treasurer, they shall so certify and file the resolutions and certificate of approval in the office of the Auditor General, who shall then draw his warrant upon the State Treasurer for the amount approved by the Governor, Auditor General and State Treasurer, and place the same in the hands of the treasurer of the State Board of Health, to be used for the purpose set forth in the resolution approved as aforesaid. and for no other purpose. If after the said epidemic shall have been suppressed, or the sickness or danger averted, there shall still be a balance of the amount drawn left in the hands of the treasurer of the State Board of Health, he shall, without delay, return the same to the State Treasurer, and it shall become a part of that said emergency fund. He shall also file with the Auditor General a specifically itemized statement, made under oath, of the expenditures of said moneys, as soon as possible.

When money is needed Board of Health shall transmit resolution to Governor, stating amount necessary.

Who shall approve resolution.

Auditor General shall draw warrant for amount approved and place same in hands of treasurer of Board of Health.

Unexpended balances shall revert to the State Treasury.

Itemized statement shall be filed.

APPROVED—The 2d day of June. A. D. 1893.

ROBT. E. PATTISON.

No. 220.

AN ACT

Making an appropriation to the State Asylum for the Chronic Insane, for furnishing, insuring and equipping the said institution, and for defraying the expense of transferring patients thereto.

SECTION 1. *Be it enacted, &c.*, That the sum of fifty thousand dollars is hereby specifically appropriated to the trustees of the State Asylum for the Chronic Insane of Pennsylvania, when appointed, or so much thereof as may be necessary, for furnishing, insuring and equipping said institution.

$50,000.00 appropriated for furnishing, &c.

$5,000.00 for transfering chronic insane patients.

SECTION 2. That the further sum of five thousand dollars is hereby specifically appropriated to the trustees aforesaid, or so much thereof as may be necessary, for the purpose of defraying the expense of transferring chronic insane patients from the State hospitals, county almshouses and poor houses to said asylum.

How payable.

The said appropriation to be paid on the warrant of the Auditor General on a settlement made by him and the State Treasurer, but no warrant shall be drawn on settlement made until the trustee of said institution shall have made, under oath to the Auditor General,

Itemized statement.

a report containing a specifically itemized statement of the receipts from all sources and expenses of said institution during the previous quarter, with the cash balance on hand, and the same is approved by him and the State Treasurer, nor until the Treasurer shall have sufficient money in the treasury, not otherwise appropriated, to pay the quarterly instalments due said in-

Unexpended balances shall revert to the State Treasury.

stitution; and unexpended balances of sums appropriated for specific purposes shall not be used for other purposes, whether specific or general, and shall revert to the State Treasury at the close of the two fiscal years.

APPROVED—The 2d day of June. A. D. 1893.

ROBT. E. PATTISON.

No. 221.

AN ACT

Making an appropriation to the Commissioners of Fisheries for the propagation of fish, the protection and distribution thereof.

$30,000.00 appropriated.

SECTION 1. *Be it enacted, &c.*, That the sum of thirty thousand dollars, or so much thereof as may be necessary, be and the same is hereby specifically appropriated to the State Fishery Commissioners for the two fiscal years beginning June first, one thousand eight hundred and ninety-three, for the purpose of hatching, propagat-

Purpose.

ing and distributing useful food and game fishes, and to stock and supply all the streams, lakes and waters of the Commonwealth with the same by distributing the young or fry to all parts of the State, and for the dissemination of any varieties of fish in the waters of the State, and to employ the necessary labor, service, materials and implements therefor, and to pay the necessary and reasonable expenses of the said Fishery Commissioners, and to pay for any improvements and repairs necessary in the

$10,000.00 for salaries of Water Bailiffs.

State hatcheries. And the further sum of ten thousand dollars, or so much thereof as may be necessary, is hereby specifically appropriated for the salaries and expenses of the water bailiffs the commissioners may appoint, or may have appointed, the said sum to cover the salaries and expenses of the same for the two years aforesaid.

The said apppropriation to be paid on the warrant of *How payable* the Auditor General on a settlement made by him and th(State Treasurer, but no warrant shall be drawn on settlement made until the officers of said commission shall have made, under oath to the Auditor General, a report containing a specifically itemized statement of the *Itemized statement.* expenses of said commission during the previous quarter, and the same is approved by him and the State Treasurer, nor until satisfactory proof shall have been made to the Auditor General that no fish or fry have been shipped or furnished to any person from the State fisheries or hatcheries upon any application unless the same shall have been endorsed by the Senator or Repré- *Endorsement of application for fish or fry.* sentative or Representatives from the county or district for which the said fish or fry shall have been furnished, nor until the Treasurer shall have sufficient money in the treasury, not otherwise appropriated, to pay the quarterly instalments due said commission; and unexpended bal- *Unexpended balances shall revert to the State Treasury.* ances of sums appropriated for specific purposes shall not be used for other purposes, whether specific or general, and shall revert to the State Treasury at the close of the two fiscal years.

APPROVED—The 2d day of June, A. D. 1893.

ROBT. E. PATTISON.

No. 222.

AN ACT

Making an appropriation for the South Western Normal School, located at California, Washington county, Pennsylvania.

SECTION 1. *Be it enacted, &c.,* That the sum of fifteen *$15,000.00 appropriated.* thousand dollars, or so much thereof as may necessary, is hereby specifically appropriated to the South Western State Normal School, located at California, Washington county, Pennsylvania, for the two fiscal years commencing June first, one thousand eight hundred and ninety-three, to cover the deficiency of a new building already completed: *Provided,* That before any part said appropriation shall be paid, the trustees of said school shall cause a mortgage to be placed upon said ground and *Mortgage shall be placed on grounds and buildings* building for the amount of money hereby appropriated, to be executed to the Commonwealth, creating a lien upon said property: *Provided further,* That a policy of insurance shall be placed upon the said school *Property shall be insured.* property in favor of the Commonwealth for a sum of not less than two-thirds of the value of the same.

The said appropriation to be paid on the warrant of *How payable.* the Auditor General on a settlement made by him and '⌐ State Treasurer, but no warrant shall be drawn on ⌐lement made until trustees of said institution shall ⌐ave made, under oath to the Auditor General, a report containing an itemized statement of the receipts from all *Itemized statement*

17—LAWS.

sources during the previous quarter, and an itemized statement showing cause of deficiency, the same is approved by him and the State Treasurer, nor until the Treasurer shall have sufficient money in the treasury, not otherwise appropriated, to pay the quarterly instalments due said institution; and unexpended balances of the sums appropriated for specific purposes shall not be used for other purposes, whether specific or general, and shall revert to the State Treasury at the close of the two fiscal years.

APPROVED—The 2d day of June, A. D. 1893.

ROBT. E. PATTISON.

Unexpended balances shall revert to the State Treasury.

No. 223.

AN ACT

Making an appropriation to the York Hospital and Dispensary.

$2,000.00 appropriated.

SECTION 1. *Be it enacted, &c.,* That the sum of two thousand dollars, or so much thereof as may be necessary, is hereby specifically appropriated to the York Hospital and Dispensary Association, for the purpose of maintenance, for the two fiscal years commencing June first, one thousand eight hundred and ninety-three.

How payable.

The said appropriation to be paid quarterly on the warrant of the Auditor General on a settlement made by him and the State Treasurer, but no warrant shall be drawn on settlement made until the directors or managers of said institution shall have made, under oath to the Auditor General, a report containing a specifically

Itemized statement

itemized statement of the receipts from all sources and the expenses of said institution during the previous quarter, with the cash balance on hand, and the same is approved by him and the State Treasurer, nor until the Treasurer shall have sufficient money in the treasury, not otherwise appropriated, to pay the quarterly instal-

Unexpended balances shall revert to the State Treasury.

ments due said institution; and unexpended balances of sums appropriated for specific purposes shall not be used for other purposes, whether specific or general, and shall revert to the State Treasurer at the close of two fiscal years.

APPROVED—The 2d day of June, A. D. 1893.

ROBT. E. PATTISON.

No. 224.

AN ACT

Making an appropriation for the relief of the State Normal School of the Sixth district, located at Bloomsburg, Pennsylvania.

$50,000.00 appropriated.

SECTION 1. *Be it enacted, &c.,* That the sum of fifty thousand dollars, or so much thereof as may be necessary, be and the same is hereby specifically appropriated to the State Normal School, located at Bloomsburg, Columbia county, for the two fiscal years beginning June first, one thousand eight hundred and ninety-three, for the purpose of paying for erection, furnishing, heating and lighting of a building now in process of construction, which is to supply additional class rooms, dormitories and a gymnasium: *Provided*, That no part of the said appropriation shall become available until the trustees of said Normal School shall have caused a mortgage to be placed upon the grounds and buildings for the amount of money hereby appropriated, to be executed to the Commonwealth, creating a lien upon said property: *Provided further*, That the school property shall be insured, for the benefit of the Commonwealth, for a sum not less than two-thirds of the value of the same. *Purpose*

Mortgage shall be placed on grounds and buildings.

Property shall be insured.

The said appropriation to be paid on the warrant of the Auditor General on a settlement made by him and the State Treasurer, but no warrant shall be drawn on settlement made until the trustees of said Normal School shall have made, under oath to the Auditor General, a report containing a specifically itemized statement of the receipts from all sources and expenses of said Normal School, together with a specifically itemized statement of the cost of said building, furnishing et cetera during the previous quarter, with cash balance on hand, and the same is approved by him and the State Treasurer, nor until the Treasurer shall have sufficient money in the treasury, not otherwise appropriated, to pay the quarterly instalments due said Normal School; and unexpended balance of sums appropriated for specific purposes shall not be used for other purposes, whether specific or general, and shall revert to the State Treasury at the close of the two fiscal years. *How payable.*

Itemized statement.

Unexpended balances shall revert to the State Treasury.

APPROVED—The 2d day of June, A. D. 1893.

ROBT. E. PATTISON.

No. 225.

AN ACT

Making an appropriation to the State Normal School, located at Kutztown, Berks county, Pennsylvania.

SECTION 1. *Be it enacted, &c.*, That the sum of seventeen thousand five hundred dollars, or so much thereof as may be necessary, be and the same is hereby specifically appropriated to the State Normal School, located at Kutztown, Berks county, Pennsylvania, for the two fiscal years commencing June first, one thousand eight hundred and ninety-three, for the purpose of completing and equipping the male dormitory building: *Provided*, That before any part of the said money shall be paid, the trustees of said school shall cause a mortgage to be placed upon the grounds and buildings for the amount *$17,500.00 appropriated.*

Mortgage shall be placed on grounds and buildings.

of money hereby appropriated, to be executed to the Commonwealth, creating a lien upon said property: *Pro vided further,* That a policy of insurance shall be placed upon the school property, in favor of the Commonwealth, for a sum not less than two-thirds of the value of the same.

Property shall be Insured.

How payable.

The said appropriation to be paid on the warrant of the Auditor General on a settlement made by him and the State Treasurer, but no warrant shall be drawn on settlement made until the trustees of said Normal School shall have made, under oath to the Auditor General,

Itemized statement.

a report containing a specifically itemized statement of the receipts from all sources and expenses of said Normal School, together with a specifically itemized statement of the cost of building and equipping said dormitory building during the previous quarter, with the cash balance on hand, and the same is approved by him and the State Treasurer, nor until the Treasurer shall have sufficient money in the treasury not otherwise appropriated, to pay the quarterly instalments due

Unexpended balances shall revert to the State Treasury

said Normal School; and unexpended balances of sums appropriated for specific purposes shall not be used for other purposes, whether specific or general, and shall revert to the State Treasury at the close of the two fiscal years.

APPROVED—The 2d day of June, A. D. 1893.

ROBT. E. PATTISON.

No. 226.

AN ACT

Making an appropriation for the maintenance of the Pennsylvania Soldiers and Sailors' Home at Erie.

$176,000.00 appropriated

SECTION 1. *Be it enacted, &c.,* That the sum of one hundred and seventy-six thousand dollars, or so much thereof as may be necessary, be and the same is hereby specifically appropriated to the Pennsylvania Soldiers and Sailors' Home at Erie for the two fiscal years beginning June first, one thousand eight hundred and ninety-three, for the maintenance of four hundred members of

Purpose.

said home, being at the annual rate of two hundred and twenty dollars per capita, and a further sum of twenty

$20,000.00 appropriated for improvements

thousand dollars, or so much thereof as may be necessary, is hereby specifically appropriated for the improvement of the buildings and grounds of said home and for the repairs of the same on account of the damage caused by the recent heavy rains and floods.

How payable.

The said appropriation to be paid on the warrant of the Auditor General on a settlement made by him and the State Treasurer, but no warrant shall be drawn or settlement made until the directors or managers of said institution shall have made, under oath to the Auditor

General, a report containing a specifically itemized statement of the receipts from all sources and expenses of said institution, together with the names and residence of the members of said home chargeable under this act during the previous quarter, with the cash balance on hand, and the same is approved by him and the State Treasurer, nor until the Treasurer shall have sufficient money in the treasury, not otherwise appropriated, to pay the quarterly instalments due said institution; and unexpended balances of sums appropriated for specific purposes shall not be used for other purposes, whether specific or general, and shall revert to the State Treasury at the close of the two fiscal years.

APPROVED—The 2d day of June, A. D. 1893.

ROBT. E. PATTISON.

Itemized statement.

Unexpended balances shall revert to the State Treasury.

No. 227.

AN ACT

Making an appropriation to the Indiana Normal School of Pennsylvania, located at Indiana, Indiana county, Pennsylvania.

SECTION 1. *Be it enacted, &c.,* That the sum of forty-four thousand dollars, or so much thereof as may be necessary, be and the same is hereby specifically appropriated to the Indiana Normal School of Pennsylvania, located at Indiana, county of Indiana, for the two fiscal years beginning June first, one thousand eight hundred and ninety-three, for the following purposes, namely:

The sum of two thousand dollars, for a new roof to present buildings; for kitchen and laundry additions, four thousand dollars; for interior changes in present building, one thousand five hundred dollars; for model school building, twelve thousand five hundred dollars; for boys' dormitory, twenty thousand dollars; for equipment of last two, four thousand dollars: *Provided,* That before any part of the money herein appropriated shall become available, the trustee of said school shall cause a mortgage to be placed upon the grounds and buildings for the amount of money herein appropriated, to be executed to the Commonwealth, creating a lien upon said property: *Provided further,* That the school property shall be insured, for the benefit of the Commonwealth, for a sum not less than two-thirds of the value of the same.

The said appropriation to be paid on the warrant of the Auditor General on a settlement made by him and the State Treasurer, but no warrant shall be drawn on settlement made until the trustees of said Normal School shall have made, under oath to the Auditor General, a report containing a specifically itemized statement of the receipts from all sources and expenses of said Nor-

$44,000.00 total appropriation.

Items.

Mortgage shall be placed on grounds and buildings.

Property shall be insured.

How payable

Itemized statement.

mal School, together with a specifically itemized statement of the cost of said new buildings and the equipment of the same during the previous quarter, with the
cash balance on hand, and the same is approved by him
and the State Treasurer, nor until the Treasurer shall
have sufficient money in the treasury, not otherwise appropriated, to pay the quarterly instalments due said
Normal School; and unexpended balances of sums appropriated for specific purposes shall not be used for
other purposes, whether specific or general, and shall
revert to the State Treasury at the close of the two fiscal
years.

APPROVFD—The 2d day of June, A. D. 1893.

ROBT. E. PATTISON.

No. 228.

AN ACT

Making an appropriation to the Pennsylvania State Normal School
of the Second district, located at Millersville, Lancaster county.

SECTION 1. *Be it enacted, &c.,* That the sum of forty
thousand dollars, or so much thereof as may be necessary,
be and the same is hereby specifically appropriated to
the Pennsylvania Normal School of the Second district
at Millersville, Lancaster county, for the two fiscal years
beginning June first, one thousand eight hundred and
ninety-three, for the following purposes, namely:

The sum of ten thousand dollars, or so much thereof as
may be necessary, for the completion of a building for
library purposes, study hall et cetera.

The sum of twenty thousand dollars, or so much thereof
as may be necessary, for the completion of a building for
scientific purposes, including a chemical laboratory, and
for manual training.

And the sum of ten thousand dollars, or so much
thereof as may be necessary, for a system of electric
lighting: *Providing,* That before said money shall be
paid, the trustees of said school shall cause a mortgage
to be placed on the grounds and buildings for the amount
of money hereby appropriated, to be executed to the
Commonwealth, creating a lien upon said property:
Provided further, That the school property shall be insured, for the benefit of the Commonwealth, for a sum of
not less than two-thirds of the value of the same.

The said appropriation to be paid on the warrant of
the Auditor General on a settlement made by him and the
State Treasurer, but no warrant shall be drawn on settlement made until the trustees of said Normal School shall
have made, under oath to the Auditor General, a report
containing a specifically itemized statement of the receipts from all sources and expenses of said Normal
School, together with a specifically itemized statement

of the cost of library building, study hall, building for scientific purposes, chemical laboratory and electric lighting et cetera, during the previous quarter, with the cash balance on hand, and the same is approved by him and the State Treasurer, nor until the Treasurer shall have sufficient money in the treasury, not otherwise appropriated, to pay the quarterly instalments due said Normal School; and unexpended balances of sums appropriated, for specific purposes shall not be used for other purposes, whether specific or general, and shall revert to the State Treasury at the close of the two fiscal years.

Unexpended balances shall revert to the State Treasury.

APPROVED—The 2d day of June, A. D. 1893.

ROBT. E. PATTISON.

No. 229.

AN ACT

Making an appropriation to the Veterinary Hospital Department of the University of Pennsylvania.

SECTION 1. *Be it enacted, &c*, That the sum of five thousand dollars, or so much thereof as may be necessary, be and the same is hereby specifically appropriated to the trustees of the University of Pennsylvania, in trust for the veterinary hospital department of said institution, for the purpose of maintenance, for the two fiscal years beginning June first, one thousand eight hundred and ninety-three.

\$5 000 00 appropriated.

The said appropriation to be paid on the warrant of the Auditor General on a settlement made by him and the State Treasurer, but no warrant shall be drawn on settlement made until the directors or managers of said institution shall have made, under oath to the Auditor General, a report containing a specifically itemized statement of the receipts from all sources and expenses of said institution during the previous quarter, with the cash balance on hand, and the same is approved by him and the State Treasurer, nor until the Treasurer shall have sufficient money in the treasury, not otherwise appropriated, to pay the quarterly instalments due said institution; and unexpended balances of sums appropriated for specific purposes shall not be used for other purposes, whether specific or general, and shall revert to the State Treasury at the close of the two fiscal years.

How payable.

Itemized statement.

Unexpended balances shall revert to the State Treasury.

APPROVED—The 2d day of June, A. D. 1893.

ROBT. E. PATTISON.

No. 230.

AN ACT

Making an appropriation to the House of Refuge.

SECTION 1. *Be it enacted, &c.,* That the sum of one hundred and twenty-five thousand dollars, or so much thereof as may be necessary, be and the same is hereby specifically appropriated to the House of Refuge, situate in the Eastern district of the State, for the following purposes, namely:

The sum of one hundred twenty thousand dollars, or so much thereof as may be necessary, towards the support of the said institution for the two fiscal years commencing on the first day of June, one thousand eight hundred and ninety-three; and the sum of five thousand dollars, or so much thereof as may be necessary, for the purpose of erecting a barn and stable, and fitting up the same, at the boys' department of said institution.

The said appropriation to be paid on the warrant of the Auditor General on a settlement made by him and the State Treasurer, but no warrant shall be drawn on settlement made until the directors or managers of said institution shall have made, under oath to the Auditor

General, a report containing a specifically itemized statement of the receipts from all sources and expenses of said institution, together with a specifically itemized statement of the cost of said barn and stable during the previous quarter, with the cash balance on hand, and the same is approved by him and the State Treasurer, nor until the Treasurer shall have sufficient money in the treasury, not otherwise appropriated, to pay the quar-

terly instalments due said institution; and unexpended balances of sums appropriated for specific purposes shall not be used for other purposes, whether specific or general, and shall revert to the State Treasury at the close of the two fiscal years.

APPROVED—The 2d day of June, A. D. 1893.

ROBT. E. PATTISON.

No. 231.

AN ACT.

Making an appropriation to the Pennsylvania Memorial Home at Brookville, Pennsylvania.

SECTION 1. *Be it enacted, &c.,* That the sum of seven thousand five hundred dollars, or so much thereof as may be necessary, be and the same is hereby specifically appropriated to the Pennsylvania Memorial Home at Brookville, for the following purposes, namely:

For the maintenance of said home, the sum of six thousand dollars, or so much thereof as may be necessary; for the education of the inmates of said home, the sum of one thousand and five hundred dollars, or so much thereof as may be necessary, for the two fiscal years beginning June first, one thousand eight hundred and ninety-three.

The said appropriation to be paid on the warrant of the Auditor General on a settlement made by him and the State Treasurer, but no warrant shall be drawn on settlement made until the directors or managers of said institution shall have made, under oath to the Auditor General, a report containing a specifically itemized statement of the receipts from all sources and expenses of said institution, together with a specifically itemized statement of the cost of the education of the inmates during the previous quarter, with the cash balance on hand, and the same is approved by him and the State Treasurer, nor until the Treasurer shall have sufficient money in the treasury, not otherwise appropriated, to pay the quarterly instalments due said institution; and unexpended balances of sums appropriated for specific purposes shall not be used for other purposes, whether specific or general, and shall revert to the State Treasury at the close of the two fiscal years.

APPROVED—The 2d day of June, A. D. 1893.

ROBT. E. PATTISON.

How payable.

Itemized statement

Unexpended balances shall revert to the State Treasury.

No. 232.

AN ACT

To provide for the current expenses of the State Board of Health and Vital Statistics for the two fiscal years commencing on the first day of June, Anno Domini one thousand eight hundred and ninety-three.

SECTION 1. *Be it enacted, &c.*, That the following sums, or so much thereof as may be necessary, be and are hereby specifically appropriated to defraying the expenses of the State Board of Health and Vital Statistics for the two fiscal years commencing on the first day of June, Anno Domini one thousand eight hundred and ninety-three:

For salary of secretary and executive officer for two years, four thousand dollars, or so much thereof as may be necessary.

For employment of necessary clerical aid in the office of the board, for postage, telegrams, express charges, rent, incidental office expenses, for traveling and other necessary expenses of the members and secretary of the board while engaged in the actual duties of the board, and for sanitary inspections, protection of water supplies and laboratory investigations and analysis, for two years, eight thousand dollars, or so much thereof as may be necessary.

The amounts expended from the above appropriation

$4,000 00 for salary

$8,000.00 for clerical aid, postage, &c.

Distribution of money

shall be distributed by the said board in accordance with the requirements of the sanitary service of the Commonwealth, and with reference to such emergencies as may arise.

The said appropriation to be paid on the warrant of the Auditor General on a settlement made by him and the State Treasurer, upon properly itemized vouchers, certified to by the president and secretary of said board. All moneys appropriated under this act and remaining unexpended at the close of the two fiscal years shall revert to the State Treasury.

APPROVED—The 2d day of June, A. D. 1893.

ROBT. E. PATTISON.

No. 233.

AN ACT

Making an appropriation to the Pennsylvania Training School for Feeble Minded Children at Elwyn, Delaware county.

SECTION 1. *Be it enacted, &c.,* That the sum of one hundred and ninety-two thousand five hundred dollars, or so much thereof as may be necessary, be and the same is hereby specifically appropriated to the Pennsylvania Training School for Feeble Minded Children, for the maintenance and training of five hundred and fifty feeble-minded children, for the two fiscal years beginning June first, one thousand eight hundred and ninety-three: *Provided,* That the amount herein appropriated shall be paid in proportion to the number of indigent children received from the various counties of this Commonwealth, at the rate of one hundred and seventy-five dollars per annum for each child, the evidence of which is to be furnished to the Auditor General.

The said appropriation to be paid on the warrant of the Auditor General on a settlement made by him and the State Treasurer, but no warrant shall be drawn on settlement made until the directors or managers of said institution shall have made, under oath to the Auditor General, a report containing a specifically itemized statement of the receipts from all sources and expenses of said institution during the previous quarter, with the cash balance on hand, and the same is approved by him and the State Treasurer, nor until the Treasurer shall have sufficient money in the treasury, not otherwise appropriated, to pay the quarterly instalments due said institution; and unexpended balances of sums appropriated for specific purposes shall not be used for other purposes, whether specific or general, and shall revert to the State Treasury at the close of the two fiscal years.

APPROVED—The 2d day of June, A. D. 1893.

ROBT. E. PATTISON.

No. 234.

AN ACT

Making an appropriation to the Pennsylvania Oral School for the Deaf.

SECTION 1. *Be it enacted,* &c., That the sum of ninety-two thousand three hundred and sixty-six dollars, or so much thereof as may be necessary, be and the same is hereby specifically appropriated to the Pennsylvania Oral School for the Deaf for the two fiscal years beginning June first, one thousand eight hundred and ninety-three, for the following purposes, namely: $92,366.00 total appropriation

For the maintenance and education of State pupils at the annual rate of two hundred and sixty dollars per capita, the sum of forty-five thousand five hundred, dollars, or so much thereof as may be necessary. $45,500.00 for maintenance and education.

For the completion of wing of building now being erected as per plans submitted to and approved by the State Board of Public Charities, the sum of seven thousand five hundred dollars, or so much thereof as may be necessary. $7,500.00 for completion of building

For building a new wing as per plans submitted to and approved by the State Board of Public Charities, the sum of thirty thousand dollars, or so much thereof as may be necessary. $30,000.00 for building new wing

For the erection of a laundry and boiler house, the sum of seven thousand dollars, or so much thereof as may be necessary. $7,000.00 for laundry and boiler house.

For the payment of a deficit in the maintenance account of said institution for the fiscal years of one thousand eight hundred and ninety-one and one thousand eight hundred and ninety-two, the sum of two thousand three hundred and sixty-six dollars, or so much thereof as may be necessary: *Provided,* That no part of this appropriation shall become available until the management of this institution shall have filed with the State Board of Public Charities and the Auditor General a declaration that hereafter all pupils received into this institution under sixteen years of age, who have not been pupils in another institution of a similar character, shall be taught exclusively the oral methods, unless physically incapable of being taught by such methods. $2,366.00 for deficit in maintenance account.

Teaching by oral method required, except in certain cases.

The said appropriation to be paid on the warrant of the Auditor General on a settlement made by him and the State Treasurer, but no warrant shall be drawn on settlement made until the directors or managers of said institution shall have made, under oath to the Auditor General, a report containing a specifically itemized statement of the receipts from all sources and expenses of said institution, together with a specifically itemized statement of the names and residence of the pupils chargeable under this act, and an itemized statement of the cost of buildings et cetera during the previous quarter, with the cash balance on hand, and the same is ap- How payable.

Itemized statement

proved by him and the State Treasurer, nor until the Treasurer shall have sufficient money in the treasury, not otherwise appropriated, to pay the quarterly instalments due said institution; and unexpended balances of sums appropriated for specific purposes shall not be used for other purposes, whether specific or general, and shall revert to the State Treasury at the close of the two fiscal years.

Unexpended balances shall revert to the State Treasury.

APPROVED—The 2d day of June, A. D. 1893.

ROBT. E. PATTISON.

No. 235.

AN ACT

Making an appropriation to the Home for the Training in Speech of Deaf Children, before they are of school age, in Philadelphia.

SECTION 1. *Be it enacted, &c.,* That the sum of thirty-six thousand dollars, or so much thereof as may be necessary, be and the same is hereby specifically appropriated to the Home for Training in Speech of Deaf Children, before they are of school age, in Philadelphia, for the two fiscal years beginning June first, one thousand eight hundred and ninety-three, for the following purposes, namely: For the maintenance and education of State pupils at the annual rate of two hundred and sixty dollars per capita, the sum of sixteen thousand dollars, or so much thereof as may be necessary; for grading of grounds and necessary additions to the buildings and furnishing the same, the sum of five thousand dollars, or so much thereof as may be necessary; for the erection of a new cottage building, furnishing the same, and incidentals thereto, the sum of fifteen thousand dollars, or so much thereof as may be necessary: *Provided,* That no part of this appropriation shall become available until the management of this institution shall have filed with the State Board of Public Charities and the Auditor General a declaration that hereafter all pupils received into this Institution under sixteen years of age, who have not been pupils in another institution of a similar character, shall be taught exclusively by the oral method, unless physically incapable of being taught by such method.

The said appropriation to be paid on the warrant of the Auditor General on a settlement made by him and the State Treasurer, but no warrant shall be drawn on settlement made until the directors or managers of said institution shall have made, under oath to the Auditor General, a report containing a specifically itemized statement of the receipts from all sources and expenses of said institution, together with a statement of the names and residences of the pupils chargeable under the provisions of this act, and an itemized statement of the cost of buildings and improvements made during the previous quar-

$36,000.00 total appropriation.

Items

Oral method shall be taught.

How payable

Itemized statement.

ter, with the cash balance on hand, and the same is approved by him and the State Treasurer, nor until the Treasurer shall have sufficient money in the treasury, not otherwise appropriated, to pay the quarterly instalments due said institution; and unexpended balances of sums appropriated for specific purposes shall not be used for other purposes, whether specific or general, and shall revert to the State Treasury at the close of the two fiscal years. *Unexpended balances shall revert to the State Treasury.*

APPROVED—The 2d day of June, A. D. 1893.

ROBT. E. PATTISON.

No. 236.

AN ACT

Making an appropriation to the State Normal School of the First District, located at West Chester, Chester county, Pennsylvania.

SECTION 1. *Be it enacted, &c.,* That the sum of thirty-five thousand dollars, or so much thereof as may be necessary, is hereby specifically appropriated to the State Normal School of the first Normal School District of Pennsylvania, located at West Chester, Chester county, Pennsylvania, for the two fiscal years commencing June first, one thousand eight hundred and ninety-three, for the following purposes, namely: *$35,000.00 total appropriation.*

The sum of twenty-five thousand dollars, or so much thereof as may be necessary, for the erection and completion of recitation hall and infirmary. *Items*

The sum of ten thousand dollars, or so much thereof as may be necessary, for the altering and refitting of the school building: *Provided,* That before said money shall be paid, the trustees of said school shall execute to the Commonwealth a mortgage for the amount of this appropriation upon the same conditions and premises as contained in the mortgages now held by the Commonwealth against said school: *Provided further,* That the school property shall be perpetually insured in reliable companies for a sum equal to the total amount of the mortgages held by the Commonwealth against said school and including the mortgage herein required. *Mortgage shall be placed on grounds and buildings.* *Property shall be insured.*

The said appropriation to be paid on the warrant of the Auditor General on a settlement made by him and the State Treasurer, but no warrant shall be drawn on settlement made until the trustees of said Normal School shall have made, under oath to the Auditor General, a report containing a specifically itemized statement of the income and expenses of said Normal School during the previous quarter, with the cash balance on hand, and the same is appr⸱⸱⸱ ⸱v him and the State Treasurer, nor until the Trea⸱⸱⸱⸱⸱ shall have sufficient money in the treasury, not otherwise appropriated, to pay the quarterly instalments due said Normal School; and *How payable* *Itemized statement.*

unexpended balances of sums appropriated for specific
purposes shall not be used for other purposes, whether
specific or general, and shall revert to the State Treasury.
APPROVED—The 2d day of June, A. D. 1893.

ROBT. E. PATTISON.

No. 237.

AN ACT

Making an appropriation for the reimbursing of the Commissioners for the Promotion of Uniformity of Legislation in the United
States.

SECTION 1. *Be it enacted, &c.*, That the sum of two
thousand dollars, or so much thereof as may be necessary, be and the same is hereby specifically appropriated
for the reimbursing of the Commissioners for the Promotion of Uniformity of Legislation in the United States
for the actual disbursements made by them for necessary
expenses in performing the duties of the appointment;
also for the actual disbursements made by them for expenses incident to holding any meeting or meetings, or
transacting any affairs of the Conference of State Boards
of Commissioners for Promoting Uniformity of Law in
the United States.

The said appropriation to be paid on the warrant of
the Auditor General on a settlement made by him and
the State Treasurer, but no warrants shall be drawn on
settlement made until the commissioner claiming reimbursement shall have rendered, under oath to the Auditor

General, a bill containing a specifically itemized statement of his actual disbursements for which reimbursement is claimed, nor until the Treasurer shall have sufficient money in the treasury, not otherwise appropriated,
to pay said commissioners.
APPROVED—The 2d day of June, A. D. 1893.

ROBT. E. PATTISON.

No. 238.

AN ACT

To carry out the provisions of acts of assembly relating to the care
and treatment of the indigent insane, approved the thirteenth
day of June, one thousand eight hundred and eighty-three, and
the twenty-second day of June, one thousand eight hundred and
ninety-one, and making an appropriation therefor.

SECTION 1. *Be it enacted, &c.*, That the sum of nine
hundred and fifty thousand dollars, or so much thereof
as may be necessary, be and the same is hereby specifically appropriated for the care and treatment of the indigent insane as prescribed by acts of assembly, approved the thirteenth day of June, one thousand eight
hundred and eighty-three, and the twenty-second day of

June, one thousand eight hundred and ninety-one, for the two fiscal years commencing on the first day of June, one thousand eight hundred and ninety-three.

The said appropriation to be paid quarterly on the warrant of the Auditor General on a settlement made by him and the State Treasurer, but no warrant shall be drawn on settlement made until the directors or managers of the respective hospitals or asylums for the insane shall have made, under oath to the Auditor General, a quarterly report containing the actual number and names of indigent insane persons received and maintained in said hospitals or asylums for the insane during the quarter, with date of admission, date of discharge or death, and showing the actual time each indigent insane person was treated and cared for. Such quarterly report or account shall be accompanied by a specifically itemized statement, made under oath, by the directors or managers, of the receipts and income from all sources whatever, and of the expenditures for all purposes whatsoever, during the quarter, together with the cash balance on hand at the beginning of or available at any time during the quarter. And any such cash balance on hand at the beginning of any quarter, or that is available during the quarter, shall be deducted from the amount chargeable for maintenance to the State for such quarter.

SECTION 2. It shall be the duty of the county commissioners, of the directors or overseers of the poor of the different counties or poor districts of the State, to report, under oath to the Auditor General, on the first days of September, December, March and June of each year, the number of indigent insane persons transferred as provided by law to the State hospitals or asylums for insane in their respective districts; said reports shall contain the name of every indigent insane person, when admitted, length of time cared for in said State hospital or asylum, and date of discharge or death.

SECTION 3. That for the neglect or refusal of the county commissioners or directors of the poor of county poor houses or almshouses or otherwise controlling the custody of such indigent insane persons, or of the directors or managers of the State hospitals or asylums wherein the indigent insane are treated and cared for, to make report to the Auditor General, as required by this act, said counties, hospitals or asylums, shall forfeit the whole amount due for the quarter in which no report was made : *Provided,* That all insane persons who apply for admission to any of said hospitals with proper papers, and are willing and able to pay their expenses be admitted, and that accommodations shall be furnished for said insane : *Provided also,* That no payment shall be made no account of the care and treatment of the insane until the Secretary of the Board of Charities shall have certified

How payable.

Quarterly report must be made.

Itemized statement.

Cash on hand at be ginning of quarter.

Reports of county commissioners and poor directors to Auditor General.

Contents of report.

If no report is made amount due for quarter shall not be paid.

Patients can pay their own expense.

When payment shall be made.

to the Auditor General that the quarterly report of the
cost of such care and treatment contains no charge except for maintenance.

APPROVED—The 2d day of June, A. D. 1893.

ROBT. E. PATTISON.

No. 239.

AN ACT

To extend the duties of the Secretary of the State Board of Agriculture.

SECTION 1. *Be it enacted, &c.*, That the Secretary of the
State Board of Agriculture shall be ex-officio a member
of the Board of Agriculture and of the Board of Trustees
of the Pennsylvania State College.

APPROVED—The 2d day of June, A. D. 1893.

ROBT. E. PATTISON.

No. 240.

AN ACT

To amend the fifth section of an act, entitled "An act making an
appropriation for the erection of a home for the training in
speech of deaf children before they are of school age," approved
June twentieth, one thousand eight hundred and ninety-one,
providing for the appointment of trustees before the actual completion of the home.

SECTION 1. *Be it enacted, &c.*, That section five of said
act which reads as follows:

Section 5, Act of
June 20, 1891, cited
for amendment.

"SECTION 5. Upon the completion of said home, the
Governor shall appoint five persons as trustees thereof,
one for one year, one for two years, one for three years,
one for four years, and one for five years, and shall thereafter at the expiration of the terms of such appointments respectively appoint a trustee for the term of five
years. Said trustees shall organize by the election of
one of their number as president, one as secretary, and
one as treasurer, and shall have charge of the management of said home and shall adopt such rules and regulations for its government as they may deem proper, and
shall report on or before the first day of November of
each year to the Auditor General of the financial condition and management of said home," be and the same is
hereby amended so as to read as follows:

Governor shall ap-
point 5 trustees.

SECTION 5. When said home shall have been sufficiently
advanced in construction to accommodate pupils, the
Governor shall appoint five persons as trustees thereof,
one for one year, one for two years, one for three years,
one for four years, and one for five years, and shall thereafter at the expiration of the terms of such appointments

respectively appoint a trustee for the term of five years. Said trustees shall organize by the election of one of their number as president, one as secretary, and one as treasurer, and shall have charge of the management of said home and shall adopt such rules and regulations for its government as they may deem proper, and shall report on or before the first day of November of each year to the Auditor General of the financial condition and management of said home.

APPROVED—The 2d day of June, A. D. 1893.

ROBT. E. PATTISON.

Organization of trustees.

Duties.

No. 241.

AN ACT

To provide for the punishment of persons wilfully procuring the publication of false statements.

SECTION 1. *Be it enacted, &c.,* That any person who wilfully states, delivers or transmits by any means whatever to the manager, editor, publisher or reporter of any newspaper, magazine, publication, periodical or serial for publication therein any libelous statement concerning any person or corporation, and thereby secures the actual publication of the same, is hereby declared guilty of a misdemeanor, and upon conviction shall be sentenced to pay a fine not exceeding five hundred dollars and undergo imprisonment for a period not exceeding two years, or either, or both, at the discretion of the court.

APPROVED—The 3d day of June, A. D. 1893.

ROBT. E. PATTISON.

Securing the publication of libelous statement a misdemeanor.

Penalty.

No. 242.

AN ACT.

To enable the surety of any trustee, committee, guardian, assignee, receiver, administrator, executor, or other trustee, or any person interested in the trust, to require the filing of statements exhibiting the manner of the investment of the trust funds, and providing for the removal of such trustee, committee, guardian, assignee, receiver, administrator, executor, or other trustee, by the court.

SECTION 1. *Be it enacted, &c.,* That in case any surety or sureties, or the representatives of any surety or sureties upon the bond of any trustee, committee, guardian, assignee, receiver, administrator, executor, or other person having trust funds in his hands, or any person interested in the trust, shall apply to the trustee, committee, guardian, assignee, receiver, administrator, executor, or other person having trust funds, in his hands, for a complete and detailed statement of the nature and char-

Request for statement of trust funds.

18—LAWS.

acter of the securities in which the said trust funds are
invested, and the said trustee, committee, guardian, assignee, receiver, administrator, executor, or other person
having trust funds in his hands, shall fail for the space
of ten days to furnish such statement, or if such statement having been furnished, it shall appear to the said
surety or sureties, or the representatives of said surety
or sureties, or other person interested in said trust, that
the funds in the hands of the said trustee, committee,
guardian, assignee, receiver, administrator, executor, or
other person having trust funds in his hands, are badly
invested so as to be likely to result in a loss to the trust,
the said surety or sureties or the representatives of said
surety or sureties, or other person interested in the trust,
may present a petition to the court having jurisdiction
of said trust, praying that an order issue requiring the
said trustee, committee, guardian, assignee, receiver, administrator, executor, or other person having trust funds
in his hands, to file in said court a complete and detailed
statement of the manner and securities in which said
trust funds are invested within twenty (20) days after
service of said order, unless the time be enlarged by the
court, whereupon the said court shall issue said order,
and if, upon such statement being filed, it shall appear
to the court that the said trustee, committee, guardian,
assignee, receiver, administrator, executor, or other person having trust funds in his hands, has used the said
trust funds himself, or has invested them in securities
outside of the State of Pennsylvania, or in securities
which are likely to cause a loss to the trust, shall order a
final account, and upon payment of the fund to his successor, or into court, the said court shall remove the said
trustee, committee, guardian, assignee, receiver, administrator, executor, or other person having trust funds in
his hands, unless in the case of investments of the fund
outside of this State it shall appear to the court that
such investments are safe and good, and not likely to result in a loss to the trust, in which case the court may by
its decree approve such investments.

SECTION 2. This act shall apply to all trusts, whether
the same be within the jurisdiction of the orphans'
court, of common pleas, or of a court of equity.

SECTION 3. All acts or parts of acts inconsistent with
this act are repealed.

APPROVED.—The 3d day of June, A. D. 1893.

ROBT. E. PATTISON.

No. 243.

A FURTHER SUPPLEMENT

To an act, entitled "An act to accept the grant of public lands by the United States for the endowment of agricultural colleges," approved April first, one thousand eight hundred and sixty-three, and making appropriations for carrying same into effect.

SECTION 1. *Be it enacted, &c.,* That in order to carry into effect the act of Congress approved July second, one thousand eight hundred and sixty-two, granting public lands to the several States for educational purposes, and the act of the Legislature of Pennsylvania, approved April first, one thousand eight hundred and sixty-three, accepting the provisions and conditions of said act of Congress, the following sums be and the same are hereby specifically appropriated to the trustees of the Pennsylvania State College for the two fiscal years beginning June first, one thousand eight hundred and ninety-three, for the following purposes, namely:

For fuel, light and water supply, the sum of seven thousand five hundred dollars, or so much thereof as may be necessary. $7,500.00 for fuel, light and water.

For repairs to buildings, the sum of eight thousand five hundred ($8,500) dollars, or so much thereof as may be necessary. $8,500.00 for repairs.

For insurance on buildings, the sum of one thousand five hundred dollars, or so much thereof as may be necessary. $1,500.00 for insurance.

For the maintenance of the department of mining engineering, including equipment and salaries of professors, the sum of sixteen thousand dollars, or so much thereof as may be necessary. $16,000.00 for department of mining engineering.

For the maintenance of the department of electrical engineering, the sum of eight thousand dollars, or so much thereof as may be necessary. $8,000.00 for department of electrical engineering.

For the maintenance of the department of chemistry, the sum of two thousand dollars, or so much thereof as may be necessary. $2,000.00 for department of chemistry.

For the maintenance of the department of civil engineering, the sum of two thousand dollars, or so much thereof as may be necessary. $2,000.00 for civil engineering.

For the maintenance of the department of agriculture, the sum of four thousand dollars, or so much thereof as may be necessary. $4,000.00 for agriculture.

For the erection of three fire escapes, the sum of one thousand seven hundred and twenty ($1,720) dollars, or so much thereof as may be necessary. $1,720.00 for fire escapes.

For equipping the new engineering building now being erected with the proper equipment for the instruction of the students in the several engineering departments, the sum of thirty thousand ($30,000) dollars, or so much thereof as may be necessary. $30,000.00 for new engineering building.

For completing the smoke stack for boiler house, three thousand five hundred dollars, or so much thereof as may be necessary. $3,500 for smoke stack.

For the maintenance and improvement of athletic grounds, one thousand dollars.

For improving the ventilation of the main college building so that a complete system of ventilation may be obtained in the said building, the sum of five thousand dollars, or so much thereof as may be necessary.

The said appropriation to be paid on the warrant of the Auditor General on a settlement made by him and the State Treasurer, but no warrant shall be drawn on settlement made until the trustees of said college shall have made, under oath to the Auditor General, a report containing a specifically itemized statement of the receipts from all sources and expenses of said college, together with a specifically itemized statement of the cost of fuel, light and water supply, repairs, insurance, fire escapes, equipment of departments and improvement of ventilation, et cetera, during the previous quarter, with the cash balance on hand, and the same is approved by him and the State Treasurer, nor until the Treasurer shall have sufficient money in the treasury, not otherwise appropriated, to pay the quarterly installments due said college ; and unexpended balances of sums appropriated for specific purposes shall not be used for other purposes, whether specific or general, and shall revert to the State Treasury at the close of the two fiscal years.

APPROVED—The 3d day of June, A. D. 1893.

ROBT. E. PATTISON.

No. 244.

AN ACT

"To regulate the employment and provide for the safety of women and children in manufacturing establishments, mercantile industries, laundry or renovating establishments, and to provide for the appointment of inspectors to enforce the same, and other acts providing for the safety or regulating the employment of said persons."

SECTION 1. *Be it enacted, &c.*, That no minor shall be employed at labor or detained in any manufacturing establishment or mercantile industry, or any laundry or renovating establishments, for a longer period than twelve hours in any day, nor for a longer period than sixty hours in any week.

SECTION 2. No child under thirteen years of age shall be employed in any factory, manufacturing or mercantile establishment, renovating works or laundry within this State. It shall be the duty of every person so employing children to keep a register in which shall be recorded the name, birth place, age and place of residence, name of parent or guardian, and date when employment ceases, of every person so employed by him under the age of sixteen years. And it shall be unlawful for any factory, manufacturing or mercantile establishment to hire or employ any child under the age of sixteen years, without there is first provided, and placed on file an affidavit made by the parent or guardian, stating the age, date and place of birth of said child. If said child have no parent or guardian then such affidavit shall be made by the child, which affidavit shall be kept on file by the employer, and which said register and affidavit shall be produced for inspection on demand by the inspector or any of the deputies appointed under this act. *Affidavit of child.*

SECTION 3. Every person, firm or corporation, employing women or children, or either, in any factory, manufacturing or mercantile establishment, or renovating works or laundry, shall post and keep posted, in a conspicuous place in every room where such help is employed, a printed notice, stating the number of hours per day for each day of the week required of such persons, and in every room where children under sixteen years of age are employed, a list of their names with their age. *Printed notice of number of hours per day.* *List of names and ages of children.*

SECTION 4. No person, firm or corporation, employing less than five persons, shall be deemed a factory, manufacturing or mercantile establishment, within the meaning of this act. *What shall be deemed a factory*

SECTION 5. The Governor shall, immediately after the passage of this act, appoint, with the advice and consent of the Senate, a Factory Inspector, at a salary of three thousand dollars per year, whose term of office shall be three years, at the expiration of which the Governor shall appoint his successor. The said inspector shall be empowered to visit and inspect at all reasonable hours and as often as practicable, the factories, workshops and other establishments in the State employing women and children. It shall also be the duties of said inspector to enforce the provisions of this act and to prosecute all violations of the same before any magistrate or any court of competent jurisdiction in the State. It shall be the duty of the Factory Inspector to report to the Governor, on or before the thirtieth day of November of each year, the names of factories inspected, the number of hands employed in each, the maximum number of hours work performed each week. Of these reports five thousand shall be published, five hundred of which shall be furnished to the Governor, two thousand to the House of Representatives, one thousand to the Senate, and fifteen hundred to the Factory Inspector's Department. *Governor shall appoint Factory Inspector.* *Salary and term* *Power of Inspector.* *Shall enforce provisions of act.* *Shall make annual report to Governor.* *Reports shall be printed.*

SECTION 6. All necessary expenses incurred by said inspector in the discharge of his duty shall be paid from the funds of the State, upon the presentation of proper vouchers for the same: *Provided,* That not more than four thousand dollars shall be expended by him therefor in any one year. *Expenses incurred by inspector.*

SECTION 7. It shall be the duty of the owner, agent or lessee of any such factory, manufacturing or mercantile establishment, where hoisting shafts or well holes are used, to cause the same to be properly and substantially enclosed or secured, if, in the opinion of the inspector, it *Shafts or well holes shall be enclosed.*

is necessary to protect the life or limbs of those employed in such establishments. It shall be the duty of the owners, agent or lessee, to provide, or cause to be provided, such proper trap or automatic doors so fastened in or at all elevator ways as to form a substantial surface when closed, and so constructed as to open and close by action of the elevator in its passage either ascending or descending.

SECTION 8. It shall also be the duty of the owner of such factory, mercantile industry of manufacturing establishment, or his agent, superintendent or other person in charge of the same, to furnish and supply, or cause to be furnished and supplied, in the discretion of the inspector, where dangerous machinery is in use, automatic shifters, or other mechanical contrivances, for the purpose of throwing on or off belts or pulleys. And no minor under sixteen years of age shall be allowed to clean machinery while in motion. All gearing and belting shall be provided with proper safe guard.

SECTION 9. It shall be the duty of the owner or superintendent to report, in writing, to the Factory Inspector all accidents or serious injury done to any person employed in such factory within twenty-four hours after the accident occurs, stating as fully as possible the cause of such injury.

SECTION 10. A suitable and proper wash and dressing room and water closets shall be provided for females, where employed, and the water closets used by females shall not adjoin those used by males, but shall be built entirely away from them, and shall be properly screened and ventilated and at all times kept in a clean condition.

SECTION 11. Not less than forty-five minutes shall be allowed for the noonday meal in any manufacturing establishment in this State. The Factory Inspector, his assistant or any of his deputies, shall have power to issue permits in special cases, allowing a shorter meal time at noon, and such permit must be conspicuously posted in the main entrance of the establishment, and such permit may be revoked at any time the inspector deems necessary, and shall only be given where good cause can be shown.

SECTION 12. That if the Inspector of Factories find that the heating, lighting, ventilation or sanitary arrangement of any shop, or factory, is such as to be injurious to the health of persons employed therein, or that the means of egress in case of fire or other disaster is not sufficient or in accordance with all the requirements of law, or that the belting, shafting, gearing, elevators, drums and machinery, in shops and factories are located so as to be dangerous to employés and not sufficiently guarded, or that the vats, pans or structures filled with molten metal or hot liquid are not surrounded with proper safe guards for preventing accident or injury to those employed at or near them, he shall notify the proprietor of such factory or workshop to make the alterations or additions necessary within sixty days, and any factory requiring exits or other safe guards provided for in fire escape law in case of fire, the same shall be erected by order of Factory Inspector regardless the exemption granted by any board of county commissioners, fire marshals or other authorities, and if such alterations and additions are not made within sixty days from the date of such notice, or within such time as said alterations can be made with proper diligence upon the part of such proprietors, said proprietors or agents shall be deemed guilty of violating the provisions of this act. ^{*(margin: May be made by Inspector.)*}

SECTION 13. The Factory Inspector, now or hereafter appointed under and by virtue of the provisions of this law, is hereby authorized to appoint such number of persons as in his judgment may be deemed necessary, not exceeding twelve, five of whom shall be females, who shall be known as deputy factory inspectors, either or any one or more of whom may be appointed to act as clerk in the main office, and whose duties it shall be to enforce the provisions of this act and of the several acts relating to factories and manufacturing establishments. The powers of said deputies shall be the same as the powers of the Factory Inspector, subject to the supervision and direction of the Factory Inspector. *(margin: Inspector may appoint twelve deputies. Clerk. Powers of deputies.)*

SECTION 14. The traveling expenses of each of said deputies shall be approved by the Inspector and audited by the Auditor General of the State before payment, and said deputy inspectors shall have an annual salary of twelve hundred dollars, to be paid monthly by the Treasurer of the State out of any moneys not otherwise appropriated. *(margin: Traveling expenses of deputies. Salary.)*

SECTION 15. Said Factory Inspector shall have power to divide the State into districts and to assign one of said deputies to each district, and may transfer any of the deputies to other districts in case the best interests of the State require it. The Inspector shall have the power of removing any of the deputy inspectors at any time. *(margin: State may be divided into districts. Removal of deputies.)*

SECTION 16. An office shall be furnished in the capitol, as soon as practicable, which shall be set apart for the use of the Factory Inspector. The Factory Inspector and his deputies shall have the same power to administer oaths or affirmations as is now given to notaries public in cases where persons desire to verify documents connected with the proper enforcement of this act. *(margin: Office for Inspector. Power to administer oaths.)*

SECTION 17. Any person who violates any of the provisions of this act, or who suffers or permits any child or female to be employed in violation of its provisions, shall be deemed guilty of a misdemeanor, and on conviction, shall be punished by a fine of not more than five hundred dollars. *(margin: Violation of act shall be a misdemeanor. Penalty.)*

SECTION 18. A printed copy of this act shall be furnished by the Inspector for each work room of every factory, manufacturing or mercantile house, where persons are employed who are affected by the provisions of this *(margin: Inspector shall furnish printed copies of this act to factories.)*

act, and it shall be the duty of the employer of the people employed therein to post and keep posted said printed copy of the law in each room.

Repealing clause.

SECTION 19. All the acts or parts of acts inconsistent with the provisions of this act are hereby repealed. Approved the twentieth day of May, Anno Domini one thousand eight hundred and eighty-nine.

APPROVED—The 3d day of June, A. D. 1893.

ROBT. E. PATTISON.

245.

AN ACT

To provide for the payment of the cost and expense of trying prisoners convicted in the courts of Huntingdon county for the violation of law while inmates of the Pennsylvania Industrial Reformatory, and for their maintenance in the county prison or penitentiary after their conviction.

Costs of trying certain inmates in Huntingdon county shall be paid by county in which they were sentenced.

SECTION 1. *Be it enacted, &c.*, That whenever any inmate of the Pennsylvania Industrial Reformatory at Huntingdon, not having been sentenced thereto by the court of Huntingdon county, shall be convicted in either of the courts of Huntingdon county of any misdemeanor or felony committed while an inmate of the said reformatory, the costs and expenses of trying such convicted inmate and of his maintenance after conviction and sentence either to the county prison of Huntingdon county or either of the penitentiaries of the State shall be paid by the county from which the said convicted inmate was sentenced.

Costs shall first be paid by Huntingdon county.

SECTION 2. The costs and expenses of the trial of such convicted inmate shall, in the first instance, be paid by the county of Huntingdon, whose commissioners are thereupon authorized to draw their warrant upon the treasurer of the county from which said convicted inmate was sentenced to the said reformatory for the amount so paid by the county of Huntingdon for said costs and expenses, which warrant it shall be the duty of the treasurer upon whom it may be drawn to forthwith pay.

Who shall pay cost of maintenance in prison to which sentenced.

SECTION 3. Whenever such convicted inmate shall be sentenced either to the county prison of Huntingdon county or to either of the penitentiaries of the State it shall be lawful for the authorities of either of such penal institutions to annually draw a warrant upon the treasurer of the county from which said inmate was originally sentenced for the costs and expense of his maintenance, and the treasurer upon whom such warrant may be drawn shall forthwith pay the same.

APPROVED—The 3d day of June, A. D 1893.

ROBT. E. PATTISON.

No. 246.

AN ACT

To authorize the retention of the two additional clerks in the office of the Adjutant General appointed with a view to the perservation of the muster rolls of the late civil war, and making an appropriation for the payment of the same.

SECTION 1. *Be it enacted, &c.*, That the Adjutant General be and he is hereby empowered to retain the two additional clerks in said department, for two years further, at a salary of twelve hundred dollars each, per year, who shall be employed to continue the work of copying these rolls in books prepared for this purpose. And the sum of forty-eight hundred dollars, or so much thereof as may be necessary, is hereby appropriated to be paid by the State Treasurer out of any moneys in the State Treasury not otherwise appropriated.

The said appropriation to be pa d on the warrant of the Auditor General on a settlement made by him and the State Treasurer upon the certified voucher of the Adjutant General.

APPROVED—The 3d day of June, A. D. 1893.

ROBT. E. PATTISON.

Margin notes: Two additional clerks. Salary. $4,800.00 appropriated. How payable

---

No. 247.

A SUPPLEMENT

To "An act empowering councils in cities of the first-class to revise and establish the line for wharves and piers and low water mark or bulkhead lines on the Delaware river in front of cities of the first class," approved June eighth, one thousand eight hundred and ninety-one, and to further authorize the acquisition by said cities of wharves, piers, bulkheads and riparian rights, and to prescribe and carry out the plans for the construction of said wharves, piers and bulkheads.

SECTION 1. *Be it enacted, &c.*, That it shall and may be lawful for cities of the first class to purchase and hold in fee simple any and all properties and improvements extending into the navigable streams in front of said cities and the rights and privileges appertaining thereto, and to totally remove, alter or modify the location, dimensions, or character of construction of the same in conformity with the plans and lines established by the Secretary of War under the authority of Congress, in order to improve and further the commercial interests of the said cities and of this Commonwealth : *Provided*, That such action shall be taken only in pursuance to and in conformity with the recommendation of the Board of Harbor Commissioners, approved by the Board of Port Wardens : *And provided further*, That such action shall be taken only in pursuance to ordinances therefor duly enacted by the councils of said cities, which said ordi-

Margin notes: May purchase and hold property extending into navigable streams. Proviso. Ordinances must be duly enacted.

nances shall clearly define the character and extent of the treatment of said properties and improvements respectfully so to be acquired for said purposes.

SECTION 2. That before such recommendation shall be made by the said boards, they shall give due notice to the owner or owners of the properties to be affected that such recommendation is contemplated and that the parties will be heard in relation thereto, and when such recommendation as aforesaid, after such hearing, shall have been made to councils and an ordinance passed in pursuance thereto, the owner or owners of the properties to

be affected shall have notice, in writing, given to him or them by the Department of Public Works of the fact that such properties will have to be removed, altered or modified, and of all the particulars of the treatment to be accorded to the same as embraced in the said ordi-

nance; and should the owner or owners, after the receipt of said notice, fail, for the period of six months thereafter, to commence and prosecute the work of removal or reconstruction as prescribed in the said notice, said cities shall have power to condemn and appropriate said properties and improvements and riparian rights, and the fee simple thereto shall become vested in the said cities for the purposes as recited in the first section of

this act: *Provided*, That the owner or owners of said properties and rights so purchased or taken shall receive compensation therefor in the mode provided for ascertaining damages by reason of change of grade of streets in cities of the first class, excepting that there shall be no assessment of benefits upon properties in the immediate vicinity.

SECTION 3. That within thirty days after the passage of the ordinance or ordinances above recited, said owner or owners shall have the right to petition the court of common pleas of the county in which such city may be situated, setting forth, the facts of the case and the ground of the petitioner's complaint, and thereupon said court, after having caused due notice of the presentation of said petition and of the time fixed for the hearing

thereof to be given to the parties in interest, shall proceed to hear and determine said matter of said petition and shall declare either that said ordinance shall be operative or inoperative and make such order for the payment of costs as justice may require, said decision to be

subject to review by the Supreme Court in the same manner as now provided with reference to proceedings in equity.

SECTION 4. In all cases where the treatment of the respective properties involves merely the removal of an existing wharf or pier to the bulkhead or arbitrary low water line and the owners of the wharf or pier so to be removed is also the owner of the bulkhead wharf or riparian rights adjoining to and extending beyond the riparian rights attached and belonging to such wharf or pier so to be removed, the condemnation proceedings

above referred to shall extend only to the acquisition of
the materials composing said wharf or pier so to be re
moved, and damages for the appropriation and removal
of the same only shall be assessed and paid, the purpose
of this provision being to leave in the riparian owner or
owners all the legal rights and privileges appertaining
to said bulkheads, the same to be exercised by him or
them under the laws of this Commonwealth.
APPROVED—The 3d day of June, A. D. 1893.

ROBT. E. PATTISON.

No. 248.

A SUPPLEMENT

To an act, entitled "An act for the compilation and publication of
the laws of the province and Commonwealth of Pennsylvania
prior to the year one thousand eight hundred," approved the
nineteenth day of May, Anno Domini one thousand eight hundred and eighty-seven amending the third section thereof and
providing for the expenses therein referred to.

SECTION 1. *Be it enacted, &c.*, That the third section
of the act of the General Assembly, entitled "An act for
the compilation and publication of the laws of the Province and Commonwealth of Pennsylvania prior to the
year one thousand eight hundred," which reads as follows: "The said commissioners shall receive no compensation for their own services, but are authorized to
employ such clerical aid as may be necessary, and the
sums of fifteen hundred dollars a year, for a period not
exceeding four years, is hereby appropriated for clerk
hire and traveling expenses, the said sums to be paid by
the State Treasurer, from time to time, upon warrants
drawn by the Auditor General upon certificates of the commissioners of the services performed, approved by the
Secretary of the Commonwealth, and filed in the office
of the Auditor General," be and the same is hereby
amended so that the same shall read as follows:

SECTION 2. The said commissioners shall receive no
compensation for their own services but are authorized
to employ such clerical aid as may be necessary, and
the sum of four thousand five hundred dollars a year,
for a period not exceeding four years from and after the
passage of this act, is hereby appropriated for clerk
hire and traveling expenses, provided that the same shall
complete the work, the sums to be paid by the State
Treasurer, from time to time, upon warrants drawn by
the Auditor General upon certificates of the commissioners of the services performed, approved by the
Secretary of the Commonwealth, and filed in the office
of the Auditor General.
APPROVED—The 3d day of June, A. D. 1893.

ROBT. E. PATTISON.

Section 3. Act of May 19, 1887, cited for amendment

Commissioners shall receive no compensation.

$4,500.00 per year appropriated for clerical aid.

How payable.

No. 249.

AN ACT

To provide for the establishing and ascertaining the lines and boundaries between two or more cities, boroughs or townships, cities and boroughs, townships and boroughs, or cities and townships, within this Commonwealth, and regulating the proceedings thereof.

Courts of quarter sessions shall have authority.

SECTION 1. *Be it enacted, &c.*, That the several courts of quarter sessions shall have authority within their respective counties to cause disputed lines and boundaries between two or more cities, boroughs or townships, cities and boroughs, townships and boroughs, or cities and townships, to be ascertained and established.

Upon application by petition court shall appoint viewers.

SECTION 2. Upon application by petition to the court of quarter sessions for the purpose of ascertaining and establishing disputed lines or boundaries between two or more cities, boroughs or townships, cities and boroughs, townships and boroughs, or cities and townships, the court shall appoint three impartial men, one of whom

Shall give notice and view lines.

shall be a competent surveyor who, after having given notice as directed by court, shall view the said lines or boundaries; and it shall be the duty of the said commissioners so appointed, or any two of them, to make a plot or draft of the lines proposed to be ascertained and established, if the same cannot be fully designated by natural lines or boundaries, all of which they, or any two of them, shall report to the next court of quarter sessions, together with their opinion of the same, and at the term

Shall make report. Review.

after that at which the report shall be made, the court shall take such order thereupon as to it shall be just and reasonable: *Provided*, That upon petition a review may

Appeal may be taken.

be ordered by said court: *And provided further*, That an appeal may be taken from the decision of said commissioners of view or review and the question of fact in dispute determined by a feigned issue to be framed by the court after the manner of framing feigned issues under existing laws, to be certified to the court of common pleas of the proper county.

Pay of commissioners.

SECTION 3. That the commissioners so appointed shall each receive three dollars per day, except the surveyor, who shall receive five dollars per day, and mileage at the rate of ten cents per mile for every mile necessarily traveled, for each and every day necessarily employed while in the performance of their duties, to be paid out of the county funds.

Lines shall be marked with stone monuments.

SECTION 4. That whenever a line is finally established by virtue of this act the court shall cause the same to be marked with stone monuments to be placed at intervals, not exceeding fifteen hundred feet from each other, the

Expenses of same.

expense thereof to be reasonable and to be first approved by the court, and to be borne equally by the municipalities interested, and the court shall compel the payment of the same according to law.

APPROVED—The 3d day of June, A. D. 1893.

ROBT. E. PATTISON.

No. 250.

AN ACT

To amend an act, entitled "A supplement to an act, entitled 'An act to create a board of public charities,' approved the twenty-fourth day of April, Anno Domini one thousand eight hundred and sixty-nine," approved the fifth day of April, Anno Domini one thousand eight hundred and seventy-two, fixing compensation of accounting officers.

SECTION 1. *Be it enacted, &c.*, That section two of an act, entitled "A supplement to an act, entitled 'An act to create a board of public charities,' approved the twenty-fourth day of April, Anno Domini one thousand eight hundred and sixty-nine," approved the fifth day of April, Anno Domine one thousand eight hundred and seventy-two, which reads as follows: "That it shall be the duty of said inspectors, sheriffs or other persons, to make return of the statements required by the first section of this act to the said board of public charities within ten days after the first day of January, April, July and October, in each year, if required by said board, and upon neglect or refusal to make statements in the manner and at the times required by this act, such inspector, sheriff or other person, so neglecting or refusing, shall forfeit and pay a fine of not less than one hundred dollars, to be sued for and collected by the general agent in the name of the board of public charities for the use of the Commonwealth," be and the same is hereby amended so as to read as follows:

That it shall be the duty of the said inspectors, sheriffs or other persons, to make return of the statements required by the first section of this act to the said board of public charities within ten days after the first day of January, April, July and October, in each year, if required by said board, for each of which statements the officer making the same shall receive the sum of ten dollars, to be paid out of the county funds of the county for which said statements shall be made, and upon neglect or refusal to make statements in the manner and at the times required by this act, such inspector, sheriff or other person so neglecting or refusing, shall forfeit and pay a fine of not more than one hundred dollars, to be sued for and collected by the general agent in the name of the board of public charities for the use of the Commonwealth.

APPROVED—The 3d day of June, A. D. 1893.

ROBT. E. PATTISON.

Section 2, Act of April 5, 1872 cited for amendment

Returns to Board of Public Charities.

Fee for making return.

Penalty for neglecting to make such return.

No. 251.

AN ACT

To amend the one hundred and eightieth section of an act, entitled "An act to consolidate, revise and amend the penal laws of this Commonwealth," approved the thirty-first day of March, eighteen hundred and sixty, so as to make the said section applicable to all penal laws of this Commonwealth.

Section 180, Act of March 31. 1860. cited for amendment.

SECTION 1. *Be it enacted, &c.*, That the one hundred and eightieth section of the act, entitled "An act to consolidate, revise and amend the penal laws of this Commonwealth," approved the thirty-first day of March, eighteen hundred and sixty, which reads: "Every principal in the second degree, or accessory before the fact, to any felony punishable under this act for whom no punishment has been hereinbefore provided, shall be punishable in the same manner as the principal in the first degree is by this act punishable; every accessory after the fact to any felony punishable under this act for whom no punishment has been hereinbefore provided, shall, on conviction, be sentenced to a fine not exceeding five hundred dollars and to undergo an imprisonment, with or without labor at the discretion of the court, not exceeding two years, and every person who shall counsel, aid or abet the commission of any misdemeanor punishable under this act for whom no punishment has been hereinbefore provided, shall be liable to be proceeded against and punished as the principal offender," be amended so as to read as follows:

Applicable to all penal laws of Pennsylvania.

Every principal in the second degree, or accessory before the fact, to any felony punishable under any act of Assembly of this Commonwealth for whom no punishment is provided, shall be punishable in the same manner as the principal in the first degree is by such act punishable; every accessory after the fact to any felony punishable under any act of Assembly of this Commonwealth for whom no punishment is provided, shall, on conviction, be sentenced to pay a fine not exceeding five hundred dollars and to undergo an imprisonment, with or without labor at the discretion of the court, not exceeding two years, and every person who shall counsel, aid or abet the commission of any misdemeanor punishable under any act of Assembly of this Commonwealth for whom no punishment is provided, shall be liable to be proceeded against and punished as the principal offender.

APPROVED—The 3d day of June, A. D. 1893.

ROBT. E. PATTISON.

No. 252.

AN ACT

To provide for the appropriate representation of the soldiers of the Pennsylvania Continental Line on the Battle Monument now being erected at Trenton, New Jersey.

WHEREAS, On the great historic battlefield of Trenton in the War of the Revolution the soldiers of this State, consisting of the First Regiment, Continental foot, Colonel Edward Hand; the First Rifle Regiment volunteers, Major Ennion Williams commanding; the German Regiment, Continental infantry, Colonel Nicholas Haussegger commanding; the Second Company, State Artillery battalion, Captain Thomas Forest commanding; the Second Company of Artillery, Philadelphia Associators, Captain Joseph Moulder commanding; and the Philadelphia Troop of Light Horse, Captain Samuel Morris commanding, took a most active and glorious part in the attack upon the town and in the great surrender of the Hessian force which followed; therefore,

SECTION 1. *Be it enacted, &c.*, That the sum of two thousand five hundred dollars, or so much thereof as may be necessary, be and the same is hereby specifically appropriated to pay for a bronze tablet to be placed on the monument erected on the battlefield of Trenton, at Trenton, New Jersey, to commemorate the deeds of the soldiers of the Pennsylvania line who participated in the battle. *$2,500.00 appropriated.* *Purpose.*

The said appropriation to be paid on the warrant of the Auditor General on a settlement made by him and the State Treasurer, but no warrant shall be drawn on settlement made until the Adjutant General of the State of New Jersey shall have furnished an itemized statement of the expense of said tablet, and that the same has been placed in position, nor until the Treasurer shall have sufficient money in the treasury not otherwise appropriated to pay the same. *How payable* *Itemized statement.*

APPROVED—The 3rd day of June, A. D. 1893.

ROBT. E. PATTISON.

No. 253.

AN ACT

To amend an act, entitled "An act to provide for the incorporation and regulation of certain corporations," approved the twenty-ninth day of April, Anno Domini one thousand eight hundred and seventy-four, as amended by the act approved the seventeenth day of April, Anno Domini one thousand eight hundred and seventy-six, providing for the incorporation of companies for the manufacture and production of silverware, plated ware, jewelry, works of ornament and art, and pictures, and the buying and selling of such articles.

SECTION 1. *Be it enacted, &c.*, That sub-division seventeen, class second, corporations for profit, in the act, en-

Sub-division 17.
Class 2d. Act of
April 29, 1874, as
amended by Act of
April 17, 1876, cited
for amenment.

titled "An act to provide for the incorporation and regulation of certain corporations," approved the twenty-ninth day of April, Anno Domini one thousand eight hundred and seventy-four, as amended by the act approved the seventeenth day of April, Anno Domini one thousand eight hundred and seventy-six, which reads as follows:

"The manufacture of iron or steel, or both, or of any other metal, or of any article of commerce from metal or wood, or both," be and the same is hereby amended to read as follows:

Providing for the
incorporation of
additional companies for profit.

The manufacture of iron or steel, or both, or of any other metal, or of any article of commerce from metal or wood, or both, and the manufacture and production of silverware, plated ware, jewelry, works of ornament and art, and pictures, and the buying and selling of such articles.

APPROVED—The 3d day of June, A. D. 1893.

ROBT. E. PATTISON.

No. 254.

AN ACT.

To repeal an act approved the twenty-sixth day of April, one thousand eight hundred and seventy, entitled "An act of Assembly relative to the election of supervisors in the township of Salem in the county of Westmoreland."

Act of April 26, 1870,
repealed.

SECTION 1. *Be it enacted, &c.*, That the act of Assembly approved the twenty-sixth day of April, Anno Domini one thousand eight hundred and seventy, entitled "An act of Assembly relative to the election of supervisors in the township of Salem in the county of Westmoreland," which reads as follows:

"SECTION 1. That hereafter the qualified voters of the township of Salem, in the county of Westmoreland, shall elect two supervisors of roads instead of four as now provided by the act of Assembly of the fifteenth of March, one thousand eight hundred and fifty-nine.

"SECTION 2. That it shall be the duty of the supervisors, elected in pursuance of the provisions of this act, to meet within ten days after their election and divide the township into two divisions as nearly equal as possible, taking into consideration the number of roads and the amount of work to be done in each division.

"SECTION 3. That at the next election at which township officers are to be elected, and at every such election thereafter under the provisions of this act, the qualified voters of said township shall vote for but one person for supervisor, and the two persons having the highest number of votes shall be declared elected to said office.

"SECTION 4. All acts and parts of acts inconsistent

with this act are hereby repealed," be and the same is hereby repealed.

APPROVED—The 3d day of June, A. D. 1893.

ROBT. E. PATTISON.

No. 255.

AN ACT

To repeal an act "Relating to the sale of seated lands in the county of Pike," approved the twelfth day of February, Anno Domini one thousand eight hundred and seventy.

SECTION 1. *Be it enacted, &c.*, That an act, entitled "An act relating to the sale of seated lands in the county of Pike," approved February twelfth, one thousand eight hundred and seventy, be and the same is hereby repealed.

APPROVED—The 3d day of June, A. D. 1893.

ROBT. E. PATTISON.

No. 256.

AN ACT.

To provide for the selection of a site and the erection of a State institution for the feeble minded, to be called the Western Pennsylvania State Institution for the Feeble Minded, and making an appropriation therefor.

SECTION 1. *Be it enacted, &c.*, That the Governor shall appoint five commissioners, who shall serve without compensation, to select a site and build an institution for the accommodation of the feeble minded children of Western Pennsylvania. Governor to appoint five commissioners to serve without compensation.

SECTION 2. Said commissioners shall select, within four months of the date of their appointment, a tract of land not less than five hundred or more than one thousand acres in extent, so located as to be most accessible by railroad facilities to the counties of Western Pennsylvania, to wit: Duties of commissioners. Location

SECTION 3. The tract of land so selected shall be good arable land, well adapted to the preservation of the health and the occupation and maintenance of the inmates of said institution, with an adequate supply of good water and natural facilities for drainage from the institution buildings, and the said tract of land so selected, and the cost thereof, shall be approved in writing by the Governor and the State Board of Public Charities before the purchase money shall be paid, and the deed for the same shall be taken in the name of the Commonwealth, but nothing herein contained shall prevent said commissioners from receiving a deed to the Commonwealth in fee for any land donated for the purpose aforesaid. Tract of land to be selected. Selection and cost thereof to be approved. Site to be deeded to the State.

19—LAWS.

Plans.

SECTION 4. The plans for said institution shall be prepared by said commissioners and approved by the State

Buildings.

Board of Public Charities. The buildings shall be of the best design for the construction of such institution, and without expensive architectural adornments, or unduly large or costly administrative accommodations,

Change of plans.

and no change shall be made in said plans of construction without the consent of the State Board of Public Charities.

Commissioners, upon approval, to select superintendent of construction, &c., and fix salaries.

SECTION 5. The said commissioners shall, with the approval of the Governor and State Board of Public Charities, have power to select a superintendent of construction and fix the salary thereof, and of such other persons as they may think necessary to employ, in order to secure the proper economical construction of said

Cost of buildings and grounds not to exceed $500,000.

buildings: *Provided*, That the total cost of said buildings and grounds shall not exceed the sum of five hundred thousand dollars.

$250,000 appropriated.

SECTION 6. To enable the commissioners to purchase the land and to erect said buildings, the sum of two hundred and fifty thousand dollars, or so much thereof as may be necessary, is hereby specifically appropriated,

How payable.

to be drawn from the treasury as the same may be required, on warrants drawn by the Auditor General in the usual manner, vouchers or statements to be furnished approved by the Secretary of the State Board of Public Charities before any warrant is issued.

Department buildings.

SECTION 7. The buildings shall be in two groups, one for the educational and industrial department, and one for the custodial or asylum department, with such other

Sub-divisions.

sub-divisions as will best classify and separate the many diverse forms of the infirmity to be treated, and shall embrace one or more school houses, a gymnasium and drill hall, a work shop, and an isolating hospital, all on

Accommodation for eight hundred inmates.

such scale as will create an institution to accommodate not less than eight hundred inmates or patients, planned and located for easy and natural additions as population demands.

Building to be completed within three years.
Report of progress to be made.

SECTION 8. Said commissioners shall proceed to erect said buildings and complete the same within three years from the passage of this act, and shall make report to the State Board of Public Charities of the amount of money expended by them, and of the progress made in the erection of the buildings, semi-annually at least, and

Semi-annually or oftener.

oftener if so required by the Board.

Upon completion of institution Governor to appoint board of trustees to take charge.

SECTION 9. The said commissioners, upon the completion of the said institution, shall surrender their trust to a board of trustees, to consist of nine members, who shall serve without compensation, and be appointed by the Governor by and with the advise and consent of the Senate. Said trustees shall be a body politic or corpor-

Name.
Duties of trustees.

ate of the name and style of the State Institution for Feeble Minded of Western Pennsylvania. They shall manage and direct the concerns of the institution, and make all necessary by-laws and regulations not inconsistent with the Constitution and laws of the Commonwealth. Of the trustees first appointed three shall serve for one year, three for two years, and three for three years, and at the expiration of the respective periods the vacancies shall be filled by the Governor by appointment for three years, as hereinbefore provided, and should any vancacy occur by death or resignation, or otherwise, of any trustee, such vacancy shall be filled by appointment, as aforesaid, for the unexpired term of such manager.

SECTION 10. That this institution shall be entirely and specially devoted to the reception, detention, care and training of idiotic and feeble-minded children, and shall be so planned in the beginning and construction as shall provide separate classification of the numerous groups embraced under the terms idiotic and imbecile or feeble-minded. Cases afflicted with either epilepsy or paralysis shall have a due proportion of space and care in the custodial department. It is specifically determined that the processes of an agricultural training shall be primarily considered in the educational department, and that the employment of the inmates in the care and raising of stock and the cultivation of small fruits, vegetables, roots et cetera, shall be made largely tributary to the maintenance of the institution.

SECTION 11. There shall be received into the institution feeble-minded children, under the age of twenty years, whose admission may be applied for as follows:

First. By the father if father and mother are living together.

Second. If father and mother are not living together then by one having custody of the child.

Third. By the guardian duly appointed.

Fourth. By the superintendent of any county orphanage.

Fifth. By the person having the management of any other institution or asylum where children are cared for.

Under items three, four and five, consent of parents if living is not required.

All inmates are subject to such rules and regulations as the board of trustees may adopt.

SECTION 12. The form of application for admission into the institution and the necessary checks to improper admissions shall be such as the board of trustees, with the approval of the State Board of Charities, may prescribe, and each application shall be accompanied by answers, under oath, to such interrogatories as the trustees shall by rule require to be propounded.

SECTION 13. Any parent or guardian who may wish to enter a child into said institution for treatment, culture or improvement, and pay all expenses of such care, may do so under terms, rules and regulations prescribed by the superintendent and approved by the trustees.

SECTION 14. Said board shall receive as inmates of said institution feeble-minded children, residents of this State under the age of twenty years, who shall be incapable of receiving instruction in the common schools of this State. Said board shall prescribe and cause to be printed instructions and forms of application for the admission of such, and shall include therein interrogatories to which they shall require answers, under oath, showing such facts as they may be needed for the information of said trustees. Such printed instructions and forms shall be furnished to all applicants for the admission of any person or patient in whole or in part as a State beneficiary,

and shall be endorsed by the board of commissioners or directors of the poor of the county in which he or she resides at the time of the making of the application.

SECTION 15. Adults who may be determined to be feeble-minded, and who are of such inoffensive habits as to make them proper subjects for classification and discipline in an institution for the feeble-minded, can be admitted on pursuing the same course of legal commitment as govern admission to the State Hospital for the Insane.

SECTION 16. The board of commissioners or directors of the poor of a county in approving an application for the admission of a person to said institution, shall state whether or not such child has an estate of sufficient value, or a parent or parents of sufficient financial ability to defray the expense in whole or in part of supporting such child in said institution, and if there be such means of support, in part only, then the amount per month which the parents or parent or the legal guardian of such child may be able to pay, and the person or persons who make the application for such admission shall therein make

statement under oath as to such means of support. Said board of trustees in accepting an application for the admission of any person shall fix the amount, if any, which shall be paid for such support according to the ability of the parents or parent of the person or according to the value of such person's estate, if any, and shall require payment for such support, so far as there may be ability to pay, as a condition to the admission or retention of said person. Said amount may at any time be changed

by said trustees according to their information concerning such means of support. Where the indigence of the

child or its family be such as to require its admission upon the full beneficiary fund of the State, the ascertainment of the facts shall be as hereinbefore stated, and the

support at the institution shall be provided for by annual appropriations at such per capita rates as shall be appropriated by the Legislature on the application of the trustees, after submission and approval of the same by the State Board of Public Charities.

SECTION 17. Said board shall have authority to receive for the use of said institution such gifts, legacies, devises and conveyances of property, real or personal, that may be made, given or granted to or for such institution or in its name or the name of said board.

SECTION 18. The said board of trustees shall appoint a skillful physician who shall be superintendent and shall be competent to oversee and direct the medical, hygienic, educational and industrial interests of the institution, and shall have charge and supervision of the entire institution, both professional and otherwise. He shall name for appointment such and so many assistants, attendants and employes, as may be considered necessary by the said board of trustees, and, with the approval of the trustees, shall appoint a steward who shall have charge, under the direction of such superintendent, of the employment of the inmates of said institution and the purchase, production and distribution of all supplies, under such rules and regulations as may be established by such trustees.

Board of trustees to appoint a physician as superintendent of entire institution.

He shall name, with approval of trustees, his assistant, and shall appoint a steward.

The salaries of the superintendent, matrons, teachers, assistants and attendants of the institution, shall be fixed by the board of trustees.

Salaries of superintendent &c., to be fixed by board of trustees.

SECTION 19. The said trustees shall make, under oath, by their president or treasurer, a quarterly report to the Auditor General of the State and to the State Board of Public Charities, containing an itemized statement of the receipts from all sources and the expenses of the institution during the previous quarter, and unless such itemized report is made and approved by the State Board of Public Charities, Auditor General and State Treasurer, the State Treasurer is hereby directed not to pay any more money to said institution until such report is made as aforesaid.

Itemized quarterly statement of receipts and expenses to be made to the Auditor General, unless approved, State Treasurer not to pay more money.

SECTION 20. The Governor, judges of the several courts of the Commonwealth, members of the Legislature and the Board of Public Charities shall be ex-officio visitors of said institution.

Ex-officio visitors.

APPROVED—The 3d day of June, A. D. 1893.

ROBT. E. PATTISON.

No. 257.

A SUPPLEMENT

To an act, entitled "An act to establish a health office and to secure the city and port of Philadelphia from the introduction of pestilential and contagious diseases, and for other purposes," approved the twenty-ninth day of January, one thousand eight hundred and eighteen (1818,) empowering the Governor to suspend the State Quarantine creating a Quarantine Board, authorizing the Governor to appoint a Quarantine Physician, and to purchase or lease or acquire land for a State Quarantine Station, and thereupon to abandon the present Lazaretto.

WHEREAS, Congress has recently enacted a general quarantine law, dated fifteenth of February, one thousand eight hundred and ninety-three, to be administered by federal officers stationed in foreign countries, and by the

Federal Marine Hospital service acting as quarantine officers at stations on or near the navigable waters of the United States, and there is reason to believe that the Federal Quarantine for the Delaware Bay and River will be fully equipped and in effective operation during the coming summer;

And whereas, The multiplication of quarantine visits and inspections on board ship during one and the same entry into the port of Philadelphia cannot fail to interfere with the expeditious movements of maritime commerce, causing hindrance and delay, and possible conflict among the Federal and State Quarantine authorities; therefore,

Governor may suspend operations of State quarantine.

SECTION 1. *Be it enacted, &c.,* That whenever it shall be shown to the satisfaction of the Governor of Pennsylvania that the government of the United States has established, and is maintaining at the Delaware Bay entrance to the port of Philadelphia, an effective and sufficient quarantine to secure this Commonwealth against the introduction of pestilential, contagious or infectious diseases, as is contemplated by the act of January twenty-ninth, one thousand eight hundred and eighteen, and its supplements, and other quarantine laws of the State, it shall be lawful for the Governor, and he is hereby em powered, to suspend by public proclamation the operation of the State Quarantine in part or in whole in his discretion as he shall deem it best for the public health and safety.

And may re-establish complete quarantine service.

In any and every case the Governor shall have, and is hereby given, discretionary power and authority to re-establish and maintain a complete quarantine service whenever through the failure of the Federal Government to maintain an efficient service, or from any other cause such action may be necessary.

Whenever State shall possess quarantine station, present Lazaretto shall be abandoned and turned over to city of Philadelphia.

SECTION 2. Whenever the State shall acquire and possess a quarantine station, other than the Lazaretto, to be used for the same or similar purposes, and be declared by the Governor to be ready for occupancy and use as a quarantine station sufficient for the use and necessities of the port of Philadelphia in guarding against the introduction of pestilential, contagious or infectious diseases into said port, said new station shall be brought into use in lieu of the Lazaretto, and the present Lazaretto shall thereafter be abandoned and turned over to the city of Philadelphia.

Lazaretto shall be discontinued after July 1, 1895.

But in any event the present Lazaretto shall, from and after July first, one thousand eight hundred and ninety-five, be discontinued for quarantine purposes. To the end that the quarantine station contemplated in this and the last preceding section shall be established at as early

Governor authorized to acquire suitable place.

a day as practicable, the Governor of this Commonwealth is hereby authorized and empowered to negotiate for and purchase, lease or acquire by eminent domain, on Reedy Island, or failing that at some suitable place on the waters of Delaware river or bay, either within or without the territorial limits of the State, if a concession from a State

bordering on Delaware Bay shall be obtained, land suffi- Where located
cient and suitable for the purpose, which, if on the main-
land, shall not be within two miles of any incorporated
city or borough, and to invite bids and make contracts Shall invite bids for construction of suitable buildings &c
for the construction of all necessary and suitable build-
ings for the uses and duties of the station and for the furnishing and full equipment of the same, with all suitable
and necessary furniture and appliances, subject however
to appropriations to be made according to law. Subject
to the provisions of this section, the Governor may use May use present Lazaretto station.
the present Lazaretto station in Tinicum township, if
satisfactory arrangements for the use of the same can be
made with the city of Philadelphia. For this purpose
the Governor is hereby authorized and empowered to Governor empowered to lease Lazaretto.
lease the said Lazaretto, upon such terms as shall be sat-
isfactory to him and the city of Philadelphia, or if such
terms cannot be agreed upon, the Governor may, if the
said city will consent thereto, agree to an arbitration to
fix the rental to be paid therefor, the Governor to name
one arbitrator, the mayor of the said city of Philadelphia
to name another, and the two thus chosen to select a third.
The sum agreed upon by the arbitrators thus chosen, or
by any two of them, to be final and conclusive.

The State Quarantine Board hereafter designated shall, Steam tug shall be leased or purchased.
if satisfactory terms can be made with the city, purchase
the steam tug now used by the quarantine officers. If
satisfactory terms cannot be made the said board shall
lease or purchase another tug.

The said board shall appoint, and at pleasure discharge, Board shall appoint pilots, engineers &c.
the pilots, engineers, firemen, tugmen, stewards, nurses,
gardners, watchmen and other servants and employés
necessary to man the said tug and carry on the said
station.

The said board shall further have power to purchase Board may purchase materials &c.
from the city of Philadelphia such of the material, ap-
paratus and supplies now on hand at the Lazaretto station
as they shall require.

SECTION 3. The following shall constitute a State Quar- State Quarantine Board, who shall constitute.
antine Board for the port of Philadelphia: The President
of the College of Physicians of Philadelphia, or a member
of said college to be designated by the President; the
Secretary of the State Board of Health; the President of
the Philadelphia Maritime Exchange, or a member of
said Exchange to be designated by the president; the
health officer appointed in pursuance of the act to which
this is a supplement; the quarantine physician provided
for in this act; a sixth member to be appointed by the
mayor of the city of Philadelphia; and a seventh member to be appointed by the Governor of Pennsylvania.
The members of the board as above constituted shall Terms of members of board.
serve for the following terms, respectively: The sixth
and seventh members of the aforesaid board appointed by
the Governor of Pennsylvania and the mayor of Philadelphia shall hold office for the term of two years, respectively, from the dates of their respective appointments,

and their successors shall hold office for like periods; the Secretary of the State Board of Health, the Quarantine Physician and the Health officer shall hold office as members of the board during their respective terms as Secretary of the State Board during their respective terms as Secretary of the State Board of Health, as Quarantine Physician and as Health Officers. If the President of the College of Physicians of Philadelphia and the President of the Maritime Exchange of Philadelphia serve upon the board, they shall hold office during their respective terms as President of the College of Physicians and as President of the Maritime Exchange; but should a member of the College of Physicians or a member of the Maritime Exchange serve upon the board in place of the presidents of these bodies such members shall hold office for a term of three years from the dates of their respective appointments, and their successors shall hold office for like periods respectively.

Board shall make rules and regulations.

The board thus constituted, shall, from and after the date when this act goes into effect, make such rules and regulations not inconsistent with the laws of the United States and of this Commonwealth, as they may deem necessary for the government and management of the quarantine station, and for the detention of vessels, their crews and passengers, the disinfection of vessels and their crews, passengers, baggage and cargo: *Provided*,

Which shall be approved by the Governor.

That the general rules and regulations established by such board shall first receive the approval of the Governor, and shall be published in such manner as the Governor shall direct.

Meetings of board.

They shall meet at certain stated periods as they may elect, at least once in every month, and also upon such special occasions as the health and safety of the Commonwealth may require, and also upon call of the Governor.

Office of board.

The said board shall rent an office in the city of Philadelphia and may, if it be deemed necessary, employ a clerk. All the necessary expenses of the said board, office rent, clerk hire, stationery, fuel and care of office, shall be paid by the State.

Officers of board.

The said board shall elect a president and secretary, define their duties, fix their term of office, and make such rules for their own government as they deem proper.

Governor shall appoint quarantine physician.

SECTION 4. The Governor is hereby authorized and required to appoint one physician who shall be denominated the quarantine physician. The quarantine physician shall be the executive officer of the quarantine station.

Requirements.

He shall be a practicing physician and a graduate of at least ten (10) years standing.

Powers.

He shall enforce all laws, rules and regulations, as provided for in this act, or as may be provided by the rules and regulations of the State Quarantine Board, respecting the detention, inspection and disinfection of vessels and their crews, passengers, baggage and cargoes, bound to any place within the Commonwealth of Pennsylvania on the Delaware river. The quarantine physician shall keep a record in book form of all vessels inspected by him, showing the date of inspection and the disposition made of each vessel. He shall also keep a hospital record in the usual form. He shall have the assistance of two deputies, to be appointed by himself, who shall receive as compensation the sum of two thousand dollars each, and the said quarantine physician, or one of his deputies, shall be on duty continuously at the quarantine station. The quarantine physician shall receive an annual salary of five thousand dollars. His salary and that of his deputies shall be paid by the State.-

The said deputies shall have and exercise all the powers and duties by this act, or by the rules and regulations of the State Quarantine Board, imposed upon the quarantine physician. They shall be graduates of at least three years' standing.

SECTION 5. The Health Officer appointed in pursuance of the act to which this is a supplement shall establish a public office at or within three squares of the custom house in said city, to be known as the quarantine office, which shall be open from nine Ante Meridian until five Post Meridian throughout the year, Sundays and holidays excepted, whereat all masters and captains of vessels may deliver the health certificate required by law, or make affidavit as to the health of the vessel as hereinafter provided. All certificates shall be filed and preserved in good order and a register shall be kept of all vessels and the names of captains or masters to whom the same are granted and the ports from which the vessels respectively sailed. He shall collect all fees, as hereafter provided, and issue a health ticket. All fees collected by him shall be paid over monthly to the State Treasurer. He shall receive a salary of five thousand dollars per annum, to be paid by the State, as the salaries of other State officers are paid. He shall perform all services now required of him by existing laws, except as they are altered by this act, for which he shall continue to receive the salary now provided by law. He shall have the authority to appoint three clerks, one to be paid a salary of one thousand two hundred dollars by the State, one to be paid a salary of one thousand two hundred dollars by the city of Philapelphia, and one a salary of eight hundred dollars to be paid by the city, in equal monthly payments.

SECTION 6. All vessels coming from any port or place outside this Commonwealth and bound to any place on the Delaware river, or its tributaries, within this Commonwealth shall submit to such detention, disinfection, or other regulation at the said quarantine station as may be deemed necessary by the Quarantine Physician, or as may be provided by the rules and regulations of the State Quarantine Board for the protection of the people of this

Margin notes:
Shall keep records.

Deputies and their compensation.

Salary of quarantine physician.

Powers of deputies.

Health officer shall establish a public office.

Certificates and register of vessels.

Fees and salary.

Duties.

Clerks and their salaries.

Detention of vessels.

Quarantine physi-
cian shall give cer-
tificate permitting
vessel to proceed.
Commonwealth. When the Quarantine Physician shall be satisfied that the admission of such vessel into the port shall not be dangerous to the health of the people of this Commonwealth, he shall give a certificate permitting such vessel to proceed to the place of destination, which certificate the captain or master of such vessel shall present at the quarantine office in the city of Philadelphia, within twenty-four hours after her arrival, who shall thereupon,

Fees and health
ticket.
upon payment by him of the fees herein provided for, have delivered to him by the officer in charge thereof a receipt or health ticket. Whenever the State Quarantine

Proceedings when
Governor shall sus-
pend the State
quarantine service.
service shall be suspended by the Governor in accordance with the provisions of this act, the master of every vessel arriving from a port without this Commonwealth, excepting ports on the Delaware river and bay above Reedy Island, shall, within twenty-four hours after the arrival of his vessel, appear at the quarantine office in the city of Philadelphia, and shall make an affidavit, under oath or affirmation to be administered by the said health officer, or in his absence by the clerk in charge of such quarantine office, who are hereby severally empowered to administer the same, setting forth the name of his vessel, the port from which he has sailed, that a certificate of health has been granted to him by the officers in charge of the Federal Quarantine station, and that the same has been deposited with the collector of the port in compliance with the regulations of the Federal authorities, and that no contagious or infectious diseases has developed on said vessel after her release from the Federal Quarantine, and shall thereupon pay to the person in charge of the quarantine office the fees herein specified, and shall receive a receipt or health ticket. Failure to report his vessel will subject the vessel to a fine of two hundred and fifty dollars, to be recovered as such fines are now recoverable by law, the action thereof to be brought by the health officers. If it shall appear either by said affidavit or otherwise that any contagious or infectious disease has developed on any vessel after her release from the Federal Quarantine, the Quarantine Physician may order such vessel back to said Federal quarantine station for further inspection and treatment. On receiving from the captain or master of any vessel the certificate of health as directed by this act, or upon making and filing the affidavit as to the health of the vessel herein required, such captain or master shall pay to the health officer, or the person in charge of said quarantine

Fees to be paid on
receipt of certificate
of health.
office, a fee according to the following rates: Any steam vessel arriving from a foreign port shall pay the sum of ten dollars; any sailing vessel arriving from a foreign port shall pay the sum of five dollars; and any coasting vessel, sail or steam, arriving from a port south of Saint Mary river shall pay the sum of two dollars and fifty cents. No fee shall be collected from vessels other than specified.

SECTION 7. The expense and charge of boarding, lodging, medicines, nursing and maintenance, and other necessaries provided for the persons landed and sent to the State Quarantine station, and all other expenses, salaries or wages, incident to the maintenance of said quarantine station, and of the persons detained there, and of the tug boat, and of the said quarantine office in the city of Philadelphia, and of the office of the State Quarantine Board, shall be paid and discharged by the Commonwealth. Expense of boarding, &c., of persons sent to State quarantine station shall be paid by the Commonwealth.

SECTION 8. If any person landed and sent to the State Quarantine station by any officer having authority to do so, or any person arriving in any vessel and detained at the quarantine station as aforesaid, shall refuse or neglect to obey the directions of the quarantine physician, or any deputy of his, and the rules and regulations established by the State Quarantine Board, from time to time agreeably to the provisions of this act, the person so neglecting or refusing shall for each and every offense, on being thereof legally convicted, forfeit and pay a fine of not more than five hundred dollars to be recovered by the health officer. Penalty for refusing to obey directions of quarantine physician.

SECTION 9. If any master, commander or pilot, shall permit any part of the cargo or baggage of any person arriving in any vessel to be landed on either shore of the Delaware bay or river, except at a Federal or State quarantine station, or suffer any person except the pilot to come on board before a certificate shall have been obtained as herein provided, unless by permission of the quarantine physician, or one of his deputies, or unless imminent danger of the loss of the vessel or lives of the crew shall render assistance necessary, the person or persons permitting, and the person or persons so landed or going on board, shall, upon conviction, forfeit and pay a fine of not more than five hundred dollars to be recovered by the health officer. Penalty for permitting cargo or persons to be landed before a certificate is obtained.

SECTION 10. This act shall go into effect on July first, one thousand eight hundred and ninety-three, from and after which date the offices of lazaretto physician and quarantine master shall cease to exist. When act shall go into effect.

SECTION 11. If the State Quarantine is suspended by the Governor, the Board of Health of any municipality shall, when notified by the Quarantine physician, or if the Quarantine physician is not on duty, or cannot at once be found, without such notification, have power, if any vessel shall arrive with contagious or infectious disease on board, to deal with the said vessel, its cargo, its passengers, the crew and their baggage, as may be deemed best to protect the people of this Commonwealth against the introduction of the disease then infecting the vessel, cargo, passengers or crew. When State quarantine is suspended board of health of any municipality may act.

SECTION 12. For the purpose of this act and of the act to which this is a supplement, the port of Philadelphia shall include all the counties that abut upon the navigable waters of the Delaware river and the navigable tributaries thereof within this Commonwealth. Territory to be included in Port of Philadelphia.

Repeal

SECTION 13. All acts or parts of acts inconsistent with this act are hereby repealed: *Provided however*, That nothing herein contained shall repeal, alter or amend,
Shall not repeal Act of April 2, 1821 and supplements
the act of second April, one thousand eight hundred and twenty-one, entitled "A supplement to the act, entitled 'An act for establishing a health office and to secure the city and port of Philadelphia from the introduction of pestilential and contagious disease, and for other purposes,'" or the several supplements thereto:
Nothing in act shall interfere with duties of port physician.
And provided further, That nothing in this act contained shall interfere in any wise with the duties now devolving on the officer known as the Port Physician, so far as they relate to the administration of the health laws of the city of Philadelphia, but from and after the date
Who shall appoint port physician.
at which this act goes into effect, he shall be appointed by the Director of the Department of Public Safety of the city of Philadelphia and receive such salary as the councils of said city shall designate:
Shall not alter powers of Board of Health of Philadelphia.
And provided further, That nothing herein contained shall abridge, alter or repeal, any of the powers now vested in the Board of Health of the city of Philadelphia, relating to the health laws of said city, but the power of said board over *Maratime* Quarantine shall cease.

APPROVED—The 5th day of June, A. D. 1893.

ROBT. E. PATTISON.

No. 258.

AN ACT

To provide for the ordinary expenses of the Executive, Judicial and Legislative departments of the Commonwealth, interest on the public debt, and for the support of the Public Schools, for the years Anno Domini one thousand eight hundred and ninety-three and one thousand eight hundred and ninety-four.

Appropriations for two years commencing June 1, 1893.
SECTION 1. *Be it enacted, &c.*, That the following sums be and the same are hereby specifically appropriated to the several objects hereinafter named for the fiscal years commencing the first day of June, one thousand eight hundred and ninety-three, and the first day of June, one thousand eight hundred and ninety-four, to be paid out of any moneys in the Treasury not otherwise appropriated.
Salaries of State officers, clerks, expenses. &c.
SECTION 2. For the payment of the salaries of the several State officers, the clerks and employés in the several departments of the State government, and for the incidental expenses of the said departments, the sum of five hundred and fifty-two thousand six hundred and fifty-nine dollars and twenty-six cents, or so much thereof as may be necessary, the same to be paid by the State Treasurer in the amounts as follows and in the manner prescribed by law.

EXECUTIVE DEPARTMENT.

For the payment of the salary of the Governor, two years, twenty thousand dollars, or so much thereof as may be necessary. Governor.

For the payment of the salary of the Lieutenant Governor, two years, eight thousand dollars, or so much thereof as may may be necessary. Lieutenant Governor.

For the payment of clerk hire, two years, sixteen thousand four hundred dollars, or so much thereof as may be necessary. Clerk hire

For the payment of contingent expenses, two years, four thousand dollars, or so much thereof as may be necessary. Contingent expenses.

For the payment of a clerk to Lieutenant Governor to June first, one thousand eight hundred and ninety-one, inadvertently omited from act of one thousand eight hundred and ninety-one, the sum of four hundred and fifty-eight dollars and thirty cents. Clerk to Lieutenant Governor.

For the payment of a clerk to the Lieutenant Governor, for two years, the sum of twenty-two hundred dollars, or so much thereof as may be necessary.

STATE DEPARTMENT.

For the payment of the salary of the Secretary of the Commonwealth, two years, eight thousand dollars, or so much thereof as may be necessary. Secretary of the Commonwealth.

For the payment of the salary of the Deputy Secretary of the Commonwealth, two years, five thousand dollars, or so much thereof as may be necessary. Deputy Secretary

For the payment of clerk hire, two years, forty-two thousand dollars, or so much thereof as may be necessary. Clerk hire

For the payment of contingent expenses, two years, six thousand dollars, or so much thereof as may be necessary. Contingent expenses.

For indexing pamphlet laws, one hundred dollars, or so much thereof as may be necessary. Indexing laws.

For indexing titles of corporations for publication with the laws, one hundred dollars, or so much thereof as may be necessary. Indexing corporations.

For the payment of postage and other expenses incident to the distribution of copies of the laws of one thousand eight hundred and ninety-three to the prothonotary of each court of common pleas in the State as required by the act of Assembly of May the eighteenth, one thousand eight hundred and ninety-three, six hundred dollars, or so much thereof as may be necessary. Distributing laws to prothonotaries.

For the payment of expenses in enforcing the provisions of the laws requiring foreign corporations and certain other corporations to file statements and returns in said department, two years, one thousand dollars, or so much thereof as may be necessary. Enforcing laws relating to foreign corporations.

For the payment of clerical and other expenses, including postage and express charges of the Secretary of the Commonwealth in receiving, filing and keeping for Clerical and other expenses of Secretary of Commonwealth in filing nomination papers.

public inspection, the certificates of nomination and nomination papers required by law to be filed in his office, and in the preparation and furnishing of duplicate official lists of all candidates nominated as required by law, two years, the sum of three thousand dollars, or so much thereof as may be necessary.

AUDITOR GENERAL'S DEPARTMENT.

Auditor General.

For the payment of the salary of the Auditor General, two years, six thousand dollars, or so much thereof as may be necessary.

Clerk hire.

For the payment of clerk hire, two years, forty-nine thousand eight hundred dollars and ninety-six cents, or so much thereof as may be necessary.

Execution of corporation tax laws.

For the payment of execution of corporation tax laws, two years, two thousand dollars, or so much thereof as may be necessary.

Contingent expenses.

For the payment of contingent expenses, two years, four thousand dollars, or so much thereof as may be necessary.

Stenographer. &c.

For the payment of a stenographer and typewriter and temporary clerical assistance, for two years, five thousand dollars, or so much thereof as may be necessary: *Provided*, Services as such shall be required for said time.

TREASURY DPAPTMENT.

State Treasurer.

For the payment of the salary of the State Treasurer, two years, ten thousand dollars, or so much thereof as may be necessary.

Clerk hire.

For the payment of clerk hire, two years, twenty-one thousand four hundred dollars, or so much thereof as may be necessary.

Stenographer &c.

For the payment of a stenographer and typewriter, for two years, two thousand dollars, or so much thereof as may be necessary: *Provided*, Services as such shall be required for the said time.

Temporary clerical assistance

For temporary clerical assistance in transferring and re-indexing the accounts of corporations and other accounts in the State Treasurer's office, the sum of three thousand dollars, or so much thereof as may be necessary.

Contingent expenses

For the payment of contingent expenses, two years, two thousand dollars, or so much thereof as may be necessary.

ATTORNEY GENERAL'S DEPARTMENT.

Attorney General.

For the payment of the salary of the Attorney General, two years, seven thousand dollars, or so much thereof as may be necessary.

Deputy Attorney General.

For the payment of the salary of the Deputy Attorney General, two years, eight thousand dollars, or so much thereof as may be necessary.

Clerk hire

For the payment of clerk hire, two years, seven thousand four dollars, or so much thereof as may be necessary.

For the payment of contingent expenses, two years, two thousand dollars, or so much thereof as may be necessary.

Contingent expenses.

For the payment of associate counsel fees and other expenses incurred by the Attorney General's department in the prosecution of the cases against the Philadelphia and Reading Railroad Company, Philadelphia and Reading Coal and Iron Company, the Lehigh Valley Railroad Company, and other coal producing and coal transporting companies, the sum of three thousand five hundred dollars, or so much thereof as may be necessary, to be paid on the warrant of the Auditor General upon vouchers properly certified to and approved by the Attorney General.

Associate counsel fees.

DEPARTMENT OF INTERNAL AFFAIRS.

For the payment of the salary of the Secretary of Internal Affairs, two years, six thousand dollars, or so much thereof as may be necessary.

Secretary of Internal Affairs

For the payment of clerk hire, two years, sixty-two thousand dollars, or so much thereof as may be necessary.

Clerk hire.

For the payment of contingent expenses, for two years, five thousand dollars, or so much thereof as may be necessary.

Contingent expenses.

For the payment of traveling and other incidental expenses for the collection of statistics by the Bureau of Industrial Statistics of the Department of Internal Affairs, for each of the fiscal years commencing June first, one thousand eight hundred and ninety-three and one thousand eight hundred and ninety-four, the sum of six thousand dollars, or so much thereof as may be necessary; said amount to cover the contingent fund provided by the act of one thousand eight hundred and seventy-four, in addition thereto the expenses of the collectors of statistics appointed under the act of April fourth, one thousand eight hundred and eighty-nine. (Pamphlet Laws page twenty-six.)

Expenses of Bureau of Industrial Statistics.

For the payment of the services rendered and the expenses incurred in the collection and compilation of the tax statistics as required by the act of May ninth, one thousand eight hundred and eighty-nine. (Pamphlet Laws 157), the following amounts, or so much thereof as may be necessary :

For services, &c., incurred in collection and compilation of tax statistics.

For the fiscal year ending May thirty-first, one thousand eight hundred and ninety-four, the sum of five thousand dollars, and for the fiscal year ending May thirty-first, one thousand eight hundred and ninety-five, the sum of five thousand dollars, to be paid upon the warrant of the Auditor General upon specifically itemized vouchers properly certified to by the Secretary of Internal Affairs.

For the payment of the services and expenses to be incurred in the examination and repairs of the boundary line monuments between the State of Pennsylvania and

Expenses, repairs, &c., to boundary line monuments

other States as required by the second section of the act
approved May fourth, one thousand eight hundred and
eighty-nine (Pamphlet Laws eighty-two), for the two
fiscal years ending May thirty-first, one thousand eight
hundred and ninety-five, the sum of two thousand dollars, or so much thereof as may be necessary, to be paid
upon the warrant of the Auditor General upon specifically itemized vouchers properly certified to by the Secretary of Internal Affairs.

BANKING DEPARTMENT.

Superintendent of Banking. For the payment of the salary of the Superintendent
of Banking, for two years, eight thousand dollars, or so
much thereof as may be necessary.

Deputy superin-tendent. For the payment of the salary of the Deputy Superintendent of Banking, for the two years, five thousand dol-
lars, or so much thereof as may be necessary,

Stenographer. For the payment of a stenographer and typewriter,
two years, one thousand eight hundred dollars, or so
much thereof as may be necessary.

Clerk hire. For the payment of clerk hire, for two years, eight
thousand two hundred dollars, or so much thereof as may
be necessary.

Contingent expenses. For the payment of contingent expenses, for two years,
three thousand six hundred dollars, or so much thereof
as may be necessary.

DEPARTMENT OF PUBLIC INSTRUCTION.

Superintendent of Public Instruction. For the payment of the salary of the Superintendent
of Public Instruction, two years, five thousand dollars, or
so much thereof as may be necessary.

Clerk hire. For the payment of clerk hire, two years, seventeen
thousand four hundred dollars, or so much thereof as may
be necessary.

Contingent expenses. For the payment of contingent expenses, two years, six
thousand dollars, or so much thereof as may be neces-
sary.

Circulating school journal. For the payment of circulating the Pennsylvania
School Journal, two years, five thousand dollars, or so
much thereof as may be necessary.

ADJUTANT GENERAL'S DEPARTMENT.

Adjutant General. For the payment of the salary of the Adjutant General,
two years, five thousand dollars, or so much thereof as
may be necessary.

Clerk hire. For the payment of clerk hire in Adjutant General's
office and employés at the State Arsenal, two years,
twenty-four thousand eight hundred dollars, or so much
thereof as may be necessary.

Contingent expenses. For the payment of contingent expenses, including
shipping of arms and so forth, two years, seven thousand
eight hundred dollars, or so much thereof as may be
necessary.

For repairs to State Arsenal buildings, fences and grounds, two thousand dollars, or so much thereof as may be necessary.

Repairs to State Arsenal.

STATE LIBRARY.

For the payment of the salary of the State Librarian, two years, five thousand dollars, or so much thereof as may be necessary.

State Librarian.

For the payment of the salary of the First Assistant State Librarian, two years, three thousand six hundred dollars, or so much thereof as may be necessary.

First assistant.

For the payment of the salary of the Second Assistant State Librarian, two years, three thousand dollars, or so much thereof as may be necessary.

Second assistant.

For the payment of the salary of the messenger, two years, two thousand dollars, or so much thereof as may be necessary.

Messenger.

For salary of night-watchman, two years, eighteen hundred dollars, or so much thereof as may be necessary.

Watchman.

For freight, expressage, postage, cleaning room and miscellaneous expenses, four thousand dollars, or so much thereof as may be necessary.

Sundry expenses.

For purchase of law books and exchanges, three thousand dollars, or so much thereof as may be necessary.

Law books.

For purchase of miscellaneous books, five thousand dollars, or so much thereof of each as may be necessary.

Miscellaneous books.

For the proper arranging and indexing the paper books of the Supreme Court deposited in the State Library, the sum of one thousand dollars, or so much thereof as may be necessary.

Arranging and indexing paper books.

For annual subscription to at least one leading newspaper in each county of the Commonwealth for permanent preservation, one thousand dollars, or so much thereof as may be necessary.

Newspaper subscriptions.

For the purchase of such of the English Parliamentary papers as may be deemed advisable by the Librarian and the Trustees of the State Library, five hundred dollars, or so much thereof as may be necessary.

English parliamentary papers.

For the payment of the salaries of two cataloguers for completing a catalogue of the State Library, the sum of four thousand dollars, or so much thereof as may be necessary: *Provided,* That said cataloguers shall not receive more than one hundred dollars each per month for the time actually employed.

Cataloguers.

DEPARTMENT OF PUBLIC PRINTING AND BINDING.

For the payment of the salary of the Superintendent of Public Printing and Binding, two years, four thousand dollars, or so much thereof as may be necessary.

Superintendent.

For the payment of contingent expenses, two years, six hundred dollars, or so much thereof as may be necessary.

Contingent expenses.

For the payment of rent of office, two years, two hundred dollars, or so much thereof as may be necessary.

Office rent

20—LAWS.

Clerk hire.

For salary of a clerk and bookkeeper, for two years, one thousand dollars, or so much thereof as may be necessary.

STATE REPORTER.

State Reporter.

For the payment of the salary of State Reporter, two years, six thousand dollars, or so much thereof as may be necessary.

Clerk hire and stationary.

For stationery, clerk hire and assistance, two years, six thousand dollars, or so much thereof as may be necessary.

PUBLIC BUILDINGS AND GROUNDS.

Superintendent.

For the payment of the salary of Superintendent of Public Buildings and Grounds, two years, two thousand eight hundred dollars, or so much thereof as may be necessary.

Watchmen.

For the payment of the salary of five watchmen, two years, nine thousand dollars, and for uniforms for the

Uniforms.

said five watchmen and elevator man as prescribed by the Board of Public Buildings and Grounds, three hundred dollars, or so much thereof as may be necessary.

Attendant at elevator.

For the person in charge of the elevator, two years, eighteen hundred dollars, or so much thereof as may be necessary.

BOARD OF SINKING FUND COMMISSIONERS.

Commissioners.

For the payment of the salaries of three commissioners, two years, one thousand eight hundred dollars, or so much thereof as may be necessary.

Clerk.

For the payment of the salary of clerk, two years, two thousand dollars, or so much thereof as may be necessary.

BOARD OF PARDONS.

Members of board.

For the payment of the salaries of the members of the board, two years, four thousand dollars, or so much thereof as may be necessary.

Recorder

For the payment of the salary of the recorder of the board, two years, one thousand dollars, or so much thereof as may be necessary.

Clerk.

For the payment of the salary of clerk, two years, one thousand dollars, or so much thereof as may be necessary.

Messenger.

For the payment of the salary of messenger, two years, eight hundred dollars, or so much thereof as may be necessary.

BOARD OF REVENUE COMMISSIONERS.

Members of board.

For the payment of salaries of the three members of the board, two years, one thousand eight hundred dollars, or so much thereof as may be necessary.

Clerk.

For the payment of the salary of clerk, two years, six hundred dollars, or so much thereof as may be necessary.

FACTORY INSPECTORS AND DEPUTIES.

For the payment of the Factory Inspector, two years, six thousand dollars, or so much thereof as may be necessary. Factory Inspector.

For the payment of twelve Deputy Factory Inspectors, two years, twenty-eight thousand eight hundred dollars, or so much thereof as may be necessary. Deputy Inspectors.

For the payment of contingent expenses of the Factory Inspector, two years, eight thousand dollars, or so much thereof as may be necessary. Contingent expenses.

For the payment of the traveling expenses of the deputies, two years, twelve thousand dollars, or so much thereof as may be necessary. Traveling expenses.

HARBOR OFFICERS, PHILADELPHIA.

For the payment of salary of harbor master, two years, five thousand dollars, or so much thereof as may be necessary. Harbor Master.

For the payment of the salaries of the deputies, messenger, engineer and fireman of the steam launch, for two years, the sum of twelve thousand dollars, or so much thereof as may be necessary. Deputies and other employes.

For rent and care of office, stationery, telephone and official expenses of harbor master, for two years, one thousand dollars, or so much thereof as may be necessary. Sundry expenses.

For repairs, coal oil and equipment of steam launch, for two years, fifteen hundred dollars, or so much thereof as may be necessary. Steam launch.

For payment to executrix of the estate of Robert S. Patterson, deceased, late harbor master of Philadelphia, to reimburse for expenditures made by the late harbor master Patterson, in relation to purchase and repairs to steam launch, "Galatea," one thousand dollars, or so much thereof as may be necessary. To be paid upon the warrant of the Auditor General upon a specifically itemized statement approved by him. Estate of Robert S Patterson.

For the payment of the salary of the port warden, two years, five thousand dollars, or so much thereof as may be necessary. Port warden.

For the payment of salary of the Quarantine Physician, for two years, ten thousand dollars, or so much thereof as may be necessary. Quarantine Physician.

For the payment of the salary of the Health Officer, for two years, the sum of ten thousand dollars, or so much thereof as may be necessary. Health officer.

For the payment of the salaries of the two deputy Quarantine Physicians and one clerk for the Health Officer, for two years, the sum of ten thousand four hundred dollars. Deputy Quarantine Physicians.

For rent of an office for the State Quarantine Board, care of office, stationery, clerk hire, telephone and official expenses of the Board, for two years, the sum of two thousand dollars. Sundry expenses of State Quarantine Board.

Sundry expenses of Health Officer.

For rent and care of office for the Health Officer, for two years, the sum of one thousand dollars.

Sundry expenses of Quarantine Station.

For rent of the State Quarantine Station, salaries and wages of all employes, and cost of the maintenance of said Quarantine Station as required by law, for two years, the sum of twenty-six thousand dollars, or so much thereof as may be necessary.

JUDICIARY DEPARTMENT.

Judiciary.

SECTION 3. For the payment of the salaries of the judges of the Supreme Court and the salaries and mileage of the president and other law judges of the several courts of common pleas in the Commonwealth and the judges of the separate orphans' courts and for the compensation of common pleas judges holding courts in other districts and for the payment of the salaries and mileage of associate judges, the sum of one million one hundred and eighty-five thousand two hundred dollars, or so much thereof as may be necessary, for the fiscal years one thousand eight hundred and ninety-three and one thousand eight hundred and ninety-four.

Payable quarterly.

Payments to be made quarterly on August thirty-first, November thirtieth, February twenty-eighth, and May thirty first, of each year, but when in case of

Payment in case of death, &c.

death, resignation or expiration of term of office of a judge, salary for a fraction of a quarter is due him, the same shall be computed so as not to increase or diminish the salary he is entitled to receive under the several acts of Assembly fixing the compensation of judges.

SUPREME COURT JUDGES.

Supreme Court Judges.

For the payment of the salaries of the Supreme Court judges, two years, one hundred and thirteen thousand dollars, or so much thereof as may be necessary.

Clerk hire.

For the payment of the salaries of seven clerks, two years, fourteen thousand dollars, or so much thereof as may be necessary.

Additional clerk hire.

For the payment of the salary of a clerk in the offices of the prothonotaries of the Supreme Court for the eastern and western districts, respectively, two years, the sum of four thousand eight hundred dollars, or so much thereof as may be necessary.

Contingent expenses.

For cleaning and contingent expenses of the Supreme Court room at Harrisburg, the sum of four hundred dollars, or so much thereof as may be necessary.

COMMON PLEAS JUDGES.

Common Pleas judges in Philadelphia.

For the payment of the salaries of the twelve common pleas judges in the county of Philadelphia, two years, one hundred and sixty-eight thousand dollars, or so much thereof as may be necessary.

In Allegheny county.

For the payment of the salaries of the nine common pleas judges in the county of Allegheny, two years, one hundred and eight thousand dollars, or so much thereof as may be necessary.

For the payment of the salaries of the two common pleas judges in the county of Dauphin, two years, twenty thousand dollars, or so much thereof as may be necessary, and for the payment of the salary of the common pleas judge of the county of Westmoreland, for two years, ten thousand dollars, the same being the only district in the Commonwealth with but one judge and having, according to the last United States census, a population exceeding ninety thousand.

For the payment of the salaries, at the rate of four thousand dollars each per annum, of the other sixty-four common pleas judges (as now provided by law) in the other districts of the State, two years, five hundred and twelve thousand dollars, or so much thereof as may be necessary.

ORPHANS' COURT JUDGES.

For the payment of the salaries of the four orphans' court judges in the county of Philadelphia, two years, fifty-six thousand dollars, or so much thereof as may be necessary.

For the payment of the salaries of the two orphans' court judges in the county of Allegheny, two years, twenty-four thousand dollars, or so much thereof as may be necessary.

For the payment of the salary of one orphans' court judge in the county of Luzerne, two years, eight thousand dollars, or so much thereof as may be necessary.

For the payment of the salary of one orphans' court judge in the county of Berks, two years, eight thousand dollars, or so much thereof as may be necessary.

ASSOCIATE JUDGES.

For the payment of the salaries of associate judges, sixty-four thousand dollars, or so much thereof as may be necessary.

MILEAGE AND EXTRA SERVICES.

For the payment of mileage of common pleas and as- sociate judges and compensation of common pleas judges holding courts in other districts, seventy-five thousand dollars, or so much thereof as may be necessary.

LEGISLATIVE DEPARTMENT.

SECTION 4. For the payment of the expenses of the Legislature for the year Anno Domini one thousand eight hundred and ninety-three, the sum of five hundred forty-four thousand three hundred and fifty-eight dollars and ninty cents, or so much thereof as may be necessary: *Provided*, That the salary, stationery, postage and mileage of the members of the Legislature shall be paid by the State Treasurer on the warrant of the President *pro tempore* of the Senate and Speaker of the House, respectfully.

SENATE.

Senate.

SECTION 5. For the payment of the salaries, mileage, stationery and postage of the Senators, the salaries and mileage of the officers and employés, the salary of the chaplain and the postage for the Lieutenant-Governor, the sum of one hundred and thirty-four thousand eight hundred and sixty-two dollars (or so much thereof as may be necessary), in detail as follows, all warrants subject to deductions for advances made by the State Treasurer.

Salaries of Senators.

Salaries of the Senators, seventy-five thousand dollars, or so much thereof as may be necessary.

Mileage.

Mileage for the Senators, three thousand two hundred and fifty-five dollars and twenty cents, or so much thereof as may be necessary.

Stationery.

Stationery allowed by law to fifty Senators, fifty dollars each, twenty-five hundred dollars, or so much thereof as may be necessary.

Postage for Senators.

Postage allowed by law to fifty Senators, five thousand dollars.

Estate of Senator John N. Neeb.

For the payment of the salary, mileage, stationery and postage of the late Senator John N. Neeb of the Forty-second Senatorial district, the sum of one thousand seven hundred and fifty dollars, or so much thereof as may be necessary, to be paid to his legal representatives.

Postage for chief clerk.

Postage for chief clerk and assistants allowed by law, one hundred dollars.

Postage for Lieutenant Governor. Salaries of officers, &c.

Postage for Lieutenant Governor, one hundred dollars.

Salaries of the officers and employés of the Senate (except librarian, watchmen and pages), thirty thousand eight hundred and fifty dollars, or so much thereof as may be necessary.

Mileage.

Mileage for officers and employés of the Senate, twelve hundred and six dollars and ninety cents, or so much thereof as may be necessary.

Chaplain.

For the salary of chaplain, four hundred and fifty dollars, or so much thereof as may be necessary.

Janitor.

For the chief clerk of the Senate for the payment of a janitor and keeping in order the apartments of the Lieutenant Governor, for two years, at two hundred and fifty dollars each year, five hundred dollars, or so much thereof as may be necessary.

Returning officers of Senate.

For the pay of the returning officers of the Senate at beginning of session, one thousand eight hundred and ninty-three, three hundred dollars, or so much thereof as may be necessary.

Mileage.

For mileage of returning officers, one hundred ninety-one dollars and ninety cents, or so much thereof as may be necessary.

Watchman and pages.

For the payment of one watchmen at three dollars per day, and ten pages at two dollars per day for the time actually employed as provided by law, five thousand one hundred and ninety dollars, or so much thereof as may be necessary.

Engineer

For the payment of an engineer of the capitol building

for the time actually employed during the recess ending the first Tuesday in January, one thousand eight hundred and ninety-five, as provided by law, the sum of one thousand seven hundred and thirty-four dollars, or so much thereof as may be necessary.

For the payment of the cellar fireman of the Senate for the time actually employed during the recess ending the first Tuesday in January, one thousand eight hundred and ninety-five, as provided by law, the sum of one thousand seven hundred and thirty-four dollars, or so much thereof as may be necessary. *Cellar fireman.*

For the payment of the librarian of the Senate, for two years ending the first Tuesday of January, one thousand eight hundred and ninety-five, as provided by law, the sum of four thousand dollars, payable quarterly as provided by an act, entitled "An act supplementary to the several acts relating to the State Treasurer and to the commissioners of the sinking fund," approved the ninth day of May, Anno Domini one thousand eight hundred and seventy-four. *Librarian of Senate.*

For the payment of the chief clerk of the Senate, for the year ending the first Tuesday of January, one thousand eight hundred and ninety-five, as provided by law, the sum of one thousand dollars, payable quarterly as provided in the case of the librarian of the Senate. *Chief clerk of Senate.*

HOUSE OF REPRESENTATIVES.

SECTION 6. For the payment of the salaries, mileage, stationery and postage of the members of the House of Representatives, the salaries and mileage of the officers and employés, and the salary of the chaplain, the sum of four hundred and ten thousand and twenty-one dollars and ninety cents, or so much thereof as may be necessary, in detail as follows: All warrants subject to deductions for advances made by the State Treasurer. *House of Representatives.*

Salaries of two hundred and four members, three hundred and six thousand dollars, or so much thereof as may be necessary. *Salaries of members.*

Mileage of the members, thirteen thousand five hundred and ninety-five dollars and forty cents, or so much thereof as may be necessary. *Mileage.*

Stationery allowed by law, fifty dollars each, ten thousand two hundred dollars, or so much thereof as may be necessary. *Stationery.*

Postage allowed by law, one hundred dollars each, twenty thousand four hundred dollars. *Postage for members.*

Postage for chief clerk and assistants allowed by law, one hundred dollars. *Postage for clerks.*

Salaries of officers and employés of the House (except resident clerk, watchmen and pages), forty-two thousand four hundred dollars, or so much thereof as may be necessary. *Salaries of officers and employes.*

Mileage for officers and employés, one thousand six hundred and ninety-three dollars and thirty cents, or so much thereof as may be necessary. *Mileage.*

Chaplain.

For salary of chaplain, four hundred and fifty dollars, or so much thereof as may be necessary.

Salaries of returning officers.

For the payment of salaries of returning officers of the House at beginning of session, one thousand eight hundred and ninety-three, three hundred and fifty dollars, or so much thereof as may be necessary.

Mileage of returning officers.

Mileage of returning officers, two hundred and eighty-one dollars and twenty cents, or so much thereof as may be necessary.

Watchmen and pages.

For the payment of one watchman at three dollars per day and fifteen pages at two dollars per day, for the time actually employed, as provided by law, six thousand six hundred and eighty-four dollars, or so much thereof as may be necessary.

Cellar fireman.

For the payment of the cellar fireman, for the time actually employed during the recess ending the first Tuesday of January, one thousand eight hundred and ninety-five, as provided by law, the sum of one thousand seven hundred and forty-three dollars, or so much thereof as may be necessary.

Charles H. Mentzer, for services.

For the payment of Charles H. Mintzer, for services as clerk to Judiciary General Committee of the House during the session of one thousand eight hundred and ninety-three, the sum of eight hundred dollars.

John Harner, for services.

For the payment of John Harner, for services as messenger for the Judiciary General and other committees of the House during the session of one thousand eight hundred and ninety-three, the sum of five hundred dollars.

M. R. Longstreth, for services.

For the payment of M. R. Longstreth, for services as clerk to the Ways and Means Committee of the House during the session of one thousand eight hundred and ninety-three, the sum of six hundred dollars.

Resident clerk.

For the payment of the resident clerk of the House of Representatives, for the year ending the first Tuesday of January, one thousand eight hundred and ninety-four, the sum of two thousand dollars, and for the year ending the first Tuesday of January, one thousand eight hundred and ninety-five, fifteen hundred dollars, as provided

Payable quarterly.

by law, payable quarterly as provided by an act, entitled "An act supplementary to the several acts relating to the State Treasurer and to the commissioners of the sinking fund," approved the ninth day of May, Anno Domini one thousand eight hundred and seventy-four.

Chief clerk.

For the payment of the chief clerk of the House of Representatives, for the year ending on the first Tuesday of January, one thousand eight hundred and ninety-five, the sum of one thousand dollars, as provided by

Payable quarterly.

law, payable quarterly as in the case of the resident clerk of the House of Representatives.

Legislature Record and wrappers.

SECTION 7. For the payment of the publication of the Legislative Record, the sum of four dollars and ninety-cents per page, in accordance with contract relating thereto; for printing the wrappers for the Record, the sum of two dollars and fourteen cents per set; and for making an index for the Legislative Record, the sum of three hundred dollars, or so much thereof as may be necessary: *Provided*, That the number of the copies of the indexes furnished by the contractor shall be equal to the number of copies of the Record printed by him.

SECTION 8. For the incidental expenses of the two Houses of the Legislature, for the year commencing December first, one thousand eight hundred and ninety-two, such sum as may be necessary to be expended by the chief clerks of the two Houses, who shall render to the Auditor General accounts therefor from time to time, with proper specifically itemized vouchers to be settled in the same manner as other accounts, but neither chief clerk shall have in his hands at any time more than two thousand dollars for which accounts have not been rendered and settled, and the whole amount expended by each chief clerk shall not exceed the sum of six thousand nine hundred dollars, for the chief clerk of the Senate, and the sum of eight thousand dollars, for the chief clerk of the House of Representatives, out of which sum shall be paid for such necessary extra labor in the Senate and House of Representatives during the session one thousand eight hundred and ninety-three as shall be certified to by the presiding officers and chief clerks thereof.

SECTION 9. For the payment of postage, labor, express charges and other expenses of the office of the resident clerk of the House of Representatives during the recess, the sum of one thousand six hundred dollars, or so much thereof as may be necessary, and for like services and expenses in the office of Librarian of the Senate, who is made by the act of June twelfth, one thousand eight hundred and seventy-nine, the custodian and distributor of all stationery and supplies for the Senate, House of Representatives and the several departments, the sum of fifteen hundred dollars, or so much thereof as may be necessary, and like sums for the year one thousand eight hundred and ninety-four, to be audited and settled by the Auditor General and State Treasurer in the usual manner. And the resident clerk shall receive from the Public Printer the bound copies of the Legislative Record and forward them to the members of the House; he shall also receive from the contractor for publishing the Legislative Record the back numbers due the members of the House, after the adjournment, and fold and mail them to the address of the persons to whom they have been mailed by the members during the session; he shall also receive, after the adjournment, from the Public Printer any documents and other printed matter authorized by law to be printed and have the same promptly forwarded by the contractor; and for the necessary expenses in the office of the chief clerks of the Senate and House of Representatives during the recess of one thousand eight hundred ninety-three, each the sum of six hundred dollars, or so much thereof as may be necessary, to be settled by the Auditor General in the usual man-

Marginal notes:

Incidental expenses of the two Houses for the year commencing December 1, 1892.

How settled.

Total amount payable to each of the chief clerks.

To include extra labor in session of 1893.

Expenses in office of Resident clerk.

And in office of Senate Librarian.

Like sums for 1894. How audited.

Duties of the Resident clerk of the House.

Expenses in offices of chief clerks of Senate and House during recess of 1893.

Like sums for 1894.

ner, and like sums for the year one thousand eight hundred and ninety-four.

For winding and care of clock on dome.

For winding and oiling the clock on the dome, the sum of one hundred dollars, for the year one thousand eight hundred and ninety-three, and a like sum for the year one thousand eight hundred and ninety-four, to be audited and settled by the Auditor General in the usual manner.

Indexes of journals.

For the chief clerks of the Senate and House of Representatives, the sum of two hundred dollars each, for making indexes for the journals of the two houses. For

Janitor of Senate basement.

the pay of Josiah Higgins, as janitor in the Senate basement during the recess at the rate of three dollars per day, for the time actually employed, in keeping in order the Senate bath-room for the use of the several departments, the sum of one thousand seven hundred and thirty-four dollars, or so much thereof as may be necessary, to be settled monthly by the Auditor General on the certificate of the chief clerk of the Senate.

Common schools.

SECTION 10. For the support of the public schools of this Commonwealth for the years commencing on the first Monday of June, one thousand eight hundred and ninety-three and the first Monday of June, one thousand eight hundred and ninety-four, each year, the sum of five million five hundred thousand dollars, to be paid on warrants of the Superintendent of Public Instruction in favor of the several school districts of the Commonwealth:

Payable on warrants of superintendent of Public Instruction.

Philadelphia to receive a proper proportion.

Provided, That the city of Philadelphia shall be entitled to a proper portion of this appropriation, and out of the amount received by the city of Philadelphia there shall be paid the sum of three thousand dollars to the teachers' institute of the said city, the sum of three thousand dollars to the Philadelphia School of Design for women, for their corporate purposes, and the sum of ten thousand dollars to the Teachers' Annuity and Aid Association of the said city: *Provided also,* That warrants for

Warrants to issue as State Treasurer designates.

the above and all other unpaid appropriations for common school purposes shall be issued in amounts designated by the State Treasurer, and whenever he shall notify the Superintendent of Public Instruction in writing there are sufficient funds in the State Treasury to pay the same.

County superintendents.

SECTION 11. For the payment of the salaries of the county superintendents of the public schools, the sum of ninety-five thousand dollars annually, or so much thereof as may be necessary, each year, to be paid on the warrant of the Superintendent of Public Instruction, and

Education of teachers in normal schools.

for the education of teachers in the normal schools, the sum of ninety-eight thousand dollars annually, or so much thereof as may be necessary, to be applied on the same conditions and under the same restrictions as are set forth in section three of the general appropriation act, approved March twenty-third, Anno Domini one thousand eight hundred and seventy-seven: *Provided,* That each student in a normal school drawing an allowance from the State must receive regular instruction in the science and art of teaching in a special class devoted to that object for the whole time such an allowance is drawn.

Students drawing allowance must receive instruction in art of teaching.

SECTION 12. The State Treasurer is hereby authorized and directed to pay out of any moneys in the treasury, not otherwise appropriated, on accounts to be audited by the Auditor General and the State Treasurer in the usual manner for the years commencing June first, one thousand eight hundred and ninety-three and June first, one thousand eight hundred and ninety-four, such sum as may be required by contract made in pursuance of law for the payment of stationery, printing, paper and material required for the public printing, for supplies and heat or fuel furnished to the two houses of the Legislature and the several departments of the government, and for the printing, binding and distribution of the laws, journals and department reports, and for the miscellaneous printing, folding, stitching and binding, and for repairs to and furnishing of the chambers and committee rooms of the two houses of the Legislature and the several departments of the government, which shall be done only on the written orders of the Board of Commissioners of Public Grounds and Buildings, and that the watchman of each house now authorized by law be required to keep an account and make report in writing to the chief clerk of each house of the number of tons of coal and the number of cords of wood delivered on said contracts.

State Treasurer to pay accounts when audited.

Stationery, printing paper, fuel, &c., for Legislature and Departments, &c.

Repairs, &c.

Duty of watchman.

SECTION 13. For the payment of the interest on the funded debt of the Commonwealth which falls due on the first day of August, Anno Domini one thousand eight hundred and ninety-three and the first day of February Anno Domini one thousand eight hundred and ninety-four, the sum of three hundred and thirty-three thousand dollars, or so much thereof as may be necessary, and for the payment of like interest due on the first day of August, Anno Domini one thousand eight hundred and ninety-four and the first day of February Anno Domini one thousand eight hundred and ninety-five, the sum of two hundred and seventy-one thousand dollars, or so much thereof as may be necessary, and for the compensation to the fiscal agent, the Farmers' and Mechanics' National Bank of Philadelphia, the sum of six thousand dollars, or so much thereof as may be necessary, each year.

Interest on funded debt.

Compensation of fiscal agents.

SECTION 14. For the payment of the salaries of the inspectors of coal mines as provided by law, for two years, from June first, one thousand eight hundred and ninety-three, the sum of eighty thousand dollars, or so much thereof as may be necessary, and for the actual traveling expenses of the inspectors and for their office rent and for stationery, postage, telegrams, express charges, instruments and other actual and necessary expenses, for two years, from June first, one thousand eight hundred and ninety-three, the sum of sixteen thousand dollars, or so much thereof as may be necessary.

Inspectors of coal mines.

Expenses, &c.

Expenses attending
examination of can-
didates for in-
spectors, &c.

For compensation and expenses attending the examina
tion of candidates for inspectors of coal mines, mine foreman and mine boss, as provided by acts of Assembly relating thereto, approved the thirteenth day of June, one
thousand eight hundred and eighty-five, for two years,
from June first, one thousand eight hundred and ninety-
three, such sums as may be necessary therefor, not exceeding in the aggregate the sum of twelve thousand
dollars.

PUBLIC BUILDINGS AND GROUNDS.

$15,000.00 for each
year for grounds
and buildings.

SECTION 15. For the expenses of keeping the public
grounds and buildings in order, repairing and improving
the same, and for paying the salaries of mechanics, flor-
ists and laborers employed by the Board of Commissioners of Public Grounds and Buildings, for the year commencing June first, Anno Domini one thousand eight
hundred and ninety-three, the sum of fifteen thousand
dollars, or so much thereof as may be necessary, and the
like sum of fifteen thousand dollars, or so much thereof
as may be necessary, for the same purpose, for the year
commencing June first, Anno Domini one thousand eight
hundred and ninety-four.

This item disap-
proved.

For electric current for operation of elevator motors,
Senate and House of Representatives, exhaust ventilating fans, Diehl ventilating fans, etc., in the several departments for portions of the years one thousand eight
hundred and ninety-one, one thousand eight hundred and
ninety-two, one thousand eight hundred and ninety-
three, and one thousand eight hundred and ninety-four,
the sum of one thousand nine hundred and forty-two
dollars, as per itemized statement in the hands of the
Board of Commissioners of Public Grounds and Buildings.

$4,8000.00 for re-
wiring buildings

For re-wiring public buildings for incandescent electric
light, as per contract with the Board of Commissioners
of Public Grounds and Buildings, the sum of four thousand eight hundred dollars, or so much thereof as may
be necessary.

$500.00 for water
pipe to arsenal.

For laying water pipe from the city line to the State
Arsenal and furnishing three hydrants and such stops as
may be required, the sum of five hundred dollars, or so
much thereof as may be necessary.

$1,000 00 item dis-
approved.

For the payment of rent for the upper portion of the
building on the corner of Second and Locust streets, now
occupied by the Bank Examiner, World's Fair Commission and Factory Inspector, from the first day of September, Anno Domini one thousand eight hundred and
ninety-two, to the thirty-first day of May, Anno Domini
one thousand eight hundred and ninety-three, the sum
of one thousand dollars, or so much thereof as may be

$2,400.00 for rent for
additional offices.

necessary, and the sum of one thousand two hundred dollars, or so much thereof as may be necessary, for the
same purpose for the fiscal year commencing June first,

Anno Domini one thousand eight hundred and ninety-three, and a like sum of one thousand two hundred dollars, or so much thereof as may be necessary, for the same purpose for the fiscal year commencing June first, Anno Domini one thousand eight hundred and ninety-four. For the erection of grand stone stairway and approaches thereto, including fountains in front of main building facing West State street, and a stone stairway at North street facing Elder street, as per plans selected by the Board of Commissioners of the Public Grounds and Buildings, the sum of twenty thousand dollars, or so much thereof as may be necessary.

$20,000.00 for stone stairway.

All contracts to be awarded and all moneys to be expended under the direction of the Board of Commissioners of Public Grounds and Buildings, and all work to be under the supervision of the superintendent of the same, who shall certify that contracts have been carried out in a satisfactory manner to the Board of Commissioners of Public Grounds and Buildings before warrants shall be drawn. The said superintendent shall file quarterly, with the Auditor General, within ten days after the close of each quarter, for settlement, proper itemized vouchers for all sums expended by him under this section.

Contracts how awarded.

Supervision of work.

Itemized vouchers must be filed.

SECTION 16. For the payment to the city of Harrisburg for supplying the public buildings and grounds with water for the years commencing June first, Anno Domini one thousand eight hundred and ninety-three, and June first, Anno Domini one thousand eight hundred and ninety-four, one thousand dollars, or so much thereof as may be necessary, each year; and also for electric lights and steam heat for the public buildings and grounds such amount as shall be found due on the contract made for furnishing such electric light and steam heat, upon the account rendered and settled by the Auditor General in the usual manner; and also for such amount for gas as may be found due the gas company when supplied on the contract with the company and upon a regular account being rendered to the Auditor General and settled in the usual manner in accordance with existing laws.

$2,000.00 for water.

For electric lights and steam heat.

For gas.

SECTION 17. For the payment of official fees, witness fees and serving process, and for such other costs as the Commonwealth may be liable to pay in cases which the Commonwealth is or may be a party to, for two years commencing June first, Anno Domini one thousand eight hundred and ninety-three, for each year, the sum of three thousand dollars, or so much thereof as may be necessary, to be paid on the warrant of the Attorney General.

$6,000.00 for official fees, &c.

SECTION 18. For the several fire companies of the city of Harrisburg, for two years commencing June first, Anno Domini one thousand eight hundred and ninety-three, for each year, the sum of eleven hundred dollars, to be distributed in equal amounts to and among said companies.

$2,200.00 for fire companies.

SECTION 19. For the payment of postage, express

charges and other incidental expenses of the Board of Pardons, for two years commencing June first, Anno Domini one thousand eight hundred and ninety-three, each year, the sum of one thousand dollars, or so much thereof as may be necessary, and for the payment of postage, express charges and other incidental expenses in the office of the State Treasurer, Auditor General, Secretary of the Commonwealth, Attorney General and Secretary of Internal Affairs, the sum of fifteen hundred dollars each, or so much thereof as may be necessary, for each year, and for the Lieutenant Governor, the sum of five hundred dollars, or so much thereof as may be necessary, for each year commencing June first, Anno Domini one thousand eight hundred and ninety-three and one thousand eight hundred and ninety-four, in addition to the amount fixed by the act of May fourteenth, one thousand eight hundred and seventy-four. Also four thousand dollars, or so much thereof as may be necessary, for the Executive Department of the said two years.

For the payment of the traveling and other expenses attending the opening and counting the votes for State Treasurer in the year one thousand eight hundred and ninety-four, the sum of ten hundred dollars, or so much thereof as may be necessary, to be paid on warrants drawn by the Auditor General.

SECTION 20. For the payment of mileage of the appraisers of mercantile and other license taxes of the several counties and cities of this Commonwealth, and for the payment of the cost for which the Commonwealth is liable in suits against delinquent dealers under the act of March thirteenth, Anno Domini one thousand eight hundred and forty-seven, for the year commencing June first, Anno Domini one thousand eight hundred and ninety-three and June first, one thousand eight hundred and ninety-four, such sum as shall be found due therefor upon accounts filed in the Auditor General's office and settled according to law.

SECTION 21. For the purpose of paying the necessary expenses of persons appointed in pursuance of law to examine the accounts of city or county officers, or individuals required by law to make report to the Auditor General of moneys due for fees or taxes received for use of the Commonwealth, such sum as may be necessary to be expended under the joint direction of the State Treasurer and the Auditor General, for the year commencing June first, Anno Domini one thousand eight hundred and ninety-three, to be paid only on separate accounts filed in the Auditor General's office and settled according to law by the Auditor General and State Treasurer, and the like sum for the year commencing June first, Anno Domini one thousand eight hundred and ninety-four: Provided, The sum shall not exceed one thousand dollars for any one year.

SECTION 22. For the payment of such advertisements as are required by law to be published by the accounting officers in the newspapers for the years commencing June first, Anno Domini one thousand eight hundred and ninety-three and one thousand eight hundred and ninety-four, so much as may be necessary to pay the same on settlement of the accounts in the Auditor General's office, not to exceed five hundred dollars for each year.

SECTION 23. For the payment of the commissions of such military State agents at Washington as have been or may be employed by the accounting officer, under the acts of one thousand eight hundred and seventy-one and seventy-two, to collect the claims due the Commonwealth from the Government of the United States for the years one thousand eight hundred and ninety-three and one thousand eight hundred and ninety-four, so much as may be necessary, not exceeding ten per centum on the amount collected through such agent or agents and paid into the treasury. *Commissions of military State agents at Washington.*

SECTION 24. For the payment of military claims in pursuance of the act of the General Assembly, approved the sixteenth day of April, one thousand eight hundred and sixty-two, and the several supplements thereto, the sum of two thousand dollars, or so much thereof as may be necessary, for the two years beginning June first, one thousand eight hundred and ninety-three. *$2,000.00 for military claims.*

SECTION 25. For the payment of extra expenses incurred in revising the schedule for stationery, supplies, furniture et cetera, for the several departments of the State government, and equalizing the price of all articles of the same kind or class, as directed to be furnished by the several departments, for the two years beginning June first, one thousand eight hundred and ninety-three, the sum of nine hundred dollars, or so much thereof as may be necessary. *$900.00 for revising schedule.*

SECTION 26. For the payment of the funeral expenses of the late Senator John N. Neeb, of the Forty-second Senatorial district, the sum of three hundred and nineteen dollars and ninety-eight cents, or so much thereof as may be nececsary, to be paid upon the warrant of the Auditor General upon the presentation of specifically itemized vouchers duly certified and approved by the Hon. J. S. P. Gobin, President pro tem. of the Senate. *$319.98 for funeral expenses of Senator John N. Neeb.*

SECTION 27. For the payment of the stenographer, witness fees and sergeant-at-arms expenses for the joint committee of the Senate and House of Representatives, appointed upon the recommendation of the Governor to investigate the State printing, the sum of nine hundred and seventy-five dollars and seventy-four cents, or so much thereof as may be necessary, to be paid upon the warrant of the Auditor General upon the presentation of specifically itemized vouchers duly approved and certified to by the chairman of the joint committee. *$975.74 for stenographer for committee &c., investigate State printing.*

SECTION 28. For the payment of the expenses of the Senate Committee on Mines and Mining in investigating the condition of the coal mines in the anthracite region in connection with a joint resolution of the Senate and *$170.40 for expenses of Senate committee on mines and mining.*

House of Representatives for a commission to investigate the causes of recent disasters at Nanticoke, Jeansville, Laurel Ridge, York Farm, Lytle Neilson shaft and Scottdale, the sum of one hundred and seventy dollars and forty cents, or so much thereof as may be necessary, to be paid upon the warrant of the Auditor General upon the presentation of specifically itemized vouchers duly approved and certified to by the chairman of said committee.

$61.00 for serving writs for special election in 42d Senatorial district.

SECTION 29. For the payment of the serving of the writs for a special election in the Forty-Second Senatorial district, the sum of sixty-one dollars, or so much thereof as may be necessary, to be paid to J. H. Myers, sergeant-at-arms of the Senate, upon the warrant of the Auditor General upon the presentation of the proper voucher.

This item disapproved.

SECTION 30. For the payment of serving special election writs subsequent to the session of one thousand eight hundred and ninety-one in the following cases, namely: In the Sixth Legislative district of Philadelphia, the sum of fifty dollars, or so much thereof as may be necessary; in the Twenty-first Legislative district of Philadelphia, the sum of fifty dollars, or so much thereof as may be necessary; in the county of Blair, the sum of seventy-one dollars, or so much thereof as may be necessary, to be paid to George R. Hoopes, sergeant-at-arms of the House of Representatives, upon the warrant of the Auditor General on the presentation of specifically itemized vouchers approved by him.

$100.00 for attendance upon Hon. William McGill,

SECTION 31. For the payment of George R. Hoopes, sergeant-at-arms of the House of Representatives, for attendance upon Honorable William McGill during his serious illness and removing him to his home in Crawford county, the sum of one hundred dollars, and for attendance upon A. W. Hayes, assistant postmaster of the House of Representatives, during his serious illness, and removing him to his home in Erie county, the sum of one hundred dollars, to be paid upon the warrant of the Auditor General on the presentation of specifically itemized vouchers approved by him.

$100.00 for attendance upon A. W. Hays.

This section disapproved.

SECTION 32. For the payment of serving a special election writ subsequent to the session of one thousand eight hundred and ninety-one, in the Nineteenth Senatorial District, the sum of seventy-five dollars and seventy cents, or so much thereof as may be necessary, to be paid to George G. Hutchinson, sergeant-at-arms of the Senate, upon the warrant of the Auditor General upon the presentation of specifically itemized vouchers approved by.

This section disapproved.

SECTION 33. For the payment to George G. Hutchinson, sergeant-at-arms of the Senate, for the session of one thousand eight hundred and ninety-one, for attendance upon the Appropriation Committee of the Senate, the sum of three hundred and ninety-one dollars, or so much thereof as may be necessary, to be paid upon the warrant of the Auditor General upon the presentation of specifically itemized vouchers duly approved by him.

SECTION 34. To William H. Ulrich of Hummelstown, late prothonotary of the court of common pleas of Dauphin county, for costs and fees due him by the State in cases in which the State of Pennsylvania was plaintiff, the sum of nine hundred and thirty-six dollars and fifty-five cents, or so much thereof as may be necessary, to be paid on the warrant of the Auditor General upon the presentation of a properly itemized account and vouchers approved by the Attorney General. *This section disapproved.*

SECTION 35. For the payment of the expenses incurred by the commission appointed under the provisions of the act, approved June fifteenth, one thousand eight hundred and eighty-seven, known as the Gettysburg Battlefield Monumental Association, the sum of two thousand dollars, or so much thereof as may be necessary, to be paid by the State Treasurer upon proper certified statements by the chairman of said commission approved by the Auditor General. *Expenses of commission Gettysburg Battlefield Memorial Association.*

SECTION 36. To the Office Specialty Manufacturing Company for base for filing case in the Senate transcribing room, the sum of three hundred dollars, or so much thereof as may be necessary, to be paid by the State Treasurer on warrant of the Auditor General when vouchers are filed approved by the Chief Clerk of the Senate. *Office Specialty Manufacturing Company.*

SECTION 37. The sum of twenty-five hundred dollars, or so much thereof as may be necessary, to the Gettysburg Battlefield Monumental Association, for the purpose of keeping the Pennsylvania monuments in repair, guarding them from desecration and preserving them in good order. *Keeping Pennsylvania monuments in repair at Gettysburg.*

APPROVED—The 6th day of June, A. D. 1893, except as to the following items:

PUBLIC BUILDINGS AND GROUNDS.

SECTION 15. "For electric current for operation of elevator motors, Senate and House of Representatives, exhaust ventilating fans, Diehl ventilating fans, etc., in the several departments for portions of the years one thousand eight hundred and ninety-one, one thousand eight hundred and ninety-two, one thousand eight hundred and ninety-three, and one thousand eight hundred and ninety-four, the sum of one thousand nine hundred and forty-two dollars, as per itemized statement in the hands of the Board of Commissioners of Public Grounds and Buildings."

This item is disapproved because the title to the present bill limits all appropriations made by it to the ordinary expenses of the State government for the years 1893 and 1894, and no appropriations for previous years can be properly embraced in this bill. Whatever deficiencies exist on that account must, under the provisions of the Constitution, be provided for in some other manner

21—LAWS.

For the same reason I disapprove of the following
item, also, in section fifteen: "For the payment of rent
for the upper portion of the building on the corner of
Second and Locust streets, now occupied by the Bank
Examiner, World's Fair Commission and Factory Inspector, from the first day of September, Anno Domini one
thousand eight hundred and ninety-two to the thirty-
first day of May, Anno Domini one thousand eight hundred and ninety-three, the sum of one thousand dollars,
or so much thereof as may be necessary."

For like reason I disapprove of the whole of section
thirty: " For the payment of serving special election writs
subsequent to the session of one thousand eight hundred
and ninety-one, in the following cases, namely: In the
Sixth legislative district of Philadelphia, the sum of fifty
dollars, or so much thereof as may be necessary; in the
Twenty-first legislative district of Philadelphia, the sum
of fifty dollars, or so much thereof as may be necessary;
in the county of Blair, the sum of seventy-one dollars, or
so much thereof as may be necessary, to be paid to George
R. Hoopes, sergeant-at-arms of the House of Representatives, upon the warrant of the Auditor General on
the presentation of specifically itemized vouchers approved by him." the same being for expenses which were
no part of the expenses of the government for the years
covered by the title of this bill.

For like reasons I disapprove the following items:

SECTION 32. "For the payment of serving a special
election writ subsequent to the session of one thousand
eight hundred and ninety-one, in the Nineteenth Senatorial district, the sum of seventy-five dollars and seventy
cents, or so much thereof as may be necessary, to be paid
to George G. Hutchinson, sergeant-at-arms of the Senate,
upon the warrant of the Auditor General upon the presentation of specifically itemized vouchers approved by
him."

. SECTION 33. "For the payment to George G. Hutchinson, sergeant-at-arms of the Senate, for the session of one
thousand eight hundred and ninety-one, for attendance
upon the Appropriation Committee of the Senate, the
sum of three hundred and ninety-one dollars, or so much
thereof as may be necessary, to be paid upon the warrant of the Auditor General upon the presentation of
specifically itemized vouchers duly approved by him."

SECTION 34. I disapprove of the following item: "To
William H. Ulrich of Hummelstown, late prothonotary
of the court of common pleas of Dauphin county, for
costs and fees due him by the State in cases in which the
State of Pennsylvania was plaintiff, the sum of nine hundred and thirty-six dollars and fifty-five cents, or so much
thereof as may be necessary, to be paid on the warrant
of the Auditor General upon the presentation of a properly itemized account and vouchers approved by the
Attorney General," for the reason that it relates to a deficiency incurred by the Commonwealth for years previous

to those embraced in the title of this bill and, if a just
obligation of the State, should have been provided for
by a separate bill properly entitled in accordance with
the constitutional requirements.

ROBT. E. PATTISON.

No. 259.

AN ACT

To amend an act, entitled "Relative to notaries public," approved
the fourth day of February, Anno Domini one thousand eight
hundred and fifty-six, extending the limits of residence and
powers of notaries public.

SECTION 1. *Be it enacted, &c.*, That an act, entitled
"Relative to notaries public," approved the fourth day
of February, Anno Domini one thousand eight hundred
and fifty-six, which reads as follows, namely: "That it
shall be lawful for any person heretofore appointed, or
who shall hereafter be appointed, a notary public, and
whose commission shall direct him to reside in any city
or borough in any of the counties of this Commonwealth
in which any said city or borough may be located, to
have his domicile in any part of said county: *Provided*,
That he shall keep an office in the said city or borough
named in his commission," be and the same is hereby
amended to read as follows: That it shall be lawful for
any person heretofore appointed, or who shall hereafter
be appointed, a notary public, and whose commission
direct him to reside in any city or borough in any of the
counties of this Commonwealth in which any said city or
borough may be located, to have his domicile in any part
of said county or of the adjoining counties: *Provided*,
That he shall keep an office in the said city or borough
or county named in his commission.

SECTION 2. That all notorial acts heretofore or hereafter
performed by notaries public of this Commonwealth,
when a notary is not within the county for which he was
commissioned, shall be as valid and legal as if he were at
the place for which he is commissioned: *Provided*, That
nothing in this section contained shall apply to or affect
any case now pending in or heretofore decided by any
court of the Commonwealth.

APPROVED—The 6th day of June, A. D. 1893.

ROBT. E. PATTISON.

Marginal notes:
Act of February 4. 1856, cited for amendment.

May have domicile in county for which appointed or in the adjoining counties.

Proviso as to office.

Acts of Notary outside of county for which appointed, legalized.

Shall not apply to case now pending in or heretofore decided by any court.

No. 260.

AN ACT

Relating to corporations organized for religious, educational, literary, scientific or charitable purposes.

May file petition in court setting forth that amount of property allowed to be held is insufficient

SECTION 1 *Be it enacted, &c.*, That it shall be lawful for any corporation formed for a religious, educational, literary, scientific or charitable purpose to file its petition in the court of common pleas of the county where the principal office or place of business of such corporation is located, setting forth that the amount of property, real and personal, which said corporation by law is authorized to hold, is insufficient to enable it to fully and properly accomplish the religious, educational, literary, scientific or charitable work or purpose for which it was formed,

Court shall make inquiry.

and thereupon it shall be the duty of the court to which said petition is presented to make inquiry into the truth of the matters alleged in the petition, and if, upon such inquiry, the court is satisfied of the truth of the matters so alleged, and that the prayer of the petition can be allowed without injury to the public welfare, then it shall

May make decree extending amount of property to be held.

be lawful for the court to enter a decree extending and defining the amount of property, real and personal, which such corporation shall be permitted to hold.

APPROVED—The 6th day of June, A. D. 1893.

ROBT. E. PATTISON.

No. 261.

AN ACT

Amending the eighty-fourth section of an act, entitled "An act regulating election districts, and for other purposes," approved the fourth day of March, Anno Domini one thousand eight hundred and forty-two, providing for the appointment of judges and inspectors of elections in case of tie votes in elections for said judges and inspectors.

SECTION 1. *Be it enacted, &c.*, That the eighty-fourth section of an act, entitled "An act regulating election districts, and for other purposes," approved the fourth day of March, Anno Domini one thousand eight hundred and forty-two, which reads as follows:

Section 84, Act of March 4, 1842, cited for amendment.

"SECTION 84. That from and after the passage of this act, in all township elections where a tie shall exist in the said election of judges, the inspector who shall have the highest number of votes in said election shall appoint a judge for that purpose," be and the same is hereby amended to read as follows:

Tie vote for judge of elections; how decided.

SECTION 84. That from and after the passage of this act, in all township elections of this Commonwealth for judges of the general and township elections where a tie shall exist in the said election for judges, the inspector who shall have the highest number of votes in said election shall appoint a judge for that purpose. And where ties shall exist in said election for judges and also for two inspectors, the two candidates who received the same number of votes for inspector shall determine by lot which of them shall be the majority inspector, and the other candidate shall be the minority inspector, and the person so determined to be the majority inspector shall appoint a judge of elections.

For judge and two inspectors

APPROVED—The 6th day of June, A. D. 1893.

ROBT. E. PATTISON.

No. 262.

AN ACT

To amend an act, entitled "An act to authorize incorporated cemetery or burial associations to purchase other grounds, and to sell and convey in fee simple such portions of their land not used or conveyed by them for burial purposes, or which may have been reconveyed to them," approved the twenty-sixth day of May, Anno Domini one thousand eight hundred and ninety-one, so as to authorize incorporated or unincorporated churches owning burial grounds to purchase other grounds, and to sell and convey such portions of their lands not used or conveyed by them for burial purposes, or which may have been reconveyed to them.

SECTION 1. *Be it enacted, &c.,* That section one of the act of Assembly, approved the twenty-sixth day of May, Anno Domini one thousand eight hundred and ninety-one, which reads as follows:

"That whenever any incorporated cemetery or burial association own grounds located wholly or in part in any cities, townships or boroughs, and by reason of the growth thereof and the consequent increasing number of interments of the dead, as well as for sanitary purposes, it is deemed necessary or desirable to change the location thereof, or where the further interment of the dead within the limits of such municipalities has been prohibited, it shall be lawful for such incorporated cemetery or burial associations, and they are hereby authorized and empowered to purchase new and more suitable ground in the vicinity, of such extent and area as they shall deem expedient, for the burial of the dead. And such incorporated cemetery or burial associations are hereby further authorized and empowered to sell and convey in fee simple, and unrestricted as to use, all such portion of their lands not used or conveyed by them for burial purposes, or which shall have been reconveyed to them, and from which all bodies shall have been removed, and to make, execute and deliver a deed or deeds for the same to the purchaser or purchasers as though owned by individuals," be and the same is hereby amended so as to read:

Section 1, Act of May 26, 1891, cited for amendment.

That whenever any incorporate or unincorporated church, cemetery or burial associations own grounds located wholly or in part in any cities, township or boroughs, and by reason of the growth thereof and the consequent increasing number of interments of the dead, as well as for sanitary purposes, it is deemed necessary or desirable to change the location thereof, or where the further interment of the dead within the limits of such municipalities has been prohibited, it shall be lawful for such incorporated or unincorporated church, cemetery or burial associations, and they are hereby authorized and empowered to purchase new and more suitable ground in the vicinity, of such extent and area as they shall deem expedient, for the burial of the dead. And such incorporated or unincorporated church, cemetery or burial associations are hereby further authorized
and empowered to sell and convey in fee simple, and unrestricted as to use, all such portions of their lands not used or conveyed by them for burial purposes, or which shall have been reconveyed to them, and from
which all bodies shall have been removed, and to make, execute and deliver a deed or deeds for the same to the purchaser or purchasers as though owned by individuals.

APPROVED—The 6th day of June, A. D. 1893.

ROBT. E. PATTISON.

No. 263.

A SUPPLEMENT

To an act, entitled "An act in relation to the imprisonment, government and release of convicts in the Pennsylvania Industrial Reformatory at Huntingdon," approved the twenty-eighth day of April, Anno Domini one thousand eight hundred and eighty-seven.

SECTION 1. *Be it enacted, &c.,* That whenever an inmate of the Pennsylvania Industrial Reformatory at Huntingdon shall be paroled and thereafter, when on his parole, shall in any manner violate the same and be declared a delinquent by the Board of Managers of said reformatory, he shall be liable to arrest and return at any time, and upon his return be required to serve the unexpired term of his
possible maximum sentence, at the discretion of the Board of Managers, and the time from the date of his declared delinquency to the date of his return to the said Reformatory shall not be counted as any part or portion of such sentence.

SECTION 2. Whenever any such paroled inmate shall, as aforesaid, so violate his said parole and be declared a delinquent by the said Board of Managers, it shall be lawful for the president of the Board of Managers of the said Reformatory to issue his warrant to detective or person authorized by law to execute criminal process, whose duty it shall be to arrest and deliver such paroled prisoner to the Reformatory at Huntingdon, the cost of executing such warrant and delivering the prisoner to the said Reformatory to be paid by the Board of Managers.

Cost of same.

SECTION 3. Whenever any inmate of the said Industrial Reformatory shall violate his parole and go into any other State, it shall be the duty of the Governor of the Commonwealth to issue his requisition for the return of such paroled inmate as being a fugitive from justice.

Requisition for paroled inmate who leaves the State.

SECTION 4. Whenever any paroled inmate of the said Industrial Reformatory shall violate his parole and be returned to the institution, the time when he was on parole may, in the discretion of the Board of Managers, be added to the maximum sentence which he could be required to serve, and in their discretion, the said paroled inmate may be compelled to serve, in addition to the maximum sentence, a period of time equal to the time that he was on parole.

Time which an inmate violating parole may be compelled to serve.

SECTION 5. If any inmate should escape from the said Industrial Reformatory, or from a keeper or any officer having him in charge while engaged in working outside of the walls, the time during which said escaped inmate may be at large may, in the discretion of the Board of Managers, be added to his maximum sentence upon his return to the institution, and in their discretion, such escaped inmates may be required to serve, in addition to his maximum sentence, a further period of time equal to the time that he was at large.

Time which an escaped inmate may be compelled to serve after his return.

APPROVED—The 6th day of June, A. D. 1893.

ROBT. E. PATTISON.

No. 264.

AN ACT

Authorizing the appointment of policemen in the boroughs of this Commonwealth, defining their powers and duties, and providing for their compensation and discharge.

SECTION 1. *Be it enacted, &c.*, That the council of any incorporated borough of this Commonwealth may appoint one or more suitable persons, citizens of this Commonwealth, who shall act as policemen in such borough and shall have the power to make arrest now possessed by the constables and policemen of this Commonwealth to arrest persons violating any ordinance of such borough, the violation of which may subject persons to arrest. And the keepers of the jails, lock-ups or station houses in the counties where the offense was committed for which an arrest may be made are required to receive all persons arrested by such policemen.

Council may appoint policemen.

Powers of such policemen

Keepers of jails, &c., must receive all persons arrested

SECTION 2. Such policemen shall, when on duty, severally wear a shield or badge with the words "Borough Police" and the name of the borough for which they are appointed inscribed thereon.

Badge of policemen.

Policemen shall be under control of the council.

SECTION 3. Such policemen shall be under the control and direction of the council of the borough in which they shall be appointed as to the time during which and the place where they shall perform their duties, and they shall receive such compensation (to be paid from the

Compensation.

borough treasury) as may be agreed upon between them and the council and be subject to removal or discharge at the discretion of the council of such borough.

APPROVED—The 6th day of June, A. D. 1893.

ROBT. E. PATTISON.

No. 265.

AN ACT

To regulate proceedings in applications for the discharge on habeas corpus of persons confined in either of the penitentiaries of the State.

Proof of notice of intended application must be submitted to judge hearing the application.

SECTION 1. *Be it enacted, &c.*, That hereafter when application shall be made to any court of this Commonwealth, or a judge thereof, by an inmate of either of the penitentiaries of the State for a writ of habeas corpus for the discharge of such inmate, the court or judge directing such writ to issue and before whom the application shall be heard, shall, before the hearing of such application and the discharge of any such inmate, have submitted to it or him proof of notice of the intended application to the authority or authorities that may have committed such inmate to the said penitentiary, and it shall not be lawful for such court or judge to order the discharge of such inmate without proof of notice as aforesaid to the said authority or authorities.

APPROVED—The 6th day of June, A. D. 1893.

ROBT. E. PATTISON.

No. 266.

AN ACT

Providing for the relief of needy, sick, injured, and in case of death, burial of indigent persons whose legal place of settlement is unknown.

Overseers of poor districts shall provide necessary support, &c., to needy persons.

SECTION 1. *Be it enacted, &c.* That in each and every county of this Commonwealth in which a poor or almshouse for the support, care and shelter of the needy and indigent is not maintained by and at county expense, it shall be the duty of the poor directors or overseers of the poor of the several poor districts in such counties to provide all needy, sick and injured indigent person or persons in their said several districts with necessary support, shelter, medicine, medical attendance, nursing, and

Also burial

in case of death, burial, whether said needy, sick and injured indigent person or persons have a legal settlement in the poor district in which they thus require and receive assistance or not; but all expenses thus incurred for the relief, support, nursing, care or burial of such indigent person or persons whose legal settlement is unknown shall be borne by the county in which the poor district furnishing such relief is located. Expenses so incurred shall be borne by the county.

And in the event of any such poor district having assumed or paid the expenses thus incurred for the relief or burial of any indigent person or persons whose legal settlement is unknown, the county in which such poor district is located shall be liable to such poor district in an action of assumpsit in a civil court for the amount thus expended or incurred, and the want of an order of relief or approval order shall not be a bar to recovery. Action of assumpsit against county for expenses incurred.

SECTION 2. All acts or parts of acts inconsistent herewith be and the same are hereby repealed. Repeal.

APPROVED—The 6th day of June, A. D. 1893.

ROBT. E. PATTISON.

No. 267.

AN ACT

To prohibit the erection of toll houses and toll gates within the limits of any borough.

SECTION 1. *Be it enacted, &c.,* That from and after the passage of this act it shall not be lawful for any turnpike road company to erect any toll house or toll gate within the limits of any borough, now incorporated or hereafter to be incorporated within this Commonwealth.

APPROVED—The 6th day of June, A. D. 1893.

ROBT. E. PATTISON.

No. 268.

AN ACT

To provide for the acknowledgment and recording of plots of land or lots.

SECTION 1. *Be it enacted, &c.,* That when the owner or owners of land or lots have divided the same into lots or sub-divisions and made plots or maps thereof, and any or all of such owners are deceased, the purchaser or purchasers or their successors in title of any such lots or subdivisions may apply to the court of common pleas of the county where the land is situated for leave to prove the same. If owners of land are dead, purchasers may apply to court for leave to prove plot or plan.

When satisfied by the evidence, the court shall direct the map or plot to be recorded in the office of the recorder of deeds of the proper county, and the record thereof shall have the same form and effect as if the map had been originally acknowledged and recorded. Court may direct plan or plot to be recorded.

SECTION 2. If the map has been lost it may be proved, as in the first section, and a duplicate made and recorded with the same form and effect.

SECTION 3. This act shall not affect adversely any persons who were not parties to the proceeding in court, but they shall be at liberty to show facts or titles different from those of the recorded plot in any contest between claimants.

APPROVED—The 6th day of June, A. D. 1893.

ROBT. E. PATTISON.

No. 269.

AN ACT

To provide for the appointment of one or more deputy coroners and defining their power and duties in the several counties of this Commonwealth.

SECTION 1. *Be it enacted, &c.*, That from and after the passage of this act, the regularly elected and duly qualified coroner in counties of this Commonwealth may appoint one or more deputies to act in his place and stead as he may deem proper and necessary.

SECTION 2. Such deputy or deputies so appointed shall have like power to hold inquests, to select, summon and compel the attendance of jurors and witnesses and to administer oaths.

APPROVED—The 6th day of June, A. D. 18 93.

ROBT. E. PATTISON.

No. 270.

AN ACT

To authorize the courts of common pleas to appoint a competent person to inspect school houses on complaint of taxable citizens of any school district in which boards of school directors or controllers have failed to provide and maintain proper and adequate school accommodations for the children who are lawfully entitled to school privileges in the district, and prescribing a penalty for neglect of duty on the part of school boards.

SECTION 1. *Be it enacted, &c.*, That whenever the school directors or controllers of any city, borough, township or independent school district shall willfully neglect or refuse to provide suitable houses, rooms or buildings in and for any school district within their jurisdiction, and under their supervision and control, with ample room and seating capacity for the reasonable and convenient accommodation of all the school children residing within the district who may be in attendance, or who desire to attend the school or schools therein, then ten or more taxable citizens, residents of the said district, may set forth in writing the facts in the case, under oath or affirmation of at least six persons who sign the statement, and petition the court of common pleas of the county in which said school district is situated, or in vacation any judge of the said court, for the appointment of a competent inspector, and the court or judge thereof may appoint such inspector, whose duty it shall be to visit the district by order of the court or judge thereof, and inquire into the facts set forth in the complaint submitted, giving due notice to the members of the board of directors against whom the complaint for neglect of duty is made, and to other persons concerned, and the said inspector shall report to the court or proper judge thereof, under oath or affirmation, of the result of his personal inspection and investigation, accompanied by statements of facts and proofs obtained in the case.

Inspector may be appointed.

Duty of inspector.

Shall report to the court result of personal inspection, &c.

SECTION 2. If, after hearing the allegations and proofs offered to substantiate the charges set forth in the complaint or to disprove them, and after having fully and diligently inquired into all the facts and circumstances bearing on the case in point, the aforesaid inspector finds that the directors or controllers have refused, neglected or failed, without valid cause for such refusal, neglect or failure on their part to provide and maintain suitable and adequate accommodations for the school children of the district as the law requires, he shall so report to the court or to the judge appointing him, and the court in such case is hereby authorized and empowered to grant a rule upon the directors or controllers then having jurisdiction in the district, or such of them as have willfully neglected or failed without justifiable excuse to perform the duties enjoined upon them by law, to show cause why the court or the judge thereof should not remove them from office and appoint others in their stead, until the next annual election for directors.

He shall hear allegations and proofs.

If he finds no valid cause for neglect of directors, he shall so report.

Court empowered to grant a rule upon directors to show cause why they should not be removed.

APPROVED—The 6th day of June, A. D. 1893.

ROBT. E. PATTISON.

No. 271.

AN ACT

Authorizing railroad companies organized under the laws of Pennsylvania and operating railroads either in whole within, or partly within and partly without, the State to increase or diminish the par value of the shares of their capital stock.

SECTION 1. *Be it enacted, &c.*, That it shall be lawful for any railroad company or corporation organized under the laws of this Commonwealth, and operating a railroad either in whole within, or partly within and partly without, this State under authority of this and any adjoining State or States, to change the par or face value of the shares into which its capital stock is divided from fifty

May change par value of shares.

dollars to one hundred dollars, or from one hundred dollars to fifty dollars, but not otherwise. Such change shall be authorized by a vote of a majority of the stockholders of any such company present in person or by proxy at any annual meeting or any special meeting duly called.

Shall not change
par value of capital
stock.

Such change of the par value of the capital stock shall not be taken to increase or diminish or change in any way the total aggregate par value of the capital stock which said company may be authorized to issue, or may have issued, but only to change the number of shares into which the same may be divided.

Certificate of such
change shall be
filed in the office of
the Secretary of the
Commonwealth.

SECTION 2. In case the stockholders so present at such meeting shall vote to increase or diminish the par value of the shares of the capital stock of the company as above provided, it shall be the duty of the proper officers of the company to file a certificate of the fact in the office of the Secretary of the Commonwealth under the seal of the corporation, and thereupon the proper officers of

Company may then
issue shares of the
new par value for
outstanding shares.

such company shall issue to its stockholders the proper number of shares of the capital stock of the new par value in exchange for outstanding shares of the former par value, upon the surrender of such outstanding shares by the respective holders and the cancellation thereof.

APPROVED—The 6th day of June, A. D. 1893.

ROBT. E. PATTISON.

No. 272.

AN ACT

For the relief of the heirs of Richard Hogan, late of the city of Harrisburg, Pennsylvania, deceased, for reimbursement of certain moneys expended by the said Richard Hogan for the forage and quarters and subsistence of the men and their horses composing the "Norris Cavalry," Pennsylvania Militia, during the year one thousand eight hundred and sixty-two.

WHEREAS, Richard Hogan, of the city of Harrisburg, now deceased, was ordered under authority of Captain E. C. Wilson, assistant quartermaster, United States Army, dated the twentieth day of September, one thousand eight hundred and sixty-two, to furnish forage and quarters for fifty horses of Captain D. H. Mulvany's troop of cavalry, Pennsylvania Militia, known as the " Norris Cavalry," and also subsistence for forty-one men of the same troop, and in obedience to said order did contract the following necessary expenses which he personally paid as he was instructed to do, and he was promised at the time being that he would be reimbursed therefor, namely:

Forage and quarters for forty-one horses of Captain D. H. Mulvany's troop, "Norris Cavalry," Pennsylvania Militia, for order of Captain E. C. Wilson, assistant quartermaster, United States Army, for four nights and days, to wit: September twentieth, twenty-first, twenty-second and twenty-third, Anno Domini one thousand eight hundred and sixty-two, at fifty cents per night and day for each horse, sixty-one dollars and fifty-cents.

To subsistence of men composing said troop, including officers, forty-one men for same period furnished with seventy-eight meals on September twenty-first, eighty-four meals on September twenty-second, and eighty-four meals on September twenty-third, one thousand eight hundred and sixty-two, amounting to two hundred and forty-six meals, at twenty-five cents for each meal, sixty-six dollars and fifty cents. Total one hundred and twenty-eight dollars; therefore,

SECTION 1. *Be it enacted, &c.,* That the proper officer or officers of the Commonwealth of Pennsylvania are hereby authorized and directed to pay out of the State Treasury the sum of one hundred and twenty-eight dollars to the heirs or legal representatives of the aforesaid Richard Hogan.

$128.00 appropriated

APPROVED—The 6th day of June, A. D. 1893.

ROBT. E. PATTISON.

No. 273.

AN ACT

To authorize the election of tax collectors for the term of three years in the several boroughs and townships of this Commonwealth.

SECTION 1. *Be it enacted, &c.,* That the qualified voters of every borough and township in the Commonwealth of Pennsylvania shall, on the third Tuesday of February after the passage of this act and triennially thereafter, vote for and elect one properly qualified person for tax collector in each of said districts, who shall serve for the term of three years, and shall give a bond annually to be approved by the court.

SECTION 2. All acts or parts of acts inconsistent herewith are hereby repealed.

APPROVED—The 6th day of June, A. D. 1893.

ROBT. E. PATTISON.

No. 274.

AN ACT

To repeal an act, entitled "An act relative to roads in Choconut township, Susquehanna county," approved the eighteenth day of February, Anno Domini one thousand eight hundred and sixty-nine.

SECTION 1. *Be it enacted, &c.,* That the act, entitled "An act relative to roads in Choconut township, Susquehanna county," approved the eighteenth day of February, Anno Domini one thousand eight hundred and sixty-nine, be and the same is hereby repealed.

APPROVED—The 6th day of June, A. D. 1893.

ROBT. E. PATTISON.

No. 275.

AN ACT

To repeal an act, entitled "An act authorizing certain commissioners therein named to review and relay out part of the Edgmont Great Road in Delaware county; relative to the estate of William Wollerton, in Chester county; and relative to tax on dogs in certain townships in said county, so far as the same relates to taxing dogs in the township of East Pikeland, Chester county, Pennsylvania."

Part of Act of March 24, 1851 repealed.

SECTION 1. *Be it enacted, &c.*, That so much of the act of Assembly, approved the twenty-fourth day of March, Anno Domini one thousand eight hundred and fifty-one, entitled "An act authorizing certain commissioners therein named to review and relay out parts of the Edgmont Great Road in Delaware county; relative to the estate of William Wollerton in Chester county; and relative to tax on dogs in the townships of East Pikeland and West Vincent, East Vincent, Londongrove and West Whiteland, in the said county of Chester, as far as relates to taxing dogs in the township of East Pikeland, county of Chester and State of Pennsylvania," be and the same is hereby repealed.

APPROVED—The 6th day of June, A. D. 1893.

ROBT. E. PATTISON.

No. 276.

AN ACT

To repeal an act, entitled "An act authorizing certain commissioners therein named, to review and relay out part of the Edgmont Great Road in Delaware county; relative to the estate of William Wollerton in Chester county; and relative to tax on dogs in certain townships in said county," so far as the same relates to taxing dogs in the township of East Vincent, Chester county, Pennsylvania.

Part of Act of March 24, 1851, repealed.

SECTION 1. *Be it enacted, &c.*, That so much of the act of Assembly, approved the twenty-fourth day of March, Anno Domini one thousand eight hundred and fifty-one, entitled "An act authorizing certain commissioners therein named to review and relay out parts of the Edgmont Great Road in Delaware county; relative to the estate of William Wollerton in Chester county; and relative to tax on dogs in the townships of East Pike-

land and West Vincent, East Vincent, Londongrove and
and West Whiteland, in the said county of Chester," as
far as relates to taxing dogs in the township of East
Vincent, county of Chester and State of Pennsylvania, be
and the same is hereby repealed.

APPROVED—The 6th day of June, A. D. 1893.

ROBT. E. PATTISON.

No. 277.

AN ACT

Authorizing the Governor to purchase, in the name of the Commonwealth, for the use of the Western State Penitentiary, a
piece of land in the city of Allegheny, with authority to exercise
the right of eminent domain in making such purchase, if deemed
advisable for the best interests of the State, and making an appropriation therefor.

SECTION 1. *Be it enacted &c.*, That the Governor be and
he is hereby authorized to purchase in the name of the
Commonweath, for the use of the Western State Penitentiary, a piece of land, situated in the city of Allegheny,
bounded and described as follows, namely : Commencing
at the intersection of Kerr and Matilda streets, thence
along the line of Matilda street to Hanover street, thence
along Hanover street to the prison wall, thence by said
prison wall to Kerr street, and thence along Kerr street
to the place of beginning, being a piece or parcel of
land now or recently owned by Hartman & Petrel, front-
ing about five hundred and forty feet on Matilda street
by about one hundred feet in depth, and the authority
to exercise the right of eminent domain, if deemed for
the best interest of the State in making this purchase, is
hereby expressly granted, and the sum of thirty thousand dollars, or so much thereof as may be necessary, is
hereby specially appropriated for this purpose, to be
paid out of any moneys in the State Treasury, not otherwise appropriated.

The said appropriation to be paid on the warrant of
the Auditor General on a settlement made by him and
the State Treasurer upon filing of proper vouchers.

APPROVED—The 6th day of June, A. D. 1893.

ROBT. E. PATTISON.

Marginal notes: Governor author- ised to purchase land. Description of land. May exercise the right of eminent domain. $30,000.00 appro- priated. How payable.

No. 278.

AN ACT

To provide for the consolidation of boroughs and the government
and regulation thereof.

SECTION 1. *Be it enacted, &c.*, That whenever two or
more boroughs duly incorporated under the laws of this

Marginal note: Two or more bor- oughs may be con- solidated.

Commonwealth shall be adjacent thereto and of such compact and contiguous territory as to form one municipal division, it shall and may be lawful for the said boroughs to be consolidated into one borough, so that all the property, rights, franchises and privileges, then by law vested in either and both of said boroughs, may be transferred to and vested in the borough formed by such consolidation.

Rights, franchises, &c., vested in new borough.

SECTION 2. Such consolidation shall be made under the following conditions, that is to say :

Consolidation, how made.

First. The town council of each borough may enter into a joint agreement, under the corporate seals of each borough, for the consolidation thereof into one borough, which joint agreement shall set forth the name of the new corporation, the number of wards into which such consolidated borough shall be divided, not exceeding nine, and the territorial boundaries thereof.

Boroughs may enter into joint agreement

What the agreement shall set forth

Second. Said agreement shall be submitted to the vote of the qualified electors of each of the said boroughs at a special election to be held on a day to be designated in the said joint agreement, which election shall be held by the regularly constituted election officers in and for said boroughs, and in accordance with the provisions of the laws of this Commonwealth regulating elections by the people. If such special election shall be ordered within ninety days of any general election or election for municipal officers, the election shall be held on the day now fixed for the holding of such elections. Such election shall be by ballots which shall be marked "Proposed Consolidation," and below shall be printed the words "For Consolidation" and "Against Consolidation," and the elector shall designate with a X his desire to vote for or against such consolidation. Notice of such election shall be given by proclamation by the constables of the respective boroughs in the manner provided for proclamations for elections for municipal officers, and if the majority of the votes cast at such election in each of the said boroughs shall be in favor of the ratification of said agreement, then that fact shall be certified to the town council of each of the said boroughs by the respective election boards or return judges, and the chief burgess and town clerk of the respective boroughs shall cause a declaration of the result of such election to be endorsed upon said joint agreement, and the agreement so adopted, or a certified copy thereof, with all its endorsements shall be filed in the office of the Secretary of the Commonwealth, and a copy of such agreement and act of consolidation, duly certified by the Secretary of the Commonwealth under the seal of his office, shall be evidence of the existence of said new corporation, and upon the filing thereof, the Governor shall cause Letters Patent to be issued under the great seal of this Commonwealth, erecting the said consolidated boroughs into one corporation by the name set forth in said joint agreement.

It shall be submitted to a vote

When such election shall be held on day of general election.

How ballots shall be printed and marked.

Notice of such election.

Vote shall be certified to council of each borough

Declaration of result shall be endorsed on agreement.

Agreement so endorsed shall be filed in the office of Secretary of the Commonwealth.

Governor shall issue letters patent.

SECTION 3. Upon the issuance of such Letters Patent

the several boroughs, parties to said joint agreement, shall be deemed and taken to be one municipal corporation by the name provided in said agreement, possessing all the rights, privileges and franchises of the respective boroughs and to be governed and controlled in accord- ance with the provisions of the acts of Assembly theretofore governing and controlling the affairs of the borough which shall have been first incorporated.

SECTION 4. Upon the consummation of the consolida- tion as aforesaid all and singular, the rights, privileges and franchises of each of said boroughs and all the property real, personal and mixed, and all debts due on whatever account and other things in action belonging to each of said boroughs shall be taken and deemed to be transferred to and vested in such new borough, without further act or deed, and all property, all rights of way and all and every other interest shall be as effectually the property of the new borough as they were of the former boroughs, parties to said agreement, and the title to real estate, whether by deed or otherwise, under the laws of this Commonwealth vested in either of said boroughs shall not be deemed to revert or be in any way impaired by reason of this act: *Provided,* That all the rights of creditors and all liens shall be preserved unimpaired, and the respective boroughs may be deemed to continue in existence to preserve same, and all debts, liabilities and duties of either of said boroughs shall henceforth attach to said borough and be enforced against it to the same extent as if said debts, liabilities and duties had been incurred by or contracted by it.

SECTION 5. The chief burgess of that borough which shall have been first incorporated shall be the chief burgess of the new borough, to serve as such until a chief burgess shall have been elected and duly qualified in accordance with the laws of this Commonwealth. The chief burgess of the other borough shall become a member of the town council of the new borough from that ward in which he shall reside and shall continue a member thereof until the expiration of his term of office. The members of the town council of each of the said boroughs shall be members of the town council of the new borough from the wards in which they respectively reside, and no election for members of the council shall be held in any of the wards of the new borough until the number of members from such ward shall have been reduced to three by the expiration of the terms of service of members in office at the time of such consolidation, and thereafter, an- nually, there shall be elected in each ward one member of council for the term of three years, and all vacancies in the office of chief burgess or member of the town council shall be filled in the manner provided by law.

SECTION 6. The chief burgess elected in such new bor- ough shall hold his office for the term of three years, and thereafter, triennially, the qualified electors of said borough shall elect one person to be chief burgess at the time and in the manner now provided by law.

SECTION 7. The chief burgess of such borough shall not be a member of the town council or entitled to a seat therein, but shall have the power to veto any ordinance or resolution passed by the said council, and no ordinance or resolution enacted by the said council shall become effective until signed by the burgess unless the same shall be passed over his veto by the affirmative vote of two thirds of all of the members of such council. The chief burgess shall either consent or disapprove, with his reasons for such disapproval, of every ordinance or resolution passed by said council, within ten days thereafter. And the vote upon passing any ordinance or resolution over the veto of the chief burgess shall be taken at the next stated session of the town council thereafter.

SECTION 8. Every such consolidated borough shall form one school district, and the members of the school board of each of the boroughs shall continue members of the school board of the new borough until the expiration of their terms of service, and no member of the school board shall be elected to serve in any ward until the number shall have been reduced to three by the expiration of the terms of office, and thereafter there shall be elected in each ward one person to serve as school director for the term of three years. All vacancies in the office of school director shall be filled at the time and in the manner now provided by law.

SECTION 9. The overseers of the poor and street commissioners of each of the said boroughs shall continue in office as officers of the new borough until the expiration of their respective terms of office, and no elections shall be held in such borough for overseer of the poor or street commissioner until the number shall have been reduced to two by the expiration of the terms of office of the present incumbents, and thereafter, annually, there shall be elected by concurrent votes of the electors of such borough, one person as overseer of the poor and one person as street commissioner, each of whom shall hold their office for the term of two years, or until their successors are duly qualified. Vacancies in the office of overseer of the poor and street commissioner shall be filled in the manner provided by law.

SECTION 10. The town council of the new borough at their first session after the consummation of the consolidation shall designate by ballot which of the treasurers of the two boroughs shall be treasurer of the new borough, which of the high constables shall be the high constable of the new borough, and which of the auditors shall be the auditors of the new borough. They shall also select some suitable person to be clerk of the council, and thereafter, annually, the qualified electors of such borough shall elect one person as high constable, one person as borough treasurer and three persons as auditors, and the town council shall select the clerk of the council.

SECTION 11. Justices of the peace in office in each of such boroughs shall continue in office until the expiration of their respective commissions, and no election for justices of the peace shall be held in such borough until the number has been reduced to two by the expiration of the commissions of the persons in office, and thereafter there shall be two justices of the peace in such new borough, who shall hold their offices for the term and be elected and qualified in the manner provided by law. Justices of the peace.

SECTION 12. The respective tax collectors of said boroughs shall continue in office until the expirations of their respective terms of service, and shall respectively have all the authority of collectors of taxes within the limits of such new borough for the collection of taxes set forth in their respective duplicates, and at the first municipal election after such consolidation, and thereafter triennally, the qualified electors of such borough shall elect one person to be collector of taxes of such borough, who shall have all the power and authority of collectors of State and county taxes under the general laws of this Commonwealth, and shall also be the collector of the borough, road, poor and school taxes levied by the proper authorities of said borough, and all precepts and duplicates shall be issued and delivered to said collector of taxes, who shall give security for the faithful performance of duties in the manner provided by the laws of the Commonwealth relative to collectors of taxes. Tax collectors. When tax collector shall be elected. Powers. What taxes he shall collect. Bond.

APPROVED—The 6th day of June, A. D. 1893.

ROBT. E. PATTISON.

No. 279.

AN ACT

To require boards of school directors and controllers to provide for the better protection of the health and morals of school children in their respective school districts.

SECTION 1. *Be it enacted, &c.*, That boards of school directors and controllers shall provide suitable and convenient water closets for each of the schools under their official jurisdiction, not less than two for each school or school building where both sexes are in attendance, in their respective school districts, with separate means of access for each, and unless placed at a remote distance one from the other, the approaches or walks thereto shall be separated by a substantial, close fence, not less than seven feet in height, and it shall be the duty of the directors or controllers to make provisions for keeping the water closets in a clean, comfortable and healthful condition. Water closets for each school. How they shall be arranged.

SECTION 2. Any failure on the part of school directors or controllers to comply with the provisions of this act

Removal of directors for failure to comply with requirements of this act.

shall make them liable to be removed from office by the court of quarter sessions of the county in which the schools are located, upon complaint made to the court, under oath or affirmation, of not less than five taxable citizens resident in the school district in which the school is located.

APPROVED—The 6th day of June, A. D. 1893.

ROBT. E. PATTISON.

No. 280.

AN ACT

To abolish all fees and commissions now allowed and received by the treasurer of any county, co-extensive in boundary with a city of the first class, for services rendered in the receipt, collection, payment and disbursement of revenues on behalf of this Commonwealth.

SECTION 1. *Be it enacted, &c.*, That all fees and commissions now allowed, received or collectible by the treasurer of any county, co-extensive in boundary with a city of the first class, for service rendered by him in the receipt, collection, payment and disbursement of revenues for or on behalf of this Commonwealth, be and the same are hereby repealed and abolished.

SECTION 2. That all laws or parts of laws inconsistent herewith be and the same are hereby repealed.

APPROVED—The 6th day of June, A D. 1893.

ROBT. E. PATTISON.

No. 281.

AN ACT

To provide for the registration of births and deaths in the several counties of the Commonwealth.

Record of births and deaths shall be kept.

SECTION 1. *Be it enacted, &c.*, That it shall be the duty of the clerk of the orphans' court of each county of the Commonwealth to keep a separate record of all births and of all deaths occurring within their respective counties. Said record shall be kept from data and in suitable books, both to be furnished as hereinafter provided, and

Births, contents of record of.

shall contain in separate columns as to births, the full name of the child, sex and color, full names of father and mother, with their residence and occupation of the father, date and place of birth, with street and number, when

Deaths, contents of record of.

possible, and date of making the record; and as to deaths, the full name of the deceased, color, sex and age, whether married or single, place of birth, occupation, date and place of death, with street and number, when possible, cause of death, duration of last illness, place and date of interment. When a minor, the name of the father and mother, and the date of making the record. Said record shall be alphabetically indexed and shall be open at all times to the inspection of physicians, clergymen and attorneys-at-law, without charge.

Arrangement and inspection of records.

SECTION 2. It shall be the duty of the assessors of the several townships, boroughs and wards within the Commonwealth to obtain, semi-annually, at the time of making their assessments now provided by law, and it shall be the duty of parents, guardians and other persons having knowledge to furnish to such assessors, the information necessary to keep the record specified in the preceding section. Said assessors shall return said information to the clerk of the orphans' court, upon blanks to be furnished as hereinafter provided, at the time of making their semi-annual returns to the county commissioners, and to each return shall be attached the oath or affirmation of the assessor that he made diligent inquiry as to the births, deaths and other information herein referred to, within his ward, borough or township, and that his return is true to the best of his knowledge, information and belief.

Assessors shall obtain the information necessary to keep records.

Shall return information to clerk of orphans' court.

Oath or affirmation shall be attached.

SECTION 3. It shall be the duty of the county commissioners to furnish to the clerk of the orphans' court in their respective counties suitable books in which to keep the record herein provided for, and to furnish to the assessors of the several wards, boroughs and townships appropriate blanks upon which to enter the information necessary to make said record.

County commissioners shall furnish record books and assessors blanks.

SECTION 4. The fees to be allowed for services rendered pursuant to the provisions of this act shall be as follows: The clerk of the orphans' court shall receive for making the record of each birth and each death, with all other information referred to in section one hereof, the sum of five cents, to be paid out of the county funds; for furnishing a certified copy of the record of each birth or death, the sum of fifty cents, to be paid by the party applying therefor; for making search for each birth or death, where a certified copy is not required, the sum of ten cents, to be paid by the party applying therefor. The assessors shall receive for each birth and for each death returned as provided by the second section hereof, the sum of five cents, to be paid out of the county funds upon a certificate given under the hand and seal of office of said clerk as to the number of births and deaths returned.

Fees allowed to clerk of orphans' court.

Fees allowed to assessors.

Fees shall be paid out of county funds.

SECTION 5. The record of births and deaths herein provided for, or duly certified copies of the same, shall be prima facie evidence of all matters therein contained and shall be admissible in all judicial proceedings.

Records or certified copies of same admissable in judicial proceedings.

SECTION 6. Every person who shall violate any of the provisions of this act shall forfeit and pay the sum of ten dollars for each offense, to be recovered in the name of the Commonwealth as debts of like amount are by law recoverable: *Provided,* That the provisions of this act

Penalty for violation of provisions of act.

Shall not affect
cities having estab-
lished system.

Repeal.

shall not affect cities where a system for the registration of births and deaths has already been established.

SECTION 7. All laws or parts of laws inconsistent herewith be and the same are hereby repealed.

APPROVED—The 6th day of June, A. D. 1893.

ROBT. E. PATTISON.

No. 282.

AN ACT

Authorizing and regulating the taking, use and occupancy of certain public burial places, under certain circumstances, for purposes of common school education.

Directors may declare intention to occupy certain public burial ground.

SECTION 1. *Be it enacted, &c.,* That whenever the board of directors or controllers of any school district in this Commonwealth shall deem it desirable to occupy for purposes of common school education any ground therein used as a public burial place, or conveyed in fee to a municipal corporation to be kept as a public burial place, such board may, by resolution passed by the affirmative vote of at least four-fifths of all the members thereof, and duly entered on the minutes, declare its intention to take, use and occupy the same for the purposes aforesaid, designating the same in said resolution by metes and bounds:

Only half acre can be taken.
Certain burial grounds not included.

Provided, No more than one-half acre of ground shall at any one time be so taken, used or occupied: *And provided,* This act shall not apply to burial grounds of religious societies, churches or congregations, or of private corporations or associations, nor to portions thereof devoted to public use or the burial of the poor, nor to burial grounds on or connected with almshouse properties.

Board shall make application to court.

SECTION 2. After the passage of said resolution, the court of common pleas of the proper county shall, on application of said board through its president, appoint three discreet citizens of the county in which said school district is located as viewers to view and ascertain the damages done, and likely to be done, by reason of such taking, use and occupancy, and shall appoint a time, not less than thirty nor more than sixty days thereafter, for said viewers to meet at or upon the premises so to be taken, used and occupied, of which time and place notice shall be given by said board of said viewers and to all parties interested, by publication for four successive weeks prior to the day of meeting, in not more than four nor less than two newspapers published in said county. The said viewers or any two of them having been first duly sworn or affirmed faithfully, justly and impartially to decide and a true report to make concerning all matters and things submitted to them, and in relation to which they are authorized by law to inquire, and having viewed the premises shall establish and determine the quantity of said land so to be taken, used and occupied for the purposes aforesaid, and after having made a fair and just

Viewers appointed.

Notice of meeting of viewers.

Viewers shall be sworn or affirmed.

Shall determine quantity of land to be taken

comparison of the advantages and disadvantages, they shall estimate and determine whether any, and if any, what amount of damages has been and seems likely to be sustained by reason of such taking, use and occupancy, and to whom payable, and make report thereof to said court; and if damages be awarded and the report be confirmed by the said court, judgment shall be entered thereon and execution to enforce the collection thereof may be issued as in other cases of judgment against school districts, and each viewer shall be entitled to two dollars per day for every day necessarily employed in the duties herein prescribed, to be paid by the school district. *[Shall estimate amount of damages.]* *[Shall report to the court.]* *[Collection of damages awarded.]* *[Pay of viewers.]*

SECTION 3. Upon the report of said viewers or any two of them being filed in said court, any party interested may, within thirty days thereafter, except to the same, or file his, her, its or their appeal from the same to said court. Such appeal shall be in writing and accompanied by an affidavit of the appellant, or his, her, its or their agent, chief officer or attorney, that the same is not taken for the purpose of delay, but because the affiant firmly believes that injustice has been done; after such appeal either party may put the cause at issue in the form directed by said court, and the same may be tried by said court and a jury, and said proceedings shall be with the same right of appeal to the Supreme Court as in other cases. *[Appeal from report of viewers.]* *[How made.]* *[Contents.]* *[Form of issue.]* *[Trial and appeal to Supreme Court.]*

SECTION 4. After the damages so finally determined upon, if any there be, shall have been paid to the parties in whose favor they are adjudged, or to the persons legally entitled thereto, such school district may, by its board of directors or controllers as the case may be, or by any person, contractor, agent, employé or officer thereto authorized by said board, enter upon, take, use and occupy such ground and erect building thereon, and do all things necessary and convenient for the purposes aforesaid: *Provided*, That before entering upon, using or occupying the same, four weeks' notice shall be given by the board by publication in manner hereinbefore set forth, within which time any person having any relative or kindred buried in such burial place may designate where the same are buried and make demand upon said board or the president thereof that the remains of such relative or kindred be removed therefrom and separately interred elsewhere and marked with substantial stones, with appropriate inscriptions thereon, at the proper expense and charge of said school district, which said demand shall be complied with before the commencement of the erection of any building on said grounds, and said school district shall, if necessary, purchase other land, not more than twice the amount so to be taken, for the purpose of re-interring therein the remains of persons buried in the ground to be taken, and all remains so far as they can be found shall be removed to the grounds so purchased, or elsewhere, and interred in an orderly and decorous manner at expense of said district, and any grounds so purchased *[After damages have been paid, land may be occupied.]* *[Removal of bodies of persons buried therein.]* *[Expenses of removal.]*

may thereafter be used as a public burial place in like manner as the property taken.

APPROVED—The 6th day of June, A. D. 1893.

ROBT. E. PATTISON.

No. 283.

AN ACT

To prevent entering of trotting or pacing horses out of their classes.

SECTION 1. *Be it enacted, &c.*, That it is hereby made unlawful for any person or persons to enter or cause to be entered for competition, or to compete for any purse, prize, premium, stake or sweepstake offered or given by any agricultural or other society, association or person or persons, in the State of Pennsylvania, any horse, mare or gelding, colt or filly, under an assumed name, or out of its proper class, when such prize, purse, premium, stake or sweepstake is to be decided by a contest, in trotting or pacing races.

Penalty for violation of act.

SECTION 2. That any person or persons found guilty of a violation of section one of this act shall, upon conviction thereof, be imprisoned not exceeding six months, or fined not exceeding five hundred dollars, or both, or either, at the discretion of the court.

When act shall take effect.

SECTION 3. That this act shall take effect from the date of its passage.

APPROVED—The 6th day of June, A. D. 1893.

ROBT. E. PATTISON.

No. 284.

AN ACT

Relating to husband and wife, enlarging her capacity to acquire and dispose of property, to sue and be sued, and to make a last will, and enabling them to sue and to testify against each other in certain cases.

Right of a married woman to acquire or dispose of property.

SECTION 1. *Be it enacted, &c.*, That hereafter a married woman shall have the same right and power as an unmarried person to acquire, own, possess, control, use, lease, sell, or otherwise dispose of any property of any kind, real, personal or mixed, and either in possession or expectancy, and may exercise the said right and power in the same manner and to the same extent as an unmarried person, but she may not mortgage or convey her real property, unless her husband join in such mortgage or conveyance.

Husband must join in mortgage or conveyance.

May make contract.

SECTION 2. Hereafter a married woman may, in the same manner and to the same extent as an unmarried person, make any contract in writing, or otherwise, which is necessary, appropriate, convenient or advantageous to the exercise or enjoyment of the rights and powers granted by the foregoing section, but she may not become accommodation endorser, maker, guarantor or surety for another, and she may not execute or acknowledge a deed, or other written instrument, conveying or mortgaging her real property, unless her husband join in such mortgage or conveyance.

SECTION 3. Hereafter a married woman may sue and be sued civilly in all respects and in any form of action and with the same effect and results and consequences as an unmarried person, but she may not sue her husband, except in a proceeding for divorce, or in a proceeding to protect or recover her separate property whensoever he may have deserted or separated himself from her without sufficient cause, or may have neglected or refused to support her, nor may he sue her, except in a proceeding for divorce, or in a proceeding to protect or recover his separate property whensoever she may have deserted him, or separated herself from him without sufficient cause, nor may she be arrested or imprisoned for her torts.

SECTION 4. In any proceeding brought by either under the provisions of section three to protect or recover the separate property of either, both shall be fully competent witnesses, except that neither may testify to confidential communications made by one or the other, unless this privilege be waived upon the trial.

SECTION 5. Hereafter a married woman may dispose of her property, real and personal, by last will and testament, in writing signed by her or by her direction, or attested by her mark made by her or by her direction, at the end thereof in the same manner as if she were unmarried: *Provided*, That nothing in this act shall affect her husband's right as tenant by the courtesy, nor his right to take against her will, as provided by existing laws.

SECTION 6. The married persons property act, approved June three, one thousand eight hundred and eighty-seven, and all other acts inconsistent herewith are hereby repealed.

APPROVED—The 8th day of June, A. D. 1893.

ROBT. E. PATTISON.

Marginal notes:
Shall not become endorser or surety.
Husband must join in mortgage or conveyance.
May sue and be sued.
Shall not sue husband except in divorce or to recover separate property.
Husband shall not sue wife except in divorce or to recover separate property.
Arrest for her torts.
Both may testify in proceedings under section three, except as to confidential communications unless waived.
She may dispose of property by will.
Shall not effect certain rights of husband.
Repeal of certain acts.

No. 285.

AN ACT

Relating to Mandamus.

SECTION 1. *Be it enacted, &c.*, That the several courts of common pleas shall, within their respective counties, have the power to issue writs of mandamus to all officers and magistrates elected or appointed in or for the respective county, or in or for any township, district or

Marginal note: Courts of common pleas shall have power to issue writs of mandamus to officers, magistrates and corporations in the respective counties.

place within such county, and to all corporations being or having their chief place of business within such county; and the court of common pleas of the county in which the seat of government is or may be located shall have the power, and it shall be required, to issue the writ of mandamus to the Lieutenant Governor, Secretary of the Commonwealth, Attorney General, Secretary of Internal Affairs, Superintendent of Public Instruction, State Treasurer, Auditor General, Insurance Commissioner, and Commissioners of the Sinking Fund.

Court at seat of government shall issue writs to certain State officers.

SECTION 2. Any person desiring to obtain a writ of mandamus shall present his petition therefor, verified by affidavit, to the judge or judges of the proper court, either in session or at chambers, setting forth the facts upon which he relies for the relief sought, the act or duty whose performance he seeks, his interest in the result, the name of the person or body at whose hands performance is sought, demand or refusal to perform the act or duty, and that the petitioner is without other adequate and specific remedy at law. If such petition presents the substance of a case for mandamus, the court shall direct that such writ issue in the alternative form: *Provided however*, That if the right to require the performance of the act is clear, and it is apparent that no valid excuse can be given for not performing it, a peremptory mandamus may be awarded in the first instance and directed to issue forthwith.

Petition for mandamus.

Contents.

If sufficient, court shall direct writ to issue.

When peremptory mandamus may be awarded.

SECTION 3. The writ of mandamus may issue upon the application of any person beneficially interested.

Who may make application.

SECTION 4. When the writ is sought to procure the enforcement of a public duty, the proceeding shall be prosecuted in the name of the Commonwealth on the relation of the Attorney General: *Provided however*, That said proceeding in proper cases shall be on the relation of the district attorney of the proper county: *Provided further*, That when said proceeding is sought to enforce a duty affecting a particular public interest of the State, it shall be on the relation of the officer entrusted with the management of such interest. In all other cases the party procuring the alternative writ shall be plaintiff, the party to whom said writ is directed shall be defendant, and the action shall be docketed as in ordinary cases, namely: . . . . . . , plaintiff, versus . . . . . , defendant.

Proceedings on relation of Attorney General.

Of District Attorney.

When proceeding affects particular interest of the State.

Who shall be parties in all other cases.

SECTION 5. All writs in the alternative form shall be in force for three months from their date and may be served by the plaintiff, or any one by him authorized, or by any sheriff or deputy sheriff in any county of the Commonwealth in which the defendant may be, by giving the defendant personally a copy thereof, attested by the prothonotary of the court awarding the writ. They shall be returnable at such time, not less than five days after the service thereof, as the court may direct.

Writs in alternative form, how long in force and how served.

When returnable.

SECTION 6. When the writ is sought against a municipal corporation, the alternative writ shall be directed to such

Writ against a municipal corporation.

of the corporate authorities in their official capacity as are concerned in the execution of the thing required, and service thereof upon any of such officers shall be sufficient.

SECTION 7. When the writ is sought against a private corporation, domestic or foreign, the alternative writ shall be directed against the corporation by name, and also against any particular person or body of persons connected therewith whom it may be sought to coerce, and service thereof upon any officer or agent of the corporation and upon such particular person or chief officer of such body of persons shall be sufficient. The peremptory writ may be directed to the said corporation, or to the person or body of persons who have the power and whose duty it is to do the act required, or to such superior officer as would be expected to execute the order.

Writ against a private corporation.

To whom peremptory writ may be directed.

SECTION 8. When the writ is sought against a board or body other than a corporation, it shall be directed to such board or body in their official capacity, and service shall be made upon a majority of the members thereof, unless the board or body was created by law and has a chairman or other presiding officer appointed pursuant to law, in which case service upon him shall be sufficient.

Writ against a board or body other than a corporation.

SECTION 9. It shall be lawful for the court, when applied to for the writ, or upon and after the issuing of the first writ on the petition of any person having or claiming a right or interest in the subject matter, other than the person to whom the writ is prayed to be or has issued, setting forth his right or interest in or to the subject matter of the controversy, to authorize in proper cases such person, even though he could not have been made original defendant, to frame the return and conduct the subsequent proceedings at his own expense, or to take such part therein and on such terms as to the court may seem just; and in such cases, if judgment is given for or against the party suing the writ, such judgment shall be given against or for the party to whom the writ shall have been directed, but the court may authorize the person permitted as aforesaid to frame the return and conduct the subsequent proceedings to use the name of the party to whom such writ shall have been directed for the recovery of costs and the enforcing of the judgment, and also for the purpose of an appeal to the Supreme Court, with like force and effect as though the party to whom such writ shall have been directed had sought to recover costs and to enforce the judgment or to appeal to the Supreme Court: *Provided however*, That when, in such cases, judgment is given in favor of the plaintiff, the court may order that damages and costs, or either, adjudged in favor of such party, shall be paid in whole or in part by the person permitted as aforesaid to conduct the proceedings.

Court may order who shall frame return and conduct proceedings at his own expense.

Judgment. for or against whom given.

Proviso as to judgment in favor of plaintiff.

SECTION 10. The court may direct what notice shall be given of all papers filed in the proceeding subsequent to the granting of the alternative writ.

Court may direct what notice shall be given.

Appearance de bene esse.

SECTION 11. Appearance *de bene esse* shall enable the defendant to take advantage of defective service of the alternative writ. The defendant may move to supersede or quash said writ; if he fails he shall be permitted to file his return as in this act mentioned, and to proceed if such motion had not been made.

Defendant may file return to alternative writ.

Judgment in default of return.

SECTION 12. The defendant shall file in the office of the prothonotary of the court awarding the alternative writ, a return thereto, verified by affidavit, within the time specified in the writ, and in default thereof, judgment shall be given against him with the same effect as if he had filed a return and such return had been adjudged insufficient.

Certainty required in such return.

SECTION 13. In such return, certainty to a certain intent in general, and no more, shall be required. If the return is uncertain, vague or evasive or informal in any respect, such opportunity may be afforded for the correction thereof as to the court shall seem just and reasonable.

Court shall allow parties time to make return, plead, &c.

SECTION 14. The court applied to for the writ shall allow the plaintiff and defendant respectively, such convenient time to make return, plead, reply, rejoin or demur as shall be just and reasonable.

Plaintiff and defendant, duty of.

SECTION 15. The plaintiff may demur to the return or he may plead to or traverse all or any of the material facts therein contained; the defendant shall reply, take issue or demur and like proceedings shall be had as in other actions at law.

Recovery of damages and costs if judgment is entered for plaintiff.

SECTION 16. If a verdict is found for the plaintiff and judgment is entered thereon, or if a judgment is given for him upon a demurrer or by *nihil dicit* or for want of an answer by *non sum informatus* or other pleading, he shall recover his damages and costs.

Costs of defendant.

SECTION 17. If judgment is given for the defendant he shall recover his costs.

When action for making return is debarred.

SECTION 18. If damages are recovered against any person making return as aforesaid, such recovery shall debar every other action for making such return.

Court may give or refuse costs.

SECTION 19. The costs of the application for a writ of mandamus, whether such writ is granted or not, also the costs of the writ if issued and obeyed or not prosecuted to judgment as aforesaid, may be given or refused according to the discretion of the court.

Execution for damages and costs.

SECTION 20. Damages and costs may be levied by execution as in other cases.

Damages sustained by plaintiff, how ascertained.

SECTION 21. Damages sustained by the plaintiff shall be ascertained by the jury trying any issue in fact; if no such issue is tried they shall be ascertained by the court in such manner as may be deemed just and reasonable.

Peremptory mandamus and judgment for damages and costs, when judgment is given for plaintiff.

SECTION 22. Whenever, in accordance with act, judgment is given for the plaintiff, the court may award that a peremptory mandamus shall issue in that behalf and shall also enter judgment for damages and costs, and thereupon such peremptory writ of mandamus may be issued accordingly at any time after twenty days from the signing of the judgment, and not before, unless the exigence of the case, in the discretion of the court, requires it, in which event the court may direct that said writ shall issue forthwith.

SECTION 23. When the writ is sought by a public officer in his official capacity for the public benefit, the action shall not abate by the termination of his office but may be prosecuted by his successor.

SECTION 24. When the writ is sought by an executor, administrator or trustee, the death of the plaintiff or his removal from position by resignation or otherwise shall not abate the writ, but the action may be continued by his successor.

SECTION 25. The death, resignation or removal from office by lapse of time or otherwise, of any defendant, shall not have the effect to abate the suit, but his successor may be made a party thereto and any peremptory writ shall be directed against him.

SECTION 26. Defects in substance in the alternative writ may be taken advantage of at any stage of the proceeding. Amendments may be allowed as in other civil actions save as hereinafter mentioned.

SECTION 27. The peremptory writ shall be directed to the same person as the alternative writ save as herein authorized; it shall be served in the same manner as the alternative writ and it shall be made returnable at such time as to the court awarding it may seem just and reasonable.

SECTION 28. The peremptory writ, though issued, may be superseded or quashed for such cause as to the court may seem just, but no amendment thereto shall be allowed.

SECTION 29. The party aggrieved by the proceedings had in any court of common pleas upon any writ of mandamus may remove the same at any time within twenty days after final judgment, order, decree, or in cases where the granting of said writ is required by the first section of this act, at any time within twenty days after refusal to grant said writ, into the Supreme Court by appeal as in other actions at law, and such appeal shall supersede any peremptory writ awarded by the court and also any execution for damages or costs, upon bail to be given as in other civil cases.

SECTION 30. Such appeal shall also supersede any peremptory writ issued within twenty days after final judgment, order or decree: *Provided however*, That the *certiorari* in consequence of such appeal be lodged in the office of the prothonotary of the court awarding the writ before the mandate thereof shall have been fully complied with: *Provided further*, That said appeal shall be made returnable forthwith.

SECTION 31. Every such appeal may be made returnable forthwith, and, if thus made returnable, it shall be heard and decided by the Supreme Court in any district in which it may be in session, as in this act provided in

Writ sought by public officer shall not abate by expiration of term.

Death or removal of plaintiff shall not abate writ when sought by executor or trustee.

Death or removal of defendant shall not abate his suit.

Defects in substance in alternative writ.

Amendments. Peremptory writ, to whom directed. Service and return of.

Peremptory writ may be superseded or quashed, but not amended.

Proceedings may be removed into the Supreme Court by appeal.

Appeal shall supersede peremptory writ and execution for costs, &c.

Shall supersede peremptory writ issued within twenty days. Proviso as to filing of certiorari.

Return of appeal.

Supreme court shall hear and decide appeal.

District in which it
shall be heard.

cases originating in said court, and if not thus returnable it shall be heard and decided by said court when in session in the proper district at the term to which it shall have been made returnable.

Supreme Court shall
exercise original
jurisdiction.

SECTION 32. The Supreme Court in any district shall exercise, throughout the State, original jurisdiction in the cases authorized by the organic law of the State, and if not decided before the close of its session in said

If case is not de-
cided before close
of session, it shall
be certified to and
filed to next dis-
trict.

district shall cause the same to be certified to and filed for action with the prothonotary of said court in the district within which it shall be next in session, and so to be certified from district to district until finally decided.

Supreme Court,
duties and powers
of, in such cases.

SECTION 33. The Supreme Court in such cases shall dispose of all issues of fact arising therein in such manner as may be deemed just and reasonable, and shall enter such judgments, orders or decrees and in such manner and on such terms as to it may seem proper, and to that

Damages and costs,
recovery of.

end may make all necessary rules and regulations. Damages and costs allowed by this act and awarded by the Supreme Court shall be recovered in the manner said court may direct.

Repeal.

SECTION 34. All acts or parts of acts inconsistent herewith be and the same are hereby repealed.

APPROVED—The 8th day of June, A. D. 1893.

ROBT. E. PATTISON.

No. 286.

AN ACT

Authorizing the courts of common pleas to direct the filing of bonds to the Commonwealth, by railroad and canal companies to secure payment of damages for taking land and materials, in cases where there is a disputed, doubtful or defective title, or where any party interested is absent, unknown, covert, not of full age, of unsound mind, or from any cause cannot be bargained with or served with notice or have a bond tendered to them, and appoint guardians ad litem or trustees for such persons.

Proceedings in case
railroad or canal
companies take
lands. &c., where
there is a disputed
title.

SECTION 1. *Be it enacted, &c.*, That in any case where any railroad or canal company has or shall have authority, under any act of Assembly, to take and appropriate lands and materials, and in any case where such company is or shall be required to give security for the payment of damages to or for the taking of any land or materials, and when it shall be made known to the court of common pleas of the proper county by petition, affidavit or otherwise that there is a disputed, doubtful or defec-

Or where party in-
terested in lands,
&c., is absent, un-
known, &c.

tive title, or that any party interested in such land or materials is absent, unknown, covert, not of full age, or of unsound mind, or from any cause cannot be bargained with or served with notice or have a bond tendered to them within the county where the land or materials are situated, the court which shall have jurisdiction of the appointment of viewers and assessment of damages in such case shall, on application of such company, direct the filing of a bond to the Commonwealth of Pennsylvania in an amount and with security to be approved by the court, for the use of the person or persons who may be found to be entitled to the damages for the taking and appropriation of such land or materials or for the damage or injury to such land, and when such bond shall be so approved and filed, and when, upon the petition of such company, viewers to assess the said damages shall be appointed, the said court shall direct notices of the approval and filing of said bond and of appointment and time and place of meeting of said viewers, respectively, to be published in two newspapers published in the county where the land or materials are situated, if two are published, twice a week for two weeks after the bond is filed and before the day appointed for the meeting of the viewers, and the bond so filed and the notice or notices so published shall have the like effect as if the said bond had been given or tendered to the parties entitled, and as if personal notice had been served on the party or parties owning or claiming such lands or materials: *Provided however*, That when the residences of any such parties shall be known to such company a copy of such published notices shall be sent to them by mail or otherwise.

Filing of bond.

Viewers shall be appointed on petition of company.

Publication of notice.

Effects of filing bond and publishing notice.

Proviso.

SECTION 2. It shall be the duty of the court having jurisdiction of the appointment of viewers and assessment of damages, at the time of the application of such company for the appointment of viewers, to appoint a guardian ad litem or trustee, as the circumstances of the case shall require, for such interested party who is absent, unknown, covert, not of full age, or of unsound mind, or from any cause cannot be bargained with or served with notice or have a bond tendered to them, and such guardian ad litem or trustee shall represent the interests of the person of whom he is guardian ad litem or trustee in all the subsequent proceedings.

Court shall appoint guardian at litem or trustee.

Powers of guardian or trustee.

APPROVED—The 8th day of June, A. D. 1893.

ROBT. E. PATTISON.

No. 287.

˙AN ACT

To provide for the manner of reducing the capital stock of corporations.

SECTION 1. *Be it enacted, &c.*, That the capital stock of any corporation may be reduced from time to time by the consent of the persons or bodies corporate holding the larger amount in value of the stock of such company, provided that such reductions shall not be below the amount of capital stock required by law for the formation of such company.

Capital stock of corporations may be reduced.

Meeting of stockholders to be called.

SECTION 2. That any corporation desirous of reducing its capital stock as provided by this act shall, by a resolution of its board of directors, call a meeting of its stockholders therefor, which meeting shall be held in its chief office or place of business in this Commonwealth,

Notice to be published.

and notice of the time, place and object of said meeting shall be published once a week for sixty days prior to such meeting in at least one newspaper published in the county, city or borough wherein such office or place of business is situate.

Election for or against reduction to be held

SECTION 3. At the meeting called pursuant to the second section of this act, an election of the stockholders of such corporation shall be taken for or against such reduction, which shall be conducted by three judges, stockholders of said corporation, appointed by the board of directors to hold said election, and if one or more of said judges be absent, the judge or judges present shall appoint a

Election judges to be sworn

judge or judges who shall act in the place of the judge or judges absent, and who shall respectively take and subscribe an oath or affirmation before an officer authorized by law to administer the same well and truly and according to law, to conduct such elections to the best of their ability, and the said judges shall decide upon the

Qualification of voters.

qualification of voters, and when the election is closed, count the number of shares voted for and against such reduction, and declare whether the persons or bodies corporate holding the larger amount of the stock of such corporation have consented to such reduction or refused

Result of election to be declared.

to consent thereto, and shall make out duplicate returns of said election, stating the number of shares of stock that voted for such reduction and the number that voted against such reduction, and subscribe and deliver the same to one of the chief officers of said company.

Ballots to be endorsed with num of shares.

SECTION 4. Each ballot shall have endorsed thereon the number of shares thereby represented, but no share or shares transferred within sixty days shall entitle the holder or holders thereof to vote at such election or meeting, nor shall any proxy be received or entitle the holder

Proxies shall bear date and have been executed three months preceding election.

to vote unless the same shall bear date and have been executed within three months next preceding such election or meeting, and it shall be the duty of such corporation to furnish the judges at said meeting with a state-

Statement of capital stock and shareholders to be furnished judges.

ment of the amount of its capital stock with the names of persons or bodies corporate holding the same, and number of shares by each respectively held, which statement shall be signed by one of the chief officers of such corporation with an affidavit thereto annexed that the same is true and correct to the best of his knowledge and belief.

Copy of return and notice to be filed with Secretary of Commonwealth.

SECTION 5. That it shall be the duty of such corporation, if consent is given to such reduction, to file in the office of the Secretary of the Commonwealth, within thirty days after such election or meeting, one of the copies of the return of such election provided for by the third section of this act with a copy of the resolution and notice calling the same thereto annexed, and upon the reduction of the capital stock of such corporation made pursuant thereto, it shall be the duty of the president or treasurer of such corporation, within thirty days thereafter, to make a return to the Secretary of the Commonwealth, under oath, of the amount of such reduction, and in case of neglect or omission so to do, such corporation shall be subject to a penalty of five thousand dollars, which penalty shall be collected on an account settled by the Auditor General and State Treasurer as accounts for taxes due the Commonwealth are settled and collected, and the Secretary of the Commonwealth shall cause said return to be recorded in a book kept for that purpose and furnish a certified copy of the same to the Auditor General.

Duty of President or Treasurer.

Penalty for neglect

Duty of Secretary of Commonwealth.

APPROVED—The 8th day of June, A. D. 1893.
ROBT. E. PATTISON.

No. 288.

AN ACT

Being a further supplement to an act, entitled "An act to provide revenue by taxation," approved the seventh day of June, Anno Domini one thousand eight hundred and seventy-nine, amending the amendment of the supplement thereto which became a law on the first day of June, Anno Domini one thousand eight hundred and eighty-nine, which amendment herein amended, was approved the eighth day of June, Anno Domini one thousand eight hundred and ninety-one, relating to the tax on capital stock.

SECTION 1. *Be it enacted, &c.,* That the twenty-first section of an act which became a law on the first day of June, Anno Domini one thousand eight hundred and eighty-nine, entitled "A further supplement to an act, entitled 'An act to provide revenue by taxation,' approved the seventh day of June, Anno Domini one thousand eight hundred and seventy-nine, as the said section is amended by an act approved the eighth day of June, Anno Domini one thousand eight hundred and ninety-one," which reads as follows, to wit:

"SECTION 21. That every corporation, joint-stock association, limited partnerships and company whatsoever, from which a report is required under the twentieth section hereof, shall be subject to and pay into the treasury of the Commonwealth annually a tax at the rate of five mills upon each dollar of the actual value of its whole capital stock of all kinds, including common, special and preferred, as ascertained in the manner prescribed in said twentieth section, and it shall be the duty of the treasurer or other officers having charge of any such corporation, joint-stock association or limited partnership, upon which a tax is imposed by this section to transmit

Section 21, Act of June 8 1891, cited for amendment.

the amount of said tax to the treasury of the Commonwealth within thirty days from the date of settlement of the account by the Auditor General and State Treasurer: *Provided,* That for the purposes of this act interests in limited partnerships or joint-stock associations shall be deemed to be capital stock taxable accordingly: *Provided also,* That corporations, limited partnerships and joint-stock associations liable to tax on capital stock under this section, shall not be required to make any report or pay any further tax on the mortgages, bonds and other securities owned by them in their own right, but corporations, limited partnerships and joint-stock associations holding such securities as trustees, executors, administrators, guardians or in any other manner, shall return and pay the tax imposed by this act upon all securities so held by them as in the case of individuals: *And provided further,* That the provisions of this section shall not apply to the taxation of the capital stock of corporations, limited partnerships or joint-stock associations, organized exclusively for manufacturing purposes and actually carrying on manufacturing within the State, excepting companies engaged in the brewing or distilling of spirits or malt liquors and such as enjoy and exercise the right of eminent domain: *Provided further,* In case of fire and marine insurance companies the tax imposed by this section shall be at the rate of three mills upon each dollar of the actual value of the whole capital stock," be and the same is hereby amended so as read as follows:

SECTION 21. That every corporation, joint-stock association, limited partnership and company whatsoever, from which a report is required under the twentieth section hereof, shall be subject to and pay into the treasury of the Commonwealth, annually, a tax at the rate of five mills upon each dollar of the actual value of its whole capital stock of all kinds, including common, special and preferred, as ascertained in the manner prescribed in said twentieth section, and it shall be the duty of the treasurer or other officers having charge of any such corporation, joint-stock association or limited partnership, upon which a tax is imposed by this section, to transmit the amount of said tax to the treasury of the Commonwealth within thirty days from the date of settlement of the account by the Auditor General and State Treasurer: *Provided,* That for the purposes of this act, interests in limited partnerships or joint-stock associations shall deemed to be capital stock and taxable accordingly: *Pi vided also,* That corporations, limited partnerships a1 joint-stock associations, liable to tax on capital sto under this section, shall not be required to make any port or pay any further tax on the mortgages, bonds a other securities owned by them in their own right; t corporations, limited partnerships and joint-stock ciations holding such securities as trustees, executo administrators, guardians, or in any other manner, sh return and pay the tax imposed by this act upon all securities so held by them as in the case of individuals : *And provided further,* That the provisions of this section shall not apply to the taxation of so much of the capital stock of corporations, limited partnerships or joint-stock associations, organized for manufacturing purposes, which is invested in and actually and exclusively employed in carrying on manufacturing within the State, except companies engaged in the brewing or distilling of spirits or malt liquors and such as enjoy and exercise the right of eminent domain; but every manufacturing corporation, limited partnership or joint-stock association shall pay the State tax of five mills herein provided, upon such proportion of its capital stock, if any, as may be invested in any property or business not strictly incident or appurtenant to its manufacturing business, in addition to the local taxes assessed upon its property in the districts where located, it being the object of this proviso to relieve from State taxation only so much of the capital stock as is invested purely in the manufacturing plant and business : *Provided further,* In case of fire or marine insurance companies the tax imposed by this section shall be at the rate of three mills on each dollar of the actual value of the whole capital stock.

APPROVED—The 8th day of June, A. D. 1893.

ROBT. E. PATTISON.

Marginal notes:
- Shall not apply to taxation of capital stock exclusively employed within this State.
- Except brewing and distilling companies and such as have right of eminent domain.
- Tax shall be paid on capital stock not strictly engaged in manufacturing business.
- Object of this proviso.
- Tax on fire and marine insurance companies shall be three mills on capital stock.

No. 289.

AN ACT

To regulate the change of location of the principal office, the place of annual and other meetings of stockholders, and the time of such annual meetings of corporations of this Commonwealth.

SECTION 1. *Be it enacted, &c.,* That it shall be lawful for any corporation of this State, now existing or hereafter created, to change the location of its principal office, the place of its annual and other meetings of stockholders, or the time for holding such annual meetings, or either, or all, by resolution of its board of directors, adopted by a two-thirds vote thereof, approved at any annual meeting or special meeting duly called of the stockholders, by a two-thirds vote thereof. Upon such approval of the stockholders, it shall be the duty of the president of such corporation to file in both the offices of the Secretary of the Commonwealth and the Auditor General of this Commonwealth a report, under the seal of the company, specifying the change or changes so made. Nothing in this act, however, shall authorize the location of the principal office or the holding of the annual or other meetings of stockholders outside of the limits of this Commonwealth.

APPROVED—The 8th day of June, A. D. 1893.

ROBT. E. PATTISON.

Marginal notes:
- Principal office and time of meetings may be changed.
- Duty of president.
- Principal office and meetings outside of State.

No. 290.

AN ACT

Regulating the satisfaction, extinguishment or discharge of dowers, legacies or other charges upon land, by judicial decree where the legal presumption of payment of the same exists from lapse of time, or where payment of the same has been made in full and no satisfaction, extinguishment, release thereof appears of record.

Proceedings by judicial decree for satisfaction, extinguishment or discharge of dowers, legacies or other charges upon land.

SECTION 1. *Be it enacted, &c.*, That in all cases where any dower, legacy or other charge upon land shall have been paid, or wherever the legal presumption of payment shall exist from lapse of time and no satisfaction or release of such dower, legacy or other charge appears of record, it shall be lawful for the owner or owners of the lands bound by the said dower, legacy or other charge to apply by petition to the orphans' court of the county where the said lands are situate, setting forth the premises and also the name or names of the holder or holders of such dower, legacy or other charge, if known, and if not known then stating that fact, whereupon the said court shall direct the sheriff of the said county to serve a notice, stating the facts set forth in the petition, on the holder or holders of the said dower, legacy or other charge, if to be found in said county, and in case the parties aforesaid cannot be found in said county, then the

Publication of notice by sheriff.

said sheriff shall give public notice as aforesaid in one or more newspapers published within or nearest to said county once a week for four weeks successively prior to the then next term after the petition as aforesaid shall have been presented, requiring said parties to appear at said term and answer the petition as aforesaid, at which term, should any person or persons appear claiming to be the holder or holders of the said dower, legacy or other

Citations to issue.

charge, the said court shall issue a citation on the person or persons so claiming, to proceed forthwith in the manner provided by the act of twenty-fourth February, one thousand eight hundred and thirty-four, section fifty-nine, (P. L. 84), relating to legacies charged upon lands, to which it shall be lawful for any party to appear and defend, and in default of compliance with said citation, and in the event of the non-appearance of any person or persons to answer the petitions as aforesaid, the said court being satisfied of the truth of said petition, are

Decree to be entered by court.

Proceedings to be recorded.

hereby authorized and required to enter a decree that said dower, legacy or other charge be satisfied, extinguished and discharged, and said proceedings and decree, upon payment of the costs, shall be recorded in the office of the recorder of deeds of said county, and thereupon the said dower, legacy or other charge shall be satisfied, extinguished and released, and all actions thereon forever barred.

APPROVED—The 8th day of June, A. D. 1893.

ROBT. E. PATTISON.

No. 291.

AN ACT

To provide for the partial payment of per diem compensation to Monroe Bassett and Frank Williams, members of the National Guard of Pennsylvania, during the time of their disability, produced by typhoid fever which they contracted in the service of the State at Homestead, Pennsylvania.

WHEREAS, Monroe Bassett, principal musician of the Sixteenth regiment, and Frank Williams, a private of Company A of said regiment of the National Guard of Pennsylvania, who were called into the service of the State during the recent riots at Homestead, Allegheny county, were taken ill with typhoid fever as a result of their exposure during their said service in the National Guard, and were confined to their homes on account of such illness until about the first of January, one thousand eight hundred and ninety-three,

And whereas, The Adjutant General in paying them for their services only gave them compensation to the tenth day of October, one thousand eight hundred and ninety-two, the date at which they were relieved from duty,

And whereas, By reason of such service and the sickness referred to they were unable to do any duty until January, one thousand eight hundred and ninety-three, thereby losing their time and their opportunities to earn a daily compensation, therefore,

SECTION 1. *Be it enacted, &c.,* That the State Treasurer be and he is hereby authorized and empowered to pay to the said Monroe Bassett the sum of one hundred dollars, being a part of his allowance as chief musician of said regiment from the tenth day of October, one thousand eight hundred and ninety-two, until the first day of January, one thousand eight hundred and ninety-three, and the State Treasurer is further authorized and empowered to pay to the said Frank Williams, a private in the company and regiment aforesaid, the sum of eighty-seven dollars, such amount being part of his per diem allowance of pay from October tenth, one thousand eight hundred and ninety-two, until the fifth day of January, one thousand eight hundred and ninety-three. Said sums of money to be paid out of any money in the treasury, not otherwise appropriated, upon warrants to be drawn by the Auditor General in the usual manner, it being understood that the amount of money provided to be paid in this bill is to cover the amount to which said musician and soldier are justly entitled on account of the sickness which they contracted in the service, and which, after their discharge, rendered them unable to perform any manual labor between the dates for which provision is herein made for their payment.

APPROVED—The 8th day of June, A. D. 1893.

ROBT. E. PATTISON.

Compensation to Monroe Bassett, guardsman.

Compensation to Frank Williams, guardsman.

How payable.

No. 292.

AN ACT

To repeal the act, entitled "An act to limit the pay of the commissioners of Crawford county," approved fourteenth February, Anno Domini one thousand eight hundred and sixty-three, and to repeal the act, entitled "An act to increase the pay of the county auditors and commissioners of the county of Crawford," approved twenty-first March, Anno Domini one thousand eight hundred and sixty-five, and to repeal the act, entitled "An act to increase the fees of the commissioners of Crawford county as directors of the poor," approved tenth April, Anno Domini one thousand eight hundred and sixty-seven.

Act of February 14, 1863, cited for repeal. SECTION 1. *Be it enacted, &c.*, That the act, entitled "An act to limit the pay of commissioners of Crawford county," approved the fourteenth day of February, Anno Domini one thousand eight hundred and sixty-three, which reads as follows:

"That in lieu of the daily payment now allowed the commissioners of Crawford county, by law, they shall each receive a salary of three hundred dollars ($300) per annum, and no more, which shall be compensation in full for all their services: *Provided,* That their actual and reasonable expenditures for transportation, while attending to the construction and repairing of bridges, shall be allowed, on the settlement of their accounts," be and the same is hereby repealed.

Act of March 21, 1865, cited for repeal. SECTION 2. That the act, entitled "An act to increase the pay of the county auditors and commissioners of the county of Crawford," approved the twenty-first day of March, Anno Domini one thousand eight hundred and sixty-five, which reads as follows:

"That from and after the passage of this act, the per diem allowance of the county auditors, of the county of Crawford, to three dollars ($3), to be paid as now provided by law; and that the Pennsylvania commissioners shall each be allowed one hundred dollars ($100), per annum, in addition to the compensation now allowed them," the same is hereby repealed.

Act of April 10, 1867, cited for repeal. SECTION 3. That the act, entitled "An act to increase the fees of the commissioners of Crawford county as directors of the poor," approved the tenth day of April, Anno Domini one thousand eight hundred and sixty-seven, which reads as follows:

"That the commissioners of Crawford county shall, on and after the passage of this act, receive one hundred dollars ($100) per annum, for their services as directors of the poor; and thereafter they shall receive one hundred dollars ($100) in addition to their present annual salaries, to continue only during the construction and completion of a new court house, in Crawford county," be and the same is hereby repealed.

Act of May 7, 1889, extended to Crawford county. SECTION 4. That the act, entitled "An act regulating the compensation of county commissioners within this Commonwealth," approved the seventh day of May, Anno Domini one thousand eight hundred and eighty-nine, be and the same is hereby extended to the county of Crawford.

APPROVED—The 8th day of June, A. D. 1893.

ROBT. E. PATTISON.

No. 293.

AN ACT

To provide for the payment of per diem compensation to Corporal Phillip C. Hockenbury and Private Fred. W. Rathbun, members of Company C, Fifteenth Regiment, National Guard of Pennsylvania, during the time of their disability produced by chronic diarrhœa and fever which they contracted in the service of the State at Homestead.

WHEREAS, Phillip C. Hockenbury, a Corporal of Company C, and Private Fred. W. Rathbun of said company of the Fifteenth regiment of the National Guard, who were called into service of the State during the recent riots at Homestead, Allegheny county, were taken ill with diarrhœa and fever as a result of their exposure during their said service in the National Guard and were confined to their homes on account of such illness until about October eighth, one thousand eight hundred ninety-two,

And whereas, The Adjutant General, when paying them for their services, only gave them compensation to the eighth day of September, one thousand eight hundred and ninety-two, the date at which their pay ceased and they were relieved from duty,

And whereas, By reason of such service and the sickness referred to they were unable to do any duty until October the eighth, one thousand eight hundred and ninety-two, thereby losing their time and their opportunities to earn a daily compensation, therefore,

SECTION 1. *Be it enacted, &c.,* That the State Treasurer be and he is hereby authorized and empowered to pay to said Corporal Phillip C. Hockenbury, the sum of fifty-two dollars and fifty cents, his pay at the rate per diem as if in the service of the State, although his salary at his regular business would have been one hundred dollars, from the eighth day of September till the eighth day of October, the time at which he was able to attend to his regular avocation, and the State Treasurer is further authorized and empowered to pay the said private Fred. W. Rathbun of Company C, Fifteenth Regiment, the sum of forty-five dollars, such amount being his pay at the rate per diem as a private in the service of the National Guard, although his expenses were fully one hundred dollars during his illness and subsequent troubles attending his illness, being now a victim of chronic diarrhœa, such amount being for services a part of his pay from the

Compensation to Phillip C. Hockenbury, guardsman.

Compensation to Fred. W. Rathbun, guardsman.

eighth day of September till the eighth day of October, one thousand eight hundred and ninety-two, said sums of money to be paid out of any money in the treasury, not otherwise appropriated, upon warrants to be drawn by the Adjutant General in the usual manner, it being understood that the amount of money provided to be paid in this bill is to cover the amount for which said corporal and private are justly entitled on the account of the sickness which they contracted in service, and which, after being relieved from duty, rendered them unable to perform any manual labor between the dates for which provision is herein made for their payment.

How payable. *(margin)*

APPROVED—The 8th day of June, A. D. 1893.

ROBT. E. PATTISON.

No. 294.

AN ACT

Amending section one of article three of an act, entitled "An act for the better government of cities of the first class in this Commonwealth," approved the first day of June, Anno Domini one thousand eight hundred and eighth-five, regulating the construction, maintenance and inspection of buildings.

SECTION 1. *Be it enacted, &c.,* That so much of section one of article three of an act, entitled "An act for the better government of cities of the first class in this Commonwealth," approved June first, one thousand eight hundred and eighty-five, which read as follows:

"SECTION 1. The Department of Public Safety shall be under the charge of one director who shall be the head thereof," be amended so as to read as follows:

SECTION 1. *Be it enacted by the Senate and House of Representatives of the Commonwealth of Pennsylvania in General Assembly met, and it is hereby enacted by the authority of the same:* That there shall be in the cities of the first class, a Bureau of Building Inspection attached to the Department of Public Safety, and under the supervision and control of the Director of Public Safety.

Shall be a Bureau of Building Inspection. *(margin)*

SECTION 2. The chief officer of said Bureau shall be called the Chief of the Bureau of Building Inspection, and shall be either a practical builder, civil engineer, bricklayer or carpenter; the other officers of the said Bureau shall consist of such number of inspectors, clerks and messengers as the city councils may, from time to time, by ordinance, determine. All of said officers shall be appointed by the Director of Public Safety. All of the Inspectors shall be either practical builders, civil engineers, carpenters or bricklayers, but shall not all be of the same occupation. None of the aforesaid officers shall be employed or engaged in any other business or be interested in any contract for building or furnishing materials to be used for building in the said cities. The city council shall, from time to time, fix their salaries.

Requirements for chief of bureau. *(margin)*

Officers of bureau, and who shall appoint. *(margin)*

Requirements for inspectors. *(margin)*

Salaries. *(margin)*

SECTION 3. In case of the temporary absence or disability of the Chief of the Bureau, the Director of Public Safety may appoint one of the inspectors as his deputy, and such deputy shall, during such absence or disability, exercise all the powers of the Chief of the Bureau. The Clerk of the Bureau shall, under the direction of the Chief, keep a record of the business of the said Bureau and perform such other duties as shall be imposed on him by the Chief. *When deputy shall have power of chief of bureau. Clerk shall keep record, &c.*

SECTION 4. The Chief or his Inspectors shall examine all buildings in the course of erection or alteration as often as practicable, and make a record of all violations of this act, with the street and number where such violations are found, the names of the owner, architect and master mechanic, and all other matters relative thereto. The Chief or his Inspectors shall examine all buildings reported dangerous or damaged by fire or accident, and make a record of such examinations, stating the nature and amount of such damage, the name of the street and number of the building, the names of the owner and occupant and purpose for which it is occupied. They shall examine all buildings for which applications have been made for permits to raise, enlarge, alter, build upon or tear down, and make a record of such examinations. The records required by this section shall always be open to the inspection of the Chief Engineer of the Bureau of Fire or any officer of the city and by any other parties, the value of whose property may be affected by the matters to which such records relate. *Examination of buildings. Record of violations. Examination of dangerous buildings. Record. Examination of buildings to be altered. Records shall be open to inspection.*

SECTION 5. The Chief of the Bureau shall require such plans and specifications of any proposed erections or alterations of buildings as sufficiently set forth and record the intent of the builder to comply with the requirements of this act to be filed with him, and shall grant permits for such erections or alterations when in conformity with the requirements of this act. He shall not give a permit for the erection of any building until he has carefully inspected the plans and specifications thereof, ascertained that the building has sufficient strength and that the means of ingress and egress are sufficient. A copy of the plans and specifications of every public building shall be deposited in the office of the Bureau. The Chief may require any applicant for a permit to give notice of the application to any persons whose interests may be affected by the proposed work. No building shall be hereafter erected or altered and no work affecting the strength or fire-risk of any wall, structure or building in any city of the first class shall be done without a permit from the Bureau of Building Inspection, nor except in conformity with the provisions of this act; such permit shall be granted or refused within ten days after the application and the submission of the said plans and specifications. *Plans and specifications required. Granting of permits. Plans &c., of public buildings. Notice to persons affected by proposed work. Permit must be obtained in all cases. Permit shall be granted or refused within ten days.*

Any applicant for a permit from the Bureau of Building Inspectors required by the act, whose application *Appeal from decision of inspector.*

has been refused, or any person who has been ordered by
the Inspector to incur any expense, may appeal from the
decision of the Inspector by giving to the Inspector notice in writing that he does so appeal. If the appeal
shall be from an order refusing a permit it shall be taken
within fifteen days from the refusal of such permit and
not thereafter. If the appeal is from an order to take
down and remove a dangerous building or structure
or a dangerous wall or walls it shall be taken within
three days from the issuing of such order and not thereafter. In computing the time within which an appeal
may be taken, if the last day shall fall on Sunday or on
a legal holiday, the appeal shall be taken on the preceed-
ing day. Notice of appeal may be given to the Inspector
by leaving the same at the office of the Bureau of Building Inspectors, either with the Inspector or with the
Chief of the Bureau or with the clerk.
Any person, the value of whose property may be affected by work done or to be done under any permit
granted by the Inspector of Buildings, may, within three
days after the issuing of such permit, appeal by giving
the Inspector notice in writing that he does so appeal.
All cases in which appeals have been taken as above provided shall be referred to the entire corps of Building
Inspectors as a board of appeal. The said board of appeal shall, after hearing, direct the Inspector to issue his
permit under such conditions, if any, as they may require, or to withhold the same or make such other and
further order in the premises as to the board shall seem
proper: *Provided*, That should any party aggrieved object to the decision of the board of appeal, he, she or
they may further appeal in writing to the Director of the
Department of Public Safety within three days of the
decision of the board of appeals, specifying in such appeal the reasons and ground therefor and accompanying
the same by the sum of thirty (30) dollars. The Director
of the Department of Public Safety shall thereupon appoint an examining commission to consist of three disinterested experts, who shall be either master builders, engineers or architects, who shall, within such time as the
said Director shall specify, carefully consider the said
appeal and make decision thereon. The decision of any
two shall be the decision of the commission. They shall
be paid for their services ten (10) dollars each.
The decision of a building inspector, unappealed from,
shall be final and conclusive in any subsequent proceeding on the matter in question in court or otherwise. The
decision of the Board of Building Inspectors as a board
of appeal, in case such decision is not appealed from as
above provided, shall be final and conclusive in any subsequent proceeding in court or otherwise. The decision
of the examining commission in case of appeal to such
commission shall be final and conclusive when certified
to the Building Inspectors, both upon said Building Inspectors and upon the court in case any proceedings

touching the matter shall be begun in court: *Provided however*, That no commission, named in accordance with this act, shall have any power or authority to set aside or nullify or alter any of the provisions herein, or order or require any permit to be issued for a building to be constructed otherwise than is herein required. *(Commission cannot nullify provision of act.)*

SECTION 6. That all buildings not of wood, hereafter erected within said cities, shall have all outside or division walls constructed of stone, brick, iron or other non-combustible material properly bonded and solidly put together, and all such walls shall be built to a line and carried up plumb and straight, and the several component parts of such buildings shall be constructed in such manner as herein provided: *Provided however*, That councils may, by a general ordinance, permit the erection of frame sheds on wharves not exceeding twenty-seven in height, or elevators or sheds of wood for the storage of grain, coal or lumber, and bay windows and fences; but all the external parts of said sheds and elevators (except sheds for the storage of lumber) shall be covered with slate, tile, metal or other equally incombustible material, and their mode of construction and location shall be subject to the approval of the inspector: *And provided further*, That councils may, by a general ordinance, permit the erection of frame buildings in the rural portions of said cities, within such limits as may be designated in said ordinance: *And provided further*, That this section shall not be construed as prohibiting the erection of such frame bath rooms or sheds as may be hereinafter provided for. *(Erection of buildings not of wood. Councils may permit erection of frame sheds on wharves. Frame buildings in rural portions of cities. Proviso as to frame bath rooms or sheds.)*

SECTION 7. All foundation walls shall be laid not less than three feet below the exposed surface of the earth on a good, solid bottom and in case the nature of the earth should require it, a bottom of driven piles or caissons filled with concrete or footing stones or iron shall be laid to prevent the walls from settling, and all piers, columns, posts or pillars resting upon the earth shall be set upon a bottom in the same manner as the foundation walls. Whenever the foundation wall or walls of any building shall be placed on a rock bottom the said rock shall be benched or leveled to receive the same. In buildings built to the street grade the foundation shall not be built above the curb level: *Provided*, That the Bureau of Building Inspectors may exempt buildings from this requirement when it appears to the bureau that the buildings are located on a street which is not likely to be used for business purposes and that the said bureau may make necessary rules and regulations for such exemption: *And further provided*, That no wooden piles shall be driven except where they can be cut off and built upon below the permanent water line. *(Foundation walls, how laid. Foundation not to be laid above curb level. Buildings may be exempt from above requirement. When wooden piles shall be driven.)*

SECTION 8. Whenever the owner or owners of property wish to excavate to a depth not exceeding ten feet below the top of the curb in front of the wall to be under-pinned, and there shall be any party or other walls wholly or *(Regulations as to underpinning of walls, when excavation does not exceed ten feet.)*

partly upon adjoining land and standing upon or near the boundary line of said lot, and the owner or owners refuse to under-pin or protect said walls after having had notice of twenty-four hours from the Bureau of Building Inspection so to do, the Inspector may enter upon the premises and employ such labor and take such steps, as in his judgment may be necessary to make the same safe and secure or to prevent the same from becoming unsafe or dangerous, at the expense of the person or persons owning said wall or building of which it may be a part, and any person or persons doing said work or any part thereof, under and by the direction of said Inspector, may bring and maintain an action against the owner or owners, or any one of them, of the said wall or building of which it may be a part for any work done or materials furnished in and about the said premises in the same manner as if he had been employed to do the work by the owner or owners of the premises. Should any owner or owners desire to excavate to a greater depth than ten feet he or they shall protect and under-pin the wall of any adjoining structure at his or their own expense: *Provided however*, That this section shall not apply to buildings now erected or to dwelling houses.

SECTION 9. Inspectors of Buildings shall, upon the application of any owner or owners of any building or their authorized agents or upon the application of any person or persons about to erect any new building or buildings, examine any or all existing party or division walls, and if they are deemed by the Inspector to be defective, out of repair or insufficient and unfit for the purpose of new buildings about to be erected such party or division wall or walls shall be repaired or made good or taken down by the parties building, as the Inspector's decision may be, the cost and expense of which repair or removal, together with the expense of the new wall or walls to be erected in lieu thereof, shall be borne a paid exclusively by the parties building, and they shall also make good all damages occasioned thereby to the adjoining premises.

SECTION 10. The footing or base course under all foundation walls, piers, columns, posts or pillars resting on the earth shall be of brick, stone or concrete, and if brick or concrete be used under a foundation wall, if practicable it shall be at least twelve inches wider than said walls, and if under piers, columns, posts or pillars shall be at least twelve inches wider on all sides than the bottom of said piers, columns, posts or pillars and not less than sixteen inches in thickness. If built of stone the stones thereof shall not be less than three by three feet and at least six inches in thickness, and all base courses shall be well bedded and laid edge to edge, and if the walls be built of piers and the nature of the soil and requirements of the superstructure render it necessary, then there must be iron rails or beams of sufficient area, or inverted arches, at least twelve inches thick, turned under and between

Marginal notes:

When excavation exceeds ten feet.

Certain buildings not included in above requirements.

Inspector shall examine party or division walls.

If unfit for new building they shall be repaired by parties building.

Expense of new walls shall be paid by parties building.

Footing or base covered under foundation walls, &c.
If brick or concrete be used.

If stone be used.

If walls be built of piers.

the piers or two footing courses of large stone at least eight inches thick in each course. This section shall not apply to dwelling houses. *Dwelling houses exempt.*

SECTION 11. All foundation walls and cellars shall be built of stone or brick laid in cement; if constructed of stone, they shall be at least six inches thicker than the wall next above them to the depth of twelve feet below said wall, and shall be increased six inches in thickness for every additional ten feet in depth below the said twelve feet, and if of brick, they shall be at least four inches thicker than the wall next above them to a depth of twelve feet below the said wall and shall be increased four inches in thickness for every additional ten feet below said twelve feet; if there be cellars or excavations, foundation walls shall start at least twelve inches below cellar bottom; this shall not apply to dwelling houses. *Foundation walls, how built. How built if stone is used. If brick is used. Where walls shall start if there be cellars.*

Minimum thickness of brick, enclosing and division wall for business buildings shall be as follows: *Minimum thickness of brick, enclosing and division wall for business buildings seventy-five by twenty-four feet span or less.*

Enclosing and division walls for business buildings seventy-five feet by twenty-four feet span, or less:

	First story.	Second story.	Third story.	Fourth story.	Fifth story.	Sixth story.
One story building,	13					
Two " "	13	13				
Three " "	13	13	13			
Four " "	18	13	13	13		
Five " "	18	18	13	13	13	
Six " "	18	18	18	13	13	13

Enclosing and division walls for business buildings seventy-five feet to one hundred and fifty feet by twenty-four feet span, or less: *Seventy-five to one hundred and fifty by twenty-four feet span or less.*

	First story.	Second story.	Third story.	Fourth story.	Fifth story.	Sixth story.
One story building,	13					
Two " "	13	13				
Three " "	13	13	13			
Four " "	18	13	13			
Five " "	18	18	18	13	13	
Six " "	22	18	18	18	13	13

Enclosing and division walls for business buildings over one hundred and fifty feet by twenty-four feet span, or less: *Over one hundred and fifty by twenty-four feet span or less.*

	First story.	Second story.	Third story.	Fourth story.	Fifth story.	Sixth story.
One story building,	18					
Two " "	18	18				
Three " "	22	18	18			
Four " "	22	18	18	18		
Five " "	22	22	18	18	18	
Six " "	22	22	22	18	18	18

Enclosing and division walls for business buildings seventy-five feet, or less, by twenty-four to thirty-one feet span: *Seventy-five feet or less, by twenty-four to thirty-one feet span.*

	First story.	Second story.	Third story.	Fourth story.	Fifth story.	Sixth story.
One story building,	13					
Two " "	13	13				
Three " "	18	13	13			
Four " "	18	18	13	13		
Five " "	18	18	18	13.	13	
Six " "	22	18	18	18	13	13

Enclosing and division walls for business buildings seventy-five to one hundred and fifty feet by twenty-four to thirty-one feet span:

	First story.	Second story.	Third story.	Fourth story.	Fifth story.	Sixth story.
One story building, . .	18					
Two " " . .	18	18				
Three " " . .	18	13	13			
Four " " . .	18	18	13	13		
Five " " . .	22	18	18	13	13	
Six " " . .	22	22	18	18	13	13

Enclosing and division walls for business buildings over one hundred and fifty feet by twenty-four to thirty-one feet span:

	First story.	Second story.	Third story.	Fourth story.	Fifth story.	Sixth story.
One story building, . .	18					
Two " " . .	22	18				
Three " " . .	22	18	18			
Four " " . .	22	22	18	18		
Five " " . .	26	22	22	18	18	
Six " " . .	26	26	22	22	18	18

Enclosing and division walls for business buildings seventy-five feet, or less, by thirty-one to thirty-four feet span:

	First story.	Second story.	Third story.	Fourth story.	Fifth story.	Sixth story.
One story building, . .	18					
Two " " . .	18	18				
Three " " . .	22	18	18			
Four " " . .	22	22	18	18		
Five " " . .	22	22	22	18	18	
Six " " . .	26	22	22	22	18	18

Enclosing and division walls for business buildings seventy-five to one hundred and fifty feet by thirty-one to thirty-four feet span:

	First story.	Second story.	Third story.	Fourth story.	Fifth story.	Sixth story.
One story building, . .	18					
Two " " . .	22	18				
Three " " . .	22	18	18			
Four " " . .	22	22	18	18		
Five " " . .	26	22	22	18	18	
Six " " . .	26	26	22	22	18	18

Enclosing and division walls for business buildings over one hundred and fifty feet by thirty-one to thirty-four feet span:

	First story.	Second story.	Third story.	Fourth story.	Fifth story.	Sixth story.
One story building, . .	18					
Two " " . .	22	18				
Three " " . .	26	22	18			
Four " " . .	26	26	22	18		
Five " " . .	30	26	26	22	18	
Six " " . .	30	30	26	26	22	18

For every fifty feet additional over one hundred and fifty, add four inches in thickness; front and rear walls built of small piers shall be increased at least four inches wider than the above table; where trusses are used the walls upon which they rest shall be at least four inches thicker than is otherwise required by this section; for every addition of twenty-five feet or part thereof to the length of the truss, over thirty feet, the amount of the materials specified may be used either in piers or buttresses in outside and division or party walls: *Provided*, That the amount of materials in no case be less than are specified in the aforesaid tables: *Provided*, That the chief of the bureau may, if in his judgment occasion demands it, require the walls increased to a greater thickness than above specified: *And provided further*, That in case the buildings constructed of a framework of iron or steel carrying the structure, and where the walls are simply used to enclose the building and do not carry its weight, the Bureau of Building Inspection shall have authority to fix the proper thickness of walls required in any particular case and may designate the thickness of walls at pilasters and between pilasters, as in its judgment may seem proper: *And provided further*, That nothing in this section shall prevent the erection of light walls constructed of a framework of iron or steel filled in with glass.

Chief of bureau may require thicker walls.

Framework of iron or steel.

SECTION 12. No brick partition wall shall be less in thickness than two-thirds of the thickness required in the preceding table for enclosing and division walls, and no wall shall be deemed a partition wall unless it is carried up two-thirds the height of the said enclosing or division walls, and this shall not apply to dwelling houses: *Provided*, That this section and section eleven shall not apply to the enclosure of fire escapes, stairways, elevator shafts and light wells.

Partition walls of brick.

Sections 11 and 12 shall not apply to fire escapes, stairways, &c.

SECTION 13. All buildings over thirty-four feet span shall be supported by trusses or have either brick partition walls or girders supported by columns, piers, pillars of posts; recesses and openings may be made in the external walls: *Provided*, That the backs of such recesses are not less than thirteen inches in thickness, and that the areas of such recesses and openings do not, taken together, exceed one-half of the whole area of the wall in which they are made, and this restriction shall not apply to street fronts properly constructed of iron or iron and masonry. No recess for water or other pipes shall be made in any wall more than one-third of its thickness, and the recesses around said pipe or pipes shall be filled up with solid masonry for the space of one foot at the top and bottom of each story.

Buildings over thirty-four feet span.

Recesses and openings.

Street fronts.

Recess for water or other pipes.

SECTION 14. The height of stories for all given thicknesses of walls must not exceed eleven feet in the clear for basement, eighteen feet in the clear for the first story, fifteen feet in the clear for the second story, fourteen feet in the clear for the third and fourth stories, and fourteen feet in the clear average height for any upper story, and if any story exceeds these heights respectively the walls of such story and all the stories below the same shall be increased four inches in thickness additional to the thickness already mentioned.

Height of stories.

SECTION 15. In all dwellings hereafter to be erected with a front of sixteen feet or less—providing they do not exceed sixty feet in length and thirty-five feet in

Dwellings with front of sixteen feet, or less, walls of.

height—the cellar or foundation wall shall not be less than eighteen inches in thickness, the front and rear walls not less than nine inches, and the party walls not less than nine inches; walls binding on the street, lane or alley shall not be less than thirteen inches to the top of the first floor joist; in all dwellings over sixteen and not over twenty feet front nor more than forty-five feet high the foundation walls shall not be less than eighteen inches in thickness, the front walls not less than thirteen inches, the party walls not less than thirteen inches, and for all dwellings over twenty feet front the party walls shall not be less than thirteen inches, and the front and rear walls shall not be less than thirteen inches the entire height; if there be a stone ashlar used three inches thick or less it shall not be reckoned in the thickness of any wall herein specified. No party wall where built of stone shall be less than sixteen inches in thickness: *Provided*, That when an application is made for a permit to erect an additional story upon a one or two-story building used or to be used for a dwelling, and the party walls of the said buildings are but nine inches thick, the Bureau of Building Inspection may, in their judgment, issue such permit without requiring any additional thickness for the party wall: *Provided further*, In all dwellings hereafter erected the cellars shall extend underneath the whole house and be ventilated from both ends, and in low, damp or made ground the bottom of all cellars shall be covered with brick or concrete or asphalt at least three inches thick, or such material as shall be approved by the Bureau of Building Inspection. Every new dwelling house shall have at least fourteen feet front: *Provided however*, That this limitation shall not apply to lots of less than fourteen feet in width on which buildings are now erected, nor to lots less than fourteen feet in width which are bounded on each side by ground belonging to other owners at the time of the approval of this act; and every such new dwelling house and shall have an open space attached to it in the rear or at the side equal to at least one hundred and forty-four square feet clear space, unobstructed by any overhanging structure.

All party walls shall be built solidly from the cellar bottom to the top of the fire wall: *Provided*, That with the approval and under the supervision of the Bureau of Building Inspection openings may be made in the party walls of contiguous buildings.

SECTION 16. In all vault walls of not a greater depth than twelve feet below the curb, the front or bank wall shall not be less than thirty inches at the bottom and eighteen inches at the top, and the side or party walls not less than eighteen inches; the front wall to be battered from the inside face, and where vaults are of a greater depth than above described, the thickness of the wall shall be determined by the Bureau of Building Inspection.

No area shall extend more than one-fourth of the width

Marginal notes:

Over sixteen and not over twenty feet.

Over twenty feet.

Stone ashlar.

Party wall of stone.

Additional story on one or two story building.

Cellars, extent, ventilation and construction of.

14 feet front for new dwelling. Lots less than 14 feet in width.

Open space at rear or side of new dwelling.

Party wall shall be built solid.

Vault walls not more than twelve feet below curb.

More than twelve feet below curb.

Area, width of.

of the pavement, nor in any case more than three feet, measuring from the inside face of the area wall, to the building line, and when areas are constructed on narrow streets the Inspector is to designate the distance from the building line, and every area shall be covered with a safe and substantial cover, the said cover in no case to extend above the grade of the sidewalk. On narrow streets. Cover of area.

SECTION 17. Where iron or wooden girders supported upon iron or wooden columns are substituted in place of partition walls, they shall be made of sufficient strength to bear safely not less than two hundred pounds for every square foot of the floor or floors that rest upon them exclusive of the weight of the material employed in their construction, and the columns shall have a footing course not less than eighteen inches in thickness, the lower footing course to be not less than nine square feet greater in area than the size of the column; and every temporary support placed under any structure, wall, girder or beam during erection, alteration or repairing of any building or part thereof shall be equal in strength to the weight which it is required to support. Girders, strength of. Footing of columns. Tempory support, strength of.

SECTION 18. All stone walls twenty-four inches or less in thickness shall have at least one header extending through the walls in every three feet in height from the bottom of the wall and in every four feet in length, and if over twenty-four inches in thickness shall have one header for every six superficial feet on both sides of the wall. All headers shall be at least eighteen inches in width and shall consist of good, flat, square stones, and in brick walls at least every eighth course of brick shall be a heading course, except where walls are faced with face brick, in which case at least every eighth course shall be bonded with Flemish headers or by cutting the corners of the face brick and putting diagonal headers behind the same or iron ties. In all buildings where the walls are built hollow the same amount of stone or brick shall be used in their construction as if they were solid, as heretofore set forth, and no hollow-bearing walls shall be built unless the two walls forming the same shall be connected by vertical ties of the same material as the walls or stone or iron, if iron to be galvanized and not over two feet apart, or if not bearing walls they may be bonded or tied with anchors not more than two feet apart in every direction. Stone walls twenty-four inches or less in thickness, how constructed. Headers, size and quality of. Brick walls, how constructed. Walls built hollow, how constructed. Hollow bearing walls. Not bearing walls.

SECTION 19. All brick work shall be of merchantable well-shaped brick, well laid and bedded with well-filled joints, in lime or cement mortar, and flushed up with every course of same brick when laid shall be wet or dry as the inspector may direct. All walls of brick shall be thoroughly bonded and solidly put together, and shall be built to a line plumb-level and straight. All bed-joints not covered are to be struck. All mortar used in the construction or repair of any building shall be of the best quality for the purpose for which it is applied. All Quality of bricks and how laid. Brick walls shall be bonded. Mortar, quality of.

Sand and cement.

sand must be clean, sharp and free from loam, and no cement shall be used that has been mixed over night.

Side, end or party walls how far carried up.

SECTION 20. In no case shall the side, end or party wall be carried up more than one story in advance of the front and rear walls, unless the said walls be secured to the side, end or party walls by iron anchors at least one and one-half inches wide by three-eighth inches thick and four feet long; and all stone used for the facing of any building, except where built with alternate headers and stretchers as hereinbefore set forth, shall be strongly anchored with iron anchors in each stone, and all such anchors shall be let into the stone at least one inch; the front, rear, side or party walls shall be anchored at each tier of joists at intervals of not more than ten feet apart, and the ends of all such joists, beams or girders so anchored to the walls that a falling joist, beam or girder will free its own anchorage and may fall without injury to the wall, and where the joists are supported by the girders, the ends of the joists resting on the girders may lap each other, and each joist covering the entire width of the girder and strapped by wrought iron straps not less than one and a half inches by three-eighths of an inch and not less than eighteen inches long, and at the same distance apart and on the same line of joists as the wall anchors, and this shall not prohibit hanging joists in iron stirrups from the girders, but in such cases the joists must be strapped as before described.

Stone facing of buildings, shall be strongly anchored.

Anchoring of front, rear, side or party walls.

Of joints, beams or girders.

Joists supported by girders.

Joists in iron stirrups

SECTION 21. All front, side or rear party walls not corniced and where no gutter is required shall be built up and extended at least ten inches above the roof, and coped with stone or metal or other incombustible material; and where the roof is of the kind known as Mansard or French or of any style excepting as above specified, unless the same is constructed of fire-proof material throughout, the party walls shall be carried up to a height of not less than ten inches above the flat or slope of said roof, and shall extend through the lower slope at least six inches distant and parallel with the roof covering, and be corbelled out at least six inches or to the outer edge of all projections, and shall be coped with incombustible material. Where a wall is finished with a stone cornice the greatest weight of material of such cornice shall be on the inside of the face of the wall. All exterior cornices and gutters hereafter erected shall be of some fire-proof material, and in every case, except where sheet metal is used, the greatest weight of the material of which the cornice shall be constructed shall be on the inside of the outer line of the wall, allowance being made for the leverage produced by the projection of the cornice beyond the face of the wall; and in all cases the walls shall be carried up to the under side of the roof planking and where the cornice projects above the roof the wall shall be carried to the top of the cornice; all exterior wooden cornices that may be or shall hereafter become unsafe shall be taken down, and if replaced shall

Walls not corniced, how built·

If roof is Mansard or French

Walls finished with a stone cornice.

Exterior cornices and gutters, material and construction of.

Exterior wooden cornices hereafter becoming unsafe.

be constructed of some fire-proof material. All exterior wooden cornice or gutters that may hereafter be damaged by fire or by decay to the extent of one-half the value thereof shall be taken down, and if replaced shall be constructed of some fire-proof material, but if not damaged to this extent may be repaired with the same kind of material of which originally constructed. *If damaged by fire or decay.*

SECTION 22. All exterior openings for doors and windows in all cases, except as otherwise provided, shall have a good and sufficient arch of stone or brick, well built and keyed, and with sufficient abutments, or a lintel of stone or iron, as follows: For an opening not more that four feet in width the lintel, if made of stone, shall not be less than seven and one-half inches in height and three inches in thickness; for an opening of not more than six feet in width the said lintel shall not be less than ten inches in height and four inches in thickness; for an opening more than six feet and less than eight feet in width the said lintel shall not be less than twelve inches in height and four inches in thickness; all lintels eight feet and over in width shall be iron beams or girders. No lintels shall have a bearing of less than four and a half inches on the walls, and on the inside of all openings in which the lintels shall be less than the thickness of the wall to be supported, there shall be a good and proper size timber lintel which shall rest at each end not less than four and a half inches on the wall and shall be beveled on each end and shall have a double counter or dead arch turned over the same when practicable. All arches over openings and fire places shall be built of good, hard brick laid with close joints and well keyed: *Provided*, That this shall not apply to single plank front frames in dwelling houses. *Exterior opening for doors and windows, must have arch or lintel. For opening not more than four feet. Not more than six feet. Not more than eight feet. Over eight feet. Bearing of lintels. Arches over openings.*

SECTION 23. All iron beams or girders used to span openings eight feet or over in width and not exceeding twelve feet, upon which a wall rests, when not supported by iron jam boxes shall have a bearing of at least nine inches at each end by the thickness of the wall supported, and for every additional foot of span over and above the said twelve feet, if the supports are of iron plates or solid, cut stone the bearings shall be increased half an inch at each end, but if supported at the ends by walls or piers built of brick or stone and when so supported at the ends by brick walls or piers shall rest upon a cut granite, blue or other stone blocks of equal strength not less than seven and a half inches thick by the full size of the bearing, and when the opening is more than twelve feet the plate or stone shall be proportionately increased, and all iron beams or girders used in any building shall be throughout not less in width than the thickness of the wall to be supported. *Iron beams or girders spanning openings between eight and twelve feet. If over twelve feet. If suppoted at ends by walls or piers Width of iron beams.*

SECTION 24. Before any iron column, post, beam, lintel or girder intended to support a wall built of brick or stone, or any floor or part thereof, or to span any opening eight feet or over in width in any building hereafter to be erected or altered shall be used for that purpose, the *Iron column. post, &c., must have distinctive name or title stamped thereon.*

manufacturer or founder thereof shall have a distinctive name or title properly stamped, rolled or cast in a conspicuous place thereon, and no greater weight shall be placed on any column, post, beam, lintel or girder than the published tables of said manufacturer or founder show it to be capable of sustaining with safety. The inspector may require columns to be drilled for inspection.

SECTION 25. In all buildings hereafter to be constructed or altered, where masonry walls with iron beams or girders and columns are used in the interior, the following rules must be observed:

First. That the ends of all metal columns shall be faced off at right angles to their axis by machinery, and where iron bed plates and caps are used they shall be faced off true at point of contact with column; if brick arches are used between beams they shall have a rise of at least one and one-fourth inches to each foot of space between them.

Second. That under the ends of all iron beams where they rest upon the walls a stone, slate or iron templet must be built in the wall of sufficient size and thickness.

Third. That all brick arches shall be at least four inches thick at the crown and shall be solidly backed up to a point above the theoretic joint of rupture.

Fourth. That said arches shall be laid to a line on nters with close joints, the same to be filled with cement mortar, bricks to be wet when laid.

SECTION 26. In all stores, warehouses and factories hereafter to be erected or altered, and all warehouses, storehouses, factories, workshops and stores where heavy materials are kept or stored or machinery introduced, the weight that each floor will safely sustain upon each superficial foot shall be estimated by an architect or civil engineer, with the date thereof, and posted by the owner in a conspicuous place on each floor thereof within one year from the date of the passage of this act, the said calculation to consider, in all cases, the beams or girders as loaded in the center. All floors shall be constructed to bear a safe weight per superficial foot exclusive of material as follows: For dwellings, seventy pounds; if used for public assembly, one hundred and fifty pounds; for storehouses, warehouses or manufactories, two hundred pounds and upward, and all roofs shall be constructed to bear a weight of at least thirty pounds per superficial foot. In all calculations of the strength of materials to be used in any building, the proportion between the safe weight and breaking weight shall be as one to four for all beams, girders and other parts subjected to cross strains, and shall be as one to six for all posts, columns and other vertical supports as also for all tie rods, tie beams and other parts subjected to a tensile strain, and the requisite dimensions of each piece of material are to be ascertained by computation by the rules of standard authors on the strength of materials, using for constants in the rules only such numbers as have been reduced from actual experi-

---

Sidenotes:

Weight to be placed on column, post, &c.

Columns may be drilled.

Rules to be observed in construction of masonry walls with iron beams or girders and columns.

Weight to be sustained by each floor shall be estimated and posted by owner.

Floors, construction of to bear a safe weight

Proportion between safe and breaking weight.

Dimensions how ascertained.

ments on materials of like kinds with that proposed to be used.

SECTION 27. All buildings to be hereafter erected or altered to be used as a school house, church, public building, hall, place of assembly or resort, tenement house, hotel, lodging house, factory or workshop more than two stories in height, shall have at least one stairway, accessible from each apartment, which shall be enclosed with brick walls or partitions made of incombustible materials and shall have no interior openings other than the doors of the apartments from which it is an exit. All stores to be hereafter erected or altered to the extent of twenty-five per centum of the assessed valuation, when more than three stories in height and in which any one of the stories above the second shall have a clear floor space of not less than four thousand square feet, shall be provided with a tower fire escape enclosed in incombustible material adjoining one of its fronts, and such fire escape from the first to the second story may be a spiral staircase. Such fire escape shall be held and taken as a fire escape under the terms of the act approved June eleventh, one thousand eight hundred and seventy-nine, entitled "An act to provide for the better security of life and limb in cases of fire in hotels and other buildings," and the several supplements and amendments thereto. And in the case of such stores in which the clear floor space of any story above the second shall be over ten thousand square feet, the Board of Fire Escapes may require one or more additional tower fire escapes as above described. And all mills, more than two stories high, of the floor area per story of three thousand square feet or more, shall have such brick enclosed fire escape or escapes as shall be approved by the Board of Fire Escapes. No obstruction shall be placed upon any way of egress from any building. No explosives or inflammable compound or combustible material shall be stored or placed under any stairway of any building or be used in any such place or manner as to obstruct or render egress hazardous in case of fire.

SECTION 28. In any hoistway elevator or well-hole not enclosed in walls of brick or other fire proof materials the openings through and upon each floor shall be provided with and protected by a substantial guard or gate or with good and sufficient automatic trap-doors to close the same. Outside windows or openings of every elevator shaft shall have such sign or device to indicate the existence of the said shaft as shall be approved by the Bureau of Fire. No passenger elevator shall be operated, unless a certificate, signed by some reputable elevator builder that the elevator is safe and in good order, has been furnished within six months and is posted in the car at the entrance.

SECTION 29. In buildings hereafter erected, altered or repaired all chimneys shall be built of brick, stone or other incombustible material. Brick chimneys shall have

Stairways, how constructed, if building is of more than two stories.

Interior openings

Fire escapes on stores.

Fire escapes on mills.

Explosives shall not be stored under any stairway, &c.

Guard or gate for elevator or well hole,

Outside openings of elevator shaft.

Certificate that passenger elevator &c. is safe, must be posted at entrance.

Chimneys, construction thereof.

walls at least nine inches thick, unless terra cotta flue linings are used, in which case four and one-half inches of brickwork may be omitted. No chimney breast shall be started or built upon any wood floor or joists. All chimneys or smoke flues shall have a wall nine inches thick at the back, and when corbelled out shall be supported by at least five courses of brick, and if supported by piers the same shall start from the foundation on the same face with the breast above. All chimneys shall be bonded to the walls at every course from the bottom to the top. The inside of all brick flues shall be built of hard brick and have struck joints: no wood furring shall be used against or around any chimney but the plastering shall be directly on the masonry or on metal lathing. All chimneys shall be topped out at least four feet above the highest point of contact with the roof flues or ranges, and boilers and other similar flues shall have the outside exposed to the height of the ceiling or be plastered directly to the bricks.

Hearths, how supported.

SECTION 30. All hearths shall be supported by trimmer arches of brick, stone, iron or concrete, or be of single stone at least six inches thick built into the chimney and supported by iron beams, one end of which shall be securely built into the masonry of the chimney or an adjoining wall, or which shall otherwise rest upon incombustible support; the brick jambs of every fireplace or grate opening shall be at least nine inches wide each, and the backs of such openings shall be at least nine inches thick. All hearths and trimmer arches shall be at least twelve inches longer on either side than the width of such openings, and at least eighteen inches wide in front of the chimney-breast; brickwork over fireplaces and grate openings shall be supported by iron bars or brick or stone arches; no chimney in any building already erected or hereafter to be built shall be cut off below in whole or in part and supported by wood, but shall be wholly supported by stone, brick or iron, and all chimneys in any building already erected or hereafter to be erected, which shall be dangerous in any manner whatever, shall be repaired and made safe or taken down.

Brick jambs of fireplace or grate.

Length and width of hearths and trimmer arches.

Brick work over fireplaces.

Chimney shall not be cut off.

Dangerous chimneys.

Smoke pipes.

SECTION 31. No smoke pipe in any building with combustible floors and ceilings shall hereafter enter any flue nearer than twelve inches from the floor or ceiling, and in all cases when smoke pipes pass through the stud or wooden partitions floor or roof, whether plastered or not, they shall be guarded by either a double collar of metal with at least two inches air space all around and holes for circulation of air, or by a soapstone ring or solid casting of plaster of paris not less than three inches in thickness and extending through the partition, or by an earthenware ring one inch from the pipe at every point.

Furnace smoke pipe.

SECTION 32. In all cases where hot water, steam, hot air or other furnaces are used the furnace smoke pipe shall be at least two feet below the joists or ceiling above the same, unless said joists or ceiling shall be properly protected by a shield or metal plate suspended above the said pipe, with at least three inches space for the free circulation of air above and below the said shield, in which case the smoke pipes shall be kept at least ten inches from the aforesaid joists or ceiling; and the tops of all furnaces set in brick must be covered with brick, slate or metal, supported by iron bars and so constructed as to be perfectly tight, said covering to be in addition to and at least six inches from the ordinary covering to the hot air chamber; the tops of all heating furnaces not set in brick shall be at least ten inches below the joists or ceiling with a shield of metal plate made tight and suspended below the said joists or ceiling at least three inches and extending one foot beyond the furnace on all sides. No boiler to be used for steam or motive power and no furnace shall be placed on any floor above the cellar floor, unless the same is set on non-combustible beams and arches or an incombustible platform, and in no case without a permit from the inspector. *[Tops of furnaces set in brick how covered.]* *[Tops of furnaces not set in brick.]* *[Boiler or furnace on floor above cellar.]*

SECTION 33. All hot-air registers set in the floor of any building shall be set in a border of soapstone or other fire-proof material, and all floor or register boxes to be made of sheet metal with flange on top to fit the groove in the border, the register to rest upon the same, and there shall also be an open space of two inches on all sides of the register box, extending from the under side of the ceiling to the border of the floor, the outside of the said space to be covered with a casing of metal made tight on all sides and to extend from the under side of the aforesaid ceiling up to and turn under the said border. No tin or other metal flue or flues or pipe or pipes or register-box or boxes of a single thickness of metal used and intended to convey heated air in any building hereafter to be built, altered or repaired shall be allowed, unless the same be built in a wall of brick or stone, in all other cases the said flue or flues pipe or pipes, register box or boxes shall be made double, that is two pipes, one inside the other, at least one-half inch apart, or covered with wire lathing and the studding covered within tin or other fire-proof material so as to be thoroughly fireproof: *Provided*, That this shall not apply to pipes leading from a heater to the hot air flue. No wood furring or lath shall be placed against any flue, metal pipe or pipes used to convey heated air or steam in any building. No permanent or stationery heating apparatus of any kind whatever shall be introduced in any building now erected without a permit from the Bureau of Building Inspection *[Hot air registers set in floor of building.]* *[Flues or pipes for heated air.]* *[Wood furring or lath against flue or pipe.]* *[Permit for introducing heating apparatus.]*

SECTION 34. In no building shall any wooden girders, joist or timbers be placed nearer than four inches of the outside of any smoke, hot-air or other flue, and all joists or other timbers in the party walls of any building hereafter erected, whether built of stone, brick or iron, shall be separated from the joists or timbers entering into the opposite side of the wall by at least four inches of solid mason work. Every trimmer over four feet long, except *[Wooden girders, &c., placing of near smoke, hot air or other flue.]*

in a dwelling, shall be hung in wrought or malleable iron stirrups of suitable dimensions, and no timber shall be used in any wall of any building where stone, brick or iron is commonly used, except bond timbers and lintels as hereinbefore provided for, or as may be approved by the Inspector, and no exposed bond timber in any wall shall, in width and thickness, exceed that of a course of brick. Where stud partitions are paralleled with the joists, the joists supporting them are to be doubled in cases, and in addition, the size of joist to be used in dwelling houses sixteen feet front or less shall be, for the first floor, not less than three by nine inches, and shall be no more than eighteen inches from center to center, for upper floors they shall not be less than three by eight inches and shall be placed not more than sixteen inches from center to center, and must be properly bridged, and all joists that are used must be sound and well seasoned. No floor joists shall be blocked up or leveled on more than one dry course of brick.

SECTION 35. The planking and sheathing of the roof of every building hereafter to be erected or altered shall in no case be extended across the party wall thereof, and every such building, and the tops and sides of every dormer window thereon, shall be covered with slate, tin, zinc, iron, copper or such other equally good fire-proof material as the Bureau of Building Inspection may authorize, and the outside of every dormer window hereafter placed on any building as aforesaid shall be made of some fire-proof material, and wooden buildings which require roofing shall not be roofed with any other roof covering except as aforesaid: *Provided*, That this shall not apply to roofs and dormers in rural and suburban districts. Nothing in this section shall be construed to prohibit the repairing of a shingle roof, provided the repairs do not amount to over one-half of the value of said roof, in which case the whole must be replaced by some fire-proof material. All buildings shall be kept provided with proper metallic leaders for conducting water from the roof to the ground or sewer in such manner as shall protect the walls and foundations from damage.

SECTION 36. All buildings of three or more stories hereafter to be built with two or more stories back buildings shall have scuttle frames and covers or bulkheads and doors, and be covered with some fire-proof material, to be opened outward. All scuttles shall have stationary ladders leading to the same, and all such scuttles and ladders shall be kept so as to be ready for use at all times; all scuttles shall be in size of opening at least eighteen by thirty inches, and if a bulkhead is used in any building in place of a scuttle it shall have stairs with a sufficient guard or hand-rail leading to the roof, and in case the building be a tenement house the doors or covers to the scuttles or bulkheads shall at no time be locked, but may be bolted or secured by hooks on the inside.

SECTION 37. Whenever the owner of any lot of ground

is desirous of improving the same by the erection of a new building or buildings thereon, the Bureau of Building Inspection may permit the owner of such lot, or the contractor for the erection of such building or buildings, to put up a wooden shed on the same or neighboring lot for the use of the mechanics employed on said building or buildings while preparing their work: *Provided however*, That such permission shall not extend to a longer time than until the building or buildings proposed to be erected shall be entirely finished, at which time the owner or contractor shall take down and remove the said shed.

Wooden shed allowed when new building is being erected.

Removal of such shed.

SECTION 38. No frame bath room projecting from the upper story of any dwelling house shall be erected within five feet of any similar construction composed wholly or partly of wood, unless the end of said bath room facing such structure shall be covered with some fire-proof material, and in no case shall the distance dividing said structures be less than three feet, unless the ends shall have division walls of masonry not less than nine inches thick built from the foundations of the building and carried up above the roof as hereinbefore provided for party walls; it shall not be lawful to build a frame bath room, other than a projecting bath room as provided for in this section, and no such bath room shall be greater in area than fifty superficial feet; it shall not be lawful to build such bath room unless the plumbing fixtures for bath purposes be placed therein.

Frame bath room projecting from upper story of building.

SECTION 39. It shall only be lawful to erect frame sheds to be attached to dwellings as follows: The said shed shall not exceed twelve feet in height nor have any floor or loft between the ground floor and the roof, and must not connect with a frame bath room projecting from an upper story; said sheds shall not be erected within five feet of any similar construction composed wholly or in part of wood, unless the side of said shed facing such structure shall be covered with fire-proof material, and in no case shall the distance dividing such structures be less than three feet, unless the ends shall have division walls of masonry not less than nine inches thick built from the foundations of the building and carried up above the roof as hereinbefore provided for party walls; the said shed may be opened or enclosed, but in no case shall it be lathed and plastered or lined with wood so as to constitute a room to be occupied as a habitation; the roof of said shed must be covered with metal or other fire-proof material; no such shed shall extend to a greater distance than ten feet in a direct line from the rear wall to which it is attached. All permits granted for the erection of frame sheds may be revoked and the shed shall be removed within thirty days after notice from the Director of Public Safety.

Frame sheds attached to buildings how constructed.

Permits for same may be revoked. Theatre or similar building how constructed.

SECTION 40. Every theatre or opera house or other building intended to be used for theatrical or operatic purposes or for public entertainments of any kind, where stage scenery and apparatus are employed, hereafter erected

Buildings must be made to conform to requirements of this section.

or altered shall be built to comply with the requirements
of this section. No building, which at the time of the
passage of this act is not in actual use for theatrical or
operatic purposes and no building hereafter erected not
in conformity with the requirements of this section, shall
be used for theatrical or operatic purposes or for public entertainments of any kind where stage scenery
and apparatus are employed, until the same shall have
been made to conform to the requirements of this sec-

**Mayors shall not
issue license until
certificate of ap-
proval is given by
Building and Fire
Bureaus.**
tion. And no building hereinbefore described shall be
opened to the public for theatrical or operatic purposes
or for public entertainments of any kind where stage
scenery or apparatus are employed, until the Bureau of
Building Inspection and the Bureau of Fire, respectively, shall have approved the same in writing as conforming to the requirements of this section, and the
Mayors of the said cities shall refuse to issue any license
for any such building and shall close the same and prevent its opening, until a certificate in writing of
such approval shall have been given by the Bureau of
Building Inspection and the Bureau of Fire, respectively.

**Front construction
of. and entrances
and exits.**
Every such building shall have at least one front on the
street, which front shall be as wide as the widest part of
the auditorium or assembly hall, and in such front there
shall be suitable means of entrance and exit for the audience. In addition to the aforesaid entrances and exits
on the street there shall be reserved for service, in case

**Open court or
space.**
of an emergency, an open court or space on the side not
bordering on the street where said building is located,
or a corner lot, and on both sides of said building where

Width of same.
there is but one frontage on the street. The width of
such open court or courts shall be not less than seven
feet where the seating capacity is not over one thousand
people, above one thousand nor more than eighteen hundred people eight feet in width, and above eighteen hun-

**Construction and
extent of same.**
dred people ten feet in width. Said open court or courts
shall begin on a line with or near the proscenium wall
and shall extend the length of the auditorium proper
to or near the wall separating the same from the
entrance, lobby or vestibule, and said open court,
or a separate and distinct corridor from each open
court, shall continue to the street through such superstructure as may be built on the street side of the auditorium, with continuous walls of brick or fire-proof
materials on each side the entire length of said corridor
or corridors, and the ceiling and floors shall be fire-proof.
Said corridor or corridors shall not be reduced in width,
except by the thickness of the outer wall, and there shall

**Doors or gates for
outer openings.**
be no projection in the same, the outer openings to be
provided with doors or gates opening toward the street.

**When doors and
gates must be kept
open.**
During the performance the doors or gates in the corridors shall be kept open by proper fastenings, at other
times they may be closed and fastened by movable bolts

**Courts and corri-
dors shall not be
used for storage
purposes.**
or locks. The said open courts and corridors shall not
be used for storage purposes or for any purpose whatso

ever, except for exit and entrance from and to the auditorium and stage, and must be kept free and clear during performances. The level of said corridors at the front entrance to the building shall not be greater than one step above the level of the side walk where they begin at the street entrance, and the entrance of the main front of the building shall not be on a higher level from the sidewalk than four steps, unless approved by the Bureau of Building Inspection. To overcome any difference of level existing between exits from the parquet into courts and the level of the said corridors, gradients shall be employed of not over one foot in ten feet with no perpendicular rises. From the auditorium opening into the said open courts or on the side street there shall be not less than two exits on each side in each tier from and including the parquet and each and every gallery. Each exit shall be at least five feet in width in the clear and provided with doors of iron or wood, if of wood the doors shall be constructed as hereinbefore in this bill described. All of said doors shall open outwardly and must be fastened with movable bolts, the bolts to be kept drawn during performances. There shall be balconies not less than four feet in width in the said open court or courts at each level or tier above the parquet on each side of the auditorium, of sufficient length to embrace the two exits and from said balconies; there shall be staircases extending to the ground level with a rise of not over eight and one-half inches to a step and not less than nine inches tread, exclusive of the nosing. The staircase from the upper balcony to to the next below shall not be less than thirty inches in width in the clear, and from the first balcony to the ground three feet in width in the clear where the seating capacity of the auditorium is for one thousand people or less, three feet and six inches in the clear where above one thousand and not more than eighteen hundred people, and four feet in the clear where above eighteen hundred people and not more than twenty-five hundred people, and less than four feet six inches to the clear where above twenty-five hundred people. All the before mentioned balconies and staircases shall be constructed of iron throughout, including the floors, and of ample strength to sustain the load to be carried by them, and they shall be covered with a metal hood or awning to be constructed as shall be directed by the Inspector of Buildings. Where one side of the building borders on a street there shall be balconies and staircases of like capacity and kind as before mentioned carried to the ground. When located on a corner lot that portion of the premises bordering on the side street and not required for the uses of the theatre may, if such portion be not more than twenty feet in width, be used for offices, stores or apartments, provided the walls separating this portion from the theatre proper are carried up solidly to and through the roof, and that a fire-proof exit is provided from the theatre on each tier equal to the combined

Level of corridors at front entrance.

Level of entrance.

To overcome difference of level.

Exits into open courts.

Exit, construction of.

Doors shall open outwardly.

Balconies at each tier

Staircases from same.

Width of staircase.

Balconies and staircases shall be of iron.

Covering of.

If building is on corner lot, part on side street may be used for offices, stores, &c.

width of exits opening on opposite sides in each tier communicating with balconies and staircases leading to the street in a manner provided elsewhere in this section; said exit passages shall be entirely cut off by brick walls from said offices, stores or apartments and the floors and ceilings in each tier shall be fire-proof. Nothing herein contained shall prevent a roof garden, art gallery or rooms for similar purposes being placed above a theatre or public building, provided the floor of the same, forming the roof over such theatre or building, shall be constructed of iron or steel and fire-proof materials and that said floor shall have no covering boards or sleepers of wood, but be of tile or cement. Every roof over said garden or rooms shall have all supports and rafters of iron or steel and be covered with glass or fire-proof materials, or both, but no such roof garden, art gallery or room of any public purpose shall be placed over or above that portion of any theatre or other building which is used as a stage. No workshop, storage or general property room shall be allowed above the auditorium or stage or under the same or in any of the fly galleries. All of said rooms or shops may be located in the rear or at the side of the stage, but in such cases they shall be separated from the stage by a brick wall and the openings leading into said portions shall have fire-proof doors on each side of the openings hung to iron eyes built into the wall. No portion of any building hereafter erected or altered, used or intended to be used for theatrical or other purposes, as in this section specified, shall be used or occupied as a hotel, boarding or lodging house, factory, workshop or manufactory, or for storage purposes, except as may be hereafter specially provided for. Said restriction relates not only to that portion of the building which contains the auditorium and the stage, but applies also to the entire structure in connection therewith. No store or room contained in the building, or the offices, stores or apartments adjoining as aforesaid, shall be let or used for carrying on any business dealings in articles designated as specially hazardous in the classification of the board of fire underwriters, or for manufacturing purposes. No lodging accommodation shall be allowed in any part of the building communicating with the auditorium. Interior walls built of fire-proof materials shall separate the auditorium from the entrance vestibule and from any room or rooms over the same, also from any lobbies, corridors, refreshment or other rooms. All staircases for the use of the audience shall be enclosed with walls of brick or of fire-proof materials, approved by the Inspector of Buildings, in the stories through which they pass, and the openings to said staircases from each tier shall be the full width of said staircase. A fire-wall built of brick shall separate the auditorium from the stage and the same shall extend at least four feet above the stage roof or the auditorium roof, if the latter be the higher, and shall be coped. Above the proscenium opening there

Roof garden, art gallery, &c., above theater, construction of.

Work shop, storage room, &c., where located.

No portion of building to be used as hotel, factory, &c.

Business dealings prohibited in the offices and store rooms.

Lodging accommodations.

Auditorium shall be separated from other rooms.

Staircase for use of audience

Separation of auditorium from stage.

shall be an iron girder covered with fire-proof materials to protect it from the heat. There shall also be constructed a relieving arch over the same, the intervening space being filled in with hard-burnt brick of the full thickness of the proscenium wall. Should there be constructed an orchestra over the stage, above the proscenium opening, the said orchestra shall be placed on the auditorium side of the proscenium fire-wall and shall be entered only from the auditorium side of said wall. The molded frame around the proscenium opening shall be formed entirely of fire-proof materials, if metal be used the metal shall be filled in solid with non combustible material and securely anchored to the wall with iron. The proscenium opening shall be provided with a fireproof metal curtain or a curtain of asbestos or similar fire-proof material, approved by the Inspector of Buildings, sliding at each end within iron grooves securely fastened to the brick wall and extending into such grooves not less than six inches on each side. Said fire-proof curtain shall be raised at the commencement of each performance and lowered at the close of said performance, and be operated by approved machinery for that purpose. The proscenium curtains shall be placed at least three feet distant from the footlights at the nearest point. There shall be no opening through the proscenium wall, except the curtain opening, and not more than two others, which shall be located at or below the level of the stage. These latter openings shall not exceed twenty-one superficial feet each, which shall have doors of iron or wood in each face of the wall, if of wood the door shall be lined with tin and securely hung to rabbeted iron frames or rabbets in the brick wall. They shall be hung so as to be opened from either side at all times. Direct access to these doors shall be provided on both sides, and the same shall always be kept free from any incumbrance. Iron ladders or stairs securely fixed to the wall on the stage side shall be provided to overcome any difference of level existing between the floor or galleries on the stage side of the fire-wall and those on the side of the auditorium. There shall be provided, immediately under the glass of said skylights there shall be a wire netting, unless the glass contains a wire netting within itself over the stage, metal skylights of an area or combined area of at least one-eighth of the area of said stage, fitted up with sliding sash and glazed with double-thick sheet glass not exceeding one-eighth of an inch thick and each pane thereof measuring not less than three hundred square inches, and the whole of which skylight shall be so constructed as to open instantly on the cutting or burning of a hempen cord which shall be arranged to hold said skylights closed, or some other equally simple approved device for opening them may be provided. All that portion of the stage not comprised in the working of scenery traps and other mechanical apparatus for the presentation of a scene usually equal to the width of the prosce-

Marginal notes:
Proscenium opening, protection of.

Orchestra over stage.

Frame around proscenium opening.

Curtain, use and arrangement of.

Openings through proscenium wall.

Access to doors.

Iron ladders to overcome difference of level.

Wire netting under skylights.

Metal skylights, construction of.

Construction of part of stage not used for scenery, traps, &c,

nium opening shall be built of iron or steel beams, filled
in between with fire-proof material, and all girders for
the support of said beams shall be of wrought iron or
rolled steel.   The fly galleries entire, including pin rails,
shall be constructed of iron or steel, and the floors of
said galleries shall be composed of iron or steel beams
filled with fire-proof materials, and no wood boards or
sleepers shall be used as covering over beams, but the
said floors shall be entirely fire-proof.   The rigging loft
shall be fire-proof, except the floor covering the same.
All stage scenery, curtains and decorations made of combustible material and all woodwork on or about the stage
shall be saturated with some non-combustible material or
otherwise rendered safe against fire to the satisfaction of
the Bureau of Fire.   The roof over the auditorium and
the entire main floor of the auditorium and vestibule, also
the entire floor of the second story of the front superstructure over the entrance lobby and corridors, and all
galleries in the auditorium, shall be constructed of iron
or steel and fire-proof materials not excluding the use of
wooden floor boards and necessary sleepers to fasten the
same to, but such sleepers shall not mean timbers of support.   The fronts of each gallery shall be formed of fire-
proof materials, excepting the capping, which may be
made of wood.   The ceiling under each gallery shall be
entirely formed of fire-proof materials.   The ceiling of the
auditorium shall be formed of fire-proof materials.   All
lathing whenever used shall be of metal.   The partitions
in that portion of the building which contains the auditorium, the entrance vestibule and every room and passage devoted to the use of the audience shall be constructed
of fire-proof materials including the furring of outside or
other walls.   None of the walls or ceilings shall be
covered with wood sheathing, canvass or any combustible
material, but this shall not exclude the use of wood wainscoting to a heighth not to exceed six feet which shall be
filled in solid between the wainscoting and the wall with
fire-proof materials.   The wall separating the actors' dressing rooms from the stage and the partitions dividing the
dressing rooms, together with the partitions of every
passage-way from the same to the stage, and all other
partitions on or about the stage, shall be constructed of
fire-proof material approved by the Inspector of Buildings.   All doors in any of said partitions shall be of
iron or of wood constructed as hereinbefore described.
All the shelving and cupboards in each and every dressing room, property room or other storage rooms shall be
constructed of metal, slate or some fire proof material.
Dressing rooms may be placed in the fly galleries: _Pro-
vided_, That proper exits are secured therefrom to the
fire-escapes in the open courts, and that the partitions
and other matters pertaining to dressing rooms shall conform to the requirements herein contained, but the stairs
leading to the same shall be fire-proof.   All seats in the
auditorium, excepting those contained in the boxes, shall

Side notes (left margin):

Fly galleries, con-struction of.

Rigging loft.

Scenery, &c., shall be saturated with non-combustible material.

Roof, floor and gal-eries, construction of.

Front of gallery.

Ceiling under gal-lery and auditorum.

Lathing and parti-tions.

Material prohibited for covering of walls or ceilings.

Walls of dressing rooms and parti-tions, construction of.

Doors in partitions.

Shelving and cup-boards.

Dressing rooms in fly galleries.

Seats in audito-rium.

be firmly secured to the floor, and no seat in the auditorium shall have more than six seats intervening between it and an aisle on either side, and no stool or seats shall be placed in any aisle. All platforms in galleries formed to receive the seats shall not be more than twenty-one inches in height of riser nor less than thirty inches in width of platform. All aisles on the respective floors in the auditorium having seats on both sides of same shall be not less than three feet wide where they begin, and shall be increased in width towards the exits in the ratio of one and one-half inches to five running feet. Aisles having seats on one side only shall be not less than two feet wide at their beginning and increased in width the same as aisles having seats on both sides   The aggregate capacity of the foyers, lobbies, corridors, passages and rooms for the use of the audience, not including aisle space between seats, shall, on each floor or gallery, be sufficient to contain the entire number to be accommodated on said floor or gallery in the ratio of one hundred and fifty superficial feet of floor room for every one hundred persons. Gradients or inclined planes shall be employed instead of steps, where possible, to overcome slight difference of level in or between aisles, corridors and passages. Every theatre accommodating three hundred persons shall have at least two exits; when accommodating five hundred persons at least three exits shall be provided; these exits not referring to or including the exits to the open court at the sides of the theatre. Doorways of exit or entrance for the use of the public shall not be less than five feet in width, and for every additional one hundred persons, or portion thereof to be accommodated in excess of five hundred an aggregate of twenty inches additional exit width must be allowed. All doors of exit or entrance shall open outwardly and be hung to swing in such manner as not to become an obstruction in a passage or corridor, and no such doors shall be closed and locked during any representation or when the building is open to the public. Distinct and separate places of exit and entrance shall be provided for each gallery above the first. A common place of exit and entrance may serve for the main floor of the auditorium and the first gallery, provided its capacity be equal to the aggregate capacity of the outlets from the main floor and the said gallery. No passage leading to any stairway communicating with any entrance or exit shall be less than four feet in width in any part thereof. All stairs within the building shall be constructed of fireproof material throughout. Stairways serving for the exit of fifty people must, if straight, be at least four feet wide between railings or between walls, and, if curved or winding, five feet wide, and for every additional fifty people to be accommodated six inches must be added to their width. In no case shall the risers of any stairs exceed seven and a half inches in height nor shall the treads, exclusive of nosings, be less than ten and one-half inches

Platform in galleries.

Aisles in auditorium.

Aggregate capacity of foyers, lobies, &c.

Gradients or inclined planes, when to be used.

Exits, regulation of number of.

Door ways of same, width of.

Doors shall open outwardly.

Exits and entrance for gallery

For main floor and first gallery.

Width of passage way.

Stairways, width of.

Risers and treads.

In circular stairs, staircases, number of regulated.

wide in straight stairs. In circular or winding stairs the width of the tread at the narrowest end shall not be less than seven inches. Where the seating capacity is for more than one thousand people there shall be at least two independent staircases with direct exterior outlets provided for each gallery in the auditorium, where there are not more than two galleries, and the same shall be located on opposite sides of said gallery. Where there are more than two galleries, one or more additional staircases shall be provided, the outlets from which shall communicate directly with the principal exit or other exterior outlets. All said staircase shall be of width proportioned to the seating capacity as elsewhere herein prescribed. Where the seating capacity is for one thousand people or less, two direct lines of staircases only shall be required, located on opposite sides of the galleries, and in both cases shall extend from the sidewalk level to the upper gallery with outlets for each gallery to each of said staircases. At least two independent staircases with direct exterior outlets shall also be provided for the service of the stage and shall be located on the

Inside stairways, construction of.

opposite side of the same. All inside stairways leading to the upper galleries of the auditorium shall be enclosed on both sides with walls of fire-proof materials. Stairs

Stairs open on one side.

leading to the first or lower gallery may be left open on one side, in which case they must be constructed as herein provided for a similar stairs leading from the entrance hall to the main floor of the auditorium. But in

Not open on both sides. Landings of stairs.

no case shall stairs leading to any gallery be left open on both sides. When straight stairs return directly on themselves, a landing of the full width of both flights without any steps shall be provided. Stairs turning at

When two side of flights connect.

an angle shall have a proper landing without winders introduced at said turn. In stairs when two side flights connect with one main flight no winders shall be introduced and the width of the main flight shall be at least equal to the aggregate width of the side flights. Circular or winding stairs shall have proper landings introduced

Landing of circular stairs. Hand rails on inclosed staircases.

at convenient distances. All enclosed staircases shall have on both sides strong hand rails firmly secured in the wall about three inches therefrom and about three feet above the stairs, but said hand rails shall not run on level platforms and landings where the same is more in length

Centre hand rails. when used and how constructed.

than the width of the stairs. All staircases six feet and over in width shall be provided with a center hand rail of hard wood or metal not less than two inches in diameter, placed at a height of about three feet above the center of the treads, and supported on wrought iron or brass standards of sufficient strength, placed not nearer than four feet apart and securely bolted to the treads or risers or stairs or both, and at the head of each flight of stairs on each landing the post or standard shall be at least six feet in height to which the rail shall be secured.

Steam boiler, location of.

Every steam boiler which may be required for heating or other purposes shall be located outside of the building,

and the space allotted to the same shall be enclosed by How inclosed.
walls of masonry on all sides, and the ceiling of such
space shall be constructed of fire-proof material. All
doorways in said walls shall have iron doors. No floor Floor register not allowed.
register for heating shall be permitted. No coil or rad- Placing of coils or radiators.
iator shall be placed in any aisle or passageway used as
an exit where it forms an obstruction, but all said coils
and radiators shall be placed in recesses formed in the
wall or partition to receive the same. All supply, return Supply pipes, &c., how protected.
or exhaust pipes shall be properly incased and protected
where passing through floors or near woodwork. Stand- Stand pipes, number and arrangement of.
pipes of two and one-half inches diameter shall be pro-
vided with hose attachments on every floor and gallery,
as follows, namely: One on each side of the auditorium
in each tier, also one on each side of the stage in each
tier, and at least one in the property room and one in the
carpenter's shop, if the same be contiguous to the building. All such standpipes shall be kept clear from ob-
struction. Said standpipes shall be separate and dis- Supply of water for and coupling of.
tinct, receiving their supply of water direct from the
steam pumps, and shall be fitted with the regulation
couplings of the fire department and shall be kept constantly filled with water by means of an automatic steam
pump or pumps of sufficient capacity to supply all the
lines of hose when operated simultaneously, and said
pump or pumps shall be supplied from the street main
and be ready for immediate use at all times during a
performance in said buildings. A separate and distinct Automatic sprinkler, how supplied and where placed.
system of automatic sprinklers, with fusible plugs, ap-
proved by the Bureau of Fire, supplied with water from
a tank located on the roof over the stage and not connected in any manner with the standpipes shall be placed
up and around the proscenium opening and on the ceiling or roof over the stage, at such intervals as will protect every square foot of stage service when said sprinklers are in operation. Automatic sprinklers shall also
be placed wherever practicable under the stage and in
the carpenter shop, paint room, store rooms and prop-
erty rooms. A proper and sufficient quantity of two and Hose and attachments.
one-half inch hose fitted with the regulation couplings of
the fire department, and with nozzles attached thereto'
and with hose spanners at each outlet, shall always be
kept attached to each hose attachment. There shall al- Water casks and buckets for use on stages.
ways be kept in readiness for immediate use on the stage
at least four casks full of water and two buckets to each
cask. Said casks and buckets shall be painted red.
There shall also be provided hand-pumps or other porta- Hand pumps, axes and hooks.
ble fire extinguishing apparatus, and at least four axes
and two twenty-five feet hooks, two fifteen feet hooks and
two ten feet hooks on each tier or floor of the stage.
Every portion of the building devoted to the uses or ac- Lighting of building and outlets.
commodation of the public, also all outlets leading to the
streets and including the open courts and corridors, shall
be well and properly lighted during every performance,
and the same shall remain lighted until the entire audi-

25—Laws.

Oil lamps in audito-
rium.

Oil to be used.

Separate shut-off
for lights in halls,
corridor and lobby.

Connections of gas
mains.

Appliances for In-
terior lights.

Wire netting for
lights.

Lights not to be in-
serted in walls, &c.

Foot lights, pro-
tection of.

Stage light, how
supplied and con-
struction of.

Duct or shafts for
heated air from
chandelier.

Wire screens for
stage lights.

Control and charge
of pipes, wires,
hose, footlights and
fire apparatus.

Diagram of tier,
gallery or floor
must be on pro-
gram.

Word EXIT painted
over each exit.

'ence has left the premises. At least two or more oil lamps on each side of the auditorium in each tier shall be provided on fixed brackets not less than seven feet above the floor. Said lamps shall be filled with whale or lard oil and shall be kept lighted during each perform-ance, or in place of said lamps candles shall be provided. All gas or electric lights in the halls, corridors, lobby or any other part of the said buildings used by the audi-ence, except the auditorium, must be controlled by a sep-arate shut-off located in the lobby and controlled only in that particular place. Gas mains supplying the building shall have independent connections for the auditorium and the stage, and provision shall be made for shutting off the gas from the outside of the building. When in-terior gas lights are not lighted by electricity, other suit-able appliances, to be approved by the Bureau of Fire, shall be provided. All suspended or bracket lights sur-rounded by glass in the auditorium or in any part of the building devoted to the public, shall be provided with proper wire netting underneath. No gas or electric light shall be inserted in the walls, woodwork, ceilings or in any part of the buildings unless protected by fire-proof materials. All lights in passages and corridors in said buildings, and wherever deemed necessary by the Bureau of Fire, shall be protected by proper wire net-work. The footlights, in addition to the wire net work, shall be pro-tected by a strong wire guard not less than two feet dis-tant from said footlights, and the trough containing said footlights shall be formed of and surrounded by fire-proof materials. All stage lights shall be incandescent electric lights, where the current can be obtained, and shall be constructed according to the best known methods and subject to the approval of the Bureau of Fire, and shall be suspended for ten feet by wire rope. All ducts or shafts used for conducting heated air from the main chandelier, or from any other light or lights, shall be constructed of metal and made double with an air space between. All stage lights shall have strong metal wire guards or screens not less than ten inches in diameter, so constructed that any material in contact therewith shall be out of reach of the flames of said stage lights, and must be soldered to the fixture in all cases. The stand-pipes, gas pipes, electric wires, hose, footlights and all apparatus for the extinguishing of fire or guarding against the same, as in this section specified, shall be in charge and under control of the Bureau of Fire, Depart-ment of Public Safety, and the said department is hereby directed to see that the arrangements in respect thereto are carried out and enforced, and councils may, by ordi-nance, fix a reasonable compensation for such service. A diagram or plan of each tier, gallery or floor, showing distinctly the exits therefrom, shall be printed in a legi-ble manner on the programme of the performance. Every exit shall have over the same on the inside, the word EXIT, painted in legible letters not less than eight inches high. It shall be within the power of the mayor, after full report from the Department of Public Safety, to cause the closing up of any theatre, opera house or public hall where, in the judgment of the mayor and the Department of Public Safety that the ingress and egress is not reasonably safe for the safe and speedy exit of the audience in case of fire or panic. Closing of theatre, opera house or hall shall be in power of Mayor.

SECTION 41. The cities of the first class may, by ordinance, regulate and determine the license fee for the permits as required by the provisions of this act, the said fees to be paid by them into the city treasury in the manner and form as is now provided for by law. All ordinances or parts of ordinances of the cities of the first class now in force relating to the building limits and the inspection and survey of buildings shall remain in force until amended or repealed by said cities. Said cities may, by ordinance, regulate the management and inspect'on of elevator hoistways and elevator shafts in said cities. License fee for permits how regulated.

Payment of said fee.

Ordinances relating to building limits.

Inspection of elevators &c., l ow regulated.

SECTION 42. In any case of final decision, either of an inspector or of the bureau or of an examining commission, such decision or order may be at once, if not complied with, certified to any court of common pleas, which court shall, upon application of the Director of the Department of Public Safety by bill or complaint, issue a mandatory injunction requiring compliance with such order or decision within five days, or within a shorter time if the relief sought is the removal of a dangerous wall, ceiling or structure, and the court sees proper to fix a shorter time. Court may issue a mandatory injunction if final decision of inspector, bureau or commission is not complied with.

Limit of time for compliance.

If said injunction is not complied with within the time specified by the court, or if it cannot, for any reason, be served, the court shall have power to enforce its order by attachment or to issue an order to any sheriff commanding him to remove the wall, building or structure condemned by the building inspectors, (either as contrary to the provisions by this act or as dangerous), under the supervision of the Bureau of Building Inspectors or such inspector as the chief of the bureau shall designate. The sheriff shall have power to employ such competent builders, riggers and workmen as shall be necessary to carry out the order of the court. He shall certify to the court when he has performed the work required to be done, the cost incurred, and such bill being approved by the court and not being paid by the owner of the premises, the court shall have power, by mandamus execution, to compel the city to pay such cost. The court shall, upon the issuing of such mandamus execution, direct that the prothonotary of the court shall enter the amount thereof as a lien against the premises whereon the order was enforced, and the costs incurred, and the city paying such costs may thereafter proceed in the case wherein the order was made to collect such bill of costs and the proper docket costs thereon, by the same process and proceedings and under the same restrictions as are now If injunction is not complied with, court may order its enforcement by attachment or order to sheriff.

Power of sheriff.

When work is done, how cost incurred shall be collected and paid, and by whom.

Penalty for refusal to comply with decision of bureau.

provided for or required by law for the collection of claims for the removal of nuisances in such city; and in case of wilful and persistent refusal to comply with the decision of the Bureau of Building Inspection the said court shall have power to impose a fine not exceeding three hundred dollars.

Repeal.

SECTION 43. All acts or parts of acts inconsistent herewith be and the same are hereby repealed.

APPROVED—The 8th day of June, A. D. 1893.

ROBT. E. PATTISON.

No. 295.

AN ACT

To provide for the partial payment of per diem compensation to Henry Shade, junior, member of the National Guard of Pennsylvania during the time of his disability produced by typhoid fever, which he contracted in the service of the State at Homestead, Pennsylvania.

WHEREAS, Henry Shade, junior, a private of Company "C," Fifteenth Regiment of the National Guard of Pennsylvania, was called into the service of the State during the riots at Homestead, Allegheny county, was taken ill with typhoid fever as a result of exposure during his said service in the National Guard, and was confined in hospitals and to his home on account of such illness until the thirteenth day of December, one thousand eight hundred and ninety-two;

And whereas, The Adjutant General in paying him for his service only gave him compensation to the twentieth day of September, one thousand eight hundred and ninety-two, the date at which he was relieved from duty;

And whereas, By reason of such service and the sickness referred to he was unable to resume his labors until the thirteenth day of December, one thousand eight hundred and ninety-two, thereby losing his time and opportunity to earn a daily compensation; therefor,

Compensation to Henry Shade, guardsman.

SECTION 1. *Be it enacted, &c.,* That the State Treasurer be and he is hereby authorized and empowered to pay to said Henry Shade, junior, the sum of one hundred and twenty-six dollars, being his per diem allowance of pay as a private of Company "C," Fifteenth Regiment National Guard of Pennsylvania from the twentieth day of September, one thousand eight hundred and ninety-two, to the thirteenth day of December, one thousand eight hundred and ninety-two. Said sum of money to be paid

How payable.

out of any money in the treasury, not otherwise appropriated, upon warrant to be drawn by the Auditor General in the usual manner, it being understood that the amount of money provided to be paid in this bill is to cover the amount to which said private is justly entitled on account of the sickness which he contracted in the service and which, after his discharge, rendered him unfit to perform any manual labor between the dates for which provision is herein made for his payment.

APPROVED—The 8th day of June, A. D. 1893.

ROBT. E. PATTISON.

No. 296.

A SUPPLEMENT

To a supplement to an act, entitled "A supplement to an act authorizing companies incorporated under the laws of any other State of the United States for the manufacture of any form of iron, steel or glass to erect and maintain buildings and manufacturing establishments, and to take, have and hold real estate necessary and proper for manufacture purposes," approved the ninth day of June, one thousand eight hundred and eighty-one, authorizing companies incorporated under the laws of any other State of the United States for the conversion, dyeing and cleansing of cotton and other fabrics to erect and maintain buildings for such manufacturing purposes, and for offices and salesrooms, or either, and to take, have and hold real estate necessary and proper for such purposes, approved the twenty-fifth day of June, Anno Domini one thousand eight hundred and eighty-five, conferring similar powers upon companies incorporated under the laws of any other State of the United States for the manufacture of lumber and wood products and pyroligneous acids, acetate of lime and charcoal by the process of destructive distillation, or the preparation of cattle hair for use, approved the twenty-eighth day of April, one thousand eight hundred and eighty-seven, conferring similar power upon companies incorporated under the laws of any other State of the United States for the manufacture of carbon dioxide and magnesia and the products thereof, and compositions, articles and apparatus from and in connection therewith, and for the manufacture of cotton velvet and other fabrics, and for the manufacture of extracts out of wood, bark, leaves and roots, or any other extracts for tanning, cleansing, dyeing or other purposes," approved the thirtieth day of April, Anno Domini one thousand eight hundred and ninety-one, conferring similar powers upon companies incorporated under the laws of any other State of the United States for the manufacture or printing of wall paper, lithographs or prints, and for mining and manufacture of clay into brick tile and various other articles and products produced from clay, and from clay and other substances mixed therewith.

SECTION 1. *Be it enacted, &c.*, That the first section of an act, entitled "A supplement to a supplement to an act, entitled 'A supplement to an act authorizing companies incorporated under the laws of any other State of the United States for the manufacture of any form of iron, steel or glass to erect and maintain buildings and manufacturing establishments, and to take, have and hold real estate necessary and proper for manufacturing purposes, approved the ninth day of June, one thousand eight

Act of April 30, 1891, supplementary to the acts of June 9, 1881, June 25, 1885 and April 28, 1887, cited for amendment.

hundred and eighty-one, authorizing companies incorporated under the laws of any other State of the United States for the conversion, dyeing and cleansing of cotton and other fabrics to erect and maintain buildings for such manufacturing purposes, and for offices and salesrooms, or either, and to take, have and hold real estate necessary and proper for such purposes, approved the twenty-fifth day of June, Anno Domini one thousand eight hundred and eighty-five, conferring similar powers upon companies incorporated under the laws of any other State of the United States for the manufacture of lumber and wood products, and pyroligneous acids, acetate of lime or charcoal by the process of destructive distillation, or the preparation of cattle hair for use, approved the twenty-eighth day of April, one thousand eight hundred and eighty-seven, conferring similar powers upon companies incorporated under the laws of any other State of the United States for the manufacture of carbon dioxide and magnesia and the products thereof, and compositions, articles and apparatus from and in connection therewith, and for the manufacture of cotton velvet and other fabrics, and for the manufacture of extracts out of wood, bark, leaves and roots, or any other extracts for tanning, cleansing, dyeing or other purposes," approved the thirtieth day of April, Anno Domini one thousand eight hundred and ninety-one, conferring similar powers upon companies incorporated under the laws of any other State of the United States for the manufacture or printing of wall paper, lithographs or prints, which reads as follows:

"That it shall and may be lawful for any company incorporated under the laws of any other State of the United States for the manufacture of any form of iron, steel, glass, lumber or wood, or for the conversion, dyeing and cleaning of cotton and other fabrics, or for the manufacture of cotton or velvet or other fabrics, or for the manufacture of pyroligneous acids, acetate of lime and charcoal by the process of destructive distillation, or the preparation of cattle hair for use, or for the manufacture of carbon dioxide and magnesia and the products thereof and compositions and articles and apparatus from and in connection therewith, or for the manufacture of extracts out of wood, bark, leaves and roots, or any other extract for tanning, cleansing, dyeing or other purposes to erect and maintain buildings for such manufacturing purposes, and for offices and salesrooms, or either, within this Commonwealth, and to take, have and hold real estate, not exceeding one hundred acres, necessary and proper for such manufacturing purposes, and for offices, dwellings and salesrooms, or either, and to mortgage, bond, lease or convey the same or any part thereof: *Provided*, That nothing herein contained shall be deemed to prevent or relieve any real estate taken and held by any such foreign corporation under the provisions of this statute from being taxed in like manner with other real estate within this Commonwealth: *And provided further*, That no such foreign corporation shall be entitled to employ any greater amount of capital in such business in this State than the same kind of corporations organized under the laws of this State are entitled to employ : *And provided further*, That every such foreign corporation doing business as aforesaid in this Commonwealth shall be liable to taxation to an amount not exceeding that imposed on corporations organized for similar purposes under the laws of this State, and every such foreign corporation taking the benefit of this act shall make the same returns to the Auditor General that are required by law to be made by corporations of this State under similar circumstances," be and the same is hereby amended so as to read as follows:

That it shall be may be lawful for any company incorporated under the laws of any other State of the United States for the manufacture of any form of iron, steel, glass, lumber or wood, or for the conversion, dyeing and cleansing of cotton and other fabrics, or for the manufacture of cotton or velvet or other fabrics, or for the manufacture of pyroligneous acids, acetate of lime and charcoal by the process of destructive distillation, or the preparation of cattle hair for use, or for the manufacture of carbon dioxide and magnesia and the products thereof and compositions, articles and apparatus from and in connection therewith, or for the manufacture of extracts out of wood, bark, leaves and roots, or any other extract for tanning, cleansing, dyeing or other purposes, or for the manufacture or printing of wall paper, lithographs or prints, and mining and manufacture of any clay into brick tile and various other articles and products produced from clay, and from clay and other substances mixed therewith, to erect and maintain buildings for such manufacturing purposes, and for offices and salesrooms, or either, within this Commonwealth, and to take, have and hold real estate, not exceeding one hundred acres, necessary and proper for such manufacturing purposes, and for offices, dwellings and salesroom, or either, and to mortgage, bond, lease or convey the same or any part thereof : *Provided*, That nothing herein contained shall be deemed to prevent or relieve any real estate taken and held by any such foreign corporation under the provisions of this statute from being taxed in like manner with other real estate within this Commonwealth : *And provided further*, That no such foreign corporation shall be entitled to employ any greater amount of capital in such business in this State than the same kind of corporations organized under the laws of this State are entitled to employ : *And provided further*, That every such foreign corporation doing business as aforesaid in this Commonwealth shall be liable to taxation to an amount not exceeding that imposed on corporations organized for similar purposes under the laws of this State, and every such foreign

Margin notes:
Powers of certain foreign corporations.

Similar powers conferred upon certain other corporations.

Proviso.

Proviso.

Proviso.

corporation taking the benefit of this act shall make the same returns to the Auditor General that are required by law to be made by corporations of this State under similar circumstances.

Title to real estate confirmed.

SECTION 2. That the title to any real estate in this Commonwealth now held by, or in trust for, any such foreign corporations for the purpose aforesaid is hereby confirmed to the same effect as if the said real estate has been purchased, held or owned under the provisions of this act.

Repeal.

SECTION 3. That all acts or parts of acts inconsistent herewith be and the same are hereby repealed.

APPROVED—The 8th day of June, A. D. 1893.

ROBT. E. PATTISON.

No. 297.

AN ACT

To limit the duration of the lien of the debts of decedents other than those of record on their real estate.

Certain debts not to remain a lien on real estate longer than two years.

SECTION 1. *Be it enacted, &c.*, That no debts of a decedent dying after the passage of this act, except they be secured by mortgage or judgment, shall remain a lien on the real estate of such decedent longer than two years

Action for recovery must be begun within two years.

after the decease of such debtor, unless an action for the recovery thereof be commenced against his heirs, executors or administrators within the period of two years after his decease, and duly prosecuted to judgment, or a copy or particular written statement of any bond, covenant, debt or demand, where the same is not payable within the said period of two years, shall be filed within the period of two years in the office of the prothonotary of the county where the real estate to be charged is situate, and then to be a lien only for the period of two years after said bond, covenant, debt or de-

Duty of prothonotary.

mand becomes due. And it shall be the duty of the prothonotary of said county, when a statement as aforesaid is filed in his office, to index the same in the judgment docket as other liens are indexed.

Proceedings by executor, &c., to have real estate relieved from any lien.

SECTION 2. It shall and may be lawful for any executor, administrator, trustee, or any party interested in the real estate of any decedent, to present his, her or their petition to any court having jurisdiction of the settlement of such estate, setting forth all the particulars, and also that there are just and reasonable grounds for believing that said decedent left no debts not of record, and that it is desirable to have the real estate of said decedent relieved from any lien now given by law for such debts.

Power of court.

SECTION 3. It shall be lawful for said court having jurisdiction as aforesaid to hear and determine the same, and shall have power to refer such petition to an exam-

Duty of examiner or master, if appointed.

iner or master whose duty it shall be to diligently inquire into the facts and circumstances alleged in any such petition, and report the same to said court, and the said court may in its discretion direct such notices to be given of such application either by publication or otherwise as may be deemed necessary. *Notice to be given.*

SECTION 4. It shall be the duty of said court, upon being fully satisfied as to the truth and justice of the matters alleged in any such petition and application, to decree and direct that the real estate of any such decedent shall be held and enjoyed free and clear of any lien of debts not of record of said decedent. *Decree of court.*

SECTION 5. All acts or parts of acts inconsistent herewith are hereby repealed. *Repeal.*

APPROVED—The 8th day of June, A. D. 1893.

ROBT. E. PATTISON.

No. 298.

AN ACT

Creating the office of county controller in counties of this Commonwealth containing one hundred and fifty thousand inhabitants and over, prescribing his duties.

SECTION 1. *Be it enacted, &c.,* That the qualified voters of each of the counties of this Commonwealth containing one hundred and fifty thousand inhabitants and over, as shown by the last preceding decennial census, shall elect, on the first Tuesday after the first Monday of November, one thousand eight hundred and ninety-three, and triennially thereafter, in place of county auditor, one citizen of each of said counties to serve as controller of said county for a term of three years, or until his successor shall be qualified, if he so long shall behave himself well: *Provided,* This act shall not apply to cities coextensive with counties. *Controller to be elected in counties containing 150,000 inhabitants.* *Term.* *Proviso.*

SECTION 2. No person holding office under the United States or this State, or in any city or county therein, shall be eligible to the office of county controller during his continuance in office as aforesaid, nor until one year thereafter, and the county commissioner, county treasurer, prothonotary, register of wills, clerk of the courts, recorder of deeds, sheriff and district attorney and their chief clerks or deputies, shall be ineligible for two years to the office of county controller, provided the said controller shall always be eligible to re-election or appointment. *Certain persons ineligible.* *Proviso.*

SECTION 3. Before entering on the duties of his office, the controller shall give bond to the county for which he may be elected, with at least two sureties, in the sum of fifty thousand dollars, to be approved by the court of common pleas of said county, conditioned for the faithful performance of his duties and those of his chief clerk. The controller and his clerks shall also each take and subscribe the oath or affirmation as prescribed by article seventh, section first of the Constitution of the Commonwealth, a wilful violation of which shall be per- *Bond.* *Oath.*

jury. Said oaths and bonds to be recorded in the recorder's office of the proper county, and then filed and kept in the commissioner's office, and the records thereof or certified copies of the same shall be used in evidence in all judicial proceeding with the same effect as the originals.

SECTION 4. The said controller shall have a general supervision and control of the fiscal affairs of the county and of the accounts and official acts of all officers or other persons who shall collect, receive or distribute the public moneys of the county, or who shall be charged with the management or custody thereof, and he may at any

time require from any of them in writing an account of all moneys or property which may have come into their

control, and he shall immediately on the discovery of any default or delinquency report the same to the commissioners and the court of common pleas of the county,

and shall take immediate measures to secure the public moneys or property and remove the delinquent party, if in office, and not removed by the commissioners.

SECTION 5. He shall cause to be kept a full and regular set of books in detail by double entry of all the fiscal operations of the county, embracing as many accounts under appropriate titles as may be necessary to show distinctly and separately all the property of the county its receipts and expenditures, and all debts and accounts due by the county officers or others, the amount raised from each source of revenue and the expenditures in detail and classified by reference to the objects thereof; he

shall prescribe the form and manner of keeping the books and papers used by each of the officers of said county in connection with the fiscal affairs of the county, and he shall on or before the first day of February, annually, communicate to the commissioners in writing a

detailed estimate of and for the legitimate purpose of the county for the current year, including interests due and to fall due on all lawful debts of the county bearing interest, and the commissioners shall on or before the

fifteenth day of February, thereafter, fix such rate of taxation upon the valuation of the property of the county as will raise sufficient sum to meet the said expenditures,

and the commissioners shall not by contract or otherwise increase the expenditures of the county in any year to an amount beyond the taxes assessed as aforesaid for said year.

SECTION 6. That he shall in the month of January in every year make a report, verified by oath or affirmation, to the court of common pleas of said county, of all receipts and expenditures of the county for the preceding year in detail and classified as required in the fifth section of this act, together with a full statement of the

financial conditions of the county, which report shall thereupon be published one time in such newspapers published in said county as the court may direct; the ag-

gregate cost of which shall not exceed one thousand dollars in any one year; to be paid for out of the county treasury, which publication shall be in lieu of that re quired by the twenty-seventh section of the act of fifteenth of April, Anno Domini one thousand eight hundred and thirty-four.

SECTION 7. That the controller shall keep his office in a room or rooms of the court house of the county, to be furnished at the expense of the county, and shall furnish the commissioners of the county, whenever required by them, a detail account of any officer or other person having in his possession, or under his control, funds belonging to the county, and shall at all times between the hours of ten o'clock ante meridian and two o'clock post meridian give information respecting any of said accounts to any taxpayer of the county demanding the same.

SECTION 8. That he shall scrutinize, audit and decide on all bills, claims and demands whatsoever against the county, and all persons having such claims shall first present the same to the controller and, if required, make oath or affirmation before him to the correctness thereof; he may, if he deems it necessary, require evidence by oaths or affirmation of the claimant and otherwise that the claim is legally due and that the supplies or services for which payment is claimed have been furnished or performed under legal authority; he may inquire or ascertain whether any officer or agent of the county is interested in the contract under which any claim may arise, or has received or is to receive any commission, consideration or gratuity relating thereto, or whether there has been any evasion of the tenth section of this act by making two or more contracts for small amount which should have been in one; and if he shall find that there has been any evasion, or that any such officer or agent is so interested, he shall refuse to approve the claim; all claims which he shall find legally due he shall certify to the commissioners. He shall countersign all receipts given by the county treasurer to persons paying money into the treasury and keep an accurate record of the same.

SECTION 9. That after the controller shall have assumed the duties of his office under this act, the commissioners of said county shall draw no warrant on the treasury for any debt, claim or demand whatsoever, not audited and approved by the controller as provided for in the foregoing section, except for the fees of jurors, witnesses, criers, and tipstaves of the several courts of the county, the amount of said fees to be ascertained by said courts and entered on the records thereof, and duly certified by their respective clerks to the commissioners, being first sworn to before the controller, and said certificates shall be delivered by the commissioners to the controller for preservation as soon as the warrants are issued.

SECTION 10. That from and after the passage of this act, all contracts made by the commissioners of said county involving an expenditure exceeding twenty dollars shall be in writing and shall immediately after their execution be filed with the controller, but no contract shall be made nor the payment thereof certified by the controller for over one hundred dollars, unless when made with the lowest and best bidder after due notice to be published by the controller when directed by the commissioners; if he approve the purpose of the proposals invited all bids to be received by the controller under seal and to be in his presence opened by the commissioners and the contracts awarded, of which awards the controller

shall keep a record, and he shall certify no warrants for contracts not made agreeably thereto.

SECTION 11. That all warrants drawn on the county treasury by the commissioners on certificates as provided for in the eighth, ninth and tenth section of this act shall be countersigned by the controller, who shall keep a correct register thereof, noting the number, date and amount of each, the date of payment, and to whom and

for what issued, and shall report to the commissioners monthly, or oftener if required by them, the amount of outstanding warrants registered and the amount of money in the treasury.

SECTION 12. That controller shall have the custody of all official bonds (except his own) given to the county, and of all title deeds to real estate owned by the county, and of all contracts entered into by or on behalf of the county, and of all books, documents and papers relating to its financial affairs, and of all bonds and other obligations issued by said county when paid, which bonds and other obligations when so paid shall be distinctly can-

celled by him and carefully and regularly be filed, a register of which cancellation shall be kept by him in a book to be provided for that purpose.

SECTION 13. The treasurer of said county shall pay no money out of the county treasury except on warrants drawn by a majority of the commissioners and countersigned by the controller. His books shall at all times

during office hours be open to the inspection of the controller, and he shall report daily to the controller all

moneys received by him from the county, the person by whom and on what account they were paid; he shall cancel all warrants when made by distinctly spearing or cutting them; he shall also report daily all moneys paid out by him, giving the number of the warrant and the party to whom paid, and shall deliver the warrants to the controller who shall cancel the same, and all outstanding warrants issued before the controller enters upon the duties of his office shall be presented to him as other claims against the county. But in the counties to which this applies wherein the poor tax is paid into the county treasury the county treasurer shall also keep a separate account of the said county poor tax received by him, and pay out of the same upon warrants drawn by a majority of the directors of the poor of the county.

Section 14. The controller shall, if he deems it necessary, appoint a chief clerk whose salary shall be fixed by the commissioners and the controller as provided by section seven of the act of thirty-first of March, one thousand eight hundred and seventy-six. The chief clerk shall, during the necessary or temporary absence of the controller, perform all his duties, and also in case of a vacancy, until a successor is qualified, but in the latter case neither the controller or his sureties shall be liable on his official bond, or otherwise, for acts done or neglected more than one month after the vacancy occurred, and the court may, if the public interest demand it, on the application of any taxpayer of the county, declare the said office vacant at any time when the duties of the controller shall, under the provisions of this section, have devolved on the chief clerk for a period exceeding three consecutive weeks, unless new sureties be given or the sureties on the official bond of the controller shall agree to be liable on said bond, notwithstanding the preceding provision in this section releasing them from liability, which agreement shall be made a record of said court, and the jurisdiction conferred by the act of the twenty-first of April, one thousand eight hundred and forty-six, entitled "An act in relation to certain public officers and their sureties," may in all cases be exercised by the court of common pleas of the county, whenever the said court may deem the public interests to require it, either with or without the petition required by the first section of this act.

Section 15. That all duties devolved on the county auditors by the act of April fifteenth, one thousand eight hundred and thirty-four, and all powers conferred on them by said act shall be performed and exercised by the county controller so far as regards county accounts, and State taxes for which the county is or may be liable, and all other accounts with the treasurer with the Commonwealth shall be audited by the auditor of the accounts of prothonotaries, clerks, et cetera, appointed by the court of common pleas under the act of twenty-first of April, one thousand eight hundred and forty-six, and its supplements. And the report required by the seventh section of this act shall have the same effect as the report of the auditors under said act of the fifteenth of April, one thousand eight hundred and thirty-four, with like rights of appeal therefrom.

Approved—The 8th day of June, A. D. 1893.

ROBT. E. PATTISON.

Marginal notes:

- Controller may appoint a chief clerk. Salary.
- Duties of chief clerk.
- Surety
- Court may declare office vacant.
- Agreement.
- To be made record of court. Jurisdiction conferred by act of April 21, 1846, may be exercised by court.
- Certain duties of county auditors to be performed by county controller.
- Report to have same effect as report of auditors.

No. 299.

AN ACT

Making an appropriation for the payment of the expenses incurred and the services rendered on account of the location of the circle of New Castle, being the boundary line between the States of Pennsylvania and Delaware, as provided by the act of May fourth, one thousand eight hundred and eighty-nine.

$3,000.00 appropriated.

Itemized vouchers.

SECTION 1. *Be it enacted, &c.*, That the sum of three thousand dollars, or so much thereof as may be found necessary by the Auditor General upon the presentation of specifically itemized vouchers duly certified under oath, be and the same is hereby specifically appropriated for the payment of the expenses incurred and the services rendered on account of the location of the circle of New Castle, being the boundary line between the States of Pennsylvania and Delaware, as provided by the act of May fourth, one thousand eight hundred and eighty-nine. Said amount being in addition to the amount appropriated in said act, and which amount is now found necessary to complete the work provided for therein.

How payable.

The said appropriation to be paid on the warrant of the Auditor General on a settlement made by him and the State Treasurer.

APPROVED—The 8th day of June, A. D. 1893.

ROBT. E. PATTISON.

No. 300.

AN ACT

Making an appropriation to enable the Governor to acquire and equip a State Quarantine Station for the Port of Philadelphia.

$35,000.00 appropriated.

SECTION 1. *Be it enacted, &c.*, That the sum of thirty-five thousand dollars, or so much thereof as may be necessary, is hereby specifically appropriated out of any money in the treasury, not otherwise appropriated, to be expended by the Governor of this Commonwealth in the acquisition of land, either by lease or purchase, for a State Quarantine Station for the port of Philadelphia, and the erection of buildings and purchase of the necessary equipment for said station as authorized by law:

Cost of surveys, &c.

Provided, That the Governor shall have power to use a portion of the money hereby appropriated to pay the cost of preliminary surveys and examination of sites.

How payable.

The said appropriation to be paid on the warrant of the Auditor General and on a settlement made by him and

Itemized vouchers.

the State Treasurer upon itemized vouchers duly certi-

Unexpended balance.

fied to by the Governor. All moneys appropriated under this act and remaining unexpended at the close of the fiscal year ending June first, one thousand eight hundred and ninety-five, shall revert to the State Treasury.

APPROVED—The 8th day of June, A. D. 1893.

ROBT. E. PATTISON.

No 301.

AN ACT

Authorizing the commitment of minors by magistrates, justices of the peace or judges, of certain charitable societies, and providing for the method of such commitment and the cost of the visitation of such minors.

SECTION 1. *Be it enacted, &c.*, That it shall be lawful for any society duly incorporated, having for one of its objects the protection of children from cruelty or the placing of children not otherwise provided for in families, to receive into its care and guardianship, at its discretion, minors committed to such care and guardianship by any justice of the peace, magistrate or judge of any court, upon complaint and due proof made, first, that such minor by reason of incorrigible, unmanageable, vicious or wayward conduct is beyond the control of the parent or guardian of such infant, or, second, that the parents of such minor by reason of vagrancy, incorrigible or vicious conduct, criminal offense, moral depravity or cruelty, are unfit to have the training and control of such minor, or, third, that the said minor is a vagrant and has no parent or guardian capable or willing to restrain, manage or take proper care of such minor, or the said society may receive under its care and guardianship any minor as aforesaid, when such minor has been committed to its care and guardianship by the judge of any court after said minor shall have been duly convicted of any criminal offense. *Certain charitable societies may receive minors committed to their care by proper officer.*

Proofs necessary before commitment.

Judge may commit minor, after conviction.

SECTION 2. It shall be lawful for any justice of the peace, magistrate or judge of any court to commit minors to any society duly incorporated, having for one of its objects the protection of children from cruelty or the placing of children not otherwise provided for in families, upon complaint and due proof made of facts such as are set forth in the first section of this act after the said minors have been duly convicted of any criminal offense. *Minor may be committed to care of society after a conviction.*

SECTION 3. It shall be the duty of the justice of the peace or magistrate aforesaid committing a vagrant or incorrigible or vicious minor as aforesaid, or any minor as provided in section one of this act, to annex to his commitment the names and residences of the different witnesses examined before him and the substance of the testimony given by them respectively on which the said adjudication was founded. *What shall be annexed to commitment by the officer.*

SECTION 4. It shall be the duty of any magistrate or justice of the peace making a commitment as provided in the first and second sections of this act of a minor to *Commitment, &c., shall be transferred to district attorney.*

any society to transfer his commitment, together with the various matters annexed thereto as provided in the third section of this act, to the district attorney of the county in which said commitment shall be made, and it shall be the duty of the district attorney when the same shall be placed in his hands, or as soon as it is possible thereafter, to place the said commitment, with the matters annexed, in the hands of a judge sitting at quarter sessions, who shall examine the same and shall endorse thereon an order for the detention of the said minor by the said society, or if he shall be of the opinion that the said minor has been wrongfully committed, he shall endorse upon the commitment an order for the discharge of the said minor: *Provided*, That nothing in this act contained shall be construed to interfere with the provisions of an act, entitled "An act for the better securing of personal liberty and preventing unlawful imprisonment," passed on the eighteenth day of February, one thousand seven hundred and eighty-five, commonly called the habeas corpus act.

SECTION 5. It shall be the duty of the duty of the society to whom a commitment shall be made in accordance with the provisions of the first section of this act, when the minors so committed to it are placed in respectable families subject to the visitation and supervision of such person as may from time to time be appointed for such purpose by the judges of the court of common pleas of the county in which such commitment shall be made, to select, so far as it may be possible, families of the same religious denomination as that to which the parents of children committed to its care shall belong.

SECTION 6. It shall be the duty of the judges of the several courts of common pleas within this Commonwealth to appoint visitors to visit the children committed in accordance with the provisions of this act by any magistrate, justice of the peace or judge in their respective counties, the said visits to be made at intervals not longer than once every six months, and the said visitors shall report upon the character of the home in which said child shall be placed, and the expense of said visitation shall be fixed by the court and borne by the counties aforesaid

SECTION 7. Authority is hereby given to every city of the first and second classes, in the discretion of the councils thereof, to make appropriations from the treasury thereof to any society having for one of its objects the protection of children from cruelty or the placing of children not otherwise provided for in families, to which society children of the citizens of said city may by law be committed by the magistrate or judges of the county within which said city may be situated, and all laws and parts of laws inconsistent herewith are hereby repealed.

APPROVED—The 8th of June, A. D. 1893. The general purpose of this bill as embodied in its first six sections meets with my hearty approval. The seventh section is not covered by the title to the bill and is not cognate to its general purposes. I am of the opinion that so much of it is therefore unconstitutional, and will be so held by the courts when submitted to the test; inasmuch, however, as it has been well settled by a line of judicial decisions that the invalid portions of a statute may be declared inoperative without affecting the remainder of the law, I have given this act my approval with this timely notice that its seventh and concluding section is in my judgment inaffective.

ROBT. E. PATTISON.

No. 302.

AN ACT

Making an appropriation to the State College to establish and maintain experimental stations for the purpose of making experiments in the culture, curing and preparation of tobacco, and providing for the publication of the report thereof.

SECTION 1. *Be it enacted, &c.,* That the sum of four thousand dollars, or so much thereof as may be necessary, for two fiscal years, beginning on the first day of June, one thousand eight hundred and ninety-three, be and the same is hereby specifically appropriated to the trustees of the Pennsylvania State College for the purpose of conducting experiments and investigations in the culture, curing and preparation of tobacco, under the management of the tobacco growers' society duly incorporated, et cetera, of Lancaster county, and such other responsible associations as may desire to engage in such work, but subject to the direction and control of the Agricultural Experiment Station of said college. The selection of locations for the proper conduct of the experiments and the determination of methods of carrying them on shall be such as shall be agreed upon between the director of said station and the managers of said society or associations respectively. The actual work of experimentation shall be carried on by the respective associations, but the analysis and investigations connected therewith shall be made by said station, and the results of the experiments together with the itemized financial statement shall be published in the annual report presented by said station to the Governor of the Commonwealth: *Provided,* That no part of the appropriation herein made shall be used for the purchase of land, and that experiments shall be carried on under this act in not less than two nor more than five separate localities.

SECTION 2. That an amount not exceeding two (2) per centum of the sums appropriated by this act may be used by the station for the purpose of printing and distributing the results of the experiments herein provided

Marginal notes:
$4,000.00 appropriated.

Investigations to be made by tobacco growers society of Lancaster county.

Control of same.

Selection of locations for experiments.

Work of experiments. Analyses, by whom made. Results and financial statement reported to Governor.

Use of appropriation.

Number of localities.

Amount allowed for printing results.

26—LAWS.

for in the form of bulletins, one copy of each which shall be sent to every newspaper published in the State, and to such individuals as may request the same so far as the means of the station may permit.

SECTION 3. That the money hereby appropriated shall be paid to said trustees by the State Treasurer on the warrant of the Auditor General in such sums as may from time to time be required, and as the condition of the treasury will allow, on the representation of a sworn statement showing in detail the purposes for which such sums have been expended under the provisions of this act.

APPROVED—The 8th day of June, A. D. 1893.

ROBT. E PATTISON.

No. 303.

AN ACT

To provide for the partial payment of per diem compensation to Albert M. Luther, a member of the National Guard of Pennsylvania, during the time of his disability produced by typhoid fever which he contracted in the service of the State at Homestead, Pennsylvania.

WHEREAS, Albert M. Luther, a private of the Fifteenth regiment, Company C, of the National Guard of Pennsylvania, who was called into service of the State during the recent riots at Homestead, Allegheny county, was taken ill with typhoid fever as a result of exposure and bad food during his said service in the National Guard, and was sent to the Hermot hospital at Erie, Pennsylvania, on account of such illness until about November eighth, one thousand eight hundred and ninety-two;

And whereas, The Adjutant General in paying him for his service only gave him compensation to the nineteenth day of September, one thousand eight hundred and ninety-two, the date at which he was relieved from duty;

And whereas, By reason of such service and the sickness referred to he was unable to do any duty until November twenty-eighth, Anno Domini one thousand eight hundred and ninety-two, thereby losing his time and opportunity to earn a daily compensation; therefore,

SECTION 1. *Be it enacted, &c.,* That the State Treasurer be and is hereby authorized and empowered to pay to the said Albert M. Luther the sum of one hundred and seventeen dollars and twenty-five cents, being a part of his allowance as a private with second enlistment pay in said regiment from the twentieth day of September, one thousand eight hundred and ninety-two, to the eighth day of November, one thousand eight hundred and ninety- two, inclusive, and hospital bill of thirty dollars, for six weeks, at five dollars per week, also loss of time when unable to work from November eighth, one thousand eight hundred and ninety-two, to November twenty-eighth, one thousand eight hundred and ninety-two, and that the State Treasurer be authorized to pay the said Albert M. Luther, a private in the company and regiment aforesaid, the full sum of one hundred and seventeen dollars and twenty-five cents, such amount being part of his per diem allowance of pay and hospital charges. Said sums of money to be paid out of any money in the treasury, not otherwise appropriated, upon warrant to be drawn by the Auditor General in the usual manner, it being understood that the amount of money provided to be paid in this bill is to cover the amount to which said private is justly entitled to on account of the sickness which he contracted in the service and which after his discharge rendered him unable to perform any manual labor between the dates for which provision is herein made for payment.

APPROVED—The 8th day of June, A. D. 1893.

ROBT. E. PATTISON.

How payable.

No. 304.

AN ACT

To continue the State Weather Service in this Commonwealth for the purpose of increasing the efficiency of the United States Weather Bureau by disseminating more speedily and thoroughly the weather forecasts, storm and frost warnings, for the benefit of the citizens of this State, and for the purpose of maintaining in each county thereof meteorological stations for the collection of climatic data and making an appropriation therefor.

SECTION 1. *Be it enacted, &c.*, That the sum of six thousand dollars, or so much thereof as may be necessary, be and the same is hereby appropriated to be expended during the two fiscal years, beginning June first, one thousand eight hundred and ninety-three, according to the provisions of an act, entitled "An act to establish a State Weather Service in this Commonwealth," approved the thirteenth day of May, Anno Domini one thousand eight hundred and eighty-seven: *Provided*, That in order to carry into effect more completely the purpose of said act, the necessary traveling expenses of the assistant in charge which may be designated and approved by the Franklin Institute shall be paid out of the sum hereby appropriated: *And provided further*, That the clerical expenses chargeable upon this appropriation shall be limited to the cost of such clerical work as may be necessary in keeping up the correspondence and compiling records and reports for publication. The amounts to be paid and work done under this appropriation shall be such as may be designated and approved by the Franklin Institute.

The said apropriation to be paid on the warrant of the Auditor General on a settlement made by him and the State Treasurer, but no warrant shall be drawn on settlement made until the directors or managers of said

$6,000.00 appropriated.

Traveling expenses of assistant to be approved by Franklin Institute.

Clerical expenses, limit of cost of.

How payable.

Itemized statement.

Franklin Institute shall have made, under oath to the Auditor General, a report containing a specifically itemized statement of the receipts from all sources and expenses of said State Weather Service during the previous quarter, with the cash balance on hand, and the same is approved by him and the State Treasurer, nor until the Treasurer shall have sufficient money in the treasury, not otherwise appropriated, to pay the quarterly instalments due said institution; and unexpended balances of sums appropriated for specific purposes shall not be used for other purposes, whether specific or general, and shall revert to the State Treasury at the close of the two fiscal years.

Unexpended balance shall revert to the State Treasury.

APPROVED—The 8th day of June, A. D. 1893.

ROBT. E. PATTISON.

No. 305.

AN ACT

To provide for the partial payment of per diem compensation to Frank I. Sprankle, a member of the National Guard of Pennsylvania, during the time of his disability produced by typhoid fever which he contracted in the service at Homestead, Pennsylvania.

WHEREAS, Frank I. Sprankle, a private in the Sheridan Troop of Cavalry, National Guard of Pennsylvania, who was called into the service of the State during the recent riots at Homestead, Allegheny county, was taken ill with typhoid fever as a result of his exposure during his said service in the National Guard, and was confined to his home on account of such illness until about the first day of October, one thousand eight hundred and ninety-two:

And whereas, The Adjutant General in paying him for his services gave him compensation to the third day of August, one thousand eight hundred and ninety-two, the date at which he was relieved from duty;

And whereas, By reason of such service and the sickness referred to he was unable to do any duty until October, one thousand eight hundred and ninety-two, thereby losing his time and his opportunity to earn a daily compensation; therefore,

$75.00 appropriated.

SECTION 1. *Be it enacted, &c.,* That the State Treasurer be and he is hereby authorized and empowered to pay the said Frank I. Sprankle seventy-five dollars, being a part of his allowance as a private of said troop from the third day of August, one thousand eight hundred and ninety-two, until the first day of October, one thousand eight hundred and ninety-two, said sum of money to be paid out of any money in the treasury, not otherwise appropriated, upon warrants to be drawn by the Auditor General in the usual manner, it being understood that the

How payable

amount of money provided to be paid in this bill is to cover the amount to which said soldier is justly entitled on account of the sickness which he contracted in the service and which after being relieved from duty rendered him unable to perform any manual labor between the dates for which provision is herein made for his payment

APPROVED—The 8th day of June, A. D. 1893.

ROBT. E. PATTISON.

No. 306.

AN ACT

Making an appropriation to the trustees of the Cottage State Hospital for Injured Persons of the bituminous and semi-bituminous coal regions of Pennsylvania, located at Philipsburg, Centre county, for necessary improvements and for current expenses.

SECTION 1. *Be it enacted, &c.,* That the sum of eighteen thousand ($18,000) dollars is hereby specifically appropriated to the trustees of the Cottage State Hospital for Injured Persons of the bituminous and semi-bituminous coal regions of Pennsylvania, located in Philipsburg, Centre county, out of any money in the Treasury, not otherwise appropriated, for the following purposes: $18,000 total appropriation.

Fourteen thousand ($14,000) dollars, or so much thereof as may be necessary, for the purpose of maintaining said hospital for the two fiscal years one thousand eight hundred and ninety-three and one thousand eight hundred and ninety-four, to be paid in quarterly instalments during the years named. $14,000 for maintenance.

Also the sum of four thousand ($4,000) dollars shall be appropriated and paid for the following specific purposes: $3,000 for laundry.

The sum of three thousand ($3,000) dollars to be used in erecting and equipping with proper appliances a laundry building, purchasing engines and boilers for the same, and making necessary improvements in connection therewith.

For isolating ward and furnishing same, one thousand ($1,000) dollars. $1,000 for isolating ward.

The said appropriation to be paid on the warrant of the Auditor General on a settlement made by him and the State Treasurer, but no warrant shall be drawn on settlement made until the directors or managers of said institution shall have made, under oath to the Auditor General, a report containing an itemized statement of the expenses of said institution during the previous quarter, and the same is approved by him and the State Treasurer, nor until the Treasurer shall have sufficient money in the treasury, not otherwise appropriated, to pay the quarterly instalments due said institution. How payable Itemized statement.

APPROVED—The 8th day of June, A. D. 1893. The amounts included in the foregoing are in excess of those originally recommended by the Board of Public Charities, but in a written communication from the Board sent to me under date of June 7, 1893, the amount appropriated as above have, after further consideration, been recommended by the Board.

ROBT. E. PATTISON.

No. 307.

AN ACT

Making an appropriation to the Easton Hospital, Easton, Pennsylvania.

$6,000 appropriated. SECTION 1. *Be it enacted, &c.*, That the sum of six thousand dollars, or so much thereof as may be necessary, be and the same is hereby specifically appropriated towards the maintenance of the Easton Hospital for the two fiscal years commencing on the first day of June, Anno Domini one thousand eight hundred and ninety-three.

How payable. The said appropriation to be paid on the warrant of the Auditor General on a settlement made by him and the State Treasurer, but no warrant shall be drawn on settlement made until the directors or managers of said institution shall have made, under oath to the Auditor **Itemized statement.** General, a report containing a specifically itemized statement of the receipts from all sources and expenses of said institution during the previous quarter, with the cash balance on hand, and the same is approved by him and the State Treasurer, nor until the Treasurer shall have sufficient money in the treasury, not otherwise appropiated, to pay the quarterly instalments due said in- **Unexpended balance shall revert to the State Treasury.** stitution; and unexpended balances of sums appropriated for specific purposes shall not be used for other purposes, whether specific or general, and shall revert to the State Treasury at the close of the two fiscal years.

APPROVED—The 8th day of June, A. D. 1893. The amounts included in the foregoing are in excess of those originally recommended by the Board of Public Charities; but in a written communication from the Board sent to me under date of June 7, 1893, the amounts appropriated as above have, after further consideration, been recommended by the Board.

ROBT. E. PATTISON.

No. 308.

AN ACT

Making an appropriation to the Home for Colored Children, located in the city of Allegheny.

$7,500 appropriated. SECTION 1. *Be it enacted, &c.*, That the sum of seven thousand five hundred dollars, or so much thereof as may be necessary, be and the same is hereby specifically appropriated to the Home for Colored Children, located in the city of Allegheny, for the two fiscal years beginning June first, one thousand eight hundred and ninety-three, for the following purposes, namely: Four thousand dollars, or so much thereof as may be necessary, for the purpose of maintenance; one thousand dollars, or so much thereof as may be necessary, for the education of the children of said home; one thousand eight hundred dollars, or so much thereof as may be necessary, for repairs to buildings, fences and ground; and seven hundred dollars, or so much thereof as may be necessary, for hospital purposes. *Items.*

The said appropriation to be paid on the warrant of the Auditor General on a settlement made by him and the State Treasurer, but no warrant shall be drawn on settlement made until the directors or managers of said institution shall have made, under oath to the Auditor General, a report containing a specifically itemized statement of the receipts from all sources and expenses of said institution, together with a specifically itemized statement of the cost of said education, repairs, etcetera, during the previous quarter, with the cash balance on hand, and the same is approved by him and the State Treasurer, nor until the Treasurer shall have sufficient money in the treasury, not otherwise appropriated, to pay the quarterly instalments due said institution; and unexpended balances of sums appropriated for specific purposes shall not be used for other purposes, whether specific or general, and shall revert to the State Treasury at the close of the two fiscal years. . *How payable. Itemized statement. Unexpended balance shall revert to the State Treasury.*

APPROVED—The 8th day of June, A. D. 1893. The amounts included in the foregoing are in excess of those originally recommended by the Board of Public Charities, but in a written communication from the Board, sent to me under date of June 7, 1893, the amounts appropriated as above have, after further consideration, been recommended by the Board.

ROBT. E. PATTISON.

No. 309.

AN ACT

Making an appropriation to the Children's Home of Pottsville, Schuylkill county.

SECTION 1. *Be it enacted, &c.,* That the sum of fifteen hundred dollars, or so much thereof as may be necessary, be and the same is hereby specifically appropriated to the Children's Home of Pottsville toward the maintenance, education and support of the homeless, destitute and vagrant children in said home for the two *$15,000 appropriated.*

fiscal years beginning June first, one thousand eight hundred and ninety-three.

How payable.

The said appropriation to be paid on the warrant of the Auditor General on a settlement made by him and the State Treasurer, but no warrant shall be drawn on settlement made until the directors or managers of said institution shall have made, under oath to the Auditor

Itemized statement.

General, a report containing a specifically itemized statement of the receipts from all sources and expenses of said institution during the previous quarter, with the cash balance on hand, and the same is approved by him and the State Treasurer, nor until the Treasurer shall have sufficient money in the treasury, not otherwise appropriated, to pay the quarterly instalments due said insti-

Unexpended balance shall revert to the State Treasury

tution; and unexpended balances of sums appropriated for specific purposes shall not be used for other purposes, whether specific or general, and shall revert to the State Treasury at the close of the two fiscal years.

APPROVED—The 8th day of June, A. D. 1893. The amounts included in the foregoing are in excess of those originally recommended by the Board of Public Charities, but in a written communication from the Board sent to me under date of June 7, 1893, the amounts appropriated as above have, after further consideration, been recommended by the Board.

ROBT. E. PATTISON.

No. 310.

AN ACT

Making an appropriation to the Wilkes-Barre City Hospital.

$60,000 total appropriation.

SECTION 1. *Be it enacted, &c.,* That the sum of sixty thousand dollars, or so much thereof as may be necessary, be and the same is hereby specifically appropriated to the Wilkes-Barre City Hospital, beginning June first, one thousand eight hundred and ninety-three, for the follow-

Items.

ing purposes, namely: For the support and maintenance of said hospital, the sum of twenty thousand dollars, or so much thereof as may be necessary. For new hospital buildings, the sum of twenty thousand dollars, or so much thereof as may be necessary. For steam heating and power plants and buildings for the same, the sum of ten thousand dollars, or so much thereof as may be necessary. For furnishing and lighting, the sum of ten thousand dollars, or so much thereof as may be necessary.

How payable.

The said appropriation to be paid on the warrant of the Auditor General on a settlement made by him and the State Treasurer, but no warrant shall be drawn on settlement made until the directors or managers of said institution shall have made, under oath to the Auditor

General, a report containining a specifically itemized statement of the receipts from all sources and expenses of said institution, together with a specifically itemized statement of the cost of said buildings and improvements during the previous quarter, with the cash balance on hand, and the same is approved by him and the State Treasurer, nor until the Treasurer shall have sufficient money in the treasury, not otherwise appropriated, to pay the quarterly instalments due said institution; and unexpended balances of sums appropriated for specific purposes shall not be used for other purposes, whether specific or general, and shall revert to the State Treasury at the close of the two fiscal years.

Itemized statement.

Unexpended balance shall revert to the State Treasury.

APPROVED—The 8th day of June, A. D. 1893. The amounts included in the foregoing are in excess of those originally recommended by the Board of Public Charities; but in a written communication from the Board sent to me under date of June 7, 1893, the amounts appropriated as above have, after further consideration, been recommended by the Board.

ROBT. E. PATTISON.

No. 311.

AN ACT

Making an appropriation to the Medico Chirurgical Hospital of the city of Philadelphia.

SECTION 1. *Be it enacted, &c.,* That the sum of one hundred thousand dollars, or so much thereof as may be necessary, be and the same is hereby specifically appropriated to the Medico Chirurgical Hospital of the city of Philadelphia for the two fiscal years beginning June first, one thousand eight hundred and ninety-three, for the following purposes, namely:

$100,000 total appropriation.

The sum of twenty thousand dollars, or so much thereof as may be necessary, for the purpose of maintenance.

Items.

The sum of twenty-five thousand dollars, or so much thereof as may be necessary, for the purpose of building and furnishing an operating room and for repairs to said hospital.

The sum of ten thousand dollars, or so much thereof as may be necessary, for the building of rooms and dormitories for nurses.

The sum of forty-five thousand dollars, or so much thereof as may be necessary, for the purpose of building and furnishing maternity wards in the said hospital.

The said appropriation to be paid on the warrant of the Auditor General on a settlement made by him and the State Treasurer, but no warrant shall be drawn on settlement made until the directors or managers of said institution shall have made, under oath to the Auditor

How payable.

General, a report containing a specifically itemized statement of the receipts from all sources and expenses of said
institution, together with a specifically itemized statement of the cost of buildings, repairs and furnishing during the previous quarter, with the cash balance on hand,
and the same is approved by him and the State Treasurer, nor until the Treasurer shall have sufficient money
in the treasury, not otherwise appropriated, to pay the

quarterly instalments due said institution; and unexpended balances of sums appropriated for specific purposes shall not be used for other purposes, whether specific or general, and shall revert to the State Treasury at
the close of the two fiscal years.

APPROVED—The 8th day of June, A. D. 1893.   The
amounts included in the foregoing are in excess of those
originally recommended by the Board of Public Charities; but in a written communication from the Board
sent to me under date of June 7, 1893, the amounts appropriated as above have, after further consideration,
been recommended by the Board.

ROBT. E. PATTISON.

No. 312.

AN ACT

Making an appropriation to the Conoquenessing Valley Hospital
Association, located in the borough of Butler, Pennsylvania.

SECTION 1. *Be it enacted, &c.*, That the sum of twelve
thousand five hundred dollars, or so much thereof as may
be necessary, be and the same is hereby specifically appropriated to the Conoquenessing Valley Hospital Association located in the borough of Butler, Pennsylvania,
as follows:

The sum of ten thousand dollars, or so much thereof
as may be necessary, to aid in the erection and furnishing a suitable hospital building for the medical and surgical care of sick and injured persons, indigent or otherwise, and without discrimination in respect to religion,
nationality or color, for the two fiscal years beginning
June first, one thousand eight hundred and ninety-three;

and the further sum of two thousand five hundred dollars, or so much thereof as may be necessary, for the
maintenance of said hospital for the fiscal year beginning June first, one thousand eight hundred and ninety-

four; *Provided*, That no part of the money herein appropriated for building and furnishing shall become
available until the treasurer of said institution shall have
certified, under oath to the Auditor General, that the
sum of five thousand dollars, exclusive of the value of
the ground, has been subscribed and paid in cash into
the treasury of said institution by private subscription

for the purpose of assisting in the erection and furnishing of said hospital building. Upon the filing of said certificate, the sum of five thousand dollars of the sum herein appropriated to aid in the erection and furnishing shall become available, and when the treasurer of said institution files a further certificate with the Auditor General, certifying that an additional sum of five thousand dollars, exclusive of the value of the ground, has been subscribed and paid in cash into the treasury of said institution by private subscriptions for the purpose of assisting in the erection and furnishing of said hospital, then the balance of the sum herein appropriated to assist in the erection and furnishing shall become available.

The said appropriation to be paid on the warrant of the Auditor General on a settlement made by him and the State Treasurer, but no warrant shall be drawn on settlement made until the directors or managers of said institution shall have made, under oath to the Auditor General, a report containing a specifically itemized statement of the income and expenses of said institution together with a specifically itemized statement of the cost of said building and furnishing the same during the previous quarter, with the cash balance on hand, and the same is approved by him and the State Treasurer, nor until the Treasurer shall have sufficient money in the treasury, not otherwise appropriated, to pay the quarterly instalments due said institution; and unexpended balances of sums appropriated for specific purposes shall not be used for other purposes, whether specific or general, and shall revert to the State Treasury at the close of the two fiscal years.

How payable.

Itemized statement.

Unexpended balance shall revert to the State Treasury.

APPROVED—The 8th day of June, A. D. 1893. The amount included in the foregoing was not recommended by the Board of Public Charities in their published report, but in a written communication from the Board sent to me, under date of June 7, 1893, the amount appropriated as above has, after consideration, been recommended by the Board.

ROBT. E. PATTISON.

No. 313.

AN ACT

Making an appropriation to the Bradford Hospital of the city of Bradford.

SECTION 1. *Be it enacted, &c.,* That the sum of six thousand dollars, or so much thereof as may be necessary, be and the same is hereby specifically appropriated to the Bradford Hospital of the city of Bradford for the two

$6,000 appropriated.

fiscal years beginning June first, one thousand eight hundred and ninety-three, for the purpose of maintenance.

How payable. The said appropriation to be paid on the warrant of the Auditor General on a settlement made by him and the State Treasurer, but no warrant shall be drawn on settlement made until the directors or managers of said institution shall have made, under oath to the Auditor

Itemized statement. General, a report containing a specifically itemized statement of the receipts from all sources and expenses of said institution during the previous quarter, with the cash balance on hand, and the same is approved by him and the State Treasurer, nor until the Treasurer shall have sufficient money in the treasury, not otherwise appropriated, to pay the quarterly instalments due said institution;

Unexpended balance shall revert to the State Treasury. and unexpended balances of sums appropriated for specific purposes shall not be used for other purposes, whether specific or general, and shall revert to the State Treasury at the close of the two fiscal years.

APPROVED—The 8th day of June, A. D. 1893. The amounts included in the foregoing are in excess of those originally recommended by the Board of Public Charities, but in a written communication from the General Agent and Secretary of the Board sent to me under date of June 8, 1893, the amounts appropriated as above have, after further consideration, been recommended.

ROBT. E. PATTISON.

No. 314.

A FURTHER SUPPLEMENT

To an act approved April twenty-ninth, Anno Domini one thousand eight hundred and seventy-four, entitled "An act to provide for the incorporation and regulation of certain corporations," amended by an act approved the tenth day of April, Anno Domini one thousand eight hundred and seventy-nine, and further amended by act approved the twenty-second day of June, Anno Domini one thousand eight hundred and eighty-three, and further amended by act approved the twenty-first day of May, Anno Domini one thousand eight hundred and eighty-nine, providing for a further amendment of the eighteenth paragraph of section two of the original act, and amending the second section of said act so as to authorize the formation of corporations for the purpose of driving and floating logs, lumber and timber upon all streams not exceeding thirty-five miles in length, and the heads of all streams not exceeding thirty-five miles in length from their sources.

SECTION 1. *Be it enacted, &c.*, That the eighteenth paragraph of section two of an act, entitled "An act to provide for the incorporation and regulation of certain corporations," approved the twenty-ninth day of April, Anno Domini one thousand eight hundred and seventy-four, which reads, as further amended by the act approved the

twenty-first day of May, Anno Domini one thousand eight
hundred and eighty-nine, as follows:

"Paragraph 18. The carrying on of any mechanical, manufacturing, mining, or quarrying business, including all purposes covered by the provisions of the acts of the General Assembly, entitled 'An act to encourage manufacturing operations in this Commonwealth,' approved April seventh, Anno Domini one thousand eight hundred and forty-nine, entitled 'An act relating to corporations for mechanical, manufacturing, mining and quarrying purposes,' approved July eighteenth, Anno Domini one thousand eight hundred and sixty-three, and the several supplements to each of said acts, including the incorporation of grain elevators, storage house and storage yard companies, and also including companies for the storage, transportation and furnishing of water, with the right to take rivulets and land and erect reservoirs for holding water for manufacturing and other purposes, and for the creation, establishing, furnishing, transmission and using of water power therefrom, the construction of dams in any stream, and the driving and floating of saw logs, lumber and timber on and over any stream, not exceeding twenty miles in length, and the heads of all streams not exceeding twenty miles in length from their source, by the usual methods of driving and floating logs, timber and lumber on stream, and so as not to obstruct the descending navigation by rafts and boats, and also including the manufacture and brewing of malt liquors, but excluding the distilling and manufacture of spirituous liquors," be and the same is hereby amended and extended so as to read as follows:

Paragraph 18 of section 3 of act of April 29, 1874, as amended by act of May 31, 1889, cited for amendment.

Paragraph 18. The carrying on of any mechanical, mining, quarrying or manufacturing business, including all of the purposes covered by the provisions of the acts of the General Assembly, entitled "An act to encourage manufacturing operations in this Commonwealth," approved April seventh, one thousand eight hundred and forty-nine, entitled "An act relating to corporations for mechanical, manufacturing, mining and quarrying purposes," approved July eighteenth, one thousand eight hundred and sixty-three, and the several supplements to each of said acts, including the incorporation of grain elevators, storage house and storage yard companies, and also including companies for the storage, transportation and furnishing of water, with the right to take rivulets and land and erect reservoirs for holding water for manufacturing and other purposes, and for the creation, establishing, furnishing, transmission and using of water power therefrom, the construction of dams in any stream, and the driving and floating of saw logs, lumber and timber on and over any stream not exceeding thirty-five miles in length, and the heads of all streams not exceeding thirty-five miles in length from their source, by the usual methods of driving and floating logs, timber and

Corporations authorized for the purpose of driving and floating logs, lumber and timber upon all streams not exceeding 35 miles in length, and the heads of all streams not exceeding 35 miles in length from their sources.

lumber on streams, and so as not to obstruct the descending navigation by rafts and boats, and also including the manufacture and brewing of malt liquors, but excluding the distilling and manufacture of spirituous liquors.

ection 2 of act of ay 21. 1889, cited or amendment.

SECTION 2. That the second section of the act approved the twenty-first day of May, Anno Domini one thousand eight hundred and eighty-nine, which reads as follows:

"SECTION 2. That corporations organized for the purpose of erecting reservoirs for the storage of water, construction of dams, transmission of power and the driving and floating of logs, timber and lumber on streams not exceeding twenty miles in length, or on the heads of all streams not exceeding twenty miles in length from their source, shall have power to clear out, improve and use any stream or the head of any stream not exceeding in length twenty miles from its source, to purchase dams and erect new dams thereon, may straighten, deepen, curb and widen such stream, or the head of any stream for the distance aforesaid as they deem proper, and may generally use and manage the streams and the head of streams for the distance aforesaid and their improvements thereon, for the floating of logs, lumber and timber thereon, both by natural and artificial floods in their discretion, but in such manner as not to obstruct the descending navigation by rafts and boats: *Provided*, That in case where the heads of streams more than twenty miles in length are improved under the provisions of this act, no tax or tolls shall be charged on timber or logs passing through, banked or floated from below such improvements: *Provided further*, That the corporation owning such improvements shall not be required to operate or furnish the use of such improvements for driving or floating timber or logs, unless the owners of such timber or logs consent to pay the tolls provided for in this act: *Provided further*, That a majority of the stock in any such corporation shall at all times be held by the persons owning lands drained by such streams," be and the same is hereby amended and extended so as to be and read as follows:

xtension of power f certain corpora- ons to clear out, nprove and use y stream, or the ead of any stream ot exceeding in ength 35 miles from s source, to pur- hase dams, &c., pon such stream r the head of any tream for the dis- nce aforesaid.

SECTION 2. That corporations organized for the purpose of erecting reservoirs for the storage of water, construction of dams, transmission of power, and the driving and floating of logs, timber and lumber on streams not exceeding thirty-five miles in length from their source, shall have power to clear out, improve and use any stream, or the head of any stream, not exceeding in length thirty-five miles from their source, shall have power to clear out, improve and use any stream, or the head of any stream, not exceeding in length thirty-five miles from its source, to purchase dams and erect new dams thereon, may straighten, deepen, crib and widen such stream, or the head of any stream, for the distance aforesaid, as they deem proper, and may generally use and manage the streams and the head of streams for the distance aforesaid and their improvements thereon for the floating of logs, lumber and timber thereon, by both natural and artificial floods, in their discretion, but in such manner as not to obstruct the descending navigation by rafts and boats: *Provided*, That in case where *Proviso.* the heads of streams more than thirty-five miles in length are improved under the provisions of this act, no tax or tolls shall be charged on timber or logs passing through, banked or floated from below such improvement: *Provided further*, That the corporation owning such improve- *Proviso.* ments shall not be required to operate or furnish the use of such improvements for driving or floating timber or logs, unless the owners of such timber or logs consent to *Proviso.* pay the tolls provided for in this act: *Provided further*, That a majority of the stock in any such corporation shall at all times be held by the persons owning lands drained by such streams.

APPROVED—The 10th day of June, A. D. 1893.

ROBT. E. PATTISON.

No. 315.

AN ACT

To provide for the quieting of titles to land.

SECTION 1. *Be it enacted, &c.*, That in all cases where an *Easement on land,* easement on land has been acquired under proceedings *how terminated.* in condemnation by any corporation possessing the right of eminent domain, and the same has been vacated and ceased to be used and occupied by any such corporation for a period of fifteen years or upwards, then and in that case said easement shall be held to have terminated and the original owner, his heirs and assigns, shall hold the title to the said land divested of said easement: *Pro-* *Proviso.* *vided*, That nothing in this act shall be held to apply to or affect any case where the fee simple title has been vested in the corporation ceasing to use or occupy said land, nor to effect, qualify, alter or repeal the act of the General Assembly of this Commonwealth, entitled "An act relating to straightened or improved lines of rail- road," approved the third day of April, one thousand eight hundred and seventy-two.

SECTION 2. When any person or persons, natural or *Proceedings where* artificial, shall be in possession of any lands or tenements *possession of lands* in this Commonwealth, claiming to hold or own posses- *puted or denied.* sion of the same by any right or title whatsoever, which right or title or right of possession shall be disputed or denied by any person or persons as aforesaid, it shall be lawful for any such person to apply by bill or petition *May apply by bill or* to the court of common pleas of the county where such *where land is situ-* land is situate, setting forth the facts of such claim of *ate.* title and right of possession and the denial thereof by the person or persons therein named, and thereupon the said court shall grant a rule upon such person or persons, so denying such right, title or right of possession, to appear at a time to be therein named and show cause why an issue shall not be framed in said court, between the parties, to settle and determine their respective rights and title in and to said land. Twenty days' notice of such rule shall be given.

And if, upon the hearing of such rule, it shall appear to the court that the facts set forth in such petition are true, it shall be the duty of the court thereupon to frame an issue of such forms as the court shall deem proper between the respective parties, to settle and determine the right and title of the respective parties to said land, and the verdict of the jury in such issue shall have the same force and effect upon the right and title and right of possession of the respective parties in and to said land as a verdict in ejectment upon an equitable title.

In case the person or persons denying such right, title or right of possession in such lands or any of them are not residents within the jurisdiction of the court, such court may make an order for service of said rule and a copy of said bill or petition upon such persons at their residence or place of business outside of the county or State where the land lies, in the same manner as service is made of a summons in a personal action, giving at least twenty days' notice of such hearing.

If any person or persons shall neglect or refuse to appear at such return day, after twenty days' service of such rule and copy of petition, or having appeared shall refuse to join in such issue, the court may proceed to determine the rule and award and proceed with the issue in like manner as if such persons had appeared therein, and any judgment obtained in such issue shall as fully and finally conclude and determine the rights and title of such defaulting party as if such persons had appeared and joined in such issue: *Provided*, That if, upon the return of such rule, any of the persons served shall disclaim, by writing filed, any right, title or interest in said land, all further proceedings as to such persons shall cease and such disclaimer shall forever bar such person from ever setting up or claiming any such right or title in any court. The decree of the court in refusing the rule or issue in any such case and the judgment in such issue shall be subject to appeal by either party to the Supreme Court, in like manner as appeals are allowed to judgments and decrees of the said court of common pleas.

APPROVED.—The 10th day of June, A. D. 1893. The purpose of this bill, as expressed in its title and provided for in the text of its second section, meets my approval, and in consideration thereof, I have affixed my signature to it. I am very doubtful whether the purpose of section one is cognate to the avowed purpose of the bill or is expressed in its title, but if this view should be

Marginal notes:

Court shall grant a rule to show cause why an issue shall not be framed.

Notice to be given.

Duty of the court.

Force and effect of the verdict of the jury.

In case persons denying such right, &c., are not residents.

Court may make an order for service of said rule, &c.

Notice to be given. In case of neglect or refusal to appear, the court may determine the rule and award and proceed with the issue.

Judgment thus obtained to have same effect as if such persons had appeared. Proviso.

Decree of court shall be subject to appeal.

entertained by the courts it will not affect, in my judgment, the second section of the bill, and I therefore, with this notice, waive objections to the form of the bill, seeing no objectionable features in its substance and purpose.

ROBT. E. PATTISON.

No. 316.

AN ACT

To authorize corporations to increase their capital stock for corporate purposes.

SECTION 1. *Be it enacted, &c.,* That any corporation created by special or general law shall, notwithstanding any limitation upon the amount of its capital stock by such special or general law, have authority, with the consent of the persons holding the larger amount in value of its stock, to increase its capital stock to accomplish enlarge the objects and purposes of its incorporation to the amount of thirty millions dollars in the aggregate; such increase may be made at once or from time to time as the stockholders aforesaid shall determine.

APPROVED—The 10th day of June, A. D. 1893.

ROBT. E. PATTISON.

Corporations may increase capital stock to $30,000.00 in the aggregate.

No. 317.

AN ACT

To provide for the incorporation of certain kinds of real estate companies having for their primary object the encouragement of trade, commerce and manufactures.

SECTION 1. *Be it enacted, &c.,* That in addition to the corporations for profit of the second class authorized to be created by the second section of an act, entitled "An act to provide for the incorporation and regulation of certain corporations," approved April twenty-ninth, one thousand eight hundred and seventy-four, corporations may be created for the purpose of erecting and maintaining a bourse or exchange hall or other building, to be used in whole or in part as a bourse or exchange hall or as a meeting place for merchants or other business men or for the exhibition of manufactured articles or natural products, and such corporations shall be governed as to the amount of their capital stock and as to the par value of the shares thereof, as may be provided by the aforesaid act and the several supplements thereto.

SECTION 2. Any corporation incorporated under the provisions of this act, or any corporation heretofore incorporated, for the purchase and sale of real estate or for holding, leasing and selling real estate, and accepting the

Corporations may be created for the purpose of erecting and maintaining a bourse or exchange hall.

Capital stock and par value of shares.

Corporations incorporated under this act or accepting provisions of this act, to file certificate with Secretary of the Commonwealth.

27—LAWS.

Contents of certifi-
cate.

provisions of this act, shall file in the office of the Secretary of the Commonwealth a certificate specifying the date of incorporation and the act of Assembly under which they were incorporated and the lot or building or the part or parts thereof to be used as a bourse or exchange hall or for an exhibition hall for the display of manufactured articles or natural products and the value thereof, and what proportion the value of the real estate used as a bourse or exchange hall or for an exhibition hall for the display of manufactured articles or natural products bears to the entire capital stock of such corpo-

What proportion of
capital stock shall
be exempt from
taxation.

ration, and upon such proportion of their capital stock, corporations incorporated under this act or heretofore incorporated for the purchase and sale of real estate or for holding, leasing and selling real estate and accepting the provisions of this act shall be exempt from taxation.

How tax upon capi-
tal stock shall be
assessed.

SECTION 3. In assessing the tax upon the capital stock of corporations accepting the provisions of this act as provided in the second section thereof, that part of the capital stock of the corporation exempt from taxation shall bear the same proportion to its whole capital stock as the value of the real estate occupied as such bourse or exchange hall or exhibition hall for the display of manufactured articles or natural products bear to the entire capital stock of such corporations.

Duty of Auditor
General.

SECTION 4. It shall be the duty of the Auditor General to determine what part of the capital stock of such corporations shall be exempt from taxation, and from his decision an appeal shall lie as now provided by law in other cases involving questions of taxation.

When entire capital
stock shall be sub-
ject to taxation.

SECTION 5. Any corporation accepting the provisions of this act, which shall in any year declare a dividend upon its entire capital stock, shall first file in the office of the Auditor General, a certificate setting forth the intent of such corporation to pay a dividend as aforesaid, and thereupon the entire capital stock of such corporation shall be subject to taxation for such year.

Proceedings in case
of sale, &c., of any
real estate.

SECTION 6. It shall be unlawful for any corporation accepting the provisions of this act to sell, transfer, let or lease any real estate specified in the certificate filed with the Secretary of the Commonwealth as required by the second section of this act as intended to be used as a bourse or exchange hall, without first filing in the office of the Secretary of the Commonwealth a certificate setting forth the intent of such corporation to sell, transfer,

Entire capital
stock subject to
taxation.
Proviso.

let or lease such real estate, and thereupon the entire capital stock of such corporation shall thereafter be subject to taxation: *Provided,* That if any corporation accepting the provisions of this act shall sell, transfer, let or lease the real estate or the part thereof specified in the certificate filed with the Secretary of the Commonwealth as required by the second section of this act as intended to be used as such bourse or exchange hall, or shall declare a dividend without first filing a certificate in the office of the Auditor General as provided in the fifth section of this act, the entire capital stock of such corporation shall thereupon be liable to taxation, together with a penalty of twelve per centum upon that portion of the capital stock theretofore exempt from taxation under the provisions of this act.

APPROVED—The 10th day of June, A. D. 1893.

ROBT. E. PATTISON.

Penalty.

No. 318.

AN ACT

To regulate the nomination and election of public officers, requiring certain expenses incident thereto to be paid by the several counties, and punishing certain offenses in regard to such elections.

SECTION 1. *Be it enacted, &c.*, That all ballots cast in elections for public officers within this Commonwealth shall be printed and distributed at public expense as hereinafter provided. The printing of the ballots and of the cards of instruction for the elections in each county, and the delivery of the same to the election officers as hereinafter provided, and all other expenses incurred under the provisions of this act shall be a county charge, unless herein otherwise provided, the payment of which shall be provided for in the same manner as the payment of other election expenses. It shall be the duty of the Secretary of the Commonwealth to prepare forms for all the blanks made necessary or advisable by this act, and to furnish copies of the same to the county commissioners of each county, who shall procure further copies of the same at the cost of the county and furnish them to the election officers or other persons by whom they are to be used, in such quantities as may be necessary to carry out the provisions of this act.

Ballots to be printed and distributed at public expense.

Shall be a county charge, unless otherwise provided. To be paid for as other election expenses.

Secretary of the Commonwealth to prepare forms for all blanks, and furnish copies of same to county commissioners. County commissioners to procure further copies at cost of county and furnish them to election officers.

SECTION 2. Any convention of delegates, or primary meeting of electors, or caucus held under the rules of a political party, or any board authorized to certify nominations representing a political party, which, at the election next preceding, polled at least two per centum of the largest entire vote for any office cast in the State, or in the electoral district or division thereof for which such primary meeting, caucus, convention, or board, desires to make or certify nominations, may nominate one candidate for each office which is to be filled in the State, or in the said district or division, at the next ensuing election by causing a Certificate of Nomination to be drawn up and filed as hereinafter provided. Every such Certificate of Nomination shall be signed by the presiding officer and the secretary or secretaries of the convention, or primary meeting, or caucus, or board, who shall add thereto their

Who may nominate, vis: convention, primary meeting or caucus, or by board authorized to certify nominations of party having two per centum of entire vote.

Certificate of Nomination to be drawn up.

places of residence, and shall be sworn or affirmed to by them before an officer qualified to administer oaths, to be true to the best of their knowledge and belief, and a certificate of the oath shall be annexed to the Certificate of Nomination.

SECTION 3. Nominations of candidates for any public office may also be made by Nomination Papers, signed by qualified electors of the State, or of the electoral district or division thereof for which the nomination is made, and filed in the proper office as provided in section five of this act.

Where the nomination is for any office to be filled by the voters of the State-at-large, the number of qualified electors of the State signing such Nomination Paper, shall be at least one-half of one per centum of the largest vote for any officer elected in the State at the last preceding election at which a State officer was voted for.

In the case of all other nominations the number of qualified electors of the electoral district or division, signing such Nomination Paper, shall be at least two per centum of the largest entire vote for any officer elected at the last preceding election in the said electoral district or division for which said Nomination Papers are designed to be made.

Each elector signing a Nomination Paper shall add to his signature his place of residence and occupation, and no person may subscribe to more than one nomination for each office to be filled.

The signatures to each Nomination Paper and the qualification of the signers shall be vouched for by the affidavit of at least five of the signers thereof, which affidavit shall accompany the Nomination Paper.

SECTION 4. All Certificates of Nomination and Nomination Papers shall specify: One (1). The party or policy which such candidate represents, expressed in not more than three words; in the case of electors of President and Vice President of the United States, the names of the candidates for President and Vice President shall be added to the party or political appellation. Two (2).

The name of each candidate nominated therein, his profession, business or occupation, if any, and his place of residence, with street and number thereon, if any. Three

(3). The office for which such candidate is nominated: *Provided*, That no words shall be used in any Nomination Papers to describe or designate the party or policy, or political appellation, represented by the candidate named in such Nomination Papers as aforesaid, identical with the words used for the like purpose in Certificates of Nominations made by a convention of delegates of a political party, which, at the last preceding election, polled two per centum of the largest vote cast: *And pro-*

vided further, That any objections filed to a nomination certificate or paper on account of the party or political appellation used therein, or involving the right as defined by sections two and three of this act, to file such certificate or paper, shall be decided by the court of common pleas on hearing as hereinafter provided.

SECTION 5. Certificates of Nomination for candidates for the offices of presidential electors and members of the House of Representatives of the United States, and for State offices, including those of Judges and Senators, shall be filed with the Secretary of the Commonwealth at least thirty-five days before the day of the election for which the candidates are nominated, and Nomination Papers for candidates for the said offices shall be filed with the said Secretary at least twenty-eight days before the day of such election. Certificates of Nomination and Nomination Papers for candidates for all other offices, except township and borough offices, shall be filed with the county commissioners of the respective counties at least twenty-eight and twenty-one days respectively before the day of the election. Certificates of Nomination and Nomination Papers for candidates for township and borough offices, and election officers and school directors in the same, shall be filed with the county commissioners at least eighteen and fifteen days respectively before the day of election. In determining or reckoning any period of time mentioned in this act, the day upon which the act is done, paper filed or notice given, shall be excluded from, and the day of election shall be included in the calculation or reckoning.

SECTION 6. It shall be the duty of the officer or officers to whom any nomination certificate or paper is brought for the purpose of filing, to examine the said certificate or paper, and if it lack sufficient signatures or be otherwise manifestly defective, it shall not be filed, but the action of the said officer or officers in refusing to receive a certificate or paper, may be reviewed by the court of common pleas of the county upon an application for a mandamus to compel its reception as of the date when it was brought to the office. All nomination certificates and papers which have been filed shall be deemed to be valid, unless objections thereto are duly made by writing filed in the court of common pleas of the county in which the certificate or paper objected to has been filed, and within the following periods.

First. In the case of certificates and papers filed with the Secretary of the Commonwealth, at least twenty-one days before the day of the election.

Second. In the case of other certificates and papers, except those designed for borough and township officers, at least eighteen days before the day of the election.

Third. In the case of certificates and papers designed for borough and township officers, at least twelve days before the day of the election.

In case the court is in session, one or more judges thereof shall proceed to hear such objections without unnecessary adjournment or delay, and shall give such hearing precedence over all other business before him or them. In case the court is not in session, any judge thereof, on the presentation to him of the certificate of

Marginal notes:

Certain certificates shall be filed with the Secretary of the Commonwealth.

Time of filing.

Time of filing Nomination Papers.

What papers shall be filed with county commissioners and when.

With township and borough auditors and when to be filed.

How time is to be reckoned.

Proper officer to examine nomination paper or certificate and if defective it shall not be filed.

Actions of officers subject to review

When certificates and papers to be deemed valid.

How objections to be made.

As to certificates and papers filed with Secretary of the Commonwealth.

For all others except borough and township.

For boroughs and townships.

Hearing of objections when court in session.

When court is not in session.

the prothonotary, that such objections have been filed as aforesaid, shall proceed to hear such objections as aforesaid. No objection of any nature whatever shall be filed, unless accompanied by proof of service of notice of the proposed objection upon at least one of the candidates named in the certificate or paper objected to; nor shall any objection be heard in the absence of any of the said candidates without proof of service of notice of the hearing upon him. If the court decide that the certificate or

paper objected to was not filed by parties entitled under this act to file the same, it shall be wholly void; but if it be adjudged defective only, the court shall indicate the matters as to which it requires amendment and the time within which such amendment must be made, and every certificate or paper amended after the time when the names therein contained should have been sent to the

sheriff, shall be subject to the provisions of this act concerning substituted nominations. The officers with whom nomination certificates and papers have been filed,

shall permit the parties who have filed them to amend them of their own motion at any time prior to the printing of the ballots.

SECTION 7. Any person whose name has been presented as a candidate may cause his name to be withdrawn from nomination, by request in writing signed by him and acknowledged before an officer qualified to take acknowledgments of deeds, and filed in the office where his nomination certificate or paper is on file fifteen days, or in the case of township and borough elections twelve days, previous to the day of the election; and no name so withdrawn shall be printed upon the ballots.

Where any office not in court of record shall for any cause become vacant after the time for making nominations for such office shall have elapsed, or when a writ for a special election to supply a vacancy shall direct such election to be held at a date which would prevent the making of nominations in time to comply with section five of this act, nominations for the office to be filled may still be made in accordance with sections two and three of this act, but in other respects the provisions of section twelve of this act shall apply to such nominations.

SECTION 8. All Certificates of Nomination and Nomination Papers when filed shall be open under proper regulations to public inspection, and shall be preserved not less than two years in the offices where they have been filed.

SECTION 9. The Secretary of the Commonwealth shall, fourteen days at least previous to the day of any election of United States or State officers, or for the adoption of

amendments to the Constitution of this Commonwealth, transmit to the county commissioners and the sheriff in each county in which such election is to be held, duplicate official lists, stating the names and residences of and parties or policies represented by all candidates whose nomination certificates or papers have been filed with him as herein provided for such election, and have not been found and declared to be invalid as provided in section six, and to be voted for at each voting place in each such county respectively, substantially in the form of the ballots to be used therein, duplicate copies of the text of all proposed constitutional amendments to be voted upon at such election. The county commissioners of each county shall also send to the sheriff of their county, at least ten days prior to the day of any general election, an official list containing the names and party or political appellations of all candidates whose nomination certificates or papers have been filed with the said commissioners as herein provided for such election and to be voted for at each voting place in the county, substantially in the form of the ballots to be used therein. *Form of certificate.*

County commissioners shall send list to sheriff.

Contents.

SECTION 10. It shall be the duty of the sheriff of every county, at least ten days before any general election to be held therein, to give notice of the same by proclamation, posted up in the most public places in every election district, or by advertisements in at least two newspapers, if there be so many published in the county, representing so far as practicable the political parties which at the preceding election cast the largest and next largest number of votes, and in every such proclamation or advertisement shall, *Sheriff shall give notice by proclamation and advertisement at least ten days before any election, in two newspapers representing the largest and next largest number of votes cast.*

Contents of proclamation, and advertisement.

I. Enumerate the officers to be elected and give a list of all the nominations made as provided in this act, and to be voted for in such county as far as may be in the form in which they shall appear upon the ballots, and the full text of all constitutional amendments submitted to a vote of the people, but the proclamations posted in each election district need not contain the names of any candidates but those to be voted for in such district. *Enumerate the officers to be elected.*

II. Designate the place at which the election is to be held. *Place of election.*

III. He shall give notice that every person, excepting justices of the peace, who shall hold any office or appointment of profit or trust under the government of the United States, or of this State, or of any city, or incorporated district, whether a commissioned officer or otherwise, a subordinate officer or agent who is or shall be employed under the legislative, executive or judiciary department of this State, or of the United States, or of any city, or incorporated district, and also that every member of Congress and of the State Legislature, and of the select or common council of any city, or commissioners of any incorporated district, is by law incapable of holding or exercising at the same time the office or appointment of judge, inspector or clerk of any election of this Commonwealth, and that no inspector, judge or other officer of any such election shall be eligible to any office to be then voted for, except that of an election officer. *Who shall be eligible to the several offices.*

How vacancy shall
be filled.

SECTION 11. In case of the death or withdrawal o. any candidate nominated as herein provided, the party convention, primary meeting, caucus, or board, or the citizens who nominated such candidate, may nominate a substitute in his place, by filing in the proper office at any time before the day of election, a nomination certificate or paper which shall conform to all the requirements of this act in regard to original certificates or papers: *Provided*, That if the said convention or citizens shall have authorized any committee, or if any executive committee of any political party be authorized by the rules of said party, to make nominations in the event of the death or withdrawal of candidates, the said convention shall not be required to reconvene nor the said citizens to sign a new Nomination Paper, but the said committee shall have power to file the requisite nomination certificate or paper, which shall recite the facts of the appointment and powers of the said committee, (naming all its members,) of the death, or withdrawal of the candidate, and of the action of the committee thereon, and the truth of these facts shall be verified by the affidavit annexed to the certificate, or paper of two members of the committee, and also of at least two of the officers of the convention who made affidavit in support of the original certificate, or two of the citizens who made affidavit to the original paper: *And provided also*, That in case of a substituted Nomination Paper not filed by a committee, but signed by citizens, it shall only be necessary that two-thirds of the signers of the said paper shall have been signers of the original paper.

Substituted nomi-
nation papers and
certificates and ob-
jections thereto.

SECTION 12. All substituted nomination certificates or papers may be objected to as provided in section six of this act, and if a substituted certificate or paper be filed after the last day for filing the original certificate or paper, objections must be made within four days after the filing, and no objections as to form and conformity to law shall be received after the time set for printing the ballots.

Substitution of
candidate.

As soon as any substituted candidate shall have been duly nominated, his name shall be substituted by the proper officers in the place of that of the candidate who has died or withdrawn so far as time may allow, and in case a substituted nomination be filed with or transmit-

If made after
ballots have been
printed, slips shall
be prepared.

ted to the county commissioners after the ballots have been printed, the said commissioners shall prepare and distribute with the ballots suitable slips of paper bearing the substituted name, together with the title of the office, and having adhesive paste upon the reverse side, which shall be offered to each voter with the regular ballot and may be affixed thereto.

County commis-
sioners to cause all
ballots to be
printed.
Commissioners
shall be responsible
for accurate print-
ing and safe
keeping.

SECTION 13. The county commissioners of each county shall cause all the ballots to be used therein to be printed. The said commissioners shall ascertain the offices to be filled and shall be responsible for the accurate printing of the ballots in accordance with this act, and for the safe keeping of the same while in their possession, or that of their subordinates or agents.

SECTION 14. The face of every ballot which shall be printed in accordance with the provisions of this act shall contain the names of all candidates whose nomination for any office specified in the ballot shall have been duly made, except such as may have died or withdrawn, arranged as hereinafter provided.

How ballots shall be printed.

The names of the candidates of each political party or body of electors shall be arranged under the titles of the offices for which they are nominated in parallel columns, with the party or political appellation at the head of each column. The said columns shall be enclosed by heavy lines and separated from each other by a clear space of at least one-eighth of an inch and shall be printed in the order as nearly as possible of the votes obtained in the State at the last State election by the parties or bodies nominating, beginning with the party or body which obtained the highest vote for the candidate, at the head of its column, at such election.

How names of candidates shall be arranged

When presidential electors are to be voted for, there shall be printed above each of the said columns, the names of the candidates for presidential electors nominated by the party or body of citizens named in the column, arranged in groups with the party or political appellation, and the surnames of the candidates for President and Vice President at the head of each group. There shall be printed above each column of candidates of a political party, a circle three-fourths of one inch in diameter, and there shall be printed around but without the circle the following words: "For a straight ticket mark within this circle."

How names of presidential electors shall be arranged.

Surnames of candidates for President and Vice President at the head of each group.

A circle to be printed at the head of each column "For a straight ticket."

There shall be left at the right of the groups of candidates for presidential electors, and of the lists of candidates for other officers, (or under the title of the office itself for which an election is to be held in case there be no candidates legally nominated therefor,) as many blank spaces as there are persons to be voted for, by each voter for such office, in which spaces the voter may insert the name of any person whose name is not printed on the ballot as a candidate for such office, and such insertion shall count as a vote without the cross-mark hereinafter mentioned.

Blank spaces to be left at the right of the groups of electors and list of candidates.

Names written in need not be marked with x.

Whenever the approval of a constitutional amendment or other question is submitted to the vote of the people, such question shall be printed upon the ballots in a brief form and followed by the words, "yes" and "no," and if such question be submitted at an election of public officers, it shall be printed below the lists of candidates.

How printed when a vote is to be taken on a constitutional amendment or other question.

The ballots shall be so printed as to give to each voter a clear opportunity to designate his choice of candidates by a cross-mark (x) in a square of sufficient size at the right of the name of each candidate and inside the line enclosing the column, and in like manner answers to the

Ballot shall be so printed as to give to each voter opportunity to designate his choice.

questions submitted by similar marks in squares at the right of the words "yes" and "no," and on the ballot may be printed instructions how to mark, and such words as will aid the voter to do this, as "mark one," "mark three," and the like: *Provided,* That a voter may designate his choice of an entire group of candidates for presidential electors by one cross-mark in a larger square, which shall be placed at the right of the surnames of the candidates for President and Vice President at the head of such group, and such mark shall be equivalent to a mark against every name in the group: *Provided further,* That a voter may designate his choice of all the candidates of a political party by one cross in the circle above such column, and such mark shall be equivalent to a mark against every name in the column.

SECTION 15. All the ballots used at the same voting place at any election shall be alike, and shall be at least six inches long and four inches wide. They shall be printed with the same kind or kinds of type, (which shall not be smaller than the size known as "brevier" or "eight-point body,") upon white paper without any impression or mark to distinguish one from another, and of sufficient thickness to prevent the printed matter from showing through. Each ballot shall be attached to a stub or counterfoil, and all the ballots for the same voting place shall be bound together in convenient numbers in books in such manner that each ballot may be detached and removed separately.

A diagonal folding line shall be printed on the right hand upper corner of the back of each ballot, and the said corner shall be edged with adhesive paste so that the corner when folded at the folding-line can be securely fastened down over the number now required by the Constitution of this Commonwealth, so that the said number cannot be seen without unfastening or cutting open the part so fastened down. The top of each ballot shall have a margin of equal size on both back and face, and the said folding-line shall be upon this margin, and the space between the folding-line and the paste shall be filled in with solid printing, and nothing else shall be printed on the margin except instructions how to mark: *Provided,* That if at any time the said Constitution shall cease to require ballots to be numbered, the foregoing requirements as to the folding-line, the margin and the adhesive paste shall be void.

On the back of each ballot, or on the right hand side of the back, if the ballot is printed in two columns, there shall be printed as a caption, "official ballot for," followed by the designation of the voting place for which the ballot is prepared, the date of the election and a fac-simile of the signatures of the county commissioners of the respective counties who have caused the ballots to be printed. A record of the number of ballots printed and furnished to each voting place, shall be kept and preserved by the county commissioners of the several counties. When it is shown by affidavit that mistake or omission has occurred in the publication of names or description of candidates, or in the printing of the ballots, the court of common pleas of the district or county, or any judge thereof, may upon the application of any qualified elector of the district or county require the county commissioners to correct the mistake or omission, or to show cause why they should not.

SECTION 16. The county commissioners of each county shall provide for each election district in which an election is to be held, one set of such ballots of not less than seventy-five for every fifty and fraction of fifty voters therein, as contained upon the assessors list. They shall also prepare full instructions for the guidance of voters, as to obtaining ballots, as to the manner of marking them and the method of gaining assistance, and as to obtaining new ballots in place of those accidentally spoiled; and they shall respectively cause the same, together with copies of sections thirty to thirty-five inclusive of this act, to be printed in large clear type on separate cards to be called Cards of Instruction. They shall also, in addition to the number of tickets required to be printed for general distribution, have printed five hundred official and one hundred sample ballots for every five thousand voters within the county, which tickets shall be kept at the office of the commissioners for the use of any district or districts, the tickets for which may be lost or destroyed. They shall also cause to be printed on tinted paper and without the fac-simile endorsements, copies of the form of the ballot provided for each voting place at each election therein, which shall be called Specimen Ballots, and at each election they shall furnish to each voting place, together with the ballots to be used there, a sufficient number of cards of instruction and specimen ballots for use as required in section twenty-one of this act. They shall also provide for each election district at every election therein, two copies of the assessor's lists of voters, and shall deliver the same as such lists are now delivered, one copy to be called the "ballot check list," for the inspectors in charge of the ballots, and the other copy to be called the "voting check list," to be used in marking the name of those who have voted and the number of their ballots as now required by law.

SECTION 17. The ballots, together with the specimen ballots and cards of instruction printed by the county commissioners as herein provided, shall be packed by them in separate sealed packages with marks on the outside clearly designating the election districts for which they are intended, and the number of ballots of each kind enclosed.

They shall then be sent by the county commissioners of the respective counties to the judges of election at the several voting places so as to be received by them on the

How mistakes in publication of names shall be corrected.

Number of ballots for each election district.
To be provided by county commissioners.

Shall prepare instructions for guidance of voters.

How cards of instruction shall be printed.

Official and sample ballots

Certain ballots to be kept at office of county commissioners.

Specimen ballots.

Cards of instruction and specimen ballots shall be furnished.
Shall also provide two copies of the assessor's list of voters.

Ballot check list.
Voting check list.

How ballots, etc., shall be packed for delivery.

How delivered to judges of election.

Saturday or Monday before the day of election. The respective judges of election shall on delivery to them of such packages, return receipts therefor to the commissioners, who shall keep a record of the time when and the manner in which the several packages are sent, and shall preserve for the period of one year, the receipts of the said judges of election.

The commissioners of any county may, if they prefer, instead of sending the packages to the judges or any number of them in the manner aforesaid, notify the judges of the election districts for which the said commissioners are required to provide ballots, to come to the said commissioners' office on the day before the election, at a time specified, and it shall be the duty of each of the said judges to come to the said office at that time, and there on presentation of his certificate of election as judge, to receive and receipt for one package of ballots, specimen ballots and cards of instruction, for use in his election district. He shall keep the said package sealed and shall be responsible for the safe keeping thereof until the ballots are used at the election. In case a judge of the elections is prevented by illness from performing the duties aforesaid, he shall depute one of the inspectors to act in his place.

SECTION 18. In case the ballots to be furnished to any voting place in accordance with the provisions of this act shall fail for any reason to be duly delivered, or in case after delivery they shall be destroyed or stolen, it shall be the duty of the judge of election of such voting place to cause other ballots to be prepared substantially in the form of the ballots so wanting, and upon receipt of such other ballots from him accompanied by a statement under oath that the same have been so prepared and furnished by him, and that the original ballots have so failed to be received, or have been so destroyed or stolen, the election officers shall cause the ballots so substituted to be used in lieu of the ballots wanting as above. It shall be the duty of the county commissioners of each county to mail complete specimens of the ballots and other necessary papers by registered letter to the judge of elections of each election district, at least four days before the election, to enable him to comply with the directions of this section.

SECTION 19. The county commissioners of each county shall provide for each election district therein, at each election, a room large enough to be fitted up with voting shelves and a guard rail as hereinafter provided. If in any district no such room can be rented or otherwise obtained, the said commissioners shall cause to be constructed for such district a temporary room of adequate size to be used as a voting room. They shall also cause all the said rooms to be suitably provided with heat and light, and with a sufficient number of voting shelves or compartments, at or in which voters may conveniently mark their ballots, with a curtain, screen or door at the upper part of the front of each compartment, so that in the marking thereof they may be screened from the observation of others, and a guard-rail shall be so constructed and placed that only such persons as are inside said rail can approach within six feet of the ballot box and of such voting shelves or compartments. The arrangment shall be such that neither the ballot box nor the voting booths shall be hidden from view of those just outside the said guard-rail. The number of such voting shelves or compartments shall not be less than one for every seventy-five names on the assessor's lists; but shall not in any case be less than three for the voters qualified to vote at such voting place. No persons other than the election officers and voters admitted as hereinafter provided, shall be permitted within the said rail, except by authority of the election officers for the purpose of keeping order and enforcing the law. Each voting shelf or compartment shall be kept provided with proper supplies and conveniences for marking the ballots.

SECTION 20. At the opening of the polls in each voting place the seals of the packages shall be publicly broken and the said package shall be opened by the judge of elections. The cards of instruction shall be immediately posted at or in each voting shelf or compartment provided in accordance with this act for the marking of the ballots, and not less than three such cards and not less than five specimen ballots shall be immediately posted in or about the voting room outside the guard-rail; and such cards and specimen ballots shall be given to any voter at his request.

SECTION 21. Any person desiring to vote shall give his name and residence to one of the election officers in charge of the ballots, who shall thereupon announce the same in a loud and distinct tone of voice, and if such name is found upon the ballot check list by the inspector or clerks in charge thereof, he shall likewise repeat the said name, and the voter shall be allowed to enter the space enclosed by the guard-rail, unless his right to vote be challenged. No person whose name is not on the said list or whose right to vote shall be challenged by a qualified citizen, shall be admitted within said guard-rail until he has established his right to vote in the manner now provided by law, and his name, if not on the check lists, shall then be added to both lists. As soon as a voter is admitted within the rail the election officer having charge of the ballots shall detach a ballot from the stub and give it to the said voter, but shall first fold it so that the words printed on the back and outside, as provided in section fifteen of this act, shall be the only wording visible and no ballot shall be voted unless folded in the same manner. Not more than one ballot shall be given to a voter except as is provided in section twenty-five of this act. As soon as a voter receives a ballot the letter "B" shall be marked against his name on the margin of

Construction of guard rail.

Fixing distance persons inside rail may approach ballot box and shelves.

Arrangement of ballot box and voting booths.

Number of voting booths.

Persons permitted within rail.

Supplies for marking ballots.

Duty of judge of election on opening of the polls.
Cards of instruction to be posted at or in compartment.
Cards of instruction and specimen ballots to be posted at or in compartment.
Cards of instruction and specimen ballots to be posted outside guard rail and given to voters on request.

Manner of voting.

No person shall be admitted within guard-rail until he has established his right to vote.

How ballot shall be delivered to voter.

Only one ballot shall be given to a voter, unless he inadvertently spoil a ballot.

the ballot-check-list; but no record of the number of the ballots shall be made on the said lists. Besides the election officers and such supervisors as are authorized by the laws of the United States or overseers appointed by the courts of this Commonwealth, not more than four voters in excess of the number of voting shelves or compartments provided, shall be allowed in said enclosed space at one time.

SECTION 22. On receipt of his ballot the voter shall forthwith and without leaving the space enclosed by the guard-rail retire to one of the voting shelves or compartments, and draw the curtain or shut the screen or door, and shall prepare his ballot by marking, if he desires to vote for every candidate of a political party, a cross in the circle above the column of such party, if otherwise he shall mark in the appropriate margin or place a cross (x) opposite the party name or political designation, or a group of candidates for presidential electors, and opposite the name of the candidate of his choice for each other office to be filled, according to the number of persons to be voted for by him for each office, or by inserting in the blank space provided therefor any name not already on the ballot; and in case of a question submitted to the vote of the people, by marking in the appropriate margin or place a cross (x) against the answer which he desires to give. In all cases where by existing laws a voter is entitled to cast more than one vote for a single candidate, he shall place in the appropriate square, instead of a cross, a number which shall indicate the number of votes to be counted for the candidate whose name is so marked. Before leaving the voting shelf or compartment the voter shall fold his ballot without displaying the marks thereon, in the same way it was folded when received by him, and he shall keep the same so folded until he has voted.

After leaving the voting shelf and before leaving the enclosed space, he shall give his ballot to the election officer in charge of the ballot box, who shall without unfolding the ballot number it as required by the Constitution of this Commonwealth, placing the said number in the right hand upper corner of the back of the ballot immediately to the left of the folding line printed thereon and nowhere else, and shall then at once fold the corner at the folding line and fasten it securely down with the adhesive paste so as to cover the number on the ballot so that it cannot be seen without unfastening or cutting open the part so fastened down, and shall then deposite the ballot in the box. The voter shall mark and deliver his ballot without undue delay and shall quit the enclosed space as soon as his ballot has been deposited: *Provided*, That if at any time the Constitution of this Commonwealth shall cease to require ballots to be numbered, no number shall be marked on the ballot, and it shall be deposited in the ballot box by the voter himself.

SECTION 23. No voter shall be allowed to occupy a voting shelf or compartment already occupied by another, except when giving the help allowed by section twenty-six of this act, nor to remain within said compartment more than three minutes in case all of such compartments are in use, and other voters are waiting to occupy the same. No voter not an election officer shall be allowed to re-enter the enclosed space after he has once left it, except to give help as hereinafter described. Each voter's name shall be checked on the voting check-list by the officer having charge thereof, as soon as he has cast his vote in the manner now provided by law. It shall be the duty of the judge of election to secure the observance of the provisions of this section, to keep order in the room in which the voting is held and to see that no more persons are admitted within the enclosed space than are allowed by this act. Each party which has by its primary meeting, caucus, convention or board, sent to the proper office a Certificate of Nomination, and each group of citizens which has sent to the proper office a Nomination Paper as provided in sections two and three of this act, shall be allowed to appoint three electors to act as watchers in each voting place without expense to the county, one of whom shall be allowed to remain in the room outside of the enclosed space. Each watcher shall be provided with a certificate from the county commissioners, stating his name, the names of the persons who have appointed him and the party or policy he represents; and no party or policy shall be represented by more than one watcher in the same voting room at any one time. Watchers shall be required to show their certificates when requested to do so. Until the polls are closed, no persons shall be allowed in the room outside of the said enclosed space except these watchers, voters not exceeding ten at any one time who are awaiting their turn to prepare their ballots, and peace officers when necessary for the preservation of the peace. No person when within the voting room shall electioneer or solicit votes for any party or candidate, nor shall any written or printed matter be posted up within the said room except as required by law. When the hour for closing the polls shall arrive all persons within the enclosed space who have received ballots but have not yet deposited them, shall be required to mark and deposit their ballots forthwith, but no other person shall be allowed to vote.

SECTION 24. No list or memorandum of the names of voters, except such lists as are expressly authorized by law, shall be made within the voting room by any person or officer, nor shall any list or memorandum of the numbers marked upon the ballots be made or kept except such lists as are expressly authorized by law: *Provided*, That any voter may make a memorandum of the number of his own ballot, and the watchers may keep their poll books and challenge lists. After the closing of the polls and before the ballot boxes are opened, all the lists of voters upon which the numbers of the ballots are recorded

Length of time voter may remain in compartment.

No voter shall be allowed to re-enter enclosed space after leaving it.

Checking of name.

Duty of judge of election.

Watchers may be appointed and by whom.

County commissioners to provide certificates.

Only one watcher of each party shall be allowed in the voting room.

Watchers must show certificate.

Who may be allowed in room outside of rail.

Soliciting of votes not allowed in room, nor any written or printed matter not authorized.

Who may vote on the closing of the polls.

No lists or memorandum of voters shall be made in voting room, except such as are authorized.

Voter may keep his own number, and watchers their poll books.

as now required by law shall be placed in separate sealed covers properly marked, and the stubs of all the ballots used, together with all unused ballots and the ballot-check list, shall also be enclosed in a sealed package properly designating the voting place, which package shall be sent to the proper office as required by law in the case of the ballots cast, and neither the said package, nor the said lists of voters shall thereafter be opened except by the return judges, or in the case of a contest, or upon the order of a court of a competent jurisdiction.

SECTION 25. No person other than the election officers shall take or remove any ballot from the voting place. If any voter inadvertently spoils a ballot he may obtain another upon returning the spoiled one. The ballots thus returned shall be immediately canceled and at the close of the polls shall be secured in an envelope, sealed and sent to the proper office as required by law in the case of the ballots cast.

SECTION 26. If any voter declares to the judge of election that by reason of any disability he desires assistance in the preparation of his ballot, he shall be permitted by the judge of election to select a qualified voter of the election district to aid him in the preparation of his ballot, such preparation being made in the voting compartment.

SECTION 27. If a voter marks more names than he is entitled to vote for, for an office, or if for any reason it is impossible to determine the voter's choice for any office to be filled, his ballot shall not be counted for such office, but the ballot shall be counted for all other offices for which the names of candidates have been properly marked.

No ballot without the official endorsement shall, except as herein otherwise provided, be allowed to be deposited in the ballot-box, and none but ballots provided in accordance with the provisions of this act shall be counted; ballots not marked, or improperly or defectively marked, shall be endorsed as defective, but shall be preserved with the other ballots. If any ballot appears to have been obtained otherwise than as provided in this act, the judge of elections shall transmit such ballot to the district attorney without delay, together with whatever information he may have tending to the detection of the person who deposited the same.

SECTION 28. After the polls are closed the election officers only shall remain in the voting room within the guard rail, and shall there at once proceed to count the votes. Such counting shall not be adjourned or postponed until it shall have been fully completed. A record shall first be made of the number of the last ballot cast; the officers in charge of the voting check list shall, in the presence of the other officers and watchers, count in a distinct and audible voice the names checked on the said list and announce the whole number thereof, and the lists of voters, the stubs of ballots used, and all unused ballots shall then be sealed up as required by section twenty-five of this act. The ballot-box shall then be opened by the inspectors, the ballots taken therefrom and audibly counted one by one by them, and when the count is completed the whole number of ballots cast shall be announced, and the counting of the number of votes received by each person voted for shall then proceed. The judge, in the presence of the inspectors, shall read aloud the name or names marked or inserted upon each ballot, and the answers marked thereon to the questions submitted, if any, and the clerks shall each carefully enter each vote as read, and keep account of the same on tally papers prepared for the purpose. It shall be unlawful for either judge or inspector, while counting the ballots or the votes thereon, to have in his hand any pen, pencil, or stamp for marking ballots.

All ballots after being removed from the box shall be kept within the unobstructed view of those present in the voting room, so that they may be able to see all the marks on each ballot, but out of their reach until they are placed in the ballot-box as required by law. A full return shall be made in the manner now provided by law of all votes cast, and the total vote, as soon as counted, shall be publicly announced.

It shall be the duty of the police officers, constables and deputy constables now required by law to be present at the polls to remain within the voting room, but outside the guard-rail, while the votes are being counted, and to preserve order therein. No person except the said peace officers, when necessary for the preservation of the peace, or persons acting by their authority for the same end, shall enter the space within the guard-rail, or communicate with any election officer in any way after the polls are closed, and until the counting of the votes has been completed.

SECTION 29. Whenever in any contested election the tribunal trying the case shall decide that the ballots used in one or more election districts were, by reason of the omission, addition, misplacing, mis-spelling or mis-statement of one or more titles of offices, or names of candidates, or parties or policies represented by them, so defective as to the office in contest as to be calculated to mislead the voters in regard to any of the candidates nominated for the said office, and that the defective condition of the said ballots may have effected the result of the entire election for the said office, the said tribunal shall declare the election to be invalid as regards the said office, and shall report their decision to the Governor of the Commonwealth.

The Governor on receiving the report of the said decision, shall without delay cause a writ or writs of election for the office in contest to issue, and appoint a day within four weeks from the date of the writ for the holding of a new election, to be held according to the provisions of this act for the office in contest.

28—LAWS.

Marginal notes:

Unused ballots to be sealed up.

Ballot-boxes to be opened and votes counted.

Announcement of result.

Ballot-box to be opened by judge and count to proceed.

Clerks to keep tally.

Neither judge nor inspector allowed to have pen, pencil or stamp in his hand.

Ballots to be kept in view of those in voting room.

A full return and public announcement.

Duties of police officers, constables, etc.

Peace officers alone allowed within guard-rail to preserve peace during count.

Contested election.

When ballots are defective tribunal shall declare election invalid and so report to Governor.

Governor shall issue writ for new election.

SECTION 30. A voter who shall allow his ballot to be seen by any person with an apparent intention of letting it be known how he is about to vote, or shall cast or attempt to cast any other ballot than the official ballot which has been given to him by the proper election officer, or shall falsely declare to a judge of election that by reason of any disability he desires assistance in the preparation of his ballot, or shall wilfully violate any other provision of this act, or any person who shall interfere with any voter when inside said enclosed space, or when marking his ballot, or who shall endeavor to induce any voter before depositing his ballot to show how he marks or has marked his ballot, or who shall disclose the contents of any ballot that has been marked by his help, or who, except when lawfully commanded by a return judge or a competent court, shall loosen, cut, or unfasten the corner pasted down over the number on any ballot, shall be guilty of a misdemeanor, and upon conviction shall be sentenced to pay a fine not exceeding one hundred dollars, or to undergo an imprisonment for not more than three months, or both, at the discretion of the court.

SECTION 31. Any person who shall, prior to an election, wilfully deface or destroy any list of candidates posted in accordance with the provisions of this act, or who, during an election, shall wilfully deface, tear down, remove or destroy any card of instruction, or specimen ballot, printed or posted for the instruction of voters, or who shall, during an election, wilfully remove or destroy any of the supplies or conveniences furnished to enable a voter to prepare his ballot, or shall wilfully hinder the voting of others, shall be guilty of a misdemeanor, and upon conviction shall be sentenced to pay a fine not exceeding one hundred dollars, or to undergo an imprisonment for not more than three months, or both, at the discretion of the court.

SECTION 32. Any person who shall falsely make or wilfully deface or destroy any Certificate of Nomination, or Nomination Paper, or any part thereof, or any letter of withdrawal, or file any Certificate of Nomination, or Nomination Paper, or letter of withdrawal, knowing the same or any part thereof to be falsely made, or suppress any Certificate of Nomination, or Nomination Paper, or any part thereof which has been duly filed, or forge, or falsely made the official endorsement on any ballot, or wilfully destroy or deface any ballot, or wilfully delay the delivery of any ballots, shall be guilty of a misdemeanor, and upon conviction shall be sentenced to pay a fine not exceeding one thousand dollars, or to undergo an imprisonment for not more than one year, or both, at the discretion of the court.

SECTION 33. Any public officer upon whom a duty is imposed by this act, who shall negligently or wilfully fail to perform such duty, or who shall negligently or wilfully perform it in such a way as to hinder the objects of this act, or who shall negligently or wilfully violate any of the provisions thereof, shall be guilty of a misdemeanor, and upon conviction shall be sentenced to pay a fine not exceeding one thousand dollars, or to undergo an imprisonment for not more than one year, or both, at the discretion of the court.

SECTION 34. Any printer employed by the commissioners of any county to print any official ballots, or any person engaged in printing the same, who shall appropriate to himself, or give or deliver or knowingly permit to be taken any of said ballots by any other person than such commissioners, or their duly authorized agent, or shall wilfully print, or cause to be printed any official ballot in any other form than that prescribed by such commissioners, or with any other names thereon, or with the names spelled otherwise than as directed by them, or the names or printing thereon arranged in any other way than that authorized and directed by this act, shall be guilty of a misdemeanor, and upon conviction shall be sentenced to pay a fine not exceeding one thousand dollars, or to undergo an imprisonment for not more than five years, or both, at the discretion of the court.

SECTION 35. Any person other than an officer charged by law with the care of ballots, or a person entrusted by any such officer with the care of the same for a purpose required by law, who shall have in his possession outside the voting room any official ballot, or any person who shall make or have in possession any counterfeit or an official ballot, shall be guilty of a misdemeanor, and upon conviction shall be sentenced to pay a fine not exceeding one thousand dollars, or to undergo an imprisonment for not more than one year, or both, at the discretion of the court.

SECTION 36. All laws and parts of laws inconsistent herewith, shall be and the same are hereby repealed.

APPROVED—The 10th day of June, A. D. 1893.

ROBT. E. PATTISON.

— · —

No. 319.

AN ACT

Amending an act, entitled "A supplement to an act approved April twenty-ninth, one thousand eight hundred and seventy-four, entitled 'An act to provide for the incorporation and regulation of certain corporations,' providing for the further regulation of such corporations, and for the incorporation and regulation of certain additional corporations," approved April seventeenth, one thousand eight hundred and seventy-six, authorizing the incorporation of drainage companies.

SECTION 1. Be it enacted, &c., That the second section of the act, entitled "A supplement to an act approved April twenty-ninth, one thousand eight hundred and seventy-four, entitled 'An act to provide for the incorporation and regulation of certain corporations,' providing for the further regulation of such corporations, and for the incorporation and regulation of certain additional corporations," approved April seventeenth, one thousand eight hundred and seventy-six, which reads as follows:

"Section 2. The purposes for which the said corporations may be formed shall be as follows, and shall be divided into two classes:

CORPORATIONS NOT FOR PROFIT—FIRST CLASS.

The first class those for—

First. The support of public worship.

Second. The support of any benevolent, charitable, educational or missionary undertaking.

Third. The support of any literary, medical or scientific undertaking, library association or the promotion of music, painting or other fine arts.

Fourth. The encouragement of agriculture and horticulture.

Fifth. The maintenance of public or private parks, and of facilities for skating, boating, trotting and other innocent or athletic sports, including clubs for such purposes, and for the preservation of game and fish.

Sixth. The maintenance of a club for social enjoyments.

Seventh. The maintenance of a public or private cemetery.

Eighth. The erection of halls for public or private purposes.

Ninth. The maintenance of a society for beneficial or protective purposes to its members from funds collected therein.

Tenth. The support of fire engine, hook and ladder, hose or other companies for the control of fire.

Eleventh. For the encouragement and protection of trade and commerce.

Twelfth. For the formation and maintenance of military organizations.

Each of said corporations may hold real estate to an amount the clear yearly value or income whereof shall not exceed twenty thousand dollars.

CORPORATIONS FOR PROFIT—SECOND CLASS.

The second class those for—

First. The insurance of the lives of domestic animals.

Second. The insurance of human beings against death, sickness or personal injury.

Third. The prevention and punishment of theft or willful injuries to property and insurance against such risks.

Fourth. The construction and maintenance of any species of road other than a railroad and of bridges in connection therewith.

Fifth. The construction and maintenance of a bridge over streams within this State.

Sixth. The construction and maintenance of a telegraph line.

Seventh. The establishment and maintenance of a ferry.

Eighth. The building of ships, vessels or boats, and carriage of persons and property thereon.

Ninth. The supply of water to the public.

Tenth. The supply of ice to the public.

Eleventh. The manufacture and supply of gas, or the supply of light or heat to the public by any other means.

Twelfth. The transaction of a printing and publishing business.

Thirteenth. The establishment and maintenance of an hotel and drove yard or boarding house, opera and market house, livery or boarding stable, or either.

Fourteenth. The creating, purchasing, holding and selling of patent rights of inventions and designs, with the right to issue license for the same and receive pay therefor.

Fifteenth. Building and loan associations.

Sixteenth. Associations for the purchase and sale of real estate or for holding, leasing and selling real estate, for maintaining or erecting walls or banks for the protection of low lying lands, and for safe deposit companies.

Seventeenth. The manufacture of iron or steel, or both, or of any other metal, or of any article of commerce from metal or wood, or both.

Eighteenth. The carrying on of any mechanical, mining, quarrying or manufacturing business, including all of the purposes covered by the provisions of the act of the General Assembly, entitled "An act to encourage manufacturing operations in this Commonwealth," approved April seventh, one thousand eight hundred and forty-nine, and entitled "An act relating to corporations for mechanical, manufacturing, mining and quarrying purposes," approved July eighteenth, one thousand eight hundred and sixty-three, and the several supplements to each of said acts, including the incorporation of grain elevator, storage warehouse and storage yard companies, and also including the storage and transportation of water, with the right to take rivulets and land and erect reservoirs for holding water, and excluding the distilling or manufacture of intoxicating liquors.

Nineteenth. The insurance of owners of real estate, mortgages and others interested in real estate from loss by reason of defective titles, liens and incumbrances.

Twentieth. The re-chartering of corporations of either of these classes, the charters whereof are about to expire.

Twenty-first. The construction and maintenance of a wharf or wharves, for public and private use, and the maintenance of any unincorporated wharf or wharves already constructed.

Twenty-second. The construction, erection and maintenance of observatories for public use or scientific purposes.

Twenty-third. The formation and operation of stage and omnibus lines.

Twenty-fourth. The formation and operation of inclined planes for the transportation of passengers and freight," be and the said section is hereby amended and re-enacted so as to read as follows:

SECTION 2. The purposes for which the said corporations may be formed shall be as follows, and shall be divided into two classes:

CORPORATIONS NOT FOR PROFIT—FIRST CLASS.

The first those for—

One. The support of public worship.

Two. The support of any benevolent, charitable, educational or missionary undertaking.

Three. The support of any literary, medical or scientific undertaking, library association, or the promotion of music, painting or other fine arts.

Four. The encouragement of agriculture and horticulture.

Five. The maintenance of public or private parks, and of facilities for skating, boating, trotting and other innocent or athletic sports, including clubs for such purposes, and for the preservation of game and fish.

Six. The maintenance of a club for social enjoyments.

Seven. The maintenance of a public or private omnibus lines.

Twenty-fourth. The formation and operation of inclined planes for the transportation of passengers and freight, be the said section is hereby amended and re-enacted so as to read as follows:

SECTION 2. The purposes for which the said corporations may be formed shall be as follows, and shall be divided into two classes:

CORPORATIONS NOT FOR PROFIT—FIRST CLASS.

First class

The first those for—

One. The support of public worship.

Two. The support of any benevolent, charitable, educational or missionary undertaking.

Three. The support of any literary, medical or scientific undertaking, library association, or the promotion of music, painting or other fine arts.

Four. The encouragement of agriculture and horticulture.

Five. The maintenance of public or private parks, and of facilities for skating, boating, trotting and other innocent or athletic sports, including clubs for such purposes, and for the preservation of game and fish.

Six. The maintenance of a club for social enjoyments.

Seven. The maintenace of a public or private cemetery.

Eight. The erection of halls for public or private purposes.

Ninth. The maintenance of a society for beneficial or protective purposes to its members, from funds collected therein.

Tenth. The support of fire engine, hook and ladder, hose or other companies for the control of fire.

Eleventh. For the encouragement and protection of trade and commerce.

Twelfth. For the formation and maintenance of military organizations.

Each of said corporations may hold real estate to an amount the clear yearly value or income whereof shall not exceed twenty thousand dollars.

CORPORATIONS FOR PROFIT—SECOND CLASS.

The second class those for—

Second class.

One. The insurance of the lives of domestic animals.

Two. The insurance of human beings against death, sickness or personal injury.

Three. The prevention and punishment of theft or willful injuries to property, and insurance against such risks.

Fourth. The construction and maintenance of any species of road other than a railroad, and the bridges in connection therewith.

Fifth. The construction and maintenance of a bridge over streams within this State.

Sixth. The construction and maintenance of a telegraph line.

Seventh. The establishment and maintenance of a ferry.

Eighth. The building of ships, vessels or boats, and carriage of persons and property thereon.

Ninth. The supply of water to the public.

Tenth. The supply of ice to the public.

Eleventh. The manufacture and supply of gas, or the supply of light or heat to the public by any other means.

Twelfth. The transaction of a printing and publishing business.

Thirteenth. The establishment and maintenance of an hotel and drove yard, or boarding house, opera and market house, livery or boarding stable, or either.

Fourteenth. The creating, purchasing, holding and selling of patent rights for inventions and designs, with the right to issue license for the same and receive pay therefor.

Fifteenth. Building and loan associations.

Sixteenth. Associations for the purchase and sale of real estate, or for holding, leasing and selling real estate, for maintaining or erecting walls or banks for the protection of low lying lands, and for safe deposit companies.

Seventeenth. The manufacture of iron or steel, or both, or of any other metal, or of any article of commerce from metal or wood, or both.

Eighteenth. The carrying on of any mechanical, mining, quarrying or manufacturing business, including all of the purposes covered by the provisions of the act of the General Assembly, entitled "An act to encourage manufacturing operations in this Commonwealth," approved April seventh, one thousand eight hundred and forty-nine, and entitled "An act relating to corporations for mechanical, manufacturing, mining and quarrying purposes," approved July eighteenth, one thousand eight hundred and sixty-three, and the several supplements to each of the said acts, including the incorporation of grain elevator, storage warehouse and storage yard companies, and also including the storage and transportation of water, with the right to take rivulets and lands and erect reservoirs for holding water, and excluding the distilling or manufacture of intoxicating liquors.

Nineteenth. The insurance of owners of real estate, mortgages and others interested in real estate from loss by reason of defective titles, liens and incumbrances.

Twentieth. The re-chartering of corporations of either of these classes, the charters whereof are about to expire.

Twenty-first. The construction and maintenance of a wharf or wharves for public and private use, and the maintenance of any unincorporated wharf or wharves already constructed.

Twenty-second. The construction, erection and maintenance of observatories for public use or scientific purposes.

Twenty-third. The formation and operation of stages and omnibus lines.

Twenty-four. The formation and operation of inclined planes for the transportation of passengers and freight.

Twenty-fifth. The construction and maintenance of sewers, culverts, conduits and pipes, with all necessary inlets and appliances for surface, under-surface and sewage drainage for the health, comfort and convenience of inhabitant, and sanitary improvement in cities, boroughs and townships of the Commonwealth, and for this purpose to enter upon and occupy any public highway with the consent of the local authorities.

APPROVED—The 10th day of June, A. D. 1893. I have given my approval to this bill, notwithstanding certain clumsiness and carelessness on the part of the transcribing clerks, by which, in the copy presented for my signature, certain paragraphs in the re-enacting clauses have been unnecessarily repeated. In the copy as prepared for my approval, the first seven classes of corporations not for profit and the twenty-fourth have been written into the bill in addition to such re-enactments as were required. The real purpose of the bill, viz: To provide for the incorporation of sewer and drainage companies, is one which meets my approval and I, therefore, have affixed my signature to the bill, notwithstanding the defects to which I call attention, and which can do no greater harm than to disfigure the statute books. None the less the existence of them reflects on the competency of the transcribing clerks, if not on the strict attention to duty reasonably expected of the committees to compare bills.

The condition of this and some other bills submitted to me, with like defects, affords additional grounds for condemnation of the usual procedure of passing bills with undue haste and recklessness during the closing days of the session.

ROBT. E. PATTISON.

No. 320.

AN ACT

Making it unlawful for any person to engage in the practice or assume the title of doctor of dental surgery, or advertise himself as a doctor of dental surgery, without first procuring a diploma from a reputable institution, recognized by the National Board of Dental Examiners, and defining who shall be understood as practicing dentistry, and authorizing State Board of Dental Examiners to charge and collect certain fees.

SECTION 1. *Be it enacted, &c.*, That from and after the passage of this act, it shall not be lawful for any person in the State of Pennsylvania to engage in the practice of dentistry, or assume the title of Doctor of Dental Surgery, or advertise himself or herself as Doctor of Dental Surgery, without first having graduated and receiving a diploma conferring the degree of Doctor of Dental Surgery, or other recognized dental degree, from a reputable institution recognized as of good repute by the National Board of Dental Examiners, and legally competent to confer the same, and having said diploma endorsed by the State Board of Dental Examiners and recorded according to requirement of the act of June twenty, one thousand eight hundred and eighty-three: *Provided*, That physicians and surgeons may, in the regular practice of their profession, extract teeth for the relief of pain, or make applications for such purpose.

[margin note: Who may practice dentistry or assume the title of Doctor of Dental Surgery.]
[margin note: Proviso.]

SECTION 2. Every person shall be understood as practicing dentistry within the meaning of this act, who shall, for fee, salary or other reward, either to himself or another person, operate upon human teeth, furnish artificial substitutes or perform those acts as assistant or principal usually understood as and called dental operations: *Provided*, That bona fide students of dentistry, under the immediate supervision of a preceptor who is

[margin note: Dental practice defined.]
[margin note: Proviso.]

in lawful practice, may assist him in operations during the usual term of pupilage, not to exceed two and one-half years from the date of commencement.

SECTION 3. The State Board of Dental Examiners is hereby authorized to collect a fee of not less than one dollar for each endorsement of a diploma required by the act of June twentieth, one thousand eight hundred and eighty-three, said amount to be paid by the holder of diploma as a prerequisite to endorsement. In all

cases the members of the State Dental Examiner's Board shall, by written or oral examination or otherwise, satisfy themselves as to the fitness and qualifications of the holder of a diploma before endorsement is made, and, in their discretion, refuse to endorse the diploma of an applicant who is found incompetent.

When an examination is considered necessary, the said board is authorized to collect from the applicant a fee of five dollars, which sum shall be refunded in case his diploma is not endorsed.

SECTION 4. In case a graduate of one of the dental schools of this State shall desire and intend to begin the practice of dentistry in a foreign country beyond the bounds of the United States, and shall make affidavit, duly certified, as to the fact, and shall ask for the endorsement of the State Board of Dental Examiners, then said State Board being satisfied as to the character and qualifications of the applicant and the good repute of the institution issuing said diploma may endorse the same,

and for each such endorsement shall collect a fee of not less than ten dollars.

SECTION 5. Any violation of the provisions of this act shall constitute a misdemeanor and shall subject the party violating it to a penalty of not more than one

hundred dollars for each offense.

SECTION 6. This act shall not apply to persons who have been engaged in the active practice of dentistry in Pennsylvania from the date of the passage of the act of June twenty, one thousand eight hundred and eighty-three.

SECTION 7. It shall not not be lawful for any recorder to place upon record any diploma of date later than September twentieth, one thousand eight hundred and eighty-three, unless said diploma has been endorsed and approved by the State Board of Dental Examiners or the secretary of said board.

SECTION 8. All acts or parts of acts inconsistent with the provisions of this act are hereby repealed.

APPROVED—The 10th day of June, A. D. 1893.

ROBT. E. PATTISON.

No. 321.

AN ACT

To amend an act approved the thirteenth day of April, one thousand eight hundred and eighty-seven, entitled "An act to provide for the organization, discipline and regulation of the National Guard of Pennsylvania, and the several supplements thereto," providing for the more efficient organization and government of the National Guard of Pennsylvania.

SECTION 1. *Be it enacted, &c.,* That section two, which reads as follows, namely:

SECTION 2. In the time of peace, the National Guard shall consist of not more than one hundred and fifty companies of infantry, five troops of cavalry and five batteries of artillery, fully armed, uniformed and equipped, to be allotted and apportioned in such localities of the State as the necessity of the service, in the discretion of the Commander-in-Chief may require, and organized in such divisions, brigades, regiments, battalions,

AN ACT

To amend an act approved the thirteenth day of April, one thousand eight hundred and eighty-seven, entitled "An act to provide for the organization, discipline and regulation of the National Guard of Pennsylvania, and the several supplements thereto."

SECTION 1. *Be it enacted, &c.,* That section two, which reads as follows, namely:

"SECTION 2. In the time of peace, the National Guard shall consist of not more than one hundred and fifty companies of infantry, five troops of cavalry and five batteries of artillery, fully armed, uniformed and equipped, to be allotted and apportioned in such localities of the State as the necessity of the service, in the discretion of the Commander-in-Chief may require, and organized in such divisions, brigades, regiments, battalions and unassigned companies, with power to make such alterations in the organization and arrangement thereof, from time to time, as he may deem necessary: *Provided,* That there shall not be more than one major general and five brigadier generals of the line. But the Commander-in-Chief shall have power, in case of war, invasion, insurrection, riot or imminent danger thereof, to increase the said force and organize the same as the exigencies of the occasion may require: *Provided,* That whenever an officer shall be re-commissioned within six months after the expiration of his original commission, in the same grade, or in a lower grade than that in which he has served in the National Guard, his new commission shall bear even date with and he shall take rank from the date provided for in his former commission," be and it is hereby amended so that it shall read as follows, namely:

Section 2, act of April 13, 1887, cited for amendment.

Organisation in
time of peace.

SECTION 2. In the time of peace the National Guard shall consist of not more than one hundred and fifty companies of infantry, five troops of cavalry and five batteries of artillery, four companies of engineers and a signal corps of one company, fully armed, uniformed and equipped, to be allotted and apportioned in such localities of the State as the necessity of the service, in the discretion of the Commander-in-Chief, may require, and organized in such divisions, brigades, regiments, battalions and unassigned companies, with power to make such alterations in the organization and arrangement thereof from time to time as he may deem necessary: *Provided*, That

Generals of the
line.

there shall not be more than one major general and five brigadier generals of the line. But the Commander-in-

Increase of force by
Commander-in-
Chief in time of
war, &c.

Chief shall have power in case of war, invasion, insurrection, riot or imminent danger thereof, to increase the said force and organize the same as the exigencies of the occasion may require: *Provided*, That whenever an officer

Certain re-com-
missioned officers
to rank from date
of former commis-
sion.

shall be re-commissioned within six months after the expiration of his original commission, in the same grade or in a lower grade than that in which he has served in the National Guard, his new commission shall bear even date with and he shall take rank from the date provided for in his former commission.

Section seven which reads as follows, namely:

Section 7, cited for
amendment.

"SECTION 7. To each regiment of infantry, one colonel, one lieutenant colonel, not to exceed three majors at the discretion of the Commander-in-Chief, one surgeon with the rank of major, one chaplain with the rank of captain, one adjutant, (an extra first lieutenant), one quartermaster, (an extra first lieutenant), two assistant surgeons with the rank of first lieutenant, one inspector of rifle practice, (an extra first lieutenant), one sergeant major, one regimental quartermaster sergeant, one regimental commissary sergeant, one hospital stewart and one principal musician," be and it is hereby amended so that it shall read as follows, namely:

Officers of regiment
of infantry.

SECTION 7. To each regiment of infantry one colonel, one lieutenant colonel, not to exceed three majors, at the discretion of the Commander-in-Chief, one surgeon with the rank of major, one chaplain with the rank of captain, one adjutant, (an extra first lieutenant), one quartermaster, (an extra first lieutenant), two assistant surgeons with the rank of first lieutenant, one inspector of rifle practice, (an extra first lieutenant), one sergeant major, one regimental quartermaster sergeant, one regimental commissary sergeant, one color sergeant, one hospital steward and one principal musician.

To each battalion of not less than four companies of a regiment of infantry one major, one adjutant, (an extra second lieutenant), one sergeant major.

Section eight which reads as follows, namely:

Section 8, cited for
amendment.

"SECTION 8. To every troop of cavalry one captain, one first lieutenant, one second lieutenant, one assistant surgeon with the rank of first lieutenant, one quartermaster with the rank of second lieutenant, one first sergeant, one quartermaster sergeant, one commissary sergeant, five sergeants, eight corporals, two trumpeters, two farriers or blacksmiths, one saddler, one wagoner and twenty-eight privates minimum, thirty-eight privates maximum.

To every company of infantry one captain, one first lieutenant, one second lieutenant, one first sergeant, four sergeants, eight corporals, two musicians, thirty five privates minimum, forty-five privates maximum.

To every battery of artillery one captain, two first lieutenants, one second lieutenant, one assistant surgeon with the rank of first lieutenant, one quartermaster with the rank of second lieutenant, one first sergeant, one quartermaster sergeant, one commissary sergeant, four sergeants, eight corporals, two musicians, two artificers, one wagoner, and forty-six privates minimum, and fifty-six privates maximum.

To every company there shall be one clerk, who shall be detailed for that duty from the company.

For all the purposes of this act the word company or companies shall apply to and include the infantry, cavalry and artillery forces," be and it is hereby amended so that it shall read as follows, namely:

To every troop of cavalry one captain, one first lieutenant, one second lieutenant, one assistant surgeon with the rank of first lieutenant, one quartermaster with the rank of second lieutenant, one first sergeant, one quartermaster sergeant, one commissary sergeant, five sergeants, eight corporals, two trumpeters, two farriers or blacksmiths, one saddler, one wagoner, and twenty-eight privates minimum, thirty-eight privates maximum. Officers and privates of cavalry troops.

To every company of infantry one captain, one first lieutenant, one second lieutenant, one first sergeant, four sergeants, eight corporals, two musicians, thirty-five privates minimum, forty-five privates maximum. Officers and privates of infantry company.

To every battery of artillery one captain, two first lieutenants, one second lieutenant, one assistant surgeon with the rank of first lieutenant, one quartermaster with the rank of second lieutenant, one first sergeant, one quartermaster sergeant, one commissary sergeant, four sergeants, eight corporals, two musicians, two artificers, one wagoner, and forty-six privates minimum, and fifty-six privates maximum. Officers and privates of battery of artillery.

To every company of engineers one captain, one first lieutenant, one second lieutenant, one first sergeant, four sergeants, eight corporals, two musicians, thirty-five privates minimum, forty-five privates maximum. Officers and privates of company of engineers.

To the signal corps of one company one captain, one first lieutenant, one second lieutenant, one first sergeant, three sergeants, four corporals, two musicians, and twenty-eight privates minimum, and thirty-two privates maximum. Officers and privates of signal corps.

To every company there shall be one clerk, who shall be detailed for that duty from the company. Company clerk.

For all purposes of this act the word company or companies shall apply to and include the infantry, cavalry, artillery, engineer and signal corps forces.

Section sixteen which reads as follows, namely:

SECTION 16. Chaplains, adjutants, quartermasters and inspectors of rifle practice shall be appointed by the respective colonels, surgeons and assistant surgeons of regiments by the respective colonels and approved by the surgeon general.

Adjutants and quartermasters of battalions, by the respective majors, assistant surgeons and battalions by the respective majors, to be approved by the surgeon general.

Assistant surgeons of troops of cavalry and artillery batteries by the respective captains, to be approved by the surgeon general.

Quartermasters of cavalry and artillery batteries, by the respective captains.

Division, brigade, regimental and battalion non-commissioned staff officers, by their respective commanders.

Non-commissioned officers of companies by the respective captains, approved by their respective commanding officers.

Clerks, by the commanding officers of the respective companies, brigade quartermasters and commissaries in time of peace shall give bond in the sum of three thousand dollars.

Regimental quartermasters shall give bonds in the sum of two thousand dollars, quartermasters of battalions, not a part of a regiment, in the sum of one thousand dollars, conditioned for the faithful discharge of their office.

Section thirty-two which reads as follows, namely:

"SECTION 32. Every brigade commander of the National Guard of Pennsylvania, with his regimental commanders, or such of them as he may select, shall constitute a military board or commission, whose duty it shall be to examine the capacity, qualifications and efficiency of every commissioned officer in his brigade, or who may hereafter be elected; and upon report of said board, if adverse to said officer and approved by the Commander-in-Chief, the commission of such officer shall be vacated or denied, and a new election ordered: *Provided always*, That if any officer shall refuse to report himself, when directed, before such board, the Commander-in-Chief may, upon report of such refusal, declare his commission vacated or refuse the same, and direct a new election; and in case any company shall neglect, within thirty days after the finding of such board, approved by the Commander-in Chief, to elect a suitable officer, the Commander-in-Chief may assign a suitable officer to fill the vacancy in such organization, or disband the same, in his discretion," be and it is hereby amended so that it shall read as follows, namely:

SECTION 32. Every brigade commander of the National

Guard of Pennsylvania, or such of his regimental commanders, or such of them as he may select, shall constitute a military board or commission, whose duty it shall be to examine the capacity, qualifications and efficiency of every commissioned officer in his brigade, or who may hereafter be elected, and upon report of said board, if adverse to said officer and approved by the Commander-in-Chief, the commission of said officer shall be vacated or denied and a new election ordered: *Provided always*, That if any officer shall refuse to report himself, when directed, before such board, the Commander-in-Chief may, upon report of such refusal, declare his commission vacated or refuse the same and direct a new election; and in case any company shall neglect, within thirty days after the finding of such board approved by the Commander-in-Chief, to elect a suitable officer, the Commander-in-Chief may assign a suitable officer to fill the vacancy in such organization or disband the same, in his discretion.

When one or more companies or battalions shall report directly to the division commander, he shall constitute a military board or commission of not exceeding five officers of which he may be one, whose duties and powers shall be, to all intents and purposes, similar to those prescribed for the brigade board or commission, and any officer in commission, or hereafter to be elected or appointed in such companies or battalions, shall report to such board or commission for examination, and on failure so to report or to pass such examination, the commission of such officers shall be vacated or deemed, at the discretion of the Commander-in-Chief, and a new election or appointment shall be ordered, or the said division commander may order such officer before the brigade board with like effect as if he were in or attached to the brigade.

Section forty-eight which reads as follows, namely:

"SECTION 48. No bill or allowance, authorized by the provisions of this act, shall be approved by the military board and paid by the State Treasurer, unless the said bill or allowance is itemized and its correctness duly sworn to or affirmed before an officer authorized by law to administer oaths or affirmations: *Provided*, That the appropriation for the annual current expenses of the National Guard, under the provisions of this act, shall not exceed the sum of three hundred thousand dollars," be and the same is hereby amended to read as follows, namely:

SECTION 48. No bill or allowance authorized by the provisions of this act shall be approved by the military board and paid by the State Treasurer, unless the said bill or allowance is itemized and its correctness duly sworn to or affirmed before an officer authorized by law to administer oaths or affirmations: *Provided*, That the appropriation for the annual current expenses of the

---

Marginal notes:

Brigade military board.

Duties of.

When commission may be vacated.

When Commander-in-Chief may fill vacancies or disband organization.

Military board or commission for company or battalion.

When commission may be vacated. New election, &c.

Section 48, cited for amendment.

Bill to be itemized and sworn to.

Appropriation shall not exceed $320,-000.00.

National Guard shall not exceed the sum of three hundred and twenty thousand dollars.

Section fifty-one which reads as follows, namely:

"SECTION 51. The necessary expenses of general, division and each brigade, regimental and battalion headquarters, including clerk hire and other actual outlays, shall be paid by the Adjutant General, on the usual lawful vouchers to that effect duly sworn or affirmed to by the officer charged with the payment of such expenses; in no event to exceed one thousand dollars per annum for the division, five hundred dollars for each brigade, three hundred dollars for each regiment and one hundred and fifty dollars for each battalion," be and the same is hereby amended to read as follows, namely:

SECTION 51. The necessary expenses of general, division and each brigade, regimental and battalion headquarters, including clerk hire and other actual outlays, shall be paid by the Adjutant General on the usual lawful vouchers to that effect, duly sworn or affirmed to by the officer charged with the payment of such expenses, such expenses in no event to exceed seven hundred and fifty dollars per annum for the division, six hundred dollars for each brigade, four hundred dollars for each regiment, one hundred and fifty dollars for each battalion not a part of a regiment.

Section fifty-eight which reads as follows, namely:

"SECTION 58. The annual appropriations received by the several infantry, cavalry and artillery companies of the Commonwealth, shall be used and expended solely for military purposes and for the use and benefit of the said several organizations," be and the same is hereby amended to read as follows, namely:

SECTION 58. The annual appropriations received by the several infantry, cavalry, artillery, engineer and signal corps companies of the Commonwealth shall be used and expended solely for military purposes and for the use and benefit of the said several organizations.

Section fifty-nine which reads as follows, namely:

"SECTION 59. The commanding officer of each infantry, cavalry and artillery company shall, at each and every annual inspection, return to the Adjutant General an itemized account and statement of all disbursements of the money appropriated during the preceding year to said company, which account and statement shall be verified by the oath or affirmation of such commanding officer, and shall be accompanied by the proper vouchers for such disbursements," be and the same is hereby amended to read as follows, namely:

SECTION 59. The commanding officer of each infantry, cavalry, artillery, engineer and signal corps companies shall, at each and every annual inspection, return to the Adjutant General an itemized account and statement of all disbursements of the money appropriated during the preceding year to said company, which account and statement shall be verified by the proper vouchers for such disbursements.

Section sixty which reads as follows, namely:

"SECTION 60. In every case in which any part of the annual appropriation to the several infantry, cavalry and artillery companies of this Commonwealth shall be used in the purchase, erection or construction of any company armory, the title of the same shall be taken in the name of the State military board, for the use of the Commonwealth of Pennsylvania; and such armory, when so erected, shall be occupied solely for the use and benefit of the said company: *Provided*, That it shall not be lawful for any company to purchase, erect or construct any company armory with the funds so appropriated, either in whole, or in part, until after such company shall have received the consent and approval of its respective regimental and brigade commanders: *And provided further*, That when any such company armory shall, in the judgment and discretion of the Commander-in-Chief, become unnecessary for use as such, he shall cause the same to be sold by the State military board to the highest and best bidder, and the deed of the said State military board shall divest all title and interest of the Commonwealth, and the money so realized from such sale or sales shall be returned to the State Treasury," be and the same is hereby amended to read as follows, namely: Section 60, cited for amendment.

SECTION 60. In every case in which any part of the annual appropriation to the several infantry, cavalry, artillery, engineer and signal corps companies of this Commonwealth shall be used in the purchase, erection or construction of any company armory, the title of the same shall be taken in the name of the State military board for the use of the Commonwealth of Pennsylvania, and such armory, when so erected, shall be occupied solely for the use and benefit of the said company: *Provided*, That it shall not be lawful for any company to purchase, erect or construct any company armory with the funds so appropriated, either in whole or in part, until after such company shall have received the consent and approval of its respective regimental and brigade commanders: *And provided further*, That when any such company armory shall, in the judgment and discretion of the Commander-in-Chief, become unnecessary for use as such, he shall cause the same to be sold by the State military board to the highest and best bidder, and the deed of the said State military shall divest all title and interest of the Commonweath, and the money so realized from such sale or sales shall be returned to the State Treasury. Title to armory.
Shall be used solely for benefit of company.
Consent of commanders must be obtained.
If armory is unnecessary it shall be sold.
Deed of board shall divest title of State.
Proceeds of sale to be returned to State Treasury.

Section seventy-five which reads as follows:

"Every arm, uniform and equipment issued by the State, shall be used only in the discharge of military duty; and any non-commissioned officer or private, who shall willfully or wantonly injure or destroy any uniform, arm or equipment, or other military property belonging Section 75 cited for amendment.

29—LAWS.

to the State, or to the regiment, battalion or company,
and refuse to make good such injury or loss, or who shall
sell, dispose of, secrete or remove the same, with intent
to sell or dispose thereof, or who shall fail, within sixty
days after being notified, to return the same to the State
or his commanding officer, shall be tried by general court-
martial, and sentenced to pay a fine of not more than one
hundred dollars, or, in default of payment of same,
undergo an imprisonment in the county jail of not more
than thirty days, and all clothing, camp and garrison
equipage, ordnance, ordnance stores and quartermaster
stores, issued by the State, or fabricated from material
issued by the State, and charged against the company
allowance, or for which commutation has been paid, shall
be the property of the State of Pennsylvania," be
amended to read as follows, namely :

Use of arms and equipments.

Penalty for damaging or selling same.

SECTION 75. Every arm, uniform or equipment issued
by the State shall be used only in the discharge of military duty, and any non-commissioned officer or private
who shall willfully or wantonly injure or destroy any uniform, arm or equipment or other military property belonging to the State or to the regiment, battalion or company,
or refuse to make good such injury or loss, or who shall
sell, dispose of, secrete or remove the same with intent
to sell or dispose thereof, or who shall fail, within ten
days after being notified, to return the same to the State

Trial by court martial.

or his commanding officer, shall be tried by court-martial
and sentenced to pay a fine of not more than one hundred
dollars, or in default of payment of same undergo an imprisonment in the county jail of not more than thirty

Clothing, stores, &c to be property of the State.

days; and all clothing, camp and garrison equipage,
ordnance, ordnance stores and quartermaster stores issued
by the State or fabricated from material issued by the
State and charged against the company allowance, or for
which commutation has been paid, shall be the property
of the State of Pennsylvania.

Section eighty-two which reads as follows, namely:

Section 82 cited for amendment

"SECTION 82. General courts martial for the trial of enlisted men shall be ordered by the brigade commander
and shall consist of five officers, any three of whom sh
constitute a quorum," be and the same is hereby amended
to read as follows, namely :

Trial of enlisted men.

SECTION 82. General courts martial for the trial of en
listed men of companies and battalions which report di
rectly to the division commander shall be ordered by him
and for the trial of enlisted men of the brigade shall
ordered by the brigade commander, and shall consist
five officers, any three of whom shall constitute a quoru

Court martial for failure to perform duty.

SECTION 105. Any officer or soldier failing to ap
upon any occasion of duty to which he shall be order
by his proper commanding officer shall be subject to
trial by courtmartial, and upon conviction, failing
render good and sufficient cause therefor, he shall

Penalty.

sentenced to pay such fine or undergo such other la
punishment as such courtmartial may direct.

APPROVED—The 10th day of June, A. D. 1893. The comments embraced in the memorandum to House bill No. 147 apply, in some degree, to the present bill. In the copy submitted for my approval, and which must be strictly followed in the publication of the statutes, one page of the bill has been twice repeated, with a slight change in the title of the bill. As the bill in the form in which it should have been transcribed has no objectionable feature, I have given it my approval, and have no doubt the courts will construe and enforce it as it was the intention of the Legislature that it should be enacted. I am not willing that that intention should be defeated nor frustrated by the carelessness of the transcribing clerks, none the less deem it my duty to the public to thus call attention to these defects in the hope that it may have some effect in preventing a recurrence of such blunders.

ROBT. E. PATTISON.

No. 322.

AN ACT

Enabling the taxpayers of townships and road districts to contract for making, at their own expense, the roads, and paying salaries of township or road district officers and thereby preventing the levy and collection of road tax therein.

SECTION 1. *Be it enacted, &c.,* That from and after the passage of this act any one or more taxpayers of any township or road district may acquire the right to furnish all the materials and labor necessary for opening, making, amending and repairing the public highways and bridges of said township or road district in manner and under the conditions in the subsequent sections of this act set out. Taxpayers may acquire right to make and repair public highways and bridges.

SECTION 2. Any one or more taxpayers desirous of acquiring the said right shall, before the beginning of any township fiscal year, present to the court of quarter sessions of the county in which the township or road district is situate as to which said right is desired, setting out that he, she, it or they are the owners of property assessed and taxed for road purposes in said township or road district, the approximate number of miles of public road in said township or road district, and the desire and ability of the petitioner or petitioners to lay out, open, make, amend and repair the public highways and bridges of said township or road district wholly at his, her, its or their own expense, for the ensuing township fiscal year, and to pay the other expenses of said township as in this act provided for, without any right against or claim upon said township or road district for or by reason of the materials, labor or money so furnished: *Provided,* That the supervisor or supervisors are hereby required to view and inspect the making and

Proceedings to be had before court of quarter sessions.

Proviso.

repairing of the public roads in said townships at least
once during every month, and be fully satisfied that the
petitioners have fully complied with their contract before final settlement and expiration of contract: *And*

Proviso.

provided further, If at any time the supervisors shall
see that any portion of said road needs repair, he shall
notify said petitioners to repair the same, and in case
said petitioners shall fail to repair said road within five
days after notice as aforesaid, the supervisor is empowered to purchase such materials and employ such
men as may be necessary to repair said road and charge
the same to said petitioners.

Bond.

SECTION 3. That with the said petition shall be presented a bond in a sum equal to five hundred dollars for
each and every mile of public road in said township or
road district, to be properly executed by said petitioners,
with one or more sureties to be approved by said court,
and payable to the said township or road district conditioned for the faithful performance of said petitioner or
petitioners of his, her, its or their duty under the provisions of this act, and to save said township harmless from
any loss or claim by reason of failure so to perform said
duty.

Notice of intention
of presenting petit-
ion and bonds to be
given.

SECTION 4. Notice of the intention of presenting the
petition and bond in the preceding section set out, and
of the time when said petition and bond will be presented
to the said court shall be given at least ten days before
the same are so presented to the supervisor or supervisors and auditors of said township or to the road commissioners of said road district.

When contract shall
be entered into with
petitioners.

SECTION 5. That upon said petition, bond and proof of
the notice required in the preceding section hereof being
presented to the said court, the same shall be ordered to
be filed, and the court being satisfied of the good faith
of the petitioners and the sufficiency of the petition, bond
and notice shall order and direct the supervisor or supervisors of such township or road commissioners of such
road district, on behalf of the township or road district
they represent, to enter into a contract with the said
petitioner or petitioners whereby the said petitioner or
petitioners shall bind him, her or itself on themselves:

What contract shall
contain.

First. To open, make, amend and repair the public
highways and bridges of said township or road district
for the ensuing fiscal year thereof in a lawful and workmanlike manner, wholly at the expense of the said petitioner or petitioners, and without creating thereby any
claim upon or right against said township for or by reason of the materials, labor or money for such person employed.

Second. To indemnify and save harmless the said
township or road district from all claim, damage, cost or
expense of whatever kind for or by reason of any act or
omission of said petitioner or petitioners, whereby any
claim, suit or other demand may be set up or recovered
against said township or road district.

Third. To pay, within sixty days from the beginning of said fiscal year, to the following officers of such township or road district the following sums to be received by said officers in full for all demands against such township or road district for their respective services as such officers to said township or road district for the fiscal year for which the said contract is made with such petitioner or petitioners, namely: To the township clerk, the sum of fifty dollars; to each of the auditors of such township, the sum of twenty-five dollars; and to an attorney to be elected by such supervisors or road commissioners as counsel for said township or road district, the sum of fifty dollars; to each supervisor or road commission, the sum of two hundred and fifty dollars.

SECTION 6. In consideration of the obligations in the preceding section set out to be assumed and performed by the said petitioner or petitioners, the said supervisor or supervisors or road commissioners, on behalf of such township or road districts, shall stipulate the said township will not assess, levy or collect any tax for road purposes during the fiscal year for which such contract is made.

Taxes shall not be assessed or collected for road purposes during year for which contract is made.

SECTION 7. All acts or parts of acts of Assembly in conflict with any of the provisions of this act are hereby repealed.

Repeal.

APPROVED—The 12th day of June, A. D. 1893.

ROBT. E. PATTISON.

No. 323.

AN ACT

Providing a system whereby cities may pave streets and alleys, pay the cost thereof by the issue of bonds and collect the same from the property benefited, in instalments.

SECTION 1. *Be it enacted, &c.,* That in addition to the present method provided by law for the payment and collection of the costs and expense of the permanent paving and improvement of any streets, alleys and other highways, or parts thereof, by the cities of this Commonwealth, said cities shall have power to ordain that said costs and expense may be paid and collected in accordance with the provisions of this act.

Additional powers given cities in the collection of costs, &c., for paving, &c.

SECTION 2. In order to provide for the payment of the cost and expense of such improvements, the councils of the cities of this Commonwealth may, from time to time, issue their bonds in such sums as may be required, in all to an amount not exceeding the cost and expense of such improvement and interest thereon.

Councils may issue bonds.

Said bonds shall bear the name of the street or alley to be improved. They shall be payable at a period not less than five years from the date of their issue, to be provided in the ordinance directing the improvement, and

Bonds shall bear name of street. Time of payment.

bear interest at a rate not exceeding six per centum per annum, payable semi-annually, on the first day of July and January.

SECTION 3. In all cases where it may be necessary to obtain the assent of the electors to an issue of bonds, the question of thus increasing the city debt shall be so submitted to the electors that they shall have the opportunity of voting for or against the issue of bonds for the improvement of any particular street or alley, separately and apart from the question of increasing the city debt for the improvement of any other street or alley.

SECTION 4. Said bonds shall be negotiated at not less than par as other bonds of said cities are negotiated, and the proceeds thereof applied solely to the payment of the cost of said improvement. The contract price of the same and interest thereon to the first day, when interest thereon is payable, shall be taken as the cost of said improvement, to be assessed on the property benefitted, according to existing laws in each of said cities.

SECTION 5. Such assessments shall be entered in the proper municipal lien and judgment docket in the prothonotary's office, and shall, if filed within six months from the completion of the improvements, without the issuing of a *scire facias* to revive, remain a first lien upon the property assessed until fully paid, having precedence of all other liens, except taxes, and shall not be diverted by any judicial sale, unless the payment of the same is provided for from the proceeds of such sale.

The assessment shall state the name of the city claimant, the name of the owner or reputed owner, a reasonable description of the property, the amount claimed to be due, for what improvement the claim is made, and the time when the assessment was finally confirmed or made.

SECTION 6. Such assessment shall be payable at the city treasurer's office in equal, semi-annual instalments, with interest, at the rate provided in said bonds, from the date to which interest was computed on the amount of the assessments, or so much as remains unpaid from time to time, until all said assessments and interest are fully paid. The money so received by the city treasurer shall be applied to the sinking fund.

SECTION 7. In case of default in the payment of any semi-annual instalment of said assessment and interest for a period of sixty days after the same shall become due and payable, the entire assessment and accrued interest shall become due and payable and the city solicitor shall proceed to collect the same under the provisions of general laws creating and regulating municipal liens and proceedings thereon.

SECTION 8. Any owner of property against whom an assessment shall have been made for such improvement shall have the right to pay the same, or any part remaining unpaid, in full with interest thereon to the next semi-annual payment due on said assessment; such payment shall discharge the lien. If any owner shall sub-divide any property after such lien attaches, he, in like manner, may discharge the same upon any sub-divided portion thereof by paying the amount for which said part would be liable.

APPROVED—The 12th day of June, A. D. 1893. The main purposes of this bill seem to be proper and commendable, and its effect will be to relieve, in some measure, the hardships occasionally resulting from inordinate assessments upon real estate for municipal street improvements; but if it was the intention of the framers of the bill, in the language of section five, to make municipal liens filed under this bill take precedence of mortgages and other liens of record before the filing of such municipal claims, I am of the opinion that such a provision is and will be held by the courts to be invalid, as tending to disturb the validity of liens and to impair existing contracts. It is likely, however, that this section will be construed by the courts to apply only to liens of record entered after the municipal liens contemplated by this bill.

ROBT. E. PATTISON.

———

No. 324.

AN ACT

Entitled "A further supplement to the act regulating elections in this Commonwealth", approved the thirtieth day of January, Anno Domini one thousand eight hundred and seventy-four, as amended by the act of May twenty-ninth, one thousand eight hundred and ninety-one, fixing the place at which the assessors shall sit to perform the duties imposed upon them by the second section of the said supplement of May twenty-ninth, one thousand eight hundred and ninety-one, in all voting districts or precincts in this Commonwealth where temporary voting places are or may be established.

SECTION 1. *Be it enacted, &c.*, That it shall be the duty of the assessor in all voting districts or precincts in this Commonwealth, where temporary voting places are or may be established, to be present at his place of residence in said election district or precinct during the two secular days next preceding the day fixed by the third section of the act of May twenty-ninth, one thousand eight hundred and ninety-one, being a supplement to the act of January thirtieth, Anno Domini one thousand eight hundred and seventy-four, for returning the list to the county commissioners, from ten ante meridian to three post meridian, and from six post meridian to nine post meridian of each of said days, to perform all the duties as set forth in section two of the act of May twenty-ninth, one thousand eight hundred and ninety-one, being a supplement to the act of January thirtieth, one thousand eight hundred and seventy-four.

Assessor shall sit at his residence, when temporary voting place is established.

APPROVED—The 12th day of June, A. D. 1893.

ROBT. E. PATTISON.

No. 325.

AN ACT

Making an appropriation to the Adrian Hospital Association, Jefferson county, Pennsylvania.

$16,000.00 total appropriation.

SECTION 1. *Be it enacted,* &c., That the sum of sixteen thousand dollars, or so much thereof as may be necessary, be and the same is hereby specifically appropriated to the Adrian Hospital Association in Jefferson county, Pennsylvania, for the following purpose, namely : The sum of ten thousand dollars, or so much thereof as may be necessary, for the support and maintenance of the hospital for the two fiscal years beginning June first, one thousand eight hundred and ninety-three.

$10,000.00 for maintenance.

$6,000.00 for new buildings.

And the sum of six thousand dollars, or so much thereof as may be necessary, for the purpose of assisting in the erection and furnishing of new hospital buildings: *Provided,* That no part of the appropriation for building and furnishing shall become available, until the treasurer of said association shall have certified, under oath to the Auditor General, that the association has become the owner, in fee simple, of a site upon which to erect a hospital building and are prepared to build thereon, and that the sum of six thousand dollars, exclusive of the value of the ground, has been subscribed by private contributions and paid in cash into the treasury of said hospital association for the purpose of assisting in the erection and furnishing said hospital building.

When amount for buildings shall become available.

How payable.

The said appropriation to be paid on the warrant of the Auditor General on a settlement made by him and the State Treasurer, but no warrant shall be drawn on settlement made until the directors or managers of said institution shall have made, under oath to the Auditor General, a report containing a specifically itemized statement of the receipts from all sources and expenses of said institution, together with a specifically itemized statement of the cost of erection and furnishing said new hospital building during the previous quarter, with the cash balance on hand, and the same is approved by him and the State Treasurer, nor until the Treasurer shall have sufficient money in the treasury, not otherwise appropriated, to pay the quarterly instalments due said institution ; and unexpended balances of sums appropriated for specific purposes shall not be used for other purposes, whether specific or general, and shall revert to the State Treasury at the close of the two fiscal years.

Itemized statement.

Unexpended balances shall revert to the State Treasury.

APPROVED—The 12th day of June, A. D. 1893. The amounts included in the foregoing are in excess of those originally recommended by the Board of Public Charities; but in a written communication from the Board sent to me under date of June 7, 1893, the amounts appropriated as above have, after further consideration, been recommended by the Board.

ROBT. E. PATTISON.

No. 326.

AN ACT

Making an appropriation to the Home for Friendless Children of the city of Reading, Pennsylvania.

SECTION 1. *Be it enacted, &c.*, That the sum of two thousand dollars, or so much thereof as may be necessary, be and the same is hereby specifically appropriated to the Home for Friendless Children of the city of Reading, Pennsylvania, for the maintenance of the inmates of the said home for the two fiscal years commencing June first, one thousand eight hundred and ninety-three. *$2,000.00 appropriated*

The said appropriation to be paid on the warrant of the Auditor General on a settlement made by him and the State Treasurer, but no warrant shall be drawn on settlement made until the directors or managers of said institution shall have made, under oath to the Auditor General, a report containing a specifically itemized statement of the receipts from all sources and expenses of said institution during the previous quarter, with the cash balance on hand, and the same is approved by him and the State Treasurer, nor until the Treasurer shall have sufficient money in the treasury, not otherwise appropriated, to pay the quarterly instalments due said institution ; and unexpended balances of sums appropriated for specific purposes shall not be used for other purposes, whether specific or general, and shall revert to the State Treasury at the close of the two fiscal years. *How payable.* *Itemized statement.* *Unexpended balances shall revert to the State Treasury.*

APPROVED—The 12th day of June, A. D. 1893. The amount included in the foregoing was not recommended by the Board of Public Charities in their published report ; but in a written communication from the Board sent to me under date of June 7, 1893, the amount appropriated as above has, after consideration, been recommended by the Board.

ROBT. E. PATTISON.

No. 327.

AN ACT

To provide for the erection, maintenance and regulation of public morgues in the several counties of this Commonwealth, for the care and disposal of bodies removed thereto, and providing for the payment of certain expenses of the same by the proper county or district or by the estate of the deceased person, and providing for the disposal of the personal effects of unclaimed dead.

SECTION 1. *Be it enacted, &c.*,

First. That the county commissioners of each and every county in the Commonwealth shall be and are hereby authorized, upon presentment of two successive *County commissioners under certain conditions, to erect and maintain a morgue.*

grand juries of the county, to buy or rent real estate and erect and maintain a morgue thereon at the expense of said county for the reception and care of the bodies of all deceased persons upon whom it may be necessary to hold a coroner's inquest, and such other bodies as may be received by permit of the coroner of the county, the location of said morgue to be approved by the county commissioners and a judge of the court of common pleas of said county and the coroner of the county.

Second. Whenever a dead body may be found in any public place, or the body of any deceased person who is unknown or having no residence convenient to the place where found, the same shall be removed to the morgue so established, unless the coroner or his deputy shall direct its removal to some other place

Third. The coroner of any county in which a morgue shall be established shall make general rules and regulations for its government and control, and shall appoint a suitable person or persons to have charge of the same, who shall be removable at the pleasure of the coroner, and he shall receive a salary to be fixed by the county commissioners (or salary board if such exists) and approved by a judge of the court of common pleas for said county and payable out of the general funds of the county as the balance of county officers are by law payable: *Provided,* That no more than one person shall be appointed, except by the approval of the county commissioners.

Fourth. All bodies received at said morgue shall, if the coroner deems it necessary, be properly embalmed or prepared for preservation for such length of time as he may think proper, (and shall be subjected to examination and inspection by such persons as he may, in writing, authorize to view the same or who may be admitted in his presence,) and said body or bodies shall be removed for burial only upon his certificate.

Fifth. The county commissioners, where any such morgue shall have been established, shall purchase and maintain an ambulance with one or more horses for the removal of bodies to and from said morgue, and for the burial of unknown or unclaimed bodies, the cost of maintaining which shall be paid out of the funds of said county.

Sixth. That all clothing and personal property of deceased persons received in such morgue, who are unknown or unclaimed, shall be retained at said morgue under charge of the coroner for the period of one year, unless sooner claimed by the legal representatives of the deceased, and at the end of one year may be sold at public sale, after advertisement by publication in one or more newspapers in said county once a week for three weeks, and by not less than six hand bills posted in the neighborhood of said morgue.

Seventh. All fees received for services or connected with said morgue and the proceeds of all sales of per-

Marginal notes

Location of morgue.

Deceased persons to be removed to morgue.

Coroner to make rules for government of morgue.

And to appoint a person or persons to have charge of same.

Salary.

How payable.

Proviso.

Care of bodies.

Subject to examination and inspection.

To be removed for burial only upon certificate.

County commissioners to furnish ambulance and horses for removal and burial of bodies.

Cost of same, how paid.

Unclaimed clothing and personal property to be retained by coroner for one year.

After one year may be sold py public sale after advertisement by publication.

Fees for services and proceeds of all sales to be paid into the county treasury.

sonal property as provided in this act shall be paid into the county treasury of the proper county upon the first day of each month, of which the coroner of the county shall make report in writing, under oath, at the time of said payment. *Coroners shall make report.*

APPROVED—The 12th day of June, A. D. 1893.

ROBT. E. PATTISON.

No. 328.

AN ACT

To regulate the confinement and trial of infants under the age of sixteen years.

SECTION 1. *Be it enacted, &c.,* That no child under restraint or conviction, under sixteen years of age, shall be placed in any apartment or cell of any prison or place of confinement, or in any court room during the trial of adults, or in any vehicle of transportation in company with adults charged with or convicted of crime. *Confinement of infants under sixteen years of age.*

SECTION 2. All cases involving the commitment or trial of children for any crime or misdemeanor, before any magistrate or justice of the peace, or in any court, may be heard and determined by such court at suitable times to be designated therefor by it, separate and apart from the trial of other criminal cases, of which session a separate docket and record shall be kept. *Trial of children may be separate and apart from trial of other criminal cases.* *Separate docket and record*

APPROVED—The 12th day of June, A. D. 1893.

ROBT. E. PATTISON.

No. 329.

AN ACT

To amend the first section of an act, entitled "An act in relations to the laying out, opening, widening, straightening, extending or vacating streets and alleys, and the construction of bridges in the several municipalities of this Commonwealth, the grading, paving, macadamizing or otherwise improving streets and alleys, providing for ascertaining the damages to private property resulting therefrom, the assessment of the damages, costs and expenses thereof upon the property benefitted, and the construction of sewers and payment of the damages, costs and expenses thereof, including damages to private property resulting therefrom," approved the sixteenth day of May, Anno Domini one thousand eight hundred and ninety-one, providing for assessment of damages where streets and alleys are changed in grade or location.

SECTION 1. *Be it enacted, &c.,* That the first section of an act, entitled "An act in relation to the laying out, opening, widening, straightening, extending or vacating streets and alleys, and the construction of bridges in the

several municipalities of this Commonwealth, the grading, paving, macadamizing or otherwise improving streets
and alleys, providing for ascertaining the damages to
private property resulting therefrom, the assessment of
the damages, costs and expenses thereof upon the property benefitted, and the construction of sewers and payment of the damages, costs and expenses thereof, including damages to private property resulting therefrom,"
approved the sixteenth day of May, Anno Domini one
thousand eight hundred and ninety-one, which reads as
follows:

Section 1, of Act of
May 16, 1891, cited
for amendment.

"SECTION 1. *Be it enacted by the Senate and House of
Representatives of the Commonwealth of Pennsylvania in
General Assembly met, and it is hereby enacted by the authority of the same,* That all municipal corporations of
this Commonwealth shall have power, whenever it shall
be deemed necessary in the laying out, opening, widening, extending or grading of streets, lanes or alleys, the
construction of bridges and the piers and abutments
therefor, the construction of slopes, embankments and
sewers, the changing of water courses or vacation of
streets or alleys, to take, use, occupy or injure private
lands, property or material, and in case the compensation for the damages or the benefits accruing therefrom
have not been agreed upon, any court of common pleas
of the proper county, or any law judge thereof in vacation, on application thereto by petition by said municipal corporation or any person interested, shall appoint
three discreet and disinterested freeholders as viewers,
and appoint a time not less than twenty nor more than
thirty days thereafter when said viewers shall meet upon
the line of improvement and view the same and the
premises affected thereby. The said viewers shall give
at least ten days' notice of the time of their first meeting
by publication in one or more newspapers of said corporation of the county in which it is situate, and where the
publication is in more than than one newspaper, one of
said newspapers may be in the German language, and
by handbills posted upon the premises, or otherwise, as
the said court shall direct, having regard to the circumstances of the case," be and the same is hereby amended
to read as follows:

Extending power of
municipal corporat-
ions to change grade
or lines of streets,
lanes or alleys, and
and providing for
assessment of dam-
ages.

SECTION 1. That all municipal corporations of this
Commonwealth shall have power, whenever it shall be
deemed necessary in the laying out, opening, widening,
extending, grading or changing grade or lines of streets,
lanes or alleys, the construction of bridges and the piers
and abutments therefor, the construction of slopes, embankments and sewers, the changing of water courses or
vacation of streets or alleys, to take, use, occupy or injure private lands, property or material, and in case the
compensation for the damages or the benefits accruing
therefrom have not been agreed upon, any court of common pleas of the proper county, or any law judge thereof
in vacation, on application thereto by petition by said

municipal corporation or any person interested, shall appoint three discreet and disinterested freeholders as viewers, and appoint a time not less than twenty nor more than thirty days thereafter when said viewers shall meet upon the line of the improvement and view the same and the premises affected thereby. The said viewers shall give at least ten days' notice of the time of their first meeting by publication in one or more newspapers of said corporation of the county in which it is situate, and where the publication is in more than one newspaper, one of said newspapers may be in the German language, and by handbills posted upon the premises, or otherwise, as the said court shall direct, having regard to the circumstances of the case.

APPROVED—The 12th day of June, A. D. 1893.

ROBT. E. PATTISON.

No. 330.

AN ACT

Relating to sale of the real estate of decedents.

SECTION 1. *Be it enacted, &c.*, That whenever any person shall die seized of real estate and the parties in interest desire the same to be converted into money for distribution it shall be lawful for the orphans' court of the proper county, in its discretion, upon the joint petition of the widow and heirs and the guardians or committees of such as are minors or under disabilities, in whom the real estate of the decedent shall have vested by descent or will, setting forth the description of the property, the desire to have the same sold, to order the executor, administrator or a trustee to make sale after he shall have given bond with one or more sureties in double the appraised value of the real estate, to be approved by the court, and proceed thereafter in all respects in the manner now provided by existing laws in cases of the sale of real estate under proceedings in partition, and the proceeds of such sale after the payment of the expenses thereof shall be distributed to and among those entitled thereto, the same as real estate: *Provided*, That such sale shall have the same effect in all respects as a public sale in proceedings in partition of real estate under existing laws.

APPROVED—The 12th day of June, A. D. 1893.

ROBT. E. PATTISON.

Orphan's court may, upon petition, order sale of real estate of decedents.

Bond.

Proceeds of sale.

How distributed.

Proviso.

No. 331.

AN ACT

To provide for the election of one person to fill the offices of prothonotary, clerk of the courts of general quarter sessions and oyer and terminer, and one other person to fill the office of register of wills, recorder of deeds, and clerk of the orphans' court, in counties containing forty thousand inhabitants, and not heretofore created a separate judicial district under Constitution.

Counties containing 40,000 inhabitants not heretofore created a separate judicial district shall elect one person prothonotary, &c., and another person register, &c.

SECTION 1. *Be it enacted, &c*, That in each of the counties of the Commonwealth containing forty thousand inhabitants, and not heretofore created a judicial district under section five, article five of the Constitution, there shall be elected one person to fill the offices of prothonotary, clerk of the court of general quarter sessions and oyer and terminer, and another person to fill the offices of clerk of the orphans' court, register of wills and recorder of deeds at the expiration of the terms of the persons now filling and exercising such offices in such counties, and the persons so elected shall hold such offices for

To hold office under existing laws.

the time and under the terms provided by existing laws therefor.

APPROVED—The 12th day of June, A. D. 1893.

ROBT. E. PATTISON.

No. 332.

A SUPPLEMENT

To an act, entitled "An act to fix the salaries of the several State officers of the Commonwealth, the number of clerks to be employed in the several departments and their compensation, and providing for the incidental expenses of said departments," approved May fourteenth, one thousand eight hundred and seventy-four, providing for an increase in the salary of the Lieutenant Governor, and in the salaries of the chief clerk and corporation clerk in the Auditor General's Department and office of Secretary of the Commonwealth, and the chief clerk in the office of the Attorney General.

Increase in salary of Lieutenant Governor and certain clerks.

SECTION 1. *Be it enacted, &c.*, That the salary of the Lieutenant Governor shall be five thousand dollars per annum; the salaries of the chief clerk and corporation clerk in the Auditor General's Department shall be three thousand dollars per annum, instead of eighteen hundred dollars as heretofore provided; that the salary of the chief clerk and corporation clerk in the State Department shall be twenty-two hundred dollars each per annum instead of eighteen hundred dollars and sixteen hundred dollars, respectively, as heretofore provided, and that the salary of the chief clerk in the Attorney General's Department shall be twenty-two hundred dollars per annum, instead of sixteen hundred dollars as heretofore provided.

SECTION 2. That all acts or parts of acts, special or Repeal. general, inconsistent herewith are hereby repealed.

APPROVED—The 12th day of June, A. D. 1893.

ROBT. E. PATTISON.

No. 333.

AN ACT

To amend an act, entitled "An act limiting the time for the completion of railroads by corporations organized by purchasers at judicial sales," approved the twenty-fifth day of June, Anno Domini one thousand eight hundred and eighty-five, extending the provisions of said act so as to embrace corporations organized by purchasers of railroads at sales under or by virtue of powers of sale contained in mortgages or deeds of trust, without any process or decree of court.

SECTION 1. *Be it enacted, &c.*, That the act of Assembly entitled "An act limiting the time for the completion of railroads by corporations organized by purchasers at judicial sales," approved the twenty-fifth day of June, Anno Domini one thousand eight hundred and eighty-five, which reads as follows: "That whenever any railroad of any corporation by or under any law of this State shall have been sold, or shall hereafter be sold and conveyed under and by virtue of any process or decree of any court of this State, or of the circuit court of the United States, and the person or persons for or on whose account such railroad was purchased, or may hereafter be purchased, shall have proceeded to organize a new corporation under existing laws of this Commonwealth, such new corporation so organized shall have a period of five years from the date of the organization of such corporation for the completion of such railroad: *Provided*, Such new corporation shall, before being to the benefits of this act, duly accept the provisions of the existing Constitution of this Commonwealth in the manner provided by law," be amended so as to read as follows:

That whenever any railroad or any corporation by or under any law of this State shall have been sold, or shall hereafter be sold and conveyed, under and by virtue of any process or decree of any court of this State, or of the circuit court of the United States, or under or by virtue of a power of sale contained in any mortgage or deed of trust, without any process or decree of a court in the premises, and the person or persons for or on whose account such railroad was purchased or may hereafter be purchased, shall have proceeded to organize a new corporation under existing laws of this Commonwealth, such new corporation so organized shall have a period of five years from the date of the organization of such corporation for the completion of such railroad: *Provided*, Such new corporation shall, before being entitled to the bene-

Act of June 25. 1885, cited for amendment.

Extending provisions to purchasers at sales contained in any mortgage or deed of trust without process or decree of court.

fits of this act, duly accept the provisions of the existing Constitution of this Commonwealth in the manner provided by law.

APPROVED—The 16th day of June, A. D. 1893.

ROBT. E. PATTISON.

No. 334.

AN ACT

To validate partitions of real estate in cases of testacy made in orphans' courts prior to the act of ninth of May, one thousand eight hundred and eighty-nine.

SECTION 1. *Be it enacted, &c.*, That all valuations and partitions of real estate in cases of testacy made in any orphans' court of this Commonwealth before the act of ninth of May, one thousand eight hundred and eighty-nine, entitled "An act to enlarge the jurisdiction of the orphans' courts in cases of testacy," shall be valid and of the same effect as if the proceedings under which said valuations and partitions were made, had been commenced and instituted prior to the passage of said act of ninth of May, one thousand eight hundred and eighty-nine: *Provided however,* That this act shall not affect any judicial decrees heretofore made or apply to pending litigation.

Proviso.

APPROVED—The 16th day of June, A. D. 1893.

ROBT. E. PATTISON.

No. 335.

AN ACT

Making an appropriation to the Children's Aid Society of Pennsylvania.

$15,000.00 appropriated.

SECTION 1. *Be it enacted, &c.*, That the sum of fifteen thousand dollars, or so much thereof as may be necessary, be and the same is hereby specifically appropriated to the Children's Aid Society of Pennsylvania for the purpose of maintenance and prosecution of its work for the two fiscal years beginning June first, one thousand eight hundred and ninety-three

How payable.

The said appropriation to be paid on the warrant of the Auditor General on a settlement made by him and the State Treasurer, but no warrant shall be drawn on settlement made until the directors or managers of said society shall have made, under oath to the Auditor General, a report containing a specifically itemized statement of the receipts from all sources and expenses of said society during the previous quarter, with the cash balance on hand, and the same is approved by him and the State Treasurer, nor until the Treasurer shall have sufficient

Itemised statement.

money in the treasury, not otherwise appropriated, to pay the quarterly instalments due said society; and unexpended balances of sums appropriated for specific purposes shall not be used for other purposes, whether specific or general, and shall revert to the State Treasury at the close of the two fiscal years.

APPROVED—The 16th day of June, A. D. 1893.

ROBT. E. PATTISON.

Unexpended balances shall revert to State Treasury.

No. 336.

AN ACT

Making an appropriation to pay the indebtedness of the Children's Aid Society of Western Pennsylvania.

SECTION 1 *Be it enacted, &c.*, That the sum of two thousand dollars, or so much thereof as may be necessary, be and the same is hereby specifically appropriated to the Childrens' Aid Society of Western Pennsylvania for the purpose of paying an indebtedness incurred for the maintenance of said society and the prosecution of its work during the two fiscal years ending June first, one thousand eight hundred and ninety-three.

$2,000.00 appropriated.

The said appropriation to be paid on the warrant of the Auditor General on a settlement made by him and the State Treasurer, but no warrant shall be drawn on settlement made until the directors or managers of said society shall have made, under oath to the Auditor General, a report containing a specifically itemized statement of the indebtedness of said society and the same is approved by him and the State Treasurer, nor until the Treasurer shall have sufficient money in the treasury, not otherwise appropriated, to pay the appropriation due said society; and unexpended balance of sums appropriated for specific purposes shall not be used for other purposes, whether specific or general.

How payable.

Itemized statement.

Unexpended balance shall not be used for other purposes.

APPROVED—The 16th day of June, A. D. 1893.

ROBT. E. PATTISON.

No. 337.

AN ACT

Making an appropriation to mark with a permanent monument the point known as Cherrytree or Canoe Place.

SECTION 1. *Be it enacted, &c.*, That the sum of fifteen hundred dollars, or so much thereof as may be necessary, be and the same is hereby specifically appropriated to erect a monument, with appropriate and suitable inscriptions, marking the exact spot known as Canoe Place, being a point on the boundary of the purchase of Governor Penn from the Indians; the design of the monu-

$1,500.00 appropriated.

30—LAWS.

ment to be approved by and the money expended under the direction of the Board of Public Grounds and Buildings of this Commonwealth.

The said appropriation to be paid on the warrant of the Auditor General upon a settlement made by him and the State Treasurer, upon itemized vouchers duly certified to by the Board of Public Grounds and Buildings.

APPROVED—The 16th day of June, A. D. 1893.

ROBT. E. PATTISON.

No. 388.

AN ACT

To amend an act, entitled "An act authorizing companies incorporated under the 'aws of any other State of the United States for the manufacture of any form of iron, steel or glass to erect and maintain buildings and manufacturing establishments, and to take, have and hold real estate necessary and proper for manufacturing purposes," approved the ninth day of June, Anno Domini one thousand eight hundred and eighty-one, extending the same to companies formed for the purpose of quarrying slate, granite, stone or rocks or for dressing, polishing, working or manufacturing the same, or any of them, and to mineral springs companies incorporated for the purpose of bottling and selling natural mineral springs water.

SECTION 1. *Be it enacted, &c.,* That section one of an act, entitled "An act authorizing companies incorporated under the laws of any other State of the United States for the manufacture of any form of iron, steel or glass to erect and maintain buildings and manufacturing establishments, and to take, have and hold real estate necessary and proper for manufacturing purposes," approved the ninth day of June, Anno Domini one thousand eight hundred and eighty-one, which reads as follows:

"That it shall and may be lawful for any company incorporated under the laws of any other State for the manufacture of any form of iron, steel or glass, to erect and maintain buildings and manufacturing establishments within this commonwealth, and to take, have and hold real estate not exceeding one hundred acres necessary and proper for such manufacturing purposes: *Provided,* That nothing herein contained shall be deemed to prevent or relieve real estate taken and held by any such company under the provisions of this statute from being taxed in like manner with other real estate within this Commonwealth: *And provided further,* That no foreign corporation shall be entitled to employ any greater amount of capital in any such business in this State than the same kind of corporation organized under the laws of this State are entitled to employ: *And provided further,* That every such foreign corporation, doing business as aforesaid in this Commonwealth, shall be liable to taxation to an amount not exceeding that imposed on corporations organized for similar purposes under the laws of this State, and every such foreign corporation taking the benefit of this act shall make the same returns to the Auditor General that are now required by laws of the corporations of this State," be amended to read as follows:

That it shall and may be lawful for any company incorporated under the laws of any other State for the manufacture of any form of iron, steel or glass or for the quarrying of slate, granite, stone or rocks of any kind, or for dressing, polishing or manufacturing the same, or any of them, or for any mineral springs company incorporated for the purpose of bottling and selling natural mineral spring water, to erect and maintain buildings and manufacturing establishments within this Commonwealth, and to take, have and hold real estate not exceeding one hundred acres necessary and proper for corporate purposes: *Provided,* That nothing herein contained shall be deemed to prevent or relieve real estate taken and held by any such company under the provisions of this statute from being taxed in like manner with other real estate within this Commonwealth: *And provided further,* That no foreign corporation shall be entitled to employ any greater amount of capital in any such business in this State than the same kind of corporations organized under the laws of this State are entitled to employ: *And provided further,* That every such foreign corporation, doing business as aforesaid in this Commonwealth, shall be liable to taxation to an amount not exceeding that imposed on corporations organized for similar purposes under the laws of this State, and every such foreign corporation taking the benefit of this act shall make the same returns to the Auditor General that are now required by laws of the corporation of this State.

APPROVED—The 16th day of June, A. D. 1893.

ROBT. E. PATTISON.

Marginal note: Extending power to companies formed for the purpose of quarrying slate, granite, stone or rocks, or for dressing, polishing or manufacturing the same, and to mineral springs companies for bottling and selling natural mineral spring water.

No. 339.

AN ACT

To provide for the payment of per diem compensation to Frank B. Reese, a member of Company B, Thirteenth Regiment of the National Guard of Pennsylvania, during the time of his disability produced by typhoid fever which he contracted in the service at Homestead, Pennsylvania.

WHEREAS, Frank B. Reese, a private of Company B of said regiment of the National Guard of Pennsylvania, who was called into the service of the State during the recent riots at Homestead, Allegheny county, was taken ill with typhoid fever as a result of his exposure during his said service in the National Guard, and was confined to his home on account of such illness until the first day of November, one thousand eight hundred and ninety-two;

And whereas, The Adjutant General in paying him for his services gave him compensation to the twenty-ninth day of July, one thousand eight hundred and ninety-two, the date at which he was relieved from duty;

And whereas, By reason of such service and the sickness referred to he was unable to do any duty until November first, one thousand eight hundred and ninety-two, thereby losing his time and his opportunity to earn a daily compensation; therefore,

Compensation to Frank B. Reese.

SECTION 1. *Be it enacted, &c.,* That the State Treasurer be and is hereby authorized and empowered to pay the said Frank B. Reese one hundred and forty-one dollars, being his allowance as a private of said regiment from the twenty-ninth day of July, one thousand eight hundred and ninety-two, until the first day of November, one thousand eight hundred and ninety-two.

How paid.

Said sum of money to be paid out of any money in the treasury, not otherwise appropriated, upon warrants to be drawn by the Auditor General in the usual manner.

APPROVED—The 16th day of June, A. D. 1893.

ROBT. E. PATTISON.

No. 340.

AN ACT

To amend sections one and three of an act, entitled "An act providing for the classification of real estate for purposes of taxation and for the appointment of assessors in cities of the second class," approved the fifth day of May, Anno Domini one thousand eight hundred and seventy-six, so as to authorize councils of such cities to fix the salary of the board of assessors, and fixing the basis for the determination of classification of said real estate.

Section 1 of Act of May 5, 1876, cited for amendment.

SECTION 1. *Be it enacted, &c.,* That section one of the act of the General Assembly approved the fifth day of May, Anno Domini one thousand eight hundred and seventy-six, entitled "An act providing for the classification of real estate for purposes of taxation and for the appointment of assessors in cities of the second class," which reads as follows:

"SECTION 1. *Be it enacted by the Senate and House of Representatives of the Commonwealth of Pennsylvania in General Assembly met, and it is hereby enacted by the authority of the same,* That the city council of any city of the second class shall, immediately after the passage of this act, and every third year thereafter, elect three resident citizens of such city as a board of assessors to make, revise or alter assessments of all subjects of taxation for taxation for city purposes, who shall serve for the term of three years from the date of their appointment. One of said assessors shall be designated as chief assessor, and shall receive an annual salary of twenty-five hundred dollars. The other members of the board shall receive as compensation five dollars per day, for each day of actual service to be determined by the affidavit of the assessors before the city controller; and said board shall, immediately after their appointment, be severally sworn to faithfully perform the duties pertaining to their office. Any vacancy occurring in said board by death, resignation or otherwise, shall be filled by said council for the unexpired term: *Provided however*, That the councils shall not elect a chief assessor until the term for which the present assessor was elected shall have expired, and up to that time he shall act as chief assessor: *And provided further*, That one of said assessors shall be a resident of the rural district of said city: *And provided further*, That whenever two assessors are to be chosen for the same term of service each member of council shall vote for one only, and when three are to be elected he shall vote for no more than two," be and the same is hereby amended so as to read as follows:

That the city council of any city of the second class shall, immediately after the passage of this act, and every third year thereafter, elect three resident citizens of such city as a board of assessors to make, revise or alter assessments of all subjects of taxation for taxation for city purposes, who shall serve for the term of three years from the date of their appointment. One of said assessors shall be designated as chief assessor, and each of said assessors shall receive such annual salary as the councils of such city may ordain and establish, and said board shall, immediately after their appointment, be severally sworn to faithfully perform the duties pertaining to their office. Any vacancy occurring in said board by death, resignation or otherwise, shall be filled by said councils for the unexpired term: *Provided however*, That the councils shall not elect a chief assessor until the term for which the present assessor was elected shall have expired, and up to that time he shall act as chief assessor: *And provided further*, That whenever two assessors are to be chosen for the same term of service, each member of council shall vote for one only, and when three are to be elected he shall vote for no more than two.

SECTION 2. That section three of said act which reads as follows:

"SECTION 3. When said board shall have altered and amended the lists of all taxable property, so as to arrive at its true cash value, they shall then ascertain the aggregate amount of the value of the entire taxable property of said city, which valuation shall remain the lawful valuation for purposes of city taxation until altered as herein provided; the said board then shall proceed to classify the real estate so assessed, in such a manner and upon such testimony as may be adduced before them, so as to discriminate between built up property, rural or suburban property, and property used exclusively for agricultural or farm purposes, including untillable land, respectively,

[margin note: Authorizing councils to fix the salary of assessors.]

[margin note: Section 3 cited for amendment.]

and to certify to the councils of said city during the month of January of each year, the aggregate valuation of city, rural and agricultural property subject to taxation; it shall be the duty of said councils in determining the rate of taxation for each year, to assess a tax upon said agricultural, farm and untillable land equal to one-half of the highest rate of tax required to be assessed for said year, and upon said rural or suburban property a tax not exceeding two-thirds of the highest rate required to be assessed as aforesaid, so that upon the said classes of real estate of said city there shall be three rates of taxation," be and the same is hereby amended to read as follows:

Fixing the basis for the determination of classification of said real estate.

When said board shall have altered and amended the lists of all taxable property so as to arrive at its true cash value, they shall then ascertain the aggregate amount of the value of the entire taxable property of said city, which valuation shall remain the lawful valuation for purposes of city taxation until altered as herein provided; the said board then shall proceed to classify the real estate so assessed in such manner and upon such testimony as may be adduced before them, so as to discriminate between built up property, rural or suburban property, and property used exclusively for agricultural or farm purposes, including untillable land, respectively, and to certify to the councils of said city, during the month of January of each year, the aggregate valuation of city, rural and agricultural property subject to taxation, and in so classifying said property the character and purpose for which said property is used shall determine its classification. It shall be the duty of said councils, in determining the rate of taxation for each year, to assess a tax upon said agricultural farm and untillable land equal to one-half of the highest rate of tax required to be assessed for said year, and upon said rural or suburban property a tax not exceeding two-thirds of the highest rate required to be assessed as aforesaid, so that upon the said classes of real estate of said city there shall be three rates of taxation.

Character and purpose for which used to determine classification.

APPROVED—The 19th day of June, A. D. 1893.

ROBT. E. PATTISON.

No. 341.

AN ACT

To provide for the sale of the equitable title of the Commonwealth of Pennsylvania in the property known as the "Grove City Armory," located in the borough of Grove City, Mercer county, Pennsylvania, and for the distribution of the proceeds of the sale.

WHEREAS, In the year one thousand eight hundred and eighty-six, W. J. Neyman, captain of Company F, Fifteenth regiment, National Guard of Pennsylvania, purchased by articles of agreement made to himself, in trust for the Commonwealth of Pennsylvania, a vacant lot in the borough of Grove City, Mercer county, Pennsylvania, and erected thereon a building to be used as an armory for the said company ;

And whereas, In the erection of said building the said W. J. Neyman used certain moneys which he borrowed for the purpose upon his notes and certificates as captain of said company, which moneys in part at least remain unpaid ;

And whereas, It is now deemed unnecessary to retain said property as an armory ; therefore,

SECTION 1. *Be it enacted, &c.,* That the State Military Board shall sell the equitable title of the Commonwealth of Pennsylvania in the said property known as the Grove City Armory to the highest and best bidder, and shall make, execute and deliver to the purchaser thereof a deed for said property, which deed shall divest all title and interest of the Commonwealth in said property ; and the money realized from the sale shall be distributed first toward the moneys borrowed by the said W. J. Neyman upon his notes and certificates as captain of said company and used in the erection of said armory building, pro rata, and if any amount remains after the payment of said borrowed money, the same shall be returned to the State Treasury.

Providing for sale of the equitable title of Pennsylvania in the "Grove City Armory."

Distribution of proceeds.

APPROVED—The 20th day of June, A. D. 1893.

ROBT. E. PATTISON.

No. 342.

AN ACT

Further extending the jurisdiction of the courts of this Commonwealth in cases of divorce, and repealing an act approved the 8th day of June, Anno Domini one thousand eight hundred and ninety-one, entitled "A further supplement to an |act, entitled 'An act extending the jurisdiction of the courts of this Commonwealth in cases of divorce,'" approved the eighth day of March, Anno Domini one thousand eight hundred and fifty-five.

SECTION 1. *Be it enacted, &c.,* That it shall be lawful for the several courts of common pleas in this Commonwealth to entertain jurisdiction of all cases of divorce from the bonds of matrimony and from bed and board for the causes of adultery committed by the husband, or willful and malicious desertion on the part of the husband and absence from the habitation of the wife without reasonable cause, for and during the term and space of two years, or where any husband shall have, by cruel and barbarous treatment, endangered his wife's life or offered such indignities to her person as to render her condition intolerable and life burdensome, and thereby force her to withdraw from his house and family ; where it shall be shown to the court by any wife that she was formerly a citizen of this Commonwealth, and that having intermarried with a citizen of any other State or any

Courts to have jurisdiction in cases of divorce for certain causes.

foreign country, she has been compelled to abandon the habitation and domicile of her husband in such other State or foreign country by reason of his adultery or willful and malicious desertion and absence from the habitation of the wife without reasonable cause, for and during the term and space of two years, or by cruel and barbarous treatment endangered his wife's life or offered such indignities to her person as to render her condition intolerable and life burdensome, and thereby force her to withdraw from his house and family, and has thereby been forced to return to this Commonwealth in which she had her former domicile: *Provided*, That where, in any such case, personal service of the subpœna cannot be made upon such husband by reason of his non-residence within this Commonwealth, the court, before entering a decree of divorce, shall require proof that in addition to the publication now required by law, that actual or constructive notice of said proceedings has been to such non-resident husband, either by personal service or by registered letter to his last known place of residence, and that a reasonable time has thereby been afforded to him to appear and defend in said suit: *And provided further*, That no application for such divorce shall be made, unless the applicant therefor shall be a citizen of this Commonwealth, or shall have resided therein for the term of one year prior to filing her petition or libel as provided by the laws of this Commonwealth.

SECTION 2. Where the wife petitions the court for a divorce under the provisions of section first of this act on the ground of willful, malicious and continued desertion by the husband from the habitation of the wife without reasonable cause, it shall be lawful for the wife to make application in such case by petition or libel to the proper court at any time not less than six months after such cause of divorce shall have taken place, but the said court shall not proceed to make a final decree divorcing the said parties from the bonds of matrimony aforesaid until after the expiration of two years from the time at which such desertion took place.

SECTION 3. The proceedings in cases embraced within the provisions of this act, except so far as they are prescribed by this act, shall be the same as those prescribed by the act, entitled "An act concerning divorces," approved the thirteenth day of March, Anno Domini one thousand eight hundred and fifteen, and the several acts supplementary thereto, with the like right of appeal as is therein given.

SECTION 4. The provisions of this act shall apply to all suits or proceedings for divorce which may be pending in the courts of this Commonwealth at the time it is approved, and to all subsequent divorce proceedings.

SECTION 5. The act approved the eighth day of June, Anno Domini one thousand eight hundred and ninety-one, entitled "A further supplement to an act, entitled 'An act extending the jurisdiction of the courts of this

Commonwealth in cases of divorce,'" approved the ninth
day of March, Anno Domini one thousand eight hundred
and fifty-five, is hereby repealed.

APPROVED—The 20th day of June, A. D. 1893.

ROBT. E. PATTISON.

No. 343.

A SUPPLEMENT

To an act, entitled "An act to provide for the payment into the
State Treasury of all fees collected by the officers, agents and
employés of the State Government, for a uniform method of
keeping the accounts of the same, and for paying by warrants
of the Auditor General to the said officers, agents and employés,
the several amounts of said fees which they are respectively entitled to receive," approved the third day of June, one thousand
eight hundred and eighty-five.

SECTION 1. *Be it enacted, &c.*, That the Auditor General
is hereby authorized and directed, as soon as possible after
the passage of this act, to settle the accounts of each and
every person whose term or terms as officer, agent or
employé of the State Government shall have expired
since the passage of the act to which this is a supplement, and hereafter immediately upon the expiration of
the term of any officer, agent or employé of the State
Government, to settle his said account, in such settlement charging such person with all fees received by him
for the use of the Commonwealth and crediting him with
the salaries, fees and emoluments appropriated to him
by law, and which fees and emoluments he shall have paid
into the State Treasury during his term or terms in office
or subsequent thereto; and it shall be the duty of the
Auditor General to furnish each such person and his
sureties with a certified copy of such settlement, and in
case a balance shall appear to be due the Commonwealth,
he shall place such settlement in the hands of the Attorney General for collection from such person or his sureties in the manner provided by law, but in case a balance
shall appear to be due any such person who is now or
may have been an officer, agent or employé of the State,
the Auditor General shall draw his warrant upon the
State Treasurer in his favor for the amount so appearing
to be due to him: *Provided,* That no credit shall be allowed any such person for fees or emoluments which
shall not have been paid by him into the State Treasury,
nor until such person shall have furnished the Auditor
General with an itemized statement of the several
monthly or quarterly payments, as the case may be,
made by him to the State Treasurer during his term or
terms of office, which said statements and all other reports required by law, such person is authorized to make,
notwithstanding his term or terms of office may have expired, with like effect as if the same had been made at

the several periods provided in the act to which this is a supplement.

APPROVED—The 20th day of June, A. D. 1893.

ROBT. E. PATTISON.

No. 344.

AN ACT

Authorizing distillers of spirituous or vinous liquors to sell such liquors of their own manufacture in original packages of not less than forty gallons, without being required to take out a license as is now required by existing laws.

Distillers may dispose of spiritous or vinous liquors of their own manufacture within this Commonwealth in original packages of not less than 40 gallons without license.

Proviso.

SECTION 1. *Be it enacted, &c.*, That from and after the passage of this act it shall be lawful for distillers of spirituous and vinous liquors within this Commonwealth to sell or dispose of spirituous or vinous liquors of their own manufacture, within this Commonwealth, in their original packages of a capacity of not less than forty gallons, without obtaining a license therefor as required by existing law: *Provided however,* That if any distillers shall sell or dispose of spirituous or vinous liquors not manufactured by themselves, within the Commonwealth, or in any other than original packages, or in a less quantity than forty gallons, such distillers shall be subject to all the penalties provided by existing laws for the sale of liquor without a license.

Such distillers to pay in addition to taxes, into the State Treasury, $1,000 for city distillery.

$200 for borough distillery.

$100 for township distillery.

Repeal.

SECTION 2. Such distillers shall pay, in addition to the taxes they are now subject to by existing law, into the Treasury of the Commonwealth for the use of the Commonwealth of Pennsylvania, the annual sum of one thousand (1,000) dollars where such distillery is situated in a city, and the sum of two hundred (200) dollars where such distillery is situated in a borough, and the sum of one hundred (100) dollars where such distillery is situated in a township.

SECTION 3. All laws or parts of laws inconsistent with this act be and the same are hereby repealed.

APPROVED—The 20th day of June, A. D. 1893.

ROBT. E. PATTISON.

No. 345.

AN ACT

Making an appropriation to the Gettysburg Battlefield Memorial Association for the purpose of maintaining and keeping in repair the battlefield of Gettysburg.

$5,000 appropriated.

SECTION 1. *Be it enacted, &c.*, That the sum of five thousand dollars, or so much thereof as may be necessary, be and the same is hereby specifically appropriated to the Gettysburg Battlefield Memorial Association for the purpose of being expended by said association in maintaining and keeping in repair the battlefield of Gettysburg, for the two fiscal years beginning June first, one thousand eight hundred and ninety-three.

The said appropriation to be paid on the warrant of the Auditor General on a settlement made by him and the State Treasurer, but no warrant shall be drawn on settlement made until the directors or managers of said Gettysburg Battlefield Memorial Association shall have made, under oath to the Auditor General, a report containing a specifically itemized statement of the income and expenses of said Gettysburg Battlefield Memorial Association during the previous quarter, with the cash balance on hand, and the same is approved by him and the State Treasurer, nor until the Treasurer shall have sufficient money in the treasury, not otherwise appropriated, to pay the quarterly instalments due said Gettysburg Battlefield Memorial Association; and unexpended balances of sums appropriated for specific purposes shall not be used for other purposes, whether specific or general, and shall revert to the State Treasury at the close of the two fiscal years.

APPROVED—The 20th day of June, A. D. 1893.

ROBT. E. PATTISON.

How payable.

Itemized statement.

Unexpended balance shall revert to State Treasury.

No. 346.

AN ACT

Making an appropriation to pay the expenses incurred by the joint special committee appointed at the session of the Legislature in one thousand eight hundred and ninety-three, to consider the reports from the Quarantine Station Commission of Pennsylvania.

SECTION 1. *Be it enacted, &c.,* That the sum of one thousand seven hundred and twenty-four dollars and fifty-nine cents, or as much thereof as may be necessary, be and the same is hereby specifically appropriated out of any money in the treasury, not otherwise appropriated, for the payment of the expenses of the joint committee of the Senate and House of Representatives appointed to consider the reports of the Quarantine Station Commission, procure information from various sources and make recommendation upon the subject of quarantine on the Delaware river, authorized by joint resolution approved February sixth, one thousand eight hundred and ninety-three, (1893) as follows:

For hotel bills at Philadelphia and Washington and meals on trains and boat, three hundred and sixty-five dollars and fifteen cents.

For car fare for trip to Washington, and meeting in Philadelphia, one hundred and eighty-nine dollars and seventy-seven cents.

$1,724.59 total appropriation

Items.

For salary of secretary, telegrams, postage and type writing, one thousand and nineteen dollars and sixty-seven cents.

For salaries of sergeant-at-arms and messenger, one hundred and fifty dollars.

How payable.

Itemized vouchers.

The said appropriation to be paid on the warrant of the Auditor General on a settlement made by him and the State Treasurer, upon specifically itemized vouchers to be furnished by the chairman of said committee.

APPROVED—The 20th day of June, A. D. 1893.

ROBT. E. PATTISON.

No. 347.

AN ACT

Making an appropriation to the Spring Garden Institute of Philadelphia.

$5,000 appropriated.

SECTION 1. *Be it enacted, &c.*, That the sum of five thousand dollars, or so much thereof as may be necessary, be and the same is hereby specifically appropriated to the Spring Garden Institute of Philadelphia for the two fiscal years beginning June first, one thousand eight hundred and ninety-three, for the general maintenance of the schools of art and mechanical handiwork of the said institute; and any portion of the said appropriation may be used for the purchase of machinery and tools, models and supplies required for teaching the arts of design or the working of wood, metal, stone and other resources of Pennsylvania:

Proviso.

Provided, That in said schools of art and of mechanical handicraft there shall be maintained a free scholarship of one pupil from each county in the State, to be filled by nomination of the Governor of the Commonwealth.

How payable.

The said appropriation to be paid on the warrant of the Auditor General on a settlement made by him and the State Treasurer, but no warrant shall be drawn on settlement made until the directors or managers of said institution shall have made, under oath to the Auditor

Itemized statement.

General, a report containing a specifically itemized statement of the receipts from all sources and expenses of said institution during the previous quarter, with the cash balance on hand, and the same is approved by him and the State Treasurer, nor until the Treasurer shall have sufficient money in the treasury, not otherwise appropriated, to pay the quarterly instalments due said

Unexpended balance shall revert to State Treasury.

institution; and unexpended balances of sums appropriated for specific purposes shall not be used for other purposes, whether specific or general, and shall revert to the State Treasury at the close of the two fiscal years.

APPROVED—The 20th day of June, A. D. 1893.

ROBT. E. PATTISON.

No. 348.

AN ACT

Making an appropriation to pay the expenses of the special committee appointed April tenth, one thousand eight hundred and ninety-three, to investigate the Electric Light Trust of the city of Philadelphia.

SECTION 1. *Be it enacted, &c.*, That the sum of one thousand eight hundred and three dollars and fifty-five cents, or so much thereof as may be necessary, is hereby specifically appropriated to pay the expenses of the committees of the House of Representatives appointed to investigate the alleged electric trust in the city of Philadelphia, for the general and necessary expenses incurred in investigating said alleged electric trust, including stenographic services, extra car fare, hotel bills, typewriting and other services, the said sum so appropriated to be paid the warrant of the Auditor General, upon vouchers furnished him by the chairmen of the said committees, as follows:

Stenographer, three hundred and eighty-seven dollars and twenty cents.

Sergeant-at-arms, three hundred dollars.

Hotel bill, five hundred and ninety-one dollars and thirty-five cents.

S. A. Losch, one hundred and fifty-eight dollars.

Frank M. Riter car fare, twenty-one dollars; parlor car, three dollars; lunches and cab hire, five dollars.—Twenty-nine dollars.

George Lawrence, one hundred and forty-seven dollars.

William L. Cassin, one hundred and fifty-eight dollars.

Total, one thousand seven hundred and seventy dollars and fifty-five cents.

APPROVED—The 20th day of June, A. D. 1893

ROBT. E. PATTISON.

$1,803.55 total appropriation.

How payable.

Items.

No. 349.

AN ACT

Making an appropriation for the payment of the services and expenses incurred in the collection and compilation of the tax statistics, as required by the act of May ninth, one thousand eight hundred and eighty-nine, for the years one thousand eight hundred and eighty-nine and one thousand eight hundred and ninety.

SECTION 1. *Be it enacted, &c.*, That the sum of six thousand six hundred and seventy-five dollars, or so much thereof as may be necessary, be and is hereby specifically appropriated out of any money in the treasury, not otherwise appropriated, for the payment of the services rendered and expenses incurred in the collection and compilation of the tax statistics as required by the Act of Assembly approved the ninth day of May, Anno Domini

$6,675.00 total appropriation.

one thousand eight hundred and eighty-nine (Pamphlet Laws page one hundred and fifty-seven), as follows: For the forty-six counties making report for the year one thousand eight hundred and eighty-nine, the sum of three thousand four hundred and fifty dollars, or so much thereof as may be necessary; for the forty-three counties making report for the year one thousand eight hundred and ninety, the sum of three thousand two hundred and twenty-five dollars, or so much thereof as may be necessary.

Items.

The said appropriation to be paid upon the warrant of the Auditor General on a settlement made by him and the State Treasurer, upon properly itemized vouchers certified to by the Secretary of Internal Affairs.

How payable.

Itemized vouchers.

APPROVED—The 22d day of June, A. D. 1893.

ROBT. E. PATTISON.

No. 350.

AN ACT

Making an appropriation to the Memorial Hospital and House of Mercy of St. Timothy's church, Roxborough, twenty-first ward, city of Philadelphia.

$7,000 appropriated.

SECTION 1. *Be it enacted, &c.,* That the sum of seven thousand dollars, or so much thereof as may be necessary, be and the same is hereby specifically appropriated to the Memorial Hospital and House of Mercy of Saint Timothy's Church, Roxborough, twenty-first ward, city of Philadelphia, for the purpose of maintenance of said Hospital for the two fiscal years beginning June first, one thousand eight hundred and ninety-three.

How payable.

The said appropriation to be paid on the warrant of the Auditor General on a settlement made by him and the State Treasurer, but no warrant shall be drawn on settlement made until the directors or managers of said institution shall have made, under oath to the Auditor General, a report containing a specifically itemized statement of the receipts from all sources and expenses of said institution during the previous quarter, with the cash balance on hand, and the same is approved by him and the State Treasurer, nor until the Treasurer shall have sufficient money in the treasury, not otherwise appropriated, to pay the quarterly instalments due said institution; and unexpended balances of sums appropriated for specific purposes shall not be used for other purposes, whether specific or general, and shall revert to the State Treasury at the close of the two fiscal years.

Itemized statement.

Unexpended balance shall revert to State Treasury.

APPROVED—The 22d day of June, A. D. 1893.

ROBT. E. PATTISON.

No. 351.

AN ACT

Making an appropriation to the Philadelphia Society for Organizing Charity for the improvement and maintenance of the wayfarers' lodges operated by that society.

SECTION 1. *Be it enacted, &c.*, That the sum of ten thousand dollars, or so much thereof as may be necessary, be and the same is hereby specifically appropriated to the Philadelphia Society for Organizing Charity for the improvement and maintenance of the wayfarers' lodges operated by that society for the two fiscal years beginning June first, one thousand eight hundred and ninety-three. *$10,000 appropriated.*

The said appropriation to be paid on the warrant of the Auditor General on a settlement made by him and the State Treasurer, but no warrant shall be drawn on settlement made until the directors or managers of said society shall have made, under oath to the Auditor General, a report containing a specifically itemized statement of the receipts from all sources and expenses of said society during the previous quarter, with the cash balance on hand, and the same is approved by him and the State Treasurer, nor until the Treasurer shall have sufficient money in the treasury, not otherwise appropriated, to pay the quarterly instalments due said society; and unexpended balances of sums appropriated for specific purposes shall not be used for other purposes, whether specific or general, and shall revert to the State Treasury at the close of the two fiscal years. *How payable. Itemized statement. Unexpended balance shall revert to State Treasury.*

APPROVED—The 22d day of June, A. D. 1893.

The amounts included in the foregoing are in excess of those originally recommended by the Board of Public Charities; but in a written communication from the Board sent to me under date of June 21st, 1893, the amounts appropriated as above have, after further consideration, been unanimously recommended by the Board.

ROBT. E. PATTISON.

No. 352.

AN ACT

Making an appropriation to the Good Samaritan Hospital at Lebanon, Pennsylvania.

SECTION 1. *Be it enacted, &c.*, That the sum of fifteen thousand dollars, or so much thereof as may be necessary, be and the same is hereby specifically appropriated to the Good Samaritan Hospital at Lebanon, Pennsylvania, for the two fiscal years beginning June first, one thousand eight hundred and ninety-three, for the following purposes, namely : The sum of ten thousand dollars, or so much thereof as may be necessary, for the purpose of erecting and furnishing a hospital building, and the *$15,000 total appropriation. Items.*

sum of five thousand dollars, or so much thereof as may be necessary, for the purpose of maintenance of said hospital.

How payable. The said appropriation to be paid on the warrant of the Auditor General on a statement made by him and the State Treasurer, but no warrant shall be drawn on settlement made until the directors or managers of said institution shall have made, under oath to the Auditor **Itemized statement.** General, a report containing a specifically itemized statement of the receipts from all sources and expenses of said institution, together with a specifically itemized statement of the cost of said building and furnishing during the previous quarter, with the cash balance on hand, and the same is approved by him and the State Treasurer, nor until the Treasurer shall have sufficient money in the treasury, not otherwise appropriated, to pay the quarterly instalments due said institution; and **Unexpended balance shall revert to State Treasury.** unexpended balances of sums appropriated for specific purposes shall not be used for other purposes, whether specific or general, and shall revert to the State Treasury at the close of the two fiscal years.

APPROVED—The 22d day of June, A. D. 1893.

The amounts included in the foregoing are in excess of those originally recommended by the Board of Public Charities; but in a written communication from the Board, sent to me under date of March 3rd, 1893, the amounts appropriated as above, have, after further consideration, been unanimously recommended by the Board.

ROBT. E. PATTISON.

No. 353.

AN ACT

Making an appropriation to the Northern Home for Friendless Children.

$15,000 total appropriation. SECTION 1. *Be it enacted, &c.,* That the sum of fifteen thousand dollars, or so much thereof as may be necessary, be and the same is hereby specifically appropriated to the Northern Home for Friendless Children for the two fiscal years beginning June first, one thousand eight hundred and ninety-three, for the following purposes, namely:

Items. For necessary repairs to buildings, the sum of five thousand dollars, or so much thereof as may be necessary.

For maintenance, the sum of ten thousand dollars, or so much thereof as may be mecessary.

How payable. The said appropriation to be paid on the warrant of the Auditor General on a settlement made by him and the State Treasurer, but no warrant shall be drawn on settlement made until the directors or managers of said institu- **Itemized statement.** tion shall have made, under oath to the Auditor

General, a report containing a specifically itemized statement of the receipts from all sources and an itemized statement of expenditures for repairs and expenses of said institution during the previous quarter, with the cash balance on hand, and the same is approved by him and the State Treasurer, nor until the Treasurer shall have sufficient money in the treasury, not otherwise appropriated, to pay the quarterly instalments due said institution; and unexpended balances of sums appropriated for specific purposes shall not be used for other purposes, whether specific or general, and shall revert to the State Treasury at the close of the two fiscal years.

Unexpended balance shall revert to State Treasury.

APPROVED—The 22d day of June, A. D. 1893.

The amounts included in the foregoing are in excess of those originally recommended by the Board of Public Charities; but in a written communication from the Board sent to me under date of June 21st, 1893, the amounts appropriated as above have, after further consideration, been unanimously recommended by the Board.

ROBT. E. PATTISON.

No. 354.

AN ACT

Making an appropriation to the Reading Hospital.

SECTION 1. *Be it enacted, &c.*, That the sum of fifteen thousand dollars, or so much thereof as may be necessary, be and the same is hereby specifically appropriated to the Reading Hospital of the city of Reading, for the purpose of maintenance during the two fiscal years beginning June first, one thousand eight hundred and ninety-three.

$15,000 appropriated

The said appropriation to be paid on the warrant of the Auditor General on a settlement made by him and the State Treasurer, but no warrant shall be drawn on settlement made until the directors or managers of said institution shall have made, under oath to the Auditor General, a report containing a specifically itemized statement of the receipts from all sources and expenses of said institution during the previous quarter, with the cash balance on hand, and the same is approved by him and the State Treasurer, nor until the Treasurer shall have sufficient money in the treasury, not otherwise appropriated, to pay the quarterly instalments due said institution; and unexpended balances of sums appropriated for specific purposes shall not be used for other purposes, whether specific or general, and shall revert to the State Treasury at the close of the two fiscal years.

How payable.

Itemized statement.

Unexpended balances shall revert to the State Treasury.

APPROVED—The 22d day of June, 1893.

The amounts included in the foregoing are in excess of those originally recommended by the Board of Public

31—LAWS.

Charities; but in a written communication from the
Board sent to me under date of June 21st, 1893, the amounts
appropriated as above have, after further consideration,
been unanimously recommended by the Board.

ROBT. E. PATTISON.

No. 355.

AN ACT

Granting an annuity of Frank Marshall, of Scranton, Pennsylvania,
a private of Company "B," Thirteenth Regiment, National Guard
of Pennsylvania.

nuity to Frank
rshall, guards-
·

SECTION 1. *Be it enacted, &c.*, That the State Treasurer is hereby authorized and required to pay to the said
Frank Marshall an annuity of two hundred and forty dollars, payable semi-annually, commencing on the first day
of July, Anno Domini one thousand eight hundred and
ninety-three.

APPROVED—The 22d day of June, A. D. 1893.

This act is carelessly drawn, in that neither in any preamble attached nor in the body of the bill, is there any
statement or explanation of the ground upon which the
annuity provided is to be granted. No well defined system of examining applications for pensions for injuries
received in the service of the National Guard has yet
been established in our Commonwealth, though the attention of the Legislature has been repeatedly called to
this subject.

These reasons might warrant Executive disapproval
of this bill; but lest injustice might be done to a worthy
sufferer, I have caused examination to be made into the
merits of this case, and have been satisfied from evidence
laid before me, that the beneficiary of this act has been
permanently disabled by disease incurred while in the
military service of the State. Such claims are expressly
recognized and warranted by the Constitution. The
sworn evidence of the comrades of this soldier, of his attending physicians and the Colonel of his regiment, presented in support of this bill, has fully satisfied me as to
its merits, and I therefore waive technical objections and
give my approval to the measure.

ROBT. E. PATTISON.

No. 356.

AN ACT

Making an appropriation to the Pittsburg and Allegheny Home
for the Friendless, of the city of Allegheny.

appropriated.
w payable.

SECTION 1. *Be it enacted, &c.*, That the sum of four
thousand dollars, or so much thereof as may be neces-

sary, be and the same is hereby specifically appropriated to the Pittsburg and Allegheny Home for the Friendless, of the city of Allegheny, for the purpose of maintenance for the two fiscal years beginning June first, one thousand eight hundred and ninety-three.

The said appropriation to be paid on the warrant of the Auditor General on a settlement made by him and the State Treasurer, but no warrant shall be drawn on settlement made until the directors or managers of said institution shall have made, under oath, a report to the Auditor General, containing a specifically itemized statement of the receipts from all sources and the expenses of said institution during the previous quarter, with the cash balance on hand, and the same is approved by him and the State Treasurer, nor until the Treasurer shall have sufficient money in the treasury, not otherwise appropriated, to pay the quarterly instalments due said institution; and unexpended balances of sums appropriated for specific purposes shall not be used for other purposes, whether specific or general, and shall revert to the State Treasury at the close of the two fiscal years.

APPROVED—The 22d day of June, A. D. 1893.

The amounts included in the foregoing are in excess of those originally recommended by the Board of Public Charities; but in a written communication from the Board sent to me under date of June 21st, 1893, the amounts appropriated as above have, after further consideration, been unanimously recommended by the Board.

ROBT. E. PATTISON.

Marginal notes: How payable. Itemized statement. Unexpended balance shall revert to State Treasury.

No. 357.

AN ACT

Making an appropriation to the Charity Hospital Association of Honesdale, Wayne county.

SECTION 1. *Be it enacted, &c.,* That the sum of five thousand dollars, or so much thereof as may be necessary, be and the same is hereby specifically appropriated to the Charity Hospital Association of Honesdale, Wayne county, Pennsylvania, for the two fiscal years beginning June first, one thousand eight hundred and ninety-three, for the purpose of assisting in the erection of a new hospital building for the medical and surgical care of sick and injured persons, indigent or otherwise, and without discrimination in respect to religion, nationality or color: *Provided,* That no part of the money herein appropriated shall become available until the treasurer of said institution shall have certified, under oath to the Auditor General, that the sum of five thousand dollars, exclusive of the value of the ground, has been subscribed and paid in cash into the treasury of said institution by private contributions for the purpose of assisting in the erection of

Marginal notes: $5,000 appropriated. Proviso.

said hospital building, and that said association has become the owner in fee simple, clear of all incumbrances, of ground of the assessed value of one thousand five hundred dollars.

How payable.

The said appropriation to be paid on the warrant of the Auditor General on a settlement made by him and the State Treasurer, but no warrant shall be drawn on settlement made until the directors or managers of said institution shall have made, under oath to the Auditor General, a report containing a specifically itemized state-

Itemized statement.

ment of the income and expenses of said institution, together with a specifically itemized statement of the cost of said hospital building during the previous quarter, with the cash balance on hand ,and the same is approved by him and the State Treasurer nor until the Treasurer shall have sufficient money in the treasury, not otherwise appropriated, to pay the quarterly instalments due said

Unexpended balance shall revert to State Treasury.

institution; and unexpended balances of sums appropriated for specific purposes shall not be used for other purposes, whether specific or general, and shall revert to the State Treasury at the close of the two fiscal years.

APPROVED—The 22d day of June, A. D. 1893.

The amounts included in the foregoing are in excess of those originally recommended by the Board of Public Charities; but in a written communication from the Board sent to me under date of May second, 1893, the amounts appropriated have, after further consideration, been recommended by the Board.

ROBT. E. PATTISON.

No. 358.

AN ACT

Making an appropriation for the "German Protestant Home for the Aged," at Fair Oaks, Allegheny county, Pennsylvania.

$5,000 appropriated.

SECTION 1. *Be it enacted, &c.,* That the sum of five thousand dollars, or so much thereof as may be necessary, be and the same is hereby specifically appropriated for the maintenance of the "German Protestant Home for the Aged," at Fair Oaks, Allegheny county, Pennsylvania, for the two fiscal years commencing June first, one thousand eight hundred and ninety-three.

How payable

The said appropriation to be paid on the warrant of the Auditor General on a settlement made by him and the State Treasurer, but no warrant shall be drawn on settlement made until the directors or managers of said institution shall have made, under oath to the Auditor

Itemized statement.

General, a report containing a specifically itemized statement of the receipts from all sources and expenses of said institution during the previous quarter, with the cash balance on hand, and the same is approved by him and the State Treasurer, nor until the Treasurer shall have sufficient money in the treasury, not otherwise appropriated, to pay the quarterly instalments due said institution; and unexpended balances of sums appropriated for specific purposes shall not be used for other purposes, whether specific or general, and shall revert to the State Treasury at the close of the two fiscal years. Unexpended balances shall revert to State Treasury.

APPROVED—The 22d day of June, A. D. 1893.

The amounts included in the foregoing are in excess of those originally recommended by the Board of Public Charities; but in a written communication from the Board sent to me under date of June 21st, 1893, the amounts appropriated as above have, after further consideration, been unanimously recommended by the Board.

ROBT. E. PATTISON.

No. 359.

AN ACT

Making an appropriation to pay the salary, postage, mileage, stationery, counsel fees and personal expenses of Charles I. Baker, in the contested election case of Taggart versus Baker, in the House of Representatives, from the county of Montgomery, during the session of one thousand eight hundred and ninety-three.

SECTION 1. *Be it enacted, &c.*, That the sum of two thousand seven hundred and twenty dollars, or so much thereof as may be necessary, be and the same is hereby specifically appropriated to Charles I. Baker, out of any money in the treasury, not otherwise appropriated, for the following purposes, namely: $2,720 total appropriation.

For salary as a member of the House of Representatives returned as elected from Montgomery county for the session of one thousand eight hundred and ninety-three, the sum of one thousand five hundred dollars, or so much thereof as may be necessary; for postage, the sum of one hundred dollars, or so much thereof as may be necessary; for mileage, the sum of seventy dollars, or so much thereof as may be necessary; for stationery, the sum of fifty dollars, or so much thereof as may be necessary. Items.

For counsel fees in the contested election case of Taggart versus Baker, in the House of Representatives, from the county of Montgomery, during the session of one thousand eight hundred and ninety-three, the sum of five hundred dollars, or so much thereof as may be necessary; for personal expenses incurred during the said contest of Taggart versus Baker, the sum of five hundred dollars, or so much thereof as may be necessary, the same to be in full of all claims against the Commonwealth for salary, mileage, postage, stationery, counsel fees and expenses incurred during said contested election case.

The said appropriation to be paid on the warrant of How payable.

Itemized vouchers

the Auditor General on a settlement made by him and the State Treasurer, upon specifically itemized vouchers rendered under oath to the Auditor General.

APPROVED—The 29th day of June, A. D. 1893.

ROBT. E. PATTISON.

No. 360.

AN ACT

Making an appropriation to pay the counsel fees and personal expenses of Austin L. Taggart in the contested election case of Taggart versus Baker, in the House of Representatives, from the county of Montgomery, during the session of one thousand eight hundred and ninety-three.

$1,000 total appropriation.

SECTION 1. *Be it enacted, &c.,* That the sum of one thousand dollars, or so much thereof as may be necessary, be and the same is hereby specifically appropriated out of any money in the treasury, not otherwise appropriated, to Austin L. Taggart for the following purposes, namely:

Items.

For the payment of counsel fees in the contested election case of Taggart versus Baker, in the House of Representatives, from the county of Montgomery, during the session of one thousand eight hundred and ninety-three, the sum of five hundred dollars, or so much thereof as may be necessary.

For personal expenses during the said contest of Taggart versus Baker, the sum of five hundred dollars, or so much thereof as may be necessary, the same to be in full of all claims against the Commonwealth on account of said contested election case.

How payable.

Itemized vouchers.

The said appropriation to be paid on the warrant of the Auditor General on a settlement made by him and the State Treasurer, upon specifically itemized vouchers rendered under oath to the Auditor General.

APPROVED—The 29th day of June, A. D. 1893.

ROBT. E. PATTISON.

No. 361.

AN ACT

Making an appropriation to pay the salary, mileage, postage and stationery of Eli Waughman while a member of the House of Representatives from Westmoreland county, during the session of one thousand eight hundred and ninety-three.

$1 721.30 total appropriation.

SECTION 1. *Be it enacted, &c.,* That the sum of one thousand seven hundred and twenty-one dollars and thirty cents, or so much thereof as may be necessary, be and the same is hereby specifically appropriated to

Eli Waughman out of any money in the treasury, not otherwise appropriated, for the following purposes, namely:

For salary as a member of the House of Representatives returned as elected from Westmoreland county for the session of one thousand eight hundred and ninety-three, the sum of one thousand five hundred dollars, or so much thereof as may be necessary. *Items.*

For postage, one hundred dollars, or so much thereof as may be necessary.

For mileage, eighty-one dollars and twenty cents, or so much thereof as may be necessary.

For stationery, fifty dollars, or so much thereof as may be necessary.

The same to be in full of all claims against the Commonwealth on account of salary, mileage, postage, stationery and expenses of contested election case.

The said appropriation to be paid on the warrant of the Auditor General on a settlement made by him and the State Treasurer, upon specifically itemized vouchers rendered under oath to the Auditor General. *How payable.* *Itemized vouchers.*

APPROVED—The 29th day of June, A. D. 1893.

ROBT. E. PATTISON.

No. 362.

AN ACT

Making an appropriation to pay the salary, mileage, postage and stationery of William R. Barnhart, a member of the House of Representatives from Westmoreland county, during the session of one thousand eight hundred and ninety-three.

SECTION 1. *Be it enacted, &c.,* That the sum of one thousand seven hundred and thirty-eight dollars, or so much thereof as may be necessary, be and the same is hereby specifically appropriated to William R. Barnhart out of any money in the treasury, not otherwise appropriated, for the following purposes, namely: *$1,738 total appropriation.*

For salary as a member of the House of Representatives returned as elected from Westmoreland county for the session of one thousand eight hundred and ninety-three, the sum of one thousand five hundred dollars, or so much thereof as may be necessary. *Items*

For mileage, eighty-eight dollars, or so much thereof as may be necessary.

For postage, one hundred dollars, or so much thereof as may be necessary.

For stationery, fifty dollars, or so much thereof as may be necessary; the same to be in full of all claims against the Commonwealth on account of salary, mileage, postage, stationery and expenses of contested election case.

The said appropriation to be paid on the warrant of *How payable.*

the Auditor General on a settlement made by him and the State Treasurer, upon specifically itemized vouchers rendered under oath to the Auditor General.

Approved—The 29th day of June, A D. 1893.

ROBT. E. PATTISON.

Itemized vouchers.

No. 363.

AN ACT

Making an appropriation to pay the counsel fees and personal expenses of W. P. Higby in the contested election case of Higby versus Andrews, in the House of Representatives, from Crawford county, during the session of one thousand eight hundred and ninety-three.

$2.000 total appropriation.

Section 1. *Be it enacted, &c.,* That the sum of two thousand dollars, or so much thereof as may be necessary, be and the same is hereby specifically appropriated to W. P. Higby out of any money in the treasury, not otherwise appropriated, for the following purposes, namely:

Items.

For counsel fees in the contested election case of Higby versus Andrews, in the House of Representatives, from Crawford county, during the session of one thousand eight hundred and ninety-three, the sum of one thousand dollars, or so much thereof as may be necessary.

For personal expenses incurred during the said contest, the sum of one thousand dollars, or so much thereof as may be necessary, the same to be in full of all claims against the Commonwealth on account of said contest.

How payable.

The said appropriation to be paid on the warrant of the Auditor General on a settlement made by him and the State Treasurer, upon specifically itemized vouchers rendered under oath to the Auditor General.

Itemized vouchers.

Approved—The 29th day of June, A. D. 1893.

ROBT. E. PATTISON.

No. 364.

AN ACT

Making an appropriation to pay the counsel fees and personal expenses of W. H. Andrews in the contested election case of Higby versus Andrews, in the House of Representatives, from Crawford county, during the session of one thousand eight hundred and ninety-three.

$1.000 total appropriation.

Section 1. *Be it enacted, &c.,* That the sum of one thousand dollars, or so much thereof as may be necessary, be and the same is hereby specifically appropriated to W. H. Andrews out of any money in the treasury, not otherwise appropriated, for the following purposes. namely :

Items.

For counsel fees in the contested election case of Higby

versus Andrews, in the House of Representatives, from
Crawford county, during the session of one thousand
eight hundred and ninety-three, the sum of five hundred
dollars, or so much thereof as may be necessary.

For personal expenses incurred during the said contest, the sum of five hundred dollars, or so much thereof
as may be necessary.

The same to be in full of all claims against the Commonwealth on account of said contest.

The said appropriation to be paid on the warrant of *How payable.*
the Auditor General on a settlement made by him and
the State Treasurer, upon specifically itemized vouchers *Itemized vouchers.*
rendered under oath to the Auditor General.

APPROVED—The 29th day of June, A. D. 1893.

ROBT. E. PATTISON.

No. 365.

AN ACT

Making appropriation to pay the counsel fees and personal expenses of Frank T. Okell in the contested election case of Okell
versus Quinnan, in the House of Representatives, from the
county of Lackawanna, during the session of one thousand eight
hundred and ninety-three.

SECTION 1. *Be it enacted, &c.,* That the sum of one *$1,000 total appro-*
thousand dollars, or so much thereof as may be neces- *priation.*
sary, be and the same is hereby specifically appropriated
to Frank T. Okell out of any money in the treasury, not
otherwise appropriated, for the following purposes,
namely:

For the payment of counsel fees in the contested elec- *Items.*
tion case Okell versus Quinnan, in the House of Representatives, from the Second Legislative district of the
county of Lackawanna, during the session of one thousand eight hundred and ninety-three, the sum of five
hundred dollars, or so much thereof as may be necessary.

For personal expenses incurred during the contest
of Okell versus Quinnan, the sum of five hundred dollars,
or so much thereof as may be necessary, the same to be
in full of all claims against the Commonwealth on account of said contested election case.

The said appropriation to be paid on the warrant of *How payable.*
the Auditor General on a settlement made by him and
the State Treasurer, upon specifically itemized vouchers *Itemized vouchers.*
rendered under oath to the Auditor General.

APPROVED—The 29th day of June, A. D. 1893.

ROBT. E. PATTISON.

No. 366.

AN ACT

Making an appropriation to pay the salary, mileage, postage, stationery, counsel fees and personal expenses of John P. Quinnan, in the contested election case of Okell versus Quinnan, in the House of Representatives, in the contested election case from the Second Legislative district of the county of Lackawanna, during the session of one thousand eight hundred and ninety-three.

$2,720 total appropriation.

SECTION 1. *Be it enacted, &c.,* That the sum of two thousand seven hundred and twenty dollars, or so much thereof as may be necessary, be and the same is hereby specifically appropriated to John P. Quinnan out of any money in the treasury, not otherwise appropriated, for the following purposes, namely:

Items.

For salary as a member of the House of Representatives returned as elected from the Second Legislative district of the county of Lackawanna, for the session of one thousand eight hundred and ninety-three, the sum of one thousand five hundred dollars.

For mileage, the sum of seventy dollars, or so much thereof as may be necessary.

For postage, the sum of one hundred dollars, or so much thereof as may be necessary.

For stationery, the sum of fifty dollars, or so much thereof as may be necessary.

For counsel fees in the contested election case of Okell versus Quinnan in the House of Representatives from the county of Lackawanna, during the session of one thousand eight hundred and ninety-three, the sum of five hundred dollars, or so much thereof as may be necessary.

For personal expenses incurred during said contested election case, the sum of five hundred dollars, or so much thereof as may be necessary; the same to be in full of all claims against the Commonwealth on account of said contested election case for salary, counsel fees and expenses incurred.

How payable.

Itemized vouchers.

The said appropriation to be paid on the warrant of the Auditor General on a settlement made by him and the State Treasurer, upon specifically itemized vouchers rendered under oath to the Auditor General.

APPROVED—The 29th day of June, A D. 1893.

ROBT. E. PATTISON.

No. 367.

AN ACT

Making an appropriation to pay the salary, postage, mileage, stationery, counsel fees and personal expenses of George Forrest in the contested election case of Franklin versus Forrest, in the House of Representatives, from the county of Lancaster, during the session of one thousand eight hundred and ninety-three.

$2,664.40 total appropriation.

SECTION 1. *Be it enacted, &c.,* That the sum of two thousand six hundred and sixty four dollars and forty cents, or so much thereof as may be necessary, be and the same is hereby specifically appropriated to George Forrest out of any money in the treasury, not otherwise appropriated, for the following purposes, namely:

For salary as a member of the House of Representa- Items. tives returned as elected from Lancaster county for the session of one thousand eight hundred and ninety-three, the sum of one thousand five hundred dollars, or so much thereof as may be necessary; for postage, the sum of one hundred dollars, or so much thereof as may be necessary; for mileage, the sum of fourteen dollars and forty cents, or so much thereof as may be necessary; for stationery, the sum of fifty dollars, or so much thereof as may be necessary.

For counsel fees in the contested election case of Franklin versus Forrest, in the House of Representatives, from the county of Lancaster, during the session of one thousand eight hundred and nine-three, the sum of five hundred dollars, or so much thereof as may be necessary; for personal expenses incurred during the said contest of Franklin versus Forrest, the sum of five hundred dollars, or so much thereof as may be necessary; the same to be in full of all claims against the Commonwealth for salary, mileage, postage, stationery, counsel fees and expenses incurred during said contested election case.

The said appropriation to be paid on the warrant of How payable. the Auditor General on a settlement made by him and the State Treasurer, upon specifically itemized vouchers Itemized vouchers. rendered under oath to the Auditor General.

APPROVED—The 29th day of June, 1893.

ROBT. E. PATTISON.

No. 368.

AN ACT

Making an appropriation to pay the counsel fees and personal expenses of W. W. Franklin in the contested election case of Franklin versus Forrest, in the House of Representatives, from the county of Lancaster, during the session of one thousand eight hundred and ninety-three.

SECTION 1. *Be it enacted, &c.,* That the sum of one $1,000 total appro- thousand dollars, or so much thereof as may be neces- priation. sary, be and the same is hereby specifically appropriated out of any money in the treasury, not otherwise appropriated, to W. W. Franklin, for the following purposes, namely:

For the payment of counsel fees in the contested elec- Items. tion case of Franklin versus Forrest, in the House of Representatives, from the county of Lancaster, during the session of one thousand eight hundred and ninety-three, the sum of five hundred dollars, or so much thereof as may be necessary.

For personal expenses during the said contest of
Franklin versus Forrest, the sum of five hundred dollars,
or so much thereof as may be necessary; the same to be
in full of all claims against the Commonwealth on account of said contested election case.

How payable.

The said appropriation to be paid on the warrant of
the Auditor General on a settlement made by him and

Itemized vouchers.

the State Treasurer, upon specifically itemized vouchers
rendered under oath to the Auditor General.

APPROVED—The 29th day of June, A. D. 1893.

ROBT. E. PATTISON.

No. 369.

AN ACT

Making an appropriation to pay the expenses incurred by the Finance Committee of the Senate, under a resolution of the Senate
during the session of the Legislature in one thousand eight hundred and ninety-one, instructing the said committee to ascertain
the amount of funds belonging to the Commonwealth in the custody of the city treasurer of Philadelphia, and if the Commonwealth is fully protected.

WHEREAS, Under a resolution of the Senate agreed to
May eleventh, one thousand eight hundred and ninety-
one, the Finance Committee of the Senate was instructed
to ascertain the amount of State funds in the custody of
the city treasurer of Philadelphia, where the same was
deposited, and if the State was fully protected;

And whereas, The committee faithfully performed the
duties imposed upon it and in the discharge of the said
duties, obligations and expenses were incurred and paid
by said committee and which it is proper should be defrayed by the Commonwealth.

$1,900 total appro-
priation.

SECTION 1. *Be it enacted, &c.,* That the sum of one
thousand nine hundred dollars, or so much thereof as
may be necessary, be and is hereby specifically appropriated for the payment of the expenses of the Finance
Committee of the Senate instructed to ascertain the
amount of State funds in the custody of the city treasurer of Philadelphia, where the same was deposited, and
if the State was fully protected.

Items.

For expenses paid by the committee for hotel bills,
extra car fare, sleeping berths, telegrams, carriages et
cetera, one thousand five hundred dollars.

For clerk and messenger, two hundred dollars.

For stenographer and typewriter, two hundred dollars.

How payable.

To be paid by warrant drawn by the Auditor General
in favor of the chairman of the committee, upon specifi-

Itemized state
ment.

cally itemized statement furnished by the chairman.

APPROVED—The 29th day of June, A. D. 1893.

ROBT. E. PATTISON.

No. 370.

AN ACT

Making an appropriation to pay the necessary and general expenses incurred in investigating and preparing reports upon appropriation bills for the session of the Legislature of one thousand eight hundred and ninety-three.

SECTION 1. *Be it enacted, &c.*, That the sum of two thousand five hundred and fifty-seven dollars and ninety-four cents, or so much thereof as may be necessary, is hereby specifically appropriated out of any moneys, not already appropriated, to pay the expenses of the committee on appropriations of the Senate of the session of one thousand eight hundred and ninety-three, for the general and necessary expenses incurred in investigating appropriation bills, and other services; the said sum so appropriated to be paid on the warrant of the Auditor General, upon vouchers furnished him by the chairman of said committee, as follows: $2,557.94 total appropriation to Senate appropriation committee.

How payable.

For service of Pullman hotel car and supplies furnished, one thousand two hundred and thirty-two dollars and ninety cents. Items.

For entertainment at Hotel Lafayette, three hundred and twenty-two dollars and seventy-one cents.

John Waller, bill, twenty dollars.

W. S. Smith, sixty-five dollars.

Luther B. Keefer, fifty dollars.

W. B. Crawford, fifty dollars.

N. C. Critchfield, fifty dollars.

John Upperman, fifty dollars.

Ellwood Becker, fifty dollars.

W. B. Meredith, fifty dollars.

A. F. Bannon, fifty dollars.

Milton C. Heringer, fifty dollars.

H. D. Green, fifty dollars.

James S. Fruit, fifty dollars.

D. D. Markley, fifty dollars.

S. J. Logan, fifty dollars.

J. H. Myers, sergeant-at-arms of Senate, three hundred and seventeen dollars and thirty-three cents.

SECTION 2. For the payment of the general and necessary expenses of the committee on appropriations of the House of Representatives of the session of one thousand eight hundred and ninety-three, incurred in visiting and examining schools, asylums, hospitals, reformatories and prisons, supported wholly or in part by the State, including clerical services, extra car fares, hotel bills, carriage hire, type-writing and other services, the sum of ten thousand two hundred and twenty-four dollars and eighty-two cents. The said sum so appropriated to be paid on the warrant of the Auditor General, upon vouchers furnished him by the chairman of said committee, as follows: $10,224.82 total appropriation to House of Representatives appropriation committee.

How payable.

William T. Marshall, four hundred and sixty dollars. Items.

Ephraim D. Miller, three hundred and ninety-seven dollars and forty-five cents.

W. E. Burdick, three hundred and sixty-nine dollars and seventy-five cents.

C. M. Wheeler, three hundred and twenty-eight dollars.

M. T. Burke, three hundred and forty-eight dollars.

C. B. Seely, three hundred and sixty-one dollars and fifty cents.

D. H. Branson, three hundred and fifty-eight dollars.

E. W. Toole, three hundred and sixty-five dollars.

S. M. Wherry, three hundred and ninety-six dollars and fifty cents.

Jno. H. Fow, four hundred and one dollars.

H. N. Hess, three hundred and forty six dollars and sixty cents.

W. T. Zeigler, three hundred and fifty-five dollars.

M. B. Lemon, three hundred and eighty-one dollars.

W. O. Smith, three hundred and sixty-eight dollars and ten cents.

P. M. Lytle, three hundred and eighty-one dollars and eighty cents.

H. F. James, three hundred and seventy-nine dollars and twenty cents.

M. L. Hershey, three hundred and twenty-nine dollars.

J. H. McClintic, three hundred and sixty-one dollars.

W. F. Stewart, three hundred and fifty-seven dollars and fifteen cents.

Philo Burritt, three hundred and sixty-eight dollars.

A. S. Stayer, three hundred and sixty-nine dollars.

Wm. R. Jeffrey, three hundred and fifty-two dollars and fifty cents.

S. B. Cochrane, four hundred and two dollars.

J. C. Quiggle, three hundred and thirty-four dollars and seventy-seven cents.

T. M. Patterson, three hundred and fifty-one dollars.

Harry E. Armstrong, one thousand dollars.

APPROVED—The 29th day of June, A. D. 1893.

ROBT. E. PATTISON.

No. 371.

AN ACT

Making an appropriation to Charles A. McCarty, a member of the the House of Representatives of Pennsylvania from Wayne county, during the session of eighteen hundred and eighty-seven, for balance of expenses of contested election.

$1 000 appropriated.

SECTION 1. *Be it enacted, &c.*, That the sum of one thousand dollars be and the same is hereby specifically appropriated to Charles A. McCarty, a member of the House of Representatives of the Commonwealth of Pennsylvania from Wayne county, during the session of one thousand eight hundred and eighty-seven, for the balance of expenses of contest due him and in full of all claims against the Commonwealth.

The said appropriation to be paid on the warrant of How payable. the Auditor General on a settlement made by him and the State Treasurer.

Approved—The 29th day of June, A. D. 1893.

ROBT. E. PATTISON.

CONCURRENT RESOLUTIONS

PASSED AT THE SESSION OF ONE THOUSAND EIGHT HUNDRED
AND NINETY-THREE.

No. 1.

IN THE SENATE, *January* 12, 1893.

Resolved, (if the House of Representatives concur,)
That five hundred copies of the Memorial Services upon
the death of Senator Thomas M. Mehard be printed for
the use of the Senate.

E. W. SMILEY,
Chief Clerk of the Senate.
IN THE HOUSE OF REPRESENTATIVES,
January 12, 1893.
CHARLES E. VOORHEES,
Chief Clerk of the House of Representatives.
APPROVED—January 18th, A. D. 1893.
ROBT. E. PATTISON.

No. 2.

IN THE SENATE, *January* 17, 1893.

Preamble No. 1.

WHEREAS, Under the provisions of the Act of Assembly approved May 7th, 1891, provision was made for the publication of the proceedings of the dedication of the Pennsylvania Monuments at Gettysburg in one volume;

Preamble No. 2.

And whereas, It has become evident that the aforesaid proceedings will be of such interest that the books should be convenient for use, which they will not be if all bound in one volume, but be cumbersome and unwieldy; therefore, be it

Proceedings of dedication of Pennsylvania Monuments to be bound in two volumes.

No additional cost.

Resolved, (if the House concur,) That the Superintendent of Public Printing be and is hereby authorized and directed to have the aforesaid proceedings bound in two volumes instead of one: *Provided*, The additional cost shall only be such as is involved in the additional binding.

E. W. SMILEY,
Chief Clerk of the Senate.

The foregoing resolution concurred in by the House
of Representatives.

CHARLES E. VOORHEES,
Chief Clerk of the House of Representatives.
APPROVED—The 23d day of January, A. D. 1893.
ROBT. E. PATTISON.

No. 3.

IN THE HOUSE OF REPRESENTATIVES,
January 18, 1893.

Resolved, (if the Senate concur,) That the National flag be raised over the Capitol buildings at all times, and that the Superintendent of Public Grounds and Buildings be required to carry this resolution into effect.

Extract from the Journal of the House of Representatives.

CHARLES E. VOORHEES,
Chief Clerk of the House of Representatives.

IN THE SENATE, *January 19, 1893.*

The foregoing resolution concurred in.

E. W. SMILEY,
Chief Clerk of the Senate.

APPROVED—The 25th day of January, A. D. 1893.

ROBT. E. PATTISON.

No. 4.

IN THE HOUSE OF REPRESENTATIVES,
January 18, 1893.

WHEREAS, The Legislature of the Commonwealth of Pennsylvania, in General Assembly met, have this eighteenth day of January, A. D. 1893, heard of the death of Rutherford B. Hayes, ex-President of the United States: therefore, *Preamble No. 1.*

Resolved, (if the Senate concur,` That the National flag over the Capitol buildings be lowered to half mast till after the funeral of said Rutherford B. Hayes, ex-President of the United States. *Flag to be lowered to half mast.*

Extract from the Journal of the House of Representatives.

CHARLES E. VOORHEES,
Chief Clerk of the House of Representatives.

IN THE SENATE, *January 19, 1893.*

The foregoing resolution concurred in.

E. W. SMILEY,
Chief Clerk of the Senate.

APPROVED—The 25th day of January, A. D. 1893.

ROBT. E. PATTISON.

No. 5.

IN THE SENATE, *January* 18, 1893.

WHEREAS, Rumors are prevalent that the material and workmanship of the foundations of the State Lunatic *Preamble No. 1.*

32—LAWS.

Asylum for the Chronic Insane at Wernersville, are insufficient and unsatisfactory, therefore, be it

Committee of eight to be appointed to investigate works, &c.

Resolved, (if the House concur), That a joint committee of three Senators and five members of the House of Representatives be appointed to make a personal examination of the condition of the work at the State Lunatic Asylum for the Chronic Insane located at Wernersville, and report as early as practicable upon the material used and character of the workmanship thus far employed.

E. W. SMILEY,
Chief Clerk of the Senate.

The foregoing resolution concurred in January 19, 1893.

CHARLES E. VOORHEES,
Chief Clerk of the House of Representatives.

APPROVED—The 25th day of January, 1893.
ROBT. E. PATTISON.

No. 6.

IN THE SENATE, *January* 19, 1893.

State Printing, investigation of.

Resolved, (if the House concur,) That in accordance with the message of His Excellency the Governor, of this date, a committee of three on the part of the Senate, and five on the part of the House of Representatives be appointed, to whom said message is referred, to investigate the matters set forth in said message and report to this Legislature, the investigation to apply to no person but the present State Printer.

E. W. SMILEY,
Chief Clerk of the Senate.

The foregoing concurred in January 24, 1893.
CHARLES E. VOORHEES,
Chief Clerk of the House of Representatives.

APPROVED—The 25th day of January, 1893.
ROBT. E. PATTISON.

No. 7.

IN THE HOUSE OF REPRESENTATIVES,
January 23, 1893.

Ship canal.

Resolved, (if the Senate concur,) That the Representatives from Pennsylvania in the House of Representatives in the Congress of the United States, be requested to vote for and advocate the passage of Senate bill No. 894, now pending in Congress, requiring the Secretary of War to cause a survey to be made for a ship canal, connecting the waters of Lake Erie and the Ohio river.

Extract from the Journal of the House of Representatives.

CHARLES E. VOORHEES,
Chief Clerk of the House of Representatives.

IN THE SENATE, *January 24, 1893.*
The foregoing resolution concurred in.

E. W. SMILEY,
Chief Clerk of the Senate.

APPROVED—The 1st day of February, A. D. 1893.

ROBT. E. PATTISON.

No. 8.

IN THE HOUSE OF REPRESENTATIVES,
January 27, 1893.

Resolved, (if the Senate concur,) That the concurrent resolution requesting the Legislature of Delaware to consent to the acquisition of land for quarantine purposes, be recalled from the Governor.

Extract from the Journal of the House of Representatives.

CHARLES E. VOORHEES,
Chief Clerk of the House of Representatives.

IN THE SENATE, *January 31, 1893.*
The foregoing resolution concurred in.

E. W. SMILEY,
Chief Clerk of the Senate.

APPROVED—The 1st day of February, A. D. 1893.

ROBT. E. PATTISON.

No. 9.

IN THE HOUSE OF REPRESENTATIVES,
January 31, 1893.

Resolved, (if the Senate concur,) That a committee to consist of three members of the House of Representatives and two on the part of the Senate be appointed for the purpose of reporting suitable resolutions to the Legislature in reference to the death of the Hon. James G. Blaine, and to recommend such further action as may be deemed proper in relation thereto.

Extract from the Journal of the House of Representatives.

CHARLES E. VOORHEES,
Chief Clerk of the House of Representatives.

IN THE SENATE, *January 31, 1893.*
The foregoing resolution concurred in.

E. W. SMILEY,
Chief Clerk of the Senate.

APPROVED—The 1st day of February, A. D. 1893.

ROBT. E. PATTISON.

No. 10.

Pensions.

Resolved, (if the Senate concur,) That we view with alarm the proclaimed purpose to strike down the pensions of the patriotic men who saved this country from disruption, and declare that instead of a reduction of pensions we are in favor of placing every honorably discharged soldier on the pension rolls, under the terms of the Pennsylvania service pension bill, introduced in the United States Senate by Senator J. D. Cameron, or a modification thereof, whereby every honorably discharged soldier of the war of the rebellion shall be treated as the veterans of all other wars of the United States have been. We further enter our solemn protest against the effort now being made to deprive the armless and legless veterans of their right, under the present law, to an exchange of their artificial limbs. We believe the preservation of this nation is worth all it cost in blood and treasure, including the money heretofore paid and to be paid to its veteran soldiers as pensions, and we earnestly request the Pennsylvania Senators and members of the House of Representatives to use their best efforts to secure the immediate pensioning of every honorably discharged soldier, and to prevent the threatened injustice to our armless and legless veterans.

Extract from the Journal of the House of Representatives.

CHARLES E. VOORHEES,
Chief Clerk of the House of Representatives.

IN THE SENATE, *January* 31, 1893.
The foregoing resolution concurred in.

E. W. SMILEY,
Chief Clerk of the Senate.

APPROVED—The 6th day of February, A. D. 1893.
ROBT. E. PATTISON.

No. 11.

IN THE SENATE, *January* 31, 1893.

Joint special committee on quarantine report. &c.

Resolved, (if the House of Representatives concur,) That a joint special committee of three members of the Senate and six members of the House of Representatives be appointed, to which the report of the Quarantine Station Commission be referred, with instructions to visit the various sites referred to by the Commission; make inquiry as to the probable cost of establishing a new State quarantine station; obtain the views of the pilot, captains and shipping interests on the subject; consult with the officials of the United States Marine Hospital Service and with the authorities of Delaware so that the plans of the National Government with reference to the National Quarantine for the Delaware Bay

and river may be ascertained, and make report concerning the same, together with such recommendation as they may deem proper, within twenty-one days from this date.
E. W. SMILEY,
Chief Clerk of the Senate.

The foregoing concurred in January 31, 1893.
CHARLES E. VOORHEES,
Chief Clerk of the House of Representatives.

APPROVED—The 6th day of February, A. D. 1893.
ROBT. E. PATTISON.

No. 12.

IN THE SENATE, *January* 31, 1893.

WHEREAS, A revolution has occurred in the Sandwich Islands and Commissioners have been appointed to submit propositions of annexation to the government of the United States,

And whereas, The patriotic sentiment of the American people, the rapidly increasing necessities of the United States and the great development promised in the near future for our merchant and naval marine, demand that this opportunity shall be boldly and firmly met:

Resolved, (if the House concur,) That our Senators and Representatives in Congress be requested to make every effort to secure the acceptance of the propositions of the Commissioners of the Sandwich Islands to the United States, on such terms and conditions as may be hereafter agreed upon.
E. W. SMILEY,
Chief Clerk of the Senate.

The foregoing concurred in February 1, 1893.
CHARLES E. VOORHEES,
Chief Clerk of the House of Representatives.

APPROVED—The 7th day of February, A. D. 1893.
ROBT. E. PATTISON.

Marginal notes: Preamble No. 1. Preamble No. 2. Propositions of Sandwich Island Commissioners should be accepted.

No. 13.

IN THE SENATE, *February* 2, 1893.

Resolved, (if the House of Representatives concur,) That the five hundred copies of the memorial proceedings on the death of the late Senator Mehard, which were ordered to be printed by the resolution approved January 18, 1893, shall be bound in cloth in the usual manner.
E. W. SMILEY,
Chief Clerk of the Senate.

The foregoing concurred in February 6, 1893.
CHARLES E. VOORHEES,
Chief Clerk of the House of Representatives.

APPROVED—The 7th day of February, A. D. 1893.
ROBT. E. PATTISON.

No. 14.

IN THE HOUSE OF REPRESENTATIVES,
February 3, 1893.

Resolved, (if the Senate concur,) That 2,500 copies of
the report of the Quarantine Commission, be printed in
pamphlet form, 1,200 for the use of the House; 800 for
the use of the Senate, and 500 for the use of the Governor.

CHARLES E. VOORHEES,
Chief Clerk of the House of Representatives.

E. W. SMILEY,
Chief Clerk of the Senate.

APPROVED—The 8th day of February, A. D. 1893.

ROBT. E. PATTISON.

No. 15.

IN THE HOUSE OF REPRESENTATIVES,
January 23, 1893.

Against the repeal or modification by Congress of the
act requiring the World's Columbian Exposition to be
closed on Sunday.

Preamble No. 1.

WHEREAS, Efforts are being made to secure the repeal
of that part of the act of Congress, passed at its last session, making an appropriation of two million five hundred thousand dollars from the National Treasury, in aid
of the Columbian Exposition at Chicago, commonly
known as the World's Fair, which prescribes the condition that the gates of said exposition shall be closed on
the Lord's day, commonly called Sunday,

Preamble No. 2.

And whereas, The directors of said exposition have
formally accepted the appropriation upon the condition
aforesaid, therefore, be it

Representatives in
Congress requested
to vote against re-
peal of act closing
gates of World's
Fair on Sunday.

Resolved, (if the Senate concur,) That the members of
the House of Representatives from Pennsylvania and the
Senators in the Senate of the United States, from this
State, be requested to vote against any proposition that
may be introduced for the repeal or modification of the
conditions upon which the appropriation was made, and
be it further

Copy of resolution
to be sent each mem-
ber.

Resolved, That the Governor cause a copy of the foregoing preamble and resolution be forwarded to each
member in the Senate and House of Representatives in
Congress from Pennsylvania.

Extract from the Journal of the House of Representatives.   CHARLES E. VOORHEES,
Chief Clerk of the House of Representatives.

IN THE SENATE, *February 8, 1893.*

E. W. SMILEY,
Chief Clerk of the Senate.

APPROVED—The 11th day of February, A. D. 1893.

ROBT. E. PATTISON.

No. 16.

In the House of Representatives,
February 8, 1893.

Resolved, (if the Senate concur,) That five thousand copies of the proceedings on the adoption of the memorial resolutions relating to the late Hon. James G. Blaine be printed in pamphlet form; three thousand for the use of the House, one thousand for the use of the Senate, and one thousand for the use of the Executive and other departments.

Extract from the Journal of the House of Representatives.

CHARLES E. VOORHEES,
Chief Clerk of the House of Representatives.
In the Senate, *February* 8, 1893.
E. W. SMILEY,
Chief Clerk of the Senate.
Approved—The 11th day of February, A. D. 1893.
ROBT. E. PATTISON.

No. 17.

In the House of Representatives,
February 10, 1893.

Resolved, (if the Senate concur,) That the five thousand (5,000) copies of the proceedings on the adoption of the memorial resolutions relating to the late Hon. James G. Blaine which were ordered to be printed by the resolution approved February 11, 1893, shall be bound in cloth in the usual manner.

Extract from the Journal of the House of Representatives.

CHARLES E. VOORHEES,
Chief Clerk of the House of Representatives.
In the Senate, *February* 15, 1893.
The foregoing resolution concurred in.
E. W. SMILEY,
Chief Clerk of the Senate.
Approved—The 15th day of February, A. D. 1893.
ROBT. E. PATTISON.

No. 18.

In the House of Representatives,
February 10, 1893.

Resolved, (if the Senate concur,) That the Board of Commissioners of Public Grounds and Buildings are hereby authorized to loan the Women's Silk Culture Association, under such conditions as to their safe keeping and return as the Board shall impose, the set of flags presented by that association to the State of Pennsylvania in 1885, for the purpose of exhibiting the same with the other silk exhibits, at the World's Columbian Exposition.

Extract from the Journal of the House of Representatives.

CHARLES E. VOORHEES,
Chief Clerk of the House of Representatives.

IN THE SENATE, *February* 15, 1893.

The foregoing resolution concurred in.

E. W. SMILEY,
Chief Clerk of the Senate.

APPROVED—The 15th day of February, A. D. 1893.
ROBT. E. PATTISON.

No. 19.

IN THE SENATE, *February* 14, 1893.

5000 apportionment maps to be furnished.

Resolved, (if the House concur,) That the Superintendent of Public Printing be and is hereby instructed to prepare and furnish, for the use of the Senate and members, five thousand apportionment maps of Pennsylvania;

How printed, and contents of.

said maps to be in outline giving county lines, and showing population by counties, as furnished by the census of 1890, with the vote cast by each political party at the last presidential election; that upon the back of said maps there be printed maps of the cities of Philadelphia, Allegheny and Scranton, showing the wards of said cities, with their population and party vote, and maps of the counties of Allegheny, Bucks, Lackawanna, Lancaster, Luzerne, Montgomery, Westmoreland and Schuylkill, showing their township divisions, and population by townships. Two thousand for the use of the Senate, and three thousand for the use of the House.

E. W. SMILEY,
Chief Clerk of the Senate.

The foregoing concurred in, February 15, 1893.

CHARLES E. VOORHEES,
Chief Clerk of the House of Representatives.

APPROVED—The 16th day of February, A. D. 1893.
ROBT. E. PATTISON.

No. 20.

IN THE SENATE, *February* 28, 1893.

Preamble No. 1.

WHEREAS, The President of the United States will shortly have the disposition of nearly half a million dollars for quarantine purposes;

Preamble No. 2.

And whereas, The Legislature of Pennsylvania is informed that Walter Wyman, Surgeon General of the Marine Hospital Service, U. S A., has strongly recommended to the Secretary of War the extension and improvement of the quarantine service at the port of Philadelphia, by establishing a boarding and disinfecting station on Rudy Island in the Delaware river, which shall be subsidiary to the United States Marine Hospital Service at Lewes, Delaware,

And whereas, The speedy perfection of the Federal quarantine service at the port of Philadelphia is of vital importance, not only to the States bordering on the Delaware bay and river, but to every State in the Union, inasmuch as a large majority of the emigrants landing at the port are transferred direct to other sections of the country, and the danger from the admission of contagious and infectious diseases is great, therefore, be it

Resolved, (if the House concur,) That we, while standing ready to assist and co-operate with the Federal authorities in preventing the entrance of the threatened cholera scourge, and being determined to leave nothing undone to establish a thorough and vigilant quarantine guard at the port of Philadelphia, respectfully request the President of the United States to see to it, that prompt and sufficient measures are taken to put into effect the plans of the United States Marine Hospital Service for the improvement of the quarantine system in the Delaware bay and river, and be it further

Resolved, That the Governor of this Commonwealth be respectfully requested to communicate these resolutions to the President of the United States.

E. W. SMILEY,
Chief Clerk of the Senate.

Concurred in March 1, 1893.

CHARLES E. VOORHEES,
Chief Clerk of the House of Representatives.

APPROVED—The 6th day of March, A. D. 1893.

ROBT. E. PATTISON.

(margin note: Preamble No. 3.)

(margin note: Quarantine service for Delaware bay and river.)

No. 21.

IN THE SENATE, *March* 20, 1893.

Resolved, (if the House concur,) That the Governor be requested to return to the Senate, House bill No. 14, entitled "An act rendering women eligible to the office of notary public" for amendment.

E. W. SMILEY,
Chief Clerk of the Senate.

Concurred in March 21, 1893.

CHARLES E. VOORHEES,
Chief Clerk of the House of Representatives.

APPROVED—The 21st day of March, A. D. 1893.

ROBT. E. PATTISON.

No. 22.

IN THE SENATE, *March* 30, 1893.

Resolved, (if the House concur,) That the clerks of the Senate and House of Representatives be directed to furnish to the several apportionment committees, maps prepared for the session of the Legislature in 1891, for the use of such committee in the preparation of bills apportioning the State into Congressional, Senatorial and Assembly districts.

E. W. SMILEY,
Chief Clerk of the Senate.

The foregoing concurred in April 5, 1893.

CHARLES E. VOORHEES,
Chief Clerk of the House of Representatives.

APPROVED—The 10th day of April, A. D. 1893.

ROBT. E. PATTISON.

No. 23.

IN THE SENATE, *March* 27, 1893.

Resolved, (if the House concur,) That 450 copies of the memorial proceedings in the Senate, upon the death of Hon. John N. Neeb of the Forty-second Senatorial district, be printed and bound in cloth for the use of the Senate.

E. W. SMILEY,
Chief Clerk of the Senate.

The foregoing concurred in March 28, 1893.

CHARLES E. VOORHEES,
Chief Clerk of the House of Representatives.

APPROVED—The 17th day of April, A. D. 1893.

ROBT. E. PATTISON.

No. 24.

IN THE SENATE, *April* 13, 1893.

Resolved, (if the House concur,) That House bill No. 24, entitled "An act to amend an act, entitled 'An act relating to marriage licenses, providing for officers herein indicated to issue licenses for parties to marry,' approved the twenty-third day of June, Anno Domini one thousand eight hundred and eighty-five, relating to the county wherein to secure the license," be recalled from the Governor for the purpose of amendment.

E. W. SMILEY,
Chief Clerk of the Senate.

The foregoing concurred in April 13, 1893.

CHARLES E. VOORHEES,
Chief Clerk of the House of Representatives.

APPROVED—The 18th day of April, A. D. 1893.

ROBT. E. PATTISON.

No. 25.

IN THE HOUSE OF REPRESENTATIVES,
April 17, 1893.

WHEREAS, Our institutions such as hospitals, asylums, almhouses, &c., are full to overflowing, and the number of inmates are constantly increasing so as to demand the enormous sum of $14,597,000 to still further enlarge our facilities for the care and maintenance of those who become dependent upon public bounty, and with a view to ascertain, as correctly as possible, reliable statistics on the question of how many of the inmates of said institutions are aliens, therefore,

Resolved, (if the Senate concur,) That the State Board of Charities notify all institutions within the State to report to them annually, under oath or affirmation, the number of such inmates, whence they came, and how long resident in this or other States previous to their coming here, and hereafter that the Board shall include the same in its annual report to the Governor, the Senate and House of Representatives for their consideration and action thereon, as they may deem necessary.

Extract from the Journal of the House of Representatives.

CHARLES E. VOORHEES,
Chief Clerk of the House of Representatives.

IN THE SENATE, *April* 19, 1893.

The foregoing resolution concurred in.

E. W. SMILFY,
Chief Clerk of the Senate.

APPROVED—The 24th day of April, A. D. 1893.

ROBT. E. PATTISON.

No. 26.

.IN THE SENATE, *May* 1, 1893.

Resolved, (if the House concur,) That the Governor be requested to return to the Senate, Senate bill 382, entitled "A supplement to an act, entitled 'An act to fix the salaries of the several State officers of the Commonwealth, the number of clerks to be employed in the several departments and their compensation, and providing for the incidental expenses of said departments,' approved May 14, 1874, providing for an increase of the salary of the Superintendent of Public Instruction."

E. W. SMILEY,
Chief Clerk of the Senate.

The foregoing resolution concurred in May 2, 1893.

CHARLES E. VOORHEES,
Chief Clerk of the House of Representatives.

APPROVED—The 2d day of May, A. D. 1893.

ROBT. E. PATTISON.

No. 27.

IN THE HOUSE OF REPRESENTATIVES,
May 2, 1893.

Resolved, (if the Senate concur,) That House bill No. 20 be recalled from the Governor for the purpose of having clerical error made in the transcribing room corrected.

Extract from the Journal.

CHARLES E. VOORHEES,
Chief Clerk of the House of Representatives.

IN THE SENATE, *May* 2, 1893.

The foregoing resolution concurred in.

E. W. SMILEY,
Chief Clerk of the Senate.

APPROVED—The 2d day of May, A. D. 1893.
ROBT. E. PATTISON.

No. 28.

IN THE HOUSE OF REPRESENTATIVES,
May 3, 1893.

Resolved, (if the Senate concur,) That the Governor be requested to return to the House of Representatives, House bill No. 64, entitled "An act to empower boroughs and cities to establish a police pension fund, to take property in trust therefor, to contribute thereto, and regulating and providing for the regulation of the same," for the purpose of amendments.

Extract from the journal of the House.

CHARLES E. VOORHEES,
Chief Clerk of the House of Representatives.

IN THE SENATE, *May* 4, 1893.

The foregoing resolution concurred in.

E. W. SMILEY,
Chief Clerk of the Senate.

APPROVED—The 4th day of May, A. D. 1893.
ROBT. E. PATTISON.

No. 29.

IN THE HOUSE OF REPRESENTATIVES,
May 23, 1893.

Resolved, (if the Senate concur,) That the Governor be requested to return to the House of Representatives, House bill No. 225, an act, entitled "A further supplement to the act regulating elections in this Commonwealth," approved the thirtieth day of January, Anno Domini one thousand eight hundred and seventy-four, as

amended by the act of May twenty-nine, one thousand
eight hundred and ninety-one, fixing the place at which
assessors shall sit to perform their duties imposed upon
them by the second section of said supplement of May
twenty-nine, one thousand eight hundred and ninety-one,
in all voting districts or precincts in this Commonwealth,
where temporary voting places are or may be established," for amendment.

Extract from the journal of the House of Representatives.

CHARLES E. VOORHEES,
Chief Clerk of the House of Representatives.

IN THE SENATE, *May*, 24, 1893.

The foregoing resolution concurred in.

E. W. SMILEY,
Chief Clerk of the Senate.

APPROVED—The 24th day of May, A. D. 1893.

ROBT. E. PATTISON.

No. 30.

IN THE HOUSE OF REPRESENTATIVES, *May* 24, 1893.

Resolved, (if the House concur), That the Governor be
requested to return to the House of Representatives,
House bill No. 61, File Folio 181, entitled "An act requiring all public records within this Commonwealth to
be kept in the English language," for the purpose of
amendment.

Extract from the Journal.

CHARLES E. VOORHEES,
Chief Clerk of the House of Representatives.

IN THE SENATE, *May* 25, 1893.

The foregoing resolution concurred in.

E. W. SMILEY,
Chief Clerk of the Senate.

APPROVED—The 25th day of May, A. D. 1893.

ROBT. E. PATTISON.

No. 31.

IN THE SENATE, *May* 23, 1893.

WHEREAS, The people of the city of Easton, Northampton county, have alleged, by petition to this Legislature,
that they are greatly inconvenienced for want of a free
public bridge to cross the river Delaware to the city of
Philipsburg in the State of New Jersey; that a toll
bridge now occupies the only location at which a bridge
between the aforesaid cities can be erected, it is impossible to erect any such structure as the great travel and
business between these cities demand, and

Whereas, The construction and style of the present toll bridge is not designed for a great thoroughfare but is very objectionable to the people compelled to use it, and has been condemned by the Medical Society and the last Grand Jury of Northampton county as detrimental to the public health and the morals of the people;

Whereas, The petitions signed by the leading citizens of Easton alleges that the company has now a reserve fund far in excess of any allowed by their charter and is and has for years been paying a dividend averaging twenty-five per cent. annually to their stockholders, and has not for many years rendered an account of its business to the Legislature as required by law, all of which being in direct violation of the act authorizing the incorporation of the company.

Resolved, (if the House concur,) That the Legislature demand of the "Company for erecting a bridge over the river Delaware at the borough of Easton," a statement of the business of the company, to comply with the provisions of law, and hereby instruct the Attorney General of the Commonwealth to institute such legal proceedings as in his judgment will be required to bring about an annulment of the charter of the company.

E. W. SMILEY,
Chief Clerk of the Senate.

The foregoing resolution concurred in, May 24, A. D. 1893.

CHARLES E. VOORHEES,
Chief Clerk of the House of Representatives.

APPROVED—The 25th day of May, A. D. 1893.
ROBT. E. PATTISON.

No. 32.

IN THE HOUSE OF REPRESENTATIVES, *May 25,* 1893.

Resolved, (if the Senate concur,) That the Governor be requested to return to the House of Representatives, Senate bill No. 377, file folio 2403, printer's No. 601, entitled "An act to provide for the support of the indigent insane in certain counties or cities of this Commonwealth," for the purpose of amendment.

Extract from the Journal.

CHARLES E. VOORHEES,
Chief Clerk of the House of Representatives.

IN THE SENATE, *May 26,* 1893.

The foregoing resolution concurred in.

E. W. SMILEY,
Chief Clerk of the Senate.

APPROVED—The 26th day of May, A. D. 1893.
ROBT. E. PATTISON.

No. 33.

IN THE SENATE, *May* 22, 1893.

Resolved, (if the House concur,) That House bill No. 223, entitled "An act relating to costs in criminal prosecutions, limiting the amount to be allowed on separate bills of indictment in any one prosecution," be recalled from the Governor for the purpose of amendment.

E. W. SMILEY,
Chief Clerk of the Senate.

The foregoing resolution concurred in May 23, A. D. 1893. CHARLES E. VOORHEES,
Chief Clerk of the House of Representatives.

APPROVED—The 25th day of May, A. D. 1893.

ROBT. E. PATTISON.

No. 34.

IN THE SENATE, *May* 25, 1893.

Resolved, (if the House concur,) That the commercial and maritime interests of the port of Philadelphia require the speedy completion of the improvements to its harbor, by the removal of the islands and shoals opposite the city without further delay.

Resolved, That the Governor be requested to forward a copy of this resolution to the Secretary of War.

E. W. SMILEY,
Chief Clerk of the Senate.

The foregoing resolution concurred in May 29, A. D. 1893. CHARLES E. VOORHEES,
Chief Clerk of the House of Representatives.

APPROVED—The 30th day of May, A. D. 1893.

ROBT. E. PATTISON.

No. 35.

IN THE HOUSE OF REPRESENTATIVES,
May 29, 1893.

Resolved, (if the Senate concur,) That House bill No. 452, file folio 1569, entitled "An act to repeal an act relating to the sale of seated lands in the county of Pike," approved February 12, 1870, be recalled from the Governor for amendment.

Extract from the Journal of the House of Representatives. CHARLES E. VOORHEES,
Chief Clerk of the House of Representatives.

IN THE SENATE, *May* 30, 1893.

The foregoing resolution concurred in.

E. W. SMILEY,
Chief Clerk of the Senate.

APPROVED—The 30th day of May, A. D. 1893.

ROBT. E. PATTISON.

CERTIFICATE.

OFFICE OF THE SECRETARY OF THE COMMONWEALTH,
HARRISBURG, *July 1, 1893.*

I certify that, in obedience to the directions of an act of the General Assembly of the Commonwealth of Pennsylvania, I have collated with, and corrected by the original rolls on file in this office, the proof sheets of the printed copies of this edition of the Laws and Resolutions of the General Assembly, passed during the session ending the first day of June, Anno Domini one thousand eight hundred and ninety-three.

WILLIAM F. HARRITY,
Secretary of the Commonwealth.

A PROCLAMATION BY THE GOVERNOR.

In the name and by authority of the Commonwealth of Pennsylvania.

A PROCLAMATION.

I, Robert E. Pattison, Governor of the Commonwealth of Pennsylvania, have caused this proclamation to issue and in compliance with the provisions of article four, section fifteen of the Constitution thereof, do hereby give notice, that I have filed in the office of the Secretary of the Commonwealth, with my objections thereto, the following bills passed by both Houses of the General Assembly, viz:

House bill No. 43, entitled "An act to provide for an additional law judge of the several courts of the twenty-seventh judicial districts."

House bill No. 457, entitled "An act regulating constables returns to the quarter sessions court of the county of Chester."

House bill No. 338, entitled "An act granting an annuity to Thomas A. Wagner of Snyder county, Pennsylvania, a private in Company H, thirty-sixth regiment, Pennsylvania State Militia."

House bill No. 389, entitled "An act granting a pension to Hamilton Smith of Jefferson county."

House bill No. 466, entitled "An act repealing so much of section one of an act approved April twenty-fifth, one thousand eight hundred and eighty-nine, entitled 'An act to amend the provisions of the first section of an act approved May thirteen, one thousand eight hundred and eighty-seven,' entitled 'An act for the destruction of wolves and wild cats,' as provides a premium for the destruction of foxes, so far as applies to Fayette county."'

House bill No. 595, entitled "An act granting an annuity to Stephen Smith of Lehigh county, Pennsylvania, a private, afterwards second lieutenant, in Company I, Forty-first regiment, Pennsylvania Volunteers."

House bill No. 241, entitled "An act to prevent the prosecution in this State of actions, which, at the time of commencing the same, are barred by the laws of the State or country in which the cause thereof arose."

Senate bill No. 156, entitled "An act to repeal the eight section of an act, entitled 'An act to incorporate the Schuylkill County Agricultural society; relative to a school district in Schuylkill county; to an election district in said county; to the daily pay of the commissioners of Berks county; to reporter of the decisions of the Supreme Court; to the collection of school taxes in certain townships in Crawford and Allegheny counties; to the estate of Joseph Parker Norris, deceased; to the Keystone Life and Health Insurance Company; to tavern licenses in Philadelphia city and county; to the estate of Polly Dunlap of Clearfield county ; to the sale of a lot of ground by the overseers of the public school of the city and county of Philadelphia', approved the fourteenth day of April, one thousand eight hundred and fifty-one."

House bill No 518, entitled "An act repealing so much of section one of an act approved April twenth-fifth, one thousand eight hundred and eighty-nine, entitled 'An act to amend the provisions of the first section of an act approved May thirteenth, one thousand eight hundred and eighty-seven,' entitled 'An act for the destruction of wolves and wildcats as provides a premium for the destruction of foxes and minks'" so far as the same applies to Greene county.'"

Senate bill No. 54, entitled "An act to repeal the first section of an act, entitled 'An act to prohibit the issuing of licenses to sell spirituous, vinous, malt or brewed liquors in the borough of Braddock, borough of Sewickley, townships of Wilkins, Versailles, Penn, North Fayette, South Fayette, Sewickley, Leet and Kilbuck, in the county of Allegheny,' approved the ninth day of April, Anno Domini one thousand eight hundred and seventy, so far as the same relates to the borough of Verona, in the said county of Allegheny."

House bill No. 183, entitled "An act to provide for the publication of abstracts of charters and other documents, relative to corporations, filed in the office of the Secretary of the Commonwealth."

House bill No. 980, entitled "An act making an appropriation to the Waterford Academy at Waterford, in the county of Erie."

House bill No. 100, entitled "An act authorizing the Superintendent of Public Instruction to place in each public school of this Commonwealth, one copy of Smull's Legislative Hand Book, and providing for the same, and providing compensation for a more thorough revision of the work."

Senate bill No. 136, entitled "A supplement to an act, entitled 'An act granting a pension to Louis Neudoerffer,' approved April second, one thousand eight hundred and sixty-seven, extending said pension to his widow Ida Neudoerffer."

Senate bill No. 40, entitled "An act relating to debts, not of record, of decedents."

House bill No. 196, entitled "An act to amend sections two and three of an act, entitled 'A supplement to an act to provide for the appointment of a fire marshal for the county of Allegheny,' approved the fourteenth day of April, one thousand eight hundred and seventy, enlarging the duties and powers of the Fire Marshal."

House bill No. 982, entitled "An act making an appropriation to the Pennsylvania State Agricultural Society "

House bill No. 476, entitled "An act to prohibit the peddling, selling or hawking of merchandise, wares or other goods, within this Commonwealth, without a license."

Senate bill No. 525, entitled "An act making an appropriation to aid the several townships in this Commonwealth in the construction, improvement and maintenance of public roads, and providing the manner of the distribution of the same."

Senate bill No. 405, entitled "An act to authorize cities to make appropriations for the establishment and maintenance of free libraries, and to acquire, by condemnation, eligible sites for the location thereof."

Senate bill No. 277, entitled "An act to prohibit the peddling, selling or hawking of produce and merchandise in the cities of the second and third classes within this Commonwealth, without a license."

House bill No. 104, entitled "An act to make taxes assessed upon real estate by counties, townships and boroughs a lien, and to provide for the collection of such taxes and a remedy for false returns."

House bill No. 150, entitled "An act to protect the revenue of the State by preventing fire insurance companies, firms and associations incorporated by another State, or a foreign government, or organized under the laws thereof, from taking risks, issuing policies or placing insurance within this State, or upon property situate therein, except by agents or officers residing within this State, requiring for that purpose affidavit, under pain of perjury, before licenses shall be issued to any such company, firm and association, and further regulating the issuing of licenses thereto."

Senate bill No. 17, entitled "An act authorizing cities and boroughs of the Commonwealth of Pennsylvania to purchase bridges already erected, or to erect and maintain bridges over streams and rivers which may separate portions of such cities and boroughs, and providing for the condemnation of such land as may be necessary for piers, abutments, fills, slopes and approaches thereto."

Senate bill No. 98, entitled "An act to authorize the orphans' court of any county of this Commonwealth, upon petition to appoint a commissioner to inquire into the advisability of funding a charge upon any lands in this Commonwealth by last will and testament, and upon his report to decree the appointment of a trustee to hold and invest the fund, and further authorizing the court to make a decree discharging the land from the lien of the charge."

Senate bill No. 196, entitled "An act to regulate the manner of electing trustees of academies chartered by act of Assembly of the Commonwealth of Pennsylvania."

House bill No. 369 entitled "An act providing for the creation and regulation of municipal liens, and the proceedings for the collection thereof in the several boroughs of this State."

House bill No. 549, entitled "An act providing for the fencing of improved lands used for agricultural and horticultural purposes in the counties of Clearfield, Centre and Cameron."

Senate bill No. 20, entitled "An act to amend an act, entitled an act to amend clause two of section thirty-one of an act, entitled 'An act to provide for the incorporation and regulation of certain corporations,' approved the twenty-ninth day of April, Anno Domini one thousand eight hundred and seventy-four, providing for increased rates of toll upon bridges in certain cases, approved the sixth day of May, one thousand eight hundred and eighty-seven, by more particularly designating the rates of toll, by providing for increase of tolls, when authorized by the court of quarter sessions, in certain cases."

Senate bill No. 113, entitled "An act to amend the first section of an act, entitled 'An act relative to the compensation of the directors of the poor and house of employment of Lehigh county,' approved the twenty-first day of March, Anno Domini one thousand eight hundred and sixty-five, defining and fixing the per diem salary of said directors of the poor."

House bill No. 507, entitled "An act to prohibit the catching or taking, for sale, within the counties of Tioga and Bradford, any grouse or pheasant, quail or partridge, woodcock, wild pigeon, speckled trout or black bass, and also to prohibit absolutely the killing of deer or fawn for a period of three years "

House bill No. 626, entitled "An act securing to mechanics, journeymen and laborers the right to file liens against real estate for the amount

of wages due for work or labor done in and about the erection or construction thereof."

Senate bill No. 120, entitled "An act providing that every vessel pro-
pelled in whole or in part by steam, shall be deemed a steam vessel
within the meaning of this act, and providing for the inspection of the
same."

House bill No. 677, entitled "An act making an appropriation for the
improvement and repair of the bank and channel of Oil Creek in the
county of Crawford, between the bridge on the Meadville road east of
Holliday's dam and the mouth of Pine creek, and to improve the sanitary condition of the territory adjacent thereto."

House bill No. 678, entitled "An act making an appropriation for the
improvement and repair of the banks and the re-location and deepening
of the channel of Little French Creek in the county of Erie, so far as
said creek is located within the limits of the borough of Union City in
said county, and providing measures for restoring the sanitary conditions of the borough."

House bill No. 679, entitled "An act making an appropriation for the
improvement and repair of the bank and channel of Oil Creek in the
county of Venango, between the bridge on the Western New York and
Pennsylvania Railroad bridge and the mouth of Oil Creek, and to improve the sanitary condition of the territory adjacent thereto."

House bill No. 1033, entitled "An act making an appropriation for
the construction of a channel for Neeson's Run, through the city of
Meadville, in the county of Crawford, between the site of the old French
Creek Feeder Canal, at the point where the said Neeson's Run formerly
flowed into the same and French Creek, and to improve the sanitary
condition of the territory adjacent thereto."

House bill No. 90, entitled "An act to prevent the adulteration of
drugs, food and spirituous, fermented or malt liquors in the State of
Pennsylvania."

Senate bill No. 47, entitled "An act to repeal an act entitled 'A supplement to an act to extend the powers of certain officers in Allegheny
county, approved the twenty-sixth day of February, Anno Domini one
thousand eight hundred and fifty-five, and for the better regulation of
the Sabbath in said county,' approved the twenty-sixth day of April,
Anno Domini one thousand eight hundred and fifty-five."

Senate bill No. 104, entitled "An act to enable city, county, township,
ward, school and borough tax collectors to collect taxes for the payment
of which they have become personally liable, without having collected
the same, but by expiration of the authority of their respective warrants,
and to extend the time for collection of the same for a period of one
year from the passage of this act."

Senate bill No. 232, entitled "An act to amend an act, entitled 'An
act to carry into effect section five of article fourteen of the Constitution, relative to the salaries of county officers and the payment of fees
received by them into the State or county treasury, in counties containing over one hundred and fifty thousand inhabitants,' approved thirty-
first March, one thousand eight hundred and seventy-six, providing for
assistant district attorneys, and fixing the salary of the same, and increasing the salary of county solicitor, clerk of the courts, recorder of
deeds and treasurer, county commissioners, controllers, coroners, county
directors of the poor, jury commissioners and county detective, and de-
creasing the salaries of auditors and county surveyor."

House bill No. 361, entitled "An act to repeal an act, entitled 'An act to prevent the consolidation of competing pipe lines for the transportation of oil, or to hold the controlling interest in the stock or bonds of competing pipe lines, or the acquisition or control, either directly or indirectly, by purchase or otherwise, and prescribing penalties for the violation thereof,' approved the thirteenth day of June, Anno Domini one thousand eight hundred and eighty-three."

House bill No. 912, entitled "An act to make an appropriation to the Centennial and Memorial Association of Valley Forge."

Senate bill No. 377, entitled "An act to provide for the support of the indigent insane in certain counties or cities of this Commonwealth."

House bill No. 1032, entitled "An act making an appropriation for the purpose of erecting a protection wall and filling the washout caused by the erection of dam number one, and abutment thereto, of the Beaver division of the Pennsylvania canal at Bridgewater, Pennsylvania."

Senate bill No. 52, entitled "An act relating to street passenger railway companies and to traction and motor power companies, authorizing sales and leases of the franchises and property of the former to the latter, authorizing contracts between such companies for the construction of motors, cables, electric and other apparatus and appliances upon and along the lines of the former, authorizing contracts for the operation of railways by such traction and motor companies by means of such apparatus and appliances, and of all other lawful motive power, and authorizing traction and motor power companies to be lessors and grantors, and to become lessees and grantees of property and franchises."

House bill No. 788, entitled "An act making an appropriation to pay the expenses of the Committee on Elections of the House of Representatives, for investigating and preparing reports on contested elections in the counties of Crawford, Lackawanna, Lancaster and Montgomery, during the session of the Legislature of one thousand eight hundred and ninety-three."

Given under my hand and the great seal of the State at the city of Harrisburg, this twenty-ninth day of June, in the year [SEAL] of our Lord one thousand eight hundred and ninety-three, and of the Commonwealth the one hundred and seventeenth.

ROBT. E. PATTISON.

By THE GOVERNOR:
WILLIAM F. HARRITY,
Secretary of the Commonwealth.

Filed in the office of the Secretary of the Commonwealth at Harrisburg, the twenty-ninth day of June, A. D. 1893.

A. L. TILDEN,
Deputy Secretary of the Commonwealth.

LIST OF CHARTERS OF CORPORATIONS

ENROLLED IN THE OFFICE

OF THE

Secretary of the Commonwealth,

Between June 1, 1891, and June 1, 1893,

WITH AN INDEX THERETO.

LIST OF CHARTERS OF CORPORATIONS

Created and organized under Act of April 29, 1874, entitled "An act to provide for the incorporation and regulation of certain corporations," and the several supplements thereto, enrolled in the office of the Secretary of the Commonwealth. Published in pursuance of the provisions of the forty-fifth section of the aforesaid act of April 29, 1874.

1a LAWS.

STYLE AND TITLE OF CORPORATION.	PURPOSE.	LOCATION.
The Forty Fort Water Company. Capital, $5,000. June 1, 1891.	Said corporation is formed for the purpose of supplying water to the public at the borough of Forty Fort, Luzerne county, Pa., and to persons, corporations, associations and partnerships residing therein and adjacent thereto desiring the same.	Wilkes-Barre.
Pleasant Ridge Land and Improvement Company. Capital, $50,000. June 1, 1891.	Said corporation is formed for the purpose of the purchase and sale of real estate, and holding, leasing and selling same.	Philadelphia.
Bedford Mineral Springs Company. Capital, $8,000. June 1, 1891.	Said corporation is formed for the purpose of manufacturing and bottling mineral waters.	Bedford.
Wilkes Rolling Mill Company. Capital, $20,000. June 1, 1891.	Said corporation is formed for the purpose of the manufacture of iron and steel or both, or of any other metal, or of any article of commerce from metal or wood or both.	Sharon.
The Wilkinsburg Gas Company. Capital, $5,000. June 1, 1891.	Said corporation is formed for the purpose of manufacturing and supplying gas to the public at the borough of Wilkinsburg, Allegheny county, Pa., and to persons, partnerships, corporations and associations residing therein and adjacent thereto as may desire the same.	Wilkinsburg.
The Marietta Manufacturing Company. Capital, $25,000. June 1, 1891.	Said corporation is formed for the purpose of manufacturing agricultural, mechanical and other appliances and articles of merchandise, of utility and usefulness in the arts, trades and commerce, out of wood, iron, or both, or out of other materials, whether by means or use of processes secured by letters-patent or not, and generally to exercise and enjoy the right, privileges and powers enumerated and mentioned in said acts of assembly and the supplements thereto and thereof.	Marietta.

LIST OF CHARTERS OF CORPORATIONS.—*Continued.*

Style and Title of Corporations.	Purpose.	Location.
The Clifton Heights Building and Loan Association. Re-charter. Capital, $500,000. June 2, 1891.	Said corporation is formed for the purpose of conducting the business of accumulating a fund by the contributions of the members thereof, and of loaning the same to them from time to time to enable them to purchase real estate, build themselves dwelling houses, or engage in any legitimate business.	Clifton Heights.
The Lebanon Market House Company. Capital, $50,000. June 2, 1891.	Said corporation is formed for the purpose of the establishment and maintenance of a market house.	Lebanon.
Derry Sand Company. Capital, $100,000. June 2, 1891.	Said corporation is formed for the purpose of mining, quarrying, excavating, producing and preparing for market and selling sand, gravel, cobblestones and other mineral substances, and for these purposes to have, possess and enjoy all the rights, benefits and privileges of said act of assembly and the supplements thereto.	Pittsburgh.
J. B. Sheriff Manufacturing Company. Capital, $25,000. June 2, 1891.	Said corporation is formed for the purpose of the manufacture of iron or steel or both, of any other metal or of any article of commerce from wood or metal or both.	Pittsburgh.
The Sixth Ward Slater Excelsior Building Association. Capital $6,000 June 2, 1891.	Said corporation is formed for the purpose of accumulating a fund by the periodical contributions of the members thereof, and of safely investing the same.	Pittsburgh.
George S. Ferguson Company. Capital, $100,000. June 2, 1891.	Said corporation is formed for the purpose of carrying on a printing and publishing business, including electrotyping, stereotyping and book binding.	Philadelphia.
The United Lumber Company. Capital, 2 000. June 2, 1891.	Said corporation is formed for the purpose of carrying on the business of manufacturing and sale of lumber and hemlock bark.	Portage Creek.

The Bailey-Farrell Manufacturing Company. Capital, $300,000. June 3, 1891.	Said corporation is formed for the purpose of the manufacture of iron or steel or both, or of any other metal, or of any article or commerce from metal or wood or both.	Pittsburgh.
The Columbia Building and Loan Association. Re-charter. Capital, $1,000,000. June 3, 1891.	Said corporation is formed for the purpose of accumulating a fund by the periodical contributions of the members thereof, and of safely investing the same and to loan the same to them from time to time to enable them to purchase real estate, build themselves houses, or engage in any legitimate business.	Philadelphia.
R. D. Nuttall Company. Capital, $125,000. June 3, 1891.	Said corporation is formed for the purpose of manufacturing machines and machinery of any and all kinds, and selling the same, with the right to acquire patent-rights for inventions and designs relating thereto; to acquire real estate and buildings necessary therefor, and generally all and every act and thing necessary to the carrying on of the said business of manufacturing machines and machinery.	Allegheny.
Royersford Glass Company. Capital, $100,000. June 4, 1891.	Said corporation is formed for the purpose of the manufacturing and selling of glass bottles, vials and other similar ware.	Royersford.
The Delaware and Schuylkill River Steamboat Company. Capital, $5,000. June 5, 1891.	Said corporation is formed for the purpose of the building of ships, vessels or boats and the carriage of persons and property thereon.	Philadelphia.
The Mount Pleasant Building and Loan Association of Harrisburg, Pennsylvania. Capital, $500,000. June 5, 1891.	Said corporation is formed for the purpose of accumulating a fund by the periodical contributions of the members thereof, and of safely investing the same.	Harrisburg.
The Arlington Avenue Building and Loan Association of Pittsburgh, Pa. Capital, $1,000,000. June 8, 1891.	Said corporation is formed for the purpose of accumulating a fund by the periodical contributions of the members thereof, and of safely investing the same.	Pittsburgh.
The Washington Slate Company. Capital, $100,000. June 8, 1891.	Said corporation is formed for the purpose of mining and manufacturing slate and slate products of all kinds.	Slatington.

LIST OF CHARTERS AND CORPORATIONS—Continued.

Style and Title of Corporations.	Purpose.	Location.
The Rosedale Park Real Estate Company. Capital, $3,000. June 8, 1891.	Said corporation is formed for the purpose of the purchase and sale of real estate, or for holding, leasing and selling real estate.	Philadelphia.
The Scranton Lathe Turning Company. Capital, $5,000. June 8, 1891.	Said corporation is formed for the purpose of the manufacture from wood of all articles, whether round or in other shapes, which can be turned upon a lathe.	Scranton.
Standard Fuel Company. Capital, $50,000. June 9, 1891.	Said corporation is formed for the purpose of manufacturing natural and artificial fuel.	Philadelphia.
Claysville Real Estate Company. Capital, $10,000. June 9, 1891.	Said corporation is formed for the purpose of purchasing and selling real estate.	Claysvill
The Rouseville Water Company. Capital, $2,500. June 10, 1891.	Said corporation is formed for the purpose of furnishing water for domestic and commercial purposes to persons, partnerships and corporations residing in the village of Rouseville, in the county of Venango, and adjacent thereto as may desire the same at such price or prices as may be agreed upon.	Rouseville.
Westwood Coal Company. Capital, $165,000. June 10, 1891.	Said corporation is formed for the purpose of mining, shipping and selling coal and carrying on all business connected therewith and incidental thereto.	Philadelphia.
Allegheny Furnace Company. Capital, $100,000. June 10, 1891.	Said corporation is formed for the purpose of the manufacture of iron or steel or both, or of any other metal or article or commerce from metal, wood or both.	Pittsburgh.
Black Top Spanish Merino Sheep Breeders Publishing Association. Capital, $2,500. June 10, 1891.	Said corporation is formed for the purpose of printing and publishing from time to time, a register containing the history and pedigree of Black Top Spanish Merino Sheep.	Washington.

Speyerer Hotel Company. Capital $50,000. June 12, 1891.	Said corporation is formed for the purpose of establishing and maintaining a hotel in the borough of Rochester, county of Beaver and State of Pennsylvania	Rochester.
The Bloomsburg Carpet Works. Capital $100,000. June 12, 1891.	Said corporation is formed for the purpose of the manufacture of carpets and other textile fabrics.	Bloomsburg.
Standard Spinning Company. Capital, $40,000. June 15, 1891.	Said corporation is formed for the purpose of manufacturing and selling textile fabrics goods and yarns, made from cotton, wool or silk and generally to have, possess and enjoy all the rights, powers, privileges and franchises conferred by said acts of assembly upon those corporations of the second class—referred to in Clause XVIII of the Second section and specified in section thirty-nine of the corporation act of 1874.	Chester.
The Prudent Real Estate Investment Company. Capital, $10,000. June 15, 1891.	Said corporation is formed for the purpose of purchasing and selling real estate, holding and leasing the same.	Philadelphia.
The Dime Savings Building and Loan Association of Sharpsburg, Pa. Capital, $250,000. June 15, 1891.	Said corporation is formed for the purpose of accumulating a fund by the periodical contributions of the members thereof, and of safely investing the same.	Sharpsburg.
Crosier Stauffer Company. Capital, $50,000. June 15, 1891.	Said corporation is formed for the purpose of manufacturing crackers, biscuits, bread, cakes and other similar articles.	Philadelphia.
The German Daily Gazette. Capital, $50,000. June 16, 1891.	The purpose, for which the corporation is formed, is to carry on the printing and publishing business.	Philadelphia.
The Washington Pipe Line Company. Capital, $2,000. June 16, 1891.	Said corporation is formed for the purpose of transporting, storing and shipping petroleum, and for that purpose to have, possess and enjoy all the rights, benefits and privileges of the act of assembly above referred to, and the several supplements thereto.	Washington.
Sayre Electric Light, Heat and Power Company. Capital, $5,000. June 16, 1891.	Said corporation is formed for the purpose of supplying light, heat and power by means of electricity, to the public at the borough of Sayre and to persons, partnerships and associations residing therein and adjacent thereto as may desire the same.	Sayre.

LIST OF CHARTERS OF CORPORATIONS—*Continued.*

Style and Title of Corporation.	Purpose.	Location.
The Curwensville Mine Car Company. Capital, $5,000. June 16, 1891.	Said corporation is formed for the purpose of manufacturing and selling mine cars, hardware, specialties, of wood or iron, or both, and of transacting a general foundry and machine business.	Curwensville.
The Hibernia Building Association of Philadelphia. Capital, $1,000,000. June 17, 1891.	Said corporation is formed for the purpose of accumulating a fund by the periodical contributions of the members thereof, and of safely investing the same.	Philadelphia.
The A. R. Smith Chemical Company. Capital, $150,000. June 17, 1891.	Said corporation is formed for the purpose of manufacturing and selling acetates, wood spirits and other products from wood.	Bradford.
The West Girard Avenue Building & Loan Association. Capital, $1,000,000. June 18, 1891.	Said corporation is formed for the purpose of accumulating a fund by the periodical contributions of the members thereof, and of safely investing the same.	Philadelphia.
Newton Hamilton Oil and Gas Company. Capital, $3,000. June 19, 1891.	Said corporation is formed for the purpose of mining or drilling for oil or gas.	Newton Hamilton.
The Spring City Steam Paper and Box Manufacturing Company. Capital, $5,000. June 19, 1891.	Said corporation is formed for the purpose of manufacturing paper and paper boxes & envelopes and selling the same.	Spring City.
The Franklin Improvement Company. Capital, $100,000. June 22, 1891.	Said corporation is formed for the purpose of creating, purchasing, holding and selling of patent rights for inventions and designs, with the right to issue licenses for the same, and receive pay therefor.	Philadelphia.

Company	Purpose	Location
United States Iron and Tin Plate Manufacturing Company. Capital, $500,000. June 22, 1891.	Said corporation is formed for the purpose of the manufacture of iron or steel, or both, or of any other metal, or of any article of commerce from metal or wood, or both.	McKeesport.
The Ashman Steel Casting Company. Capital, $50,000. June 22, 1891.	Said corporation is formed for the purpose of the manufacture of iron or steel, or both, or of any other metal, or of any article of commerce from metal or wood, or both.	Sharon.
Somerset and Johnsonburg Manufacturing Company. Capital, $150,000. June 22, 1891.	Said corporation is formed for the purpose of the manufacture from clay, or combination of clay with other substances, or from coal dust, bricks, stove linings, tiles, paving blocks, sewer pipes, stone ware and pottery and brick-making machinery therefor.	Johnsonburg.
The Central Homestead Company of Germantown. Capital, $15,000. June 22, 1891.	Said corporation is formed for the purpose of purchasing, taking, hold ing and enjoying real estate in fee simple on lease or upon ground rent, improving, leasing, mortgaging and selling the same in fee simple; or for any less estate or upon ground rent to its sale, shareholders and others, or on such terms as to time of payment as it may determine.	Philadelphia.
The Spang Steel and Iron Company. Capital, $1,000,000. June 23, 1891.	Said corporation is formed for the purpose of the manufacture of iron or steel, or both, or of any other metal, or of any article of commerce from metal or wood, or both.	Etna.
Sampson Fertilizer and Chemical Company. Capital, $250,000. June 23, 1891.	Said corporation is formed for the purpose of manufacturing fertilizer and chemicals, their various compounds and combinations, and the sale or other disposition of the same.	Northeast borough, Erie county.
Eclipse Coal Company. Capital, $30,000. June 24, 1891.	Said corporation is formed for the purpose of mining coal and manufacturing coke.	Pittsburgh.
The Shrewsbury Water Company. Capital, $2,500. June 24, 1891.	Said corporation is formed for the purpose of supplying water to the public in the borough of Shrewsbury, York county, State of Pennsylvania, and to such persons and partnerships residing therein and adjacent thereto, as may desire the same.	Shrewsbury.
The Harrisburg Furniture Manufacturing Company. Capital, $50,000. June 24, 1891.	Said corporation is formed for the purpose of the manufacture and sale of furniture of every description.	Harrisburg.

LIST OF CHARTERS OF CORPORATIONS—*Continued.*

Style and Title of Corporation.	Purpose.	Location.
The Susquehanna Steam Heater and Manufacturing Company. Capital, $10,000. June 24, 1891.	Said corporation is formed for the purpose of to manufacture of iron or steel, or both, or of any other metal or article of commerce from metal or wood, or both.	Susquehanna Depot.
Wm. Beury & Co. Incorporated. Capital, $50,000. June 24, 1891.	Said corporation is formed for the purpose of manufacturing and selling of blasting and gun powder and other high explosives.	Shamokin.
The Philadelphia Bourse. Capital, $112,000. June 25, 1891.	Said corporation is formed for the purpose of purchasing real estate, holding, leasing and selling the same.	Philadelphia.
Auderton Brewing Company. Capital, $50,000. June 25, 1891.	Said corporation is formed for the purpose of manufacturing and brewing of malt liquors.	Beaver Falls.
The Robinson Machine Company, of Bellwood, Blair County, Pa. Capital, $20,000. June 26, 1891.	Said corporation is formed for the purpose of obtaining the powers and franchises set forth and contained in said act of assembly and the supplements thereto, pertaining to the manufacture of iron or steel, or both, or of any other metal, or of any article of commerce from metal or wood, or both, and for the purpose of manufacturing patent & other specialties in iron & steel.	Bellwood.
The First United States Excelsior Building Association. Capital, $500,000. June 29, 1891.	Said corporation is formed for the purpose of accumulating a fund by the periodical contributions of the members thereof, and of safely investing the same.	Washington.
The Pittsburgh Moccasin Company. Capital, $30,000. June 29, 1891.	Said corporation is formed for the purpose of the manufacture and sale of buck slippers, wool boots and all kinds of foot wear.	Pittsburgh.
Times Publishing Company of Norristown. Capital, $25,000. June 30, 1891.	Said corporation is formed for the purpose of the transaction of a printing and publishing business.	Norristown.

Company	Purpose	Location
California Coal Company, Capital, $50,000. July 2, 1891.	Said corporation is formed for the purpose of mining and selling coal and coke, and for that purpose to have, maintain and operate the necessary tools, appliances, steam boats, barges, flats, boats and cars incident to such business.	California.
American Vault, Safe and Lock Company, Capital, $4,000. July 3, 1891.	Said corporation is formed for the purpose of the manufacture of iron or steel, or both, or of any other metal, or of any article of commerce from metal or wood or both.	Elizabeth.
Avonmore Building and Loan Association, Capital, $1,000,000. July 6, 1891.	Said corporation is formed for the purpose of accumulating a fund by the periodical contributions of the members thereof, and of safely investing the same.	Avonmore.
The Crescent Pipe Line Company. Capital, $10,000. July 6, 1891.	Said corporation is formed for the purpose of transporting, insuring and shipping petroleum, and for that purpose to lay down, construct and maintain pipes, tubing, tanks, offices and such other machinery, devices or arrangements as may be necessary to fully carry out that right; and also with the right to enter upon take and occupy such land and other property as may be requisite for the purposes of such corporations.	Pittsburgh.
The Silverton Coal Company. Capital, $100,000. July 6, 1891.	Said corporation is formed for the purpose of mining coal and preparing the same for market.	Scranton.
Globe Ticket Company, Capital, $75,000. July 6, 1891.	Said corporation is formed for the purpose of manufacturing tickets of all sorts and kinds, including the making, coloring, printing, stamping, numbering and finishing of the same, and the transaction of all lawful business incidental and necessary thereto.	Philadelphia.
Mercantile Company, Capital, $100,000. July 6, 1891.	Said corporation is formed for the purpose of holding, leasing and selling real estate.	Pittsburgh.
Rockland Oil Company, Capital, $300,000. July 7, 1891.	Said corporation is formed for the purpose of boring, drilling, mining and operating for petroleum oil and gas and disposing of the same, the buying, selling, leasing, holding and disposing of such real and personal estate as may be necessary and convenient in the conducting of the business of such corporation.	Allegheny City.
The Bloomington Company.	Said corporation is formed for the purpose of mining, producing and ship-	

LIST OF CHARTERS OF CORPORATIONS—Continued.

STYLE AND TITLE OF CORPORATION.	PURPOSE.	LOCATION.
The Mashentuck Manufacturing Company. Capital, $100,000. July 8, 1891.	Said corporation is formed for the purpose of manufacturing cotton yarns and other cotton fabrics.	Allentown.
Marilla Gardens, Capital, $1,500. July 9, 1891.	Said corporation is formed for the purpose of establishing and maintaining the business of floral and market gardening, inclusive of the cultivation, purchase and sale of flowers, plants and trees, fruit, vegetables and seeds.	Bradford.
Nescopeck Water Company. Capital, $5,000. July 9, 1891.	Said corporation is formed for the purpose of furnishing water for domestic and manufacturing purposes to the citizens and public of Nescopeck, Luzerne county, Pennsylvania.	Nescopeck.
The Blue Ridge Land Company. Capital, $10,000. July 13, 1891.	Said corporation is formed for the purpose of the purchasing of real estate and the improvement thereof, and the selling the same, with or without improvement.	Pen Argyl.
Tioga Farmers Market Company. Capital, $40,000. July 14, 1891.	Said corporation is formed for the purpose of establishing and maintaining a market house.	Philadelphia.
Somerset Stone Company. Capital, $60,000. July 14, 1891.	Said corporation is formed for the purpose of quarrying and selling stone and manufacturing sand from stone and selling the same, and for these purposes to have, possess and enjoy all the rights, benefits and privileges of the said act of assembly and its supplements.	Johnstown.
Hanover Foundry and Machine Company, Capital, $100,000. July 15, 1891.	Said corporation is formed for the purpose of the manufacture of iron and steel, or both, or of any other metal, or of any article of commerce from metal or wood, or both.	Hanover.
Lebanon Match Company, Capital, $30,000. July 16, 1891.	Said corporation is formed for the purpose of the manufacture and sale of friction matches for igniting purposes.	Lebanon.

Company	Purpose	Location
The Devonian Oil Company. Capital, $300,000. July 16, 1891.	Said corporation is formed for the purpose of mining, drilling and operating for the production of oil and gas, with the right of acquiring property necessary therefor.	Pittsburgh.
Enterprise Homestead Company of (Germantown, Philadelphia. Capital, $15,000. July 16, 1891.	Said corporation is formed for the purpose of purchasing, taking, holding and enjoying real estate in fee simple, on lease, or upon ground rent, improving, leasing, mortgaging and selling the same in fee simple, or for any less estate or upon ground rent, to its sale, shareholders and thus upon such terms as it may determine.	Philadelphia.
The Bartlett Manufacturing Company. Capital, $20,000. July 20, 1891.	Said corporation is formed for the purpose of manufacturing preparations of shoe polish, shoe polish, laundry blues, mustard, spices, roasted coffees, flavoring extracts, sauces and condiments, and the selling of the same.	Philadelphia.
The Juniata Furnace and Foundry Company. Capital, $200,000. July 20, 1891.	Said corporation is formed for the purpose of manufacturing iron or steel, or of both, or of any other metal or of any article of commerce made from metal.	Philadelphia.
The National Homestead Loan and Trust Company of Pittsburgh, Pa. Capital, $15,000. July 20, 1891.	Said corporation is formed for the purpose of purchasing, taking, holding and enjoying real estate in fee simple, upon lease or upon ground rent, improving, leasing, mortgaging and selling the same in fee simple or for any less estate or upon ground rent to its sale shareholders and others, and on such terms as time of payment as it may determine.	Pittsburgh.
Blairsville Land Improvement Company. Capital, $50,000. July 21, 1891.	Said corporation is formed for the purpose of purchasing, leasing, improving and selling real estate.	Blairsville.
Knickerbocker Brace Company. Capital, $25,000. July 21, 1891.	Said corporation is formed for the purpose of manufacturing the "Knickerbocker brace," and other articles of merchandise, and other articles of a similar character.	Easton.
The Folmer Shoe Company. Capital, $50,000. July 21, 1891.	Said corporation is formed for the purpose of carrying on the business of manufacturing boots, shoes and other articles principally made of leather.	Orwigsburg.
The Panther Creek Water Company. Capital, $20,000. July 21, 1891.	Said corporation is formed for the purpose of supplying water for the public in the township of Fell, county of Lackawanna, Pa., and to persons, partnerships, associations and corporations residing therein and adjacent thereto as may desire the same.	Scranton.

LIST OF CHARTERS OF CORPORATIONS—*Continued.*

STYLE AND TITLE OF CORPORATION.	PURPOSE.	LOCATION.
Sterling Razor Company. Capital, $5,000. July 22, 1891.	Said corporation is formed for the purpose of manufacturing razors, cutlery, surgical instruments or any other article of commerce from metal, wood or both.	Pittsburgh.
The North Twelfth Street Land Association. Capital, $17,000. July 24, 1891.	Said corporation is formed for the purpose of purchasing, holding, leasing and selling real estate.	Philadelphia.
The Thompson Borough Water Company. Capital, $5,000. July 24, 1891.	Said corporation is formed for the purpose of supplying water to the public in the borough of Thompson, Susquehanna county, Pennsylvania, and to persons, partnerships and associations residing therein and adjacent thereto as may desire the same.	Thompson borough.
Derwent Foundry Company. Capital, $5,600. July 27, 1891.	Said corporation is formed for the purpose of manufacturing stoves and light castings.	Pittsburgh.
Foxtroll Insulated Wire Company. Capital, $200,000. July 27, 1891.	Said corporation is formed for the purpose of manufacturing insulated wires and cables, insulating materials and compounds and electrical appliances.	Philadelphia.
The Paragon Oil Can Company. Capital, $60,000. July 27, 1891.	Said corporation is formed for the purpose of carrying on the manufacture and sale of a certain oil can invented by Edwin W. Luce, to whom letters patent of the United States of America have been issued therefor, and of all improvements thereon, to which the intended corporation may become entitled.	Meadville.
The Black's Creek Improvement Company. Capital, $1,000. July 27, 1891.	Said corporation is formed for the purpose of clearing out, improving and using Black's creek, a stream not exceeding twenty miles in length and a tributary of Little Pine creek, in the counties of Tioga and Lycoming, and of purchasing dams and erecting dams on said stream, and of straightening, deepening, cribbing and widening said stream, with power generally to use and manage said stream and their improvements thereon for the floating of logs, lumber and timber thereon by both natural and artificial floods.	Williamsport.

Company	Purpose	Location
The Carbondale Water Company. Capital, $10,000. July 27, 1891.	The purpose for which said corporation is formed is to supply water to the public in the township of Carbondale, in the county of Lacka-wanna, in said commonwealth, and to such persons, partnerships, associations and corporations residing therein or adjacent thereto, as may desire the same.	Carbondale.
Artic Ice Company. Capital, $300,000. July 28, 1891.	Said corporation is formed for the purpose of manufacturing artificial ice.	Allegheny City.
The Sharon Hill Real Estate Company. Capital, $10,000. July 30, 1891.	Said corporation is formed for the purpose of holding, selling and leasing real estate.	Sharon Hill.
The Birmingham Iron and Steel Company. Capital, $5,000. July 30, 1891.	Said corporation is formed for the purpose of manufacturing of iron, steel and other metals, and articles of wood.	Pittsburgh.
Elwood Enamel Company. Capital, $5,000. July 30, 1891.	Said corporation is formed for the purpose of preparation and making of enamel and application of same to iron, steel, or both, or any other metal, or to tile brick, clay or other : sale of commerce.	Ellwood City.
The Thompson Run Coal Company. Capital, $16,000. July 31, 1891.	Said corporation is formed for the purpose of the mining of coal and the manufacturing of coke.	Newcastle.
The Shenango Valley Steel Company. Capital, $300,000. July 31, 1891.	Said corporation is formed for the purpose of the manufacture of iron or steel, or both, or of any other metal, or of any article of commerce from metal or wood or both.	Newcastle.
The Fitzgerald Plaster Company of Western Pennsylvania. Capital, $250,000. July 31, 1891.	Said corporation is formed for the purpose of the manufacture, sale and use of patent plaster.	Pittsburgh.
LaBelle Cutlery Company. Capital, $5,000. August 3, 1891.	Said corporation is formed for the purpose of manufacturing iron or steel, or both, or of any other metal, or of any article of commerce from metal or wood, or both.	Allegheny City.

LIST OF CHARTERS OF CORPORATIONS—*Continued.*

Style and Title of Corporation.	Purpose.	Location.
Columbia Avenue Building Association. Re-charter. Capital, $1,000,000. August 3, 1891.	Said corporation is formed for the purpose of accumulating a fund by the periodical contributions of the members thereof, and of safely investing the same.	Philadelphia.
Monongahela Iron and Steel Company. Capital, $100,000. August 3, 1891.	Said corporation is formed for the purpose of manufacturing iron or steel, or both, or of any other metal, or of any other article of commerce from metal or wood or both.	Pittsburgh.
LaBelle Steel Company. Capital, $5,000. August 3, 1891.	Said corporation is formed for the purpose of manufacturing iron or steel, or both, or of any other metal, or of any article of commerce from metal or wood or both.	Allegheny City.
The Ebensburg Tanning Company. Capital, $40,000. August 3, 1891.	Said corporation is formed for the purpose of manufacturing and tanning leather.	Pittsburgh.
South Greensburg Land Company. Capital, $35,000. August 3, 1891.	Said corporation is formed for the purchase and sale of real estate.	Greensburg.
J. H. Zeilin and Company, Incorporated. Capital, $300,000. August 3, 1891.	Said corporation is formed for the purpose of the manufacture of medicines, drugs and chemicals.	Philadelphia.
The Bellefield Oil & Gas Company. Capital, $5,000. August 3, 1891.	Said corporation is formed for the purpose of the mining for and the production of oil and gas.	Pittsburgh.
The Mount Vernon Coal Company. Capital, $100,000. August 4, 1891.	Said corporation is formed for the purpose of mining, preparing and shipping coal and leasing, purchasing and holding real estate by purchase or lease and to dispose of the same and necessary for the purposes connected with such business.	Scranton.

Company	Purpose	Location
The Franklin Water Company. Capital, $600. August 4, 1891.	Said corporation is formed for the purpose of the supply of water to the public, and the supply, storage, transportation of water and water power for commercial and manufacturing purposes, at the township of East Franklin, Armstrong county, Pa., and to such persons, partnerships and associations residing therein and adjacent thereto as may desire the same.	Kittanning.
Warren Real Estate Improvement Company, Capital, $60,000. August 5, 1891.	Said corporation is formed for the purpose of purchasing, taking, holding, and enjoying real estate in fee simple or upon ground rent, improving, leasing, mortgaging and selling the same in such parts and parcels and on such terms as to time of payment as said corporation may determined and to convey same to purchasers in fee simple, or for any less estate, or upon ground rents, & in like manner to mortgage, sell, convey or extinguish any ground rent reserved out of any real estate so sold.	Warren.
The Reserve Premium and Loan Association. Capital, $250,000. August 6, 1891.	Said corporation is formed for the purpose of accumulating a fund by the periodical contributions of the members thereof, and of safely investing the same.	Allegheny.
West Derry Glass Company. Capital, $140,000. August 6, 1891.	Said corporation is formed for the purpose of manufacturing glass and glassware.	Burdsville.
Oliver Coke & Furnace Company. Capital, $400,000. August 6, 1891.	Said corporation is formed for the purpose of the manufacture of iron or steel, or both, or of any other metal, or of any article of commerce from metal or wood, or both.	Pittsburgh.
The Climax Cigarette and Cigar Machine Company, Capital, $100,000. August 6, 1891.	The said corporation is formed for the purpose of manufacturing and selling the Climax cigar bunching machine and other machines for the manufacture of cigars, cheroots and cigarettes, and for the manufacture and sale of cigars, cigarettes and cheroots.	Philadelphia.
The Hughesville Electric Light and Power Company, Capital, $10,0. August 10, 91.	Said corporation is formed for the purpose of supplying electric lights and electric power to the public at the borough of Hughesville, Lycoming county, Pennsylvania, and to such persons, partnerships and corporations residing therein and adjacent thereto as may desire the same.	Hughesville.
The Langhorne Building and Loan Association. Capital, $100,000. August 10, 1891.	Said corporation is formed for the purpose of accumulating a fund by the periodical contribution of the members thereof, and of safely investing the same.	Langhorne.

LIST OF CHARTERS OF CORPORATIONS—*Continued.*

STYLE AND TITLE OF CORPORATION.	PURPOSE.	LOCATION.
The Wilson & Fenimore Company. Capital, $200,000. August 10, 1891.	Said corporation is formed for the purpose of manufacturing paper hangings, window shadings, and wall and ceiling decorations of all kinds.	Bristol.
The Atcheson Coke Company. Capital, $20,000. August 10, 1891.	Said corporation is formed for the purpose of mining and excavating coal, and the manufacture of coke therefrom.	Dunbar.
A. Hallman Stove Company. Capital, $75,000. August 10, 1891.	Said corporation is formed for the purpose of manufacturing stoves, heaters, ranges and machinery castings and selling the same.	Philadelphia.
Schoen Pressed Steel Brake Beam Company. Capital, $500,000. August 10, 1891.	Said corporation is formed for the purpose of the manufacture of iron or steel, or both, or of any other metal or article of commerce from metal, wood, or both.	Allegheny City.
The Douglas Bridge Company. Capital, $5,000. August 11, 1891.	Said corporation is formed the purpose of the construction and maintenance of a bridge over the Youghiogheny river, from a point in Elizabeth township, Allegheny county, Pennsylvania, at or near the mouth of Douglas run near Douglas station, on the Pittsburgh, McKeesport & Youghiogheny railroad, to a point in Suterville, Westmoreland county, Pennsylvania, opposite or nearly opposite thereto.	Blythesdale.
Erie Insulating Company. Capital, $10,000. August 11, 1891.	Said corporation is formed for the purpose of manufacturing insulating coverings from wool, hair and other non-conducting substances.	Erie.
Pennsylvania National Savings Fund and Loan Association. Capital, $1,000,000. August 12, 1891.	Said corporation is formed for the purpose of accumulating a fund for the benefit of its members and the transaction of such business as mutual saving fund or building and loan associations may lawfully transact under the laws of the State of Pennsylvania.	Pittsburgh.
Wainright Brewing Company. Capital, $500,000. August 13, 1891.	Said corporation is formed for the purpose of manufacturing and brewing malt liquors.	Pittsburgh.

Company	Purpose	Location
The Bellevue Homestead Loan and Trust Company. Capital, $15,000. August 18, 1891.	Said corporation is formed for the purpose of purchasing, taking, holding and enjoying real estate in fee simple on lease or upon ground rent, improving, leasing, mortgaging and selling the same in fee simple, or for any less estate, or upon ground rent, to its sale shareholders and others on such terms as to time of payment as it may determine.	Bellevue.
The Fifth Mutual Building Society. Re-charter. Capital, $1,000,000. August 18, 1891.	Said corporation is formed for the purpose of accumulating a fund by the periodical contributions of the members thereof, and of safely investing the same.	Philadelphia.
Successful Building Association. Re-charter. Capital, $500,000. August 17, 1891.	The said corporation is formed for the purpose of accumulation a fund by the periodical contribution of the members thereof, and safely investing the same.	Philadelphia.
The Columbia Gray Iron Company. Capital, $50,000. August 17, 1891.	Said corporation is formed for the purpose of the manufacture and sale of hardware, articles of commerce made from metal or metal and wood.	Columbia.
The Hyndman Water Company. Capital, $20,000. August 17, 1891.	Said corporation is formed for the purpose of supplying water to the public, or the supply, storage or transportation of water and water power for commercial and manufacturing purposes, in the borough of Hyndman, county of Bedford, and to such persons, partnerships and associations residing therein and adjacent thereto as may desire the same.	Hyndman.
The Holmes' Land Association. Capital, $12,800. August 17, 1891.	Said corporation is formed for the purpose of purchasing real estate, improved and unimproved, and the improvement thereof and the division, allotment thereof, before or after such improvement, by public or private sale to the stockholders or others, for the profit and advantage of the stockholders.	Moore's, Delaware Co.
Huntingdon Valley Building Association. Re-charter. Capital $250,000. August 18, 1891.	Said corporation is formed for the purpose of accumulating a fund from the monthly contributions of its members, fines, premiums on loans and interest on investments, to be loaned to its members on approved security, to enable said members to purchase real estate, build dwelling houses or invest in any legitimate business.	Huntingdon Valley.
The Mozart Building Association. Capital, $1,000,000. August 18, 1891.	Said corporation is formed for the purpose of accumulating a fund by the periodical contributions of the members thereof, and of safely investing the same.	Philadelphia.

2a LAWS.

LIST OF CHARTERS OF CORPORATIONS—*Continued.*

Style and Title of Corporation.	Purpose.	Location.
Quaker City Morocca Company. Capital, $100,000. August 20, 1891.	Said corporation is formed for the purpose of manufacturing leather of all kinds.	Philadelphia.
The People's Building and Loan Association, of Ridgway Pennsylvania. Capital, $1,000,000. August 20, 1891.	Said corporation is formed for the purpose of accumulating a fund by the periodical contributions of its members thereof, and of safely investing the same.	Ridgway.
Pittsburgh Collar Company. Capital, $35,000. August 20, 1891.	Said corporation is formed for the purpose of manufacturing horse collars and leather goods.	Pittsburgh.
The Cooper Excelsior Company. Capital, $75,000. August 20, 1891.	Said corporation is formed for the purpose of the manufacture of excelsior for packing out of wood.	Pittsburgh.
Davis Farrar Company. Capital, $30,000. August 20, 1891.	Said corporation is formed for the purpose of manufacturing all kinds of boilers and engines, and any articles of commerce from metal or wood, or both.	Erie.
The Pennsylvania Artificial Stone Paving Company. Capital, $80,000. August 21, 1891.	Said corporation is formed for the purpose of making artificial stone pavement for the paving of streets, sidewalks, pavements, cellars, floors, and other places, where paving with artificial stone may be desired.	Lock Haven.
The Keystone Land and Improvement Company. Capital, $80,000. August 21, 1891.	Said corporation is formed for the purpose of purchasing, improving and selling real estate.	Pittsburgh.

The Spring Hill Incline Plane Company of the City and County of Allegheny, Pennsylvania.
Capital, $50,000.
August 21, 1891.

Said corporation is formed for the purpose of locating, constructing, maintaining and operating an incline plane from Madison avenue, Twelfth ward, Allegheny City, to Haslage avenue, on Spring Hill; also, in the same ward and city, and is to be located as follows, viz: Beginning at a point on the east side of Madison avenue, in the Twelfth Mill street, and at the base of Spring Hill, thence extending up along the side of Spring Hill a distance of about eight hundred feet (800 ft.) to Haslage avenue on the crown of Spring Hill at or near a point where said Haslage / same meets with Kloper street, in the 12th ward, city of Allegheny, aforesaid and for the purpose of carrying and conveying and transporting passengers and freight or other upon and over said lane from Madison / same to Haslage avenue on Spring Hill, 12th ward, Allegheny City aforesaid, and for the fee and enjoyment of such other rights, privileges and franchises as are by law used in said incline plane companies.

} Allegheny.

The Kremer Manufacturing Company.
Capital, $25,000.
August 24, 1891.

Said corporation is formed for the purpose of manufacturing various articles of commerce from iron, steel and other metals and wood, or any or either of said materials.

} Pittsburgh.

Philadelphia Manufacturing Company.
Capital, $15,000.
August 24, 1891.

Said corporation is formed for the purpose of manufacturing upholstery goods and fabrics and furniture coverings and curtains of every kind, and for the selling of the same.

} Philadelphia.

Tichenor Hat Company.
Capital, $10,000.
August 24, 1891.

Said corporation is formed for the purpose of manufacturing soft and stiff felt hats.

} Philadelphia.

Westmoreland Fire Brick Company.
Capital, $60,000.
August 25, 1891.

Said corporation is formed for t... purpose ... manufacturing and excavating for fire-clay and sand stone, manufacturing the same in crude or manufactured forms, and for that purpose to have and possess the powers and privileges expressed and given in the 39th section of the corporation act of 1874, and the supplements thereto.

} Pittsburgh.

Camp Milling Company.
Capital, $45,000.
August 28, 1891.

Said corporation is formed for the purpose of manufacturing and selling flour and feed at their flouring mills.

} Union City.

The Avonmore Foundry and Machine Company.
Capital, $50,000.
August 31, 1891.

Said corporation is formed for the purpose of manufacting rolls, ingot moulds, rolling mill and steel mill machinery, and to conduct a general machine and foundry business.

} Avonmore.

LIST OF CHARTERS OF CORPORATIONS—*Continued.*

STYLE AND TITLE OF CORPORATION.	PURPOSES.	LOCATION.
The Plain Speaker Publishing Company. Capital, $25,000. August 31, 1891.	Said corporation is formed for the purpose of the transaction of a printing and publishing business.	Hazleton.
Middle Coal Field Real Estate Company. Capital, $5,000. August 31, 1891.	Said corporation is formed for the purpose of purchasing, holding, leasing and selling real estate.	Hazleton.
Otto Furniture Company. Capital, $170,000. August 31, 1891.	Said corporation is formed for the purpose of manufacturing and selling all kinds of furniture.	Williamsport.
Independent Deposit and Loan Association, of Pittsburgh. Capital, $1,000,000. September 1, 1891.	Said corporation is formed for the purpose of loaning money to its members out of moneys paid in by its stockholders, and for all the purposes of a building and loan association.	Pittsburgh.
Collingdale Land and Improvement Company. Capital, $6,000. September 1, 1891.	Said corporation is formed for the purpose of purchasing, holding, leasing and selling real estate.	Collingdale.
Erie Piano Company. Capital, $25,000. September 1, 1891.	Said corporation is formed for the purpose of the manufacture of iron or steel, or both, or of any other metal, or of any article of commerce from metal or wood, or both.	Erie.
Corry Chair Company. Capital, $50,000. September 2, 1891.	Said corporation is formed for the purpose of manufacturing chairs, lumber & other products of wood.	Corry.
The Republican Printing and Publishing Company, of Irwin, Pa. Capital, $5,000. September 2, 1891.	Said corporation is formed for the purpose of transacting a printing and publishing business.	Irwin.

Company	Purpose	Location
Champion Saw Company. Capital, $60,000. September 4, 1891.	Said corporation is formed for the purpose of the manufacture of iron or steel, or both, or of any other metal, or of any article of commerce from metal or wood, or both.	Beaver Falls.
National Separating and Manufacturing Company. Capital, $120,000. September 8, 1891.	Said corporation is formed for the purpose of the manufacture of iron or steel, or both, of any other metal, or of any article of commerce from wood, metal or both.	Pittsburgh.
The Hopkins Land Company. Capital, $100,000. September 8, 1891.	Said corporation is formed for the purpose of holding, leasing and selling real estate.	Lock Haven.
Stony Creek Mills Building and Loan Association. Capital, $100,000. September 8, 1891.	Said corporation is formed for the purpose of accumulating a fund by the periodical contributions of the members thereof, and of safely investing the same.	Stony Creek Mills.
The Commercial Building and Loan Association. Capital, $1,000,000. September 8, 1891.	Said corporation is formed for the purpose of accumulating a fund by the periodical contributions of the members thereof, and of safely investing the same.	Allegheny City.
Patterson Ferry Company. Capital, $600. September 8, 1891.	Said corporation is formed for the purpose of erecting, constructing and maintaining a ferry and approaches thereto over the Monongahela river from a point at or near Patterson station, on the McKeesport and Bell Vernon R. R., in Lincoln township, Allegheny county, to a point on the opposite side of said river, in Jefferson township in said county, the location of said ferry being more than 5,000 feet from any other incorporated bridge or ferry over said stream.	Elizabeth.
The West Reading Savings Fund and Loan Association No. 4. Capital, $600,000. September 9, 1891.	Said corporation is formed for the purpose of accumulating a fund by the contributions of the members thereof and to loan the same to them from time to time to enable them to purchase real estate, build themselves dwelling houses, or engage in any legitimate business.	Reading.
The Thompson-Houston Electric Light and Power Company. Capital, $30,000. September 9, 1891.	Said corporation is formed for the purpose of manufacturing and supplying light, heat and power, or any of them, by means of electricity and steam generated at its lighting plant, to the public in the borough of Sharon, Mercer county, Pennsylvania, and to such persons, partnerships and corporations residing therein or adjacent thereto as may desire the same.	Sharon.

LIST OF CHARTERS OF CORPORATIONS—*Continued.*

Style and Title of Corporation.	Purpose.	Location.
The City Storage and Supply Company. Capital, $5,000. September 9, 1891.	Said corporation is formed for the purpose of carrying on a storage warehouse business, the furnishing facilities for cold and free storage, the payment of advancements on warehouse storage certificates and such other business as may be lawfully done by said company.	Pittsburgh.
The Morrellville Building and Loan Association. Capital, $1,000,000. September 10, 1891.	Said corporation is formed for the purpose of accumulating a fund by the periodical contributions of the members thereof, and of safely investing the same.	Morrellville.
Stenographer Printing and Publishing Company. Capital, $10,000. September 10, 1891.	Said corporation is formed for the purpose of the transaction of a printing and publishing business.	Philadelphia.
Greensburg Loan and Trust Company. Capital, $15,000. September 10, 1891.	Said corporation is formed for the purpose of purchasing, taking, holding and enjoying real estate, in fee simple, on lease, or upon ground rent, improving, leasing, mortgaging and selling the same in fee simple or for any less estate, or upon ground rent, to its sale shareholders and others, on such terms as to time of payment as it may determine.	Greensburg.
People's Express and Transfer Company. Capital, $3,000. September 11, 1891.	Said corporation is formed for the purpose of transferring baggage and express and for doing a general local express business.	Williamsport.
John C. Miller Brewing Company. Capital, $300,000. September 14, 1891.	Said corporation is formed for the purpose of manufacturing and brewing malt liquors.	Philadelphia.
The Mansfield Water Company. Capital, $60,000. September 14, 1891.	Said corporation is formed for the purpose of supplying water to the public in the borough of Mansfield, Tioga county, Penna., and to persons, partnerships and associations residing therein and adjacent thereto; desiring the same.	Mansfield.

The Blossburg Water Company. Capital, $60,000. September 14, 1891.	Said corporation is formed for the purpose of supplying water to the public in the borough of Blossburg, Tioga county, Pennsylvania, and to such persons, partnerships and associations residing therein and adjacent thereto as may desire the same.	Blossburg.
The Pennsylvania Loan and Building Association. Capital, $1,000,000. September 15, 1891.	Said corporation is formed for the purpose of accumulating a fund by the periodical contributions of the members thereof, and of safely investing the same.	Allentown.
George W. Plumly Company. Capital, $100,000. September 15, 1891.	Said corporation is formed for the purpose of manufacturing boxes made from paper, card board or other material.	Philadelphia.
H. Lloyds' Sons Company. Capital, $200,000. September 16, 1891.	Said corporation is formed for the purpose of the manufacture of iron and steel, or either, and of the products thereof.	Pittsburgh.
The Patterson Water Company. Capital, $1,000. September 18, 1891.	Said corporation is formed for the purpose of supplying water to the borough of Patterson, and to such persons, partnerships and corporations residing therein and adjacent thereto who may desire the same.	Patterson.
The Mifflintown Water Company. Capital, $30,000. September 18, 1891.	Said corporation is formed for the purpose of supplying water to the borough of Mifflintown, and to such persons, partnerships and corporations residing therein and adjacent thereto who may desire the same.	Mifflintown.
Connelly Gas Engine Company. Capital, $50,000. September 18, 1891.	Said corporation is formed for the purpose of the manufacture of iron or steel, or both, or of any other metal, or of any article of commerce from metal or wood, or both.	Newcastle.
Philadelphia Carette Company. Capital, $25,000. September 18, 1891.	Said corporation is formed for the purpose of operating of stage and omnibus lines in the city of Philadelphia.	Philadelphia.
Equitable Building and Loan Association. Capital, $600,000. September 21, 1891.	Said corporation is formed for the purpose of accumulating a fund by the periodical contributions of the members thereof, and of safely investing the same.	Mauch Chunk.
Cambria Lumber Company. Capital, $1,000. September 21, 1891.	Said corporation is formed for the purpose of acquiring by purchase, lease or exchange, timber, timber lands and logs, for manufacturing lumber, doing mill work and making articles manufactured from wood, and for the purpose of selling and disposing of such lands, timber, logs and lumber and other articles made therefrom.	Philadelphia.

LIST OF CHARTERS OF CORPORATIONS—*Continued.*

STYLE AND TITLE OF CORPORATION.	PURPOSE.	LOCATION.
Emil Winter Company. Capital, $5,000. September 21, 1891.	Said corporation is formed for the purpose of manufacturing material out of and from mineral oils, and any other oils or fatty substances whether mineral, animal or vegetable and of artificial manures.	Allegheny City.
The St. Lawrence Building Saving and Loan Association. Capital, $150,000. September 22, 1891.	Said corporation is formed for the purpose of accumulating a fund by the periodical contributions of the members thereof, and of safely investing the same.	St. Lawrence, Berks county, Exeter township.
The Hercules Cement Company. Capital, $75,000. September 23, 1891.	Said corporation is formed for the purpose of manufacturing and selling cement.	Catasauqua.
The Neversink Building and Savings Association No. 4. Capital, $1,000,000. September 23, 1891.	Said corporation is formed for the purpose of accumulating a fund by the periodical contributions of the members thereof, and of safely investing the same.	Reading.
The German Building and Loan Association of Chartiers borough, Allegheny county, Pennsylvania. Capital, $1,000,000. September 24, 1891.	Said corporation is formed for the purpose of accumulating a fund by the periodical contributions of the members thereof, and of safely investing the same.	Chartiers.
The Duncannon Water Company. Capital, $25,000. September 24, 1891.	Said corporation is formed for the purpose of supplying water to the public at Duncannon, Pa., and to such persons, partnerships and associations residing therein and adjacent thereto as may desire the same.	Duncannon.
Athens Electric Light, Heat and Power Company. Capital, $5,000. September 23, 1891.	Said corporation is formed for the purpose of supplying light, heat and power by means of electricity to the public, at the borough of Athens, and to persons, partnerships and associations residing therein and adjacent thereto, as may desire the same.	Athens.
Brownsville and Bridgeport Land and Improvement Company. Capital, $25,000. September 24, 1891.	Said corporation is formed for the purpose of purchasing, holding, improving, leasing, selling, or otherwise disposing of real estate.	Brownsville.

The Carborundum Company. Capital, $150,000. September 28, 1891.	Said corporation is formed for the purpose of manufacturing carborundum and other abrasive materials.	Monongahela City.
Florence Zinc Company. Capital, $250,000. September 30, 1891.	Said corporation is formed for the purpose of the manufacture of iron or steel, or both, or of any other metal or article of commerce, from metal, wood or both.	Florence.
The Lackawanna Fertilizer and Chemical Company. Capital, $20,000. September 30, 1891.	Said corporation is formed for the purpose of the manufacture of fertilizers and chemicals.	Moosic.
The Berks County Hedge and Wire Fence Company, of Yellow House, Pa. Capital, $15,000. September 30, 1891.	Said corporation is formed for the purpose of the manufacture of hedge and wire fence, by plashing and otherwise combining hedge, wire and other materials.	Yellow House.
The New Philadelphia Building and Loan Association. Capital, $1,000,000. September 30, 1891.	Said corporation is formed for the purpose of accumulating a fund by the periodical contributions of the members thereof, and of safely investing the same.	Philadelphia.
Monongahela Fire Clay Company. Capital, $60,000. October 1, 1891.	Said corporation is formed for the purpose of mining for fire clay and coal, and manufacturing brick.	Phillipsburg.
Richland Coal Company. Capital, $50,000. October 1, 1891.	Said corporation is formed for the purpose of mining coal and the manufacture of coke and other products of coal therefrom.	Altoona.
The Pennsylvania Brass Works. Capital, $40,000. October 2, 1891.	Said corporation is formed for the purpose of the manufacture and sale of brass, malleable and grey iron goods and special tools; such as generally used by gas and steam fitters and plumbers in their business.	Erie.
The Upper Darby Building and Loan Association. Re-charter. Capital, $500,000. October 2, 1891.	Said corporation is formed for the purpose of conducting the business of accumulating a fund by the contributions of the members thereof; and of loaning the same from time to time to them, to enable them to purchase real estate, build themselves dwelling houses or engage in any legitimate business.	Upper Darby.

LIST OF CHARTERS OF CORPORATIONS—*Continued.*

STYLE AND TITLE OF CORPORATION.	PURPOSE.	LOCATION.
The Ella Coal Company. Capital, $30,000. October 5, 1891.	Said corporation is formed for the purpose of mining & transporting coal and manufacturing the same into coke and other products of coal, and transporting, marketing and selling the same, either in crude or manufactured form, and for these purposes to have, maintain and operate the necessary buildings, machinery, tools, boats, barges, steamboats and appliances necessary to said business, and to this end to have, hold, purchase, lease and acquire, either in fee simple or otherwise, real estate, coal and coal rights, and the same to sell, case exchange or otherwise dispose of, and such sale, lease or other disposition of said real estate by said corporation may be made by the board of directors of said corporation without the consent of the stockholders.	McKeesport.
The Thirty-fifth Ward Building and Loan Association. Capital, $1,000,000. October 5, 1891.	Said corporation is formed for the purpose of accumulating a fund by contributions of the members which shall enable them to purchase homesteads or other real estate or to borrow money for investment in any lawful business.	Philadelphia.
Ligonier Fire Brick Company. Capital, $40,000. October 6, 1891.	Said corporation is formed for the purpose of manufacturing brick, tile, pipe and other specialties out of fire clay and the procuring and mining of fire clay for that purpose and the transaction of all matters appertaining to the said business.	Greensburg.
Cambria Fire Brick Company. Capital, $32,000. October 9, 1891.	Said corporation is formed for the purpose of mining fire clay and coal and manufacturing fire brick and other products of all descriptions, from fire clay, and for that purpose to have and possess the powers and privileges expressed and given in the 39th section of the corporation act of 1874, and the supplements thereto.	Lock Haven.
Iron City Sand Company. Capital, $5,000. October 12, 1891.	Said corporation is formed for the purpose of mining, quarrying, excavating, dredging, producing and preparing for market, and selling sand, gravel, cobble stones, lime, limestone and other mineral substances, and for this purpose to own, possess and operate all the necessary tools, steamboats, dredgeboats and appliances necessary for the transaction of such business.	Pittsburgh.

J. H. Wilhelm Building and Loan Association. Capital, $200,000. October 5, 1891.	Said corporation is formed for the purpose of accumulating a fund by the periodical contributions of the members thereof and of safely investing the same.	Mauch Chunk.
The Wortsall and Carl Spoke and Wheel Company. Capital, $25,000. October 12, 1891.	Said corporation is formed for the purpose of manufacturing wheels and other wood work for carriages and wagons.	Doylestown.
The Ohio River Improvement Company. Capital, $36,000. October 12, 1891.	Said corporation is formed for the purpose of buying, selling & improving real estate.	Pittsburgh.
Excelsior Automatic Knitting Machine Company. Capital, $25,000. October 12, 1891.	Said corporation is formed for the purpose of manufacturing and operating knitting and other machinery.	Norristown.
The Lilly Building and Loan Association, of Lilly, Pa. Capital, $1,000,000. October 13, 1891.	Said corporation is formed for the purpose of accumulating a fund by the periodical contributions of the members thereof, and of safely investing the same.	Lilly.
John C. Johnson Soda Water Apparatus Company. Capital, $10,000. October 14, 1891.	Said corporation is formed for the purpose of manufacturing & selling soda water and all kinds of soda water apparatus.	Philadelphia.
The Schuylkill Anthracite Coal Royalty Company. Capital, $350,000. October 14, 1891.	Said corporation is formed for the purpose of the purchase and sale of real estate, or for holding, selling and leasing real estate.	Scranton.
Aliquippa Steel Company. Capital, $150,000. October 14, 1891.	Said corporation is formed for the purpose of the manufacture of iron or steel, or both, or of any other metal, or of any article of commerce from metal or wood, or both.	Pittsburgh.

LIST OF CHARTERS OF CORPORATIONS—*Continued.*

STYLE AND TITLE OF CORPORATION.	PURPOSE.	LOCATION.
Watsontown Bridge Company. Capital, $1,000. October 15, 1891.	Said corporation is formed for the purpose of erecting, constructing and maintaining a bridge, and approaches thereto, over the west branch of the Susquehanna river, from a point at or near Watsontown, in the county of Northumberland, to a point on the opposite side of said river at or near White Deer, in the county of Union. The location of said bridge is over one mile from any other incorporated bridge or ferry over said stream.	Watsontown.
Burrell Building and Loan Association. Capital, $1,000,000. October 15, 1891.	Said corporation is formed for the purpose of accumulating a fund by the periodical contributions of the members thereof, and of safely investing the same.	Kensington.
The J. C. Russell Shovel Company. Capital, $50,000. October 15, 1891.	Said corporation is formed for the purpose of the manufacture of iron or steel, or both, or of any other metal, or of any article of commerce from metal or wood, or both.	Pittsburgh.
Tomahawk Publishing and Printing Company. Capital, $3,000. October 16, 1891.	Said corporation is formed for the purpose of the transaction of a printing & publishing business and for said purpose to have and enjoy all the rights, powers & privileges granted by the said act of April, 1874, and its supplements.	Philadelphia.
The Mifflinburg Electric Light and Power Company. Capital, $1,000. October 16, 1891.	Said corporation is formed for the purpose of supplying light, heat and power by means of electricity to the public at Mifflinburg, in Union county, Penna., and to such persons, partnerships and corporations residing therein and adjacent thereto as may desire the same.	Mifflinburg.
The Beaver Valley Stone and Clay Company. Capital, $35,000. October 16, 1891.	Said corporation is formed for the purpose of quarrying stone, mining clay, and manufacturing it into any article of commerce.	New Brighton.
Thurlow Medical Company. Capital, $2,000. October 19, 1891.	Said corporation is formed for the purpose of manufacturing and selling drugs, chemicals, pharmaceutical preparations and medicines of all kinds.	South Chester.

The Lindner Shoe Company. Capital, $35,000. October 19, 1891.	Said corporation is formed for the purpose of manufacturing and selling boots and shoes, and for that purpose to have and possess the powers and privileges expressed and given in the 39th section of the corporation act of 1874, and the supplements thereto.	Carlisle.
The Provident Building and Loan Association, of Wissinoning. Capital, $1,000,000. October 19, 1891.	Said corporation is formed for the purpose of accumulating a fund by the periodical contributions of the members thereof, and of safely investing the same.	Philadelphia.
The Building and Loan Association, of Sharon. Capital, $500,000. October 20, 1891.	Said corporation is formed for the purpose of accumulating a fund by the periodical contributions of the members thereof, and of safely investing the same.	Sharon.
National Brick and Tile Company. Capital, $20,000. October 20, 1891.	Said corporation is formed for the purpose of mining shale, clay, earth and rock, and converting the same, or any of them, into brick, tile, terra-cotta, or other articles usually manufactured from said substances.	Bradford.
The Western Water Company. Capital, $1,000. October 20, 1891.	Said corporation is formed for the purpose of storing, transporting and furnishing water, with the right to take rivulets and land, and erect reservoirs for holding water for manufacturing and other purposes, and of acquiring all the rights, powers and privileges conferred upon corporations for said purposes as described in the eighteenth paragraph of the second section of the said act of April 29th, 1874, and the supplement thereto of May 21st, 1889, not including the right to supply any village, borough or city with water.	Greensburg.
Bedford Creamery. Capital, $6,000. October 20, 1891.	Said corporation is formed for the purpose of manufacturing butter, ice cream, cheese, and all goods or commodities manufactured from cream or milk, and the transacting of all business connected with a creamery.	Bedford.
Orvilla Avenue Turnpike Company. Capital, $4,000. October 22, 1891.	Said corporation is formed for the purpose of building and maintaining an artificial road or turnpike of ta, in or gravel and earth, from a point at the southeastern edge of the ld and Towamencin turn-... ad, between lands of W. lp and Abraham Sorver, to a point in the public ed known w path road opposite "the Dunl d meeting house," between lands of said Dunkar ig and John W. Rg, to extend in a southeasterly direction 300.04 perches from the point of beginning to the point of ending, and being wholly within the township of Hatfield, Montgomery county, Pennsylvania.	Orvilla.

LIST OF CHARTERS OF CORPORATIONS—*Continued.*

STYLE AND TITLE OF CORPORATION.	PURPOSE.	LOCATION.
The Esplen Fuel and Light Company. Capital, $10,000. October 22, 1891.	Said corporation is formed for the purpose of manufacturing and supplying gas for light and fuel to the public at the borough of Esplen, in the county of Allegheny, and to such persons, partnerships and corporations residing therein and adjacent thereto as may desire the same.	Pittsburgh.
The McKees Rocks Fuel and Light Company, Capital, $10,000. October 22, 1891.	Said corporation is formed for the purpose of manufacturing and supplying gas for light and fuel to the public at the township of Stowe, in the county of Allegheny, and to such persons, partnerships and corporations residing therein and adjacent thereto as may desire the same.	Pittsburgh.
The Homestead Fuel and Light Company. Capital, $10,000. October 22, 1891.	Said corporation is formed for the purpose of manufacturing and supplying gas for light and fuel to the public at the borough of Homestead, in the county of Allegheny, and to such persons, partnerships and corporations residing therein and adjacent thereto as may desire the same.	Pittsburgh.
The Mansfield and Chartiers Fuel and Light Company, Capital, $10,000. October 22, 1891.	Said corporation is formed for the purpose of manufacturing and supplying gas for light and fuel to the public at the borough of Mansfield and Chartiers, in the county of Allegheny, and to such persons, partnerships and corporations residing therein and adjacent thereto as may desire the same.	Pittsburgh.
Jeannette Textile Manufacturing Company, Capital, $100,000. October 22, 1891.	Said corporation is formed for the purpose of manufacturing plush imitation animal furs and seal skins, astrachans and other similar fabrics.	Philadelphia.
The Rose Building and Loan Association, of Pittsburgh, Pennsylvania. Capital, $1,000,000. October 26, 1891.	Said corporation is formed for the purpose of accumulating a fund by the periodical contributions of the members thereof, and of safely investing the same.	Pittsburgh.
The Washington Nut Lock and Bolt Company, Capital, $10,000. October 27, 1891.	Said corporation is formed for the purpose of the manufacture of irons or steel, or both, or of any other metal, or of any article of commerce from metal or wood, or both.	Washington.

Reynoldsville Coal Company. Capital, $10,000. October 27, 1891.	Said corporation is formed for the purpose of mining coal and manufacturing coke.	Falls Creek
The Carrotte Company. Capital, $10,000. October 27, 1891	Said corporation is formed for the purpose of the formation and operation of a stage and omnibus line.	Pittsburgh.
The Dougherty Type Writer Company. Capital, $100,000. October 27, 1891.	Said corporation is formed for the purpose of manufacturing type-writing and cash register machines, and other articles incidentally connected therewith.	Pittsburgh.
Fallston Pottery Company. Capital, $40,000. October 28, 1891.	Said corporation is formed for the purpose of mining of fire clay or other clays, the preparation of the same for use or sale; the manufacturing of such clays into stone ware, terra-cotta ware, brick, tiles or other articles that may be produced therefrom, and the sale of such products.	Fallston.
The Dispatch Building and Loan Association of Ptg., Pa. Capital, $1,000,000. October 28, 1891.	Said corporation is formed for the purpose of accumulating a fund by the periodical contributions of the members thereof, and of safely investing the same.	Pittsburgh.
Getman Glass Manufacturing Company. Capital, $75,000. October 29, 1891.	Said corporation of formed for the purpose of manufacturing glass.	Avenmore.
Montrose Electric Light and Power Company. Capital, $12,000. October 29, 1891.	Said corporation is formed for the purpose of furnishing light, heat and power by means of electricity to the public at the borough of Montrose, and to such persons, partnerships and corporations, residing therein and adjacent thereto as may desire the same.	Montrose.
The Taylor Engine Company. Capital, $130,000. November 2, 1891.	Said corporation is formed for the purpose of manufacturing iron or steel or both, or any other metal or any article of commerce in any shape or form, of metal or wood, or both, including locomotives or other engines operated by steam or other motive power.	Chambersburg.
Hostetter Connellsville Coke Company. Capital, $5,000. November 2, 1891.	Said corporation is formed for the purpose of manufacturing and selling coke, and for that purpose to purchase, own and operate the necessary lands and mines, and to construct and operate the necessary ovens, buildings, machinery and structures.	Whitney.

LIST OF CHARTERS OF CORPORATIONS—*Continued.*

STYLE AND TITLE OF CORPORATION.	PURPOSE.	LOCATION.
Shippingport Ferry Company. Capital, $1,000. November 2, 1891.	Said corporation is formed for the purpose of erecting, constructing and maintaining a ferry and approaches thereto over the Ohio river, from a point at or near Shippingport, in the county of Beaver, to a point on opposite side of said river in said county. The location of said ferry being more than three thousand feet from any other incorporated bridge or ferry over said stream.	Shippingport.
The Pattison Building and Loan Association. Capital, $1,000,000. November 2, 1891.	Said corporation is formed for the purpose of accumulating a fund by the periodical contributions of the members thereof, and of safely investing the same.	Pittsburgh.
The State Capital Building and Loan Association. Capital, $1,000,000. November 2, 1891.	Said corporation is formed for the purpose of accumulating a fund by the periodical contributions of the members thereof, and of safely investing the same.	Harrisburg.
The Fairmount Ice Manufacturing Company. Capital, $400,000. November 2, 1891.	The said corporation is formed for the purpose of manufacturing, buying, supplying and selling ice and distilled or purified water, and applying refrigeration for general cold storage purposes.	Philadelphia.
Citizens' Natural Gas Company. Capital, $25,000. November 2, 1891.	Formed for the purpose of producing, mining, dealing in, transporting, storing and supplying natural gas.	Johnsonburg.
Philadelphia Stove and Iron Foundry Company. Capital, $65,000. November 2, 1891.	Said corporation is formed for the purpose of manufacturing iron or steel, or both, or any other metal, or of any article of commerce from metal or wood, or both.	Philadelphia.
Spreckles' Steamship Company. Capital, $100,000. November 4, 1891.	Said corporation is formed for the purpose of building ships, vessels or boats, and carriage of persons and property thereon, conducting the business of a steamship company, and of doing whatever else shall be incidental to the said business.	Philadelphia.

The Unique Building and Loan Association, Capital, $1,000,000. November 4, 1891.	Said corporation is formed for the purpose of accumulating a fund by the periodical contributions of the members thereof, and of safely investing the same.	Philadelphia.
Lycoming Mining Company. Capital, $90,000. November 5, 1891.	Said corporation is formed for the purpose of quarrying and mining marble, nickel, limestone, oil, graphite, iron, tin, lead, gold and silver, and the sale of the same in crude or manufactured form and for that purpose to have and possess the powers and privileges expressed and given in the 39th section of the corporation act of 1874, and the supplements thereto.	Philadelphia.
The Victoria Oil Company. Capital, $10,000. November 5, 1891.	Said corporation is formed for the purpose of producing crude petroleum and manufacturing, compounding and mixing the products thereof.	Warren borough.
Western Plaster Board Company. Capital, $60,000. November 6, 1891.	Said corporation is formed for the purpose of the manufacture of plaster and plaster boards from vegetable, mineral and animal substances, or any of them.	Pittsburgh.
The Tyrone Opera House Company, of Tyrone, Pa. Capital, $20,000. November 9, 1891.	Said corporation is formed for the purpose of establishing and maintaining an opera house at Tyrone, Blair county, Pennsylvania.	Tyrone.
The Perfecta Building and Loan Association of Philadelphia. Capital, $1,000,000. November 9, 1891.	Said corporation is formed for the purpose of accumulating a fund by the periodical contributions of the members thereof, and of safely investing the same.	Philadelphia.
Allentown Hardware Works. Capital, $80,000. November 9, 1891.	Said corporation is formed for the purpose of the manufacture of iron or steel, or both, or of any other metal, or any other article of commerce from metal or wood, or both.	Allentown.
Birmingham Boat Works Company. Capital, $7,500. November 9, 1891.	Said corporation is formed for the purpose of building ships, vessels or boats, and carriage of persons and property thereon.	Pittsburgh.
The Backus Manufacturing Company. Capital, $250,000. November 10, 1891.	Said corporation is formed for the purpose of manufacturing, putting into operation, using and selling, the Backus Portable Steam Heater, and other mechanical contrivances, or any article of commerce from metal or wood, or both.	Williamsport.

LIST OF CHARTERS OF CORPORATIONS—*Continued.*

STYLE AND TITLE OF CORPORATION.	PURPOSE.	LOCATION.
Bovaird and Seyfang Manufacturing Company. Capital, $500,000. November 10, 1891.	Said corporation is formed for the purpose of manufacturing boilers, engines, oil well tools and supplies.	Bradford.
The Nuding Brewing Company. Capital, $150,000. November 10, 1891.	Said corporation is formed for the purpose of brewing, manufacturing and selling of lager beer, porter, all and other malt liquors.	Allentown.
Blairsville Rolling Mill and Tin Plate Company. Capital, $75,000. November 10, 1891.	Said corporation is formed for the purpose of the manufacture of iron or steel, or tin, or all of them, or of any other metal, or any article of commerce, from metal or wood, or both.	Blairsville.
York Brick, Stone and Lime Manufacturing Company. Capital, $45,000. November 11, 1891.	Said corporation is formed for the purpose of manufacturing all kinds of brick, tile and clay products, and for the manufacture of all kinds of lime and stone, and stone products therefrom.	York city.
The Burgoon Royal Medicine Company. Capital, $1,000. November 12, 1891.	Said corporation is formed for the purpose of manufacturing Dr. J. A. Burgoon's Royal Medicines.	Allegheny City.
Kopitzsch Soap Company. Capital, $100,000. November 13, 1891.	Said corporation is formed for the purpose of manufacturing all kinds of soaps and candles.	Pottsville.
F. L. John Company. Capital, $25,000. November 13, 1891.	Said cor... ...on is formed for the purpose of manufacturing and selling John's Balsamic Syrup and other drug specialties and drug sundries.	Philadelphia.
The Wilkes-Barre Gun Company. Capital, $50,000. November 13, 1891.	Said corporation is formed for the purpose of the manufacture of iron or steel, or both, or of any other metal, or of any article of commerce from metal or wood, or both.	Wilkes-Barre.

Company	Purpose	Location
The Fisher and Hinkle Company. Capital, $40,000. November 13, 1891.	Said corporation is formed for the purpose of the manufacture and sale of bread, cakes, crackers, pastry and confectionary of all kinds.	Williamsport.
First National Building and Loan Association. Capital, $1,000,000. November 16, 1891.	Said corporation is formed for the purpose of accumulating a fund by the periodical contributions of the members thereof, and of safely investing the same.	Pittsburgh.
Hatboro Loan and Building Association. Capital, $96,200. November 16, 1891.	Said corporation is formed for the purpose of accumulating a fund by the periodical contributions of the members thereof, and of safely investing the same.	Hatboro.
Analomink Paper Mills. Capital, $100,000. N ber 16, 1891.	Said corporation is formed for the purpose of manufacturing all kinds of pulp and paper, and the selling of the same with all rights incidental thereto.	Experiment Mills, Smithfield twp., Monroe Co.
Perry Homestead Loan and Trust Company. Capital, $15,000. November 16, 1891.	Said corporation is formed for the purpose of purchasing, taking, holding and enjoying real estate in fee simple, or lease, or upon ground rent, improving, leasing, mortgaging & selling the same in fee simple, or for any less estate, or upon ground rent to its sale shareholders and others, on such terms as to time of payment as its directors may determine.	Allegheny City.
The Blair Land Company. Capital, $55,000. November 16, 1891.	Said corporation is formed for the purpose of purchasing, improving, holding and enjoying real estate in fee simple, or upon ground rent or lease, and to lease, mortgage and sell the same in such parts and parcels, improved or unimproved on such terms as to time and manner of payment as may be agreed upon.	Pittsburgh.
The Co-operative Real Estate Company. Capital, $5,000. November 16, 1891.	Said corporation is formed for the purpose of buying, selling, holding and leasing real estate upon such terms and conditions as may be determined upon by said company.	Philadelphia.
The Radnor Water Company. Capital, $5,000. November 17, 1891.	Said corporation is formed for the purpose of supplying water to the public in the township of Radnor, Delaware county, Pa.	Philadelphia.

LIST OF CHARTERS OF CORPORATIONS—*Continued.*

STYLE AND TITLE OF CORPORATION.	PURPOSE.	LOCATION.
Wayne Water Works Company. Capital, $50,000. November 17, 1891.	Said corporation is formed for the purpose of supplying water to the public in that part of the township of Radnor, in the county of Delaware, lying between the old Lancaster or Conestoga road, and the King of Prussia road, and northwest of the road leading from the old Lancaster road at the Friends' Meeting House to the King of Prussia road near Radnor station.	Wayne.
Hope Church Building and Loan Association. Capital, $400,000. November 17, 1891.	Said corporation is formed for the purpose of accumulating a fund by the periodical contributions of the members thereof, and of safely investing the same.	Hope Church.
The Plymouth Bridge Company. Capital, $5,000. November 17, 1891.	Said corporation is formed for the purpose of erecting, constructing and maintaining a bridge and approaches thereto over the Susquehanna river from a point at or near the intersection of Bead and River streets, in the borough of Plymouth, county of Luzerne, Pennsylvania, to a point on the opposite side of the river, in Hanover township, county of Luzerne aforesaid.	Wilkes-Barre.
The Keystone Rattan and Novelty Works. Capital, $10,000. November 17, 1891.	Said corporation is formed for the purpose of manufacturing and selling chairs, tables, mantels, easels, stands and novelties to be made of rattan reed and other materials.	Huntingdon.
The Pittsburgh Coal Company. Capital, $25,000. November 19, 1891.	Said corporation is formed for the purpose of carrying on the business of mining and quarrying coal and manufacturing coke from coal.	Pittsburgh.
Carlisle Two Wheeler Company. Capital, $22,500. November 19, 1891.	Said corporation is formed for the purpose of manufacturing two wheeled and other vehicles and the several parts thereof.	Carlisle.
The F. A. Davis Company. Capital, $500,000. November 19, 1891.	Said corporation is formed for the purpose of the manufacture and sale of medical, scientific and other books, periodicals and publications.	Philadelphia.

The King Rock-Drill Company. Capital, $5,000. November 23, 1891.	Said corporation is formed for the purposes of manufacturing mining machinery from metal or wood, or both, and the sale of the same.	Pittsburgh.
Hardwood Door and Prim Company. Capital, $40,000. November 23, 1891.	Said corporation is formed for the purpose of doing a general planing mill business, manufacturing lumber and manufacturing articles therefrom.	Hyndman.
Tenth Street Inclined Plane. Capital, $60,000. November 23, 1891.	Said corporation is formed for the purpose of erecting, maintaining and operating an inclined plane in the city of Pittsburgh, county of Allegheny, from a point at or near the southeast corner of South 10th street and Bradford street to a point on Brownville avenue, at or near property now or late of Louis Fritz, for carrying, conveying and transporting passengers and freight.	Pittsburgh.
The Plymouth and Wilkes-Barre Turnpike Company. Capital, $1,000. November 23, 1891.	Said corporation is formed for the purpose of building and maintaining an artificial road or turnpike of stone, gravel and earth from a point on Main street, in the borough of Plymouth, county of Luzerne, Pennsylvania, at or near the northeasterly line of said borough to a point on the "River Road" in Hanover township, or the city of Wilkes-Barre, at or near the dividing line between said Hanover township and said city of Wilkes-Barre, in Luzerne county, Pennsylvania.	Wilkes-Barre.
The Lafayette Manufacturing Company. Capital, $300,000. November 24, 1891.	Said corporation is formed for the purpose of manufacturing charcoal, acetates and other products from wood.	Bradford.
Allegheny County Sanitary and Manufacturing Company. Capital, $10,000. November 24, 1891.	Said corporation is formed for the purpose of the manufacture and sale of fertilizing agents and other articles from the refuse and garbage of cities, boroughs and other localities.	Pittsburgh.
Four Mile Run Improvement Company. Capital, $1,000. November 24, 1891.	Said corporation is formed for the purpose of the construction of dams and floating of logs, timber and lumber on Four Mile run, in Cameron county, Pennsylvania, for a distance not exceeding twenty miles from its source.	Emporium.
The Fall Brook and Newton Water Company. Capital, $10,000. November 24, 1891.	Said corporation is formed for the purpose of introducing, supplying and furnishing water to the public of the city of Carbondale, county of Lackawanna, and State of Pennsylvania, and to such persons, partnerships and associations residing therein and adjacent thereto as may desire the same.	Carbondale.

LIST OF CHARTERS OF CORPORATIONS—*Continued.*

STYLE AND TITLE OF CORPORATION.	PURPOSE.	LOCATION.
The Clymer Paving Company. Capital, $10,000. November 25, 1891.	Said corporation is formed for the purpose of engaging in and carrying on the business of making and laying artificial granite pavement.	Philadelphia.
The Torresdale Electric Light and Power Company. Capital, $1,000. November 27, 1891.	Said corporation is formed for the purpose of supplying light, heat and power, or any of them, by means of electricity to the public within the Thirty-fifth ward of the city of Philadelphia, State of Pennsylvania, and to such persons, partnerships and associations residing therein and adjacent thereto as may desire the same.	Philadelphia.
The Morelton Electric Light and Power Company. Capital, $1,000. November 30, 1891.	Said corporation is formed for the purpose of supplying light, heat and power, or any of them, by means of electricity, to the public within the township of Bensalem, county of Bucks, and State of Pennsylvania, and to such persons, partnerships and associations residing therein and adjacent thereto as may desire the same.	Torresdale Mills.
The Herald Publishing Company. Capital, $10,000. November 30, 1891.	Said corporation is formed for the purpose of the transaction of a printing and publishing business.	McKeesport.
The Rittenhouse Homestead Company, of Philadelphia. Capital, $15,000. November 30, 1891.	Said corporation is formed for the purpose of purchasing, taking, holding and enjoying real estate in fee simple or lease, or upon ground rent, improving, leasing, mortgaging and selling the same in fee simple or for any less estate or upon ground rent to its sale shareholders and others, or on such terms as to time of payment as it may determine.	Philadelphia.
J. Horace McFarland Company. Capital, $10,000. November 30, 1891.	Said corporation is formed for the purpose of transacting a printing and publishing business.	Harrisburg.

South Windom Land and Improvement Company. Capital, $10,000. November 30, 1891.	Said corporation is formed for the purpose of purchasing, taking, holding and enjoying real estate in fee simple or lease, or upon ground rent: to improve, lease, mortgage and sell the same in such parts or parcels, and on such terms as to time of payment, as the said company may determine, and to convey the same to the purchasers in fee simple or for any less estate, or upon ground rent, and in like manner to mortgage, sell, convey or extinguish any ground rent reserved out of any real estate so sold.	Philadelphia.
Bloomsburg Brass and Copper Company. Capital, $7,500. December 1, 1891.	Said corporation is formed for the purpose of the manufacture of tubes, rods and other articles of commerce from wood or metal and the manufacture of brass, copper and all other metals.	Bloomsburg.
Gen. A. Macbeth Company. Capital, $5,000. December 1, 1891.	Said corporation is formed for the purpose of manufacturing glass and glassware.	Pittsburgh.
Queen City Tannery. Capital, $100,000. December 2, 1891.	Said corporation is formed for the purpose of manufacturing leather from hides and skins.	Titusville.
East Berlin Carriage and Manufacturing Company. Capital, $8,800. December 2, 1891.	Said corporation is formed for the purpose of manufacturing buggies, carriages, wagons, &c.	East Berlin.
Oakland Brick Company. Capital, $33,350. December 2, 1891.	Said corporation is formed for the purpose of manufacturing and selling brick.	Pittsburgh.
Smoky City Building and Loan Association, of the Twenty-fourth ward, city of Pittsburgh. Capital, $1,000,000. December 3, 1891.	Said corporation is formed for the purpose of accumulating a fund by the periodical contributions of the members thereof, and of safely investing the same.	Pittsburgh.
The Hastings Water Company. Capital, $5,000. December 3, 1891.	Said corporation is formed for the purpose of supplying water to and for the public, in the borough of Hastings, county of Cambria, and State of Pennsylvania, and to persons, partnerships, corporations and associations residing therein, and adjacent thereto, as may desire the same, and for these purposes to have, possess and enjoy all the rights, benefits and privileges conferred by the act of April 29th, 1874, and the supplements thereto.	Hastings.

LIST OF CHARTERS OF CORPORATIONS—*Continued.*

Style and Title of Corporation.	Purpose.	Location.
The Progressive Building and Loan Association. Capital, $800,000. December 4, 1891.	Said corporation is formed for the purpose of accumulating a fund by the periodical contributions of the members thereof, and of safely investing the same.	East Mauch Chunk.
C. M. Littleton Company. Capital, $50,000. December 4, 1891.	Said corporation is formed for the purpose of manufacturing and selling patent dress lacing.	Philadelphia.
The Exponent Publishing Company. Capital, $10,000. December 4, 1891.	Said corporation is formed for the purpose of transacting a printing and publishing business.	Pittsburgh.
Lutheran Missionary Journal Printing Company. Capital, $5,000. December 7, 1891.	Said corporation is formed for the purpose of transacting a general printing and publishing business.	York.
Mt. Pleasant and Donegal Turnpike Road Company. Capital, $5,000. December 7, 1891.	Said corporation is formed for the purpose of making and maintaining a turnpike road of wood, stone, gravel or other proper and convenient materials, such as the nature of the ground may require, from Mt. Pleasant, Westmoreland county, Pa., to Donegal in said county, a distance of nine miles, part of said distance, 2 miles, will be in Fayette county, Pa.	Mt. Pleasant.
Thayer Water Gas Furnace Company. Capital, $5,000. December 8, 1891.	Said corporation is formed for the purpose of manufacturing and selling water gas furnaces, under letters patent of the United States, numbered 299, 877, and other patents covering improvements on such furnaces, and the purchase and sale of said letters patent, and rights, and licenses thereunder.	Pittsburgh.
Stuart Brothers Company. Capital, $100,000. December 8, 1891.	Said corporation is formed for the purpose of manufacturing of blank books and all things appertaining to the same.	Philadelphia.

The Anshutz Bradberry Company. Capital, $120,000. December 8, 1891.	Said corporation is formed for the purpose of the manufacture of stoves, ranges and castings out of iron and other metals.	Allegheny City.
Friendship Building and Loan Association. Capital, $300,000. December 9, 1891.	Said corporation is formed for the purpose of accumulating a fund by the periodical contributions of the members thereof, and of safely investing the same.	Pittsburgh.
North American Oil Company. Capital, $100,000. December 10, 1891.	Said corporation is formed for the purpose of drilling, mining and operating for petroleum oil and gas.	Bradford.
The Annville Building and Loan Association. Capital, $1,000,000. December 10, 1891.	Said corporation is formed for the purpose of accumulating a fund by the periodical contributions of the members thereof, and of safely investing the same.	Annville.
The Nevin Land Company. Capital, $24,000. December 10, 1891.	Said corporation is formed for the purpose of purchasing real estate and improving the same, and sell the same in such parts and parcels, and on such terms as to time of payment as they may determine.	Easton.
The White—Ross Manufacturing Company. Capital, $25,000. December 10, 1891.	Said corporation is formed for the purpose of manufacturing novelties from iron or steel, or both, or from any other metal, and also any article of commerce from metal or wood, or both.	Carlisle.
Alpha Slate Company. Capital, $150,000. December 14, 1891.	Said corporation is formed for the purpose of mining, manufacturing and selling roofing slate and other slate products.	Bangor.
Kaufman Hat & Fur Company. Capital, $80,000. December 14, 1891.	Said corporation is formed for the purpose of manufacturing hats, fur goods and the trimmings therefor.	Pittsburgh.
Delaware Water Gap Land and Improvement Company. Capital, $3,000. December 14, 1891.	Said corporation is formed for the purpose of purchasing, taking, holding and enjoying real estate in fee simple, to improve, lease, mortgage and sell the same in such parts or parcels as they may determine, in the borough of Delaware Water Gap.	Delaware Water Gap.

LIST OF CHARTERS OF CORPORATIONS—*Continued.*

STYLE AND TITLE OF CORPORATION.	PURPOSE.	LOCATION.
The Newville Electric Light, Heat & Power Company. Capital, $5,000. December 14, 1891.	Said corporation is formed for the purpose of furnishing light, heat & power to those with whom the company may contract in the borough of Newville, & to such persons & partnership residing therein & adjacent thereto, as may desire the same.	Newville.
The Common Sense Bicycle Manufacturing Company. Capital, $100,000. December 14, 1891.	Said corporation is formed for the purpose of the manufacture of iron or steel, or both, or of any other metal, or of any article of commerce from metal or wood, or both.	Philadelphia.
Pyle Manufacturing Company. Capital, $10,000. December 14, 1891.	Said corporation is formed for the purpose of the manufacture of iron or steel or both or of any other metal or article of commerce from metal, wood or both.	Philadelphia.
Alta Manufacturing Company. Capital, $50,000. December 15, 1891.	Said corporation is formed for the purpose of manufacturing soaps, oils, essences, soap materials, candles, starch and kindred articles.	Philadelphia.
Fourth Rhein Building Association. Capital, $1,000,000. December 15, 1891.	Said corporation is formed for the purpose of accumulating a fund by the contributions of its members, which, increased by careful management and investment, will enable its members to purchase real estate or to invest the same for any lawful purposes	Philadelphia.
Central Market House Company, of Lebanon, Pennsylvania. Capital, $40,000. December 15, 1891.	Said corporation is formed for the purpose of the establishment and maintenance of a market house at Lebanon, Penna.	Lebanon.
The Eighth United States Excelsior Building Association. Capital, $500,000. December 15, 1891.	Said corporation is formed for the purpose of accumulating a fund by the periodical contributions of the members thereof, and of safely investing the same.	Pittsburgh.
Hamburg Building and Loan Association of Hamburg Berks Co., Pa. Capital, $400,000. December 15, 1891.	Said corporation is formed for the purpose of accumulating a fund by the periodical contributions of the members thereof, and safely investing the same.	Hamburg.

The Clifton Building and Loan Association of Allegheny City. Capital, $1,000,000. December 15, 1891.	Said corporation is formed for the purpose of accumulating funds by periodical contributions of its members from which loans shall be granted to members thereof to enable them to acquire homes, and to otherwise transact such business as building and loan associations are by law authorized to do.	Allegheny City.
The Néveraink Light, Heat and Power Company. Capital, $50,000. December 16, 1891.	Said corporation is formed for the purpose of supplying light, heat and power, or any of them, by electricity to the public in the city of Reading and adjacent territory.	Reading.
The Carlisle Mining and Paint Manufacturing Company. Capital, $25,000. December 18, 1891.	This corporation is formed for the purpose of mining and manufacturing metalic paint.	Carlisle.
Ramona Land Company. Capital, $60,000. December 18, 1891.	Said corporation is formed for the purpose of the purchase and sale of real estate.	Belle Vernon.
Ramona Iron and Steel Company. Capital, $60,000. December 18, 1891.	Said corporation is formed for the purpose of the manufacture of iron or steel, or both, or of any other metal or of any article of commerce from wood or metal, or both.	Belle Vernon.
Newberry Bridge Company. Capital, $16,500. December 18, 1891.	Said corporation is formed for the purpose of erecting, constructing and maintaining a bridge and approaches thereto over the Lycoming creek, from a point in the Sixth ward in the city of Williamsport, in the county of Lycoming, Pennsylvania, between the county bridges across said creek, to a point on the opposite side thereof, in the Seventh ward in the said city of Williamsport. There is no incorporated bridge or ferry over said stream.	Williamsport.
The Carlin Manufacturing Company. Capital, $50,000. December 21, 1891.	Said corporation is formed for the purpose of the manufacture of iron castings, steel, lead or brass, or of any other metal, or of any article of commerce from metal or wood, or both.	Pittsburgh.
The Landsdowne Real Estate Company. Capital, $5,000. December 21, 1891.	Said corporation is formed for the purpose of purchasing and selling real estate, and holding, leasing and selling real estate.	Philadelphia.

LIST OF CHARTERS OF CORPORATIONS—*Continued.*

STYLE AND TITLE OF CORPORATION.	PURPOSE.	LOCATION.
Greensburg Rolling Mill Company. Capital, $100,000. December 21, 1891.	Said corporation is formed for the purpose of the manufacture of iron or steel, or both, or of any other metal or of any article of commerce from metal or wood, or both.	Greensburg.
The Perfection Knitting Machine Company. Capital, $18,000. December 21, 1891.	Said corporation is formed for the purpose of manufacturing and selling knitting machines.	Clearfield.
The Vesta Coal Company. Capital, $250,000. December 22, 1891.	Said corporation is formed for the purpose of mining, producing, transporting and selling coal and its products, with power in the board of directors of said company to sell or release the real estate of the corporation without the agreement and consent of the majority in value of the stock.	Pittsburgh.
Corwin Land Company. Capital, $1,000. December 22, 1891.	Said corporation is formed for the purpose of the purchase and sale of real estate or for holding, leasing and selling real estate.	Pittsburgh.
Carlisle Peach Land Company. Capital, $15,000. December 23, 1891.	Said corporation is formed for the purpose of purchasing, holding, improving, leasing and selling real estate.	Carlisle.
Chambers Glass Company. Capital, $600,000. December 23, 1891.	Said corporation is formed for the purpose of the manufacture of glass.	Pittsburgh.
Banner Baking Powder Company. Capital, $1,000. December 23, 1891.	Said corporation is formed for the purpose of the manufacture and sale of baking powder, scourene, stove polish and grocers' specialties.	Pittsburgh.
The Grocers Baking Company. Capital, $30,000. December 24, 1891.	The said corporation is formed for the purpose of the manufacture and sale of bread and bread stuffs.	Philadelphia.

Corporation	Purpose	Location
The Chaplin Fulton Manufacturing Company, Capital, $60,000. December 28, 1891.	Said corporation is formed for the purpose of the manufacture of iron or steel, or both, or of any other metal or of any article of commerce from metal or wood, or both.	Pittsburgh.
The E. C. Penfield Company. Capital, $100,000. December 28, 1891.	Said corporation is formed for the purpose of manufacturing and selling trusses, supporters and surgical appliances.	Philadelphia.
The Gulf Brewing Company. Capital, $5,000. December 28, 1891.	Said corporation is formed for the purpose of manufacturing and brewing malt liquors.	Conshohocken.
Electric Preserving Works. Capital, $10,000. December 28, 1891.	Said corporation is formed for the purpose of manufacturing preserves, jellies, fruit butters, mince meat, vegetable extracts, condiments and all articles of commerce connected therewith and the sale of same.	Scranton.
Kensington Improvement Company. Capital, $2,000. December 28, 1891.	Said corporation is formed for the purpose of the purchase and sale of real estate and for holding, leasing and selling real estate.	Pittsburgh.
The Mount Troy Building and Loan Association of Reserve Township, Allegheny county, Pennsylvania Capital, $500,000. December 28, 1891.	Said corporation is formed for the purpose of accumulating a fund by the periodical contributions of the members thereof and of safely investing the same.	Allegheny City.
The Dunmore Building and Loan Association. Capital, $1,000,000. December 28, 1891.	Said corporation is formed for the purpose of accumulating a fund by the contributions of the members thereof, and to loan the same to them from time to time, to enable them to purchase real estate, build themselves dwelling houses or engage in any legitimate business.	Dunmore.
Troy Electric Light and Power Company. Capital, $10,000. December 28, 1891.	Said corporation is formed for the purpose of supplying light and power by means of electricity to the public at the borough of Troy, Pa., and to such persons, partnerships, corporations and associations residing therein and adjacent thereto as may desire the same.	Troy borough.
York Carriage Company. Capital, $100,000. December 28, 1891.	Said corporation is formed for the purpose of manufacturing all kinds of wagons, carriages, buggies, carts and vehicles of all kinds; also sleighs of all kinds.	York city.

LIST OF CHARTERS OF CORPORATIONS—*Continued.*

STYLE AND TITLE OF CORPORATION.	PURPOSE.	LOCATION.
Sonman Coal Mining Company. Capital, $50,000. December 28, 1891.	Said corporation is formed for the purpose of mining coal and manufacturing coke therefrom.	Philadelphia.
The Columbia Homestead Company. Capital, $15,000. December 28, 1891.	Said corporation is formed for the purpose of purchasing, taking, holding and enjoying real estate in fee simple, on lease or upon ground rent, improving, leasing, mortgaging and selling the same in fee simple, or for any less estate or upon ground rent to its shareholders and others, or on such terms, as to manner and time of payment as it may determine.	Philadelphia.
The Scranton New Tripoli Slate Company. Capital, $25,000. December 28, 1891.	Said corporation is formed for the purpose of quarrying, mining, manufacturing and selling slate.	Scranton.
North Penn Building and Loan Association of Lansdale. Capital, $500,000. December 29, 1891.	Said corporation is formed for the purpose of accumulating a fund by the periodical contributions of the members thereof, and of safely investing the same.	Lansdale.
Brown & Company (Incorporated), Capital, $5,000. December 29, 1891.	Said corporation is formed for the purpose of manufacture iron or steel, or both, or of any other metal or of any article of commerce from metal or wood, or both.	Pittsburgh.
Armstrong Brother and Company (Incorporated). Capital, $1,000,000 December 30, 1891.	Said corporation is formed for the purpose of the manufacture of cork and all articles of merchandize made from cork, and into which it enters in combination, and bungs, shovels and faucets made from wood.	Pittsburgh.
The Hensel Silk Manufacturing Company. Capital, $25,000. December 30, 1891.	Said corporation is formed for the purpose of manufacturing trimmings and textile fabrics.	Philadelphia.

Company	Purpose	Location
J. H. McEwen Manufacturing Company. Capital, $100,000. December 30, 1891.	Said corporation is formed for the purpose of manufacturing iron and steel, or any other metal, or either thereof, in all shapes and forms, and either of these metals, exclusively or in combination with other metals or with wood.	Ridgway.
The Stewart Manufacturing Company. Capital, $80,000. December 30, 1891.	Said corporation is formed for the purpose of manufacturing curtains, rugs, table covers, and other articles made of wool and silk and cotton, or any of them, and generally to do a manufacturing business.	Philadelphia.
The Duquesne Heat, Light and Power Company. Capital, $20,000. December 30, 1891.	Said corporation is formed for the purpose of supplying heat, light and power, or any of them by means of electricity, to the public in Mifflin township, Allegheny county, Penna., and to persons, partnerships and associations residing therein and adjacent thereto as may desire the same.	Duquesne.
The News Publishing Company. Capital, $5,000. December 31, 1891.	Said corporation is formed for the purpose of carrying on the news-paper and printing business.	Slatington.
The Philadelphia and Boston Petroleum Company, Capital, $20,000. December 31, 1891.	Said corporation is formed for the purpose of mining for oil, gas, coal and other mineral products.	Philadelphia.
The Scranton Supply and Machinery Company. Capital, $50,000. December 31, 1891.	Said corporation is formed for the purposes of the manufacture and sale of mining machinery and supplies.	Scranton.
The Enterprise Homestead Company No. 2, of Germantown, Philadelphia. Capital, $15,000. December 31, 1891.	Said corporation is formed for the purpose of purchasing, taking, holding and enjoying real estate in fee simple, on lease or upon ground rent, improving, leasing, mortgaging and selling the same in fee simple or for any less estate or upon ground rent to its sale shareholders and others, upon such terms as it may determine.	Philadelphia.
Scouller Milling Company. Capital, $80,000. January 4, 1892.	Said corporation is formed for the purpose of the manufacture and sale of flour and feed.	North East.
The Novelty Manufacturing Company. Capital, $10,000. January 4, 1892.	Said corporation is formed for the purpose of manufacturing and selling articles composed in whole or in part of iron, brass, metal or wood.	Allegheny.

LIST OF CHARTERS OF CORPORATIONS—*Continued.*

STYLE AND TITLE OF CORPORATION.	PURPOSE.	LOCATION.
The Wilson Oil Company. Capital, $5,000. January 4, 1892.	Said corporation is formed for the purpose of the mining for the production of oil and gas.	Washington.
The Cruikshank Brothers Company. Capital, $25,000. January 4, 1892.	Said corporation is formed for the purpose of manufacturing of vinegar, pickles, condiments and syrups.	Allegheny.
M. Ehret, Jr., & Co. (Incorporated). Capital, $300,000. January 4, 1892.	Said corporation is formed for the purpose of manufacture of coal tar products, of coal tar, of oils, of asphalt and of roofing and of paving materials composed partly or wholly of tar or asphalt, and the sale of said products thus manufactured by it.	Philadelphia.
Haverford Land and Improvement Company. Capital, $100,000. January 4, 1892.	Said corporation is formed for the purpose of purchasing and selling real estate, to hold lease and sell the same, and to purchase, take, hold and enjoy real estate in fee simple, on lease or upon ground rent, to improve, lease, mortgage and sell the same, in such parts and parcels and on such terms as to time of payment as it may determine, and to convey the same to the purchaser in fee simple or for any less estate or upon ground rents, and in like manner to mortgage, sell, convey or extinguish any ground rent reserved out of any real estate so sold.	Haverford College.
The Tamaqua Building and Loan Association. Capital, $200,000. January 4, 1892.	Said corporation is formed for the purpose of accumulating a fund by the periodical contributions of the members thereof, and of safely investing the same.	Tamaqua.
The Rankin Ten-cent Building & Loan Association. Capital, $1,000,000. January 4, 1892.	Said corporation is formed for the purpose of accumulating a fund by the periodical contributions of the members thereof, and of safely investing the same.	Rankin.
The Industrial Building and Loan Association of Bloomsburg. Capital, $500,000. January 5, 1892.	Said corporation is formed for the purpose of accumulating a fund by the periodical contributions of the members thereof, and of safely investing the same.	Bloomsburg.

American Iron Building and Loan Association of Pittsburgh, Pa. Capital, $1,000,000. January 7, 1892.	Said corporation is formed for the purpose of accumulating a fund by the periodical contributions of the members thereof, and of safely investing the same.	Pittsburgh.
Success Wire and Hedge Fence Company of Jacobus, Penna. Capital, $10,000. January 7, 1892.	Said corporation is formed for the purpose of the manufacture of wire and hedge fence.	Jacobus.
Lebanon Valley Hedge and Wire Fence Company. Capital, $20,000. January 7, 1892.	Said corporation is formed for the purpose of manufacturing hedge and wire fence by the process of plashing and wireing, and selling the same.	Annville.
Lycoming Suspender Company. Capital, $25,000. January 7, 1892.	Said corporation is formed for the purpose of manufacturing and selling suspenders and suspender supplies.	Williamsport.
Westmoreland Electric Company. Capital, $50,000. January 8, 1892.	Said corporation is formed for the purpose of supplying light, heat and power by means of electricity to the public in the borough of Greensburg, Westmoreland county, Pa., and to such persons, partnerships and corporations residing therein or adjacent thereto as may desire the same.	Greensburg.
Fidelity Dime Building and Loan Association. Capital, $1,000,000. January 8, 1892.	Said corporation is formed for the purpose of accumulating a fund by the periodical contributions of the members thereof, and of safely investing the same.	Beltzhoover.
O'Leary Glass Company. Capital, $10,000. January 8, 1892.	Said corporation is formed for the purpose of manufacturing and selling glass and glassware.	Pittsburgh.
The Overbrook Chemical Company. Capital, $25,000. January 8, 1892.	Said corporation is formed for the purpose of manufacturing drugs, chemicals and colors.	Philadelphia.
The Culler and Hawley Furniture Company. Capital, $20,000. January 8, 1892.	Said corporation is formed for the purpose of manufacturing furniture of all kinds, and of making sale of same.	Williamsport.

4a—LAWS.

LIST OF CHARTERS OF CORPORATIONS—*Continued.*

STYLE AND TITLE OF CORPORATION.	PURPOSE.	LOCATION.
People's Water Company. Capital, $10,000. January 11, 1892.	Said corporation is formed for the purpose of supplying water to the public in the borough of Chartiers, in the county of Allegheny, and State of Pennsylvania, and such individuals, associations and corporations therein and adjacent thereto, as may desire the same.	Chartiers.
Union Water Company. Capital, $10,000. January 11, 1892.	Said corporation is formed for the purpose of supplying water to the public in the borough of Mansfield, in the county of Allegheny, and the State of Pennsylvania, and such individuals, associations and corporations therein and adjacent thereto, as may desire the same.	Mansfield.
The American Chair Manufacturing Company. Capital, $40,000. Jan'ry 11, 1892.	Said corporation is formed for the purpose of manufacturing chairs and other furniture, and selling the same.	Brandt.
Williams Valley Water Company. Capital, $40,000. Jan'ry 11, 1892.	Said corporation is formed for the purpose of supplying water to the public in Williamstown borough, Pa., and to such persons and partnerships residing therein, or adjacent thereto, as may desire the same.	Williamstown.
The Elmhurst Water Company. Capital, $10,000. January 11, 1892.	Said corporation is formed for the purpose of supplying of pure water to the public of the borough of Elmhurst and vicinity, and to all persons, partnerships and corporations residing in said borough of Elmhurst, or adjacent thereto, as may desire the same.	Scranton
The Wakefield Homestead Company of Philadelphia. Capital, $15,000. January 11, 1892.	Said corporation is formed for the purpose of purchasing, taking, holding and enjoying real estate in fee simple, or lease or upon ground rent, improving, leasing, mortgaging and selling the same in fee simple or for any less estate, or upon ground rent, to its sale, shareholders and others, or on such terms as to time of payment as it may determine.	Philadelphia.
The Citizens' Electric Light, Power and Heat Company. Capital, $2,000. January 11, 1892.	Said corporation is formed for the purpose of supplying light, heat and power, or any of them, by electricity, to the public in the borough of Dubois, Clearfield county, Pennsylvania, and to such persons, partnerships and corporations residing therein, or adjacent thereto, as may desire the same.	Dubois.

Corporation	Purpose	Location
The Heptasophes Building and Loan Association. Capital, $1,000,000. January 11, 1892.	Said corporation is formed for the purpose of accumulating a fund by the periodical contributions of the members thereof, and of safely investing the same.	Pittsburgh.
The First United States Excelsior Building Association. Capital, $500,000. January 13, 1892.	Said corporation is formed for the purpose of accumulating a fund by the periodical contributions of the members thereof, and of safely investing the same.	Cannonsburg.
The Standard Burial Case and Manufacturing Company. Capital, $30,000. January 13, 1892.	Said corporation is formed for the purpose of the manufacture of iron or steel or both, or of any other metal, or of any article of commerce from metal or wood, or both.	McKeesport.
Clinton County Electric Light, Heat & Power Company. Capital, $25,000. January 14, 1892.	Said corporation is formed for the purpose of supplying light, heat and power, or any of them, by means of electricity, to the public in the city of Lock Haven, and to persons, partnerships and corporations residing therein or adjacent thereto.	Lock Haven.
The Cowley Run Logging Company. Capital, $2,000. January 15, 1892.	Said corporation is formed for the purpose of the construction of dams and the floating of logs, lumber and timber on Cowley Run and the West Branch or head thereof, for a distance not exceeding twenty miles in length from its source, in the counties of Potter and Cameron.	Sizerville.
American Paper Bag Company. Capital, $25,000. January 18, 1892.	Said corporation is formed for the purpose of manufacturing all kinds of paper bags and paper goods.	West Newton.
The Henry H. Roelofs Building and Loan Association. Capital $1,000,000 January 18, 1892.	Said corporation is formed for the purpose of accumulating a fund by the periodical contributions of the members thereof, and of safely investing the same.	Philadelphia.
Apollo Electric Light, Heat and Power Company. Capital, $20,000. January 18, 1892.	Said corporation is formed for the purpose of supplying light, heat and power, by means of electricity, and furnishing the same to the public at Apollo, Pa., and to such persons, partnerships and corporations residing therein and adjacent thereto as may desire the same.	Apollo.
The Somerset Electric Light, Heat and Power Company. Capital, $12,000. January 18, 1892.	Said corporation is formed for the purpose of supplying electricity in the borough of Somerset, Pennsylvania, and to such persons and partnerships residing therein and adjacent thereto as may desire the same.	Somerset.

LIST OF CHARTERS OF CORPORATIONS—*Continued.*

STYLE AND TITLE OF CORPORATION.	PURPOSE.	LOCATION.
Scranton Stone Company. Capital, $10,000. January 18, 1892	Said corporation is formed for the purpose of mining, quarrying and manufacturing stone	Scranton.
Westmoreland Oil Company. Capital, $6,000. January 18, 1892	Said corporation is formed for the purpose of mining for carbon oils, manufacturing, refining and selling or conveying the same to market.	Greensburg.
The Thompson Glass Company Capital, $10,000. January 18, 1892	Said corporation is formed for the purpose of manufacturing and selling glass and glassware.	Uniontown.
Central Cycle Company. Capital, $25,000. January 18, 1892	Said corporation is formed for the purpose of carrying on the business of the manufacture of bicycles, tricycles, and other wheeled vehicles and all goods appertenant to the same.	Philadelphia.
The West Philadelphia Real Estate Agency. Capital, $10,000. January 18, 1892.	Said corporation is formed for the purpose of purchasing real estate, and of holding, leasing and selling the same.	Philadelphia.
The Pen Argyl Electric Light and Power Co. Capital, $10,000. January 18, 1892	Said corporation is formed for the purpose of supplying light, heat and power by means of electricity to the public in the borough of Pen Argyl, Northampton county, Pa., and to such persons, partnerships, corporations and associations residing therein or adjacent thereto as may desire the same.	Pen Argyl.
American Railway Publishing Company. Capital, $50,000. January 21, 1892	Said corporation is formed for the purpose of conducting a general publishing, printing and lithographing business.	Philadelphia.
The "Towanda Chair Company." Capital, $35,000. January 22, 1892.	Said corporation is formed for the purpose of manufacture and sale of chairs, or any article of commerce from wood or metal, or from both, or other materials or parts thereof.	Towanda.

The Leesport Knitting Company.
Capital, $10,000.
January 22, 1892.

Said corporation is formed for the purpose of the manufacture of and sale of knit goods and all kinds of hosiery, and for that purpose to have and possess the power and privileges of said act of assembly and its supplements.

West Leesport.

The Valley Coal & Mining Company.
Capital, $15,000.
January 25, 1892.

Said corporation is formed for the purpose of mining for coal or fire-clay, lime stone and other minerals.

Kittanning.

The Penn Building and Loan Association No. 2, of Altoona, Pa.
Capital, $1,000,000.
January 28, 1892.

Said corporation is formed for the purpose of accumulating a fund by the periodical contributions of the members thereof, and of safely investing the same.

Altoona.

The Argoline Manufacturing Company.
Capital, $15,000.
January 28, 1892.

Said corporation is formed for the purpose of the manufacture and sale of the various products of crude petroleum and the medicinal and pharmaceutical admixtures and compounds thereof, and also any and all other medicinal or pharmaceutical preparations, compounds and mixtures, whether made from crude petroleum or otherwise.

Homestead.

Harrison Gas Coal Company.
Capital, $100,000.
January 28, 1892.

Said corporation is formed for the purpose of mining and selling coal.

Greensburg.

The Doylestown Electric Company.
Capital, $16,000.
January 28, 1892.

Said corporation is formed for the purpose of supplying light, heat and power by electricity to the public in the borough of Doylestown, Bucks county, Pennsylvania, and to such persons, partnerships and corporations residing therein or adjacent thereto as may desire the same.

Doylestown.

The Home Building and Loan Association of Coatsville.
Capital $500,000.
January 27, 1892.

Said corporation is formed for the purpose of accumulating a fund by the periodical contributions of the members thereof, and of safely investing the same.

Coatsville.

The Fidelity Home Purchasers' Building and Loan Association.
Capital, $1,000,000.
January 27, 1892.

Said corporation is formed for the purpose of accumulating a fund by the periodical contributions of the members thereof, and of safely investing the same.

Philadelphia.

The Avondale Lime and Stone Company.
Capital, $50,000.
January 27, 1892.

Said corporation is formed for the purpose of quarrying stone, and manufacturing lime and other mineral products.

Philadelphia and Avondale.

LIST OF CHARTERS OF CORPORATIONS—*Continued.*

STYLE AND TITLE OF CORPORATION.	PURPOSE.	LOCATION.
Quaker City Cooperage Co. Capital, $500,000. January 27, 1892.	Said corporation is formed for the purpose of manufacturing barrels, and selling the products manufactured.	Philadelphia.
United Steel Company, Capital, $1,000. January 27, 1892.	Said corporation is formed for the purpose of manufacturing iron or steel, or both, or any other metal, or of any article of commerce from metal or wood, or both.	Pittsburgh.
The Reading Paper Box Company. Capital, $25,000. January 27, 1892.	Said corporation is formed for the purpose of manufacturing boxes, cartons and other objects from straw board, wood board, paper, wood and metal.	Reading.
The Cocalico Water Company. Capital, $20,000. January 28, 1892.	Said corporation is formed for the purpose of supplying water to the public in the township of Ephrata, Lancaster county, Pennsylvania, and to such persons, partnerships and corporations residing therein or adjoining thereto as may desire the same.	Ephrata.
The Ephrata Light Company. Capital, $10,000. January 28, 1892.	Said corporation is formed for the purpose of supplying light, heat and power by means of electricity, to the public in the borough of Ephrata, Lancaster county, Pa., and to such other persons, partnerships and corporations residing therein or adjacent thereto as may desire the same.	Ephrata.
The Highland Paper Company. Capital, $250,000. January 29, 1892.	Said corporation is formed for the purpose of manufacturing paper out of wood pulp, or other materials, fibre wood pulp and wood pulp articles, and selling the same, and carrying on the business incidental thereto.	Johnsonburg.
The Keystone Brick and Terra Cotta Company, Capital, $50,000. January 28, 1892.	Said corporation is formed for the purpose of mining stone, clay and coal, and the manufacture and sale of tile, sewer pipe, brick, terra cotta ware and other building material made from clay and stone, or either of them.	Georgetown.
The North Penn Building Association of Philadelphia, Capital, $1,000,000. February 2, 1892.	Said corporation is formed for the purpose of accumulating a fund by the periodical contributions of the members thereof, and of safely investing the same.	Philadelphia.

Ridgway Publishing Company. Capital, $16,000. February 2, 1883.	Said corporation is formed for the purpose of the transaction of a printing and publishing business.	Ridgway.
Hooper Brothers Company. Incorporated. Capital, $20,000. February 2, 1892.	Said corporation is formed for the purpose of the manufacture and sale of brick.	Pittsburgh.
Pratt Food Company. Capital, $200,000. February 3, 1892.	Said corporation is formed for the purpose of the manufacture and sale of foods for cattle, animals and poultry, and other foods, and of supplies connected with the use and rearing of cattle, animals and poultry, and the transaction of all lawful business arising out of the same.	Philadelphia.
The Herndon Manufacturing Company. Capital, $7,500. February 4, 1892	Said corporation is formed for the purpose of manufacturing doors, sash, blinds, brackets and such other articles as are manufactured in a planing mill.	Herndon.
The Heller Printing Company. Incorporated. Capital, $3,500. February 4, 1892.	Said corporation is formed for the purpose of transacting a printing and publishing business.	Williamsport.
Workingmen's Building and Loan Association of Butler, Pa. Capital, $1,000,000. February 5, 1892.	Said corporation is formed for the purpose of accumulating a fund by the periodical contributions of the members thereof, and of safely investing the same.	Butler.
The Kittanning Building and Loan Association. Capital, $200,000. February 5, 1892.	Said corporation is formed for the purpose of accumulating a fund by the periodical contributions of the members thereof, and of safely investing the same.	Kittanning.

LIST OF CHARTERS OF CORPORATIONS—Continued.

STYLE AND TITLE OF CORPORATION.	PURPOSE.	LOCATION.
W. L. Mellon Pipe Lines. Capital, $200,000. February 8, 1892.	Said corporation is formed for the purpose of transporting, storing, insuring and shipping petroleum, and for that purpose to lay down, construct and maintain pipes, tubing, tanks, offices and such other machinery, services and arrangements as may be necessary to fully carry out that right; and also with the right to enter upon, take and occupy such land and other property as may be requisite for the purposes of such corporations.	Pittsburgh.
Henrietta Coal Mining Company. Capital, $50,000. February 8, 1892.	Said corporation is formed for the purpose of mining coal and manufacturing coke and other products of coal therefrom, and for these purposes to have, possess and enjoy all the rights, benefits and privileges of said act of assembly and the various supplements thereto.	Philadelphia.
Milton Electric Light and Power Company. Capital, $40,000. February 8, 1892.	Said corporation is formed for the purpose of the manufacture and supply of light and power, or either of them, by electricity to the public in the borough of Milton, Pa., and vicinity, and to such persons, partnerships and corporations residing therein or adjacent thereto as may desire the same.	Milton.
The Commodore Art Building and Loan Assoc iation. Capital, $1,000,000. February 8, $2.	Said corporation is formed for the purpose of accumulating a fund by the periodical contribution of the members thereof, and of safely investing the same.	Philadelphia.
The Columbian Building and Loan Association. Capital, $600,000. February 9, 1892.	Said corporation is formed for the purpose of accumulating a fund by the periodical contributions of the members thereof, and of safely investing the same.	Scranton.
The People's Building and Loan Association of Steelton. Capital, $1,000,000. February 9, 1892.	Said corporation is formed for the purpose of accumulating a fund by the periodical contributions of the members thereof, and of safely investing the same.	Steelton.

Company	Description	Location
The Lower Chichester Electric Light, Heat and Power Company. Capital, $1,000. February 9, 1892.	Said corporation is formed for the purpose of supplying light, heat and power by electricity to the public in the township of Lower Chichester, in the county of Delaware, and State of Pennsylvania, and to such partnerships and associations residing therein and adjacent thereto as may desire the same.	Linwood.
Marcus Hook Water Company. Capital, $1,000. February 9, 1892.	Said corporation is formed for the purpose of supplying water to the public, in the borough of Marcus Hook, in the county of Delaware, and state of Pennsylvania.	Marcus Hook.
The Wilkes-Barre and Shawnee Bridge. Capital, $10,000. February 11, 1892.	Said corporation is formed for the purpose of erecting maintaining a bridge and approaches thereto over the from a point at or near the main street in the borou ginning at Ferry street in said borough (being the convenient point as near as may be near the center of said borough from north to south), in the county of Luzerne, to a point on opposite side of said river, in the county of Luzerne aforesaid, in the township of Hanover. The location of said bridge being more than three thousand feet from any other incorporated bridge over said stream.	Wilkes-Barre.
The Acme Torpedo Company. Capital, $2,000. February 11, 1892.	Said corporation is formed for the purpose of the manufacture of nitro-glycerine, oil well torpedoes and other explosives of like nature, and the apparatus and materials for exploding the same.	Pittsburgh.
Rittersville Hotel Company. Capital, $50,000. February 11, 1892.	Said corporation is formed for the purpose of establishing and maintaining an hotel at the village of Rittersville, in Hanover township, Lehigh county, Pennsylvania.	Rittersville.
The Globe Powder Company. Capital, $5,000. February 11, 1892.	Said corporation is formed for the purpose of manufacture of mining, blasting and gunpowder.	Pittsburg.
Reading Cold Storage Company. Capital, $150,000. February 11, 1892.	Said corporation is formed for the purpose of carrying on a general storage warehouse business.	Reading.
The Newmanstown Water Company. Capital, $4,000. February 11, 1892.	Said corporation is formed for the purpose of supplying water to the public, in the village of Newmanstown, and to such persons and partnerships residing therein, and adjacent thereto, as may desire the same.	Newmanstown.

LIST OF CHARTERS OF CORPORATIONS—*Continued.*

STYLE AND TITLE OF CORPORATION.	PURPOSE.	LOCATION.
The Bessemer Homestead Loan and Trust Company No. 2. Capital, $15,000. February 12, 1892.	Said corporation is formed for the purpose of buying, holding and conveying real estate, in fee simple or any less estate, improving, leasing, mortgaging and selling the same to its shareholders and others, on such terms as to time of payment as it may determine, in fee simple or for any less estate, or for ground rent.	Homestead.
Muncy Woolen Mills Company. Capital, $100,000. February 12, 1892.	Said corporation is formed for the purpose of the manufacture of woolen goods.	Borough of Muncy.
Tremont Engine and Boiler Works. Capital, $100,000. February 15, 1892.	Said corporation is formed for the purpose of the manufacture of iron and steel, or both, or any other metal, or of any article of commerce from metal or wood, or both, and for that purpose to have and possess the power and privileges expressed in the 38th section of the corporation act of 1874, and the various supplements thereto.	Tremont.
Hunyon's Homeopathic Home Remedy Company. Capital, $25,000. February 15, 1892.	Said corporation is formed for the purpose of manufacturing and selling medicines, chemicals, pharmaceutical and other useful preparations for scientific, medical and domestic uses.	Philadelphia.
Glen Willow Ice Manufacturing Company. Capital, $200,000. February 16, 1892.	Said corporation is formed for the purpose of manufacturing ice, and of selling the ice manufactured.	Philadelphia.
New York and Middle Coal Field Railroad and Coal Company. Re-charter. Capital, $1,500,000. February 17, 1892.	Said corporation is formed for the purpose of mining, shipping and selling coal, and carrying on all business connected therewith and incidental thereto.	Philadelphia.
The Galates Building and Loan Association. Capital, $1,000,000. February 17, 1892.	Said corporation is formed for the purpose of accumulating a fund by the periodical contributions of the members thereof, and of safely investing the same.	Philadelphia.

The First United State Excelsior Building and Loan Association of Uniontown. Capital, $500,000. February 18, 1892.	Said corporation is formed for the purpose of accumulating a fund by the periodical contributions of the members thereof, and of safely investing the same.	Uniontown.
East Palestine Coal Company. Capital, $14,000. February 18, 1892.	Said corporation is formed for the purpose of mining and selling bituminous coal.	Pittsburgh.
The Cresent Coal Company. Capital, $10,000. February 18, 1892.	Said corporation is formed for the purpose of mining coal and preparing it for market.	Wilkes-Barre.
The Miller Wagon Manufacturing Company. Capital, $10,000. February 19, 1892.	Said corporation is formed for the purpose of manufacturing and sale of coaches, carriages, wagons, carts, cars, sleighs and other vehicles of like kind, with the right to hold and enjoy patent rights necessary for carrying on said business.	Pittsburgh.
Warn and McClain Company. Capital, $40,000. February 19, 1892.	Said corporation is formed for the purpose of the manufacturing lumber and timber.	Ridgway.
The Pittsburgh Tin Plate Works. Capital, $60,000. February 23, 1892.	Said corporation is formed for the purpose of the manufacture of iron or steel, or both, or of any other metal, or of any article of commerce from metal or wood, or both.	New Kensington.
Wilcox Tanning Company. Capital, $500,000. February 23, 1892.	Said corporation is formed for the purpose of manufacture and sale of leather, and such other business as may be incident thereto.	Wilcox.
Ass G. Nevill Glass Company. Capital, $50,000. February 23, 1892.	Said corporation is formed for the purpose of manufacturing glass and glassware of every description.	Blairsville.
The Summit Coal and Coke Company. Capital, $1,000. February 23, 1892.	Said corporation is formed for the purpose of mining of coal, the manufacture of coke, and the transportation thereof to market and the sale thereof.	Clearfield
Ajax Iron Works. Capital, $60,000. February 23, 1892.	Said corporation is formed for the purpose of manufacture and sale of engines, boilers, pumps and machinery of all kinds, and machinery supplies.	Corry.

LIST OF CHARTERS OF CORPORATIONS—*Continued.*

STYLE AND TITLE OF CORPORATION.	PURPOSE.	LOCATION.
Murphy-Parker Company. Capital, $15,000. February 23, 1892.	Said corporation is formed for the purpose of conducting a general book-binding business.	Philadelphia.
The Penn Steel Castings and Machine Company, Capital, $150,000. February 23, 1892.	Said corporation is formed for the purpose of the manufacture of iron or steel, or both, or of any other metal or of any article of commerce from metal or wood, or both.	Chester.
Reform Bureau, Capital, $12,000. February 24, 1892.	Said corporation is formed for the purpose of the transaction of a printing and publishing business, to wit; the printing and publishing of a paper called the Christian Statesman, and other papers, books, documents, tracts, lectures, addresses and literature advocating the great moral reforms from an evangelical standpoint.	Pittsburgh.
The Ford Boiler Cleaner Company. Capital, $5,500. February 24, 1892.	Said corporation is formed for the purpose of the manufacture and sale of boiler cleaners made under the patent granted to George R. Ford, and also for the purpose of the manufacture and sale of iron or steel, or both, or of any other metal, or of any article of commerce from metal or wood, or both.	Norristown.
Western Star Land Company. Capital, $2,500. February 24, 1892.	Said corporation is formed for the purpose of buying, holding, improving, leasing, mortgaging and selling real estate.	Carnot.
G. S. Lovell Clock Company. Capital, $50,000. February 24, 1892.	Said corporation is formed for the purpose of manufacturing clocks, watches and bronzes.	Philadelphia.
Keystone Tin Plate Company. Capital, $25,000. February 25, 1892.	Said corporation is formed for the purpose of manufacturing tin and terne plate and other metal products and the sale of such products manufactured.	Philadelphia.
The Germantown Avenue Building Association. Re-charter. Capital, $1,000,000. February 25, 1892.	Said corporation is formed for the purpose of accumulating a fund by the periodical contributions of the members thereof, and of safely investing the same.	Philadelphia.

The Acme Iron Company. Capital, $75,000. February 25, 1892.	Said corporation is formed for the purpose of manufacturing pig-iron.	Norristown.
The Raymond and Campbell Manufacturing Company. Capital $350,000. February 25, 1892.	Said corporation is formed for the purpose of manufacturing stoves, boilers, general machinery and implements of all kinds, castings of iron, steel, brass and other metals, woodwork and any article of commerce made from metal or wood, or a combination of both, and selling the same.	Middletown.
The Columbian Metallic Rod-Packing Company. Capital, $150,000. February 25, 1892.	Said corporation is formed for the purpose of the manufacture and sale of metallic rod packing, for machinery, under letters patent of the United States, No. 418,802, and other patents covering improvements on the same, and for the purchase and sale of such patents and of rights and licenses under said patents, and for the manufacture and sale of patented articles, together with all the rights and privileges granted by clause XVIII, section 2, act of April 29, 1874, and its several supplements.	Philadelphia.
The Belle Vernon Coal & Coke Company. Capital, $60,000. February 25, 1892.	Said corporation is formed for the purpose of carrying on the business of mining coal and in manufacturing coke therefrom.	Belle Vernon.
The Blaisdall Water Company. Capital, $5,000. February 26, 1892.	Said corporation is formed for the purpose of supplying the inhabitants of a portion of Bradford township, bounded north by the Bradford city line, on the east by the public highway leading up the east side of the Tunangwant creek, on the south and west by south and west lines of warrant 3,416 with pure and wholesome water for domestic and other uses.	Bradford City.
Beaver Refining Company. Capital, $25,000. February 26, 1892.	Said corporation is formed for the purpose of manufacturing refined and lubricating oils, greases, petroleum and other such products of petroleum.	Oak Grove.
The Bellwood Mutual Building and Loan Association. Capital, $1,000,000. February 26, 1892.	Said corporation is formed for the purpose of accumulating a fund by the periodical contributions of the members thereof, and of safely investing the same.	Bellwood
The Pennsylvania Building & Loan Association. Capital, $1,000,000. February 26, 1892.	Said corporation is formed for the purpose of accumulating a fund by the periodical contributions of the members thereof, and of safely investing the same.	Altoona.

LIST OF CHARTERS OF CORPORATIONS—*Continued.*

STYLE AND TITLE OF CORPORATION.	PURPOSE.	LOCATION.
The Keystone Water Company. Capital, $375,00. February 29, 1892.	Said corporation is formed for the purpose of supplying water to the public in the city of Harrisburg, Dauphin county, Pa., and to such persons, partnerships, associations and corporations residing therein and adjacent thereto, as may desire the same.	Harrisburg.
New Castle Steel and Tin Plate Company. Capital, $150,000. February 29, 1892.	Said corporation is formed for the purpose of the manufacture of iron or steel, or both, or of any other metal, or of any article of commerce from metal or wood, or both.	New Castle.
The Dauphin Water Company. Capital, $7,500. February 29, 1892.	Said corporation is formed for the purpose of supplying water to the public in the borough of Dauphin, county of Dauphin, Pa., and to such persons, partnerships, associations, and corporations residing therein and adjacent thereto, as may desire the same.	Scranton.
The Steelton Water Company. Capital, $15,000. February 29, 1892.	Said corporation is formed for the purpose of supplying water to the public in the borough of Steelton, county of Dauphin, Pa., and to such persons, partnerships, and corporations and associations residing therein and adjacent thereto, as may desire the same.	Harrisburg.
Smith Brudewold Glass Company. Capital, $75,000. February 29, 1892.	Said corporation is formed for the purpose of manufacturing glass, glassware, and its products.	Pittsburgh.
The Sterrick Creek Coal Company. Capital $100,000. February 29, 1892.	Said corporation is formed for the purpose of opening coal mines, mining and preparing coal for market, and vending the same.	Scranton.
The Kenderton Building and Loan Association. Re-charter. Capital, $250,000. February 29, 1892.	Said corporation is formed for the purpose of accumulating a fund by the contributions of the members, and to loan the same to them from time to time, to enable them to purchase real estate, build themselves dwelling or other houses, pay off and satisfy mortgages and redeem ground-rents, or engage in any legitimate business.	Philadelphia.

The Girard Building and Loan Association. Capital, $1,000,000. February 29, 1892.	Said corporation is formed for the purpose of accumulating a fund for the purchase of real estate, the purchase and erection of houses, and to aid its members by loans in acquiring real estate, making improvements thereon, and removing incumbrances therefrom, and for the transaction of the general business of a building and loan association, in accordance with the provisions of section 37 of the above-mentioned Act of assembly, and of the acts amendatory thereof and supplemental thereto.	Girard.
The Weeks Manufacturing Company. Capital, $50,000. March 1, 1892.	Said corporation is formed for the purpose of manufacturing grocers specialties and supplies.	Philadelphia.
Richards' Grate Bar Company. Capital, $12,000. March 1, 1892.	Said corporation is formed for the purpose of manufacturing and selling, grate bars and coal mine machinery of all kinds.	Catasauqua.
Wyoming Valley Lace Mills. Capital, $50,000. March 1, 1892.	Said corporation is formed for the purpose of carrying on the manufacture of lace curtains and other textile fabrics.	Wilkes-Barre.
The Brushton Building & Loan Association. Capital, $1,000,000. March 2, 1892.	Said corporation is formed for the purpose of accumulating a fund by the periodical contributions of the members thereof, and of safely investing the same.	Brushton.
The Pennsylvania Hard Vein Slate Company. Capital, $25,000. March 3, 1892.	Said corporation is formed for the purpose of mining, quarrying, manufacturing and selling slate and slate products.	Easton.
Utopia Real Estate Company. Capital, $40,000. March 3, 1892.	Said corporation is formed for the purpose of the purchase and sale of real estate, or for holding, leasing and selling real estate.	Philadelphia.
The Twelfth Ward Union Building & Loan Association. Capital, $1,000,000. March 3, 1892.	Said corporation is formed for the purpose of accumulating a fund by the periodical contributions of the members thereof, and of safely investing the same.	Pittsburgh.

LIST OF CHARTERS OF CORPORATIONS—*Continued.*

STYLE AND TITLE OF CORPORATION.	PURPOSE.	LOCATION.
The Somerton Building and Loan Association. Capital, $500,000. March 4, 1892.	Said corporation is formed for the purpose of accumulating a fund by the periodical contributions of the members thereof, and of safely investing the same.	Philadelphia.
The Peoples Mutual Building and Loan Association of Banksville. Capital, $500,000. March 4, 1892.	Said corporation is formed for the purpose of accumulating a fund by monthly contributions, to be loaned to its members to assist them in their business and aid them in procuring homes, and to transact such other business as building and loan associations are by law authorized to transact.	Banksville.
Marble Hill Quarry Company. Capital, $30,000. March 4, 1892.	Said corporation is formed for the purpose of mining, quarrying stone, clay or other substances or raw materials of a like nature, and manufacturing the same or combinations thereof, or of other substances or minerals into artificial stone, paving blocks, bricks or other forms adapted to building, paving, sewering or other like purposes.	Pittsburgh.
Rowley & Hermance Company. Capital, $325,000. March 4, 1892.	Said corporation is formed for the purpose of manufacturing iron or steel, or both, or of any other metal, or of any article of commerce from metal or wood, or both.	Williamsport.
Blue Ridge Powder Company. Capital, $15,000. March 4, 1892.	Said corporation is formed for the purpose of manufacturing dynamite and powder and to sell the same.	Allentown.
The Martinsburg Water Company. Capital, $20,000. March 4, 1892.	Said corporation is formed for the purpose of supplying water to the public in the borough of Martinsburg, Blair county, Pennsylvania, and vicinity.	Martinsburg.
The Citizens Water Company of Darby Borough. Capital, $1,000. March 7, 1892.	Said corporation is formed for the purpose of supplying water to the public in the borough of Darby, in the county of Delaware, in the State of Pennsylvania, to such persons, partnerships and corporations residing therein or adjacent thereto, as may desire the same.	Media.
The Consumers Water Company of Upper Darby. Capital, $1,000. March 7, 1892.	Said corporation is formed for the purpose of supplying water to the public in the township of Upper Darby, county of Delaware, and State of Pennsylvania, and to such persons, partnerships and corporations residing therein or adjacent thereto, as may desire the same.	Media.

The Penn Water Company of Sharon Hill Borough. Capital, $1,000. March 7, 1892.	Said corporation is formed for the purpose of supplying water to the public in the borough of Sharon Hill, in the county of Delaware, and State of Pennsylvania, and to such persons, partnerships and corporations residing therein or adjacent thereto, as may desire the same.	Media.
The Peoples Water Company of Darby Township. Capital, $1,000. March 7, 1892.	Said corporation is formed for the purpose of supplying water to the public in the township of Darby, in the county of Delaware, and State of Pennsylvania, and to such persons, partnerships and corporations residing therein or adjacent thereto, as may desire the same.	Media.
The Tinicum Water Company. Capital, $1,000. March 7, 1892.	Said corporation is formed for the purpose of supplying water to the public in the township of Tinicum, in the county of Delaware, and State of Pennsylvania, and to such persons, partnerships and corporations residing therein and adjacent thereto, as may desire the same.	Media.
The Highland Water Company of Ridley Township. Capital, $100,000. March 7, 1892.	Said corporation is formed for the purpose of supplying water to the public in the township of Ridley, county of Delaware, and State of Pennsylvania, and to such persons, partnerships and corporations residing therein or adjacent thereto, as may desire the same.	Media.
Elkins Gas Coal Company. Capital, $10,000. March 7, 1892.	Said corporation is formed for the purpose of mining and selling coal and manufacturing and selling coke.	Philadelphia.
The Farmers Creamery Company. Capital, $10,000. March 7, 1892.	Said corporation is formed for the purpose of manufacturing butter, cheese, and all other products made from milk, and for manufacturing creamery supplies.	Philadelphia.
The Mechanics Loan and Building Association of Allentown, Pa. Capital, $1,000,000. March 7, 1892.	Said corporation is formed for the purpose of accumulating a fund by the periodical contributions of the members thereof, and of safely investing the same.	Allentown.
The Huntingdon Building and Loan Association of Philadelphia. Capital, $1,000,000. March 7, 1892.	Said corporation is formed for the purpose of accumulating a fund by the periodical contributions of the members thereof, and of safely investing the same.	Philadelphia.
The Hughesville Building and Loan Association. Capital, $400,000. March 8, 1892.	Said corporation is formed for the purpose of accumulating a fund by the periodical contributions of the members thereof, and of safely investing the same.	Hughesville.

5a LAWS.

LIST OF CHARTERS OF CORPORATIONS—*Continued.*

STYLE AND TITLE OF CORPORATION.	PURPOSE.	LOCATION.
Beaver County Building and Loan Association. Capital, $1,000,000. March 10, 1892.	Said corporation is formed for the purpose of accumulating a fund by the periodical contributions of the members thereof, and of safely investing the same.	New Brighton.
Venango Building and Loan Association of Franklin. Capital, $600,000. March 10, 1892.	Said corporation is formed for the purpose of accumulating a fund by the periodical contributions of the members thereof, and of safely investing the same.	Franklin.
The Ridgway Electric Light Company. Capital, $10,000. March 11, 1892.	Said corporation is formed for the purpose of supplying light, heat and power, or any of them, by electricity to the public in the borough of Ridgway, in the the county of Elk, and to such persons, partnerships and corporations residing therein or adjacent thereto, as may desire the same.	Ridgway.
The Markleton Hotel Company Capital, $75,000. March 11, 1892.	Said corporation is formed for the purpose of establishing and maintaining an hotel at Harkleton, Somerset county, Pennsylvania.	Markleton.
The Pneumatic Fire Alarm Telegraph Company. Capital, $250,000. March 11, 1892.	Said corporation is formed for the purpose of carrying on the business of manufacturing mechanical or electrical appliances and devices, working or operating by means of compressed air.	Philadelphia.
American Carbon Black Co. Capital, $45,000. March 11, 1892.	Said corporation is formed for the purpose of manufacturing carbon black, gas black lamp black.	Warren.
The Nonpariel Cement Company. Capital, $30,000. March 11, 1892.	Said corporation is formed for the purpose of manufacturing and selling cements and plaster, enameled brick and goods of a like description.	Philadelphia.
Pittsburgh Car Wheel Company. Capital, $30,000. March 14, 1892.	Said corporation is formed for the purpose of the manufacture of iron or steel, or both, or of any other metal, or of any article of commerce from metal or wood, or both.	Pittsburgh.

Corporation	Purpose	Location
The Mack Paving Company. Capital, $100,000. March 14, 1892.	Said corporation is formed for the purpose of the grading, curbing, paving or macadamizing, construction and maintenance of any species of street, road or highway, and the furnishing of the materials and labor therefor.	Philadelphia.
The Apollo Improvement Company. Capital, $50,000. March 14, 1892.	Said corporation is formed for the purpose of the purchase and sale of real estate, and holding; leasing, improving and selling real estate.	Appollo
The Diamond Street Omnibus Company. Capital, $50,000. March 14, 1892.	Said corporation is formed for the purpose of forming and operating stage and omnibus lines in the city of Philadelphia, in said Commonwealth.	Philadelphia.
Peoples Building Company of McKeesport, Pa. Capital, $10,000. March 14, 1892.	Said corporation is formed for the purpose of purchasing and selling real estate, and for holding, leasing and selling the same.	McKeesport.
The Wadsworth Stone and Paving Company. Capital, $10,000. March 15, 1892.	Said corporation is formed for the purpose of the manufacture and sale of artificial stone and artificial stone paving.	Pittsburgh.
The West Philadelphia Steam Heat Company. Capital, $10,000. March 15, 1892.	Said corporation is formed for the purpose of supplying heat by steam to the public in the city of Philadelphia, Pennsylvania, and to such persons, partnerships and associations residing in said city, or adjacent thereto, as may desire the same.	Philadelphia.
Crescent Fire Brick Company. Capital, $50,000. March 15, 1892.	Said corporation is formed for the purpose of mining and quarrying stone, clay, fire-clay, sand, and the manufacture of the same into articles of merchandise.	Pittsburgh.
The Middletown Flouring Mills Company. Capital, $10,000. March 15, 1892.	Said corporation is formed for the purpose of manufacturing and selling flour and feed, and the products of cereals of all kinds.	Middletown.
The Safe Deposit, Building and Loan Association of Harrisburg, Pa. Capital, $1,000,000. March 15, 1892.	Said corporation is formed for the purpose of accumulating a fund by the periodical contributions of the members thereof, and of safely investing the same.	Harrisburg.

LIST OF CHARTERS AND CORPORATIONS—*Continued.*

Style and Title of Corporations.	Purpose.	Location.
Spring Mill Building and Loan Association. Capital, $1,000,000. March 16, 1892.	Said corporation is formed for the purpose of accumulating a fund by the periodical contributions of the members thereof, and of safely investing the same.	Spring Mill.
The Home Building and Loan Association of Monongahela City. Capital, $1,000,000. March 16, 1892.	Said corporation is formed for the purpose of accumulating a fund by the periodical contributions of the members thereof, and of safely investing the same.	Monongahela City.
Chambersburg Shoe Manufacturing Company. Capital, $40,000. March 17, 1892.	Said corporation is formed for the purpose of manufacturing boots, shoes and other articles out of leather and cloth.	Chambersburg.
Standard Axe and Tool Works. Capital, $10,000. March 17, 1892.	Said corporation is formed for the purpose of manufacturing articles of commerce from metal and wood.	West Ridgway.
Braddock and Homestead Bridge Company. Capital, $2,000. March 17, 1892.	Said corporation is formed for the purpose of ... , constructing and maintaining of a bridge and app roaches ... , over the Monongahela river, from a point at or near the City Farm Station, on the Baltimore and ... railroad, on the northerly bank of the Monongahela river, in the city of ... , county of Allegheny, Penna., and thence ... said river to the southerly bank thereof, to a point in the borough of Homestead, in said ... ty of Allegheny. The location of said bridge being one thousand feet from any ther ... a bridge or ferry over said river.	Pittsburgh.
The Scranton Axle Works. Capital, $150,000. March 17, 1892.	Said corporation is formed for the purpose of the manufacture of iron or steel, or both, or of any other metal or article of commerce, from metal, wood, or both, with the right to hold and enjoy such patents and patented rights as may be necessary in carrying on said business.	Scranton.

Corporation	Purpose	Location
The Columbia Coal Mining Company. Capital, $150,000. March 18, 1892.	Said corporation is formed for the purpose of the mining of coal and the manufacture of coke therefrom.	Philadelphia.
Madison Gas Coal Company. Capital, $100,000. March 21, 1892.	Said corporation is formed for the purpose of mining coal, manufacturing coke, and selling the same in crude or manufactured form.	Greensburg.
Beaver Valley Land Improvement Company. Capital, $10,000. March 21, 1892.	Said corporation is formed for the purpose of purchasing, improving, holding, leasing and selling real estate.	Beaver.
Sharpsburg Brick and Stone Co. Capital, $12,000. March 21, 1892.	Said corporation is formed for the purpose of the manufacture of brick and the quarrying of stone.	Sharpsburg.
The Eagles Mere Land Company. Capital, $8,000. March 21, 1892.	Said corporation is formed for the purpose of the purchase and sale of real estate.	Williamsport.
J. C. McCook Company. Capital, $75,000. March 21, 1892.	Said corporation is formed for the purpose of manufacturing confectionary and chocolates.	Philadelphia.
The People's Trust, Savings and Deposit Company. Capital, $250,000. March 23, 1892.	Said corporation is formed for the purpose of engaging in and carrying on the business of the insurance of owners of real estate, mortgages and others interested in real estate from loss by reason of defective liens and encumbrances and titles.	Lancaster.
Scottsdale Brick and Tile Company. Capital, $25,000. March 24, 1892.	Said corporation is formed for the purpose of manufacturing brick, sewer pipe, tile and other articles composed in whole or in part of clay, &c., and selling and disposing of the same.	Greensburg.
The Mountain City Lumber Company. Capital, $20,000. March 24, 1892.	Said corporation is formed for the purpose of manufacturing lumber and timber.	Altoona.
Standard Machine Company. Capital, $25,000. March 25, 1892.	Said corporation is formed for the purpose of manufacturing patented knitting machines and machinery of all kinds.	Philadelphia.

LIST OF CHARTERS OF CORPORATIONS—*Continued.*

STYLE AND TITLE OF CORPORATION.	PURPOSE.	LOCATION.
Charleroi Coal Co. Capital, $100,000. March 25, 1892.	Said corporation is formed for the purpose of mining coal, manufacturing coke, and sale of same in crude or manufactured state, with the right to acquire and dispose of such property, real or personal, as may be necessary or convenient in carrying on said business, and to these ends erect, maintain and use all such buildings, machinery and appliances as may be necessary for mining, manufacturing and marketing the product of the mines.	Charleroi.
T. R. Clark & Co. Incorporated. Capital, $33,300. March 25, 1892.	Said corporation is formed for the purpose of manufacturing glass, glassware, china and chinaware.	Honesdale.
The Crafton Light and Power Company. Capital, $10,000. March 28, 1892.	Said corporation is formed for the purpose of supplying light, heat and power or any of them by electricity to the public in the borough of Crafton, and to persons, partnerships and corporations residing therein or adjacent thereto, as may desire the same.	Crafton.
Standard Guage Steel Company. Capital, $21,000. March 28, 1892.	Said corporation is formed for the purpose of the manufacture and sale of drawn steel, iron and other metals, machines and articles made from steel, iron or other metallic substances, either alone or combined with other materials.	Beaver Falls.
The P. A. Swartz Company. Capital, $25,000. March 28, 1892.	Said corporation is formed for the purpose of manufacturing flour, grain and feed of all kinds, and for the transaction of all business incident thereto.	Philadelphia.
The Boston Bridge Company. Capital, $1,000. March 28, 1892.	Said corporation is formed for the pur of c ing, constructing and maintaining a highway bridge and a es thereto over the Youghiogheny river from a point in rasilles township, Allegheny county, and on the western side of the township, road at "Elrod's Ferry," to a point upon the opposite side of the Youghiogheny river, in the village of Boston, in Elizabeth township, Allegheny county, and on western side of township road leading to Elizabeth, and one hundred and fifty (150) feet west from said ferry and township road.	Boston, Pa.

Corporation	Purpose	Location
The Coatesville Electric Light, Heat and Power Company. Capital, $25,000. March 28, 1892.	Said corporation is formed for the purpose of supplying light, heat and power, or any of them by electricity to the public in the borough of Coatesville, and to such persons, partnerships and corporations residing therein or adjacent thereto, as may desire the same.	Coatesville.
Springfield Building and Loan Association. Re-charter. Capital, $1,000,000. Mh 28, 1892.	The said corporation is formed for the purpose of accumulating a fund by contributions of the members thereof, and to loan the same to them from time to time to enable them to purchase real estate, build themselves dwelling houses or engage in any legitimate business.	Media.
The W silk Iron Company. Re-charter. Capital, $250,000. March 28, 1892.	Said corporation is formed for the purpose of making and manufacturing pig-iron and malleable iron.	Pottstown.
The County Seat Building and Loan Association. Capital, $1,000,000. March 28, 1892.	Said corporation is formed for the purpose of accumulating a fund by the periodical contributions of the members thereof, and of safely investing the same.	Beaver.
John III., Sobeski, King of Poland, Ten Cent Building and Loan Association. Capital, $1,000,000. March 28, 1892.	Said corporation is formed for the purpose of accumulating a fund by the periodical contributions of the members thereof, and of safely investing the same.	Pittsburgh.
The Newcastle Car Manufacturing Company. Capital, $25,000. March 29, 1892.	Said corporation is formed for the purpose of manufacturing and selling railway passenger coaches or other cars or other articles of commerce made from wood or glass, iron, steel, brass or other metals, or any combination of them, and for preparing for market and for its own use hard and soft woods of all kinds.	Newcastle.
The Hughes Manufacturing Company. Capital, $20,000. March 30, 1892.	Said corporation is formed for the purpose of manufacturing glazed thread, and other threads and yarns.	Philadelphia.
Pennsylvania Company for Protection and Assurance against Burglary. Capital, $500,000. March 30, 1892.	Said corporation is formed for the purpose of the prevention and punishment of theft, or wilful injuries to property by means of patented burglar alarms and other methods and assurance against such risks.	Philadelphia.

LIST OF CHARTERS OF CORPORATIONS—*Continued.*

STYLE AND TITLE OF CORPORATION.	PURPOSE.	LOCATION.
Home Building and Loan Association. Capital, $1,000,000. March 30, 1892.	Said corporation is formed for the purpose of accumulating a fund by the periodical contributions of the members thereof, and of safely investing the same.	Latrobe.
The Traders' Building and Loan Association of Scranton, Pa. Capital, $400,000. March 30, 1892.	Said corporation is formed for the purpose of accumulating a fund by the periodical contributions of the members thereof, and of safely investing the same.	Scranton.
The Dauphin Centennial Bau-und Spar Verein No. 2, of Harrisburg, Pa. Capital, $1,000,000. March 31, 1892.	Said corporation is formed for the purpose of accumulating a fund by the periodical contributions of the members thereof, and of safely investing the same.	Harrisburg.
High Explosive Company. Capital, $150,000. March 31, 1892.	Said corporation is formed for the purpose of manufacturing nitro glycerine, dynamite, gun cotton, gelatine, sporting ordnances, and blasting powder, and torpedoes composed in whole or in part of some one or more of the explosives above mentioned.	Bradford.
Congo Creamery. Capital, $2,200. March 31, 1892.	Said corporation is formed for the purpose of manufacturing butter, cheese and other products of milk.	Congo.
The Penn Chemical Company. Capital, $150,000. April 1, 1892.	Said corporation is formed for the purpose of manufacturing and selling acetates, wood spirits and other articles of commerce extracted or manufactured from wood, within the counties of Susquehanna and McKean, or elsewhere within the State of Pennsylvania.	Susquehanna Depot.
The World's Columbian Exposition Transportation Company of Pittsburgh, Penns. Capital, $25,000. April 4, 1892.	Said corporation is formed for the purpose of furnishing transportation for passenges to and from the city of Pittsburg, county of Allegheny, Pennsylvania, and points adjacent thereto, to the city of Chicago, Illinois, and return during the progress of the World's Fair at said city of Chicago, Illinois, and to provide for the care and comfort of said passengers during their stay in said city of Chicago.	Pittsburgh.

The Quaker City Mortar Company. Capital, $200,000. April 4, 1892.	Said corporation is formed for the purpose of carrying on the business of manufacturing and selling machine mixed mortar and cement.	Philadelphia.
The Church Magazine Publishing Company of Philadelphia. Capital, $5,000. April 4, 1892.	Said corporation is formed for the purpose of transacting a printing and publishing business.	Philadelphia.
Germantown Brewing Company. Capital, $10,000. April 4, 1892.	Said corporation is formed for the purpose of manufacturing and brewing of malt and malt liquors and selling the same.	Philadelphia.
Hughes & Patterson. Incorporated. Capital, $300,000. April 4, 1892.	Said corporation is formed for the purpose of manufacturing iron or steel, or any other metal, and to mould, cast or construct these metals in all shapes and forms in combination with other metals, or with wood, or into any article of commerce or of trade, and to transport said articles to market, dispose of the same and do all such other acts and things, and possess the powers and privileges expressed and given in the thirty-eighth section of the corporation act of 1874, and the supplements thereto.	Philadelphia.
The Mifflintown Electric Light Company. Capital, $2,500. April 4, 1892.	Said corporation is formed for the purpose of supplying light by means of electricity to the borough of Mifflintown, Juniata county, Pennsylvania, and to such persons, partnerships and corporations residing or doing business therein and adjacent thereto, as may desire the same.	Mifflintown.
The Patterson Electric Light Company. Capital, $2,500. April 4, 1892.	Said corporation is formed for the purpose of supplying light by means of electricity to the borough of Patterson, Juniata county, Pennsylvania, and to such persons, partnerships and corporations residing therein or adjacent thereto, as may be desire the same.	Mifflintown.
The Gazette Company of Altoona, Pennsylvania. Capital, $25,000. April 4, 1892.	Said corporation is formed for the purpose of transacting a printing and publishing business.	Altoona.
The Eureka Wood Pulley Company. Capital, $30,000. April 4, 1892.	Said corporation is formed for the purpose of the manufacture of pulleys, or of any other article of commerce from metal or wood, or both.	Berlin.

LIST OF CHARTERS OF CORPORATIONS—*Continued.*

STYLE AND TITLE OF CORPORATION.	PURPOSE.	LOCATION.
The "Elect" Manufacturing Company. Capital, $5,000. April 5, 1892.	Said corporation is formed for the purpose of manufacturing pharmaceutical preparations.	Philadelphia.
The People's Building and Savings Association of Carlisle. Capital, $400,000. April 5, 1892.	Said corporation is formed for the purpose of accumulating a fund by the periodical contributions of the members thereof, and of safely investing the same.	Carlisle.
Greensburg Fire Brick Company. Capital, $30,000. April 5, 1892.	Said corporation is formed for the purpose of manufacturing fire brick, tile, sewer pipe and other articles made in whole or in part from fire clay and selling and disposing of the same.	Greensburg.
The Mill Hall Brick Works. Capital, $32,600. April 5, 1892.	Said corporation is formed for the purpose of manufacturing vitrified paving brick, building and ornamental brick, fire brick, sewer pipe, drain pipe, tiling, terra cotta ware, crockery ware and all building and other materials which they may desire to manufacture from clay, shale rock or fire clay.	Mill Hall.
The Brownsville Plate Glass Company. Capital, $75,000. April 5, 1892.	Said corporation is formed for the purpose of manufacturing glass, such as rough and ribbed plate-cathedral, polished plate, etc.	Pittsburgh.
The Stewart Wire Company. Capital, $400,000. April 5, 1892.	Said corporation is formed for the purpose of manufacturing rods, wire, the products of wire, and kindred articles from iron, steel and other metals.	South Easton.
The Williamsport Iron and Nail Company. Capital, $100,000. April 5, 1892.	Said corporation is formed for the purpose of the manufacture of iron or steel, or both, or of any other metal, or article of commerce from metal, wood, or both.	South Williamsport.
Cambria Coal Mining Company. Capital, $100,000. April 6, 1892.	Said corporation is formed for the purpose of the mining of coal and the manufacture of coke the efrom.	Williamsport.

Company	Purpose	Location
Royal Braid Company. Capital, $25,000. April 5, 1892.	Said corporation is formed for the purpose of the manufacture and sale of braids, trimmings and articles of wearing apparel.	Williamsport.
Hydraulic Machine Company. Capital, $100,000. April 6, 1892.	Said corporation is formed for the purpose of the manufacture of iron or steel, or both, or of any other metal, or of any article of commerce from metal or wood, or both, and for that purpose to have and possess the privileges expressed and given in the 36th section of the powers and corporation act of 1874, and the supplements thereto.	Pittsburgh.
The Merion Water Company. Capital, $10,000. April 6, 1892.	Said corporation is formed for the purpose of supplying water to the public in the township of Lower Merion, Montgomery county, Pennsylvania, and to persons, partnerships and associations residing therein and adjacent thereto, as may desire the same.	Bryn Mawr.
South West Connellsville Coke Company. Capital, $5,000. April 6, 1892.	Said corporation is formed for the purpose of manufacturing coke.	Mount Pleasant.
Neversink Mountain Hotel Company. Capital, $75,000. April 6, 1892.	Said corporation is formed for the purpose of establishing and maintaining a hotel on Neversink mountain, in Lower Alsace township, Berks county, Pennsylvania.	Reading.
The Bryn Mawr Water Company. Capital, $1,000. April 6, 1892.	Said corporation is formed for the purpose of supplying water for the public in the township of Lower Merion, county of Montgomery, and State of Pennsylvania, and to such persons, partnerships and associations residing in said district, or adjacent thereto, as may desire the same.	Bryn Mawr.
The First United States Excelsior Building Association of Johnstown. Capital, $500,000. April 7, 1892.	Said corporation is formed for the purpose of accumulating a fund by the periodical contributions of the members thereof, and of safely investing the same.	Johnstown.
The Northampton County Building and Loan Association. Capital, $1,000,000. April 7, 1892.	Said corporation is formed for the purpose of accumulating a fund by the periodical contributions of the members thereof, and of safely investing the same.	Easton.

LIST OF CHARTERS OF CORPORATIONS—*Continued.*

STYLE AND TITLE OF CORPORATION.	PURPOSE.	LOCATION.
Elsas Paper Company. Capital, $100,000. April 8, 1892.	Said corporation is formed for the purpose of manufacturing all kinds of paper goods and bags.	West Newton.
The Tyrone Industrial Company. Capital, $5,000. April 8, 1892.	Said corporation is formed for the purpose of manufacturing brooms.	Tyrone.
The J. O. Schimmel Works. Capital, $50,000. April 8, 1892.	Said corporation is formed for the purpose of manufacturing preserves, jellies, fruit butters, mince meat, condiments and all articles of commerce connected therewith or relating thereto.	Philadelphia.
"Beaver Building and Loan Association, No. 2." Capital, $416,000. April 8, 1892.	Said corporation is formed for the purpose of accumulating a fund by the periodical contributions of its members, and to safely invest the same, and to have such other franchises, rights and privileges as are or may be legally held and enjoyed by such associations under the said act of assembly and the several supplements thereto.	Beaver.
"J. E. Dayton Company." Capital, $64,000. April 8, 1892.	Said corporation is formed for the purpose of manufacturing boots and shoes of all kinds, and of selling the manufactured product.	Williamsport.
Cranberry Improvement Company. Capital, $20,000. April 11, 1892.	Said corporation is formed for the purpose of mining coal, iron ore and limestone, and preparing the same for market.	Philadelphia.
Chester Rubber Company. Capital, $30,000. April 11, 1892.	Said corporation is formed for the purpose of carrying on a general rubber manufacturing business.	Chester.
New Wales Hard Vein Slate Company. Capital, $30,000. April 12, 1892.	Said corporation is formed for the purpose of mining, quarrying, manufacturing and sale of slate and slate products.	Easton.

"Hanover Morocco Co.," Capital, $50,000. April 12, 1892.	Said corporation is formed for the purpose of the manufacture and sale of morocco and all kinds of leather.	Penn township, York county, Hanover.
The Pittsburgh Gas Engine and Manufacturing Company. Capital, $1,000. April 12, 1892.	Said corporation is formed for the purpose of the manufacture of iron or steel, or both, or of any other metal, or of any article of commerce from metal or wood, or both.	Pittsburgh.
Wilkes-Barre Grand Opera House Company, Capital, $30,000. April 12, 1892.	Said corporation is formed for the purpose of establishing and maintaining an opera house in the city of Wilkes-Barre, and to have and enjoy all the rights and privileges conferred by said act of assembly and its supplements upon such companies.	Wilkes-Barre.
Hamburg Electric Light, Heat and Power Company, Capital, $15,000. April 12, 1892.	Said corporation is formed for the purpose of supplying light, heat and power by electricity at the borough of Hamburg, Penna, and to such persons, partnerships, associations and corporations residing therein and adjacent thereto, as may desire the same.	Hamburg.
The Equity Building and Loan Association. Capital, $1,000,000. April 12, 1892.	Said corporation is formed for the purpose of accumulating a fund by the periodical contribution of the members thereof, and of safely investing the same.	Pittsburgh.
The Nay Aug Coal Company. Capital, $3,000. April 14, 1892.	Said corporation is formed for the purpose of mining, preparing for market and selling anthracite coal.	Scranton.
The Columbus Oil Company. Capital, $10,000. April 14, 1892.	Said corporation is formed for the purpose of drilling for, producing and mining petroleum or carbon oil and natural gas and storing, transporting and selling the same.	Pittsburgh.
Vehicle Improvement Company. Capital, $10,000. April 14, 1892.	Said corporation is formed for the purpose of manufacturing and selling certain improvements in carriage and wagon axles, and hubs.	Philadelphia.
The Manor Electric Company. Capital, $6,000. April 14, 1892.	Said corporation is formed for the purpose of supplying light, heat and power or any of them by electricity to the public in the borough of Manor, and to such persons, partnerships and corporations residing therein and adjacent thereto, as may desire the same.	Manor.
Indiana Glass Company. Capital, $50,000. April 14, 1892.	Said corporation is formed for the purpose of manufacturing glass, glassware, and the various kinds and forms of products from material used in the manufacture of glass, and selling the same.	Indiana.

LIST OF CHARTERS OF CORPORATIONS—*Continued.*

STYLE AND TITLE OF CORPORATION.	PURPOSE.	LOCATION.
The Great Bend Water Company. Capital, $25,000. April 14, 1892.	Said corporation is formed for the purpose of supplying water to the public in the borough of Great Bend, Great Bend township, Susquehanna county, Pennsylvania, and to such persons, partnerships and associations residing therein, and adjacent thereto, as may desire the same.	Great Bend.
The Roberts & Taylor Company. Capital, $50,000. April 14, 1892.	Said corporation is formed for the purpose of manufacturing W. D. Roberts, Srs', fire and water-proof paints, and paints of different character, including a liquid preparation for coating blackboards, and for the sale of said paints and blackboard surfaces.	Philadelphia.
The Hallstead Water Company. Capital, $25,000. April 14, 1892.	Said corporation is formed for the purpose of supplying water to the public in the borough of Hallstead, Great Bend township, Susquehanna county, Pennsylvania, and to such persons, partnerships and associations residing therein and adjacent thereto, as may desire the same.	Hallstead.
Jackson Building and Loan Association. Re-charter. Capital, $500,000. April 14, 1892.	Said corporation is formed for the purpose of accumulating a fund from the periodical contributions of the stockholders thereof, and loaning or advancing to them the moneys so accumulated.	Philadelphia.
Peck Lumber Manufacturing Company. Capital, $80,000. April 18, 1892.	Said corporation is formed for the purpose of manufacturing all kinds of lumber.	Scranton.
The Stoddart Coal Company. Capital, $25,000. April 18, 1892.	Said corporation is formed for the purpose of mining, preparing for market and selling anthracite coal and the products thereof.	Gilberton.
Standard Hub and Block Company. Capital, $200,000. April 18, 1892.	Said corporation is formed for the purpose of manufacturing all kinds of hubs, blocks, spokes and other timbers, and selling the said manufactured products.	Philadelphia.
The Union Cigar Manufacturing Company of Logansville, Penna. Capital, $3,000. April 18, 1892.	Said corporation is formed for the purpose of manufacturing and selling cigars and all kinds of tobacco.	Logansville.

The Globe Building and Loan Association of the city and county of Philadelphia, No. 3. Re-charter. Capital, $600,000. April 18, 1892.	Said corporation is formed for the purposes of accumulating a fund by the periodical contributions of the members thereof, and of safely investing the same.	Philadelphia.
The Pennsylvania Ammonia and Fertilizer Company. Capital, $25,000. April 19, 1892.	Said corporation is formed for the purposes of manufacturing fertilizers, chemicals and kindred products.	Harrisburg.
"The W. L. Scott Company." Capital, $1,000,000. April 19, 1892.	Said corporation is formed for the purpose of mining bituminous and anthracite coal, and all other business appertaining thereto.	Erie.
"The Demorest Manufacturing Company," Capital, $300,000. April 19, 1892.	Said corporation is formed for the purpose of the manufacture of iron or steel or both or of any other metal or article of commerce from metal, or wood or both.	Williamsport.
"Western Asphalt Block and Tile Company," Capital, $100,000. April 19, 1892.	Said corporation is formed for the purpose of manufacturing from stone and asphalt, and from other materials, blocks and tiles for pavements, curbing, sewers, buildings and other constructions.	Newcastle.
Hazleton Iron Works Company. Capital, $50,000. April 20, 1892.	Said corporation is formed for the purpose of doing a general foundry and machine shop business.	Hazleton
The First United States Excelsior Building Association of Greensburg. Capital, $500,000. April 21, 1892.	Said corporation is formed for the purpose of accumulating a fund by the periodical contributions of the members thereof, and of safely investing the same.	Greenburg.
The Allegheny Water Company. Capital, $4,000. April 22, 1892.	Said corporation is formed for the purpose of supplying water to the public of the southwestern half of the township of Logan, to persons, partnerships, associations and corporations residing therein and adjacent thereto.	Allegheny.
"Financial News and Price Current Company," Capital, $15,000. April 22, 1892.	Said corporation is formed for the purpose of issuing daily, weekly and monthly publications and bulletins, and publications having reference to the various trades, the securing advertisements and contracts therefor, and the necessary business connected therewith.	Pittsburgh.

LIST OF CHARTERS OF CORPORATIONS—*Continued.*

STYLE AND TITLE OF CORPORATION.	PURPOSE.	LOCATION.
The Kensington Ferry Company. Capital $500. April 22, 1892	Said corporation is formed for the purpose of establishing, maintaining and operating a flat boat rope, chain, wire or team ferry, and appliances thereto, and all aids, skiffs and all other necessary ferry equipage for the accommodation of the public, with all the rights and franchises conferred upon corporations of this class. The said ferry is to be over the Allegheny river, from a point at the foot of 76th street in the town of Kensington, Westmoreland city, Penna., to a point on the Pike side of the said river, near the boundary line separating the townships of East Deer and Springdale, in Allegheny county, Pa. The location of said ferry being more than one mile distant from any other incorporated bridge or ferry over said river.	Tarentum.
The Crowell and Class Cold Storage Company. Capital, $250,000. April 25, 1892.	Said corporation is formed for the purpose of the furnishing cold and general storage for produce, meats, fruits and other articles of food and perishable merchandise, the conducting of a general storage and warehouse business.	Philadelphia.
The Chalfont and Doylestown Turnpike Company. Capital, $15,000. April 25, 1892.	Said corporation is formed for the purpose of constructing, maintaining and managing an artificial road or turnpike, from an iron pin in the Doylestown and Montgomeryville road, fifty-four feet two inches from the southeast corner of the public house of Isaac Keller, where the Chalfont and Hilltown road intersects with the said road in the village of Chalfont, in New Britain township, Bucks county, to a point in the said Doylestown and Montgomeryville road at the place where said road crosses the line of the borough of Doylestown in the county of Bucks.	Chalfont.
The Lewistown Foundry and Machine Company. Capital, $20,000. April 25, 1892.	Said corporation is formed for the purpose of manufacturing and selling articles of iron and steel, or both, of any metal or of any article of commerce of wood or metal, or both.	Lewistown.

Company	Purpose	Location
Central Plaster Board Company. Capital, $100,000. April 25, 1892.	Said corporation is formed for the purpose of manufacturing and selling machine plaster boards, tiles, insulation and ceiling insulations and other plastering, fire proofing and insulating materials.	Philadelphia.
The De Frehn Chair Company, of Mount Union Pa. Capital, $35,000. April 28, 1892.	Said corporation is formed for the purpose of the manufacture and sale of chairs, shieve blocks, mine rollers, lumber, and other merchantable manufactures made from lumber.	Mount Union.
Home Building and Loan Association of Scranton, Pa. Capital, $1,000,000. April 28, 1892.	Said corporation is formed for the purpose of accumulating a fund by the periodical contributions of the members thereof, and of safely investing the same.	Scranton.
The Mechanics' Building and Savings Association. Capital, $500,000. April 27, 1892.	Said corporation is formed for the purpose of accumulating a fund by the periodical contributions of the members thereof, and of safely investing the same.	Reading.
The New Milford Water Company. Capital, $15,000. April 28, 1892.	Said corporation is formed for the purpose of supplying pure water to the citizens, partnerships, associations or corporations in the said borough of New Milford, and adjacent thereto.	New Milford.
Acme Car Coupler Company. Capital, $25,000. April 29, 1892.	Said corporation is formed for the purpose of the manufacture of iron or steel, or both, or of any other metal, or of any article of commerce from metal or wood, or both.	Pittsburgh.
The Glen Hazel Chemical Company. Capital, $100,000. April 29, 1892.	Said corporation is formed for the purpose of manufacturing wood, spirits, acetates and other articles of commerce, manufactured or extracted from wood, in the counties of Susquehanna and McKean and elsewhere within the State of Pennsylvania, and selling the same.	Susquehanna Depot.
Fayette Oil Company. Capital, $15,000. April 29, 1892.	Said corporation is formed for the purpose of mining for petroleum.	Uniontown.
Arona Gas Coal Company. Capital, $160,000. April 29, 1892.	Said corporation is formed for the purpose of the mining of coal and the manufacture of coke, and the sale of the same in crude or manufactured form.	Greensburg.
Brookville Building and Loan Association. Capital, $1,000,000. April 29, 1892.	Said corporation is formed for the purpose of accumulating a fund by the periodical contributions of the members thereof, and of safely investing the same.	Brookville.

6a LAWS.

LIST OF CHARTERS OF CORPORATIONS—*Continued.*

Style and Title of Corporation.	Purpose.	Location.
The Canton Electric Light, Heat and Power Company. Capital, $10,000. May 2, 1892.	Said corporation is formed for the purpose of supplying light, heat and power by means of electricity, to the public at the borough of Canton, Pennsylvania, and to such persons, partnerships, corporations and associations residing therein and adjacent thereto, as may desire the same.	Canton.
The Rush Grange Hall Association. Capital, $2,000. May 2, 1892.	Said corporation is formed for the purpose of establishing an opera and market house in Rushton, Northumberland county, Pennsylvania.	Rushtown.
Brookside Coal Company. Capital, $30,000. May 2, 1892.	Said corporation is formed for the purpose of the opening of coal mines, mining and preparing coal for market and vending the same.	Wilkes-Barre.
Yellow Run Coal Company. Capital, $75,000. May 2, 1892.	Said corporation is formed for the purpose of the mining of coal and the manufacture of coke, and the sale of the same in crude or manufactured form.	Greensburg.
Hop Bottom Water Company. Capital, $15,000. May 2, 1892.	Said corporation is formed for the purpose of supplying water for the public at the borough of Hop Bottom, Susquehanna county, Pennsylvania, and to persons, corporations, partnerships and associations residing therein and adjacent thereto, as may desire the same.	Hop Bottom.
The Black Lick Land and Improvement Company. Capital, $150,000. May 2, 1892.	Said corporation is formed for the purpose of the purchase and sale of real estate, or for holding, leasing and selling real estate, for maintaining or erecting walls or banks for the protection of low lying land.	Philadelphia and Ebensburg.
The Fidelity Building and Savings Association. Capital, $600,000. May 2, 1892.	Said corporation is formed for the purpose of accumulating a fund by the periodical contributions of the members thereof, and of safely investing the same.	Reading.
The First United States Excelsior Building Association of Newcastle. Capital, $500,000 May 2, 1892.	Said corporation is formed for the purpose of accumulating a fund by the periodical contributions of the members thereof, and of safely investing the same.	Newcastle.

Company	Purpose	Location
The Mahoning Building and Loan Association of Punxsutawney, Pa. Capital, $1,000,000. May 2, 1882.	Said corporation is formed for the purpose of accumulating a fund from the periodical contributions of the members thereof, and of loaning or advancing to them the moneys so accumulated from time to time.	Punxsutawney.
The Industrial Building and Loan Association. Capital, $1,000,000. May 3, 1892.	Said corporation is formed for the purpose of accumulating a fund by the contributions of the members thereof, and to loan the same to them from time to time, to enable them to purchase real estate, build themselves dwelling houses, or engage in ny legitimate business.	Scranton.
The Leghorn Mining and Manufacturing Company. Capital, $5,000. May 3, 1892.	Said corporation is formed for the purpose of mining, milling and marketing siennas, ochres and all classes of paint-materials and iron ores, and for that purpose, to have and possess the powers and privileges expressed and given in the 39th section of the corporation act of 1874, and the supplements thereto.	Reading.
DeCou Brothers' Company. Capital, $30,000. May 3, 1892.	Said corporation is formed for the purpose of manufacturing boots and shoes of all kinds.	Philadelphia.
Laurel Hill Lumber Company. Capital, $50,000. May 3, 1892.	Said corporation is formed for the purpose of manufacturing of all kinds of lumber, and of purchasing, holding, and conveying timber and timber land for that purpose, and to do and perform all such other business and acts as may be necessary to carry out the objects of association and incorporation.	Harrisburg.
The Florence Oil Company. Capital, $2,000. May 5, 1892.	Said corporation is formed for the purpose of producing, storing, transporting, selling and dealing generally in petroleum.	Pittsburgh.
National Tubular Axle Company. Capital, $30,000. May 9, 1892.	Said corporation is formed for the purpose of manufacturing articles of iron or steel, or both, or of any other metal or article of commerce from metal or wood, or both.	Emigsville.
Monongahela Investment Company. Capital, $5,000. May 9, 1892.	Said corporation is formed for the purpose of purchasing, taking, holding and enjoying real estate in fee simple, on lease, or upon ground rent, of improving, leasing, mortgaging, or selling the same in such parts or parcels, and on such terms as to time of payment as they may determine.	McKeesport.
Bradford Hardware Lumber Company. Capital, $50,000. May 9, 1892.	Said corporation is formed for the purpose of manufacturing articles of commerce from wood.	Bradford.

LIST OF CHARTERS OF CORPORATIONS—*Continued.*

Style and Title of Corporation.	Purpose.	Location.
Renner's Ferry. Capital, $100. May 9, 1892.	Said corporation is formed for the purpose of erecting, constructing and maintaining a ferry and approaches thereto over the Youghiogheny river, from a point at or near the village of Markletown, in the county of Westmoreland, to a point on the opposite side of said river, in the county of Allegheny, the location of said ferry being three thousand feet from any other incorporated bridge or ferry over said stream.	Suterville.
The Winfield Manufacturing Company. Capital, $12,000. May 10, 1892.	Said corporation is formed for the purpose of carrying on the business of manufacturing cotton and woolen goods.	Philadelphia.
A. R. Keller Company. Capital $125,000. May 10, 1892.	Said corporation is formed for the purpose of the transaction of a printing and publishing business.	Philadelphia.
Nicholson Water Company. Capital, $30,000. May 10, 1892.	Said corporation is formed for the purpose of supplying water for the public at the borough of Nicholson, Wyoming county, Pennsylvania, and to persons, partnerships, corporations and associations residing therein and adjacent thereto, as may desire the same.	Nicholson.
The Acme Powder Company. Capital, $20,000. May 10, 1892.	Said corporation is formed for the purpose of the manufacture of dynamite, nitro-glycerine and other explosives of like nature, and the transaction of business incident thereto.	Pittsburgh.
The Allegheny and McKee's Rocks Bridge Company. Capital, $5,000. May 10, 1892.	Said corporation is formed for the purpose of erecting, constructing and maintaining a bridge and approaches thereto, over the Ohio river, from a point at the foot of Wilkins street, city and county of Allegheny, to a point on the south side of the Ohio river, known as McKee's Rocks, and about 200 feet from the cliff at the upper end thereof, also in the county of Allegheny, the location of said bridge being 5,000 or more feet from any other incorporated bridge over said stream.	Pittsburgh.
The Eighteenth Ward Ten Cent Building and Loan Association. Capital, $1,000,000. May 10, 1892.	Said corporation is formed for the purpose of accumulating a fund by the periodical contributions of the members thereof, and of safely investing the same.	Pittsburgh.

Name	Purpose	Location
The Consumers Gas Company of Wilkes-Barre. Capital, $50,000. May 11, 1892.	Said corporation is formed for the purpose of the manufacture and supply of gas for the supply of light or heat to the public in the city of Wilkes-Barre, Luzerne county, Pa., and vicinity.	Wilkes-Barre.
The McLaughlin Oil Company. Capital, $8,500. May 11, 1892.	Said corporation is formed for the purpose of mining, drilling and operating for petroleum oil, with the right of acquiring and holding property necessary for the business of the corporation.	Allegheny City.
Protection Bridge Company. Capital, $5,000. May 12, 1892.	Said corporation is formed for the purpose of constructing and maintaining a bridge and causeways or approaches thereto over Oil creek in the city of Oil City, county of Venango, and State of Pennsylvania, from Sycamore street to the western bank of said Oil creek.	Oil City.
Blue Ridge Coal Company. Capital, $100,000. May 13, 1892.	Said corporation is formed for the purpose of mining coal and preparing the same for market.	Scranton.
The F. E. Okie, Company. Capital, $35,000. May 13, 1892.	Said corporation is formed for the purpose of manufacturing and selling printing inks and bronze powders.	Philadelphia.
Relief Bridge Company, Capital, $10,000. May 16, 1892.	Said corporation is formed for the purpose of constructing and maintaining a bridge and causeways or approaches thereto over the Allegheny river, in the city of Oil City, in the county of Venango, State of Pennsylvania, from Central avenue to the north bank of said river.	Oil City.
Seneca Bridge Company. Capital, $10,000. May 16, 1892.	Said corporation is formed for the purpose of constructing and maintaining a bridge and causeways or approaches thereto over the Allegheny river, in the city of Oil City, in the county of Venango, State of Pennsylvania, from Short street to the north bank of said river.	Oil City.
Fleming Brothers Company. Capital, $100,000. May 16, 1892.	Said corporation is formed for the purpose of manufacturing and selling Dr. C. McLane's celebrated vermifuge and liver pills and other proprietary medicines.	Pittsburgh.
Webster Land and Improvement Company. Capital, $50,000. May 16, 1892.	Said corporation is formed for the purpose of purchasing, holding, leasing and selling real estate.	Ehrenfold.

LIST OF CHARTERS OF CORPORATIONS—*Continued.*

STYLE AND TITLE OF CORPORATION.	PURPOSE.	LOCATION.
The McKean Building and Loan Association. Capital, $1,000,000. May 16, 1892.	Said corporation is formed for the purpose of accumulating a fund by the periodical contributions of the members thereof, and of safely investing the same.	Philadelphia.
The Bennett Public Building and Loan Association of Millvale Borough. Capital, $1,000,000. May 17, 1892.	Said corporation is formed for the purpose of accumulating a fund by the periodical contributions of the members thereof, and of safely investing the same.	Millvale.
The Old Reliable Building and Loan Association of Allegheny, Penna. Capital, $650,000. May 17, 1892.	Said corporation is formed for the purpose of accumulating a fund by the periodical contributions of the members thereof, and of safely investing the same.	Allegheny.
Glenwood and Homestead Ferry Company. Capital, $10,000. May 17, 1892.	Said corporation is formed for the purpose of erecting, constructing and maintaining a ferry and approaches thereto, over the Monongahela river from a point at or near Glenwood, in county of Allegheny, to a point on the opposite side of said river at or near Homestead, in the county of Allegheny.	Pittsburgh.
Cymbria Coal Company. Capital, $100,000. May 17, 1892.	Said corporation is formed for the purpose of the mining of coal, the manufacture of coke, and selling and shipping the same.	Philadelphia.
Incorporated Hall Association. Capital, $1,500. May 19, 1892.	Said corporation is formed for the purpose of establishing and maintaining a building to be and as an opera house, lodge room, &c., in the village of Grand Valley, Pennsylvania.	Grand Valley.
The Brownsville Electric Light Company. Capital, $7,000. May 20, 1892.	Said corporation is formed for the purpose of generating and supplying light, heat and power by means of electricity, in the borough of Brownsville, Pennsylvania, and to such persons, partnerships, associations and corporations residing therein and adjacent thereto, as may desire the same.	Brownsville.

Company	Purpose	Location
The Connoaut Lake Exposition Company. Capital, $25,000. May 20, 1892.	Said corporation is formed for the purpose of the purchase and sale of real estate, or for holding, leasing and selling real estate.	Meadville.
The Lewisburg Light, Heat and Power Company. Capital, $12,000. May 23, 1892.	Said corporation is formed for the purpose of supplying light, heat and power, or any of them to the public by electricity, in the borough of Lewisburg, Pennsylvania, and to such persons and partnerships residing therein and adjacent thereto, as may desire the same.	Lewisburg.
Ambler Spring Water Company. Capital, $25,000. May 23, 1892.	Said corporation is formed for the purpose of supplying water for the public at the borough of Ambler, in the county of Montgomery, Pennsylvania, and to persons, partnerships and associations residing in and adjacent thereto, as may desire the same.	Ambler.
The East Tyrone Water Company. Capital, $10,000. May 23, 1892.	Said corporation is formed for the purpose of supplying water for the public at the borough of East Tyrone, Blair county, Pennsylvania, and to persons, partnerships, corporations, &c., residing therein and adjacent thereto as may desire from "Deckers Run," or some other convenient course.	Tyrone.
The Huntingdon Improvement Company. Capital, $15,000. May 23, 1892.	Said corporation is formed for the purpose of the purchase and sale of real estate, or for holding, leasing and selling or improving the same.	Huntingdon.
Ellwood Patent Enamel Company. Capital, $100,000. May 23, 1892.	Said corporation is formed for the purpose of the manufacture of iron or steel, or both, or of any other metal or article of commerce from metal or wood, or both.	Ellwood City.
The Suburban Water Company. Capital, $500. May 23, 1892.	Said corporation is formed for the purpose of supplying water to the public in the township of Lower Merion, Montgomery county, State of Pennsylvania.	Bryn Mawr.
The Covington Glass Company. Capital, $30,000. May 23, 1892.	Said corporation is formed for the purpose of manufacturing and selling window glass.	Covington.
The Ebensburg Building and Loan Association. Capital, $1,000,000. May 23, 1892.	Said corporation is formed for the purpose of accumulating a fund by the periodical contributions of the members thereof, and of safely investing the same.	Ebensburg.

LIST OF CHARTERS OF CORPORATIONS—*Continued.*

STYLE AND TITLE OF CORPORATION.	PURPOSE.	LOCATION.
The Farmers and Citizens' Market Company, Capital, $10,000. May 24, 1892.	Said corporation is formed for the purpose of establishing and maintaining a market house in the borough of Columbia, county of Lancaster, and State of Pennsylvania, with stalls, to be appropriated and used as a public market house for the sale of meats, vegetables, victuals and provisions, the building and stalls to be leased or disposed of in such manner and on such terms and conditions as shall be determined by the directors.	Columbia.
The Carbondale Consumers Water Company, Capital, $30,000. May 24, 1892.	Said corporation is formed for the purpose of supplying water to the public in the city of Carbondale, and to persons, partnerships and associations residing therein and adjacent thereto, as may desire the same.	Carbondale.
The East Park Land Company. Capital, $100,000. May 24, 1892.	Said corporation is formed for the purpose of the purchase and sale of real estate, and full power and authority is given to the board of directors to sell or release the real estate of said corporation.	Carbondale.
The Rush Brook Water Company. Capital, $30,000. May 24, 1892.	Said corporation is formed for the purpose of supplying water to the public in the borough of Jermyn, and to persons, partnerships and associations residing therein and adjacent thereto, as may desire the same.	Jermyn.
The Electrical Supply and Construction Company. Capital, $100,000. May 25, 1892.	Said corporation is formed for the purpose of the manufacture and construction of electrical supplies and appliances.	Pittsburgh.
Uhlersville Paper Mill Company. Capital, $150,000. May 25, 1892.	Said corporation is formed for the purpose of manufacturing paper of every kind and description from rags, wood or other material or combinations thereof.	Uhlersville.
The Henderson Machine Tool Company.　Capital, $25,000. May 25, 1892.	Said corporation is formed for the purpose of manufacturing machine tools and general machinery of wood and metals.	Philadelphia.

Corporation	Purpose	Location
The Graham Oil Company. Capital, $5,000. May 26, 1892.	Said corporation is formed for the purpose of mining or quarrying for oil, gas, coal or other minerals.	Franklin Mills.
The Marietta Gravity Water Company. Capital, $10,000. May 27, 1892.	Said corporation is formed for the purpose of supplying water to the public at the borough of Marietta, Lancaster county, Pennsylvania, and to persons, partnerships and associations residing therein or adjacent thereto, that may desire the same.	Marietta.
Mann Edge Tool Company. Capital, $75,000. May 27, 1892.	Said corporation is formed for the purpose of the making and manufacturing axes and other edge tools.	Lewistown.
Belle Vernon Water Company. Capital, $1,000. May 27, 1892.	Said corporation is formed for the purpose of supplying water for the public at the borough of Belle Vernon, Fayette county, Pennsylvania, and to persons, partnerships and corporations residing therein and adjacent thereto, as may desire the same.	Belle Vernon.
The Marietta Water Company. Capital, $1,000. May 27, 1892.	Said corporation is formed for the purpose of supplying water to the public at the borough of Marietta, Lancaster county, Pennsylvania, that is to persons, partnerships and associations residing therein and adjacent thereto, that may desire the same.	Marietta.
Belle Vernon Electric Light Company. Capital, $1,000. May 27, 1892.	Said corporation is formed for the purpose of supplying light, heat and power by means of electricity to the public at the borough of Belle Vernon, Pennsylvania, and to such persons, partnerships and corporations residing therein and adjacent thereto, as may desire the same.	Belle Vernon.
Iron City and Hammondville Improvement Company. Capital, $72,000. May 27, 1892.	Said corporation is formed for the purpose of purchasing and selling real estate, and for holding, leasing and improving real estate.	Pittsburgh.
McKee's Rocks Modern Building and Loan Association. Capital, $1,000,000. May 27, 1892.	Said corporation is formed for the purpose of accumulating a fund by the periodical contributions of the members thereof, and of safely investing the same.	McKee's Rocks.
The People's Gas Company. Capital, $25,000. May 31, 1892.	Said corporation is formed for the purpose of manufacturing and supplying illuminating gas for light only, to the public in the borough of Parsons, Miners Mills and Plains township, in the county of Luzerne, Pennsylvania, all the districts named being continuous and forming practically one municipality, and in the judgment of the undersigned necessary to make said business a success in that locality.	Parsons.

LIST OF CHARTERS OF CORPORATIONS—*Continued.*

STYLE AND TITLE OF CORPORATION.	PURPOSE.	LOCATION.
The Belmont Mills Company Capital, $10,000. May 31, 1892.	Said corporation is formed for the purpose of manufacturing of cotton, woolen, worsted and mixed goods of every nature and kind.	West Manayunk.
The Mitchell Coal and Coke Company. Capital, $200,000. May 31, 1892.	Said corporation is formed for the purpose of mining coal and the manufacture of coke therefrom.	Tyrone
The E. R. Artman-Treichler Carpet Company. Capital, $100,000. May 31, 1892.	Said corporation is formed for the purpose of manufacturing carpets and textile fabrics, and the selling and disposing thereof.	Philadelphia.
The Juniata Valley Canning Company. Capital, $4,000. May 31, 1892.	Said corporation is formed for the purpose of canning and evaporating sweet or sugar corn, peaches, apples and other fruits, vegetables and berries.	Mifflintown.
Aliquippa Tin Plate Company. Capital, $15,000. May 31, 1892.	Said corporation is formed for the purpose of the manufacture & sale of tin & terne plate, and of all articles to be manufactured from and out of the same.	Tobyhanna Mills.
The Medix Run Lumber Company. Capital, $400,000. June 1, 1892.	Said corporation is formed for the purpose of the manufacture of logs, lumber, lath and other products of the forest.	Pittsburgh.
Grit Publishing Company. Capital, $100,000. June 1, 1892.	Said corporation is formed for the purpose of the transaction of a printing and publishing business.	Williamsport.
Pacific Coal Company. Capital, $100,000. June 1, 1892.	Said corporation is formed for the purpose of mining and transporting coal, and the manufacture of coke therefrom.	Pittsburgh.
Hubbard Publishing Company. Capital, $125,000. June 2, 1892.	Said corporation is formed for the purpose of a general printing and publishing business.	Philadelphia.

Company	Purpose	Location
The Philadelphia Crystallized Fruit Company. Capital, $6,000. June 2, 1892.	Said corporation is formed for the purpose of manufacturing dried, candied and crystallized fruits, dried, candied and crystallized vegetables, and dried, candied and crystallized food products of like nature, and for the purpose of selling the same.	Philadelphia.
The Forest City Electric Light, Heat and Power Company. Capital, $1,000. June 2, 1892.	Said corporation is formed for the purpose of supplying light, heat and power, or either of them, to the public, by means of electricity, in the borough of Forest City, county of Susquehanna, Pennsylvania, and to such persons, partnerships and corporations residing therein and adjacent thereto, as may desire the same, and for this purpose to have and enjoy all the powers and privileges conferred upon corporations of this class, by the said act and its supplements.	Forest City.
James P. Witherow Company. Capital, $1,000. June 2, 1892.	Said corporation is formed for the purpose of the manufacture of iron or steel, or both, or of any other metal, or of any article of commerce from metal or wood, or both.	Pittsburgh.
The Riverton Water Company. Capital, $40,000. June 2, 1892.	Said corporation is formed for the purpose of supplying water to the public at Riverton, in Cumberland county, Pennsylvania, and to persons, partnerships and associations residing therein and adjacent thereto, as may desire the same.	Riverton.
The Broad Top and Cambria Coal Company. Capital, $50,000. June 3, 1892.	Said corporation is formed for the purpose of mining coal, fire-clay, limestone and other minerals, and preparing the same for market in crude or manufactured form.	Harrisburg.
The West Side Gas Company. Capital, $50,000. June 3, 1892.	Said corporation is formed for the purpose of the manufacture and supply of illuminating gas for light only in the boroughs of Kingston, Edwardsville, Dorranceton, Forty-Fort and Luzerne, Luzerne county, Pa.	Kingston.
Caskey Boat Store Supply Company. Capital, $30,000. June 3, 1892.	Said corporation is formed for the purpose of the manufacture and sale of boat supplies.	Pittsburgh.
The Journal Publishing Company. Capital, $7,000. June 3, 1892.	Said corporation is formed for the purpose of transacting a printing and publishing business.	Washington.
Fairview Terrace Land Company. Capital, $10,000. June 3, 1892.	Said corporation is formed for the purpose of purchasing, taking, holding and enjoying real estate in fee simple or lease, or ground rent, or of improving, leasing, mortgaging or selling the same in such parts or parcels and on such terms as to time of payment as they may determine.	McKeesport.

LIST OF CHARTERS OF CORPORATIONS—*Continued.*

STYLE AND TITLE OF CORPORATION.	PURPOSE.	LOCATION.
The Philadelphia Machinery and Supply Co. Capital, $50,000. June 6, 1892.	Said corporation is formed for the purpose of manufacturing engines, tools, manufacturers, supplies and general hardware.	Philadelphia.
The Bellefield Land Company. Capital, $20,000. June 6, 1892.	Said corporation is formed for the purpose of "to purchase sell and lease real estate."	Pittsburgh.
The B. F. Isenberg Milling Company. Capital, $75,000. June 6, 1892.	Said corporation is formed for the purpose of manufacturing wheat, rye and other cereals into marketable products.	Huntingdon.
est Elizabeth Bridge Company. Capital, $1,892. June 6, 1892.	Said corporation is formed for the purpose of constructing, maintaining and operating a bridge over the Monongahela river from a point in, on, at or near the foot of Plum street, in the borough of Elizabeth, to a point in the borough of West Elizabeth, on the opposite side of said river, all in Allegheny county, Pennsylvania, and is distant two hundred and forty feet from any other incorporated bridge or ferry over the same stream.	Pittsburgh.
Holgate Bros. Co. Capital, $50,000. June 6, 1892.	Said corporation is formed for the purpose of manufacturing brush blocks, brush handles, wooden curry combs and other novelties in wood.	Kane.
The Landsdowne Sewage Company. Capital, $5,000. June 6, 1892.	Said corporation is formed for the purpose of manufacturing fertilizers from sewage.	Landsdowne.
Ivins, Dietz & Metzger Company. Capital, $1,000,000. June 6, 1892.	Said corporation is formed for the purpose of manufacturing and selling carpets, carpetings, rugs, art squares, mats, curtains, upholstery goods, plushes and spinning, as authorized by said act of assembly and its supplements.	Philadelphia.
Canton Mills Company. Capital, $300,000. June 6, 1892.	Said corporation is formed for the purpose of the manufacture and sale of textile fabrics, and other articles of merchandise made from cotton, wool or other fibrous substances.	Philadelphia.

The People's Mutual Savings Fund and Loan Association of Jeannette, Pa. Capital, $1,000,000. June 7, 1892.	Said corporation is formed for the purpose of accumulating a fund by the periodical contributions of the members thereof, and of safely investing the same.	Jeannette.
The McKee Water Company Capital, $20,000. June 7, 1892	Said corporation is formed for the purpose of supplying water to the public in Susquehanna township, Dauphin county, Pennsylvania, and to persons, partnerships, corporations and associations residing therein and adjacent thereto, as may desire the same.	Harrisburg.
The Lackawanna Hardware Company. Capital, $30,000. June 8, 1892	Said corporation is formed for the purpose of the manufacture and sale of hardware.	Scranton.
The J. M. Kelly Printing Company. Capital, $20,000. June 8, 1892	Said corporation is formed for the purpose of the transaction of a printing and publishing business.	Pittsburgh.
The Honeybrook Novelty Company. Capital, $50,000. June 8, 1892	Said corporation is formed for the purpose of manufacturing and selling the following patented articles, to wit: Door pocket and burglar alarms, bells, tobacco, lath holders, shears, pen, pencil and crayon holders.	Lancaster.
The Hecla Coke Company. Capital, $5,000. June 8, 1892.	Said corporation is formed for the purpose of mining coal and manufacturing coke.	Pittsburgh.
The McKinley Tin Plate Company. Capital, $50,000. June 8, 1892	Said corporation is formed for the purpose of manufacturing of tin and terne plate, iron or steel, or all of said metals, or any other metal, or of any article of commerce from metal or wood, or both.	Wilkinsburg.
St. Alban Real Estate Association. Capital, $25,000. June 9, 1892	Said corporation is formed for the purprse of the purchase and sale of real estate, or for holding, leasing and selling real estate.	Philadelphia.
The Saylorsburg Enamel and Buff Brick Manufacturing Company. Capital, $50,000. June 9, 1892.	Said corporation is formed for the purpose of manufacturing enamel and buff brick, tile, terra-cotta and other articles made from clay, kaolin and other similar substances.	Stroudsburg.

LIST OF CHARTERS OF CORPORATIONS—*Continued.*

STYLE AND TITLE OF CORPORATION.	PURPOSE.	LOCATION.
Park Incline Plane Company. Capital, $25,000. June 10, 1892.	Said corporation is formed for the purpose of erecting, maintaining and operating an inclined plane in the city of Pittsburgh, in the county of Allegheny, and State of Pennsylvania, from a point on Barkheimer street, or Arlington avenue, to a point at base of hill, between Thirteenth street and Twenty-fifth street, for carrying, conveying and transporting passengers and freight.	Pittsburgh.
The Brookville Furniture Company. Capital, $25,000. June 10, 1892.	Said corporation is formed for the purpose of carrying on the manufacture of furniture of wood, or iron, or steel, or partly of wood and partly of iron, steel or both, or any other article of commerce from metal or wood, or both, or either, or all.	Brookville.
The Wrightsville Water Company. Capital, $1,000. June 10, 1892.	Said corporation is formed for the purpose of supplying water to the public at the borough of Wrightsville, York county, Pennsylvania, that is, to persons, partnerships and associations residing therein and adjacent thereto, that may desire the same.	Wrightsville.
The Mansfield Wood Novelty Company. Capital, $20,000. June 13, 1892.	Said corporation is formed for the purpose of manufacturing and selling of toys and articles of wood.	Mansfield.
Harrisburg Ventilated Barrel Company. Capital, $37,500. June 13, 1892.	Said corporation is formed for the purpose of manufacturing and selling ventilated and other barrels, boxes and packages.	Harrisburg.
Pittsburgh Heating Supply Co. Capital, $20,000. June 13, 1892.	Said corporation is formed for the purpose of manufacturing and selling, constructing and furnishing, portable steam heaters and radiators, heating and cooking devices, and all articles, material, apparatus, equipments, structures, fixtures, supplies and appliances needful, or designed for, or relating to, the use and application of steam, electricity, water, heat, hot air, natural or manufactured gas for the scientific and sanitary heating and ventilation of public and private buildings, etc.	Pittsburgh.

Company	Description	Location
The Eynon-Evans Manufacturing Company. Capital, $60,000. June 13, 1892.	Said corporation is formed for the purpose of manufacturing steam, jet apparatus, machinery and articles of commerce made from metal, or wood, or both, and carrying on a general manufacturing and mechanical business pertaining thereto.	Philadelphia.
The Meadow Brook Land Company. Capital, $100,000. June 13, 1892.	Said corporation is formed for the purpose of purchasing, holding, improving, leasing and selling real estate, and for this purpose, to have all the rights and privileges granted and conferred in section 35 and of the general coporation act of 1874, and the several amendments and supplements thereto.	Scranton.
The North Huntingdon Gas Manufacturing Company. Capital, $1,000. June 13, 1892.	Said corporation is formed for the purpose of the manufacture and the supply of gas to the public in the township of North Huntingdon, in the county of Westmoreland, and State of Pennsylvania, and to persons, partnerships and associations residing therein and adjacent thereto, as may desire the same.	Philadelphia.
The Penn Gas Manufacturing Company. Capital, $1,000. June 13, 1892.	Said corpora tin is formed for the purpose of the manufacture ad supply of gas to the public in the tnhip of Penn, in the county of W st-moreland, ad State of Pennsylvania, ad to p ms, r tpe ad sins residing theein ad bnt th te, as my desire the m.	Philadelphia.
The Westmoreland Gas Manufacturing Company. Capital, $1,000. June 13, 1892.	Said corporation is formed for the t ge of the mrly of gas to the p blic in the unip of nd, ad State of Pennsylvania, and to ps, partnerships ad ns lilg thin ud bpnt thereto, as may desire the m.	Philadelphia.
The Improved Savings and Loan Association. Capital, $500,000. June 14, 1892.	Said corporation is formed for the purpose of the accumulation of a fund by the savings of the members thereof, sufficient to enable the stock-holders to borrow money to build or purchase for themselves respectively dwelling houses or other real estate, or for any other purposes, and in which the members shall find a sure and profitable investment for their money.	Philadelphia.
The Bloomsburg Cold Storage Company. Capital, $3,000. June 15, 1892.	Said corporation is formed for the purpose of the furnishing of cold and general storage for produce, meats, fruits and other articles of food and perishable merchandise, the conducting of a general storage and warehouse business.	Bloomsburg.
New Kensington Company. Capital, $200,000. June 15, 1892.	Said corporation is formed for the purpose of the purchase and sale of real estate, and for holding, leasing and selling real estate.	Pittsburgh.

LIST OF CHARTERS OF CORPORATIONS—*Continued.*

Style and Title of Corporation.	Purpose.	Location.
The Jacobs Creek Ferry Company. Capital, $1,000, June 15, 1892.	Said corporation is formed for the purpose of maintaining and operating a ferry over the Youghiogheny River from a p int on the east bank of said river about six hundred yards lbw the railroad bridge to a point on the opposite side of said river or Larimer's station on the Pla- burgh, McKeesport and Youghiogheny railroad, ther with the ssary approaches thereto, the termini oing entirely within the county of Westmoreland, and State of Pennsyl ania. Said ferry is to be located more t han one mile from any other incorporated bridge or ferry.	Jacobs Creek.
Coraopolis and Neville Island Bridge Company. Capital, $3,500. June 15, 1892	Said corporation is and for the purpose of erecting, constructing and maintaining a toll bridge and approaches to the same from the over of Ferree street and Fourth avenue, in the borough of and over the abk, or south channel of the Ohio river, to a point at a public highway on the property of Wm. A. Shanks, on Neville and alle township, all in the county of Allegheny, and State of othe r se, the place where it is proposed to erect the said bridge, being me than one thousand feet above and more than five miles low ay bridge or ferry chartered under the aws of Pennsylvania.	Coraopolis.
The Bloomsburg Artificial Ice Com- pany. Capital, $27,000. June 15, 1892.	Said corporation is formed for the purpose of manufacture and sale of ice.	Bloomsburg.
The Bloomsburg Furniture Com- pany. Capital, $30,000. June 15, 1892.	Said corporation is formed for the purpose of the manufacture and sale of furniture.	Bloomsburg
The Josephine Building and Loan Association No. 3, of Pittsburgh, Pa. Capital, $1,000,000. June 15, 1892.	Said corporation is formed for the purpose of accumulating a fund by the periodical contributions of the members thereof, and of safely invest- ing the same.	Pittsburgh.

Miner's Deposit Bank (Re-charter). Capital, $100,000. June 15, 1892.	Said corporation is formed for the purpose of doing a general banking business.	Lykens.
DuBois Deposit Bank. Capital, $75,000. June 16, 1892.	Said corporation is formed for the purpose of transacting a general banking business.	DuBois.
Duquesne Water Company. Capital, $10,000. June 17, 1892.	Said corporation is formed for the purpose of supplying water to the borough of Duquesne and the adjacent territory, and to the persons, partnerships, corporations and associations residing or located therein and adjacent thereto, as may desire the same.	Duquesne.
Coalport Water Company. Capital, $2,000. June 20, 1892.	Said corporation is formed for the purpose of supplying water to the public in the borough of Coalport, Pennsylvania, and to such persons, corporations and partnerships residing therein and adjacent thereto, as may desire the same.	Coalport
The Adams Radiator and Boiler Company. Capital, $30,000. June 20, 1892.	Said corporation is formed for the purpose of the manufacture of iron or steel, or both, or of any other metal, or article of commerce, from metal, wood, or both.	Reading.
Cowanshannock Ferry Co. Capital $500. June 20, 1892.	Said corporation is formed for the purpose of erecting, constructing, and maintaining a ferry and the approaches thereto, over the Allegheny river, from a point at or near the road leading down to the river above the old Monticello furnace, on lands of Campbell, to a point on the opposite side of said river, at or near a small run on lands of Brown's heirs, the location of said ferry being more than three thousand feet from any other incorporated bridge or ferry over said stream.	Gosford.
The Listie Mining and Manufacturing Company. Capital, $50,000. June 20, 1892.	Said corporation is formed for the purpose of mining coal, fire clay, limestone and other minerals from their lands in Somerset county, Pennsylvania, and preparing the same for market, in crude or manufactured form.	Listie.
The Marietta Electric Light, Heat and Power Company. Capital, $1,000. June 21, 1892.	Said corporation is formed for the purpose of supplying light, heat and power, or any of them, by electricity to the public in the borough of Marietta, Lancaster county, Pennsylvania, and to such persons, partnerships and corporations residing therein or adjacent thereto, as may desire the same.	Marietta.

7a LAWS.

LIST OF CHARTERS OF CORPORATIONS—*Continued.*

STYLE AND TITLE OF CORPORATION.	PURPOSE.	LOCATION.
The National Manufacturing Company. Capital, $50,000. June 21, 1892.	Said corporation is formed for the purpose of the purchase and sale of patents granted by the authority of the United States, and of rights and licenses under said patents, and for the manufacture and sale of patented articles.	Wilkes-Barre.
The Commonwealth Horse Collar Company. Capital, $10,000. June 22, 1892.	Said corporation is formed for the purpose of the manufacture of horse collars and horse furniture generally.	Harrisburg.
The Stoverdale Memorial Association. Capital, $20,000. June 22, 1892.	Said corporation is formed for the purpose of the purchase and sale of real estate, or for holding, leasing and selling real estate.	Hummelstown.
The Homestead and Pittsburgh Bridge Company. Capital, $25,000. June 22, 1892.	Said corporation is formed for the purpose of ... constructing and maintaining a bridge and the app ... thereto, over the Monongahela river, in the county of Allegheny, in the Commonwealth of Pennsylvania, from a point at or near the ... of Samuel S. Brown, in the ...-third ward, Pittsburgh, on the right bank of said river, about two hundred feet below Nine-Mile run, to a point on the ... side of said ... for, at or near the foot of Ann street, in the borough of Homestead, in said county. The ... ... of said bridge being more than three ... ... feet from any ther ... bridge over said ..., and about 500 feet from any incorporated ferry over said stream.	Pittsburgh.
The Susquehanna Island and Sand Company. Capital, $8,000. June 22, 1892.	Said corporation is formed for the purpose of mining and quarrying stone, sand, fossils, ores and minerals.	Midddletown.
Phillips & Mittonzwey Saw Mill & Lumber Company. Capital, $30,000. June 22, 1892.	Said corporation is formed for the purpose of the manufacture of iron or steel, or both, or of any other metal, or article of commerce from metal, wood, or both.	Pittsburgh.

Name	Purpose	Location
Manufacturers' Gas Company of Greensburg. Capital, $10,000. June 28, 1892	Said corporation is formed for the purpose of manufacturing and supplying gas to the public at the borough of Greensburg, Ludwick, Bunker Hill, East Greensburg and the village of Paradise (all of said boroughs being contiguous and adjoining), and to such persons, partnerships and associations residing therein or adjacent thereto, as may desire the same.	Greensburg.
Jamison Coal Company, Capital, $150,000. June 28, 1892.	Said corporation is formed for the purpose of mining coal and manufacturing coke and selling the same in crude or manufactured form.	Greensburg.
Joseph Wolf Land Company. Capital, $1,000. June 24, 1892.	Said corporation is formed for the purpose of the purchase and sale of real estate, or for holding, leasing and selling real estate.	Braddock.
East End Land Improvement Company. Capital, $10,000. June 24, 1892.	Said corporation is formed for the purpose of the purchase and sale of real estate, and for holding, leasing and selling real estate.	Pittsburgh.
The Mansfield Glove and Mitten Company. Capital, $10,000. June 24, 1892.	Said corporation is formed for the purpose of manufacturing and selling gloves and mittens, and articles of leather.	Mansfield.
Potter County Land Company. Capital, $30,000. June 24, 1892.	Said corporation is formed for the purpose of purchasing and selling, holding and leasing real estate.	Coudersport.
The Ledlig Manufacturing Company. Capital, $100,000. June 24, 1892.	Said corporation is formed for the purpose of the manufacture of iron or steel, or both, or of any other metal or of any article of commerce from metal or wood, or both.	Philadelphia.
The South West Water Company. Capital, $5,000. June 24, 1892.	Said corporation is formed for the purpose of supplying water for the public at the township of North Union, county of Fayette, and State of Pennsylvania, and to such persons, partnerships and associations residing therein and adjacent thereto, as may desire the same.	Uniontown.
The Reading Terminal Land Association, Logan Station, Philadelphia. Capital, $448,000. June 27, 1892.	Said corporation is formed for the purpose of purchasing, holding, leasing and selling real estate.	Philadelphia.

LIST OF CHARTERS OF CORPORATIONS—*Continued.*

STYLE AND TITLE OF CORPORATION.	PURPOSE.	LOCATION.
The Beltzhoover Water Company. Capital, $3,000. June 27, 1892.	Said corporation is formed for the purpose of supplying water to the public in the borough of Beltzhoover, and to such persons, partnerships and associations residing therein and adjacent thereto, as may desire the same.	Beltzhoover.
The St. Clair Water Company, Capital, $3,000. June 27, 1892.	Said corporation is formed for the purpose of supplying water to the public in the township of Lower St. Clair, and to such persons, partnerships and associations residing therein and adjacent thereto, as may desire the same.	Knoxville, Pa.
The Knoxville Water Company. Capital, $3,000. June 27, 1892.	Said corporation is formed for the purpose of supplying water to the public in the borough of Knoxville, and to such persons, partnerships and associations residing therein and adjacent thereto, as may desire the same.	Knoxville, Pa.
The Aqua Supply Company. Capital, $60,000. June 27, 1892.	Said corporation is formed for the purpose of mining and boring for the production of water, oil, gas, coal or any other minerals.	York.
The Enterprise Shoe Manufacturing Company. Capital, $60,000. June 27, 1892.	Said corporation is formed for the purpose of manufacturing and selling boots, shoes, slippers and other foot wear.	Lebanon.
The Hollidaysburg Electric Light and Power Company. Capital, $25,000. June 29, 1892.	Said corporation is formed for the purpose of furnishing electricity for light, heat and power to the citizens, firms and corporations in the boroughs of Hollidaysburg and Gaysport, which are contiguous, and Allegheny township, in which the same are situated, in Blair county, Pennsylvania.	Hollidaysburg.
The Carnegie Land and Loan Association of Pittsburgh, Penna. Capital, $100,000. June 29, 1892.	Said corporation is formed for the purpose of accumulating a fund by the periodical contributions of the members thereof, and of safely investing the same.	Pittsburgh.

Company	Purpose	Location
The Air Gas Stove Company. Capital, $50,000. June 28, 1892.	Said corporation is formed for the purposes of the manufacture and sale of gas stoves and patented appliances, connected therewith, and any other article of commerce composed of metal or wood, or both.	Reading.
The Pennsylvania Premium Building and Loan Association of Allegheny City. Capital, $500,000. July 1, 1892.	Said corporation is formed for the purpose of accumulating a fund by the periodical contributions of the members thereof, and of safely investing the same.	Allegheny City.
New Kensington Heat, Light and Power Company. Capital, $2,000. July 1, 1892.	Said corporation is formed for the purpose of supplying heat, light and power in the township of Lower Burrell, Westmoreland county Penna., and to persons, partnerships and associations residing therein and adjacent thereto, as may desire the same.	New Kensington.
Kensington Brick Company. Capital, $50,000. July 1, 1892.	Said corporation is formed for the purpose of the manufacture of brick, tile, clay and shale products.	New Kensington.
Walburn Land Company. Capital, $100,000. July 1, 1892.	Said corporation is formed for the purpose of the purchase and sale, or holding, leasing and selling real estate.	Ridgway.
The Daisy Shirt Company of Annville, Penn. Capital, $15,000. July 1, 1892.	Said corporation is formed for the purpose of manufacturing and selling shirts or wearing apparal, or both, or of any other article of commerce from linen, cotton and woolen fabrics.	Annville.
Mount Vernon Cigar Manufacturing Company. Capital, $20,000. July 1, 1892.	Said corporation is formed for the purpose of the manufacture and sale of cigars.	Seven Valley.
Lisbon Coal Company. Capital, $300,000. July 2, 1892.	Said corporation is formed for the purpose of the minin ufacture thereof into its products, and selling, shippi the same to markets, and for these purposes, or any have, possess and enjoy all the rights, benefits and privileges of the said act of assembly, and all acts supplemental thereto, or amendatory thereof, or otherwise lawfully accruing, including, inter alia, the right to maintain and operate the machinery, cars and the appliances incident to such business.	Philadelphia.

LIST OF CHARTERS OF CORPORATIONS—Continued.

STYLE AND TITLE OF CORPORATION.	PURPOSE.	LOCATION.
The Bellevue Water Company. Capital, $1,000. July 5, 1892.	Said corporation is formed for the purpose of supplying water to the public and to individuals, firms and corporations residing and doing business in the borough of Bellevue, and in the territory adjacent thereto, within the county of Allegheny and State of Pennsylvania.	Bellevue.
The Rising Sun Brewing Company. Capital, $60,000. July 5, 1892.	Said corporation is formed for the purpose of manufacturing and selling malt or brewed liquors.	Philadelphia.
The Benge Baking Company. Capital, $2,482. July 5, 1892.	Said corporation is formed for the purpose of the manufacture of bread, cake, ice cream and other articles usually made by bakers and confectioners.	Philadelphia.
Clinton County Saving, Loan and Building Association. Capital, $200,000. July 5, 1892.	Said corporation is formed for the purpose of accumulating a fund by the periodical contributions of the members thereof, and of safely investing the same.	Lock Haven.
The Northwood Glass Company. Capital, $75,000. July 6, 1892.	Said corporation is formed for the purpose of carrying on the business of manufacturing glass and glassware.	Ellwood.
The Willetts Company. Capital, $5,000. July 6, 1892.	Said corporation is formed for the purpose of manufacturing machinery, apparatus and supplies belonging, appertaining or incidental to work for manufacturing glass.	Pittsburgh.
The Mayfield Water Company. Capital, $15,000. July 7, 1892.	Said corporation is formed for the purpose of supplying water to the public at the borough of Mayfield, and to persons, partnerships and associations residing therein and adjacent thereto, as may desire the same.	Mayfield, Lackawanna county.
The South Lincoln Coal Company. Capital, $200,000. July 7, 1892.	Said corporation is formed for the purpose of mining and quarrying for coal, preparing the same for market, and selling the same.	Scranton.

Company	Purpose	Location
The South Lincoln Land Company. Capital, $250,000. July 7, 1892.	Said corporation is formed for the purpose of the purchase and sale of real estate, or for holding, selling and leasing real estate.	Scranton.
The Hyde Land Company. Capital, $50,000. July 8, 1892.	Said corporation is formed for the purpose of purchasing, holding, improving, leasing, selling and otherwise disposing of real estate.	Pittsburgh.
Water Circulating Grate Company. Capital, $100,000. July 11, 1892.	Said corporation is formed for the purpose of the manufacture of iron or steel, or both, or of any other metal, or of any article of commerce from metal or wood, or both.	Philadelphia.
The Sharon Hill Electric Light Company. Capital, $1,000. July 11, 1892.	Said corporation is formed for the purpose of supplying light, heat and power by means of electricity, to the public at the borough of Sharon Hill, in the county of Delaware, and State of Pennsylvania, and to persons, partnerships and associations residing therein and adjacent thereto, as may desire the same.	Sharon Hill.
The People's Water Company of Sharon Hill. Capital, $1,000. July 11, 1892.	Said corporation is formed for the purpose of supplying water to the public at the borough of Sharon Hill, in the county of Delaware, and State of Pennsylvania, and to persons, partnerships and associations residing therein and adjacent thereto, as may desire the same.	Sharon Hill.
The Duquesne Real Estate Improvement Company. Capital, $5,000. July 11, 1892.	Said corporation is formed for the purpose of purchasing, improving and selling real estate, or holding and leasing the said real estate or any part thereof.	Duquesne.
The Scranton Iron Fence and Manufacturing Company. Capital, $30,000. July 11, 1892.	Said corporation is formed for the purpose of manufacturing fences and other articles from iron, steel and wood, or either.	Scranton.
The Franklin Lead and Zinc Company. Capital, $50,000. July 11, 1892.	Said corporation is formed for the purpose of mining and quarrying for lead, zinc, coal, iron, ore and other minerals.	Franklin.
The Birmingham Dime Building & Loan Association of Pittsburgh. Capital, $1,000,000. July 11, 1892.	Said corporation is formed for the purpose of accumulating a fund by the periodical contributions of the members thereof, and of safely investing the same.	Pittsburgh.

LIST OF CHARTERS OF CORPORATIONS—*Continued.*

Style and Title of Corporation.	Purpose.	Location.
Northampton Cement Company. Capital, $250,000. July 11, 1892.	Said corporation is formed for the purpose of quarrying cement stone and manufacturing cements of all kinds, thereout and therefrom.	Stemton.
The Textile Record Company. Capital, $50,000. July 12, 1892.	Said corporation is formed for the purpose of transacting a printing and publishing business.	Philadelphia.
J. M. Rumbaugh Brick Co. Capital, $120,000. July 12, 1892.	Said corporation is formed for the purpose of manufacturing brick, tile, terra-cotta and all articles produced from clay, shale, stone.	Greensburg.
The Granite Water Company. Capital, $5,000. July 12, 1892.	Said corporation is formed for the purpose of supplying water to the public in the village of Big Mine Run, in Butler township, Schuylkill county, P nns..and to such persons and partnerships residing therein or adjacent thereto, as may desire the same.	Big Mine Run.
The St. Anthony Building and Loan Association. Capital, $1,000,000. July 13, 1892.	Said corporation is formed for the purpose of accumulating a fund by the periodical contributions of the members thereof, and of safely investing the same.	Philadelphia.
The Fort Pitt Building and Loan Association. Capital, $1,000,000. July 14, 1892.	Said corporation is formed for the purpose of accumulating a fund by the contrib tion of the members thereof, and to loan the same to them fnm me to time, to enable them to purchase real estate, build dwelling uses or engage any legitimate business.	Pittsburgh.
The Norristown Shoe Manufacturing Company. Capital, $50,000. July 14, 1892.	Said corporation is formed for the purpose of manufacturing and selling boots, shoes and brogans.	Norristown.
The Philadelphia, Chester, Wilmington, Lewes Steamboat Company. Capital, $150,000. July 14, 1892.	Said corporation is formed for the purpose of building ships, vessels or boats, and carriage of persons and property thereon.	Philadelphia.

Company	Purpose	Location
The First United States Excelsior Building Association of California. Capital, $500,000. July 15, 1892.	Said corporation is formed for the purpose of accumulating a fund by the periodical contributions of the members thereof, and of safely investing the same.	California, Washington Co.
The Rose Brothers and Hartman Company. Capital, $100,000. July 18, 1892.	Said corporation is formed for the purpose of the manufacture of umbrellas and parasols, and of all the materials used in the manufacture thereof, and of sticks, canes, runners, ribs, silks, cottons and muslins, and every manner of fabric now or hereafter employed in the manufacture of umbrellas and parasols.	Lancaster.
The West Johnson Printing and Publishing Company. Capital, $15,000. July 18, 1892.	Said corporation is formed for the purpose of the transaction of a printing and publishing business.	Easton.
The Brownsville Water Company. Capital, $20,000. July 18, 1892.	Said corporation is formed for the purpose of supplying water to the public in the borough of Brownsville, Fayette county, Pennsylvania.	Brownsville.
The Bridgeport Water Company. Capital, $10,000. July 18, 1892.	Said corporation is formed for the purpose of supplying water to the public in the borough of Bridgeport, Fayette county, Pennsylvania.	Brownsville.
Essex Enamel Company. Capital, $35,000. July 18, 1892.	Said corporation is formed for the purpose of the manufacture of iron or steel, or both, or of any other metal or article of commerce from metal, wood or both.	Pittsburgh.
The Frankstown Avenue Building and Loan Association. Capital, $1,000,000. July 19, 1892.	Said corporation is formed for the purpose of accumulating a fund by the contribution of the members thereof, and to loan the same to them from time to time, to enable them to purchase real estate, build houses or engage in any legitimate business.	Pittsburgh.
Mercantile Journal Company. Capital, $2,500. July 19, 1892.	Said corporation is formed for the purpose of transacting a printing and publishing business.	Pittsburgh.
The Cycling Publishing Company. Capital, $5,000. July 19, 1892.	Said corporation is formed for the purpose of transacting a printing and publishing business.	Philadelphia.

LIST OF CHARTERS OF CORPORATIONS—*Continued.*

STYLE AND TITLE OF CORPORATION.	PURPOSE.	LOCATION.
Peale, Peacock and Kerr. Incorporated. Capital, $75,000. July 19, 1892.	Said corporation is formed for the purpose of mining and shipping coal, manufacturing coke and other products therefrom, and selling the same in crude or manufactured form.	Philadelphia.
The Lackawanna Slate Company. Capital, $25,000. July 20, 1892.	Said corporation is formed for the purpose of mining, quarrying and manufacturing slate.	Pen Argyl.
The People's Mutual Savings Fund and Loan Association of Greensburg, Pa. Capital, $1,000,000. July 21, 1892.	Said corporation is formed for the purpose of accumulating a fund by the periodical contributions of the members thereof, and of safely investing the same.	Greensburg.
The Silver Creek Mining Company. Capital, $10,000. July 21, 1892.	Said corporation is formed for the purpose of mining and quarrying coal, preparing the same for market and selling the same.	Pottsville.
Philadelphia Car Wheel Company. Capital, $35,000. July 22, 1892.	Said corporation is formed for the purpose of the manufacture of iron or steel, or both, or of any other metal or article of commerce from metal, wood, or both, and for these purposes, to have, possess and enjoy all the rights, benefits and privileges of said act of assembly and its supplements.	Philadelphia.
George V. Cresson Company. Capital, $500,000. July 22, 1892.	Said corporation is formed for the purpose of the manufacture of iron or steel, or both, or of any other metal, or of any article of commerce from metal or wood, or both.	Philadelphia.
The Pittsburgh Rolled Car Axle Company. Capital, $5,000. July 25, 1892.	Said corporation is formed for the purpose of the manufacture of iron or steel, or both, or of any other metal, or of any article of commerce from metal or wood, or both.	Pittsburgh.
The Tannago Patent Company. Capital, $64,000. July 25, 1892.	Said corporation is formed for the purpose of creating, purchasing, holding and selling patent rights for inventions, and designs with the right to issue licenses for the same and receive pay therefor.	Philadelphia.

Hawthorne Engraving and Printing Company. Capital, $12,000. July 25, 1892.	Said corporation is formed for the purpose of the transaction of a printing and publishing business.	Pittsburgh.
The Farmers' Bank of Lebanon, Pennsylvania. Capital, $50,000. July 25, 1892.	Said corporation is formed for the purpose of carrying on the business of banking under and pursuant to the act of assembly of the Commonwealth of Pennsylvania, entitled "an act for the incorporation and regulation of banks of discount and deposit," approved the 13th day of May, A. D. 1876, and the several supplements thereto.	Lebanon.
The Renova Novelty Company, Limited. Capital, $5,000. July 26, 1892.	Said corporation is formed for the purpose of manufacturing and selling wagon jacks and other articles of commerce composed of wood and metal.	Renova.
The Excelsior Flint Glass Company. Capital, $75,000. July 26, 1892.	Said corporation is formed for the purpose of manufacturing and selling all kinds of glassware, the works being at Kensington, in the county of Westmoreland, in the State of Pennsylvania.	Pittsburgh.
The Fifth Avenue Bridge Company of McKeesport. Capital, $25,000. July 26, 1892.	Said corporation is formed for the purpose of erecting, constructing and maintaining a bridge and approaches thereto over the Youghiogheny river, from a point at or near the western end of Fifth avenue in the city of McKeesport, Allegheny county, Penna., to point on opposite side of said river, at or near the property of Benj. Coursin in the borough of Reynoldton, in aid of Railway, this bridge but 620 feet south of the railroad bridge of the Pittsburgh, McKeesport and Youghiogheny Railroad Company.	McKeesport.
N. R. Cox Company. Capital, $100,000. July 27, 1892.	Said corporation is formed for the purpose of manufacturing boots, shoes and leather and shoe materials, and disposing of the same.	Philadelphia.
Ellwood Water Company. Capital, $5,000. July 27, 1892.	Said corporation is formed for the purpose of the supply of water to the public in the township of Wayne, in the county of Lawrence, Pennsylvania, and to persons, partnerships and associations residing therein and adjacent thereto, as may desire the same.	Ellwood City.
The American Monument Company of Pittsburgh, Pa. Capital, $30,000. July 27, 1892.	Said corporation is formed for the purpose of manufacturing and selling marble, granite and metal monuments, head stones, curbing, pillars, &c., the building of vaults and other structures of marble and granite in cemeteries, and other general cemetery work.	Pittsburgh.

LIST OF CHARTERS OF CORPORATIONS—Continued.

STYLE AND TITLE OF CORPORATION.	PURPOSE.	LOCATION.
Charleroi Heat, Light and Power Company. Capital, $5,000. July 28, 1892.	Said corporation is formed for the purpose of supplying heat, light and power, or any of them, by means of electricity, to the public in the borough of Charleroi, Washington county, Pennsylvania, and to persons, partnerships and corporations residing or doing business therein or adjacent thereto, as may desire the same.	Charleroi.
The World Manufacturing Company. Capital, $15,000. July 29, 1892	Said corporation is formed for the purpose of manufacturing all kinds of paints, oils, wood fillers, varnishes and driers.	Philadelphia.
The Salem Iron Company. Capital, $50,000. July 29, 1892	Said corporation is formed for the purpose of manufacturing iron or steel in their various forms, or both, or of any other metal, or article of commerce from metal, wood, or both.	Pittsburgh.
Columbian Land Improvement Company of Harrisburg. Capital, $10,000. July 29, 1892.	Said corporation is formed for the purpose of purchasing, holding, leasing, selling and improving real estate.	Harrisburg.
The Titusville Electric Light and Power Company. Capital, $100,000. July 29, 1892.	Said corporation is formed for the purpose of supplying light, heat and power by means of electricity, at the city of Titusville, and to persons, partnerships and associations residing therein and adjacent thereto, as may desire the same.	Titusville
Northumberland Water Company. Capital, $40,000. July 29, 1892.	Said corporation is formed for the purpose of furnishing a supply of water for the private and public uses generally of the citizens of the borough of Northumberland and vicinity, and to corporations and individuals residing therein and adjacent and adjoining thereto.	Northumberland.
Citizens' Building and Loan Association No. 2, of Tyrone, Pa. Capital, $340,000. August 1, 1892.	Said corporation is formed for the purpose of accumulating a fund by the periodical contributions of the members thereof, and of safely investing the same.	Tyrone, Pa.

Company	Purpose	Location
The George W. Blabon Company. Capital, $1,000,000. August 1, 1892.	Said corporation is formed for the purpose of the manufacture of oil cloth, linoleum, cork-tile and all coverings for floors made with a cloth foundation, and made with oil and other materials, table oil cloth, stair oil cloth, enamelled oil cloth, and all oil cloths howsoever made, and linseed oil, ochre and other colors used in the manufacture of oil cloth, and for the sale of the products of such manufacture.	Philadelphia.
Prospect Land Company. Capital, $5,000. August 1, 1892.	Said corporation is formed for the purpose of purchasing, selling and leasing real estate.	Pittsburgh.
Trexler Shoe Company. Capital, $50,000. August 1, 1892.	Said corporation is formed for the purpose of the manufacture from leather and other materials, boots, shoes, gaiters, slippers, bags, pouches, receptacles and other articles of commerce.	Mertztown.
United Mining and Manufacturing Company. Capital, $100,000. August 1, 1892.	Said corporation is formed for the purpose of the manufacture of iron or steel, or both, or of any other metal, or of any article of commerce from wood or metal, or both.	Philadelphia.
Bellevue Light and Power Company. Capital, $1,000. August 1, 1892.	Said corporation is formed for the purpose of supplying light, heat or power, or any of them, to the public at the borough of Bellevue, Allegheny county, Pennsylvania, and to such persons, partnerships and associations residing therein and adjacent thereto, as may desire the same.	Pittsburgh.
J. D. Chantler Leather Company. Capital, $30,000. August 1, 1892.	Said corporation is formed for the purpose of the manufacture and sale of shoe-uppers and articles in the leather and shoe-findings line.	Pittsburgh.
Tube City Brick Company. Capital, $25,000. August 1, 1892.	Said corporation is formed for the purpose of the manufacture of brick, tile and similar products from clay, crushed rock and sand.	McKeesport.
South Fork Water Company. Capital, $15,000. August 1, 1892.	Said corporation is formed for the purpose of supplying water for the public at the borough of South Fork, and to persons, partnerships and associations residing therein and adjacent thereto, as may desire the same.	South Fork.
The Young Brothers' Machine Company. Capital, $20,000. August 2, 1892.	Said corporation is formed for the purpose of manufacturing machinery for working wood.	Williamsport.

LIST OF CHARTERS OF CORPORATIONS—*Continued.*

STYLE AND TITLE OF CORPORATION.	PURPOSE.	LOCATION.
Mehoopany Boom Company. Capital, $1,000. August 2, 1892.	This corporation is formed for the purpose of erecting reservoirs for water, construction of dams, and the driving and floating of logs, timber and lumber on the Mehoopany creek, in the county of Wyoming, Commonwealth of Pennsylvania (the said creek not exceeding twenty miles in length) as authorized by law.	Mehoopany.
The Messing Printing and Publishing Company. Capital, $1,500. August 2, 1892.	Said corporation is formed for the purpose of conducting the printing and publishing business.	Pittsburgh.
The Pennsylvania Paint and Ochre Company. Capital, $10,000. August 2, 1892.	Said corporation is formed for the purpose of manufacturing paints of all kinds out of materials, mined and quarried by this corporation and various admixtures thereof and additions thereto.	Allentown.
The Berwick Electric Light Company. Capital, $25,000. August 4, 1892.	Said corporation is formed for the purpose of furnishing light by means of electricity for the borough of Berwick, Pa., and vicinity.	Berwick.
The Berwick Gas Company. Capital, $25,000. August 4, 1892.	Said corporation is formed for the purpose of manufacturing & supplying gas to the public within the borough of Berwick, Pa., & vicinity.	Berwick.
The Juniata Building and Loan Association. Capital, $1,000,000. August 4, 1892.	Said corporation is formed for the purpose of accumulating a fund by the periodical contributions of the members thereof, and of safely investing the same.	Altoona.
Keystone National Savings Fund and Loan Association. Capital, $1,000,000. August 4, 1892.	Said corporation is formed for the purpose of accumulating a fund by the periodical contributions of the members thereof, and of safely investing the same.	Erie..

Corporation	Purpose	Location
McKeesport and Wilmerding Land Company. Capital, $200,000. August 5, 1892.	Said corporation is formed for the purpose of purchasing, taking, holding and enjoying real estate in fee simple, on lease or upon ground rent, of improving, leasing, mortgaging or selling the same in such parts or parcels and on such terms as to time of payment as they may determine.	McKeesport.
The Polish American Building and Loan Association of Pittsburgh, Penna. Capital, $1,000,000. August 8, 1892.	Said corporation is formed for the purpose of accumulating a fund by the periodical contributions of the members thereof, and of safely investing the same.	Pittsburgh.
The Iron Workers' Saving Fund Association of Johnstown, Pa. Capital, $1,000,000. August 8, 1892.	Said corporation is formed for the purpose of accumulating a fund by the periodical contributions of the members thereof, and of safely investing the same.	Johnstown.
Emporium Lumber Company. Capital, $30,000. August 8, 1892.	Said corporation is formed for the purpose of manufacturing lumber.	Emporium.
The Hallstead Land Improvement Company. Capital, $20,000. August 8, 1892.	Said corporation is formed for the purpose of purchasing and selling real estate, or holding, leasing and selling real estate, and improving the same and the transaction of business incidental thereto.	Hallstead.
The Goodwin Meter Company. Capital, $50,000. August 8, 1892.	Said corporation is formed for the purpose of manufacturing gas meters, gas engines, gas stoves and generally all kinds of gas appliances.	Philadelphia.
Brookville Manufacturing Company. Capital, $25,000. August 8, 1892.	Said corporation is formed for the purpose of manufacturing of iron or steel, or both, or of any other metal, or of any other article of commerce from metal or wood, or both.	Brookville.
The Steelton Home Water Company. Capital, $30,000. August 9, 1892.	Said corporation is formed for the purpose of supplying water to the public, at the borough of Steelton, Dauphin county, Pa., that is to persons, partnerships and associations residing therein and adjacent thereto, that may desire the same.	Steelton.
Albright Coal Company. Capital, $200,000. August 9, 1892.	Said corporation is formed for the purpose of mining and preparing coal for market and selling the same.	Llewellyn.

LIST OF CHARTERS OF CORPORATIONS—*Continued.*

STYLE AND TITLE OF CORPORATION.	PURPOSE.	LOCATION.
Sentinel Building and Loan Association of Philadelphia. Capital, $1,000,000. August 10, 1892.	Said corporation is formed for the purpose of accumulating a fund by the periodical contributions of the members thereof, and of safely investing the same.	Philadelphia.
The Point Marion Water Company. Capital, $5,000. August 10, 1892.	Said corporation is formed for the purpose of supplying water to the public at the village of Point Marion, in Springfield township, Fayette county, Pennsylvania, to such persons, partnerships and associations residing therein and adjacent thereto, as may desire.	Point Marion.
The Frett Water Company of Frett, Pa. Capital, $6,000. August 11, 1892.	Said corporation is formed for the purpose of supplying water to the public at the borough of Everett, Pa., and to persons, partnerships and corporations residing or transacting business therein or adjacent thereto.	Everett.
The Harrisburg Preserving Company. Capital, $25,000. August 12, 1892.	Said corporation is formed for the purpose of manufacturing preserved vegetables and fruits and for that purpose to have and possess the powers and privileges expressed and given in the 39th section of the corporation act of 1874, and the supplements thereto.	Harrisburg.
The Point Marion Electric Light and Power Company. Capital, $10,000. August 12, 1892.	Said corporation is formed for the purpose of light, heat and power, or any of them, by e the town of Point Marion, Fayette county, persons, partnerships and corporations resi thereto, as may desire the same (and to with the necessary appliances to utilize the same). and supplying the public in ia, and to such and adjacent d supply consumers	Point Marion.
The Monaca Water Company. Capital, $21,000. August 12, 1892.	Said corporation is formed for the purpose of supplying water for the public at the borough of Phillipsburg, in the county of Beaver, and State of Pennsylvania, and to such persons, partnerships, companies and associations residing therein and adjacent thereto, as may desire the same.	Phillipsburg.
The Columbian Land and Improvement Company. Capital, $30,000. August 12, 1892.	Said corporation is formed for the purpose of the purchase and sale of real estate, and for holding, leasing and selling real estate as well as improving the same.	Pittsburgh.

Superior Steel Company. Capital, $100,000. August 12, 1892.	Said corporation is formed for the purpose of the manufacture of iron or steel, or of both, or of any other metal or article of commerce from metal, wood, or both.	Pittsburgh.
Steelton Light, Heat and Power Company. Capital, $40,000. August 15, 1892.	Said corporation is formed for the purpose of supplying light, heat and power, by means of electricity to the public in the borough of Steelton, ... in ... ty, Pennsylvania, and to such persons, partnerships and corporations residing therein and adjacent thereto, as may desire the same.	Steelton.
Acme Worsted Company. Capital, $50,000. August 15, 1892.	Said corporation is formed for the purpose of manufacturing and vending of ... ens, cloths and cotton and woolen goods of every description.	Philadelphia.
The Central Stove Company. Capital, $100,000. August 15, 1892.	Said corporation is formed for the purpose of the manufacture and sale of iron or ... tel, or both, or of any other metal, or of any article of commerce from metal or wood, or both.	Philadelphia.
Spangler Building and Loan Association. Capital, $1,000,000. August 16, 1892.	Said corporation is formed for the purpose of accumulating a fund by the periodical contributions of the members thereof, and of safely investing the same.	Spangler.
Aramingo Building and Loan Association. Capital, $1,000,000. August 17, 1892.	Said corporation is formed for the purpose of accumulating a fund by the contributions of the members thereof, and to loan the same to them from time to time to enable them to purchase real estate, build themselves dwelling houses, or engage in any legitimate business.	Philadelphia.
The Keystone Engine and Machine Company of Williamsport, Pa. Capital, $10,000. August 18, 1892.	Said corporation is formed for the purpose of the manufacture of iron or steel, or both, or of any other metal, or of any article of commerce from metal or wood, or both.	Williamsport.
Iron Economy Fire Proofing Company. Capital, $50,000. August 18, 1892.	Said corporation is formed for the purpose of the manufacture of all kinds of cement, plaster and fire proof materials to be used in the construction of buildings of all kinds or wherever such materials may or can be used.	Pittsburgh.
The First United States Excelsior Building Association of Bell Vernon, Pa. Capital, $500,000. August 18, 1892.	Said corporation is formed for the purpose of accumulating a fund by the periodical contributions of the members thereof, and of safely investing the same.	Belle Vernon.

8 a LAWS.

LIST OF CHARTERS OF CORPORATIONS—*Continued.*

Style and Title of Corporation.	Purpose.	Location.
Carlisle Clothing Company. Capital, $15,000. August 18, 1892.	Said corporation is formed for the purpose of manufacturing clothing.	Carlisle.
American National Savings Fund Building and Loan Association. Capital, $1,000,000. August 18, 1892	Said corporation is formed for the purpose of accumulating a fund by the periodical contributions of the members thereof, and of safely investing the same.	Erie.
The People's Mutual Savings Fund and Loan Association of Mt. Pleasant, Pa. Capital, $1,000,000. August 18, 1892	Said corporation is formed for the purpose of accumulating a fund by the periodical contributions of the members thereof, and of safely investing the same.	Mt. Pleasant
The Sentinel Printing Company of Hazleton, Pa. Capital, $25,000. August 19, 1892	Said corporation is formed for the purpose of transacting a general printing and publishing business in the city of Hazleton.	Hazleton.
The Spangler Water Company. Capital, $2,000. August 19, 1892	Said corporation is formed for the purpose of supplying the inhabitants of the village of Spangler, in Cambria county, Pennsylvania, with water, for domestic and other purposes.	Spangler.
Cauldwell Iron Works. Capital, $40,000. August 19, 1892	Said corporation is formed for the purpose of the manufacture and sale of iron or steel, or both, or any other metal, or article of commerce from metal, wood, or both, and for these purposes to have, possess and enjoy all the rights, benefits and privileges of said act of assembly and supplements thereto.	Forty Fort.
Pittsburgh Novelty Company. Capital, $1,000. August 22, 1892.	Said corporation is formed for the purpose of manufacturing articles of commerce from iron and steel, or both, or of any other metal, or from metal or wood, or both.	Pittsburgh.
McMillan Sash Balance Company. Capital, $4,000. August 22, 1892.	Said corporation is formed for the purpose of the manufacture of iron and steel, or both, or of any other metal or article of commerce from metal, wood or both.	Pittsburgh.

Corporation	Purpose	Location
The State College Water Company. Capital, $1,000. August 22, 1892.	Said corporation is formed for the purpose of supplying water to the public at the township of College in the county of Centre, and to such persons, partnerships and corporations residing therein and adjacent thereto, as may desire the same.	State College.
Pennsylvania Range Boiler Company. Capital, $40,000. August 22, 1892.	Said corporation is formed for the purpose of manufacturing boilers and tanks from iron and steel, and other metals, and from combinations of metals, and also of manufacturing sheet iron specialties.	Philadelphia.
The Bedford Handle and Hartwood Company. Capital, $20,000. August 23, 1892.	Said corporation is formed for the purpose of the manufacture of various articles of commerce from wood.	Bedford.
The William Anderson Company. Capital, $100,000. August 24, 1892.	Said corporation is formed for the purpose of the manufacture of iron or steel, or both, or of any other metal, or of any article of commerce from metal or wood, or both.	Pittsburgh.
The Morris Einstein Company. Capital, $100,000. August 24, 1892.	Said corporation is formed for the purpose of compounding or manufacturing of medicines.	Allegheny.
Eclipse Bicycle Company. Capital, $200,000. August 25, 1892.	Said corporation is formed for the purpose of the manufacture of iron or steel, or both, or of any other metal, or of articles of commerce, from metal or wood, or both, and especially for the manufacture of bicycles and chain.	Beaver Falls.
The Enterprise Powder Manufacturing Company. Capital, $125,000. August 25, 1892.	Said corporation is formed for the purpose of the manufacture and sale of powder dynamite and other explosive substances.	Scranton.
The Keystone Bicycle Company. Capital, $1,000. August 25, 1892.	Said corporation is formed for the purpose of manufacturing and selling bicycles.	Scranton.
Ellwood Steel Company. Capital, $100,000. August 25, 1892.	Said corporation is formed for the purpose of the manufacture of iron or steel, or both, or of any other metal or of any article of commerce from metal or wood, or both.	Ellwood City.
The Chamberlain Coal Company. Capital $150,000. August 23, 1892.	Said corporation is formed for the purpose of mining and quarrying for coal, preparing the same for market and selling the same.	Scranton.

LIST OF CHARTERS OF CORPORATIONS—*Continued.*

STYLE AND TITLE OF CORPORATION.	PURPOSE.	LOCATION.
Harvey Coal Mining Company Capital, $30,000. August 29, 1892.	Said corporation is formed for the purpose of mining for coal and manufacturing coke therefrom.	Philadelphia.
The Fox Chase Electric Light, Heat and Power Company of Philadelphia. Capital, $25,000. August 29, 1892.	Said corporation is formed for the purpose of supplying light, heat and power, by means of electricity, to the public at the city of Philadelphia, in the State of Pennsylvania, and to persons, partnerships and associations residing therein and adjacent thereto, as may desire the same.	Philadelphia.
The Consumers' Water Company of Montrose, Pa. Capital, $40,000. August 31, 1892.	Said corporation is formed for the purpose of introducing, supplying and furnishing water to the public of the borough of Montrose, county of Susquehanna, and State of Pennsylvania, and to such persons, partnerships, corporations and associations residing therein and adjacent thereto, as may desire the same.	Montrose.
The Third Fairhill Building Association. Capital, $1,000,000. August 31, 1892.	Said corporation is formed for the purpose of accumulating a fund by the periodical contributions of the members thereof, and of safely investing the same.	Philadelphia.
Philadel hia Emery and Corundum Wheel C mpany. Capital, $10,000. September 1, 1892.	Said corporation is formed for the purpose of manufacturing emery and corundum wheels, wooden polishing wheels, brush wheels, buffing wheels, machinery for running grinding wheels, nickel salts, nickel anodes, roughes. compounds of tripoli, and generally all polishing supplies used by nickel platers and polishers.	Philadelphia.
The Wilkinson Manufacturing Company. Capital, $50,000. September 1, 1892.	Said corporation is formed for the purpose of the manufacture of boilers, furnaces, engines and machinery and portions thereof, and more particularly for the manufacture of the "Wilkinson Automatic Stocker," to have, possess, and enjoy all the rights, benefits and privileges of said act of assembly and its supplements.	Philadelphia.
The Oregon Building and Loan A- sociation No. 3, ol Pittsburgh. Capital, $25,000. September 2, 1892.	Said corporation is formed for the purpose of accumulating a fund by the periodical contributions of the members thereof, and of safely investing the same.	Pittsburgh.

Corporation	Purpose	Location
The People's Electric Company of Braddock. Capital, $35,000. September 6, 1892.	Said corporation is formed for the purpose of supplying light, heat and power, or any of them, by electricity, to the public of the borough of Braddock, and such persons, partnerships and corporations residing therein or adjacent thereto, as may desire the same.	Braddock.
The People's Mutual Savings Fund and Loan Association of Derry Station, Pa. Capital, $1,000,000. September 6, 1892.	Said corporation is formed for the purpose of accumulating a fund by the periodical contributions of the members thereof, and of safely investing the same.	Derry Station.
Dunlap Electric Company. Capital, $5,000. September 6, 1892.	Said corporation is formed for the purpose of generating and supplying light, heat and power, or any of them, by electricity, to the public in the borough of Brownsville, Fayette county, Penna., and to such persons, partnerships and corporations residing therein or adjacent thereto, as may desire the same.	Brownsville.
The Black Granite Brick Company. Capital, $2,000. September 6, 1892.	Said corporation is formed for the purpose of manufacturing brick and other products of clay.	Pittsburgh.
United States Pipe Line Company. Capital, $600,000. September 6, 1892.	Said corporation is formed for the purpose of laying down, constructing and maintaining pipes, tubing, tanks, offices and machinery, devices and arrangements necessary to enable it to carry out the right and purpose of transporting, storing, insuring and shipping petroleum between places within the State of Pennsylvania.	Bradford.
The Farmers' Voice Publishing Company. Capital, $2,000. September 6, 1892.	Said corporation is formed for the purpose of conducting and publishing a weekly and semi-weekly newspaper and doing a general publishing business.	Coudersport.
Glenmore Foundry and Machine Company. Capital, $100,000. September 6, 1892.	Said corporation is formed for the purpose of manufacturing wrought and cast iron and other metals.	Philadelphia.
The College Tract Residence Company. Capital, $5,000. September 6, 1892.	Said corporation is formed for the purpose of purchasing, holding and enjoying real estate in fee simple, upon ground rent or lease, and to improve the same by the erection of buildings thereon, of leasing, mortgaging or selling the same in such parts or parcels, improved or unimproved on such terms as to time and manner of payment as may be agreed upon.	Swarthmore.

LIST OF CHARTERS OF CORPORATIONS—*Continued.*

STYLE AND TITLE OF CORPORATION.	PURPOSE.	LOCATION.
The Uniform Stone Company. Capital, $10,000. September 6, 1892.	Said corporation is formed for the purpose of quarrying stone.	Allegheny City.
West View Land Company. Capital, $2,000. September 9, 1892.	Said corporation is formed for the purpose of purchasing, holding, improving, leasing selling, and otherwise disposing of real estate.	Bolivar.
The Waynesburg, Woodruff and Weaver Telephone Company. Capital, $1,000. September 9, 1892.	Said corporation is formed for the purpose of constructing and operating a public telephone line for the transmission of telephone messages between the points of Waynesburg & J. Weaver's store in Greene county, Pa.	Woodruff.
The Algonquin Coal Company. Capital, $300,000. September 12, 1892.	Said corporation is formed for the purpose of mining coa. and .or that purpose to have and possess the powers and privileges expressed and given in the 39th section of the corporation act of 1874, and supplements thereto.	Wilkes-Barre.
West Braddock Bridge Company. Capital, $1,000. September 13, 1892.	Said corporation is formed for the purpose of constructing, maintaining and operating a bridge over the Monongahela river from a point in or near the foot of Clara street in the borough of Braddock, to a point in Mifflin township on the opposite side of said river, all within Allegheny county, Pennsylvania, and is distant one mile from any other incorporated bridge or ferry over the same stream.	Pittsburgh.
The United States Building Association of Rochester, Pa. Capital $100,000. September 13, 1892.	Said corporation is formed for the purpose of accumulating a fund by the periodical contributions of the members thereof, and of safely investing the same.	Rochester.
The New Wilmington Water Supply Company. Capital, $10,000. September 15, 1892.	Said corporation is formed for the purpose o. supplying water for the borough of New Wilmington, Lawrence county, Pennsylvania, and to persons, partnerships and associations residing therein and adjacent thereto.	New Wilmington.

Sabine Curatine Oil Company. Capital, $3,600. September 15, 1892.	Said corporation is formed for the purpose of manufacturing all kinds of medicines, principally Sabine Curative oil and "Chapsega."	Warren.
The South Branch Manufacturing Company. Capital, $50,000. September 19, 1892.	Said corporation is formed for the purpose of manufacturing commercial products from wood.	Galeton, Potter county.
Beaver Falls Hedge Company. Capital, $150,000. September 19, 1892.	Said corporation is formed for the purpose of manufacturing all kinds of hedge fences.	Beaver Falls.
Southern Transportation Company. Capital, $30,000. September 20, 1892.	Said corporation is formed for the purpose of building ships, vessels and boats, and the carriage of persons and property thereon.	Pittsburgh.
The Paisley Woolen Company. Capital, $40,000. September 21, 1892.	Said corporation is formed for the purpose of manufacturing and selling of shawls and other woolen fabrics.	Mansfield.
The Jefferson Electric Light, Heat and Power Company. Capital, $6,000. September 23, 1892.	Said corporation is formed for the purpose of supplying light, heat and power, or any of them, by electricity to the public in the boroughs of Punxsutawney and Clayville, both in Jefferson county, Pennsylvania, and to such persons, partnerships and corporations residing therein or adjacent thereto, as may desire the same.	Punxsutawney.
Dawson Electric Light and Power Company. Capital, $20,000. September 23, 1892.	Said corporation is formed for the purpose of supplying light, heat and power by means of electricity to the public of the borough of Dawson, Fayette county, Pa., and to such persons, partnerships, associations and corporations residing therein and adjacent thereto, as may desire the same.	Dawson.
The East End Bridge Company. Capital, $20,000. September 23, 1892.	Said [illegible] is [illegible] for the [illegible] of er[illegible]ing, [illegible]ting and maintaining a [illegible] and [illegible] over the [illegible]hela [illegible], from a [illegible] on the [illegible] side of the [illegible] in North [illegible], Allegheny county, and [illegible], at or near the [illegible] of the U. S. [illegible] Pipe Mg. Co. and Brown [illegible], to a point on the opposite side of said [illegible] in the borough of Duquesne, said [illegible] the location of said bridge is not [illegible] 3,000 feet of any [illegible] or bridge, and the McK[illegible] and [illegible] being the [illegible] bridge is [illegible] thousand feet distant from said [illegible].	McKeesport.

LIST OF CHARTERS OF CORPORATIONS—*Continued.*

STYLE AND TITLE OF CORPORATION.	PURPOSE.	LOCATION.
Leechburg Ferry Company. Capital, $1,000. September 23, 1892.	Said corporation is formed for the purpose of erecting, constructing and maintaining a ferry and approaches thereto, from a point on the William Grinder farm in Allegheny township, Westmoreland Co., where the public road as laid out strikes the Kiskiminetas river to a point on the opposite side of the river on the lands of Jos. G. Beale in Gilpin township, Armstrong Co., Pa. There are no incorporated bridges or ferry companies on the Kiskiminetas river.	Leechburg.
The Industrial Homestead Loan and Trust Company of Philadelphia. Capital, $15,000. September 26, 1892.	Said corporation is formed for the purpose of purchasing, taking, holding and enjoying real estate in fee simple, on lease or upon ground rent, improving, leasing, mortgaging and selling same in fee simple, or for any less estate, or upon ground rent to its sale shareholders and others, or on such terms as to time and manner of payment as it may determine.	Philadelphia.
Maxwell, Rowland and Company. Incorporated. Capital, $100,000. September 26, 1892.	Said corporation is formed for the purpose of manufacturing shovels, spades, scoops, forks, edge tools of all descriptions, and including iron, steel and all other metal goods.	Philadelphia.
The West End Inclined Plane Company. Capital, $1,000. September 27, 1892.	Said corporation is formed for the purpose of erecting, maintaining and operating an inclined plane in the city of Pittsburgh, county of Allegheny, from a point on Greenleaf street, between West Carson street and the line dividing the Thirty-fourth and Thirty-fifth wards, to the summit of the hill, for the conveying and transporting of passengers and freight.	Pittsburgh.
The Kepp Gear Wheel and Foundry Company. Capital, $50,000. September 27, 1892.	Said corporation is formed for the purpose of manufacturing machine gearing, and machinery composed in whole or in part of metal, iron and wood.	Allegheny City.
The Downingtown Improvement Company. Capital, $35,000. September 28, 1892.	Said corporation is formed for the purpose of purchasing, holding, improving and selling real estate.	Downingtown.

Beaver Falls Improvement Company. Capital, $30,000. September 29, 1892.	Said corporation is formed for the purpose of the purchase and sale of real estate.	Beaver Falls.
The Gouldsboro' Ice Company. Capital, $10,000. September 29, 1892.	Said corporation is formed for the purpose of manufacturing ice.	Gouldsboro'.
The Hummelstown Electric Light, Heat and Power Company. Capital, $10,000. October 3, 1892.	Said corporation is formed for the purpose of supplying of light, heat and power to the public by electricity at Hummelstown, Dauphin county, Pennsylvania, and to such persons, partnerships and corporations residing therein and adjacent thereto, as may desire the same.	Hummelstown.
Rising Sun Building and Loan Association. Capital, $1,000,000. October 3, 1892.	Said corporation is formed for the purpose of accumulating a fund by the periodical contributions of the members thereof, and of safely investing the same.	West Conshohocken.
The Metropolitan Building and Loan Association No. 2, 17th ward, Pittsburgh. Capital, $975,000. October 3, 1892.	Said corporation is formed for the purpose of accumulating a fund by the periodical contributions of the members thereof, and of safely investing the same in loans to the stockholders thereof.	Pittsburgh.
Ohio Valley Building and Loan Association. Capital, $1,000,000. October 3, 1892.	Said corporation is formed for the purpose of accumulating a fund by the periodical contributions of the members thereof, and of safely investing the same.	Avalon.
The People's Mutual Savings Fund and Loan Association of Johnstown, Pa. Capital, $1,000,000. October 3, 1892.	Said corporation is formed for the purpose of accumulating a fund by the periodical contributions of the members thereof, and of safely investing the same.	Johnstown.
Morelton Inn Company. Capital, $50,000. October 3, 1892.	Said corporation is formed for the purpose of the establishment and maintenance of an hotel in the city of Philadelphia, Pennsylvania.	Philadelphia.
Hyde Park Brick Co. Capital, $10,000. October 3, 1892.	Said corporation is formed for the purpose of manufacturing brick, fire-brick, tile and other articles from clay or shale substances.	Leechburg.

LIST OF CHARTERS OF CORPORATIONS—*Continued.*

Style and Title of Corporation.	Purpose.	Location.
The People's Mutual Savings Fund and Loan Association of Irwin, Pa. Capital, $1,000,000. October 4, 1892.	Said corporation is formed for the purpose of accumulating a fund by the periodical contributions of the members thereof, and of safely investing the same.	Irwin, Pa.
The Allegheny City Premium Building and Loan Association No. 2 Capital, $300,000. October 4, 1892.	Said corporation is formed for the purpose of accumulating a fund by the periodical contributions of the members thereof, and of safely investing the same.	Allegheny City.
The Pittsburgh and Northwestern Coal Company. Capital, $40,000. October 4, 1892.	Said corporation is formed for the purpose of carrying on the business of mining coal and transporting it to market and of manufacturing coke therefrom and transporting to market and selling the same.	Bridgeville.
The Kidder Coal Company. Capital, $20,000. October 4, 1892.	Said corporation is formed for the purpose of mining, preparing for market, shipping and selling anthracite coal.	Wilkes-Barre.
The Central Real Estate Company of Philadelphia. Capital, $150,000. October 5, 1892.	Said corporation is formed for the purpose of buying and selling, holding, leasing and mortgaging and improving real estate.	Philadelphia.
The Liberty Homestead Loan and Trust Company. Capital, $15,000. October 6, 1892.	Said corporation is formed for the purpose of purchasing, taking, holding and enjoying real estate in fee simple, on lease or upon ground rent, improving, leasing, mortgaging and selling the same in fee simple or for any less estate or upon ground rent to its sale shareholders and others, upon such terms as to time of payment as it may determine.	Pittsburgh.
The Wire Glass Company Capital, $6,000. October 6, 1892.	Said corporation is formed for the purpose of manufacturing plate glass and wire glass, and to sell the same.	Philadelphia.

Company	Purpose	Location
Twenty-first Street Incline Plane Company. Capital, $300,000. October 7, 1892.	Said corporation is formed for the purpose of erecting, maintaining and operating an inclined plane in the city of Pittsburgh, county of Allegheny, and State of Pennsylvania, from point on South Twenty-first street, south of Josephine street, and running to a point on Arlington avenue, between the Brownsville road and Amanda avenue, for the carriage, conveyance and transportation of passengers and freight.	Philadelphia.
T. C. Avis Basket Company. Capital, $60,000. October 7, 1892.	Said corporation is formed for the purpose of manufacturing baskets and divers kindred articles of commerce.	Philadelphia.
The Snowdon Manufacturing Company. Capital, $15,000. October 7, 1892.	Said corporation is formed for the purpose of the manufacture of iron, or steel, or both, or of any other metal, or of any article of commerce, from metal or wood, or both.	Brownsville.
The Everett Crystal Water Company. Capital, $5,000. October 7, 1892.	Said corporation is formed for the purpose of supplying water to the public in Everett borough, county of Bedford, Pennsylvania, and to such persons, partnerships and corporations residing therein and adjacent thereto, as may desire the same.	Everett.
The M'Anulty Mill Furnishing Company. Capital, $75,000. October 7, 1892.	Said corporation is formed for the purpose of manufacturing devices, fixtures, supplies & appliances needful or designed for or relating to flour mills made out of wood & iron, and also to manufacture any other machine or contrivance for useful purposes made out of wood & iron.	Manheim.
The Ten Cent Tutor Building and Loan Association of the West End, Pittsburgh, Pa. Capital, $2,400,000. October 10, 1892.	Said corporation is formed for the purpose of accumulating a fund by the periodical contributions of the members thereof, and of safely investing the same.	Pittsburgh.
The Mt. Gretna Ice Company. Capital, $25,000. October 10, 1892.	Said corporation is formed for the purpose of supplying ice to the public.	Lebanon.
The Keystone Brewing Company. Capital, $1,000,000 October 10, 1892.	Said corporation is formed for the purpose of manufacturing and brewing malt liquors.	Pittsburgh.
The Thermo Sanitaire Company. Capital, $4,000. October 10, 1892.	Said corporation is formed for the purpose of the manufacture and sale of a certain machine to be used in the destruction and desiccation of garbage and household wastes by the utilization of heat.	Philadelphia.

LIST OF CHARTERS OF CORPORATIONS—*Continued.*

STYLE AND TITLE OF CORPORATION.	PURPOSE.	LOCATION.
Rowena Furnace Company. Capital, $100,000. October 11, 1892.	Said corporation is formed for the purpose of the manufacture of iron or steel, or both, or of any other metal, or article of commerce from metal, wood or both.	Pittsburgh.
The Helios Electric Company. Capital, $100,000. October 11, 1892.	Said corporation is formed for the purpose of manufacturing, contracting, furnishing all articles, materials, apparatus, machinery, equipment, devices, structures, fixtures, supplies and appliances needful or designed for or relating to the use and application of electricity, steam, water, heat, power and natural or manufactured gas to or for any useful purpose.	Philadelphia.
The Standard Hay Baling Company. Capital, $100,000. October 11, 1892.	Said corporation is formed for the purpose of the carrying on the mechanical business of baling hay.	Souderton.
Manville Covering Company of Norristown, Pa. Capital, $100,000. October 12, 1892.	Said corporation is formed for the purpose of manufacturing the Manville patent coverings for steam pipes and boilers, and any other coverings or protections designed for the conservation of heat and economy of fuel.	Norristown.
Thouron Coal Land Company. Capital, $360,000. October 13, 1892.	Said corporation is formed for the purpose of the purchase and sale of real estate, and for holding, leasing and improving real estate.	Scranton.
The W. J. McCahan Sugar Refining Company. Capital, $2,000,000. October 13, 1892.	Said corporation is formed for the purpose of the refining and manufacture of sugar, and the purchase of raw materials for said purposes.	Philadelphia.
The West Penn Transportation Company. Capital, $2,000. October 14, 1892.	Said corporation is formed for the purpose of transporting merchandise, or articles of whatsoever nature, passengers, or United States mails, either by land or water.	Pittsburgh.

Company	Purpose	Location
The Westinghouse Electric Light, Heat and Power Company of York, Pa. Capital, $50,000. October 14, 1892.	Said corporation is formed for the purpose of supplying light, heat or power, or any of them, by means of electricity, to the public in the city of York, and to such persons and partnerships residing therein or adjacent thereto, as may desire the same.	York.
The West Penn Coal and Coke Company. Capital, $25,000. October 14, 1892.	Said corporation is formed for the purpose of mining and selling coal, and manufacturing and selling coke and other products of coal.	Pittsburgh.
The Philip Frank Malting Company. Capital, $50,000. October 17, 1892.	Said corporation is formed for the purpose of manufacturing of malt.	Mount Joy.
Frank-Kneeland Machine Company. Capital, $150,000. October 17, 1892.	Said corporation is formed for the purpose of manufacture of iron or steel, or both, or of any other metal or article of commerce from metal, wood, or both.	Pittsburgh.
The Vulcan Works. Capital, $50,000. October 17, 1892.	Said corporation is formed for the purpose of the manufacture of iron or steel, or both, or of any other metal, or of any article of commerce from metal or wood, or both.	South Chester.
The Freemansburg Building and Loan Association. Re-charter. Capital, $1,000,000. October 20, 1892.	Said corporation is formed for the purpose of accumulating a fund by the periodical contributions of the members thereof, and of safely investing the same.	Freemansburg.
Bell Coal Company. Capital, $1,000. October 20, 1892.	Said corporation is formed for the purpose of mining, manufacturing and marketing of coal, coke and other minerals, and of the products thereof.	Greensburg.
Shenango Glass Company. Capital, $100,000. October 20, 1892.	Said corporation is formed for the purpose of the manufacture of window glass.	Newcastle.

LIST OF CHARTERS AND CORPORATIONS—*Continued.*

STYLE AND TITLE OF CORPORATIONS.	PURPOSE.	LOCATION.
The Tionesta Water Supply Company. Capital, $5,000. October 24, 1892.	Said corporation is formed for the purpose of supplying water to the public in the borough of Tionesta, Pennsylvania, and to such persons and corporations residing therein or adjacent thereto, as may desire the same.	Tionesta.
York Mutual Building and Loan Association. Capital, $375,000. October 24, 1892.	Said corporation is formed for the purpose of accumulating a fund by the periodical contributions of the members thereof, and of safely investing the same.	York.
The Hyndman Electric Light, Heat and Power Company. Capital, $15,000. October 25, 1892.	Said corporation is formed for the purpose of supplying light, heat and power, or any of them by means of electricity to the public in the borough of Hyndman, Bedford county, State of Pennsylvania, and to such persons, partnerships and associations residing therein and adjacent thereto, as may desire the same.	Hyndman.
The Workingmen's Land Company. Capital $25,000. October 25, 1892.	Said corporation is formed for the purpose of purchasing, improving, holding and enjoying real estate in fee simple, upon ground rent or lease, and for leasing, mortgaging and selling the same in such parts and parcels and on such terms as to payments as may be agreed upon.	Allegheny.
The Keystone Fuel Gas Company of Williamsport, Pa. Capital, $100,000. October 25, 1892.	Said corporation is formed for the purpose of supplying heat by means of manufactured gas in the city of Williamsport, and to such persons, partnerships and corporations residing therein or adjacent thereto desiring the same.	Williamsport.
South McKeesport Land Company. Capital, $35,000. October 25, 1892.	Said corporation is formed for the purpose of the purchase and sale of real estate, or for holding, leasing and selling real estate, for maintaining or erecting walls or banks for the protection of low lying lands.	McKeesport.
The Lewistown Shirt Manufacturing Company. Capital, $10,000. October 25, 1892.	Said corporation is formed for the purpose of manufacture and sale of shirts, drawers, overalls, skirts and other articles of clothing.	Lewistown.

The Lashell Ferry Company. Capital, $500. October 28, 1892.	Said corporation is formed for the purpose of erecting, constructing and maintaining a ferry and approaches thereto over and across the Ohio river, from a point at or near Lashell landing on said river, in Moon township, in the county of Allegheny, to a point on the opposite side of said river at or near the foot of Chestnut In the borough of Sewickley, in said county of Allegheny. The location of said ferry being more than three thousand feet from any other incorporated bridge or ferry over said stream.	Coraopolis.
Round Island Bridge Company. Capital, $2,500. October 26, 1892.	Said corporation is formed for the purpose of erecting, constructing and maintaining a bridge and the approaches thereto over the Sinnemahoning creek at Round Island, Cl......nty, Pa, to a point on the opposite side of said creek in the county of Clinton and State of Pennsylvania. The location of said bridge being at least nine miles from any other incorporated bridge or ferry over said stream.	Round Island
Stewartstown Building and Loan Association. Capital, $250,000. October 26, 1892.	Said corporation is formed for the purpose of conducting the business of a building and loan association, under the provisions of the act of assembly, approved April 29, A. D. 1874, and act of assembly of April 10, A. D. 1879, together with the powers and privileges usually and lawfully belonging to such corporations, and for these purposes to have, possess and enjoy all the rights, benefits and privileges under said acts of assembly and the several supplements thereto.	Stewartstown.
Tacony Saving Fund Safe Deposit Title and Trust Company. Capital, $150,000. October 27, 1892.	Said ...ation is ...d ...r the ... ...e of ... ...s of ... by mortgagees ... ...d in ... ... in ... by ... of def... ... ...s, to ... in ...e ...s of ... ...n, ... or ...r obli... ...n of any ... ...n, municipality, or ... , or ... ... by ... agreed ...g by ... ...d ... ...r on ... ...s granted to ...p, and to enjoy all ...e i ...s, p rivileges ...d ...e granted to ... ...e un ... ...r the ...st of 29th ...il, A. D. 1874, ...d ...e ev... ...s theeto.	Philadelphia.
The United Anthracite Collieries Company of Pennsylvania. Capital, $10,000. October 27, 1892.	Said corporation is formed for the purpose of mining, quarrying and preparing coal and transporting the same to market in crude or manufactured form.	Philadelphia.
Crouch Brothers Company. Capital, $100,000. October 27, 1892.	Said corporation is formed for the purpose of the manufacture and sale of flour and feed.	Erie.

LIST OF CHARTERS OF CORPORATIONS—*Continued.*

TITLE AND TITLE OF CORPORATION.	PURPOSE.	LOCATION.
The American Wire Glass Manufacturing Company. Capital, $100,000. October 27, 1892.	Said corporation is formed for the purpose of manufacturing wire glass and selling the same.	Philadelphia.
Beaver Falls Hotel Company. Capital, $35,000. October 28, 1892.	Said corporation is formed for the purpose of establishing and maintaining a hotel in the borough of Beaver Falls, Beaver county, Pa.	Beaver Falls.
The Ferrous Chemical Company. Capital, $30,000. October 28, 1892.	Said corporation is formed for the purpose of manufacturing and selling chemicals and acids.	Pittsburgh.
The Schnader Nagle Company. Capital, $50,000. October 31, 1892.	Said corporation is formed for the purpose of manufacturing tinware, tinners supplies, sheet iron ware, house furnishing goods, stoves, stove fixtures and appliances, tin plates, or any article of commerce from tin, sheet iron, other metals or wood.	Reading.
Allegheny and Esplen Bridge Company. Capital, $1,200. October 31, 1892.	Said ... ation is ... a bridge ... on a point in ... at or ... Pittsburgh ... in ... city of Allegheny, ... (60) feet ... mpany over ... in ny other ...	Pittsburgh.
Delta Hedge and Wire Fence Company. Capital, $18,000. October 31, 1892.	Said corporation is formed for the purpose of manufacturing hedge and wire fences.	Delta.
Hanover Match Company. Capital, $50,000. October 31, 1892.	Said corporation is formed for the purpose of the manufacture and sale of friction matches for igniting purposes.	Hanover.

The Catholic Times Publishing Company. Capital, $10,000. October 31, 1892.	Said corporation is formed for the purpose of the transaction of a printing and publishing business.	Philadelphia.
The Improved Building and Loan Association of 28th Ward, Pittsburgh. Capital, $1,000,000. October 31, 1892.	Said corporation is formed for the purpose of accumulating a fund by the periodical contributions of the members thereof, and of safely investing the same.	Pittsburgh.
The Armstrong Opera House Company. Capital, $25,000. November 1, 1892.	Said corporation is formed for the purpose of the maintenance and establishment of an opera house in the borough of Johnsonburg, Pa.	Johnsonburg.
Legnard Manufacturing Company. Capital, $3,000. November 4, 1892.	Said corporation is formed for the purpose of manufacturing commercial cleaning and washing compounds.	Pittsburgh.
People's Bank of Hanover. Capital, $50,000. November 7, 1892.	For the purpose of carrying on the business of banking and the regulation of discounts and deposits, etc.	Hanover.
The Real Estate and Improvement Company of Lancaster, Penna. Capital, $100,000. November 7, 1892.	Said corporation is formed for the purpose of purchasing, taking, holding and enjoying real estate in fee simple, on lease, or upon ground rent; to improve, lease, mortgage and sell the same in such parts and parcels and on such terms as to time of payment as may be determined, and to convey the same to the purchaser in fee simple or for any less estate, or upon ground rents, and in like manner to mortgage, sell, convey, or extinguish any ground rent reserved out of real estate so sold.	Lancaster.
Providence Gas Company. Capital, $1,000. November 7, 1892.	Said corporation is formed for the purpose of manufacturing and supplying gas to the public in the borough of Media and the townships of Nether Providence, Upper Providence, Middletown and Springfield, in Delaware county, Pennsylvania, and to such persons, partnerships and association residing therein and adjacent thereto, as may desire the same.	Chester.

a9 LAWS.

LIST OF CHARTERS OF CORPORATIONS—Continued.

STYLE AND TITLE OF CORPORATION.	PURPOSE.	LOCATION.
South West Fuel Gas Company. Capital, $5,000. November 7, 1892	Said corporation is formed for the purpose of the manufacture and supply of gas for heat and power to the public, in the borough of Connellsville, county of Fayette, and to such persons, partnerships and corporations residing therein or adjacent thereto, as may desire the same, at such prices as may be agreed upon.	Pittsburgh.
Self-Bosworth and Creighton Company. Capital, $30,000. November 10, 1892	Said corporation is formed for the purpose of manufacturing cigars and stogies from tobacco, and for that purpose to have and possess the powers and privileges expressed and given in said act of assembly and the supplements thereto.	Allegheny.
The Moosic Mountain Water Company. Capital, $10,000. November 10, 1892	Said corporation is formed for the purpose of supplying water for the public at the village of Jessup, borough of Winton, Lackawanna county, Pa., and to persons, partnerships and associations residing therein and adjacent thereto, as may desire the same.	Scranton.
The Casey and Kelly Brewing Company. Capital, $100,000. November 10, 1892	Said corporation is formed for the purpose of manufacturing and brewing ale.	Scranton.
Pittsburgh Typewriter Company. Capital, $1,500. November 10, 1892	Said ... is formed for the purpose of the manufacture of iron or steel, or ... or of any other metal, or of any article of commerce from ... or ... or both.	Pittsburgh.
The Citizens' Building and Savings Association of the city of Reading. Capital, $500,000. November 10, 1892	Said corporation is formed for the purpose of accumulating a fund by the periodical contributions of the members thereof, and of safely investing the same.	Reading.
The People's Mutual Savings Fund and Loan Association of Scottdale. Capital, $1,000,000. November 11, 1892	Said corporation is formed for the purpose of accumulating a fund by the periodical contributions of the members thereof, and of safely investing the same.	Scottdale.

Advance Building and Loan Association of Pittsburgh. Capital, $1,000,000. November 11, 1892.	Said corporation is formed for the purpose of accumulating a fund by the periodical contributions of the members thereof, and of safely investing the same.	Pittsburgh.
Riverside Land Company. Capital, $50,000. November 11, 1892.	Said corporation is formed for the purpose of buying, selling, holding and leasing real estate.	Pittsburgh.
The Patrons' National Savings and Loan Association. Capital, $1,000,000. November 14, 1892.	Said corporation is formed for the purpose of accumulating a fund by the periodical contributions of the members thereof, and of safely investing the same.	Greensburg.
The Rochester Glass Sign and Novelty Company. Capital, $3,000. November 14, 1892.	Said corporation is formed for the purpose of manufacturing glass signs and glass novelties.	Rochester.
The Joseph Kohnle Brewing Company. Capital, $100,000. November 14, 1892.	Said corporation is formed for the purpose of manufacturing and selling malt and malt liquors.	Philadelphia.
The Pocono Mountain Ice Company. Capital, $50,000. November 14, 1892.	Said corporation is formed for the purpose of manufacturing ice and carrying on the mechanical business of gathering the same.	Tobyhanna Mills.
The Lake Transit Company. Capital, $3,000. November 14, 1892.	Said corporation is formed for the purpose of the building of steamboats, and the carriage of persons and property thereon.	Wilkes-Barre.
Augusta Hotel Company. Capital, $50,000. November 14, 1892.	Said corporation is formed for the purpose of the establishment and maintenance of an hotel in Philadelphia, Pennsylvania.	Philadelphia.
The Mine Hill Coal Company. Capital, $75,000. November 15, 1892.	Said corporation is formed for the purpose of mining, quarrying and preparing anthracite coal for market in crude or manufactured form.	Scranton.

LIST OF CHARTERS OF CORPORATIONS—*Continued.*

STYLE AND TITLE OF CORPORATION.	PURPOSE.	LOCATION.
South View Land Improvement Company. Capital, $4,000. November 15, 1892	Said corporation is formed for the purpose of purchasing, improving, holding and enjoying real estate in fee simple, upon ground rent or lease, and to lease, mortgage and sell the same in such parts and parcels, improved or unimproved, on such terms as to time and manner of payment as may be agreed upon.	Pittsburgh.
Freehold Land Improvement Company. Capital, $10,000. November 15, 1892	Said corporation is formed for the purpose of purchasing, improving, holding and enjoying real estate in fee simple, upon ground rent or lease, and to lease, mortgage and sell the same in such parts and parcels, improved or unimproved, on such terms as to time and manner of payment as may be agreed upon.	Pittsburgh.
The Chartiers Creek Coal Company. Capital, $20,000. November 18, 1892	Said corporation is formed for the purpose of mining coal.	Pittsburgh.
The Citizens' Water Company of Pittsburgh. Capital, $50,000. November 18, 1892	Said corporation is formed for the purpose of supplying water for the public in that portion of the city of Pittsburgh, lying south of the Monongahela and Ohio rivers, and to persons, partnerships and associations residing therein and adjacent thereto, as may desire the same.	Pittsburgh.
The Hamilton Company. Capital, $1,000. November 21, 1892	Said corporation is formed for the purpose of purchasing and selling real estate.	Pittsburgh.
The F. Gutekunst Company. Capital, $100,000. November 21, 1892	Said corporation is formed for the purpose of manufacturing and vending of photographs of all kinds, photolypes, photogravures, picture prints, etchings, engravings, lithographs, picture frames and mats and similar products.	Philadelphia.
The Favorite Building and Loan Association of Allegheny, Pa. Capital, $500,000. November 21, 1892	Said corporation is formed for the purpose of accumulating a fund by the periodical contributions of the members thereof, and of safely investing the same.	Allegheny.

The Bushnell Manufacturing Company. Capital, $60,000. November 22, 1892.	Said corporation is formed for the purpose of manufacturing spiral springs, car seats, car berths, car chairs, spring beds and all articles of commerce from metal or wood, or both.	Easton.
Cleona Creamery Company. Capital, $5,000. November 22, 1892.	Said corporation is formed for the purpose of manufacturing butter, cheese, ice cream and other products of milk.	Cleona.
Point Township Grange Hall Association. Capital, $2,000. November 23, 1892.	Said corporation is formed for the purpose of the erection and maintenance of a boarding house, opera & market house.	Northumberland.
Columbia Electric Light Company. Capital, $100,000. November 23, 1892.	Said corporation is formed for the purpose of supplying light and power by means of electricity in the city of Philadelphia, State of Pennsylvania.	Philadelphia.
The Throop Water Company. Capital, $5,000. November 25, 1892.	Said corporation is formed for the purpose of supplying water for the public in the borough of Dickson City, county of Lackawanna, Pennsylvania, and to persons, partnerships, associations and corporations residing therein and adjacent thereto, as may desire the same.	Dickson City.
North Avenue Stair Company. Capital, $14,000. November 25, 1892.	Said corporation is formed for the purpose of manufacturing stair and mantles and hardwood store and office fixture.	Allegheny.
The Ridgway Manufacturing Company. Capital, $60,000. November 25, 1892.	Said corporation is formed for the purpose of the manufacture of iron or steel, or both, or of any other metal, or article of commerce from metal, wood, or both.	Ridgway.
Provident Building and Loan Association of Huntingdon, Pa. Capital, $1,000,000. November 25, 1892.	Said corporation is formed for the purpose of accumulating a fund by the periodical contributions of the members thereof, and of safely investing the same.	Huntingdon.
The Standard Combination Tie Plate and Brace Company. Capital, $10,000. November 28, 1892.	Said corporation is formed for the purpose of the manufacture of iron or steel, or both, or of any other metal, or of any article of commerce from metal or wood, or both, and for that purpose to have and possess the powers and privileges expressed and given in the 38th section of the corporation act of 1874, and the supplements thereto.	Philadelphia.

LIST OF CHARTERS OF CORPORATIONS—*Continued.*

Style and Title of Corporation.	Purpose.	Location.
The Economy Land Company. Capital, $5,000. November 28, 1892.	Said corporation is formed for the purpose of buying, holding, selling, leasing and improving real estate.	Pittsburgh.
Ellwood Gas Stove and Stamping Company. Capital, $5,000. November 28, 1892.	Said corporation is formed for the purpose of the manufacture of iron or steel, or both, or of any other metal, or of any article of commerce from me al or wood, or both.	Ellwood City.
Keasbey & Mattison Company. Capital, $2,000,000. November 28, 1892.	Said oration is formed for the purpose of manufacturing and selling al, pharmaceutical, chemical and technical preparations and compounds.	Ambler.
The Frink and Barcus Manufacturing Company. Capital, $20,000. November 28, 1892.	Said ation is formed for the purpose of manufacturing and selling dy, harness and leather specialties.	Philadelphia.
The Everett Light, Heat and Power Company. Capital, $15,000. November 28, 1892.	Said corporation is formed for the purpose of supplying light, heat and power at the borough of Everett, in the county of Bedford, and State of Pennsylvania, to such persons, partnerships and corporations residing therein and adjacent thereto.	Everett.
Thurlow Cotton Manufacturing Company. Capital, $50,000. November 28, 1892.	Said corporation is formed for the purpose of manufacturing cotton and woolen yarns and textile fabrics by spinning and weaving and selling the product.	Thurlow.
The Patton Coal Company. Capital, $1,000. December 1, 1892.	Said corporation is formed for the purpose of mining, quarrying and otherwise producing coal, preparing the same for market in crude or manufactured form, and of acquiring, possessing and enjoying all the rights, powers, privileges and immunifies conferred by the said act of the 29th day of April, Anno Domini 1874, and the several supplements thereto, upon corporations mentioned in the eighteenth clause of the second section of the said act,	Philadelphia.

Corporation	Purpose	Location
The Croscent Land and Improvement Company. Capital, $8,000. December 1, 1892.	Said corporation is formed for the purpose of the purchase and sale of real estate, and for holding, leasing and selling real estate, as well as improving the same.	Pittsburgh.
The Times Publishing Company of Williamsport. Capital, $25,000. December 1, 1892.	Said corporation is formed for the purpose of transacting a printing and publishing business.	Williamsport.
Fort Pitt Land Company. Capital, $10,000. December 1, 1892.	Said ... in is formed for the purpose of holding, leasing and selling al de.	Allegheny.
Specialty Manufacturing Company. Capital, $25,000. December 1, 1892.	Said ... ation is formed for the purpose of engaging in the manufac... te in ... ed or metal, or both, of any article of commerce.	Titusville.
The Allegheny Foundry Company. Capital, $20,000. December 2, 1892.	Said ... in is formed for the purpose of the manufacture of iron or tel, or both, or of any other metal, or of any article of commerce from al or ... l, or both.	Allegheny.
Montello Clay and Brick Company. Capital, $100,000. December 5, 1892.	Said corporation is formed for the purpose of the manufacture and sale of bricks of all kinds, clay, tilling, terra cotta and other articles of commerce made in whole or part of clay.	Montello.
The Washed Bar Sand Dredging Company. Capital, $25,000. December 5, 1892.	Said corporation is formed for the purpose of mining sand by dredging, washing and separating river sand for building purposes.	Philadelphia.
Welde and Thomas Brewing Company. Capital, $400,000. December 5, 1892.	Said corporation is formed for the purpose of manufacturing and brewing malt liquors.	Philadelphia.
The Keystone Building and Loan Association of the 26th Ward, Pittsburgh, Pa. Capital, $1,000,000. December 5, 1892.	Said corporation is formed for the purpose of accumulating a fund by the periodical contributions of the members thereof, and of safely investing the same.	Pittsburgh.

LIST OF CHARTERS OF CORPORATIONS—*Continued.*

STYLE AND TITLE OF CORPORATION.	PURPOSE.	LOCATION.
The Steuben Building and Loan Association No. 2, of Pittsburgh. Capital, $300,000. December 5, 1892	Said corporation is formed for the purpose of accumulating a fund by the periodical contributions of the members thereof, and of safely investing the same.	Pittsburgh.
West End Electric Company. Capital, $5,000. December 7, 1892	Said corporation is formed for the purpose of manufacturing electricity for light, heat and power, and supplying the same to the public at that portion of the city of Pittsburgh lying south of the Ohio and Monongahela rivers and west of the Pittsburgh & Castle Shannon Incline to persons, partnerships and rations residing therein and adjacent thereto, as may desire the same.	Pittsburgh.
The Munger Manufacturing Company. Capital, $1,500. December 7, 1892	Said corporation is formed for the purpose of the manufacture of metals into a badge known as Munger's World's Fair Souvenir Badge (being a badge patented by W. B. Munger, September 6, 1892), and for the general manufacture of articles of commerce from metals, wood or both.	Harrisburg.
The Ringgold Building and Savings Association No. 3. Capital, $1,000,000. December 8, 1892	Said corporation is formed for the purpose of accumulating a fund by the periodical contributions of the members thereof, and of safely investing the same.	Reading.
The Gravel Run Water Company. Capital, $5,000. December 8, 1892	Said corporation is formed for the purpose of supplying water to the public in the township of Hazle, Luzerne county, Pennsylvania, and to such persons, corporations, partnerships and associations residing therein and in the vicinity, as may desire the same.	Philadelphia.
The Milnesville Water Company. Capital, $2,500. December 8, 1892	Said corporation is formed for the purpose of the supply of water to the public at the village of Milnesville, in the township of Hazle, Luzerne county, Pa., and to persons, partnerships and associations residing therein and adjacent thereto, as may desire the same.	Hazleton.

Company	Purpose	Location
The Ambler Electric Light, Heat and Motor Company. Capital, $15,000. December 8, 1892.	Said corporation is formed for the purpose of manufacturing and supplying light, heat and power by means of electricity to the public of the borough of Ambler, county of Montgomery, and to such persons, partnerships and associations residing therein and adjacent thereto, as may desire the same.	Ambler.
The Bower Slate and Pencil Quarry Company. Capital, $125,000. December 9, 1892.	Said corporation is formed for the purpose of quarrying slate and manufacturing slate products.	Lynnport.
The Manufacturers' Water Company of Bloomsburg, Penna. Capital, $1,000. December 9, 1892.	Said corporation is formed for the purpose of supplying water to the public in the town of Bloomsburg, Columbia county, Pennsylvania, and to persons, associations, partnerships and corporations residing therein and adjacent thereto, as may desire the same.	Bloomsburg.
The Boyertown Light, Heat and Power Company. Capital, $1,000. December 9, 1892.	Said corporation is formed for the purpose of supplying light, heat or power or any of them, by means of electricity, to the public in the borough of Boyertown, Berks county, Pennsylvania, and to such persons, and partnerships residing therein and adjacent thereto, as may desire the same.	Boyertown.
The H. F. Watson Building and Loan Association. Capital, $1,000,000. December 12, 1892.	Said corporation is formed for the purpose of accumulating a fund by the periodical contributions of the members thereof, and of safely investing the same.	Erie.
The Luzerne Heat and Power Company. Capital, $2,000. December 12, 1892.	Said corporation is formed for the purpose of supplying heat or power by means of steam to the public in the borough of Luzerne, Luzerne county, Pennsylvania, and to such persons, partnerships, associations and corporations residing therein or adjacent thereto, as may desire the same.	Luzerne borough.
The Bellevue Creamery Company. Capital, $1,000. December 12, 1892.	Said corporation is formed for the purpose of the manufacture and sale of butter, cheese, ice cream and other creamery products.	Mickleys
The Sherwood Brothers Company. Capital, $100,000. December 12, 1892.	Said corporation is formed for the purpose of manufacturing earthenware, stone and terra-cotta ware and mining and selling fire-clays and other clays.	New Brighton.
Columbian Brick Company. Capital, $15,000. December 12, 1892.	Said corporation is formed for the purpose of manufacturing and selling brick, tile, sewer pipe and other similar articles.	Connellsville.

LIST OF CHARTERS OF CORPORATIONS—*Continued.*

STYLE AND TITLE OF CORPORATION.	PURPOSE.	LOCATION.
Norristown Furnace Company. Capital, $50,000. December 12, 1892.	Said corporation is formed for the purpose of the manufacture of iron or steel, or both, or of any other metal, or of any article of commerce from metal.	Philadelphia.
The Leon C. Magaw Cheese Company. Capital, $15,000. December 12, 1892.	Said corporation is formed for the purpose of manufacturing all kinds of cheese and butter from milk and the products thereof.	Meadville.
Bradford Woodenware and Enameling Company. Capital, $20,000. December 13, 1892.	Said corporation is formed for the purpose of the manufacture and sale of wares from wood and metals and combinations thereof, plain and enameled.	Bradford.
The Wilmore Coal Company. Capital, $360,000. December 14, 1892.	Said corporation is formed for the purpose of mining coal, manufacturing coke, producing and manufacturing minerals, and for these purposes to have and enjoy all the rights and privileges which are conferred by the thirty-ninth section of the act known and cited as "The Corporation Act of 1874."	Wilkes-Barre.
The Keystone Traction Device Company. Capital, $6,000. December 14, 1892.	Said corporation is formed for the purpose of creating, purchasing, holding and selling of patent rights for inventions and designs, with the right to issue license for the same and receive pay therefor, and particularly as to certain inventions in improvements in traction devices for canals and navigable water ways.	Scranton.
Hamilton Watch Company. Capital, $350,000. December 14, 1892.	Said corporation is formed for the purpose of the manufacture and sale of watches and watch movements and materials, and everything pertaining to watches from steel, brass, nickel and other metals.	Lancaster.
The Philadelphia Decorative Glass Company. Capital, $3,000. December 14, 1892.	Said corporation is formed for the purpose of carrying on the business of manufacturing and decorating glass and glassware by mechanical or chemical processes or both.	Philadelphia.

Company	Purpose	Location
The Dravosburg Light, Heat and Power Company. Capital, $20,000. December 15, 1892.	Said corporation is formed for the purpose of the manufacture and supply of light, heat and power by means of electricity in Dravosburg, Allegheny county, Pennsylvania.	Dravosburg.
The Edgerton Coal Company. Capital, $20,000. December 15, 1892.	Said corporation is formed for the purpose of mining, preparing for market and selling anthracite coal.	Scranton.
South Harrisburg Chain Works. Capital, $15,000. December 15, 1892.	Said corporation is formed for the purpose of the manufacture of chain or of any other article of commerce from metal, wood or both.	Harrisburg.
The Summit Coal company. Capital, $15,000. December 15, 1892.	Said corporation is formed for the purpose of mining, preparing for market and selling anthracite coal.	Scranton.
Sherman Manufacturing Company. Capital, $50,000. December 15, 1892.	The purpose of said corporation is to manufacture articles of commerce from wood or metal, or both, as provided in clause seventeen of the second class, in section two of the Corporation Act of 1874, and therewith to have the power and privileges conferred by the thirty-eighth section of said act.	Sherman.
Ellwood Electric Light Company. Capital, $1,000. December 16, 1892.	Said corporation is formed for the purpose of supplying light, heat and power by electricity, to the public at Ellwood City, Lawrence county, Pennsylvania, and to such persons, partnerships, corporations and associations residing therein or adjacent thereto, as may desire the same.	Ellwood.
The Home Building and Loan Association of Marietta, Pennsylvania. Capital, $500,000. December 19, 1892.	Said corporation is formed for the purpose of accumulating a fund by the periodical contributions of the members thereof, and of safely investing the same.	Marietta.
The Albro-Clem Elevator Company. Capital, $100,000. December 20, 1892.	Said corporation is formed for the purpose of manufacturing, erecting and selling elevators and hoisting machinery.	Philadelphia.
Lebanon Ice Manufacturing Company. Capital, $50,000. December 20, 1892.	Said corporation is formed for the purpose of manufacturing ice.	Lebanon.

LIST OF CHARTERS OF CORPORATIONS—Continued.

STYLE AND TITLE OF CORPORATION.	PURPOSE.	LOCATION.
Hazle Water Company. Capital, $5,000. December 20, 1892.	Said corporation is formed for the purpose of supplying water to the public in the township of Lehigh, Carbon county, and to persons, partnerships and associations residing therein and adjacent thereto.	Mauch Chunk.
The James Caven Company. Capital, $100,000. December 21, 1892.	Said corporation is formed for the purpose of manufacturing shade and rug fringes and textile fabrics.	Philadelphia.
The J. S. Thorn Company. Capital, $100,000. December 21, 1892.	Said corporation is formed for the purpose of the manufacture of articles of commerce from iron or steel, or other metal or wood, or both.	Philadelphia.
Model Heating Company. Capital, $100,000. December 21, 1892.	Said corporation is formed for the purpose of the manufacture and sale of iron or steel, or both, or of any other metal, or of any article of commerce from metal or wood, or both.	Philadelphia.
The Nations Mower and Reaper Company. Capital, $500,000. December 22, 1892.	Said corporation is formed for the purpose of the manufacture of iron or steel, or both, or of any other metal or article of commerce from metal, wood, or both.	Pittsburgh.
McKee and Bros., Incorporated. Capital, $5,000. December 22, 1892.	Said corporation is formed for the purpose of manufacturing glass and glassware.	Pittsburgh.
The Collingdale Water Company. Capital, $1,000. December 22, 1892.	Said corporation is formed for the purpose of supplying water to the public in the borough of Collingdale, in the county of Delaware, and State of Pennsylvania, and to such persons, partnerships and corporations residing therein and adjacent thereto, as may desire the same.	Media.
The Eddystone Water Company. Capital, $1,000. December 22, 1892.	Said corporation is formed for the purpose of supplying water to the public in the borough of Eddystone, in the county of Delaware, and State of Pennsylvania, and to such persons, partnerships and corporations residing therein and adjacent thereto, who may desire the same.	Media.

Company	Purpose	Location
The Grampian Land Company. Capital, $40,000. December 23, 1892.	Said corporation is formed for the purpose of purchasing and selling real estate in the township of Loyal Sock, in the county of Lycoming, and State of Pennsylvania, and holding and leasing the same.	Williamsport.
The Standard Coal Company. Capital, $300,000. December 23, 1892.	Said corporation is formed for the purpose of mining coal and manufacturing coke therefrom and transporting the same to market in crude or manufactured form.	Pittsburgh.
The Cramer Coal Coke and Stone Company. Capital, $100,000. December 23, 1892.	Said corporation is formed for the purpose of conducting the business of mining coal, manufacturing coke therefrom and quarrying stone and transporting the same in crude or manufactured form.	Cramer.
Ruhe Bros. Company. Capital, $50,000. December 23, 1892.	Said corporation is formed for the purpose of the manufacture and sale of cigars, or of any other article of commerce made either in whole or in part from tobacco.	Allentown.
The Pittsburgh Gauge Company. Capital, $50,000. December 23, 1892.	Said corporation is formed for the purpose of the manufacture of iron or steel, or both, or of any other metal, or of any article of commerce, from metal or wool, or both.	Pittsburgh.
Ingleside Water Company. Capital, $2,000. December 23, 1892.	Said corporation is formed for the purpose of supplying water for the public at the township of Allegheny, Westmoreland county, Pennsylvania, and to persons, partnerships and associations residing therein and adjacent thereto, as may desire the same	Ingleside.
The Minerva Land and Improvement Company. Capital, $10,000. December 23, 1892.	Said corporation is formed for the purpose of purchasing, taking, holding, leasing and enjoying real estate, in fee simple, or on any less estate, improving and selling the same in fee simple, or for any less estate, or upon ground rent to its shareholders and others on such terms as to time of payment as it may determine.	California.
Sellersville Building Company. Capital, $6,000. December 23, 1892.	Said corporation is formed for the purpose of the purchasing, owning, selling, renting, leasing and improving real estate.	Sellersville.
The Bramcote Manufacturing Company. Capital, $25,000. December 27, 1892.	Said corporation is formed for the purpose of mining and quarrying coal, iron ore, iron oxides, mineral paint, fire clay, sandstone, and such other substances and minerals as may in the prosecution of its business be found in and on any lands leased or otherwise acquired by it, and the manufacture and sale of said products, and transportation of the same to market in crude or manufactured form.	Pottstown.

LIST OF CHARTERS OF CORPORATIONS—*Continued.*

STYLE AND TITLE OF CORPORATION.	PURPOSE.	LOCATION.
Central Ice Company. Capital, $50,000. December 27, 1892	Said corporation is formed for the purpose of manufacturing and selling artificial ice.	Philadelphia.
The Philadelphia Printing and Publishing Company. Capital, $5,000. December 27, 1892	Said corporation is formed for the purpose of the transaction of a printing and publishing business.	Philadelphia.
R. A. Crawford Manufacturing Company. Capital, $10,000. December 27, 1892	Said corporation is formed for the purpose of manufacturing and selling Crawford's Patent Automatic Wheel and Pick-up Guards for cars.	Pittsburgh.
Home Building & Loan Association of the 32nd Ward, Pittsburg, Pa. Capital, $500,000. December 27, 1892	Said corporation is formed for the purpose of accumulating a fund by the periodical contributions of the members thereof, and of safely investing the same.	Pittsburg.
The Pennsylvania Bottling and Supply Company of Philadelphia. Capital, $100,000. December 28, 1892	Said corporation is formed for the purpose of manufacturing preserves, fruit syrups and condiments, and in connection therewith, of carrying on the mechanical business of bottling mineral waters, in which said syrups are to be used, as well also of conducting a general bottling business.	Philadelphia.
East Bangor Manufacturing Company. Capital, $10,000. December 28, 1892	Said corporation is formed for the purpose of manufacturing machinery, fences, or any article of commerce from metal, wood, or both.	East Bangor.
The Columbia Land and Improvement Company. Capital, $30,000. December 28, 1892.	Said corporation is formed for the purpose of purchasing, improving, holding, leasing and selling of real estate.	Columbia.

The Columbia Powder Company. Capital, $8,000. December 29, 1892.	Said corporation is formed for the purpose of manufacturing and selling black powder, nitro-glycerine, dynamite and all other high explosives.	Pittsburgh.
The Nay Aug Falls and Elmhurst Boulevard Company. Capital, $25,000. December 29, 1892.	Said corporation is formed for the purpose of building & maintaining an artificial road or turnpike of stone, gravel and earth, from a point at or near Arthur avenue and Mullberry street, in the city of Scranton, in the county of Lackawanna, to a point at or near Spring lane, in the Schoonmaker plot, in the borough of Elmhurst, in the county of Lackawanna, a distance of seven miles, all of said road being located in the county of Lackawanna.	Scranton
Beaver Falls Trunk Company. Capital, $20,000. December 29, 1892.	Said corporation is formed for the purpose of manufacturing trunks, valises, traveling bags and leather goods.	Beaver Falls.
The Columbia Building Association. Capital, $750,000. December 29, 1892.	Said corporation is formed for the purpose of accumulating a fund by the periodical contributions of the members thereof, and of safely investing the same.	Columbia.
East Columbia Land Company. Capital, $50,000. December 29, 1892.	Said corporation is formed for the purpose of the purchase and improvement, holding, leasing and sale of real estate.	Columbia.
The West Chester Knitting Company. Capital, $25,000. December 29, 1892.	Said corporation is formed for the purpose of manufacturing, selling and disposing of all kinds of knit goods, and for the leasing and purchasing of such buildings and real estate as may be necessary for conducting and carrying on said business.	West Chester.
Pittsburgh Barrow and Forge Company. Capital, $10,000. December 29, 1892.	Said corporation is formed for the purpose of manufacturing wheel barrows, portable forges and all articles manufactured, made or produced by any process from iron and steel, or either of them either in whole or in part.	Pittsburgh.
Standard Water Company of Crafton, Pa. Capital, $500. December 29, 1892.	Said corporation is formed for the purpose of supplying water for the public at the borough of Crafton, Allegheny county, Pennsylvania, and to persons, partnerships and associations residing therein and adjacent thereto, as may desire the same.	Crafton.
Crescent Water Company of Chartiers Township. Capital, $500. December 29, 1892.	Said corporation is formed for the purpose of supplying water for the public at the township of Chartiers, Allegheny county, Pennsylvania, and to persons, partnerships and associations residing therein and adjacent thereto, as may desire the same.	Crafton.

LIST OF CHARTERS OF CORPORATIONS—Continued.

STYLE AND TITLE OF CORPORATION.	PURPOSE.	LOCATION.
Corry Radiator Company. Capital, $75,000. December 29, 1892.	Said corporation is formed for the purpose of the manufacturing of articles of commerce from metal and wood, especially the manufacture of radiators from metal.	Corry.
Standard Coal & Coke Co. Capital, $100,000. December 30, 1892.	Said corporation is formed for and otherwise producing coal, the manufacture of the coal found in or upon any lands acquired by the said company into coke, and the sale thereof in crude or manufactured form.	Williamsport.
Grand Rapids Mining Company. Capital, $5,000. December 30, 1892.	Said corporation is formed for the purpose of mining coal and preparing coal for market.	Wyoming.
Alexander McClure Company. Capital, $40,000. December 30, 1892.	Said corporation is formed for the purpose of manufacturing and selling lumber, barges, boats, boxes, and all articles of merchandise made from lumber or wood, and into which it enters in combination.	Pittsburgh.
Bridgewater Cordage Company. Capital, $250,000. December 30, 1892.	Said corporation is formed for the purpose of manufacturing all kinds of rope, twine, cordage and other articles made thereof, or of hemp, cotton, flax, jute, manilla and kindred materials or combinations thereof.	Philadelphia.
The Warren Extension Table Company. Capital, $20,000. December 30, 1892.	Said corporation is formed for the purpose of the manufacture of extension tables, and other articles of commerce, constructed of wood or metal, or both, and the sale of the same.	Warren.
The Tisdell Camera and Manufacturing Company. Capital, $10,000. December 30, 1892.	Said corporation is formed for the purpose of the manufacturing and selling cameras, stereopticons, lanterns, lantern-slides, views and other instruments and materials used in connection with the art of photography.	Scranton.
Universal Nut Lock Company. Capital, $10,000. December 30, 1892.	Said corporation is formed for the purpose of the manufacture and sale of nut locks and other hardware.	Allegheny.

Company	Purpose	Location
The Mechanics' Building and Loan Association of Lebanon, Pa. Capital, $1,000,000. December 30, 1892.	Said corporation is formed for the purpose of accumulating a fund by the periodical contributions of the members thereof, and of safely investing the same.	Lebanon.
The Gas Company of West Chester. Capital, $150,000. January 3, 1893.	Said corporation is formed for the purpose of manufacturing and supplying gas to the public in the borough of West Chester and townships of East Bradford and West Goshen, in Chester county, Pennsylvania.	West Chester.
The Juan F. Portuondo Cigar Manufacturing Company. Capital, $300,000. January 3, 1893.	Said corporation is formed for the business of manufacturing and selling the La Flor De Portuondo Cuban hand made cigars.	Philadelphia.
Pennsylvania Beef Company. Capital, $20,000. January 3, 1893.	Said corporation is formed for the purpose of doing a general storage business.	Ridgway.
National Mineral Table Water Company. Capital, $50,000. January 3, 1893.	Said corporation is formed for the purpose of producing natural mineral table waters, and marketing and supplying the same to the public.	Cambridge borough.
Brahma M... Capital, 2,800. January 3, 1893.	Said corporation is formed for the purpose of the manufacture and sale of medical preparations and compounds.	Pittsburgh.
Girardville Electric Company. Capital, $5,000. January 4, 1893.	Said corporation is formed for the purpose of manufacturing and supplying light, heat and power, or any of them, by means of electricity, to the public in Girardville, Pa., and to such persons and partnerships residing therein and adjacent thereto, as may desire the same.	Girardville.
The Wilkes-Barre Artificial Ice Company. Capital, $60,000. January 4, 1893.	Said corporation is formed for the purpose of the manufacture of ice and the sale and supply of the same to the public.	Wilkes-Barre.
The Susquehanna Water Company. Capital, $25,000. January 4, 1893.	Said co...lic in...on is formed for the purpose of supplying water for the public in...ip of Plains, Luzerne county, Pennsylvania, and persons, partnerships and associations residing therein and adjacent thereto, as may desire the same.	Plains.

LIST OF CHARTERS OF CORPORATIONS—*Continued.*

STYLE AND TITLE OF CORPORATION.	PURPOSE.	LOCATION.
German National Building and Loan Association of Pittsburgh, Pa. Capital, $1,000,000. January 5, 1893.	Said corporation is formed for the purpose of accumulating a fund by the periodical contributions of the members thereof, and of safely investing the same.	Pittsburgh.
Williamsport Upholstering Company. Capital, $25,000. January 5, 1893.	Said corporation is formed for the purpose of manufacturing and selling furniture of all kinds.	Williamsport.
Lebanon Water Co. Capital, $1,000. January 5, 1893.	Said corporation is formed for the purpose of supplying water to the public in the borough of Mansfield, county of Allegheny, and to such persons, partnerships and associations residing therein and adjacent thereto, as may desire the same.	Knoxville.
Putnam Water Co. Capital, $1,000. January 5, 1893.	Said corporation is formed for the purpose of supplying water to the public in the borough of Chartiers, in the county of Allegheny, and to persons, partnerships and associations residing therein and adjacent thereto, as may desire the same.	Knoxville.
Breisford Packing Company of Harrisburg. Capital, $165,000. January 5, 93.	Said corporation is formed for the purpose of manufacturing and preparing for market, and selling of hams, bacon, beef, lard and all other commercial products of hogs, sheep and cattle.	Harrisburg.
The Highland Water Company of West Newton, Pa. Capital, $10,000. January 6, 1893.	Said corporation is formed for the purpose of supplying water to the public at the borough of West Newton, Pennsylvania, and to persons, partnerships and associations residing therein and adjacent thereto.	Irwin.
The Girard Saving Fund and Loan Association of Girardville, Pa. Capital, $600,000. January 9, 1893.	Said corporation is formed for the purpose of accumulating a fund by the periodical contributions of the members thereof, and of safely investing the same.	Girardville.

Queen and Company, Incorporated. Capital, $400,0. January 9, 1893.	Said corporation is formed for the purpose of the manufacture and sale of optical, mathematical and scientific instruments and apparatus.	Philadelphia.
The Hunt & Cornell Company. Capital, $60,000. January 9, 1893.	Said corporation is formed for the purpose of manufacturing of brass, copper, tin and sheet-iron ware, miner's lamps, wrought-iron nipples, plumbing, gas fitting, steam and hot water heating apparatus, glass tube cutters and articles of commerce from metal, wood or glass, or of all or either.	Scranton.
The West Hazleton Water Company. Capital, $1,000. January 9, 1893.	Said corporation is formed for the purpose of supplying water for the public at the borough of West Hazleton, Pennsylvania, and to persons, partnerships and associations residing therein and adjacent thereto, as may desire the same.	Hazleton.
Williamsport Engineering Supply Company. Capital, $15,000. January 9, 1893.	Said corporation is formed for the purpose of the manufacture of iron or steel, or both, or of any other metal or article of commerce from metal, wood or both, in accordance with act of April 29, 1874, and its supplements thereto.	Williamsport.
"John Hancock Ice Company." Capital, $250,000. January 9, 1893.	Said corporation is formed for the purpose of supplying ice to the public.	Philadelphia.
"Railway Patents Company.' Capital, $300,000. January 9, 1893.	Said corporation is formed for the purpose of creating, purchasing, holding and selling patent rights for inventions and designs, and the purchasing of copy-rights for books, publications and registered trademarks, with the right to issue license for the same and receive pay therefor.	Philadelphia.
The Security Building and Loan Association of the City of Reading. Capital, $600,000. January 10, 1893.	Said corporation is formed for the purpose of accumulating a fund by the periodical contributions of the members thereof, and of safely investing the same.	Reading.
The Pittsburgh Gas and Electric Fixture Manufacturing Company. Capital, $10,000. January 10, 1893.	Said corporation is formed for the purpose of manufacturing gas, electric and combination chandeliers and fixtures from iron, steel, brass, aluminum or any other metal, or from a combination of any or all of said metals, or other metal whatsoever, and to sell such chandeliers, fixtures and manufactured products.	Pittsburgh.
The South Side Land Company. Capital, $120,000. January 1, 1893.	Said corporation is formed for the purpose of the purchase and sale of real estate, and for holding, leasing and selling real estate.	Easton.

LIST OF CHARTERS OF CORPORATIONS—*Continued.*

Style and Title of Corporation.	Purpose.	Location.
Washington Hotel Company. Capital, $25,000. January 12, 1893.	Said corporation is formed for the purpose of the establishment and maintenance of a hotel for the use of the public.	Philadelphia.
John Dunlap Company. Capital, $200,000. January 12, 1893.	Said corporation is formed for the purpose of the manufacture of tinware, stamped and Japaned tinware, tinners' supplies, and sheet metal goods.	Pittsburgh.
The Versailles Water Company. Capital, $5,000. January 12, 1893.	Said corporation is formed for the purpose of supplying water for the public at the township of Versailles, and to persons, partnerships and associations residing therein and adjacent thereto as may desire the same, which township is situate in Allegheny county, State of Pennsylvania.	McKeesport.
The American Incinerating Company. Capital, $10,000. January 13, 1893.	Said corporation is formed for the purpose of manufacturing fertilizers from garbage and other refuse matter by incineration and other methods.	Philadelphia.
McKean Chemical Company Capital, $80,000. January 13, 1893.	Said corporation is formed for the purpose of manufacturing from wood acetate of lime, wood alcohol and charcoal.	Williamsport.
Glenwood Paint Company. Capital, $10,000. January 13, 1893.	Said corporation is formed for the purpose of manufacturing all kinds of paints, oils, varnishes, colors, and painters' materials.	Erie.
Albert Krout Co. Capital, $50,000. January 16, 1893.	Said corporation is formed for the purpose of manufacturing vegetable and mineral extracts and compounds, drugs and chemicals, and the sale thereof when manufactured, and of the ingredients thereof.	Philadelphia.
The Ajax Metal Company Capital, $150,000. January 16, 1893.	Said corporation is formed for the purpose of the manufacture and sale of metals and alloys and composition of metals, and all castings, shapes and articles composed of metals, or of their alloys or compositions.	Philadelphia.
Youghiogheny Mining Company. Capital, $30,000 January 16, 1893.	Said corporation is formed for the purpose of carrying on the business of mining bituminous coal.	Banning.

Ice Manufacturing and Cold Storage Company of Wilkes-Barre, Pa. Capital, $65,000. January 16, 1893.	Said corporation is formed for the purpose of manufacturing ice by artificial process.	Wilkes-Barre.
Central Coal and Coke Company. Capital, $110,000. January 16, 1893.	Said corporation is formed for the purpose of mining and otherwise producing coal, manufacturing coke and other products therefrom, transporting to market and selling the same in crude or manufactured form.	Philadelphia.
The Cosmos Building and Loan Association. Capital, $1,000,000. January 16, 1893.	Said corporation is formed for the purpose of accumulating a fund by the periodical contributions of the members thereof, and of safely investing the same.	Philadelphia.
The Spring Hill Premium Building and Loan Association No. 2, of Allegheny City. Capital, $500,000. January 16, 1893.	Said corporation is formed for the purpose of accumulating a fund by the periodical contributions of the members thereof, and of safely investing the same.	Allegheny City.
The Silver Brook Water Company. Capital, $10,000. January 17, 1893.	Said corporation is formed for the purpose of supplying water for the public in the township of Nescopeck, Luzerne county, Pennsylvania, and to persons, partnerships and associations residing therein or adjacent thereto, as may desire the same.	Nescopeck.
Home Electric Company. Capital, $10,000. January 17, 1893.	Said corporation is formed for the purpose of supplying of light, heat and power or any of them by electricity to the public in the borough of Coudersport and to such persons, partnerships and corporations residing therein or adjacent thereto as may desire the same, at such prices as may be agreed upon.	Coudersport.
The Sheldon Glass Company. Capital, $15,000. January 18, 1893.	Said corporation is formed for the purpose of manufacturing glass and glass-ware.	Bradford.
The Manufactured Gas Company of Johnstown, Cambria Co., Pa. Capital, $5,000. January 19, 1893.	Said corporation is formed for the purpose of manufacturing, and supplying gas to the public at the city of Johnstown, Cambria county, Pennsylvania, and to such persons, partnerships, corporations and associations residing therein and adjacent thereto, as may desire the same.	Johnstown.
The Scranton Knitting Company. Capital, $31,250. January 20, 1893.	Said corporation is formed for the purpose of the manufacture and sale of knit goods.	Scranton.

LIST OF CHARTERS OF CORPORATIONS—Continued.

STYLE AND TITLE OF CORPORATION.	PURPOSE.	LOCATION.
Rice & Robinson Soap Company. Capital, $50,000. January 20, 1883.	Said corporation is formed for the purpose of the manufacture and sale of soaps and perfumes and such other commercial products as are incidental to such manufacture and connected therewith.	Titusville.
Alliquippa & Linmore Ferry Company. Capital, $1,000. January 20, 1883.	Said corporation is formed for the purpose of erecting, constructing and maintaining a ferry and approaches thereto over the Ohio river, from a point at or near Alliquippa Grove, Hopewell township, in the county of Beaver, Pa., to a point on the opposite side of said river, in the county of Beaver. The location of said ferry being more than five miles from any other incorporated ferry over said stream.	Freedom.
Ocean Coal Company. Capital, $1,000,000. January 20, 1883.	Said corporation is formed for the purpose of mining coal in the county of Westmoreland, in the State of P̶ ̶ sylvania, and manufacturing coke therefrom, and transporting said coal and coke to market in crude or manufactured form, with power in the ̶ ̶ ̶rs of said ̶ ̶pany in ̶ ̶ir discretion of selling, leasing or otherwise disposing of any of the property of the corporation, real or personal, without the consent of a majority in value of the capital stock, or of any special authority of the stockholders, except as may be p̶ ̶ ̶d in the by-̶ ̶pany, with further ̶ ̶wer in the said directors of said company of making, altering and amending the by-laws of the corporation at any meeting of said directors to be ̶ ̶ded for t̶ ̶at purpose.	Philadelphia.
Delta Coal Mining Company. Capital, $10,000. January 23, 1883.	Said corporation is ̶ ̶ned for the purpose of mining coal, and manufacturing therefrom coke and other products of coal, and transporting the ̶ ̶me to market in crude or manufactured ̶ ̶rm, with the right to ac-quire, hold and ̶ ̶se of real ̶ ̶ate and ̶ ̶ther property necessary to carry on said ̶ ̶his, and to have and enjoy all the rights and fran-̶ ̶se, and to ̶ ̶nt all such ̶ ̶ness as mining and manufacturing companies of like kind are by law authorized to do, and for ̶ ̶ese pur-poses to ̶ ̶ake, possess and enjoy all the rights, ̶ ̶tits and privileges of said act of ̶ ̶bly, and the various supplements thereto.	Philadelphia.
Alfred M. Slocum Company. Capital, $25,000. January 23, 1883.	Said corporation is formed for the purpose of the transaction of a printing and publishing business.	Philadelphia.

Company	Purpose	Location
Schuylkill Valley Illuminating Company. Capital, $500. January 23, 1893.	Said corporation is formed for the purpose of supplying light, heat, and power by electricity to the public at the borough of Phœnixville, Chester county, Pennsylvania, and to such persons, partnerships and corporations residing therein or adjacent thereto, as may desire the same.	Philadelphia.
Uniondale Water Company. Capital, $10,000. January 23, 1893.	Said corporation is formed for the purpose of supplying water to the public at the borough of Uniondale, and to persons, partnerships and associations residing therein and adjacent thereto.	Uniondale.
Kings M Co. Capital, $50,000. January 24, 1893.	Said corporation is formed for the purpose of manufacturing and selling proprietary medicines.	Pittsburgh.
The Provident Manufacturing Company. Capital, $100,000. January 24, 1893.	Said corporation is formed for the purpose of the manufacture of mechanical and other appliances, articles of merchandise and novelties of wood, metal and other materials.	Williamsport.
The Connellsville and New Haven Bridge Company. Capital, $1,000. January 28, 1893.	Said corporation is formed for the purpose of erecting, constructing and maintaining a bridge and approaches thereto, over the Youghiogheny river, in the county of Fayette, Pennsylvania, from a point at or near Apple street, in the borough of Connellsville, to a point on the opposite side of said river, in the borough of New Haven, directly opposite the foot of said Apple street, in the county of Fayette. The location of said bridge being 800 feet from any other incorporated bridge or ferry over said river	Connellsville.
The Bellbridge Ferry Company. Capital, $500. January 26, 1893.	Said corporation is formed for the purpose of erecting, constructing and maintaining a ferry and approaches thereto over and across the Monongahela river, from a point at or near Blair on the west side of said river, in Jefferson township, in the county of Allegheny, to Bellbridge on the opposite side of said Monongahela river, in Lincoln township, in the county of Allegheny, in the Sta sylvan The location of said ferry being four thousand feet from any other in rporated bridge or ferry over said stream.	Elizabeth
The Lackawanna Chemical Company. Capital, $150,000. January 27, 1893.	Said corporation is formed for the purpose of manufacturing acetates, wood spirits and other articles of commerce extracted from wood.	Susquehanna Depot.

LIST OF CHARTERS OF CORPORATIONS—*Continued*.

STYLE AND TITLE OF CORPORATION.	PURPOSE.	LOCATION.
Standard Wire Company. Capital, $20,000. January 27, 1893.	Said corporation is formed for the purpose of the manufacture of iron or steel, or both, or of any other metal, or of any article of commerce from metal or wood, or both.	New Castle.
The McKeesport Telephone Company. Capital, $50,000. January 27, 1893.	Said corporation is formed for the purpose of constructing, maintaining and operating lines of telephone within the State of Pennsylvania.	McKeesport.
The Enterprise Glass Co. Capital, $10,000. January 27, 1893.	Said corporation is formed for the purpose of manufacturing glass bottles, vials, stoppers, flasks, and articles of glass of like character and nature, and for these purposes to have and enjoy all the rights, benefits and privileges of said act of assembly and the supplements thereto.	Pittsburgh.
Beaver Valley Theatre Company. Capital, $60,000. January 26, 1893.	Said corporation is formed for the purpose of establishing and maintaining an opera house in the borough of Beaver Falls, in the county of Beaver, State of Pennsylvania.	Beaver Falls.
Lawrence Gas Fixture Manufacturing Company. Capital, $10,000. January 30, 1893.	Said corporation is formed for the purpose of the manufacture and sale of gas pipe, gas, electric or combination fixtures, machinery and articles of commerce made from metal or wood, and carrying on a general manufacturing and mechanical business pertaining thereto.	Philadelphia.
The Twin Cities National Building and Loan Association of Pittsburgh and Allegheny, Pa. Capital, $1,000,000. January 30, 1893.	Said corporation is formed for the purpose of accumulating a fund by the periodical contributions of the members thereof, and of safely investing the same.	Pittsburgh.
Carlisle Shoe Company. Capital, $150,000. January 31, 1893.	Said corporation is formed for the purpose of manufacturing shoes.	Carlisle.
Fifth Avenue Savings and Loan Association. Capital, $1,000,000. January 31, 1893.	Said corporation is formed for the purpose of accumulating a fund by the periodical contributions of the members thereof, and of safely investing the same.	McKeesport.

Corporation	Purpose	Location
The South Easton Toll Bridge Company. Capital, $5,000. February 1, 1883.	Said corporation is formed for the purpose of erecting, constructing and maintaining a bridge and approaches thereto over the Lehigh river, from a point at or near the foot of Packer street, in the borough of South Easton, in the county of Northampton, to a point on the opposite side of said river in said county, at or near the Easton city line, said bridge being more than 3,000 feet from any other incorporated bridge or ferry over said stream.	Easton
The Milton Manufacturing Company. Capital, $8,000. February 1, 1883.	Said corporation is formed for the purpose of the manufacture of iron or steel, or both, or of any other metal, or of any article of commerce from metal or wood, or both, and of acquiring, possessing and enjoying all the franchises, rights, powers, privileges and immunities conferred by the aforesaid act of April 29, 1874, and the supplements thereto upon corporations chartered for said purpose, being of the class mentioned in clause XVII of the second section of said act.	Milton.
Harrisburg Trust Company. Capital, $400,000. February 2, 1883.	Said corporation is formed for the purpose of the insurance of owners of real estate, mortgagees and others interested in real estate from loss by reason of defective titles, liens and incumbrances.	Harrisburg.
The Lawrence Cement Company. Capital, $5,000. February 2, 1883.	Said corporation is formed to make and vend hydraulic and portland cements, hydraulic and other limes, plasters and other like materials used for building purposes.	Siegfried's Bridge.
The York Dynamite Company. Capital, $10,000. February 3, 1883.	Said corporation is formed for the purpose of the manufacture and sale of nitro-glycerine, dynamite, fuses, powder and other explosives.	York city.
The American Safety Head Match Company. Capital $100,000. February 3, 1883.	Said corporation is formed for the purpose of manufacturing the patent safety head match and other matches.	Lebanon.
Scranton Fire Brick Company. Capital, $30,000. February 3, 1883.	Said corporation is formed for the purpose of making, manufacturing and selling fire brick, ground fire clay, stove linings, flue linings and paving brick.	Scranton.
The Centennial Building and Loan Association of the City of Philadelphia. Re-charter. Capital, $5,000,000. February 3, 1883.	Said corporation is formed for the purpose of accumulating a fund by the periodical contributions of the members thereof, and of safely investing the same.	Philadelphia.

LIST OF CHARTERS OF CORPORATIONS—*Continued.*

STYLE AND TITLE OF CORPORATION.	PURPOSE.	LOCATION.
The J. E. Fricke Company. Capital, $100,000. February 3, 1883.	Said corporation is formed for the purpose of manufacturing and selling rope and twine.	Philadelphia.
The Bradenville Elgin Butter and Cheese Company. Capital, $5,500. February 6, 1883.	Said corporation is formed for the purpose of manufacturing butter and cheese and like products from cows' milk.	Bradenville.
The Cross Stitch Button Sewing Machine Company. Capital, $25,000. February 6, 1883.	Said corporation is formed for the purpose of manufacturing and selling sewing machines.	Philadelphia.
Ellwood Building and Loan Association. Capital, $1,000,000. February 7, 1883.	Said corporation is formed for the purpose of accumulating a fund by the periodical contributions of the members thereof, and of safely investing the same.	Ellwood.
The Robingson Manufacturing Company. Capital, $25,000. February 7, 1883.	Said corporation is formed for the purpose of the manufacture of iron or steel, or both, or of any other metal, or of any article of commerce from metal or wood, or both.	New Brighton.
The Jones & Spruks Company. Capital, $75,000. February 7, 1883.	Said corporation is formed for the purpose of carrying on a general storage and warehouse business.	Scranton.
Stineman Coal and Coke Company. Capital, $60,000. February 8, 1883.	Said corporation is formed for the purpose of carrying on the coal mining and coke manufacturing business and for those purposes to have and possess the powers and privileges expressed and given in the corporation act of 1874, and the supplements thereto.	Philadelphia.

Hanover Bridge Company. Capital, $6,000. February 8, 1883.	Said corporation is formed for the purpose of constructing and maintaining a bridge and approaches thereto over the Susquehanna river from a point in the borough of Plymouth, in said county of Luzerne, in the State of Pennsylvania, at or on a roadway or street which leads from Main street in said borough near or along the premises and planing mill of the Plymouth Planing Mill Company to said river, and which roadway or street is commonly called Mill street, to a point on the opposite side of said river, in Hanover township, in said county, on land of Adelaide, Jacobsky and Selig Cohen, as near as may be on Plymouth avenue as laid out on said land. The proposed bridge is located immediately on the site of the Plymouth Ferry Company's ferry and is distant twenty-three hundred feet from the site of the Wilkes-Barre and Shawnee bridge both of which are incorporated companies under the laws of this Commonwealth.	Wilkes-Barre.
The Lucyville Ferry Company. Capital, $500. February 9, 1883.	Said corporation is formed for the purpose of erecting, maintaining and operating a ferry stream or otherwise, and (a) the stream over which the ferry is proposed to be erected, maintained and operated is the Monongahela river, (b) the place and counties wherein the ferry is to be located is from a landing (or point) at or near the foot of Wayne street, in the unincorporated town of Lucyville, in Allen township, Washington county, Pennsylvania, to a point opposite over said stream in Fayette county. The distance of the ferry from the nearest incorporated ferry is more than 3,000 feet.	Lucyville.
The Carbon Coal Company of Hastings, Pa. Capital, $25,000. February 9, 1883.	Said corporation is formed for the purpose of mining, preparing for market and shipping coal, and manufacturing coke and other products of coal.	Hastings.
The South Broad Street Building and Loan Association of Philadelphia. Capital, $1,000,000. February 9, 1883.	Said corporation is formed, for the purpose of accumulating a fund by the contributions of the members thereof, and to loan the same to them from time to time, to enable them to purchase real estate, build themselves dwelling houses or engage in any legitimate business.	Philadelphia.
The Citizens' Electric Light, Heat and Power Company of Lancaster, Pa. Capital, $100,000. February 9, 1883.	Said corporation is formed for the purpose of supplying light, heat and power, by electricity to the public in the city of Lancaster, Pennsylvania, and to such persons, partnerships and corporations residing therein or adjacent thereto, as may desire the same.	Lancaster.

LIST OF CHARTERS OF CORPORATIONS—Continued.

STYLE AND TITLE OF CORPORATION.	PURPOSE.	LOCATION.
The Middleburgh Water Company. Capital, $25,000. February 9, 1893.	Said corporation is formed for the purpose of supplying water to the public in the borough of Middleburgh, Pa., and to such persons and partnerships residing therein and adjacent thereto, as may desire the same.	Middleburgh.
Neshaminy Falls Stone Company. Capital, $10,000. February 9, 1893.	Said corporation is formed for the purpose of quarrying stone and selling the same.	Philadelphia.
McGill, Wilcox and Company. Incorporated. Capital, $60,000. February 9, 1893.	Said corporation is formed for the purpose of the manufacture of iron or steel, or both, or of any other metal, or of any article of commerce from metal or wood, or both.	Pittsburgh.
Fayette Manufacturing Company. Capital, $25,000. February 9, 1893.	Said corporation is formed for the purpose of manufacturing fire brick.	Pittsburgh.
The Kennett Electric Light, Heat and Power Company. Capital, $20,000. February 10, 1893.	Said corporation is formed for the purpose of furnishing light, heat and power, by electricity to the public in the borough of Kennett Square, and to such persons, partnerships and corporations residing therein or adjacent thereto, as may desire the same.	Kennett Square.
Ferncliff Coal Company. Capital, $20,000. February 10, 1893.	Said corporation is formed for the purpose of cleaning, separating and preparing for market anthracite coal from culm.	Winton.
Power's Run Ice Company. Capital, $10,000. February 10, 1893.	Said corporation is formed for the purpose of supplying ice to the public.	Johnsonburg.
Catasauqua Electric Light and Power Company. Capital, $40,000. February 10, 1893.	Said corporation is formed for the purpose of supplying light, heat and power, or any of them, by means of electricity to the public in the borough of Catasauqua, and to such persons, partnerships, corporations and associations residing therein and adjacent thereto, as may desire the same.	Catasauqua.

Company	Purpose	Location
The Globe Gas Engine Company. Capital, $50,000. February 13, 1893.	Said corporation is formed for the purpose of the manufacture of iron or steel, or both, or of any other metal or article of commerce from metal or wood, or both, and for that purpose to have and possess the powers and privileges expressed and given in the 38th section of the corporation act of 1874, and the supplements thereto.	Philadelphia.
Mackintosh, Hemphill and Company. Capital, $1,000,000. February 14, 1893.	Said corporation is formed for the purpose of the manufacture of iron or steel, or both, or of any other metal, or of any article of commerce from metal or wood, or both.	Pittsburgh.
The Clark's Summit Water Company. Capital, $10,000. February 14, 1893.	Said corporation is formed for the purpose of supplying water for the public at the township of South Abington, and to persons, partnerships, and associations residing therein and adjacent thereto, as may desire the same.	Scranton.
The H. Sheldon Manufacturing Company. Capital, $15,000. February 14, 1893.	Said corporation is formed for the purpose of manufacturing and selling any articles of commerce from metals or woods, or a combination of both, and especially map and chart rollers and mouldings, fan handles and other novelties, or parts thereof, made from wood, iron, steel or other materials.	Canton.
The Versailles Land Company. Capital, $50,000. February 15, 1893.	Said corporation is formed for the purpose of the purchase and sale of real estate, or for holding, leasing and selling real estate.	McKeesport.
Foot and Shear Company. Capital, $40,000. February 15, 1893.	Said corporation is formed for the purpose of manufacturing house furnishing goods from wood, tin, copper, iron, steel or metal, all or either.	Scranton.
The Old's Wood Pulley Company. Capital, $1,000. February 16, 1893.	Said corporation is formed for the purpose of manufacturing pulleys and hangers.	Pittsburgh.
The Central Guarantee Trust and Safe Deposit Company. Capital, $250,000. February 16, 1893.	Said corporation is formed for the purpose of the insurance of owners of real estate, mortgagees and others interested in real estate from loss by reason of defective titles, liens and incumbrances, and of doing and performing such other matters and things as corporations formed for the purpose aforesaid are empowered to do and perform under and by virtue of the aforesaid act of Assembly and its supplements, approved May 9th A. D. 1889 (P. L., 1889, page 159, etc).	Harrisburg.

LIST OF CHARTERS OF CORPORATIONS—*Continued.*

STYLE AND TITLE OF CORPORATION.	PURPOSE.	LOCATION.
Morse, Williams & Co. Capital, $300,000. February 16, 1883.	Said corporation is formed for the purpose of the manufacture of iron or steel, or of both, or of any other metal, or of any article of commerce from metal or wood, or both.	Philadelphia.
Leader Printing and Publishing Company. Capital, $3,000. February 17, 1883.	Said corporation is formed for the purpose of the transaction of a printing and publishing business.	Carlisle.
The Philadelphia Shoe Manufacturing Company. Capital, $30,000. February 20, 1883.	Said corporation is formed for the purpose of manufacturing shoes and other articles principally made of leather.	Port Carbon.
Belle Bridge Coal Company. Capital, $75,000. February 20, 1883.	Said corporation is formed for the purpose of mining coal and transporting the same to market in a crude or manufactured form.	Belle Bridge.
The Panther Valley Electric Light, Heat and Power Company. Capital, $10,000. February 20, 1883.	Said corporation is formed for the purpose of supplying light, heat and power, or any of them by means of electricity to the public, and to persons, partnerships and corporations of the borough of Lansford and vicinity, in Carbon county, Pennsylvania.	Lansford.
The Hellertown Building and Loan Association. Capital, $500,000. February 23, 1883.	Said corporation is formed for the purpose of accumulating a fund by the contributions of the members thereof, and of safely investing the same.	Hellertown.
The Weston Mill Company. Capital, $112,000. February 23, 1883.	Said corporation is formed for the purpose of manufacturing flour, feed, meal and other products from grain.	Scranton.
The Fred. R. Miller Blank Book Company. Capital, $20,000. February 23, 1883.	Said corporation is formed for the purpose of carrying on the business of manufacturing and selling blank books and stationery, and of printing, lithographing, engraving and book-binding.	Williamsport.

The Jersey Shore Electric Light, Heat and Power Company. Capital, $5,000. February 28, 1898.	Said corporation is formed for the purpose of supplying light, heat and power, or any of them by means of electricity in the borough of Jersey Shore and vicinity.	Jersey Shore.
The Alba Butter and Cheese Manufacturing Company. Capital, $6,000. February 24, 1893.	Said corporation is formed for the purpose of manufacturing butter and cheese.	Alba Borough.
Verona Tool Works. Capital, $120,000. February 24, 1893.	Said corporation is formed for the purpose of the manufacture of iron or steel, or both, or of any other metal, or of any article of commerce from metal or wood, or both, and for that purpose to have and possess the powers and privileges expressed and given in the 38th section of the corporation act aforesaid of April 29th, A. D. 1874, and the supplements thereto.	Oakmont.
The People's Gas Company of Steelton, Pa. Capital, $5,000. February 24, 1893.	Said corporation is formed for the purpose of manufacturing and supplying gas for light and heat to the public in the borough of Steelton, in the county of Dauphin, and State of Pennsylvania, and to all such persons, partnerships & associations residing therein or adjacent thereto, as may desire the same.	Harrisburg.
Victor Dish Company. Capital, $20,000. February 27, 1893.	Said corporation is formed for the purpose of the manufacture of dishes, pail and other like wares, from wood, paper and metals and combinations thereof.	Bradford.
The East Troy Elgin Process Butter and Cheese Manufacturing Company. Capital, $6,000. February 27, 1893.	Said corporation is formed for the purpose of the manufacture and sale of butter and cheese.	East Troy.
The Veness Machine Company. Capital, $10,000. February 27, 1893.	Said corporation is formed for the purpose of the manufacture of iron or steel, or both, or of any other metal, or of any article of commerce from metal or wood, or both.	Pittsburgh.
Publishers' Press Association. Capital, $10,000. February 27, 1893.	Said corporation is formed for the purpose of manufacturing the Horgan patent printing block and plate.	Pittsburgh.
Pierpont Boiler Company. Capital, $1,000. February 28, 1893.	Said corporation is formed for the purpose of the manufacture of iron and steel, or any article of commerce from wood or metal, or both.	Pittsburgh.

LIST OF CHARTERS OF CORPORATIONS—*Continued.*

STYLE AND TITLE OF CORPORATION.	PURPOSE.	LOCATION.
The Silverdale Creamery Company. Capital, $5,000. February 28, 1893.	Said corporation is formed for the purpose of manufacturing and selling butter, cheese and other dairy products.	East Canton.
The People's Building and Loan Association of Wilkinsburg. Capital, $1,000,000. March 1, 1893.	Said corporation is formed for the purpose of accumulating a fund by the periodical contributions of the members thereof, and of safely investing the same.	Wilkinsburg.
Pennsylvania Glue Company. Capital, $160,000. March 1, 1893.	Said corporation is formed for the purpose of manufacturing and selling glue, and any other article of commerce or material which may be manufactured from waste products of tanneries and slaughter houses.	Springdale.
The Penn Tack Company. Capital, $25,000. March 1, 1893.	Said corporation is formed for the purpose of the manufacture of tacks, nails, rivets, screws and similar articles from iron, steel, copper, brass and other metals.	Norristown.
Beaver Falls Planing Mill Company. Capital, $50,000. March 2, 1893.	Said corporation is formed for the purpose of the manufacture of iron or steel, or both, or of any other metal or of any article of commerce from metal or wood, or both.	Beaver Falls.
Lawrenceville Bronze Company. Capital, $25,000. March 2, 1893.	Said corporation is formed for the purpose of the manufacture of iron or steel, or both, or of any other metal, or of any article of commerce from metal or wood, or both.	Pittsburgh.
Lebanon Boiler, Foundry and Machine Company. Capital, $70,000. March 2, 1893.	Said corporation is formed for the purpose of manufacturing boilers, engines, pumps, stills, stacks, castings, pipes, fittings and all kinds of machinery.	Lebanon.
The Bangor Co-operative Slate Works. Capital, $15,000. March 3, 1893.	Said corporation is formed for the purpose of which is the mining, manufacturing and vending of roofing slate and slate commodities of every name and nature, and for these purposes to have, possess and enjoy all the rights, benefits and privileges of the said act of Assembly, and the supplements thereto.	Bangor.

Company	Purpose	Location
Waynesboro Canning Company. Capital, $15,000. March 3, 1893.	Said corporation is formed for the purpose of carrying on the mechanical business of evaporating and preserving fruits & vegetables, and such mechanical business as is necessarily incident thereto.	Waynesboro.
The Standard Manufacturing Company. Capital, $80,000. March 6, 1893.	Said corporation is formed for the purpose of manufacturing cash registers.	East Stroudsburg.
The Chadwick Leather Company. Capital, $30,000. March 6, 1893.	Said corporation is formed for the purpose of manufacturing and selling leather from all kinds of skins and hides.	Philadelphia.
Cancos Manufacturing Company. Capital, $20,000. March 6, 1893.	Said corporation is formed for the purpose of manufacturing and selling all kinds of steam and hydraulic packing, rubber goods, waste, oils and lubricants, and any and all other articles, materials and substances out of which said packing is or may be made.	Philadelphia.
The Lehigh Mining and Manufacturing Company. Capital, $50,000. March 6, 1893.	Said corporation is formed for the purpose of mining coal, manufacturing coke, and manufacturing the same into all the products thereof.	Philadelphia.
The Roxburgh Mills Company. Capital, $40,000. March 6, 1893.	Said corporation is formed for the purpose of manufacturing carpets, mattings and other fabrics from jute, wool and other fibrous and textile materials, the manufacture of twine, thread, yarn, cords and cordage from jute, wool and other fibrous and textile materials.	Plymouth.
Wilkes-Barre Times. Capital, $30,000. March 6, 1893.	Said corporation is formed for the purpose of the transaction of a printing and publishing business.	Wilkes-Barre.
The Finch Manufacturing Company. Capital, $250,000. March 7, 1893.	Said corporation is formed for the purpose of the manufacture of iron or steel, or both, or of any other metal or article of commerce from metal, wood or both.	Scranton.
Whitehall Water Company. Capital, $5,000. March 7, 1893.	Said corporation is formed for the purpose of supplying water to the public at Whitehall, Lehigh county, Pennsylvania, and to persons, partnerships, associations and corporations residing therein and adjacent thereto, as may desire the same.	Scranton.

LIST OF CHARTERS OF CORPORATIONS—*Continued.*

STYLE AND TITLE OF CORPORATION.	PURPOSE.	LOCATION.
Tarentum Bridge Company. Capital, $2,000. March 7, 1888.	Said corporation is formed for the purpose of erecting, constructing and maintaining a bridge over the Allegheny river and the approaches thereto, from a point at or near the westerly end of Nineteenth street, in the borough of New Kensington, county of Westmoreland, and State of Pennsylvania, to a point on the opposite side of said river in East Deer township, county of Allegheny, and State aforesaid, said location being about 1,800 feet from any other bridge or ferry over said stream, heretofore incorporated under the laws of said Commonwealth.	Pittsburgh.
Creighton Bridge Company. Capital, $2,000. March 7, 1888.	Said	Pittsburgh.
Foxburg Boat Manufacturing Company. Capital, $5,000. March 7, 1888.	Said corporation is formed for the purpose of the manufacturing flat-boats and other articles of commerce from wood.	Foxburg.
The G. F. Rothacker Brewing Company. Capital, $1,000. March 7, 1888.	Said corporation is formed for the purpose of the manufacturing and brewing malt liquors and selling the products thereof.	Philadelphia.
American Safety Lamp and Mine Supply Company. Capital, $100,000. March 8, 1888.	Said corporation is formed for the purpose of manufacture and sale of mining, safety lamps, general mine and electrical supplies and steam, gas and electrical metal work.	Scranton.

The Mehoopany Lumber Company. Capital, $40,000. March 8, 1893.	Said corporation is formed for the purpose of manufacturing lumber.	Mehoopany.
A French Spring Company. Capital, $1,000. March 9, 1893.	Said corporation is formed for the purpose of the manufacture of iron or steel, or both, or of any other metal or of any article of commerce from metal or wood or both.	Pittsburgh.
Pittsburgh Trust Company. Capital, $600,000. March 10, 1893.	Said corporation is formed for the purpose of insuring owners of real estate, mortgagees and others interested in real estate, from loss by reason of defective titles, liens and encumbrances.	Pittsburgh.
The New Columbia Building & Loan Association of Pittsburgh, Pa. Capital, $998,400. March 10, 1893.	Said corporation is formed for the purpose of accumulating a fund by the periodical contributions of the members thereof, and of safely investing the same.	Pittsburgh.
The Westmoreland Building and Loan Association. Capital, $1,000,000. March 13, 1893.	Said corporation is formed for the purpose of accumulating a fund by the periodical contributions of the members thereof, and of safely investing the same.	Philadelphia.
The Knoxville Building and Loan Association. Capital, $1,000,000. March 13, 1893.	Said corporation is formed for the purpose of accumulating a fund by the periodical contributions of the members thereof, and of safely investing the same.	Knoxville borough.
The Security Title and Trust Company. Capital, $250,000. March 13, 1893.	Said corporation is formed for the purpose of the insurance of owners of real estate, mortgagees and others from loss by reasons of defective titles, liens and incumbrances.	York.
The Fair Haven Land Company. Capital, $35,000. March 13, 1893.	Said corporation is formed for the purpose of purchasing, holding, leasing, mortgaging, improving and selling real estate.	Pittsburgh.
Warren Table Works. Capital, $20,000. March 13, 1893.	Said corporation is formed for the purpose of manufacturing tables, stands, desks, chairs & other similar articles from wood, iron and other materials.	Warren.

LIST OF CHARTERS OF CORPORATIONS—*Continued.*

Style and Title of Corporation.	Purpose.	Location.
The Enterprise Manufacturing Company of Pennsylvania. Capital, $1,600,000. March 14, 1893.	Said corporation is formed for the purpose of manufacturing all kinds of hardware, machinery, metal, castings, electrical appliances and all other articles of commerce from metal, wood, or both.	Philadelphia.
James S. Kelly Company. Capital, $10,000. March 14, 1893.	Said corporation is formed for the manufacture of blank books and general paper ruling, and general book binding.	Philadelphia.
The Melrose Land and Improvement Company. Capital, $125,000. March 14, 1893.	Said corporation is formed for the purpose of buying, holding, leasing and selling real estate, and enjoying all the rights, benefits and privileges granted to real estate companies for the successful maintenance and carrying on of such business.	Philadelphia.
Mears Manufacturing Company. Capital, $80,000. March 14, 1893.	Said corporation is formed for the purpose of the manufacture of iron or steel, or both, or of any other metal or article of commerce from metal, wood, or both.	Bloomsburg.
The Bell Water Company. Capital, $20,000. March 14, 1893.	Said corporation is formed for the purpose of supplying water to the public in the town of Sabbath Rest, in the township of Antis, in the county of Blair, and State of Pennsylvania, and to such persons, partnerships, associations and corporations residing therein and adjacent thereto, as may desire the same.	Hollidaysburg.
Criterion Coal Company. Capital, $10,000. March 14, 1893.	Said corporation is formed for the purpose of mining coal and manufacturing coke therefrom, and transporting the same to market in crude or manufactured form.	Philadelphia.
Penna. Tar Manufacturing Company. Capital, $20,000. March 15, 1893.	Said corporation is formed for the purpose of manufacturing and marketing tar products.	Bradford.
The Kountz Brothers Company. Capital, $1,000. March 15, 1893.	Said corporation is formed for the ... se of the making of brick, tile, sewer pipe and all products of clay and ...ne.	Harmarville.

Company	Description	Location
The Allentown Shoe Manufacturing Company. Capital, $50,000. March 16, 1883.	Said corporation is formed for the purpose of the manufacture and sale of boots and shoes.	Allentown.
The Burnside Butter and Cheese Manufacturing Company. Limited. Capital, $4,250. March 16, 1883.	Said corporation is formed for the purpose of manufacturing butter and cheese and all other dairy products.	Burnside Borough.
Kensington Bridge Company. Capital, $2,000. March 16, 1883.	Said ... is ... for the ... of ... ding, constructing and maintaining a bridge and ... ... two ... ur the Alleg... by ... from a point on the ... ... of said ... ier, on lands of K ... ... Brick ... ... ar the ... he ... tar in the ... ... of ... ... ar the county of ... ... d, to a ... ipt on the ... ... rk of ... d ... ... e, on lands of the ... ... We ... ... ar the ... th line ... tar in the ... bship of ... at Deer, in the ... ty of Alle... ... ... y. The ... ... of ... el bridge ... king upwards of ... ... d ... ... t from ... ay ... tar ... ... ed bridge or ferry over ... ... to wit, about 1,580 ft.	Pittsburgh.
The Star Publishing Company. Capital, $10,000. March 17, 1883.	Said corporation is formed for the purpose of transacting a printing and publishing business, and especially the publishing of a daily and weekly newspaper, and doing all kinds of book and job printing, ruling and binding.	Beaver.
The Polish American Publishing Company. Capital, $10,000. March 17, 1883.	Said corporation is formed for the purpose of the transaction of a printing and publishing business.	Pittsburgh.
Pyroleum Appliance Company. Capital, $100,000. March 17, 1883.	Said corporation is formed for the purpose of purchasing and selling patents granted by the authority of the United States, and rights and licenses under said patents, and for the manufacture and sale of patented articles.	Philadelphia.
Valley Creamery. Capital, $4,000. March 20, 1883.	Said corporation is formed for the purpose of making butter, cheese and feed for stock from milk and its products.	Grand Valley.

LIST OF CHARTERS OF CORPORATIONS—*Continued.*

STYLE AND TITLE OF CORPORATION.	PURPOSE.	LOCATION.
Lake Shore Rubber Company. Capital, $5,000. March 20, 1888.	Said corporation is formed for the purpose of the manufacture and sale of rubber goods for mechanical purposes, druggists' sundries and other rubber novelties, specialties and wares.	Erie.
Scott Valley Creamery. Capital, $5,000. March 20, 1888.	Said corporation is formed for the purpose of manufacturing and preparing for market butter, milk, cream, ice cream, cheese and all other dairy products.	Scott.
The New Dunning Marble and Granite Company. Capital, $25,000. March 20, 1888.	Said corporation is formed for the purpose of manufacturing stone for monumental and building purposes.	Erie.
The Chapman Decorative Company. Capital, $30,000. March 20, 1888.	Said corporation is formed for the purpose of preparing and mechanically executing designs for the decorating and furnishing of buildings, including frescoing and painting, paper hanging and upholstering.	Philadelphia.
Clearfield Manufacturing Company. Capital, $25,000. March 20, 1888.	Said corporation is formed for the purpose of the manufacture of any article of commerce from metal or wood, or both.	Clearfield.
Henry Christian Building and Loan Association of Philadelphia. Recharter. Capital, $1,000,000. March 20, 1888.	Said corporation is formed for the purpose of accumulating a fund by the periodical contributions of the members thereof, and of safely investing the same.	Philadelphia.
Howard Hudson Building and Loan Association. Capital, $1,000,000. March 20, 1888.	Said corporation is formed for the purpose of accumulating a fund by the periodical contributions of the members thereof, and of safely investing the same.	Philadelphia.
The Churchville Building and Loan Association. Capital, $20,000. March 20, 1888.	Said corporation is formed for the purpose of accumulating a fund by the periodical contributions of the members thereof, and of safely investing the same.	Churchville.

Name / Capital / Date	Purpose	Location
The Sourin Building and Loan Association. Capital, $1,000,000. March 20, 1888.	Said corporation is formed for the purpose of accumulating a fund by the periodical contributions of the members thereof, and of safely investing the same.	Philadelphia.
Security Cash Register Company. Capital, $20,000. March 21, 1888.	Said corporation is formed for the purpose of the manufacture and sale of cash registers and other patented articles and novelties.	Hanover.
Blaisdell Paper Pencil Company. Capital, $100,000. March 21, 1888.	Said corporation is formed for the purpose of manufacturing pencils of every nature, character and description, and for the selling of the same.	Philadelphia.
The Highlands Investment Company. Capital, $100,000. March 22, 1888.	Said corporation is formed for the purpose of the purchase and sale of real estate, and for holding, leasing and selling real estate.	Pittsburgh.
The Stewart Fire Brick Company. Capital, $20,000. March 22, 1888.	Said corporation is formed for the purpose of the manufacture and sale of bricks, fire bricks and articles made of clay, stone and earth.	Pittsburgh.
Forbes Land Company, Capital, $5,000. March 23, 1888.	Said corporation is formed for the purpose of purchasing, improving, mortgaging, leasing and selling real estate.	Pittsburgh.
West Philadelphia Coal Company. Capital, $50,000. March 24, 1888.	Said corporation is formed for the purpose of the mining and selling coal, and the manufacture and sale of coke.	Philadelphia.
Security Building and Loan Association of York, Penna. Capital, $999,900. March 24, 1888.	Said corporation is formed for the purpose of accumulating a fund by the periodical contributions of the members thereof, and of safely investing the same.	York.
The Westmoreland Guarantee Building and Loan Association of Pennsylvania. Capital, $1,000,000. March 24, 1888.	The nature of the business of this corporation shall be that of a permanent building and loan association, and its object shall be to furnish to its members a safe, profitable and systematic plan of investing their savings, and to assist them in building houses, buying or improving property or real estate, and to transact all business appertaining to the proper working and management of a permanent building and loan association.	Jeannette.

LIST OF CHARTERS OF CORPORATIONS—*Continued.*

STYLE AND TITLE OF CORPORATION.	PURPOSE.	LOCATION.
The Greenfield Building and Loan Association of the 23rd Ward, Ward, Pittsburgh. Capital, $1,000,000. March 24, 1893.	Said corporation is formed for the purpose of accumulating a fund by the periodical contributions of the members thereof, and the lending of such funds so accumulated to its members, and to have and enjoy all the rights and franchises, and to do and transact all such business as building and loan associations are by law authorized.	Pittsburgh.
The Nazareth Building and Loan Association. Capital, $1,000,000. March 27, 1893.	Said corporation is formed for the purpose of accumulating a fund by the periodical contributions of the members thereof, and of safely investing the same.	Nazareth.
The Flory and Reichard Power Company. Capital, $50,000. March 27, 1893.	Said corporation is formed for the purpose of a supply, storage and transportation of water for commercial and manufacturing purposes to persons, partnerships and associations in the borough of Bangor, and adjacent thereto as may desire the same.	Bangor.
McSherrystown Water Company. Capital, $15,000. March 29, 1893.	Said corporation is formed for the purpose of the supplying water for the public, at the borough of McSherrystown, Adams county, Pennsylvania, and to persons, partnerships and associations residing therein and adjacent thereto, as may desire the same.	McSherrystown.
The Union Building and Loan Association. Capital, $1,000,000. March 29, 1893.	Said corporation is formed for the purpose of accumulating a fund by the periodical contributions of the members of the said building and loan association, and safely investing the same.	Bridgewater.
Hanover Building and Loan Association No. 7. Capital, $500,000. April 3, 1893.	Said corporation is formed for the purpose of accumulating a fund by the periodical contributions of the members thereof, and of safely investing the same.	Hanover.
National Loan and Trust Company of Wilkes-Barre, Pa. Capital, $1,000,000. April 3, 1893.	Said corporation is formed for the purpose of accumulating a fund by the periodical contributions of the members thereof, and of safely investing the same.	Wilkes-Barre.

Germania Ban und Spar Verin No. 3 of Harrisburg, Pa. Capital, $600,000. April 3, 1888.	Said corporations formed for the purpose of accumulating a fund by the periodical contributions of the members thereof, and of safely investing the same.	Harrisburg.
The Cedar Ledge Creamery Company. Capital, $5,000. April 3, 1888.	Said corporation is formed for the purpose of manufacturing and selling butter and cheese.	Cedar Ledge, Bradford county.
Pittsburgh Steel Hollowware Company. Capital, $50,000. April 3, 1888.	Said corporation is formed for the purpose of the manufacture of iron or steel, or both, or of any other metal or of any article of commerce from metal wood, or both.	Allegheny City.
Watsontown Table and Furniture Company. Capital, $20,000. April 3, 1888.	Said corporation is formed for the purpose of manufacturing all kinds of furniture.	Watsontown.
"Burk & McFetridge Company." Capital, $150,000. April 3, 1888.	Said corporation is formed for the transaction of a printing and publishing business.	Philadelphia.
"National Chemical Company." Capital, $80,000. April 3, 1888.	Said corporation is formed for the purpose of the manufacture of alcohol, acid, acetate of lime, charcoal, tar and other products from wood in the counties of McKean, Elk, Warren and Forest.	Kushequa, McKean county.
Haustetter Distilled Water Company. Capital, $5,000. April 4, 1888.	Said corporation is formed for the purpose of manufacturing distilled and carbonated waters.	Philadelphia.
The News Publishing Company. Capital, $10,000. April 4, 1888.	Said corporation is formed for the purpose of publishing a daily and weekly newspaper, and carrying on a general printing and newspaper publishing business.	Uniontown.
The Bethlehem Chenille and Tapestry Company. Capital, $80,000. April 6, 1888.	Said corporation is formed for the purpose of manufacturing textile fabrics from cotton, linen, silk and woolen yarns, and for these purposes to have, possess and enjoy all the rights, benefits and privileges of said act of Assembly.	Bethlehem.

LIST OF CHARTERS OF CORPORATIONS—*Continued.*

STYLE AND TITLE OF CORPORATION.	PURPOSE.	LOCATION.
Hanover Turnpike Company. Capital, $3,500. April 6, 1883.	Said corporation is formed for the purpose of building and maintaining an artificial road or turnpike of gravel and earth, from a point, or near the junction of Carey avenue with old river road in the city of Wilkes-Barre, in the county of Luzerne, to a point at or near Plymouth avenue, laid out on land of Adelaide Jacobosky and Selig Cohen, in the township of Hanover, in the county of Luzerne, a distance of about one mile and a half, all of said road being located in the county of Luzerne.	Wilkes-Barre.
John Gay's Sons. Incorporated. Capital, $300,000. April 10, 1883.	Said corporation is formed for the purpose of the manufacture and sale of yarns, carpets, rugs and textile fabrics.	Philadelphia.
J. K. McKee Company. Capital, $50,000. April 10, 1883.	Said corporation is formed for the purpose of the manufacture of confectionery, fruit juices, fluid extracts, tinctures and pharmaceutical preparations.	Pittsburgh.
Schurr Brothers Company. Capital, $10,000. April 10, 1883.	Said corporation is formed for the purpose of manufacture and sale of butter, cheese and other dairy products.	Philadelphia.
Millholland Tube Company. Capital, $20,000. April 10, 1883.	Said corporation is formed for the purpose of manufacturing and selling steel tubing and articles of commerce from metal or wood, or both.	Reading.
The Pennsylvania Blue Stone Company. Capital, $2,100. April 10, 1883.	Said corporation is formed for the purpose of quarrying and manufacturing all kinds of stone, including flagging, curbing, paving and building stone.	Lanesboro.
Quakertown Water Company. Capital, $1,000. April 10, 1883.	Said corporation is formed for the purpose of supplying water to the borough of Quakertown, Bucks county, Pennsylvania, and to such persons, partnerships and corporations residing therein and adjacent thereto, as may desire the same.	Quakertown.

The Folding Box Machine Company. Capital, $99,000. April 10, 1883.	Said corporation is formed for the purpose of creating, purchasing, holding and selling of patent rights for inventions and designs, with the right to issue license for same and receive pay therefor.	Honesdale.
Pennsylvania Building and Loan Association of Harrisburg, Pa. Capital, $1,000,000. April 11, 1883.	Said corporation is formed for the purpose of accumulating a fund by the periodical contributions of the members thereof, and of safely investing the same.	Harrisburg.
Crescent Electric Light Company. Capital, $25,000. April 11, 1883.	Said corporation is formed for the purpose of supplying light, heat and power, or any or all of them to the public by means of electricity, in the borough of McKees Rocks, Allegheny county, Pennsylvania, and such persons, partnerships and corporations therein or adjacent thereto, as may desire the same.	McKee's Rocks.
The Armstrong Telephone Company. Capital, $3,000. April 11, 1883.	Said corporation is formed for the purpose of constructing, maintaining and leasing lines of telegraph for the private use of individuals, firms, corporations, municipal and otherwise for general business, for police, fire alarm or messenger business, or for the transaction of any business in which electricity over or through wires may be applied to any useful purpose within the county of Armstrong in the State of Pennsylvania.	Dayton, Armstrong county.
The Columbian Building and Loan Association of Mauch Chunk. Capital, $1,000,000. April 11, 1883.	Said corporation is formed for the purpose of accumulating a fund by the periodical contributions of the members thereof, and of safely investing the same.	Mauch Chunk.
The Scranton and Hyde Park ville Coal Land Company. Capital, $300,000. April 12, 1883.	Said corporation is formed for the purpose of the purchase and sale of real estate, and for holding, leasing and improving real estate.	Scranton.
The Security Ten Cent Loan Association. Capital, $600,960. April 13, 1883.	Said corporation is formed for the purpose of accumulating a fund by the periodical contributions of the members thereof, and of safely investing the same.	Pittsburgh.
East Brady Water Company. Capital, $12,000. April 13, 1883.	Said corporation is formed for the purpose of supplying water to the borough of East Brady, Clarion county, Penna., and to persons, partnerships, corporations and associations residing therein and adjacent thereto.	East Brady.

LIST OF CHARTERS OF CORPORATIONS—*Continued.*

STYLE AND TITLE OF CORPORATION.	PURPOSE.	LOCATION.
The Stafford Water Company. Capital, $1,000. April 13, 1893.	Said corporation is formed for the purpose of supplying water for the public in the township of Tredyffrin, in the county of Chester, and State aforesaid, and to persons, partnerships and associations residing therein and adjacent thereto, as may desire the same.	Wayne.
The Millbrook Water Company. Capital, $1,000. April 13, 1893.	Said corporation is formed for the purpose of supplying water to the public in the township of Haverford, in the county of Delaware, and State aforesaid, and to persons, partnerships and associations residing therein and adjacent thereto, as may desire the same.	Wayne.
The St. Davids Water Company. Capital, $1,000. April 13, 1893.	Said corporation is formed for the purpose of supplying water for the public in the township of Radnor, in the county of Delaware, and State aforesaid, and to persons, partnerships and associations residing therein and adjacent thereto, who may desire the same.	Wayne.
The Skippack Water Company. Capital, $1,000. April 13, 1893.	Said corporation is formed for the purpose of supplying water for the public in the township of Lower Providence, in the county of Montgomery, and State aforesaid, and to persons, partnerships and associations residing therein and adjacent thereto, as may desire the same.	Wayne.
The Valley Forge Water Company. Capital, $1,000. April 13, 1893.	Said corporation is formed for the purpose of supplying water for the public in the township of Upper Merion, in the county of Montgomery, and State aforesaid, and to persons, partnerships and associations residing therein and adjacent thereto, as may desire the same.	Wayne.
The Elm Water Company. Capital, $1,000. April 13, 1893.	Said corporation is formed for the purpose of supplying water for the public in the township of Lower Merion, in the county of Montgomery, and State aforesaid, and to persons, partnerships and associations residing therein and adjacent thereto, as may desire the same.	Wayne.
The Devon Water Company. Capital, $1,000. April 13, 1893.	Said corporation is formed for the purpose of supplying water for the public in the township of Easttown, in the county of Chester, and State aforesaid, and to persons, partnerships and associations residing therein and adjacent thereto, who may desire the same.	Wayne.

Corporation	Purpose	Location
"Logan's Ferry," of Miller's Eddy, Armstrong County, Penna. Capital, $250. April 13, 1893.	Said corporation is formed for the purpose of erecting, constructing and maintaining a ferry and approaches thereto over the Allegheny river, from a point near Miller's Eddy (or Shakely's run) in Armstrong county, Penna., to a point at the east side of said river, in said county, at or near West Monterey, in Clarion county, Penna. the location of said ferry being more than one mile from any other bridge or ferry over said stream, the location of said ferry within and and at both termini being within the limits of Armstrong county.	Miller's Eddy.
The Johnson Company. Capital, $1,000,000. April 13, 1893.	Said corporation is formed for the purpose of the manufacture of iron or steel, or both, or of any other metal, or of any article of commerce from metal or wood, or both.	Johnstown.
The Allegheny Steel Company. Capital, $5,000. April 14, 1893.	Said corporation is formed for the purpose of the manufacture and sale of iron and steel in all their branches, and all articles of commerce, and sale from either or both.	Pittsburgh.
Iron City Chemical Company. Capital, $8,000. April 14, 1893.	Said corporation is formed for the purpose of the manufacture and sale of chemical, drug and proprietary specialties.	Pittsburgh.
Union Tanning Company. Capital, $50,000. April 17, 1893.	Said corporation is formed for the purpose of manufacturing leather.	Westfield.
Elk Tanning Company. Capital, $50,000. April 17, 1893.	Said corporation is formed for the purpose of manufacturing leather.	Ridgway.
Penn Tanning Company. Capital, $100,000. April 17, 1893.	Said corporation is formed for the purpose of manufacturing leather.	Sheffield.
East Warren Real Estate Company. Capital, $50,000. April 17, 1893.	Said corporation is formed for the purpose of purchasing, taking, holding and enjoying real estate in fee simple, on lease, or upon ground rent, improving, leasing, mortgaging and selling the same in such parts and parcels, and on such terms as to time of payment as said corporation may determine, and to convey the same to purchaser or purchasers in fee simple, or for any less estate, or upon ground rents, and in like manner to mortgage, sell, convey or extinguish any ground rent reserved out of any real estate so sold.	Warren.

LIST OF CHARTERS OF CORPORATIONS—*Continued.*

STYLE AND TITLE OF CORPORATION.	PURPOSE.	LOCATION.
Kensington Hand-in-Hand Building Association. Re-chartered. Capital, $1,000,000. April 14, 1893.	Said corporation is formed and is desirous of being re-chartered for the purpose of accumulating a fund by the periodical contributions of the members thereof, and to loan the same to them from time to time to enable them to purchase real estate, engage in business or build themselves dwelling houses.	Philadelphia.
The Home Building and Loan Association of Harrisburg, Pa. Capital, $1,000,000. April 14, 1893.	Said corporation is formed for the purpose of accumulating a fund by the periodical contributions of the members thereof, and of safely investing the same.	Harrisburg.
Highlands Building and Loan Association. Capital, $1,000,000. April 17, 1893.	Said corporation is formed for the purpose of accumulating a fund by the periodical contributions of the members thereof, and of safely investing the same.	Pittsburgh.
Lehigh Steel and Iron Company. Capital, $250,000. April 17, 1893.	Said corporation is formed for the purpose of manufacturing steel or iron, or both, into all the products thereof.	Allentown.
Jefferson Milling Company. Capital, $30,000. April 17, 1893.	Said corporation is formed for the purpose of manufacturing flour, feed and meal from all kinds of grain.	Brookville.
The Acme Creamery Company. Capital, $5,000. April 17, 1893.	Said corporation is formed for the purpose of manufacturing of cream, butter and cheese.	Port Allegheny.
Sterling White Lead Company. Capital, $200,000. April 17, 1893.	Said corporation is formed for the purpose of the manufacture and sale of white lead, oxides of lead and other products of pig lead, linseed oil and paints generally.	Pittsburgh.
Bradford Chemical Company. Capital, $50,000. April 18, 1893.	Said corporation is formed for the purpose of manufacturing wood alcohol, acetates, charcoal, tar and other productions from wood.	Bradford.

The Laurel Run Coal Company. Capital, $500. April 19, 1888.	Said corporation is formed for the purpose of mining coal, and for that purpose to have and possess the powers and privileges expressed and given in the 39th section of the corporation act of 1874, and supplements thereto.	Wilkes-Barre.
The West Ridge Coal Company. Capital, $100,000. April 19, 1888.	Said corporation is formed for the purpose of mining coal and preparing the same for market in crude or manufactured form.	Scranton.
Peerless Foundry Company. Capital, $10,000. April 20, 1888.	Said corporation is formed for the purpose of manufacturing hardware specialties and metal castings.	Philadelphia.
The Chestnut Hill Electric Laundry. Capital, $5,000. April 21, 1888.	The purpose for which it is formed is general laundry work by means of steam and electric machinery.	Philadelphia.
"The Pittsburgh Welding Manufacturing Company." Capital, $10,000. April 21, 1888.	Said corporation is formed for the purpose of manufacturing machines out of iron or steel for the purpose of welding boilers and pipes.	Pittsburgh.
Allegheny National Building and Loan Association. Capital, $1,000,000. April 24, 1888.	Said corporation is formed for the purpose of accumulating a fund by the periodical contributions of the members thereof, and of safely investing the same.	Allegheny.
Crystal Water Company. Capital, $10,000. April 24, 1888.	Said corporation is formed for the purpose of the supply, storage or transporting of water and water power for commercial and manufacturing purposes, as aforesaid.	Tidioute.
The Gallitzin Electric Light Company. Capital, $20,000. April 24, 1888.	Said corporation is formed for the purpose of supplying light to the public by electricity, at Gallitzen, Cambria county, Pennsylvania, and to persons, partnerships and associations residing therein and adjacent thereto, as may desire the same.	Gallitzin.
Brigg's Lock-Joint Brick Company. Capital, $150,000. April 24, 1888.	Said corporation is formed for the purpose of manufacturing brick or other materials, or articles of commerce from clay.	Pittsburgh.

LIST OF CHARTERS OF CORPORATIONS—*Continued.*

STYLE AND TITLE OF CORPORATION.	PURPOSE.	LOCATION.
The Renova Opera House Company. Capital, $12,500. April 25, 1888.	Said corporation is formed for the purpose of the establishment and maintenance of an opera house, in the borough of Renova, Clinton county, Penna.	Renova.
Messer Elastic Rotator Company. Capital, $10,000. April 26, 1888.	Said corporation is formed for the purpose of the general manufacture and sale of machinery, wheels and mechanical appliances.	Philadelphia.
"The Briesch-Hine Company." Capital, $45,000. April 26, 1888.	Said ... ny, is formed for the purpose of manufacturing of confec-	Philadelphia.
Alumina Shale Brick Company. Capital, $50,000. April 27, 1888.	Said corporation is formed for the purpose of the manufacture of brick and other articles of commerce from clay and shale.	Bradford.
Rowenna Shoe Manufacturing Company. Capital, $25,000. April 27, 1888.	Said corporation is formed for the purpose of manufacturing and selling all descriptions of shoes and carrying on a general manufacturing business in leather goods.	Rowenna.
DuBois Windmill Company. Capital, $10,000. May 1, 1888.	Said corporation is formed for the purpose of the manufacture of windmills out of iron, wood and steel and the sale thereof.	DuBois.
The Apollo Spring Water Company. Capital, $2,750. May 1, 1888.	Said corporation is formed for the purpose of the supply, storage or transportation of water and water power for commercial and manufacturing purposes in the city of Pittsburgh, Allegheny county, Pennsylvania.	Pittsburgh.
The Columbian Building and Loan Association. Capital $250,000. May 5, 1888.	Said corporation is formed for the purpose of accumulating a fund by the periodical contributions of the members thereof, and of safely investing the same.	York.

Company	Purpose	Location
The Philadelphia Advertising and Stamp Vending Company. Capital, $20,000. May 1, 1893.	Said corporation is formed for the purpose of creating, purchasing, holding and selling of a certain patent right of a new invention known and designated as the "Envelope and Stamp Vendor," designed for the automatic delivery of government postage stamps, envelopes and writing material, and to distribute proper advertising matter in connection therewith by said machine, and to issue license for the same and secure pay therefor.	Philadelphia.
Shenandoah Manufacturing Company. Capital, $25,000. May 2, 1893.	Said corporation is formed for the purpose of manufacturing hats, caps and clothing.	Shenandoah.
The Worthington Elgin Creamery. Capital, $6,000. May 2, 1893.	Said corporation is formed for the purpose of manufacturing butter and cheese.	Worthington.
The Uniontown Glass Company. Capital, $30,000. May 2, 1893.	Said corporation is formed for the purpose of manufacturing glass and glassware, and selling the said manufactures.	Uniontown.
The Allentown Ice Manufacturing Company. Capital, $30,000. May 2, 1893.	Said corporation is formed for the purpose of manufacturing ice and selling such product to the public.	Allentown.
Hanover Light, Heat & Power Co. Capital, $25,000. May 3, 1893.	Said corporation is formed for the purpose of supplying heat, light and power by means of electricity to the public at the borough of Hanover, York county, Pennsylvania, and to persons, partnerships and associations residing therein and adjacent thereto, as may desire the same.	Hanover.
The Standard Land Company Capital, $21,000. May 3, 1893.	is formed for the purpose of purchasing and holding on ground rent, or for other less estate, and for selling, mortgaging or leasing the same in such parts, improved or unimproved, and on such terms as to time and manner of payment as may be agreed upon.	Pittsburgh.
The Columbia Paint and Color Company of Pittsburgh, Pennsylvania. Capital, $5,000. May 3, 1893.	Said corporation is formed for the purpose of the manufacture of paints and colors from mineral substances as articles of commerce, and the sale of the same.	Pittsburgh.

12a—LAWS.

STYLE AND TITLE OF CORPORATION.	PURPOSE.	LOCATION.
Hartzell Concentrating Company. Capital, $100,000. May 3, 1883.	Said corporation is formed for the purpose of manufacturing steel or iron, or both, or any other metal or any article of commerce from metal or wood, or both.	Allentown.
Priceburg Electric Light Company. Capital, $20,000. May 5, 1883.	Said corporation is formed for the purpose of supplying light, heat and power by means of electricity to the public at the borough of Dickson City, and to partnerships and associations residing therein and adjacent	Dickson City.
The Crystal Springs Water Company. Capital, $1,000. May 5, 1883.	Said corporation is formed for the purpose of supplying water to the public at the borough of Austin, Potter county, Pennsylvania, and to such persons, partnerships and corporations residing therein and adjacent thereto, as may desire the same.	Austin, Potter county.
Architectural Publishing Company. Capital, $5,000. May 5, 1883.	Said corporation is formed for the purpose of carrying on the printing and publishing business, and for the purpose of printing, publishing and selling art and scientific books, prints, photographs, drawings, educational matter and text books.	Williamsport.
Boyertown Burial Casket Company. Capital, $20,000. May 8, 1883.	Said corporation is formed for the purpose of manufacturing burial caskets, coffins & furniture.	Boyertown.
The Stroudsburg Land and Improvement Company. Capital, $20,000. May 8, 1883.	Said corporation is formed for the purpose of purchasing, taking, holding and enjoying real estate in fee simple, to improve, lease, mortgage and sell the same in such parts or parcels as they may determine in the borough of Stroudsburg and township of Stroud.	Stroudsburg.
The Point Marion Ferry Company. Capital $500. May 8, 1883.	Said corporation formed for the purpose of erecting, constructing and maintaining a ferry and approaches thereto over and across the Monohngahela river, from a point at or near the foot of Main street, in the village of Point Marion, in Spring Hill township, in Fayette county, Pennsylvania, to a point on the opposite side of said river in the county of Greene, State aforesaid. The location of the said ferry is one and one-fourth miles from any other ferry or bridge over said stream.	Point Marion.

Company	Purpose	Location
The Laughead—Modisette Planing Mill Company. Capital, $70,000. May 9, 1888.	Said corporation is formed for the purpose of carrying on the business of erecting and constructing buildings and of supplying materials therefor.	Uniontown.
Benton Shirt Manufacturing Company. Capital, $5,000. May 9, 1888.	Said corporation is formed for the purpose of manufacturing shirts and waists of the various materials from which they are usually made.	Benton.
Clinton Mining Company. Capital, $2,000. May 9, 1888.	Said corporation is formed for the purpose of mining and selling of fire clay and coal.	Lock Haven.
The Waymart Water Company. Capital, $5,000. May 10, 1888.	Said corporation is formed for the purpose of supplying water to the public in the borough of Waymart, Wayne county, Pennsylvania, and to such persons, partnerships and corporations residing therein or adjacent thereto, as may desire the same.	Waymart.
The Newport Home Water Company. Capital, $1,000. May 10, 1888.	Said corporation is formed for the purpose of supplying water to the borough of Newport, Perry Co., Pa., and to such persons, partnerships and corporations residing therein and adjacent thereto, and for these purposes to have, and possess and enjoy all rights & benefits of said act of assembly and its supplements.	Newport.
Bradford Pressed Brick and Tile Company. Capital, $20,000. May 11, 1888.	Said corporation is formed for the purpose of mining shale, clay, earth and rock and converting the same into brick, tile, terra cotta and other articles usually manufactured from such substances, and for these purposes to have, possess and enjoy all the rights, benefits and privilege of said act of assembly, and the supplements thereto.	Bradford.
The Presbyterian Banner Publishing Company. Capital, $1,000. May 15, 1888.	Said corporation is formed for the purpose of printing and publishing the Presbyterian Banner, a religious newspaper, as well as for the transaction of a general printing and publishing business.	Pittsburgh.
Lackawanna Valley Electric Light and Power Company. Capital, $150,000. May 15, 1888.	Said corporation is formed for the purpose of furnishing light, heat and power by electricity to the public in Mayfield, Pennsylvania, and to such other persons, partnerships and corporations residing therein and adjacent thereto, as may desire the same.	Mayfield.

LIST OF CHARTERS OF CORPORATIONS—*Continued.*

STYLE AND TITLE OF CORPORATION.	PURPOSE.	LOCATION.
The Nazareth Electric Light and Power Company. Capital, $10,000. May 15, 1893.	Said corporation is formed for the purpose of supplying light and power by means of electricity to the public at the borough of Nazareth, in the county of Northampton, and State of Pennsylvania, and to such persons, partnerships and associations residing therein and adjacent thereto, as may desire the same.	Nazareth.
The Tower City Water Company. Capital, $1,000. May 15, 1893.	Said corporation is formed for the purpose of supplying water to the borough of Tower City, Schuylkill Co., Pa., and to such persons, partnerships and corporations residing therein and adjacent thereto, as may desire the same.	Tower City.
Juniata Park Land Association. Capital, $641,000. May 15, 1893.	Said corporation is formed for the purpose of purchasing, holding, leasing and selling real estate.	Philadelphia.
The Lorraine Hotel Company. Capital, $300,000. May 16, 1893.	Said corporation is formed for the purpose of establishing and maintaining a hotel in the city of Philadelphia, Pa.	Philadelphia.
The York Card and Paper Company. Capital, $50,000. May 16, 1893.	Said corporation is formed for the purpose of the manufacture and sale of card, wall and other paper products.	York.
The Black Manufacturing Company. Capital, $100,000. May 16, 1893.	Said corporation is formed for the purpose of manufacturing bicycles and parts thereof, and other articles of commerce made of metal or wood, or both.	Erie.
The Conemaugh and Franklin Water Company. Capital, $10,000. May 16, 1893.	Said corporation is formed for the purpose of supplying water for the public at the borough of Conemaugh, and to persons, partnerships and associations residing therein and adjacent thereto, as may desire the same.	Conemaugh.
Kittanning Burial Case Company. Capital, $40,000. May 16, 1893.	Said corporation is formed for the purpose of the manufacture of iron or steel, or both, or of any other metal, or of any article of commerce from metal or wood, or both.	Kittanning.

Company	Purpose	Location
The Snow Shoe Mining Company. Capital, $30,000. May 16, 1893.	Said corporation is formed for the purpose of mining, preparing for market and shipping coal, and manufacturing coke and other products of coal.	Bellefonte.
Haddon Coal Company. Capital, $5,000. May 17, 1893.	Said corporation is formed for the purpose of mining, shipping and selling bituminous coal.	Leechburg.
The Thornburg Stone Company. Capital, $20,000. May 18, 1893.	Srid corporation is formed for the purpose of mining, quarrying, manufacturing and selling stone in all forms.	Media.
The Big Meadows Gas Company. Capital, $10,000. May 18, 1893.	Said corporation is formed for the purpose of producing, dealing in, transporting, storing and supplying natural gas.	New Castle.
The Fair Haven Building and Loan Association of Fair Haven, Pa. Capital $1,000,000 May 14, 1893.	Said corporation is formed for the purpose of accumulating a fund by the periodical contributions of the members thereof, and of safely investing the same.	Baldwin township, Allegheny county.
The Lewis Run Pressed Brick Company. Capital, $30,000. May 19, 1893.	Said corporation is formed for the purpose of manufacturing pressed brick and tile, and other products of clay or shale.	Bradford.
The Allegheny Valley Heat, Light and Power Company. Capital, $15,000. May 22, 1893.	Said corporation is formed for the purpose of manufacturing and supplying light, heat and power, or any of them by means of electricity to the public at the borough of New Kensington, in the county of Westmoreland, Penna., and to persons, partnerships and associations residing therein and adjacent thereto, as may desire the same.	New Kensington.
The Washington & Westmoreland Ferry Company. Capital, $1,800. May 22, 1893.	Said corporation is formed for the purpose of erecting, g and maintaining a ferry and approaches thereto over Monongahela river, from a point at or near Charleroi, in the county of Washington, to a point on the opposite side of said river, in the co y of Westmoreland, and is distant from the nearest ferry now in o ration over the same stream one mile.	Charleroi.
The Tribune Publishing Company. Capital, $10,000. May 22, 1893.	Said corporation is formed for the purpose of transacting a printing and publishing business.	Uniontown.

LIST OF CHARTERS OF CORPORATIONS—*Continued.*

STYLE AND TITLE OF CORPORATION.	PURPOSE.	LOCATION.
New Process Bread Company. Capital, $10,000. May 22, 1893.	Said corporation is formed for the purpose of the manufacture of bread and other articles composed wholly or partially of flour or meal.	Scranton.
The Blue Diamond Slate Company. Capital, $25,000. May 22, 1893.	Said corporation is formed for the purpose of quarrying slate, manufacturing it into roofing, blackboards, building and other commercial forms of slate, and selling it.	Philadelphia.
The James Hay Company. Capital, $50,000. May 22, 1893.	Said poration is formed for the purpose of the manufacture of iron or steel, or both, or of any other metal, or of any other article of commerce in tal or wood, or both.	Allegheny.
The Tioga Point Electric Light & Power Company. Capital, $3,000. May 22, 1893.	Said in is formed for the purpose of furnishing light, heat and p, or any of them by electricity to the public, and to persons, and corporations within the borough of Athens, Bradford unty, and corporations within the borough of Athens, Bradford unty, P., and adjacent thereto, as may desire the same.	Athens.
The Electric Light & Power Company of Sayre, Pa. Capital, $3,000. May 22, 1893.	Said corporation is formed for the purpose of furnishing light, heat and power, or any of them, by electricity, to the public, and to such persons, partnerships and corporations within the borough of Sayre, Bradford county, Pa., and adjacent thereto, as may desire the same.	Sayre.
The Crystal Ice Company. Capital, $100,000. May 22, 1893.	Said corporation is formed for the purpose of manufacturing ice by artificial process.	Harrisburg.
The Central Market Company. Capital, $100,000. May 22, 1893.	Said corporation is formed for the purpose of establishing, conducting and maintaining a market house in the city of Erie.	Erie.
The Crafton Land Company. Capital, $50,000. May 23, 1893.	Said corporation is formed for the purpose of purchasing, improving, selling and leasing real estate, in Allegheny county, Penna.	Crafton.

Corporation	Purpose	Location
Mansfield Building and Loan Association. Capital, $1,000,000. May 23, 1893.	Said corporation is formed for the purpose of accumulating a fund by the periodical contributions of the members thereof, and of safely investing the same.	Mansfield.
The Homestead Building and Loan Association. Capital, $800,000. May 24, 1893.	Said corporation is formed for the purpose of accumulating a fund by the periodical contributions of the members thereof, and of safely investing the same.	Summit Hill.
New Bethlehem Building and Loan Association. Capital, $1,000,000. May 26, 1893.	Said corporation is formed for the purpose of accumulating a fund by the periodical contributions of the members thereof, and of safely investing the same.	New Bethlehem.
Wilmer Atkinson Company. Capital, $30,000. May 26, 1893.	Said corporation is formed for the purpose of transacting a printing and publishing business.	Philadelphia.
The Fairchance Water Company. Capital, $10,000. May 26, 1893.	Said corporation is formed for the purpose of supplying water to and for the public at the borough of Fairchance, Fayette county, Pennsylvania, and to such persons, partnerships, corporations and associations residing therein and adjacent thereto, as may desire the same.	Fairchance.
Pittsburgh & Allegheny Abattoir Company. Capital, $40,000. May 26, 1893.	Said corporation is formed for the purpose of the manufacture and sale of dressed meats, the manufacture of fertilizers and other articles of commerce from the products obtained in the slaughtering of cattle.	Pittsburgh.
Toronto Fire-Clay Manufacturing Company. Capital, $30,000. May 26, 1893.	Said corporation is formed for the purpose of manufacturing sewer pipe and other articles from "fire-clay."	Pittsburgh.
Union Refining Company. Capital, $175,000. May 29, 1893.	Said corporation is formed for the purpose of manufacturing illuminating and all other oils, and all merchantable products from and of crude petroleum.	Titusville.
The Mansfield Land Company. Capital, $5,000. May 29, 1893.	Said corporation is formed for the purpose of purchase and sale of real estate, and for holding, leasing and selling real estate.	Mansfield.

LIST OF CHARTERS OF CORPORATIONS—*Continued.*

STYLE AND TITLE OF CORPORATION.	PURPOSE.	LOCATION.
North Latrobe Land Company, Capital, $40,000. May 29, 1893.	Said corporation is formed for the purpose of the purchase and sale of real estate.	Pittsburgh.
The Church Press Association. Capital, $10,000. May 29, 1893.	Said corporation is formed for the purpose of transacting a printing and publishing business.	Philadelphia.
The Lincoln Building and Loan Association of Lansford. Capital, $240,000. May 29, 1893.	Said corporation is formed for the purpose of accumulating a fund by the periodical contributions of the members thereof, and of safely investing the same.	Lansford.
Homekeeper Publishing Company. Capital, $10,000. May 29, 1893.	Said corporation is formed for the purpose of the transaction of a printing and publishing business.	Philadelphia.
The Grain Scouring Machine Company. Capital, $100,000. May 29, 1893.	Said corporation is formed for the purpose of manufacturing improved grain hulling and scouring machines.	Philadelphia.
The Medical Gum Company. Capital, $12,000. May 29, 1893.	Said corporation is formed for the purpose of manufacturing chewing gum and marketing the product.	Bradford.
The R. C. Schmertz Glass Company Capital, $250,000. May 31, 1893.	Said corporation is formed for the purpose of the manufacture and sale of window glass, and any and all other articles, materials and substances out of which window glass is or may be made.	Pittsburgh.
The Monroe Paint Company. Capital, $10,000. May 31, 1893.	Said corporation is formed for the purpose of manufacturing colors and paints from certain iron ores, and other pigmentary materials, to dig for and mine the same, to acquire and hold such patents as may be necessary for carrying on its business, and for that purpose to have and possess the powers and privileges expressed and given in the 39th section of the corporation act of 1874, and its supplements.	Philadelphia.

Joseph Walton and Company. Incorporated. Capital, $5,000. May 31, 1883.	Said corporation is formed for the purpose of the mining of coal and the transportation thereof to market, and the sale of the same in crude or manufactured form.	Pittsburgh.
The Tuna Valley Brick Company. Capital, $60,000. May 31, 1883.	Said corporation is formed for the purpose of the manufacture of brick and other articles of commerce from clay and shale.	Bradford.
The West Branch Hosiery Company. Capital, $30,000. May 31, 1883.	Said corporation is formed for the purpose of the manufacture of all kinds silks, cotton and woolen knitted goods.	Milton.
The World Refining Company. Capital, $15,000. May 31, 1883.	Said corporation is formed for the purpose of manufacturing or compounding oils, greases, packings, dressings and such other like compounds.	Easton.
The Oltman Land & Loan Association. Capital, $50,000. May 31, 1883.	Said corporation is formed for the purpose of accumulating a fund by the periodical contributions of its members thereof, and of safely investing the same.	Pittsburgh.
The Crystal Ice Company of Pittsburgh and Allegheny. Capital, $150,000. May 31, 1883.	Said corporation is formed for the purpose of supplying ice to the public.	Allegheny City.

CERTIFICATE.

OFFICE OF THE SECRETARY OF THE COMMONWEALTH,
HARRISBURG, *June 11, 1893.*

I do hereby certify that the foregoing, as contained on the last one hundred and eighty-six pages, is a full, true, and correct list of all charters of corporations created and organized under the provisions of an act of the General Assembly of the Commonwealth of Pennsylvania, entitled "An act to provide for the incorporation and regulation of certain corporations," approved April 29, A. D. 1874, and the several supplements thereto, enrolled in this office between the 1st day of June, A. D. 1891, and the 1st day of June, A. D. 1893.

WILLIAM F. HARRITY,
Secretary of the Commonwealth.

INDEX

TO CHARTERS OF CORPORATIONS CREATED AND ORGANIZED UNDER
THE "GENERAL CORPORATION ACT OF APRIL 29, 1874," AND ITS SEV-
ERAL SUPPLEMENTS.

A.

B.

C.

13a—LAWS.

F.

J.

K.

O.

P.

Q.

R.

U.

V.

W.

Y.

INDEX TO LAWS.

A.

INDEX TO LAWS.

INDEX TO LAWS.

16a—LAWS.

B.

INDEX TO LAWS.

F.

I.

18a— LAWS

N.

Page.

S.

T.

Page.

W.